QuickBooks® 2014
IN DEPTH

Laura Madeira

que®

800 East 96th Street,
Indianapolis, Indiana 46240 USA

QUICKBOOKS® 2014 IN DEPTH

Trademarks

All terms mentioned in this book that are known to be trademarks or service marks have been appropriately capitalized. Que Publishing cannot attest to the accuracy of this information. Use of a term in this book should not be regarded as affecting the validity of any trademark or service mark.

Warning and Disclaimer

Every effort has been made to make this book as complete and as accurate as possible, but no warranty or fitness is implied. The information provided is on an "as is" basis. The author and the publisher shall have neither liability nor responsibility to any person or entity with respect to any loss or damages arising from the information contained in this book.

Special Sales

For information about buying this title in bulk quantities, or for special sales opportunities (which may include electronic versions; custom cover designs; and content particular to your business, training goals, marketing focus, or branding interests), please contact our corporate sales department at corpsales@pearsoned.com or (800)382-3419.

For government sales inquiries, please contact governmentsales@pearsoned.com.

For questions about sales outside the U.S., please contact international@pearsoned.com.

Editor-in-Chief
Greg Wiegand

Acquisitions Editor
Michelle Newcomb

Development Editor
Ginny Munroe

Managing Editor
Sandra Schroeder

Project Editor
Mandie Frank

Copy Editor
Krista Hansing Editorial
Services, Inc.

Indexer
Brad Herriman

Proofreader
Debbie Williams

Technical Editor
MB Raimondi, CPA, CITP

Editorial Assistant
Cindy Teeters

Designer
Mark Shirar

Compositor
Trina Wurst

CONTENTS AT A GLANCE

Introduction   1

What's New for QuickBooks 2014   7

1   Getting Started with QuickBooks   35

2   Getting Around QuickBooks   67

3   Accounting 101   87

4   Understanding QuickBooks Lists   107

5   Setting Up Inventory   151

6   Managing Inventory   205

7   Setting Up Vendors   231

8   Managing Vendors   265

9   Setting Up Customers   303

10   Managing Customers   381

11   Setting Up Payroll   445

12   Managing Payroll   491

13   Working with Bank and Credit Card Accounts   519

14   Reporting in QuickBooks   553

15   Reviewing Your Data   575

16   Sharing QuickBooks Data With Your Accountant   597

17   Managing Your QuickBooks Database   643

18   Using Other Planning and Management Tools   675

A   Client Data Review   695

B   QuickBooks Statement Writer   753

C   QuickBooks Enterprise Solutions Features   783

D   QuickBooks Shortcuts   835

Index   841

TABLE OF CONTENTS

Introduction 1

How This Book Is Organized 2

Conventions Used in This Book 3
Menu Commands 3
Web Pages and Manufacturer
Information 4
Special Elements 5

**What's New for
QuickBooks 2014 7**

New and Improved Features 7
Bounced Checks 7
Income Tracker 8
Inventory Min and Max Reorder
Points 9
Sent Email Tracking 10
Alerts and Reminders List on Menu
Bar 11
Bill Payment Stub Now Includes Bill
Credits 11
Assign a Sales Rep to the Job
Record 12
Job Status Reporting 12
Left Icon Bar Customization 13
Color Customization Options 14
Bank Feeds 14
Sort and Resize Billable Time and Costs
Window 15
Create Multiple Email Templates 16
Include Attachments with Email 17
More Reports on the Transaction
Ribbon 18
Print to One Page 19
Copy and Paste Line Items on Forms 20
Improved Payroll Center 20
Improved My Company Information 21
Enable or Disable Collections Center 22

For the Accounting Professional 23
Client Collaborator 23
Improved Batch Enter Transactions 24
Improved Client Data Review 25

For QuickBooks Enterprise Users 25
Add Sales Rep and Custom Fields to
Expense Transactions 25
Job Work in Process (WIP) Summary
Report 26
Committed Costs by Job Report 27
Automatically Build Subassemblies 27
Efficiently Replace or Remove
Components in Assemblies 28
Options for Automatically Calculating
the Cost Field in an Assembly
Record 29
Efficiently Edit Cost, Price, Markup, and
Margin for Inventory Items 30
Create Auto POs Now Suggests a
Quantity to Order 31

QuickBooks Enterprise with Advanced
Pricing 32
Price Rules 32
Quantity Discounts 33

**1 Getting Started with
QuickBooks 35**

Understanding QuickBooks 35

Using QuickBooks Sample Data 37

Creating a New QuickBooks File 38
Express Start 39
Advanced Setup or Detailed Start—
Formerly the EasyStep Interview 45
Creating a New File from an Existing
Company File 49

Converting from Other Accounting
Software 50
Converting from Quicken to
QuickBooks 51
Converting from Peachtree, Small
Business Accounting, or Office
Accounting to QuickBooks 52

My Company Information 54

Setting Up Users and Permissions **55**
 External Accountant **56**
 Other QuickBooks Users **57**

User Security in QuickBooks Enterprise **59**
 Overview of Comprehensive User
 Security in QuickBooks Enterprise **59**
 Set Up and Modify User Roles **60**
 Set Up Users **63**

Reporting on User Activity **65**

2 Getting Around QuickBooks 67

Home Page and Navigation **67**
 Title Bar **67**
 Menu Bar **68**
 Top Icon Bar **69**
 Left Icon Bar **72**
 Home Page **74**
 Open Windows List **77**

Tutorials **79**

Preferences **79**
 Accounting—Company Preferences **79**
 Desktop View—My Preferences **80**
 General—My Preferences **81**
 Spelling—My Preferences **82**

Help Options **82**

Selecting a Company File to Open **83**
 Opening Your Data File for the First
 Time **83**
 Choosing from a List of Multiple Data
 Files **84**

3 Accounting 101 87

Basic Principles of Accounting **87**
 The Matching Principle **87**
 Accrual Versus Cash Basis
 Reporting **89**

Basic Financial Reports **91**
 Balance Sheet **91**
 Income Statement **91**
 Statement of Cash Flows **92**

Accounting Checklist to Help You Manage
Your Financials **92**

Setting Up a QuickBooks Data File for
Accrual or Cash Basis Reporting **94**
 Cash or Accrual Basis Startup
 Transactions: Accounts Receivable **95**
 Cash or Accrual Basis Startup
 Transactions: Accounts Payable **100**
 Cash or Accrual Basis Startup
 Transactions: Bank Account Statement
 Balance **103**
 Cash or Accrual Basis Startup
 Transactions: Recording Uncleared Bank
 Checks **105**

**4 Understanding QuickBooks
Lists 107**

Chart of Accounts **108**
 Account Types **108**
 Adding a New Account **110**

Items **112**
 Understanding Items **112**
 Item Types **113**
 Adding an Item **115**

Class **117**

Customer Type **120**

Managing Lists **120**
 Chart of Account Preferences **121**
 Add/Edit Multiple List Entries **122**
 Add Your Excel Data to QuickBooks
 Utility **124**
 Importing an Intuit Interchange Format
 File (IIF) **129**

Reporting on Lists **132**

Finding and Fixing Chart of Account
Errors **132**
 QuickBooks Required Accounts **133**
 Making an Account Inactive **133**
 Merging Duplicated Accounts **134**
 Modifying an Account in the Chart of
 Accounts **135**

Assigning or Removing a Subaccount
Relationship **136**

Finding and Fixing Item List Errors **139**
Reviewing the Item List on the
Computer Screen **139**
Item Listing Report **140**
Profit & Loss Standard Report **142**
Correcting One-Sided Items **144**
Making an Item Inactive **147**
Merging Items **148**
Creating Items As Subitems **149**

5 Setting Up Inventory 151

Inventory Features by QuickBooks
Edition **152**
QuickBooks Pro 2014 **152**
QuickBooks Premier 2014 **153**
QuickBooks Enterprise Solutions
Editions **153**

Enabling Inventory Preferences **156**

Inventory Item Type Descriptions **159**
Inventory Part **160**
Non-inventory Part **160**
Group Items and Inventory
Assemblies **160**

Adding or Editing Inventory Items **161**
Adding or Editing Individual Items **162**
Using Add/Edit Multiple List
Entries **166**
Importing an Intuit Interchange Format
File (IIF) **169**
Changing Item Prices **170**
Creating Inventory Assemblies **173**
Creating Group Items **175**
Setting Up Multiple Unit of
Measurement **177**

Proper Inventory Processes **180**
Purchasing, Receiving, and Entering the
Vendor Bill **182**
Paying for Inventory **190**
Selling Inventory **193**
Working with Group Items **194**

Working with Assemblies **195**
Handling Inventory Backorders **196**
Handling Customer Inventory
Returns **200**
Handling Vendor Inventory Returns **203**

6 Managing Inventory 205

Adjusting Inventory **205**
Performing a Physical Inventory
Count **206**
Quantity Adjustments **207**
Value Adjustments **209**

Inventory Reporting **211**
Inventory Center **212**
Report Center **213**
Inventory Valuation and Your
Financials **214**
Reviewing the Recorded Average Cost
Valuation **217**
Reviewing Aged Item Receipts **219**
Reviewing Aged Accounts Payable **223**

How QuickBooks Handles Negative
Inventory **224**
When Inventory Has an Average Cost
from Prior Purchase Transactions **224**
When Inventory Does Not Have a Prior
Average Cost **227**

7 Setting Up Vendors 231

Customizing Your Home Page for Vendor
Activities **231**

Preferences That Affect Accounts
Payable **232**
Accounting **232**
Bills **233**
Calendar **234**
Checking **234**
General **235**
Reminders **236**
Reports and Graphs **237**
Tax:1099 **237**
Time & Expenses **239**

Working with the Vendor Center   240
   Adding or Modifying Vendors   242
   Finding Vendor Transactions   245

The Accounts Payable Process   247
   Accounts Payable Transactions   247
   Accounts Payable Workflow   249
   Entering a Purchase Order   251
   Recording Vendor Bills   251
   Recording Vendor Credits   254
   Paying Vendor Bills   256
   Applying Vendor Credits   259
   Taking Discounts on Vendor Bills   262

8 Managing Vendors   265

Accounts Payable Reporting   265
   Reconciling Balance Sheet Accounts
   Payable Balance to A/P Aging Summary
   Report Total   265
   Reviewing the Unpaid Bills Detail
   Report   267
   Reviewing Aged Open Item
   Receipts   268
   Reviewing Item Setup   270
   Accounts Payable Balance on Cash Basis
   Balance Sheet   272
   Tracking and Reporting Vendor 1099-
   MISC Payments   275

Correcting Accounts Payable Errors   285
   When Vendor Bills Are Paid Without
   Using the Proper Process   285
   Misapplied Vendor Credit   288
   Removing Aged Open Item Receipts or
   Vendor Bills   289
   Making General Journal Adjustments to
   Accounts Payable   290

Handling Unique Accounts Payable
Transactions   293
   Bartering Services with Your
   Vendors   293
   Recording Vendor Prepayments   295
   Entering Midyear 1099 Balances   298
   Memorizing Recurring Transactions   299
   Depositing a Vendor Refund   300

Paying and Recording a Credit Card
Bill   301

9 Setting Up Customers   303

Customizing Home Page Customer
Activities   304

Preferences That Affect Accounts
Receivable   304
   Payments   306
   Sales & Customers   307
   Checking   308
   Finance Charge   309
   Jobs & Estimates   310
   Reminders   311
   Reports & Graphs   312
   Sales Tax   314
   Send Forms   315
   Spelling   316
   Time & Expenses   316

Working with the Customer Center   318
   Adding or Modifying Customers and
   Jobs   319
   Finding Customer Transactions   323

Working with Prospects in the Lead
Center   325

Setting Up Sales Tax   327
   Creating Sales Tax Items   327
   Creating Sales Tax Group Items   328
   Creating Sales Tax Codes   329
   Assigning Sales Tax Codes to Products
   or Services   331
   Assigning Sales Tax Codes and Sales
   Tax Items to Customers   332

Creating Price Level Lists   333

Using Advanced Pricing in QuickBooks
Enterprise   334
   Price Rules   335
   Quantity Discount   336

Creating Payment Terms   338

Customizing QuickBooks Forms **339**
  Using the Customize My Forms
  Wizard **340**
  Using the Customize Data Layout
  Tool **343**

Accounts Receivable Processes **346**
  Using QuickBooks Estimates **348**
  Using QuickBooks Sales Orders **349**
  Creating Customer Invoices **350**
  Time and Expense Invoicing **363**
  Recording a Sales Receipt **367**
  Recording a Statement Charge **369**
  Recording the Customer Payment **370**
  Making the Bank Deposit **373**
  Recording and Applying a Customer
  Credit Memo **376**
  Refunding a Customer's
  Overpayment **379**

10 Managing Customers 381

Accounts Receivable Reporting **381**
  Reviewing A/R Aging Summary and
  Detail Reports **382**
  Reviewing the Open Invoices
  Report **383**
  Reconciling Accounts Receivable
  Totals **385**
  Viewing the Accounts Receivable
  Balance on a Cash Basis Balance
  Sheet **386**
  Income Tracker **388**
  Enable the Collections Center **391**
  Generating the Missing Customer
  Invoices Report **393**

Sales Tax Payable Reports **394**
  Reviewing Customer Lists for Tax Code
  and Tax Item Assigned **394**
  Reviewing the Item List for Tax Code
  Assigned **395**
  Reconciling Total Sales to Total
  Income **396**
  Reconciling Sales Tax Liability to
  Balance Sheet Sales Tax Payable **397**
  When a Check or Bill Is Used to Pay
  Sales Tax **398**

Paying Sales Tax **398**
  Paying Sales Tax Without an
  Adjustment **399**
  Paying Sales Tax with an
  Adjustment **400**

Correcting Accounts Receivable Errors **402**
  Removing an Open Balance from a
  Customer Invoice **403**
  Correcting Customer Payments **407**
  When a Credit Memo Is Applied to the
  Wrong Customer Invoice **411**
  When Deposits Were Made
  Incorrectly **412**
  Eliminating the Print Queue for
  Customer Invoices Marked to Print **418**

Correcting Sales Tax Errors **419**
  When a Check or Bill Is Used to Pay the
  Sales Tax **419**
  When the Sales Tax Liability Report
  Shows Past Sales Tax Due **420**
  When Total Sales Does Not Equal Total
  Income **422**

Correcting Undeposited Funds Account
Errors **426**
  Reviewing the Balance in the
  Undeposited Funds Account **426**
  Removing Old Dated Payments in the
  Undeposited Funds Account **429**

Unique Customer Transactions **431**
  Recording Your Accountant's Year-End
  Adjusting Journal Entry to Accounts
  Receivable **432**
  When a Customer Is Also a Vendor **432**
  Recording a Customer's Bounced
  Check **434**
  Tracking Customer Deposits in
  QuickBooks **438**

Unique Sales Tax Transactions **439**
  When Your State Imposes a Maximum
  Sales Tax **439**
  Multiple Sales Tax Rates on One
  Invoice **441**
  Issuing Credit Memos When Sales Tax
  Should Not Have Been Charged **442**

11 Setting Up Payroll 445

Getting Started 445
  Payroll Process Overview 446
  Selecting and Activating a Payroll Service Subscription 447
  Updating Payroll Tax Tables 449
  Employer Resources 450
  Creating Payroll Accounts in the Chart of Accounts 452
  Setting Up Payroll Tax Vendors 454
  Payroll Preferences 455
  Using the Payroll Setup Interview 458
  Using the Run Payroll Checkup Diagnostic Tool 466

Setting Up Employees 469
  Using the Employee Center 469
  Adding or Editing Employee Information 470
  Finding Payroll Transactions 473

Setting Up Payroll Items 475
  Adding or Editing Payroll Items 475
  Reporting About Payroll Items 478

Paying Employees 479
  Payroll Home Page Workflow 480
  Entering Employee Time 480
  Preparing Employee Paychecks 482
  Printing Paychecks or Paystubs 484
  ViewMyPaycheck 485

Preparing Payroll Liability Payments 487
  Paying Scheduled Liabilities 487
  Adjusting Payroll Liabilities 488

12 Managing Payroll 491

Report Center Payroll Reports 491

Excel Reports 492

Tax Forms and Filings 494
  Preparing and Printing Tax Forms 494
  E-Filing Tax Payments and Forms 497

Troubleshooting Payroll 497
  Comparing Payroll Liability Balances to the Balance Sheet 497

Comparing the Payroll Summary Report to Filed Payroll Returns 500
Reconciling Payroll Reports to Business Financials 500

Recording Unique Payroll Transactions 501
  Employee Loan Payment and Repayment 501
  Reprinting a Lost Paycheck 506
  Paying a Taxable Bonus 507
  Adjusting an Employee Paycheck 508
  Allocating Indirect Costs to Jobs Through Payroll 509
  Depositing a Refund of Payroll Liabilities 514
  Recording Payroll When Using an Outside Payroll Service 515

13 Working with Bank and Credit Card Accounts 519

Preferences That Affect Banking and Credit Card Management 520

Working with Write Check Transactions 520
  Using the Expenses Tab and Items Tab 521
  Writing a Check 523
  Printing Checks 526

Entering a Bank Debit Charge 529

Entering Credit Card Charges 529

Paying the Credit Card Bill 531

Transferring Funds Between Bank Accounts 532

Bank Feeds 532
  Set Up Bank Feeds 533
  Manage Bank Feeds 534
  Renaming Rules in Bank Feeds 537

Reconciling the Bank or Credit Card Account 538

Troubleshooting Reconciliations 541
  Determining Whether the Account Has Been Reconciled 541

Verifying That All Account Transactions Have Been Entered **543**

Identifying All Uncleared Transactions **544**

Completing the Multi-year or Multi-month Bank Reconciliation **545**

Reviewing Uncleared Transactions **546**

Reviewing Previous Bank Reconciliation Reports **548**

Locating Bank Account Reconciliation Discrepancies **548**

Reviewing the Voided/Deleted Transactions Reports **549**

Restarting a Previously Completed Bank Reconciliation **550**

Undoing a Previous Bank Reconciliation **550**

Reconciling with an Adjustment **551**

14 Reporting in QuickBooks 553

Using the Company Snapshot **553**
  Customizing the Company Snapshot **554**
  Defaulting the Company Snapshot as Home Page **556**

Report Center **557**

Reports & Graphs Preferences **559**
  My Preferences **559**
  Company Preferences **560**

Modifying Reports **563**
  Modifying Options Available on the Report Window **563**
  Customizing Reports **564**

Report Groups **565**
  Creating Report Groups **565**
  Using Report Groups **566**
  Managing Memorized Report List and Memorized Report Groups **568**

Memorized Reports **569**

Exporting and Importing Report Templates **570**

Exporting a Report or Report Group Template **570**

Importing a Report or Report Group Template **571**

Exporting Reports to a .CSV File or to Excel **571**

Emailing Reports **573**

15 Reviewing Your Data 575

Reviewing the Balance Sheet **575**
  Account Types **576**
  Prior Year Balances **577**
  Bank Account Balance(s) **578**
  Accounts Receivable **578**
  Undeposited Funds **579**
  Inventory **580**
  Other Current Assets **581**
  Fixed Assets **582**
  Accounts Payable **583**
  Credit Cards **584**
  Payroll Liabilities **584**
  Sales Tax Payable **585**
  Other Current Liabilities and Long-Term Liabilities **585**
  Equity **585**

Reviewing the Profit & Loss Report **586**

Other Reviews **587**
  Tracking Changes to Closed Accounting Periods **587**
  Using the Audit Trail Report **588**
  Using the Credit Card Audit Trail Report **589**
  Reporting on Voided/Deleted Transactions **591**
  Viewing the Transactions List by Date Report **592**
  Troubleshooting Opening Balance Equity Account **593**
  Closing Opening Balance Equity into Retained Earnings **593**

16 Sharing QuickBooks Data with Your Accountant 597

Overview **597**
 Benefits for the Business Owner **598**
 Benefits for the Accountant **598**

QuickBooks File Types **599**
 Choosing a Method to Share Data **599**

Data Sharing for the Business Owner **603**
 Reviewing Your QuickBooks Data **604**
 Creating an Accountant's Copy of Your Data **604**
 What the Business Owner Can and Cannot Do **609**
 Importing Your Accountant's Changes **610**
 Canceling an Accountant's Copy **616**

Data Sharing for the Accountant **616**
 File Manager 2014 **617**
 Creating an External Accountant User Type **618**
 Preparing Your Client for Data Exchange **619**
 Receiving an Accountant's Copy File **619**
 What the Accountant Can Do **623**
 What the Accountant Cannot Do **626**
 Returning the Accountant's Copy Change File to the Client **626**
 What to Request from the Client When the Import Is Complete **629**
 Converting the Accountant's Copy to a Regular Company File **629**

Other Methods of Sharing Data **630**
 Send General Journal Entries **630**
 Batch Enter Transactions **632**

Client and Accountant Collaboration **634**
 Access to Client Collaborator **635**
 How the Accountant Gets Started **636**
 How the Business Owner Gets Started **637**
 Accountant and Client Converse via Client Collaborator **638**

17 Managing Your QuickBooks Database 643

The QuickBooks Database **643**
 System Requirements **644**
 Express Installation of QuickBooks **646**
 Installing QuickBooks for Multiuser Mode **647**
 The QuickBooks Database Server Manager **648**
 Windows Permissions Required for QuickBooks **650**

Keeping Your Software Current **651**
 Upgrading Your QuickBooks Version **651**
 Installing a QuickBooks Maintenance Release **652**

Protecting Your QuickBooks Database **653**
 Creating a QuickBooks Backup **653**
 Protecting the QuickBooks Operating Environment **656**
 Using Intuit Data Protect Online Backup Service **659**

Monitoring Your QuickBooks Database **660**
 The Product Information Dialog Box **660**
 Using the Verify Data Utility **663**
 Monitoring QuickBooks Performance Using Windows Task Manager **663**

QuickBooks Database Corruption **664**
 Common Causes of Corruption **664**
 Signs of Data Corruption **665**
 The QBWin.log File **665**
 Repairing List Corruptions **668**
 Reducing Database File Fragments **669**
 Rebuilding Your Company File **670**
 Using the QuickBooks File Doctor **671**
 Resolving QuickBooks Program File Corruption Issues **673**

18 Using Other Planning and Management Tools 675

Planning and Budgeting 675
Create a Budget 676
Edit a Budget 678
Print Budget Reports 679
Delete a Budget 681

QuickBooks Loan Manager 681
Information to Collect 682
Getting QuickBooks Ready 682
Setting Up a New Loan 682
Setting Up a Loan Payment 684

Using the Year-End Guide 685

Synchronizing QuickBooks Lists with Microsoft Outlook 686

Using the QuickBooks Timer 690
Installing the QuickBooks Timer 691
Tracking Time with the Timer 691
Exporting Timer Activities 692
Importing Timer Activities into QuickBooks 693

A Client Data Review 695

Introduction: Features and Benefits 696

Accessing Client Data Review Tools and Features 698

Customizing the Accountant Center 699

Customizing the Client Data Review Center 701
Modifying the Review Date and Basis 702
Customize Cleanup Tasks 702
Minimize or Expand Task Groups 704
Assigning Status and Notes to Review Tasks 705

Account Balances 705
Troubleshoot Prior Account Balances 706
Reclassify Transactions 710
Open Working Trial Balance 712

Review List Changes 713
Chart of Accounts 713
Items 714
Fixed Asset Items 715
Payroll Items 716
Review Item Setup 717
Customers 718
Vendors 718
Change Other Name Types 718

Accounts Receivable 719
Fix Unapplied Customer Payments and Credits 719
Clear Up Undeposited Funds Account 720
Reviewing the AR Aging Summary Report 722
Write Off Invoices 724

Accounts Payable 726
Fix Unapplied Vendor Payments and Credits 727
Evaluate and Correct 1099 Account Mapping 728
Reviewing the Unpaid Bills Report 728

Sales Tax 729
Fix Incorrectly Recorded Sales Tax 729
Adjust Sales Tax Payable 732
Manage Sales Tax 733
Pay Sales Tax 733
Sales Tax Preferences 733

Inventory 734
Review Inventory Setup 734
Compare Balance Sheet and Inventory Valuation 734
Troubleshoot Inventory 736
Adjust Inventory Quantity/Value on Hand 738

Payroll 739
Find Incorrectly Paid Payroll Liabilities 739
Review Payroll Liabilities 741
Review Employee Default Settings 741
Enter After-the-Fact Payroll 741

Bank Reconciliation 742
  Reconcile Accounts 742
  Locate Discrepancies in Bank
  Reconciliation 742
  Reviewing Missing Checks 743

Miscellaneous 744
  Setting Closing Date and Password 744
  Review QuickBooks Preferences 746
  Condense Data from Previous
  Periods 747

Finishing a Client Data Review 748
  Saving the Review as a PDF 748
  Mark Review Complete 750

Reopen Completed Review 750

Reporting on Review Activity 750

Creating an External Accountant User 751

**B QuickBooks Statement
Writer 753**

Overview 753
  Terms 754
  Workflow 754
  Benefits 754

Getting Started 755
  Preferences & Formats 756

Using the Report Designer 759
  Report Content 759
  Columns 760
  Rows/Accounts 761
  Headers & Formatting 762
  Review & Finish 763

Opening a Previously Created Report 764

Creating a New Report from a Memorized
Report 764

Modifying a Statement Writer Report in
Excel 764
  Method 1: Using the Report
  Designer 765
  Method 2: Using the Document Actions
  Pane 765

Method 3: Using the Excel Add-Ins
Ribbon Icons 774

Working with Supporting Documents 774
  Overview 775
  Adding or Modifying a Supporting
  Document 775
  Using the QSW Toolbar in Word 777
  Editing an Existing QSW Supporting
  Document 777
  Creating a New QSW Supporting
  Document 779

Printing or Exporting a Statement Writer
Report 779

**C QuickBooks Enterprise Solutions
Features 783**

QuickBooks Enterprise Customization 784
  Custom Fields 784
  Customize Expense Transactions 786

QuickBooks Enterprise Inventory 788
  Accessing Inventory Features and
  Reports 788
  Auto Create Purchase Orders 791
  Working with Assemblies 793
  Sales Order Fulfillment Worksheet 798
  Enhanced Inventory Receiving 800
  Automatic Cost & Price Updates 804
  Assigning Markup Defaults per
  Item 805

QuickBooks Enterprise with Advanced
Inventory 806
  Multiple Inventory Locations 806
  Serial/Lot Numbers 813
  First-In, First-Out (FIFO) Inventory
  Costing 819
  Barcodes 821

QuickBooks Enterprise with Advanced
Pricing 826
  Price Rules 827
  Quantity Discount 829

QuickBooks Enterprise Reporting **830**
  Job Work in Process (WIP) Summary
  Report **830**
  Committed Costs by Job Report **831**
  Combine Reports from Multiple
  Companies **832**

D QuickBooks Shortcuts 835

  Editing QuickBooks Transactions and
  Lists **836**

  Opening QuickBooks Dialog Boxes and
  Lists **836**

  Memorized Transactions **837**

  Standard Text Editing **837**

  Opening QuickBooks Data Files **838**

  QuickBooks Date Shortcuts **838**

  Miscellaneous Shortcuts **839**

  Index 841

ABOUT THE AUTHOR

Laura Madeira is the owner of ACS, Inc., a software sales and consulting firm located in the greater Dallas, Texas, area. She is one of the original members of the elite Intuit Trainer/ Writer Network and a guest speaker for Intuit—she shares "What's New for QuickBooks" each fall. Laura was also a founding member of the Intuit Customer Advisory Council and a recent member of the Intuit Solution Provider Council. She is an Advanced QuickBooks Certified ProAdvisor, Enterprise and Point of Sale Certified, and is also a Sage Certified Consultant representing Sage 100 Contractor (formerly Master Builder).

Laura is the author of *QuickBooks 2013 and 2012 In Depth*, a reference and training guide. She is also the author of *QuickBooks Solutions Guide, QuickBooks Essentials: For All QuickBooks Users*, self-paced video instruction, and the co-author of *QuickBooks on Demand*—all offered by Que Publishing.

For more than 25 years, Laura has worked with companies of all sizes and from many industries. Her focus has been to help growing businesses become more successful by automating their internal accounting processes and improving their overall business financial reporting.

Additionally, Laura is a guest speaker for Intuit, providing training to thousands of consultants and accountants nationwide at numerous events. She is also a respected author for Intuit; she has written technical training materials and presentations, and has documented and reviewed competing software.

Laura earned her accounting degree from Florida Atlantic University. She enjoys photography, art, and camping with her family. When Laura is not writing, she enjoys reading a good book or two.

For more information, visit her website, www.quick-training.com, or email her at info@quick-training.com.

ABOUT THE TECHNICAL EDITOR

M. B. (Mary Beth) Raimondi, CPA, CITP, MS Taxation, is an Advanced QuickBooks Certified ProAdvisor and an Intuit Solution Provider. She holds certifications in QuickBooks Online, Enterprise, and POS, and is a Sleeter Group Certified Consultant as well as a Chapter Co-Leader/Instructor for the National Advisor Network (NAN). M. B. is also a charter member of the Intuit Training/Writing Network. She has used QuickBooks since the DOS version and has been teaching QuickBooks nationally to both end users and accountants/consultants since 1999. The focus of her practice in Trumbull, Connecticut, has migrated from a full-time tax and accounting practice to mainly QuickBooks consulting and training, specializing in strategizing, researching, and installing third-party add-ons and conversions to QuickBooks from other accounting software.

Dedication

To my husband, Victor, who willingly took care of everything for me as I recovered from total knee replacement during the edits for this edition. He needs a long break somewhere warm!

To my parents, to whom I owe everything—they are amazing examples of how to raise a child to believe they can do anything they want if they give it their best effort.

To my acquisitions editor, Michelle at Que—how could I have done this project without her constant support? I know it was not optimal that my deadlines were missed.

Acknowledgments

Another year's edition of the book could not have happened without the expertise of this year's technical editor, M. B. Raimondi. She is both a friend and a QuickBooks expert.

Her knowledge of QuickBooks helped to ensure that the details were accurate. Being a technical editor is not a "glamorous" job at all. The technical editor responsibilities include being completely familiar with the subject of the book, testing each documented step for technical accuracy, and verifying that the proper terminology is used for the specific audience.

These are just a few of the requirements. The technical editor must then communicate the change needed to the author in a clear and concise manner, while allowing the author the final word. Often weeks can go by between these reviews. Additionally, we write the original content during the beta release of the software and then retest when the final software is released.

A big thank you again to William Murphy, a certified QuickBooks consultant, whose continued review and edits helped to define the content for Chapter 17, "Managing Your QuickBooks Database."

I appreciate Charlie Russell and our many late-night emails about the new features and how they work. Charlie was instrumental in his help to learn about and document QuickBooks Enterprise features included in this edition.

Thanks to the entire Intuit Product Development Team, who continues to keep me advised of new product features and helps me collect information during the beta testing of each new year's release of QuickBooks.

To all my QuickBooks peers in the many forums I belong to, thank you! You all play a part in this book, however unknowingly. In these forums, I read your questions and answers, and it helps to guide what content I should include in the book.

For my family and friends who encouraged me to not lose sight of the goal—to share my knowledge of QuickBooks in this one-of-a-kind reference book—I could not have done this without your support.

Last, but very important, a big thanks to my acquisitions editor at Que, Michelle Newcomb, who has, after all these years, become a friend and who patiently works to keep me on schedule. (Well, she tries anyway.) And to the team at Que, including Ginny Munroe, development editor, who worked very closely with me to simplify the editing process; and Krista Hansing, copy editor, who made sure my content was grammatically accurate.

WE WANT TO HEAR FROM YOU!

As the reader of this book, *you* are our most important critic and commentator. We value your opinion and want to know what we're doing right, what we could do better, what areas you'd like to see us publish in, and any other words of wisdom you're willing to pass our way.

We welcome your comments. You can email or write to let us know what you did or didn't like about this book—as well as what we can do to make our books better.

Please note that we cannot help you with technical problems related to the topic of this book.

When you write, please be sure to include this book's title and author as well as your name and email address. We will carefully review your comments and share them with the author and editors who worked on the book.

Email: feedback@quepublishing.com

Mail: Que Publishing
         ATTN: Reader Feedback
         800 East 96th Street
         Indianapolis, IN 46240 USA

Reader Services

Visit our website and register this book at quepublishing.com/register for convenient access to any updates, downloads, or errata that might be available for this book.

Introduction

Whether you're new to QuickBooks, you're an expert user, or you fall somewhere in between, you will find this book to be a quick-start, comprehensive reference guide to help you successfully complete your day-to-day QuickBooks tasks.

Having worked with many types of businesses in the past 25 years, I know the importance of providing readers with the "how and why" of common QuickBooks tasks. For both the inexperienced and expert users, this book includes easy-to-follow quick-start, step-by-step instructions accompanied by hundreds of illustrations. Additionally, using the provided instructions, you can practice what you learn with sample data installed with your QuickBooks software. In no time at all, you will be using QuickBooks like a pro!

What truly sets this book apart from the competition is the detailed instruction for managing and troubleshooting your QuickBooks data. For the business owner, this book provides step-by-step guides, checklists, and detailed advanced discussions of what information your QuickBooks data provides.

For the accounting professional, learn how to work efficiently with your clients' QuickBooks files using Accountant's Copy, Client Data Review, QuickBooks Statement Writer, Send General Journal Entries, and other useful features included with the QuickBooks Accountant 2014 software.

For the QuickBooks Enterprise 14.0 user, Appendix C, "QuickBooks Enterprise Solutions Features," has a special focus on robust inventory features, including those available with an Advanced Inventory subscription.

How This Book Is Organized

QuickBooks 2014 In Depth offers a wealth of information gathered from the author's years of working with business and accounting professionals who use QuickBooks software. So you can find just the right information, this book is organized into specific chapters, each focused on a particular task for working with your own or a client's QuickBooks data.

- **What's New**—Learn quickly about what's new in QuickBooks 2014.

- **Chapter 1, "Getting Started with QuickBooks"**—Learn how to create a new file, convert from other software, and set up users and permissions. Learn how to set up user security in QuickBooks Enterprise.

- **Chapter 2, "Getting Around QuickBooks"**—Find out about navigating, setting preferences, using Help, and selecting a file to open.

- **Chapter 3, "Accounting 101"**—For the business owner, learn the basics of financial reporting. The included checklist helps you keep a close eye on the financial details.

- **Chapter 4, "Understanding QuickBooks Lists"**—Dive into using the chart of accounts, Items List, and class list; managing lists; and fixing list errors.

- **Chapter 5, "Setting Up Inventory"**—Learn about the different features in each version of QuickBooks, inventory preferences, and the proper inventory process.

- **Chapter 6, "Managing Inventory"**—See how to adjust inventory, review inventory reports, and handle inventory backorders.

- **Chapter 7, "Setting Up Vendors"**—Learn how to use the Home page, set vendor preferences, and use the recommended accounts payable process.

- **Chapter 8, "Managing Vendors"**—Learn about completing vendor reporting, correcting vendor transactions, and handling unique accounts payable transactions, such as prepaying a vendor.

- **Chapter 9, "Setting Up Customers"**—Check into tracking customer leads, customizing the Home page, setting preferences, and properly invoicing and collecting payment from your customers—this is an important chapter.

- **Chapter 10, "Managing Customers"**—Find a wealth of information about properly reporting your customer balances, paying sales tax, correcting transaction errors, and handling unique customer transactions.

- **Chapter 11, "Setting Up Payroll"**—Learn about the many payroll options, how to set up payroll items and employees, and the proper payroll processing steps.

- **Chapter 12, "Managing Payroll"**—Prepare your quarterly and annual payroll tax forms, troubleshoot payroll errors, and record unique payroll transactions, such as a loan made to an employee.

- **Chapter 13, "Working with Bank and Credit Card Accounts"**—Learn about entering checks, credit card transactions, and bank transfers, as well as reconciling tasks. Save time using the Online Banking Center to download transactions directly into QuickBooks.

- Chapter 14, "**Reporting in QuickBooks**"—Find out how to set preferences, use the Report Center, and modify and memorize reports in this chapter.

- Chapter 15, "**Reviewing Your Data**"—Get step-by-step guidance on reviewing the accuracy of your data. Don't miss this chapter!

- Chapter 16, "**Sharing QuickBooks Data with Your Accountant**"—Delve into instructions for the business owner and accountant, plus get a discussion of the different types of QuickBooks files.

- Chapter 17, "**Managing Your QuickBooks Database**"—See how to back up your data and upgrade your data. For the more advanced user, learn about troubleshooting database errors and monitoring your QuickBooks database.

- Chapter 18, "**Using Other Planning and Management Tools**"—Take advantage of all the tools available with your QuickBooks software, including loan management, planning, a year-end guide, Microsoft Outlook contacts sync, and the QuickBooks timer.

- Appendix A, "**Client Data Review**"—For the accounting professional, learn how to reclassify transactions in batch, track changes to lists, write off small customer balances in batch, fix beginning balance errors, and send journal entries by email, to name just a few tasks.

- Appendix B, "**QuickBooks Statement Writer**"—For the QuickBooks Enterprise user or accounting professional, learn how to prepare customized financials using Microsoft Excel and Word integration.

- Appendix C, "**QuickBooks Enterprise Solutions Features**"—Learn about managing the many unique tools available only in QuickBooks Enterprise. Value-added content details features that are included with Advanced Inventory or Advanced Pricing subscriptions.

- Appendix D, "**QuickBooks Shortcuts**"—Save time and work more efficiently with these shortcuts.

Conventions Used in This Book

The book is straightforward enough that you can easily go to a specific chapter and find the needed information. It is worthwhile, however, to let you know how information is presented in this book.

Menu Commands

QuickBooks 2014 offers a variety of methods to accomplish a task. To simplify the instructions given, many steps use the top menu bar in QuickBooks.

Sample Rock Castle Construction - QuickBooks Accountant 2014

File   Edit   View   Lists   Favorites   Accountant   Company   Customers   Vendors   Employees   Banking   Reports   Window   Help

Menu bar

For example, the instructions for preparing a report might look like the following:

1. From the menu bar, select **Reports**, **Vendors & Payables**.

This directive refers to clicking Reports on the menu bar and then selecting Vendors & Payables as a submenu of Reports.

Another instruction method utilizes the transaction ribbon toolbar in QuickBooks.

Transaction ribbon toolbar

For example, the instructions for modifying an invoice template might look like the following:

1. To continue with customizing your forms, select the **Customize Design** icon on the Formatting tab of the ribbon toolbar.

Instructions to select or type are **bolded** for easy identification in the text and might look like the following:

1. In the Item column on the next available row, select the non-inventory part **Flooring**.

2. In the Qty field, type **1**. Leave the U/M (Unit of Measure) field blank.

Additionally, for added clarity in the topic discussion, screen illustrations often accompany the written steps.

Web Pages and Manufacturer Information

A few web pages are listed in this book, mostly directing you to the www.intuit.com website. These web addresses were current as this book was written; however, websites can change.

Special Elements

As you read through this book, note several special elements, presented in what we call margin notes. Different types of margin notes are used for different types of information, as you see here.

 QuickStart

Several chapters in the book offer Quick Start directives. These references help you quickly complete the given task. When time permits, you can return to the same chapter to read more detailed information about the topic.

tip

This tip might prove useful for whatever you are in the process of doing.

note

Here you find additional related information or alternative techniques to consider.

caution

This is a caution that something you might accidentally do could have undesirable results—so take care!

Sidebars

Learn quickly how to complete a task by following along with supplied step-by-step instructions using sample data installed with your QuickBooks software.

WHAT'S NEW FOR QUICKBOOKS 2014

QuickBooks is both easy to learn and easy to use. With the improvements in QuickBooks 2014, small businesses can complete their financial and accounting responsibilities with minimal amount of effort so they can focus on growing their business.

All features detailed in this section are available in QuickBooks Pro, Premier, Accountant, and Enterprise versions unless otherwise stated.

New and Improved Features

The newest version of QuickBooks is designed to help small businesses save time managing their finances. For 2014, users will find many requested improvements that make tracking business financials more efficient than ever.

Bounced Checks

Bounced Checks (see Figure 1) efficiently records the credit of funds to the bank account and marks the original invoice as unpaid when a deposited payment is returned due to insufficient funds (NSF). Optionally, it creates a credit to the bank for the NSF fee and a new invoice to the customer for any NSF fee charged.

➡️ *To learn more about recording this type of transaction, see "Recording a Customer's Bounced Check," p. 434.*

Figure 1
Easily record bounced check transactions.

Income Tracker

With Income Tracker in Figure 2, you can view customer transactions all on one screen. Get a summary of unbilled, unpaid, and recently paid transactions on the Money Bar. Use the Money Bar to filter which transactions you see. Use the drop-down lists to filter transactions for ease in working with activities in batch. Take immediate action on customer transactions to get them paid on time. You can efficiently work in a batch when working with transactions: create new, print, or email in batch. All data in the tracker is in real time, so the information is right at your fingertips. You do not need to prepare reports to see what actions need to be pursued to get paid.

➡️ *To learn more, see "Income Tracker," in Chapter 10, p. 388.*

Figure 2
Use the
Income
Tracker to
track your
customer
transactions.

Inventory Min and Max Reorder Points

QuickBooks now provides both a Min and a Max field for suggested reorder points. See Figure 3. Earlier versions of QuickBooks included a single reorder point field. Both Min and Max data displays on stock status reports. Additionally, in QuickBooks Enterprise, this new functionality permits QuickBooks to suggest a reorder point to reach the Max level when using Auto Create Purchase Orders.

➡ To learn more about how QuickBooks uses these new reorder point fields, see "Auto Create Purchase Orders," p. 791.

Figure 3
QuickBooks provides Min and Max inventory reorder points.

Sent Email Tracking

The Customer Center shown in Figure 4, Vendor Center, and Employee Center all include a new tab that keeps a list of previously sent emails.

Figure 4
Track emails sent for Vendors, Customers, and Employees.

Alerts and Reminders List on Menu Bar

New icons on the menu bar provide easy access to data performance alerts and company file reminders. See Figure 5.

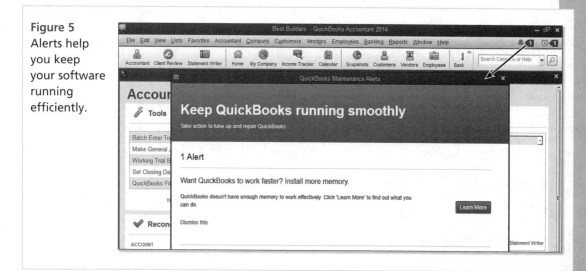

Figure 5
Alerts help you keep your software running efficiently.

Bill Payment Stub Now Includes Bill Credits

When paying a vendor bill in full with a vendor credit as in Figure 6, these paid bills and their associated credits are included on Bill Payment Stubs as in Figure 7. If the only transactions are the vendor bill and the bill credit, and they are of equal amounts, QuickBooks creates a net -0- amount check in the checkbook register.

Figure 6
Here you pay a vendor bill with a vendor credit.

☑ DATE DUE	VENDOR	REF. NO.	DISC. DATE	AMT. DUE	DISC. USED	CREDITS USED	AMT. TO PAY
☑ 12/15/2017	ABC Supplier	6231		1,000.00	0.00	1,000.00	0.00
			Totals	1,000.00	0.00	1,000.00	0.00

To learn more about this improvement, see the tip on p. 260 in Chapter 7.

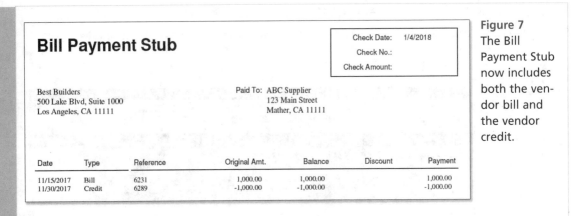

Figure 7
The Bill Payment Stub now includes both the vendor bill and the vendor credit.

Assign a Sales Rep to the Job Record

You can uniquely assign a Sales Rep to each job (see Figure 8). Previous versions of QuickBooks allowed you to assign a Sales Rep only to the Customer record, not the Job record. Additionally, you can filter many job profitability reports by Sales Rep.

Figure 8
Sales Reps can now be assigned to Job records in addition to Customer records.

 To learn more about adding a Sales Rep, see "Creating a Customer and Job Record," p. 320.

Job Status Reporting

QuickBooks users can now filter Job Profitability reports (and others) by Job Status, a field that is assigned to Customer and Job records as displayed in Figure 9.

 To learn about adding the Job Status to a Customer or Job record, see "Creating a Customer and Job Record," p. 320.

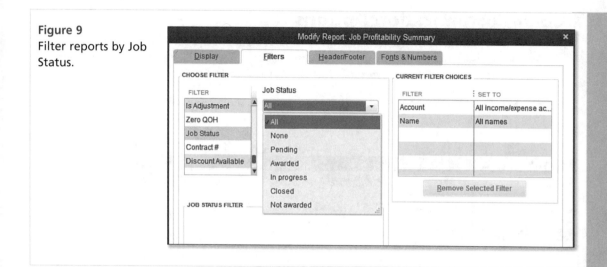

Figure 9
Filter reports by Job Status.

Left Icon Bar Customization

Previously, all bank, credit card, Accounts Receivable, and Accounts Payable accounts displayed. This feature gives you the flexibility to display only the accounts you want to view on the Left Icon Bar displayed in Figure 10.

➡ *To learn more, see "Left Icon Bar," p. 72.*

Figure 10
Customize the accounts that display on the Left Icon Bar.

Color Customization Options

QuickBooks enables individual users to switch to colored icons or a light background on the Top Icon Bar. It also permits individual users to choose a color scheme (see Figure 11) for the data file. This is particularly useful when working with multiple QuickBooks data files.

➡ *To learn more about this and other preferences, see "Desktop View—My Preferences," p. 80.*

Figure 11
Choose a Company File Color Scheme and other customizing options here.

Bank Feeds

Bank Feeds is a feature that provides more efficient recording of transactions downloaded from your bank or credit card provider. See Figure 12. With improved Renaming Rules, each successive download of QuickBooks Bank Feeds remembers the details you previously assigned to similar transactions.

➡ *To learn more, see "Bank Feeds," p. 532.*

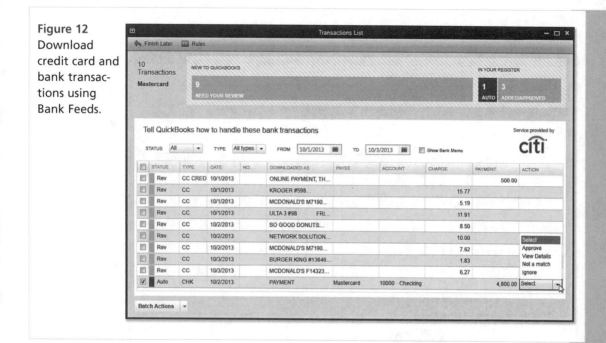

Figure 12
Download credit card and bank transactions using Bank Feeds.

Sort and Resize Billable Time and Costs Window

You can resize the Choose Billable Time and Costs window (Figure 13) and also sort each column of data. This allows greater flexibility in how the data appears on a customer invoice.

➡ *To learn more about this type of invoicing, see "Time and Expense Invoicing," p. 363.*

Click any header to sort the column details

✓	DATE	ITEM ▲	DESCRIPTION	QTY	U/M	RATE	AMOUNT	HIDE
	12/15/2017	Subs:Drywall	Install drywall	5		25.00	125.00	
	12/15/2017	Subs:Insulating	Install insulation	20		25.00	500.00	
	12/15/2017	Subs:Painting	Painting	10		25.00	250.00	
	12/15/2017	Subs:Plumbing	Plumbing	15		25.00	375.00	
	12/10/2017	Lumber:Rough	Rough lumber	1		380.00	380.00	
	12/10/2017	Lumber:Trim	Trim lumber	1		95.00	95.00	

Figure 13
The sorted order determines what displays on the customer's invoice.

Choose Billable Time and Costs

Time and Costs For: Ecker Designs:Office Expansion

Time $0.00 | Expenses $0.00 | Mileage $0.00 | Items $0.00

Select All

☐ Print selected time and costs as one invoice item

Total billable time and costs 0.00

OK   Cancel   Help

Create Multiple Email Templates

Customizable email templates (Figure 14) let you auto populate QuickBooks data such as invoice number and amount due in the body of the email, helping to ensure accurate communication.

➡️ *To learn more about creating email templates, see "Preferences That Affect Accounts Receivable," p. 304.*

Figure 14
Create
custom
email tem-
plates when
communi-
cating with
customers,
vendors,
and
employees.

Fields of data can be imbedded
in the body of the email

Include Attachments with Email

You can attach documents to transactions when emailing the transaction from within QuickBooks.
See Figures 15 and 16.

➡️ *To learn more about adding attachments, see "Creating an Invoice," p. 353.*

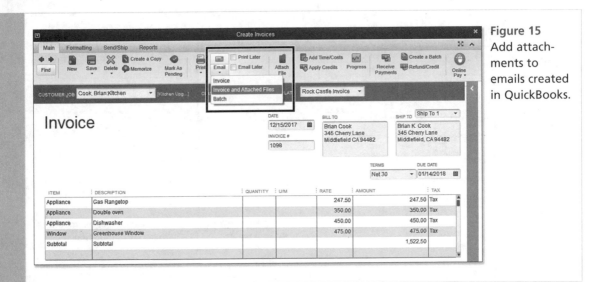

Figure 15
Add attachments to emails created in QuickBooks.

Figure 16
Browse, scan, or select from existing attachments.

More Reports on the Transaction Ribbon

You can work more efficiently with access to more transaction-specific reports (see Figure 17), accessible from the ribbon toolbar on displayed transactions.

Figure 17
The Reports tab on the ribbon toolbar offers a variety of transaction-specific reports.

Print to One Page

When printing a report, users can choose to fit the printed report to a specified number of pages(s) wide and a specified number of pages(s) high. See Figure 18.

Figure 18
Determine both the width and height of a report.

Copy and Paste Line Items on Forms

You can copy and paste transaction line data to another line in both customer and purchase transactions from the Formatting tab on the transaction ribbon toolbar. See Figure 19.

➡ *To learn more about copying and pasting rows of data on invoices, see "Creating Customer Invoices," p. 350.*

Figure 19
Right-click with your cursor on a line, or get access from the ribbon toolbar.

Improved Payroll Center

The new user interface shown in Figure 20, available in the Payroll Center, separates the details for payroll into three important groupings: Pay Employees, Pay Liabilities, and File Forms.

➡ *To learn more about working with the Payroll Center, see "Preparing Payroll Liability Payments," p. 487, and "Tax Forms and Filings," p. 494.*

Figure 20 New Payroll Center tabs make processing and reporting on payroll tasks more efficient.

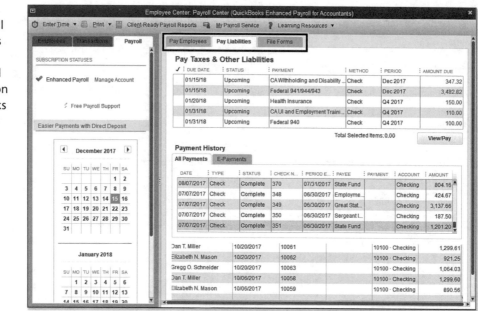

Improved My Company Information

The new My Company information window replaces the formerly titled Company Information window. See Figure 21. In addition to listing your company's address, Federal Identification Number, and other items, the window now displays your connected apps, services, and subscriptions. From this window, you can also view suggested apps, services, and subscriptions, as well as log into your Intuit Account.

➡ *To learn more, see "My Company Information," p. 54.*

Figure 21
Get easy access to subscription applications others recommend in the new My Company window.

Enable or Disable Collections Center

Company Preference settings (Figure 22) permit users to enable or disable the Collections Center. The Collections Center functionality was replaced with the Income Tracker. This capability is useful for those users who prefer to work with the Collections Center in addition to the new Income Tracker. See Figure 23.

Figure 22
QuickBooks offers the option to enable the Collections Center for users who want to continue using it in addition to the Income Tracker.

Figure 23
After enabling the Collections Center, you can access it from the Customer Center.

To learn more, see "Enable the Collections Center," p. 391.

For the Accounting Professional

QuickBooks Accountant 2014 and Enterprise Accountant 14.0 add even more tools and improvements to help you work more efficiently with your clients' data.

Client Collaborator

Client Collaborator is available exclusively with QuickBooks Accountant 2014 PLUS, free for ProAdvisors with paid membership or available for an additional fee. This feature is available with QuickBooks Enterprise Solutions Accountant with a paid Full Service Plan. The software stores online inquiries about specific transactions as displayed in Figure 24. The client needs only to use QuickBooks 2014 desktop software and be invited by the accountant to access the transaction inquiry and provide replies.

To learn more, see "Client and Accountant Collaboration," p. 634.

Figure 24
Accountants can associate questions with specific transactions for the client to reply to.

Improved Batch Enter Transactions

In addition to batch-entering Checks, Credit Card Charges, and Credits, you can now enter vendor bills, vendor bill credits, customer invoices, and customer credit memos in a spreadsheet-like interface. See Figure 25. Alternatively, you can copy and paste more than 1,000 transactions from a spreadsheet and save them at once in QuickBooks.

➡ To learn more, see "Batch Enter Transactions," p. 632.

Figure 25
You can now enter bills, bill credits, invoices, and credit memos in batch.

Improved Client Data Review

Reclassify Transactions now permits reclassifying the Source or From account, including Balance Sheet accounts. See Figure 26. The change can be only between accounts of the same type, such as between one Bank account and another Bank account.

➡️ *Accounting professionals who want to learn more can see "Client Data Review," p. 695.*

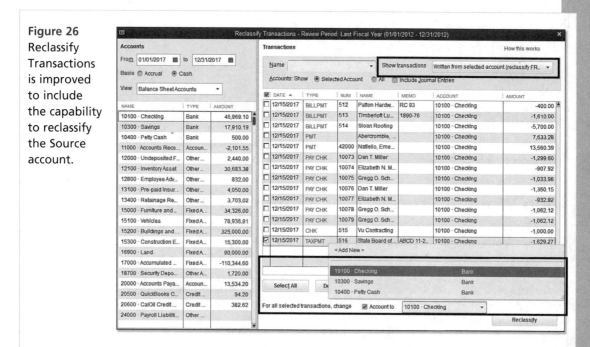

Figure 26
Reclassify Transactions is improved to include the capability to reclassify the Source account.

For QuickBooks Enterprise Users

QuickBooks Enterprise users often push the limits of software because of their transaction volume, number of users, or other complexities. In that regard, QuickBooks Enterprise 14.0 builds on its slate of advanced features with these new additions for 2014.

> 🔍 **Note**
> The remaining features discussed in this section are available only when using the QuickBooks Enterprise software.

Add Sales Rep and Custom Fields to Expense Transactions

Users can optionally add Sales Rep and custom-defined fields to the check, vendor bill, vendor credit, credit card charge, or credit card credit transactions. See Figure 27.

➡️ *To learn more, see "Customize Expense Transactions," p. 786.*

Job Work in Process (WIP) Summary Report

This new report provides much-needed details for any industry that needs to report revenue based on a percentage-of-completion computation for their jobs. See Figure 28.

Rock Castle Construction
Job Work in Progress (WIP) Summary
All Transactions

	Est. Cost	Act. Cost	(%) Complete	Est. Revenue	Earned Revenue	Act. Revenue	($) Diff.
▼ Abercrombie, Kristy							
Remodel Bathroom	3,000.00	5,416.23	100.0%	3,114.00	3,114.00	6,749.50	-3,635.50
Total Abercrombie, Kristy	3,000.00	5,416.23	100.0%	3,114.00	3,114.00	6,749.50	-3,635.50
▼ Cook, Brian							
2nd story addition	18,989.90	15,767.60	83.03%	21,331.50	17,711.54	18,061.20	-349.66
Kitchen	12,185.00	7,390.00	60.65%	13,003.00	7,886.32	12,906.45	-5,020.13
Total Cook, Brian	31,174.90	23,157.60	74.28%	34,334.50	25,503.67	30,967.65	-5,463.98
▼ Ecker Designs							
Office Repairs	5,370.00	2,910.00	54.19%	5,757.50	3,119.99	4,984.50	-1,864.51
Total Ecker Designs	5,370.00	2,910.00	54.19%	5,757.50	3,119.99	4,984.50	-1,864.51
▼ Pretell Real Estate							
75 Sunset Rd.	16,226.00	3,036.00	18.71%	18,409.93	3,444.50	23,583.14	-20,138.64
Total Pretell Real Estate	16,226.00	3,036.00	18.71%	18,409.93	3,444.50	23,583.14	-20,138.64
TOTAL	55,770.90	34,519.83	61.90%	61,615.93	38,140.26	66,284.79	-28,144.53

One industry in particular, the construction industry, uses this type of calculation to determine the amount of revenue to record in their financials at year end.

➡ *To learn more about this report, see "Job Work in Process (WIP) Summary Report," p. 830.*

Committed Costs by Job Report

This report provides a more comprehensive view of a customer or job potential profit or loss. The report includes Estimated Costs minus Actual Costs minus Committed Costs (open monetary value on purchase orders) minus Unpaid Wages to arrive at the Remaining Cost. See Figure 29.

➡ *To learn more about this report, see "Committed Costs by Job Report," p. 831.*

Figure 29
This report includes the open balance on purchase orders and a timesheet payroll estimate.

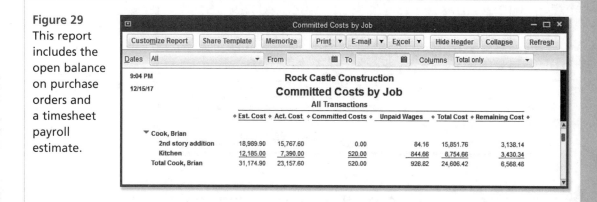

Automatically Build Subassemblies

For some industries, inventory assemblies might have subassemblies as components. To complete the final assembly, QuickBooks must have on hand the required quantity of the subassemblies; see Figure 30. QuickBooks Enterprise improves the process of working with assemblies by allowing users to first have QuickBooks build the subassemblies. In QuickBooks Premier, the other edition of QuickBooks that offers assemblies, users have to know to build the subassemblies first.

➡ *To learn more about working with subassemblies, see "Automatically Build Subassemblies," p. 793.*

Figure 30
When building assemblies, you can opt to use nested assemblies.

Efficiently Replace or Remove Components in Assemblies

QuickBooks Enterprise improves the process of adding or removing components in an assembly. Only in QuickBooks Enterprise can users choose to automatically remove or replace components in multiple assemblies easily. See Figure 31. In QuickBooks Premier, if a component is used in multiple assemblies and needs to be removed or replaced, users have to manually edit each assembly that includes that component.

➡ *To learn more about working with components of assemblies, see "Efficiently Replace or Remove Components in Assemblies," p. 794.*

Figure 31
Substitute
a new com-
ponent or
remove an
existing
component
from multiple
assemblies.

Options for Automatically Calculating the Cost Field in an Assembly Record

Another related assembly improvement included exclusively with QuickBooks Enterprise is the capability to set a default for handling the Cost field in an Assembly type item record. See Figure 32.

➡ *To learn about this feature, see "Options for Automatically Calculating the Cost Field in an Assembly Record," p. 786.*

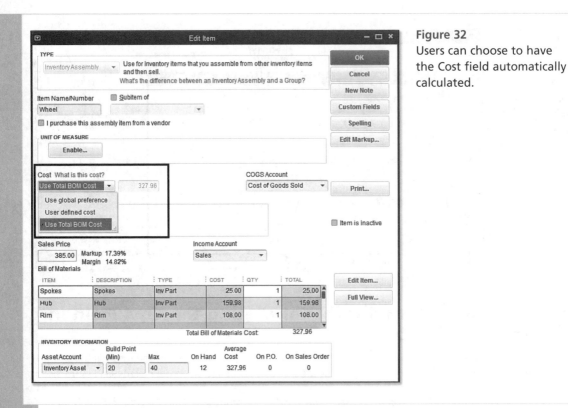

Figure 32
Users can choose to have the Cost field automatically calculated.

Efficiently Edit Cost, Price, Markup, and Margin for Inventory Items

The Inventory Center is available in QuickBooks Premier, Accountant, and QuickBooks Enterprise Solutions. In QuickBooks Enterprise, the Inventory Center includes the capability to edit the cost, sales price, markup, and margin without opening the individual item record. See Figure 33.

➡️ *To learn more, see "Inventory Center," p. 212.*

Figure 33
Conveniently edit fields while viewing inventory details in the Inventory Center.

Create Auto POs Now Suggests a Quantity to Order

The Auto Create Purchase Orders feature available exclusively in QuickBooks Enterprise can help you restock your items in record time. In earlier versions of QuickBooks, you reviewed your inventory reorder reports and then created a single purchase order at a time.

New for QuickBooks Enterprise 14.0, the Auto Create Purchase Orders suggests a quantity to purchase. The amount used for the suggested Quantity factors in the Quantity Available, Quantity on Purchase Orders and then compares this to the Reorder Point, Max value for the item. See Figure 34.

➡ *To learn more about this feature, see "Auto Create Purchase Orders," p. 791.*

Figure 34
Suggested
Qty to Order
brings up
inventory
to the Max
reorder
point.

QuickBooks Enterprise with Advanced Pricing

Exclusively for QuickBooks Enterprise 14.0 is Advanced Pricing. Advanced Pricing is a subscription-based feature that is charged annually and that also requires an active Full Service Plan. The feature replaces the free Price Levels with much more sophisticated automated price settings.

➡️ *To learn more about this new feature, see "QuickBooks Enterprise with Advanced Pricing," p. 826.*

Price Rules

Price Rules let you automate your pricing in QuickBooks; see Figure 35. No more manual updates—you can easily change your sales prices. Using multiple variables, you can set prices for scheduled promotions with future start dates, change the price charged by class (such as by location), extend a price change to certain customer or job types, and set a price to be exclusive of any other specials the customer may qualify for.

Figure 35
Create a variety of
conditions to control
the use of a Price Rule.

Quantity Discounts

Also included with the Advanced Pricing subscription is Quantity Discounts. With Quantity Discounts, you can reward your customers for making bulk purchases.

For example, QuickBooks can charge different prices when a customer buys 10 to 19 items, or 20 to 29 items, or 30 or more items. See Figure 36.

Figure 36
Advanced Pricing (Subscription) includes both Price Rules and Quantity Discount.

GETTING STARTED WITH QUICKBOOKS

This comprehensive reference book offers the reader clear and concise step-by-step written instructions accompanied by detailed illustrations for using QuickBooks Pro, Premier 2014, Premier Accountant 2014, and QuickBooks Enterprise Solutions 14.0. Written for the business owner, accountant, or bookkeeper, *QuickBooks 2014 In Depth* offers readers a complete guide to the software they use every day.

Understanding QuickBooks

The QuickBooks software comes in a version that is just right for your business needs. For more details, you can use your Internet browser to search for "QuickBooks comparison" and select any links that display. Table 1.1 details a few of the differences.

Table 1.1 QuickBooks Software Summary

Software Version	Number of Users	Invoice Customers, Pay Vendor Bills, Prepare Payroll	Industry-Specific Versions	Accountant-Specific Tools and Features
QuickBooks Online Plus	Up to 25			
QuickBooks for Mac	Up to 5	✓		
QuickBooks Pro	Up to 3	✓		
QuickBooks Premier	Up to 5	✓	✓	
QuickBooks Accountant	Up to 5	✓	Can toggle to all industry editions	✓
QuickBooks Enterprise	Up to 30	✓	✓	
QuickBooks Enterprise Accountant	Up to 30	✓	Can toggle to all industry editions	✓

This book does not cover the setup or use of QuickBooks Online or QuickBooks for Mac. The content in this comprehensive guide is for working with QuickBooks Pro, Premier, Accountant, and QuickBooks Enterprise. Most illustrations are from QuickBooks Accountant unless otherwise noted. In some sections, I note when the content or illustrations are from a specific version or industry edition of QuickBooks.

Additionally, this book is a perfect companion to the *QuickBooks Essentials LiveLessons* video training, combining the best of audio learning and book reference functionality. For more information, see the author's website, www.quick-training.com.

The primary purpose of this book is to teach business owners and accounting professionals how to use QuickBooks software quickly and accurately. Most chapters also include troubleshooting content that sets this book apart from other how-to books. This chapter helps you get started quickly and provides you with quick steps to begin using your QuickBooks software. If you would like to practice what you are learning, open one of the sample files installed with your QuickBooks software. I teach you how to do that first!

Over the years, I have helped hundreds of businesses troubleshoot problems with getting the proper financial and management information out of their QuickBooks data. I have found that improper setup of the data file is most often the primary cause of problems, second only to judgment errors in posting transactions to the incorrect account.

> **⚠ caution**
>
> It is not my intention to offer you tax advice; I make comments throughout the text encouraging you to consult your accounting or tax professional before making any data corrections that might have a significant impact on a company's financials.

Using QuickBooks Sample Data

You can open one of the sample data files installed automatically with your QuickBooks software and begin trying what this book shows you. With this data, you can test creating transactions, review how lists are set up, and process reports with ready-made data.

The number and type of sample data files installed differs, depending on the version of QuickBooks you purchased.

To open a sample file with sample data, follow these steps:

1. Launch QuickBooks from the icon on your desktop.

2. From the menu bar, select **File, Close Company.** The No Company Open dialog box displays.

3. Click the Open a Sample File button and choose a sample file from the drop-down list, as Figure 1.1 shows.

> ## ⚡ caution
>
> Do not enter your own busi-ness data into the supplied sample files; use them only for testing how to create transactions and reviewing reports populated with the sample data. Additionally, any customizing that you do with the sample data is not saved to other files, including your own business files.

Figure 1.1
Practicing with sample data can help you feel more confident about using QuickBooks.

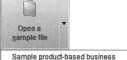

After creating your own data file, the next time you launch QuickBooks, your file (not the sample file) defaults as the file that QuickBooks opens.

If you want to quickly access previously opened QuickBooks files, including the sample file, from the menu bar, select **File, Open Previous Company**. QuickBooks displays a list of previous files to choose from.

If you do not see other files listed, you might need to change the number of files displayed on this list. To do so, first open any data file. Then, on the menu bar, select **File, Open Previous Company, Set Number of Previous Companies**, and enter a number between 1 and 20. The No Company Open dialog box displays the most recent files you have opened with the software.

> ## 🔍 note
>
> This book uses the Sample product-based business file included automatically when you install QuickBooks on the computer. The company name associated with this fictitious data file is Sample Rock Castle Construction. The images and exercises in the book are from this sample file, but you can read along and practice with any of the installed sample files.

➡ *For more information, see "Selecting a Company File to Open," p. 83.*

Click here to edit the list of company files displayed

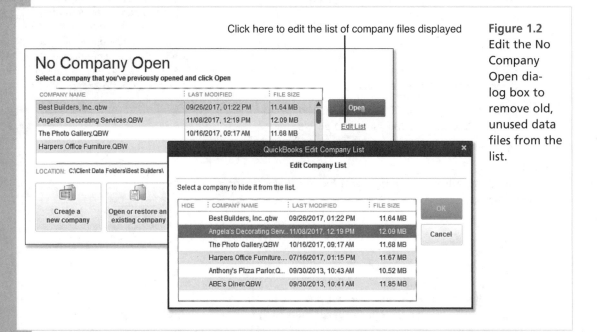

Figure 1.2
Edit the No Company Open dialog box to remove old, unused data files from the list.

Creating a New QuickBooks File

If you are new to QuickBooks, the first task is to create a data file. In the No Company Open dialog box, click the Create a New Company button. The QuickBooks Setup dialog box displays the following three options if you are using QuickBooks Pro, Premier (non-accountant), or Enterprise (non-accountant):

- **Express Start**—Create a file quickly with the least amount of initial setup time.

- **Advanced Setup**—Formerly called EasyStep Interview. Answer a series of questions to help you set up your new file. If you are using QuickBooks Accountant 2014, you will have additional methods, as this section details.

- **Other Options**—Open an Existing File, Convert Quicken Data, Convert from Other Accounting Software Data, or Set Up On Behalf of Someone Else.

➡ *To learn more about other options your accounting professional might have with QuickBooks Accountant 2014, see "Creating a New File from an Existing Company File," p. 49.*

Choose from one of the three options that best suits your needs; the following sections detail each one.

➡ *If instead of creating a new QuickBooks file you are upgrading your existing file, you can learn more about this process in "Upgrading Your QuickBooks Version," p. 651.*

Express Start

QuickBooks users have multiple ways of getting their first Quickbooks data file created. This section details working with the Express Start method, the easiest and quickest way to get started.

With Express Start, you can use your new file in just three easy steps (outlined in the following sections). Express Start guides you through the basics of entering your company information, contact information, and—optionally—contacts, products, services, and bank accounts. From the menu bar, select **File, Create a New Company**, and then click the Express Start button in the QuickBooks Setup dialog box. Alternatively, select the **Create a New Company** button in the No Company Open dialog box and then click the Express Start button.

> **note**
>
> Are you working with QuickBooks Accountant 2014 or QuickBooks Enterprise Accountant 14.0? You have the previous options for creating a new file, plus the added method of creating a new company from an existing company file.
>
> What information is copied from the existing company file to the new file? Sales tax items, chart of accounts (with the exception of bank or credit card accounts), and most preferences are copied from the existing file.
>
> What information from the existing file is not copied to the new file? Information not copied includes memorized reports that contain data file–specific filters, memorized transactions, leads, customers, vendors, other names, and employees.

Step 1—Tell Us

Enter the following information about your business (see Figure 1.3):

1. **Company Name**—This is the name that will be assigned to the file on your computer. It does not have to be your legal name.

2. **Industry**—QuickBooks uses this to provide you with a sample chart of accounts and, for some industries, a sampling of ready-made items that are used throughout QuickBooks when invoicing customers and buying services or products from vendors. Click Help Me Choose to see the choices available for Industry selections.

3. **Company Type**—QuickBooks uses this to create specific equity accounts used primarily in tax preparation. Click Help Me Choose to see the choices available for Company Type.

4. **Tax ID#**—QuickBooks uses this information when processing payroll using one of Intuit's payroll subscription offerings.

5. **Do You Have Employees?**—Select **Yes** or **No** or **No, but I Might in the Future**.

When finished, click Continue to advance to the next step in the setup.

Tell us about your business

Enter the essentials so we can create a company file that's just right for your business.

1 **Tell us** — 2 **Email address** — 3 **Contact info** → Start working

* Company Name	Best Builders, Inc.
	We'll use this on your invoices and reports, and to name your company file.
* Industry	Construction General Contractor Help me choose
	We'll use this to create accounts common for your industry.
* Company Type	S Corporation ▼ Help me choose
	We'll use this to select the right tax settings for your business.
Tax ID #	12-3456789 ❓
	We'll use this on your tax forms.

* Required

Need help? Give us a call

[Back] [Continue]

Figure 1.3
With Express Start, you can use your file in no time!

🔍 note

Should you need to change the company name or any of the legal information you entered in the Express Start, from the menu bar, select, **Company**, **My Company**. To edit or add additional information click the edit icon in the top right of the My Company dialog box.

You will be able to add or edit:

- Contact Information
- Legal Information
- Company Identification
- Report Information
- Payroll Tax Form Information
- Ship To Address
- Add Attachments

In addition, from the My Company dialog box you can view your connected applications and services, as well as see recommended applications and services.

Step 2—Contact Info

Complete the following fields of information on the Contact Info dialog box that is displayed in Figure 1.4:

1. Enter the legal name of the business. This will be used in payroll filings.

2. Enter other contact information. The zip code field and phone number field are required when setting up the file. This information is used if you choose to set up a QuickBooks Payments account, enabling you to receive payments online from your customers. More information is sent to the email address you provide in this dialog box.

3. You can choose to select the **Preview Your Settings** button. Click each of the displayed tabs to see the Features Selected, Chart of Accounts, and Company File Location QuickBooks suggests for you, based on your answers in step 1. If you need to change the location where your QuickBooks data file will be stored, on the Company File Location tab, click the Change Location button.

   Don't worry too much about the other settings just yet; you can easily modify them later in your file, and later chapters of the book address them.

4. Click OK to close the Preview Your Settings dialog box.

5. After completing the required fields, click the Create Company File button to continue to the next step. QuickBooks now creates your file and saves it on your hard drive, or to a default location or the specific location you selected in step 3. Optionally, click the Back button to review or change previous settings.

Figure 1.4
Complete the setup by entering your business contact information.

Enter your business contact information

Once you enter your contact information, you're ready to create your company file.

❶ —— ❷ —— ❸ ——▶ Start working
Tell us   Email address   Contact info

Legal Name	Best Builders, Inc. ❓
Address	123 Main Street
City	Anytown
State	TX ▼ * ZIP 11111
Country	U.S. ▼
* Phone	555-111-2222
Email	jsmith@bestbuildersinc.com
Website	www.bestbuildersinc.com

Enter basic contact information so you can instantly print and email invoices and other forms.

This will also be used to set up your QuickBooks Payments account. We will send you an email with additional details, including how to enable your account.

We value your privacy and security. This information is stored safely on Intuit servers.

* Required

[Back]   [Preview Your Settings]   [**Create Company File**]

Step 3—Add Info

Continue with the QuickBooks Setup by adding the people you do business with, your products and services, and your bank accounts to your new data file.

If you want to skip these steps, on the bottom of the displayed dialog box (see Figure 1.5), click the Start Working button to launch the QuickBooks Home page.

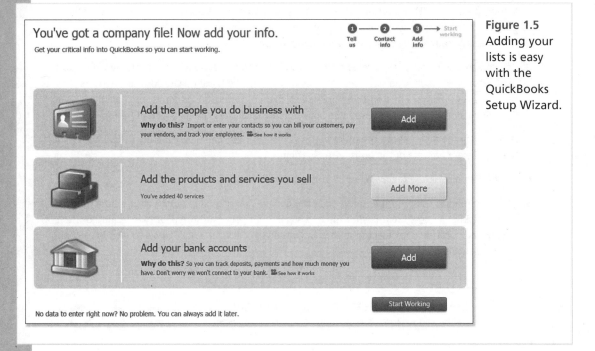

Figure 1.5 Adding your lists is easy with the QuickBooks Setup Wizard.

Adding People You Do Business With Now is the perfect time to add the people you do business with to your newly created file. This list includes customers, vendors, and employees. Adding contacts is a three-step process: Choose how to add contacts, select who to add, and review and finish. Later, to learn more about these lists, see Chapter 7, "Setting Up Vendors," and Chapter 9, "Setting Up Customers."

To add contacts using the QuickBooks Setup Wizard, follow these steps:

1. In the Add the People You Do Business With box (or click Add More if you've already entered some names), click the Add button to import or enter the names of people you do business with.

2. If you selected the Add option, you can choose how to add from these choices:

   ■ **Import from Outlook, Yahoo!, or Gmail Email**—Follow the instructions for importing from one of the listed email providers. You can specify which contacts you want imported into QuickBooks. For Outlook, if you have more than one address book, you can choose which one to use for the import. For other email providers, you might receive an email message that you have shared your address book with QuickBooks.

■ **Paste from Excel or Enter Manually**—Your imported contacts display in the spreadsheet-like form in Figure 1.6. Be sure to scroll to the right to see additional data fields. You can also copy and paste from Excel or manually enter contacts directly in the form before importing.

Figure 1.6
Adding the people you do business with is easy when getting started with QuickBooks.

Add the people you do business with							Choose how to add	② Select who to add	Review and finish		

Enter your contacts below and mark each one as a customer, vendor, or employee. You can save time by pasting from Excel. Don't worry about getting everything perfectly, we'll let you know if you need to fix anything. How does this work?

Skip	Customer	Vendor	Employee	Name	Company Name	First Name	Last Name	Email	Phone	Alt Phone	Fax
Select all	Select all	Select all	Select all								
○	○	●	○	ABC Supplier	ABC Supplier	Susan	James	sj@abcsupplier.com	555-222-333	555-666-5555	
○	●	○	○	Shores Construction							
●	○	○	○								

3. If you selected **Add More**, you return to the Add the People You Do Business With dialog box, with the same choices as in step 2.

4. After importing or entering manually, click Continue to review and finish. QuickBooks Setup checks your list for duplicate names or emails. If any duplicates are detected, you need to change the Name field (not the Company Name field) so that no duplicates are imported.

5. Click the Fix button to have QuickBooks display any contacts that have duplicate names. Change the Name field to make each unique.

6. Click Continue after fixing. QuickBooks shows how many contacts are ready to be added and how many may need to be fixed. Follow step 5 again, if needed.

7. Click Continue. QuickBooks returns to the dialog box for you to add more contacts or to add products, services, or bank accounts.

Adding the Products and Services You Sell You can add the products and services you sell in just a few steps. If your business tracks inventory, you cannot enter your inventory items here.

To add non-inventory products and services, follow these steps:

1. In the Add the Products and Services You Sell section, click Add (or click Add More, if you've already entered some items).

2. Choose an item type and click the Continue button. Non-inventory types can be changed to inventory later. Item type options include the following:

   ■ **Service**—Work you perform, such as an hour of labor

   ■ **Non-inventory part**—Products you sell but do not want to track as inventory

> **⚠ caution**
>
> If you choose, you can skip these steps of adding the people you do business with. QuickBooks makes it easy to later add or edit the information imported into your company data.

> **⊙ tip**
>
> QuickBooks does not allow you to have duplicate entries in the Name field across the various lists. For example, an employee name cannot be the same as a vendor name. An easy fix for this is to add a *V* to the end of the Name field for the vendor listing who is also included on the employee list.

3. Copy and paste from a list you already have in Excel, or manually enter the item details, including the name, description,
price, and manufacturer's part number. Click Continue.

4. QuickBooks checks for any item duplicates or to see if any items
to be imported are already in your QuickBooks file. If necessary,
click Fix. To add the items to your file, click Continue.

To learn more about setting up inventory, see Chapter 5, "Setting
Up Inventory."

Adding Bank Accounts In the Add Your Bank Accounts panel,
click Add to create accounts to track deposits, payments, and
how much money you have. Type the Account Name (required),
such as **Checking** or **Savings**, and optional Account number. You
can choose to enter your opening balance here or wait until you
have reviewed the information in Chapter 3, p. 87. If you choose
to enter your opening balance, QuickBooks offsets the entry to
the Opening Balance Equity account. Ask your accountant to help
with this entry when it is time for your tax preparation.

To add your bank accounts into your new QuickBooks file, follow
these steps:

1. In the Add Your Bank Accounts dialog box (or the Add More
dialog box, if you've already entered an account), click the
Add button.

2. Type your Account Name, Account Number (optional), Opening
Balance (optional), and Opening Balance Date (optional).

3. Click Continue. QuickBooks displays information about ordering
checks from Intuit. Select your reminder preference and click
Continue. QuickBooks adds the bank account to your data file.

You are now ready to begin working with your QuickBooks file.
Click the Start Working button. The Quick Start Center dialog box
displays with useful links to learn how to track money in and out
using QuickBooks. Click the X in the top-right corner to close this
dialog box.

Remember, everything you have entered so far is completely
modifiable in your newly created QuickBooks file.

If you used the instructions in this section, you can now skip
to the section titled "Setting Up Users and Permissions" in this
chapter. Otherwise, you should review another method for getting started using the Advanced Setup or Detailed Start discussed
in the next section.

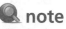 **note**

Resist the temptation to click
the Enter Opening Balances
when using this startup method.
Balances entered in this way
are listed as a single amount
due, not as individual customer invoices or vendor bill
transactions. See Chapter 3,
"Accounting 101," for more
detailed information on properly setting up these beginning
balances.

---

note

If you selected one of the available industry types (as in Figure
1.3), your file might already
contain industry-related items.
You can find more information about working with items
in Chapter 4, "Understanding
QuickBooks Lists," p. 108.

---

tip

The bank account informa-
tion you enter is necessary
for you to properly reconcile your QuickBooks bank
account. For example, if you
are going to use 10/1/17 as
your new start date, you
would enter your opening
balance, which would be the
9/30/17 statement ending
balance *not including* any
uncleared checks or deposits;
you will enter these individually later. For the opening
balance date, you would use
9/30/17 in this example.

Advanced Setup or Detailed Start—Formerly the EasyStep Interview

For help in creating a new file, earlier editions of QuickBooks did not have the Express Start option, but instead offered the QuickBooks EasyStep Interview. You can access it now from Advanced Setup in QuickBooks 2014, or from Detailed Start when using QuickBooks Accountant 2014.

If you select the **Advanced Setup** or **Detailed Start** option, QuickBooks provides a series of question-and-answer-type choices to help you properly set up your data file and certain default features.

Information to Collect

Having the following information on hand before starting the Advanced Setup or Detailed Start can help when entering the details:

- **Company Name**—This should be the company name or a name that best describes the business. By default, this is the filename given to the data file (.QBW extension) on your computer.

- **Legal Name**—The legal name displays on certain reports and federal tax forms.

- **Tax ID**—Although this ID is not required to begin using QuickBooks, it is required if you want to sign up for one of the QuickBooks payroll services or use QuickBooks to print 1099s.

- **Remaining Information**—This includes a phone number, email address, website, and so on (see Figure 1.7). You can optionally add this information in QuickBooks, such as on a customer invoice.

Figure 1.7
Selecting
Advanced
Setup or
Detailed
Start provides
access to
the EasyStep
Interview.

If you need to leave the EasyStep Interview at any time after saving the file, QuickBooks returns to the point where you left off when you open the data file again.

The EasyStep Interview now prompts you for certain information based on what industry you selected. Your answers to the remaining questions make certain features in QuickBooks the default. The purpose of this chapter is not to define each of these choices; most are self-explanatory or are included in various chapters in this book. However, discussing the effect of several important choices is useful at this time.

Using Advanced Setup or Detailed Start

You might prefer to have a bit more control of the setup process up front. This is exactly what the Advanced Setup (also known as the EasyStep Interview) offers.

To create a new file using Advanced Setup, from the menu bar, click File, Create a New Company; then, in the QuickBooks Setup dialog box, click the Advanced Setup button. Alternatively, in the No Company Open dialog box, click the Create a New Company button, and then click the Advanced Setup button.

You then enter the following information when creating the new data file:

- **Enter Your Company Information**—Enter your Company Name, Legal Name, Tax ID, and other information that can be included on customer invoices and other forms within QuickBooks. Click Next.

- **Select Your Industry**—QuickBooks can help you get started quickly by providing basic information for particular industries (see Figure 1.8). Pick an industry that closely matches your own. Click Next.

- **How Is Your Company Organized?**—Select the legal organization your company selected when obtaining your Federal Identification Number. This choice creates unique Equity accounts to match your legal selection. Click Next.

- **Select the First Month of Your Fiscal Year**—Select the month your fiscal year starts in. Some reports display the correct fiscal year dates by default when you select this option. Click Next.

> **note**
>
> Do not worry if you cannot complete the entire set of questions at one time. After QuickBooks creates the file, you can click the Leave button. QuickBooks saves your choices, and when you reopen QuickBooks, you return to where you left off.

- **Set Up Your Administrator Password**—Setting up an administrator password is recommended. If you do not set one during the EasyStep Interview, you can open a QuickBooks file with the default username of Admin and leave the password blank. Using a blank password is fine during the initial setup, but you should put more security in place after you enter sensitive information. You can also set up or change this password later. Click Next, and QuickBooks creates your company file.

- **Create Your Company File**—QuickBooks requires that you decide where to store the company data file and provide a name for the file. Click Next. Browse to select a location to store your file, or accept the default location and name QuickBooks suggests. Click Save. QuickBooks displays a progressive message that your file is being created.

Figure 1.8
QuickBooks includes customized settings for your specific industry.

■ **Customizing QuickBooks for Your Business**—After reading the information, click Next.

■ **What Do You Sell?**—Choose from Services, Products, or Both Services and Products. This preference affects the type of default invoice form that is selected when you begin using QuickBooks. Click Next.

■ **Do You Charge Sales Tax?**—Specify whether you want to charge sales tax, choosing from the Yes or No option button. (You can change this later, if necessary.) Click Next.

> **note**
>
> Not certain which choice to make when completing the Advanced Setup (EasyStep Interview)? No worries— QuickBooks selects the recommended option based on the industry you selected in step 2.

■ **Do You Want to Create Estimates in QuickBooks?**—Select either the **Yes** or **No** option button. If you provide a proposal to your clients or multiple proposals, you will want to enable this feature. Click Next.

■ **Tracking Customer Orders in QuickBooks**—Choose either the Yes or No options. (This feature is available only in QuickBooks Premier, Accountant, or QuickBooks Enterprise Solutions.) Click Next.

➡ *For more information, see "Using QuickBooks Sales Orders," p. 349.*

■ **Using Statements in QuickBooks**—Choose between Yes or No. This option enables you to print past-due statements for your customers. Click Next.

- **Using Invoices in QuickBooks and Using Progress Invoicing in QuickBooks**—Select **Yes** or **No**. Selecting Yes enables the use of customer invoices. In selected industries, you might also be prompted to enable progress invoicing. Progress invoicing is "milestone billing" (when you invoice a customer progressively during a job).

- **Managing Bills You Owe**—Choosing Yes enables the capability for you to enter vendor bills and pay those bills at a later date. Click Next.

   Working with vendors is discussed in Chapter 7, p. 232.

- **Tracking Inventory in QuickBooks**—Select either **Yes** or **No** to enable this feature. Remember, you can later enable these features in Preferences. Click Next.

   To learn more about inventory, see Chapter 5, "Setting Up Inventory," p. 151, and Chapter 6, "Managing Inventory," p. 205.

- **Tracking Time in QuickBooks**—Tracking time enables you to bill customers for time, analyze time on projects, and pay salary or hourly employees or hourly paid vendors. Select either **Yes** or **No**. Click Next.

- **Do You Have Employees?**—Choose either W-2 employees or 1099 contractors. If you selected Yes to W-2 employees, QuickBooks creates the needed chart of accounts items. You can modify this setting later. Click Next.

- **Using Accounts in QuickBooks**—Click the link "Why Is the Chart of Accounts Important?" to learn more about this list in QuickBooks. Click Next.

   This Chart of Accounts list is also discussed in Chapter 4, "Understanding QuickBooks Lists," p. 107

- **Select a Date to Start Tracking Your Finances**—Choose from Beginning of This Fiscal Year: 01/01/2016 (for example) or Use Today's Date or The First Day of the Quarter or Month. These are examples of potential start dates.

  - You start using QuickBooks immediately upon starting your business, with no prior expenses or income. This date is the easiest one to work with because you have no historical balances or transactions to consider. You begin by paying vendors and invoicing customers. Everything else falls into place.

  - You can start at the beginning of a calendar year, such as January 1, 20xx. This choice is common when the decision to begin using QuickBooks is at the end of a year or is not far into the New Year. Again, if the company has previously had business transactions, you will have beginning balances to enter.

> **tip**
>
> If you selected the incorrect first month of your fiscal year during the EasyStep Interview, you can easily change it from the menu bar by selecting **Company, My Company**. Click the edit icon and chose Report Information on the right.
>
> Changing this month does not affect individual transactions, but it does ensure that the reports that are based on a fiscal year are correct.

➡️ *To learn more, see "Setting Up a QuickBooks Data File for Accrual or Cash Basis Reporting," p. 94.*

- You can start at the beginning of your fiscal year (for companies whose tax year does not coincide with the calendar year).

  - You can begin on the first day of a month during the current calendar or fiscal year. Click Next when you're finished with this selection.

- **Review Income and Expense Accounts**—You have the opportunity to include or exclude certain default charts of account from your new data file. Click Next.

- **Congratulations**—You are finished with the Advanced (or Detailed) Setup. Click Go to Setup.

- **You've Got a Company File!**—You can now add contacts, products, services, and bank accounts, as discussed in the "Express Start" section, earlier in this chapter.

Creating a New File from an Existing Company File

Available with QuickBooks Accountant and QuickBooks Enterprise Solutions Accountant is the option to use an existing QuickBooks data file to create a new data file, as Figure 1.9 shows. Your original file remains unchanged in the process.

Figure 1.9
The Accountant version permits creating a new QuickBooks file from an existing QuickBooks file.

> **Create From Existing File** ✕
>
> Quickly create a new company file by copying the preferences and key lists like the chart of accounts from an existing company. All you need to do is...
>
> 1. Select a company to copy from   What data gets copied?
>
> C:\Client Data Folders\Best Builders\Best Builders, Inc..qbw   Browse...
>
> 2. Enter a name for the new company
>
> Shores Remodely Services, Inc.
>
> Create Company   Cancel

To create a new file from an existing file, follow these steps:

1. From the QuickBooks Setup dialog box, click the Create button. The Create from Existing File dialog displays.

2. By default, the currently opened company is selected as the file to be copied from. To select a different QuickBooks file, click the Browse button.

> 🔍 **note**
> The capability to create a new file from an existing file referenced in step 1 is available only if you are creating a new file from the Accountant 2013 or Enterprise Solutions Accountant 13.0 software or newer.

3. Type a **Name** for the new company file.

4. Click Create Company.

5. Accept the default filename and location for saving your new file, or modify as needed.

6. Click Save.

Using the Create from Existing Company File process, QuickBooks copies the following information from one file to another:

- **Preferences**—Not including those for bank or credit card accounts.

- **Items List**—Only sales tax items—no products or services.

- **Memorized Reports**—Only those that do not filter for specific accounts, customers or jobs, vendors, items, or employees.

- **Type of Tax Form**—Useful if you are going to integrate with tax preparation software.

- **Chart of Accounts**—No bank accounts copied.

If you find that you wanted more details copied from the original file, or you wanted to remove a specific year's transactions, ask your accounting professional to use QuickBooks Accountant 2014 software and provide you with a newly created Condensed Data file.

Hopefully, you found one of the three options best for your needs in starting your new QuickBooks file. The next section in this chapter covers converting other accounting software to a QuickBooks file.

> **tip**
>
> Not using the Accountant version of QuickBooks software? Or would you like to be able to copy the products and services from one file to another? Consider using the IIF (Intuit Interchange Format) export. From the menu bar, select **File, Utilities, Export, Lists to IIF Files**.
>
> With this option, you can select a specific list (not transactions) that you want to import into another QuickBooks file.

Converting from Other Accounting Software

QuickBooks has automated the process of converting files from other financial software into QuickBooks files. Other programs you can convert from include the following:

- Quicken

- Peachtree by Sage (recently renamed Sage 50)

- Microsoft Small Business Accounting

- Microsoft Office Accounting

This section provides specific details about how QuickBooks handles the conversions and what you need to consider when making the choice to convert existing data from one of the listed financial software programs to a QuickBooks data file.

Before converting your company data to QuickBooks, make sure you have QuickBooks installed and registered/licensed and updated to the latest release.

➡ *For more information, see "Managing Your QuickBooks Database," p. 643.*

Even with the automation of the process, consider finding a QuickBooks Certified ProAdvisor in your area to assist with the conversion. From the Help menu in QuickBooks, select **Find a Local QuickBooks Expert**.

Converting from Quicken to QuickBooks

To begin the conversion from Quicken, open QuickBooks and, from the menu bar, select **File**, **New Company**. Then from the Other Options drop-down list in the QuickBooks Setup dialog box, select **Convert Quicken Data**. The Conversion tool copies your Quicken data to a new QuickBooks file, leaving your original Quicken data file unchanged.

Table 1.2 shows how the Quicken accounts are converted into QuickBooks accounts.

Table 1.2   Quicken Account Conversion

This Type of Account in Quicken:	Becomes This Type of Account in QuickBooks:
Checking	Bank
Credit Card	Credit Card
Asset	Other Current Asset
Liability	Other Current Liability
Investment	Other Current Asset

Because QuickBooks does not offer the Investment tracking feature that is in Quicken, you can choose whether to include or exclude the value of your investments in the resulting QuickBooks balance sheet. If you choose to include them, QuickBooks converts the investment accounts into the Other Current Asset chart of account type.

If you choose to exclude the investments, you are given the opportunity to delete the accounts before converting to QuickBooks. Any transfers that were recorded to or from the deleted accounts are recorded to your Opening Balance Equity account. This is in keeping with the "debits equal credits" accounting that goes on behind the scenes in QuickBooks.

During the conversion process, QuickBooks asks whether a Quicken Accounts Receivable account with customer payments exists. If you click Yes, the QuickBooks Conversion tool asks you to identify your Quicken Accounts Receivable account. QuickBooks then begins converting the Quicken transactions to QuickBooks Accounts Receivable transactions. This process can take several minutes.

During the conversion:

- QuickBooks creates an Opening Balance Equity account to compensate for deleted Quicken accounts.

- Memorized Invoices in Quicken might need to be reviewed, making sure the items memorized in Quicken remain on the invoice in QuickBooks.

- Duplicate check, invoice, and credit memo numbers are stored in a QBwin.log for review. You learn more about this log in Chapter 17, "Managing Your QuickBooks Database," p. 643.

- Every payee name in Quicken must be on a QuickBooks list.

After you click OK to change the name type, you cannot undo the change. If you are not sure what list the payee belongs to, leave it as an Other Name. Because QuickBooks cannot determine which list an item belongs to, the conversion places all items on the Other Names list (see Figure 1.10).

From the menu bar, select **Lists**, **Other Names List** to open the Other Name List dialog box. Right-click this dialog box and then select **Change Other Name Types** for a one-time option to change the payee from an Other Name list item to a vendor, employee, or customer. If you do not need to use a name on a vendor transaction or customer form, you can leave the name on the Other Names list.

NAME	CUSTO...	VENDOR	EMPLO...	OTHER NA...
Annual Depreciation				✔
ATM Withdrawal				✔
Bad Check Charges				✔
Baxter, Gregory		✔		
Deposit				✔
Opening Bal Adj to Retain Earnings				✔
Tom Ferguson			✔	
Transfer from Savings				✔
Transfer to Savings				✔

Figure 1.10
After converting from Quicken, you need to reassign most of the names on the Other Names list to the Customer, Vendor, or Employee lists.

Converting from Peachtree, Small Business Accounting, or Office Accounting to QuickBooks

Just as in the Quicken conversion, QuickBooks can convert your Peachtree/Sage 50, Small Business Accounting, or Office Accounting data to QuickBooks data directly from the Options drop-down menu on the QuickBooks Setup dialog box. The conversion process leaves your original Peachtree/Sage 50, Small Business Accounting, or Office Accounting data untouched.

To download the free conversion tool, follow these steps:

1. From the menu bar, select **File**, **New Company** or, alternatively, in the No Company Open dialog box, click the Create a New Company button. The QuickBooks Setup dialog box displays.

2. From the Other Options drop-down list, select **Convert Other Accounting Software Data**; you need an Internet connection to complete this step.

3. Follow the helpful links to download the free conversion tool or to read the Conversion Tool FAQs document.

The free downloadable tool converts Peachtree/Sage 50 (2001–2011), Microsoft Small Business Accounting, or Office Accounting data. You can use the tool to convert multiple company files from any of the named software.

The technical whitepaper available when downloading the free conversion tool is outdated as of this writing, but it still provides useful information about the conversion details.

In the conversion process, you can select the specific Peachtree/Sage 50, Microsoft Small Business Accounting, Microsoft Office Accounting, or Office Accounting Express file and the QuickBooks product version to which you will be converting it. Additionally, you can specify the conversion of lists and transactions (including historical transactions) or lists only. You also choose a conversion date; any transactions dated after this date will not be converted.

Because of the differences between the two products, you also have a choice to identify customers and vendors in QuickBooks with the name of the Peachtree/Sage 50, Microsoft Small Business Accounting, Microsoft Office Accounting, or Microsoft Office Express ID value. You must choose to use the name or the ID value in QuickBooks, so it's best to make this decision before performing the conversion.

Key lists that are converted include the following:

- Chart of accounts
- Customer/prospects
- Jobs
- Employees/sales reps
- Vendors
- Inventory item
- Custom fields
- Balance information

Open transactions include the following:

- Open invoices
- Open vendor bills

Customer transactions include the following:

- Estimates
- Sales orders

- Invoices

- Payment receipts

- Deposits

- Credit memos

Vendor transactions include the following:

- Purchase orders

- Bills

- Bill payments

- Checks

- Bill credits

My Company Information

The My Company dialog (see Figure 1.11) is new and improves on the information that was stored with previous versions of QuickBooks. From the menu bar, select **Company**, **My Company**. From the My Company dialog you can:

- View your QuickBooks production information, including your license information, product #, no. of users and registration.

- View and edit your company name and address including:

  - **Contact Information**—can be added to reports and forms like a customer invoice or purchase order

  - **Legal Information**—included in QuickBooks prepared legal forms

  - **Company Identification**—your Federal Employer Identification No. or Social Security number used on payroll forms

  - **Report Information**—selecting your Fiscal Year and Tax Year and Income Tax Form Used

  - **Payroll Tax Form Information**—contact name and other details used on payroll forms prepared by QuickBooks

- Manage Your Apps, Services & Subscriptions

- View Apps, Services & Subscriptions Recommended For You

- Log into your Intuit Account to manage your applications and services

Click to edit the information

Figure 1.11
View and edit company information in the My Company dialog.

Setting Up Users and Permissions

QuickBooks always creates a default user with the username Admin. The Admin user has full rights to all settings and preferences in QuickBooks. If your company is going to have multiple users accessing the QuickBooks data file, create a unique user login for each person and assign specific permissions, if needed. With unique usernames for each person, QuickBooks will be able to tell you who entered, modified, or deleted a transaction on the Audit Trail report.

Enable multiuser access if you want to have two or more users access your QuickBooks files simultaneously.

➡ *For more information, see "Changing to Multiuser Access," p. 648.*

> **note**
>
> Table 1.1 listed the number of users who can work in a company file at the same time, based on the version of the software that you have. If you need to buy additional licenses from the menu bar, choose Help, Manage My License, Buy Additional User License.

External Accountant

Business owners who plan to share data with their accountant at tax time or for other purposes should create a unique user for their accountant. The External Accountant user type has all the controls of the Admin, except that the accountant cannot do the following:

- Add, delete, modify, or view sensitive customer credit card details

- Add, delete, or modify other QuickBooks user settings

To create a user login for your accountant, follow these steps:

1. From the menu bar, select **Company**, **Set Up Users and Passwords**, **Set Up Users**.

2. In the User List dialog box, click the Add User button.

3. Enter a User Name and Password (optional but recommended) and then enter the password again to confirm.

4. If you need to add licenses to your QuickBooks file, click the Explain link for more information about Intuit's licensing policy.

5. Click the Next button. If you didn't enter a password in step 3, QuickBooks opens the No Password Entered dialog box. Click Yes to create a password or No to skip this step.

6. Select the **External Accountant** option button, shown in Figure 1.12, and click Next to continue.

7. In the Warning dialog box, click Yes to confirm you want to give the user access to all areas of QuickBooks except credit card information.

8. Click Finish. If a Warning dialog box opens, click OK to confirm that you understand that the Admin user is being assigned to integrated applications.

9. Click Close to close the User List dialog box.

 tip

If you are an accounting professional using QuickBooks Accountant 2014, you can use QuickBooks File Manager 2014 to store your client's assigned username and password for you. When you open the client's file from within File Manager, QuickBooks automatically logs you in, bypassing the username and password dialog box. This works with QuickBooks Pro, Premier, or Enterprise 2011 or newer files.

To log in to the file as the new External Accountant user, from the menu bar, select **File**, **Close Company/Logoff**. From the No Company Open dialog box, select the file from the list. Click Open and enter the username and password.

Figure 1.12
You can create an
External Accountant
user for your account-
ing professional that
limits access to sensitive
customer information.

Other QuickBooks Users

Setting up users with permissions is recommended when you have multiple users working in the same QuickBooks file. Transactions are assigned to users, and many changes to the file are also tracked to the user who logged in to the file.

To create a user login and set permissions for additional users, follow these steps:

1. From the menu bar, select **Company**, **Set Up Users and Passwords**, **Set Up Users**.

2. From the User List dialog box, select **Add User**.

3. Enter a User Name and Password (optional but recommended) and enter the password again to confirm.

4. If you need to add licenses to your QuickBooks file, click the Explain link.

5. If you didn't enter a password, click Yes to create a password or No to skip this step.

6. Select the access option:

   - **All Areas**—Provides access to all areas of QuickBooks except those that require Admin access.

   - **Selected Areas**—Enables you to choose the options for access to each sensitive area of your QuickBooks data.

7. You now work through nine permission screens. On the 10th screen (see Figure 1.13), you can review the permission settings. Each dialog box offers details about the access levels, and most include some or all of the following permission levels:

- No Access

- Full Access

- Selective Access—Includes all or some of these options:

  - Create transactions only

  - Create and print transactions

  - Create transactions and create reports

Figure 1.13
You can review a summary of the access rights assigned to a QuickBooks user.

If you are uncertain about the limitations of a permission setting in QuickBooks Pro or Premier, I recommend that you set it for the Create Only option, the highest level of security. Then log in as that new user and attempt to access an area the employee will work in or an area an employee shouldn't be in, to determine whether the permissions assigned provide the controls you need. QuickBooks tells you what level of permission is needed for any task you attempt.

> ### 🔍 note
>
> Are you a QuickBooks Pro and Premier user intrigued by the extensive user security available in QuickBooks Enterprise? No worries—upgrade your data file to QuickBooks Enterprise with just a click. All your previous data will be available in QuickBooks Enterprise software. The user interface and menus in Enterprise are similar to those in QuickBooks Pro and Premier, so you do not have to learn to use new software. For more information, see "Upgrading Your QuickBooks Version," p. 651.

User Security in QuickBooks Enterprise

If you have users other than yourself accessing QuickBooks Enterprise data, you'll surely want to implement security controls. QuickBooks Enterprise allows granular control over user access to tasks, reports, and features.

QuickBooks Enterprise offers far more robust access control than QuickBooks Pro or Premier.

Overview of Comprehensive User Security in QuickBooks Enterprise

QuickBooks Enterprise Solutions provides the capability to safeguard sensitive business data by giving employees access only to the specific information they need. These controls are robust, with the capability to set individual user permissions for more than 115 different tasks in QuickBooks.

To use the QuickBooks Enterprise user security settings, you need to complete these steps:

1. Add to or modify the supplied user roles. Roles are permissions assigned to a specific position. For example, Accounts Payable role will have permissions assigned that relate to working with vendor transactions.

2. Set up named users.

3. Assign a role or multiple roles to the named user.

When defining access rights, you are modifying specific activity rights within an area in QuickBooks. Areas are defined as a group of related tasks. Areas include the following:

- Accounting
- Banking
- Centers
- Company
- Customers & Receivables
- Employees & Payroll
- File
- Lists
- Reports
- Time Tracking
- Vendors & Payables

The next section discusses how to set up or modify user roles in QuickBooks Enterprise.

Set Up and Modify User Roles

In QuickBooks, a user role permits, limits, or blocks a user's access to reports, transactions, lists, centers, and so on. Roles can represent positions within a company and can be assigned to multiple QuickBooks users. QuickBooks Enterprise comes with these predefined roles (similar to a position title) that can be modified (unless otherwise noted):

- Accountant
- Accounts Payable
- Accounts Receivable
- Admin (cannot be modified)
- Banking
- External Accountant (cannot be modified)
- Finance
- Full Access

- Inventory
- Payroll Manager
- Payroll Processor
- Purchasing
- Sales
- Time Tracking
- View-only

These roles have predefined, modifiable security settings for specific activities related to that feature area. With roles, you can do the following:

- Create a New Role
- Edit an Existing Role (except as noted previously)
- Duplicate an Existing Role
- Delete a Role

The first step is to review the permissions assigned for a specific role or, optionally, create a new role. It is often easier to select an existing role and modify it. To modify an existing role in your file, follow these instructions:

1. Log in to the QuickBooks file as the default Admin user, as discussed earlier in this chapter.

2. From the menu bar, select **Company**, **Users**, **Set Up Users and Roles**. The Users and Roles dialog box displays with the User List Tab selected.

3. To modify or create a Role, select the **Role List** tab. For this example, the Role Name of Accounts Payable was selected.

4. Click the Edit button on the right. The Edit Role dialog box displays with the following information, as Figure 1.14 shows:

   - **Role Name**—This is the name you see when you choose from a list of roles to assign to a user.

   - **Description**—Here you provide an overview of the role's rights and restrictions.

- **Area and Activities**—Functional groupings of QuickBooks activities. Each area's general access level is noted by the coloring of the icon in front of the area, per the following:

  - **Shaded Circle**—Indicates that all activities in this area are allowed Full Access rights for the selected role.

  - **Partially Shaded Circle**—Indicates that some activity restrictions exist in that group for the selected role.

  - **Nonshaded Circle**—Indicates no access to any of the activities in this area.

- **Area Access Level**—More granular access controls.

- **None**—No access to the selected Role Access Activity.

- **Full**—Complete, unlimited access to the selected Role Access Activity.

- **Partial**—View option, as well as access to Create, Modify, Delete, Print, View Balance, and other options unique to the selected Role Access Activity.

Figure 1.14
Edit the security settings for an existing role.

5. For this example, in the Area and Activities panel, select the minus sign (–) in front of Custom Transaction to expand the choices. Choose either Full or Partial options, and set whether the user can both View and Print the report. Your choices differ, depending on the specific activity you have selected. See Figure 1.14.

6. Make any other modifications to this Area and other Areas and Activities as needed. When finished with the changes, click OK.

After a role is created or modified, it can be assigned to one or more users of the company file. Conversely, a user can be assigned multiple roles.

> **tip**
>
> Do you want to give users the opportunity to create reports, but not have the report display information they do not have access to? When defining role access, in the Area and Activities section, select **Custom Transaction** and choose the **Custom Transaction Detail Limited** option, in Figure 1.15.

Select the activity and then choose the preferred activity access level

Figure 1.15
Define granular user security settings with QuickBooks Enterprise.

For example, to prevent a user from accessing sensitive payroll information, you must set user access levels as shown in Table 1.3 for the role assigned to the user.

🔍 **note**

Are you uncertain how many user licenses you have with your QuickBooks Enterprise software? With the file open, on your keyboard, press F2 to display the Product Information dialog box. Near the top and to the left, you can see the number of user licenses will be listed. QuickBooks Enterprise offers simultaneous use by 2–30 users.

Table 1.3 Limiting Access to Payroll

Area	Access Level
Employees & Payroll	None
Centers > Employee Center	None
Banking > Checks	None
Banking > Bank Accounts > Paycheck Bank Account	None
Reports > Company & Financial > Company & Financial Report Detail	None
Reports > Company & Financial > Company & Financial Report Summary	View only (if user needs it—otherwise, set to None)
Reports > Employees & Payroll	None
Reports > Custom Transaction	None

Now that you have set up roles with the desired security settings for Activities, you can create users and assign these roles to the users.

Set Up Users

After creating or modifying user roles, you are ready to add named users to the file and assign the user roles to them.

1. Log in to the QuickBooks file as the default Admin user, as discussed earlier in this chapter.

2. From the menu bar, select **Company**, **Users**, **Set Up Users and Roles**. The Users and Roles dialog box displays with the Users Tab selected.

3. Select **User List** tab. From this tab, you can do the following:

   ▪ Add a new user

   ▪ Edit an existing user's settings

   ▪ Duplicate an existing user's settings for ease in adding a new, similar user

   ▪ Delete a user (not recommended). If a user no longer is with the company, simply remove the user's roles

📢 **caution**

When someone no longer works for your company, resist the urge to delete the person's name. If you remove the name, transactions this user entered or modified are listed as "unknown user" on the Audit Trail reports. Instead, change the user's password and access level. Only active users in your file count toward your licensed user limit.

4. Select **New**. The New User dialog box displays.

5. Type a User Name. This is the name the user needs to type to log in to the data file. The name typed is not case sensitive, but it must be spelled exactly as it is listed here, including any spaces.

6. Type a password (optional but recommended). This password is case sensitive.

7. Type the password again to confirm.

8. From the Available Roles list, select the applicable roles for this individual's duties in the QuickBooks file. Click the Add button to assign the selected role to the Assigned Roles list to the right.

9. Click OK when you are finished assigning roles to the selected new username.

10. You might get a warning message if you have previously instructed QuickBooks to log in to the file automatically. Click OK to close the message. You return to the User and Roles list that displays the newly created user and the roles assigned (see Figure 1.16).

tip

You can print a report detailing the permissions by employee or role. From the Users and Roles dialog box, click View Permissions. You can choose to show permissions for the user or role. Click Display to view the details.

New User	✕

USER NAME AND PASSWORD

User Name: Laura

Password (optional): ••••••••

Confirm Password: ••••••••

ROLES

How do I modify a Role?

Available Roles

- Inventory
- Payroll Manager
- Payroll Processor
- Sales
- Time Tracking
- View-Only

Add >>

<< Remove

Assigned Roles

- Accounts Payable
- Accounts Receivable
- Banking
- Purchasing

Description

This role is designed for your sales staff members who need access to Sales Orders, Sales Receipts, Sales reports, Estimates, and all information in the Customer list.

OK   Cancel

Figure 1.16
From the Users and Roles dialog box, you can see who is logged in to the file and the roles assigned to each of the users.

Reporting on User Activity

Setting up users with the proper security access is important for any company that wants to have controls in place with its accounting data.

You can use these reports to track transactions that have been added, modified, or deleted using these reports accessible from the menu bar by choosing **Reports, Accountant & Taxes**:

- **Audit Trail**—This is a listing of all transactions added or modified, grouped by username. You can learn more about this report in Chapter 15, "Reviewing Your Data," p. 575.

- **Closing Date Exception Report**—Get details of when the closing date was set or removed and transactions that were altered on or before the set closing date. Chapter 16, "Sharing QuickBooks Data with Your Accountant," has more on working with the closing date.

- **Customer Credit Card Audit Trail**—If you track credit card numbers for your customers in QuickBooks, you can enable credit card security and prepare reports on who accessed this sensitive information. To enable this security for your file, from the menu bar, choose Customer Credit Card Protection.

- **Voided/Deleted Transactions Summary**—You cannot filter this report to remove the information. For more information, see Chapter 15.

- **Voided/Deleted Transactions Detail**—You cannot filter this report to remove the information. For more information, see Chapter 15.

Additionally, if you are using QuickBooks Accountant 2014 or QuickBooks Enterprise Solutions Accountant 14.0, you have access to Client Data Review, which includes a tool to track changes to lists. The previously listed reports do not report on changes to lists. See Appendix A, "Client Data Review," for more details.

With QuickBooks 2014, you have gotten off to a quick start in setting up your new file (or converting from other accounting software) and setting up users with specific permissions. You will also find it helpful to use the QuickBooks sample data when you want to practice or follow along with much of the content in this book.

GETTING AROUND QUICKBOOKS

You can make the most of your QuickBooks software when you learn how to navigate and customize the options available to meet your business's specific needs. This chapter shows you just how easy that task can be. For example, if your business does not need to track inventory, you can turn off that feature. However, as your business grows and the products and services you offer change, you can later enable these features again.

Home Page and Navigation

QuickBooks 2014 makes this easy-to-use and popular accounting software even easier to customize and navigate. Let's start by making this *your* software!

Title Bar

At the top of your open QuickBooks file is the title bar, which Figure 2.1 shows on the Home page.

The title bar indicates the following information about your file:

- The name of your file as it is assigned in the Company Name field, which is in the My Company dialog box (from the menu bar, select **Company**, **My Company** to open this dialog box).

Title bar   Top Icon Bar   Home page   Menu bar

Figure 2.1
Working with the many QuickBooks navigation points is easy.

- Your QuickBooks software year and edition, including Pro, Premier, or Enterprise. Also indicated (if applicable) is the industry specification, such as accountant, retail, professional services, and so on.

- Multiuser and the username currently logged in, if more than one user has access to the company file at a time.

🛜 **caution**

If you are following along with this text using one of the sample data files installed with your QuickBooks file, take note of any customization you do. This customization in the sample file does not affect your own QuickBooks file.

Menu Bar

The menu bar includes almost all the tasks, reports, forms, alerts, reminders, and functionality available in QuickBooks. For companies that share their data with their accountant, the new QuickBooks Client Collaboration tool is also accessible from the menu bar.

If you are a new QuickBooks user, I encourage you to review all the menus and submenus. Look at what is included in the Company menu in Figure 2.2. Discovering these features can be valuable for your business because many of these additional QuickBooks tools are beyond the scope of this book.

Figure 2.2
Review the menus for useful tools and features not shown on the Home page or icon bar.

Top Icon Bar

Users can choose to have the icon bar placed at the top (see Figure 2.1). The choice is personal and can help maximize the vertical working space for today's widescreen monitors.

The Top Icon Bar (see Figure 2.1) provides quick access to the tasks and reports you frequently use. You can customize the Top Icon Bar by selecting the color version and adding or removing shortcuts; it is uniquely customizable for each user.

The Top Icon Bar has two color choices:

- Default dark blue with white icons and text

- Colored icons with light-colored background and black text

For companies that have multiple users accessing the same data file, the choice is an individual preference setting and does not affect all users. To select the Top Icon Bar with colored icons, follow these steps:

1. On the menu bar, select **View**, **Top Icon Bar**. The Top Icon Bar displays above the Home page. By default, the icon bar is dark blue with white icons, as in Figure 2.3.

2. To change the Top Icon Bar to display with a light background and colored icons, on the menu bar, select **Edit**, **Preferences**, **Desktop View** and choose the My Preferences tab.

3. Place a checkmark next to Switch To Colored Icons/Light Background on the Top Icon Bar in the Desktop settings.

Figure 2.3
The Top Icon Bar has a default dark blue background.

4. Click OK to close the preferences dialog box. The icon bar now has color icons, as in Figure 2.4.

Figure 2.4
The Top Icon Bar looks like this after enabling the color feature in preferences.

To customize the icon bar for a particular user, make sure you are logged in to the file with that username before making any changes.

 For more information see, "Setting Up Users and Permissions," p. 55.

You can customize the icon bar by doing the following:

- Adding icons (shortcuts)

- Editing existing icons

- Rearranging the order of the icons

- Grouping icons

- Removing icons

The icon bar provides quick access to the most common tasks. You can customize the icon bar to be at the top or to the left in your QuickBooks data. Pick a style that works best for you and your specific monitor size.

> **tip**
>
> When you first begin working with QuickBooks 2014, a new tips banner might display. If you click the message to turn off the banners, you can bring them back by selecting **Help**, **What's New** from the menu bar.

Customizing the Top Icon Bar

The icon bar can be placed either on the top of your QuickBooks Home page or to the left. Follow these instructions for customizing the icon bar.

Use these steps to add the Calculator to the Top Icon Bar and reposition the new icon next to the Calendar icon:

1. From the menu bar, select **View**, **Top Icon Bar**. (If you selected the Left Icon Bar, view the instructions in the next section.)

2. On the Top Icon Bar, click the small double arrows on the far right near the search box and select **Customize Icon Bar**. The Customize Icon Bar dialog box displays your currently selected icons (see Figure 2.5).

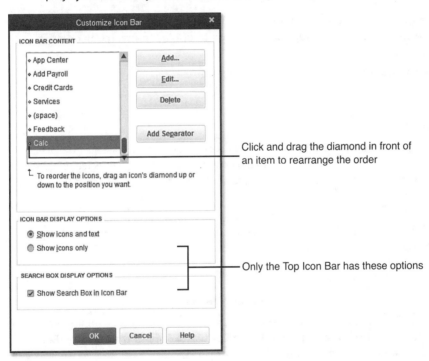

Figure 2.5
Add, remove, and reposition icons on your personal icon bar.

3. Click Add and, in the Add Icon Bar Item dialog box, select **Calculator**. The Calculator icon image is selected for you, but you can choose another icon image from the available choices.

4. Accept or edit the default Label. Keep the text as short as possible here; long labels can crowd the available space on the icon bar.

5. Accept or edit the default Description. The description displays when you hover over the icon with your cursor.

6. Click OK to close the Add Icon Bar Item dialog box.

7. To reposition the Calc icon next to the Calendar icon, click the diamond in front of the Calc item. Drag the item up the list (refer to Figure 2.5), releasing the mouse when the Calc icon is next to the Calendar icon. Look at your icon bar; you will see the Calc icon is next to the Calendar icon. How easy was that?

> **tip**
>
> Now that you know how to drag and drop a list item by clicking the diamond in front of an item, you can rearrange many other QuickBooks lists this way.

8. (Optional) If you are modifying the settings for the top display of the icon bar, keep the default Show Icons and Text option, or select Show Icons Only.

9. (Optional) If you are modifying the settings for the top display of the icon bar, select the Search Box Display Options checkbox to display the search bar on the far right of the icon bar.

10. Click OK to close the Customize Icon Bar dialog box.

Left Icon Bar

The Left Icon Bar placement takes advantage of our wider computer monitor screens by allowing more space top to bottom for your QuickBooks transactions and reports. If you selected to use the Left Icon Bar, from the View menu on the menu bar, follow the instructions provided in this section for customizing the Left Icon Bar.

The icon bar provides quick access to the most common tasks, alerts, and reminders, as well as the option to collaborate with your accountant. You can customize the Left Icon Bar similar to how you customized the Top Icon Bar.

Customizing the Left Icon Bar

The Left Icon Bar (see Figure 2.6) provides easy access to common tasks, reminders, reports, and services. Use these steps to add the Calculator icon to the Left Icon Bar and reposition the new icon next to the Calendar icon:

1. From the menu bar, select **View**, **Left Icon Bar**. (If you selected the Top Icon Bar, view the instructions in the previous section.)

2. On the Left Icon Bar, in the middle, click the My Shortcuts bar and scroll to the bottom link titled Customize Shortcuts. The Customize Icon Bar dialog box displays, as previously shown in Figure 2.5; it displays your currently selected icons.

3. Click Add and, in the Add Icon Bar Item dialog box, select **Calculator**. The Calculator icon image is selected for you, but you can choose another icon image from the available choices.

4. Accept or edit the default Label. Labels can be longer than those on the Top Icon Bar, but only the first 28 or so characters display.

5. Accept or edit the default Description. The description displays when you hover over the icon with your cursor.

6. Click OK to close the Add Icon Bar Item dialog box.

Figure 2.6
QuickBooks provides the option of using the icon bar placed to the left of the Home page.

7. To reposition the Calc icon next to the Calendar icon, click the diamond in front of the Calc item. Drag the item up the list (refer to Figure 2.5), releasing the mouse when the Calc icon is next to the Calendar icon. Look at your icon bar, and you will see that the Calc icon is next to the Calendar icon.

8. Click OK to close the Customize Icon Bar dialog box.

An added benefit to using the Left Icon Bar is the ease in customizing the balances that display on the View Balances tab. Follow these steps to customize the list of accounts displayed in the View Balances window of the Left Icon Bar:

1. From the Left Icon Bar, click View Balances.

2. Click the Customize View Balances link at the bottom of the View Balances view. The Customize Account Balances dialog box displays (see Figure 2.7).

Figure 2.7
Customize the accounts displayed in the View Balances section of the Left Icon Bar.

3. On the left, from the Available Accounts drop-down, select the type of account to display.

4. From the accounts displayed, select with your cursor the account on the left and click the Add button in the center. QuickBooks adds the account to the Selected Accounts on the right.

5. On the right, with an account selected, optionally click Move Up or Move Down to reposition the order of the account balances displayed.

6. Click OK when you are finished with this task to close the Customize Account Balances dialog box.

Complete similar steps to customize the listings on the My Shortcuts and Run Favorite Reports tab of the Left Icon Bar.

Home Page

The best place to start customizing QuickBooks specifically for your business needs is the Home page. The Home page displays by default when you create a new QuickBooks file and include tasks and workflows you can customize (refer to Figure 2.1). You can add or remove icons from the Home page. You cannot rearrange the order or placement of icons on the Home page. (Some Home page icons cannot be removed if related preferences are enabled.)

When you customize the Home page to include or remove specific icons, you are often redirected to the related preference. For more detailed instructions on working with individual preferences, see the "Preferences" section in this chapter or the related preferences section included with most chapters in this book.

To edit the Home page icons, you must be logged in to the file as the Admin or External Accountant user (see Chapter 1, "Getting Started with QuickBooks").

The Admin User in QuickBooks

What if you're not sure whether you are logged in to the file as the Admin user? If you are working with a multiuser file (see Chapter 17, "Managing Your QuickBooks Database," for more details), the title bar shows the user currently logged in to the opened file (see Figure 2.1). However, if you are in the file in single-user mode, or if you renamed the Admin user, the username might or might not display "Admin."

To determine whether you are currently logged in to the file as the originally created default Admin user, on the menu bar, select **Company, Set Up Users and Passwords, Set Up Users** to open the User List dialog box. Figure 2.8 shows how the original Admin user was renamed to Laura. A renamed Admin user still has all the same privileges as the original Admin user.

Many preferences and features require you to be logged in to the file as the Admin user. If you are not currently logged in as the Admin user, from the menu bar, you can log off by selecting **File, Close Company/Logoff**.

Not recommended to rename the Admin user as shown here

Figure 2.8
Viewing the User List shows whether the Admin user was renamed (not recommended).

Customizing Icons (Tasks)

The QuickBooks Home page displays common tasks and workflow for vendors, customers, employees, and other activities and information. You can add or remove some tasks, depending on the needs of your business.

If your Home page does not automatically display, you can always open it by clicking the Home page icon on the icon bar, as in Figure 2.1. In this section, you learn to manage the preference to display the Home page each time you launch QuickBooks.

To make changes to the Home page icons, follow these steps:

1. First, log in to your file as the default Admin or External Accountant user in single-user mode (File, Switch to Single User Mode). Enter the appropriate password, if one was set.

2. From the menu bar, select **Edit, Preferences** to open the Preferences dialog box, which displays the preferences available in your file.

3. In the left column, select the **Desktop View** preference.

4. At the top of the Preferences dialog box, select the **Company Preferences** tab. The following options are provided:

- **Customers**—Choose to add or remove the following Home page icons:

  - **Invoices**—Can be removed only if Estimates, Sales Orders, and Sales Tax tracking is disabled. Either Sales Receipts or Statement and Statement Charges must be enabled to remove Invoices from the Home page.

  - **Sales Receipts**—Remove the checkmark if you do not want Sales Receipts included on the Home page.

  - **Statements and Statement Charges**—Remove the checkmark if you do not want these included on the Home page.

- **Vendors**—Here you have the option to remove both the Enter Bills and Pay Bills icons. If this option is grayed out, it is because another preference is enabled that depends on using vendor bills. For example, if Inventory is enabled, you cannot remove the vendor icons of Enter and Pay Bills.

- **Related Preferences**—Click the corresponding links to enable or disable features globally for all users. These preference settings are discussed in more detail in their related chapters.

  - **Estimates**—See Chapter 9, "Setting Up Customers."

  - **Sales Tax**—See Chapter 9.

  - **Sales Orders**—See Chapter 9.

  - **Inventory**—See Chapter 5, "Setting Up Inventory."

  - **Payroll**—See Chapter 11, "Setting Up Payroll."

  - **Time Tracking**—See Chapter 11.

5. Click OK to close the Preferences dialog box.

If you know you want to remove an icon (task) from the Home page by deselecting it in the Preferences dialog box, you can safely do that. You can later reinstate these icons to your Home page.

> ### 🔺 caution
> Read the referenced chapter before adding a new Home page icon. Often you need to define other unique settings when adding a new icon to your Home page.

Customizing Data Displayed on the Home Page

If you have chosen to use the Top Icon Bar, the right side of the Home page (see Figure 2.1) displays several additional panels of information (see Figure 2.9). Click the upward-facing arrow to expand or collapse the detail displayed.

Figure 2.9
When using the Top Icon Bar, you can expand or collapse each panel of information.

Click here to collapse or expand

These panels include the following:

- **Account Balances**—Click the column headers to sort the accounts by the Name or Balance column.

- **Do More with QuickBooks**—Follow these links to other products or services offered for QuickBooks users.

- **Backup Status**—Get notifications on when the last backup was completed and links to information on storing your data online.

- **Reminders and Alerts**—Check out these links to view the reminders and alerts you have enabled in your QuickBooks file.

Open Windows List

Are you ready for another personal preference for navigating in QuickBooks? Try the Open Windows list. The Open Windows list will show each QuickBooks form or report you currently have open. With computer monitors getting larger, you will most likely have plenty of room to use it with your QuickBooks file. This feature works with both the Top and Left Icon Bars; how you access the feature depends on which icon bar you are using.

When Using the Top Icon Bar

From the menu bar, select **View**, **Open Window List**. The Open Windows list displays on the left side of your Home page (see Figure 2.10), which enables you to move among many open reports or transactions easily by clicking on their name in this list.

Figure 2.10
The Open
Windows
List view
looks like
this when
using the
Top Icon
Bar.

Your open windows might cascade over the top of another open window. If you find this distracting, select **View**, **One Window** from the menu bar to make all the windows use the full QuickBooks desktop area. You can also resize an open window by dragging its top, bottom, sides, or corners.

When Using the Left Icon Bar

Some users with wide monitors might prefer to use the Left Icon Bar. As instructed previously, from View on the menu bar, you can choose which icon bar to use. If you selected the Left Icon Bar, use these instructions to enable the same Open Windows list in Figure 2.11.

1. With the Left Icon Bar displayed, click the Open Windows bar. The Left Icon Bar lists any currently opened windows.

2. Optionally, from the menu bar, select **View**, **One Window** or **Multiple Windows**. Choosing Multiple Windows floats multiple open windows on top of each other. You can also resize an open window by dragging its top, bottom, sides, or corners.

3. Click any displayed icon in the Open Windows box to jump to that selected item.

Figure 2.11
The Open
Windows List
view looks
like this
when using
the Left Icon
Bar.

Having the icon bar display the open windows makes it easy to work with multiple transactions or tasks at the same time.

Tutorials

Included in your QuickBooks software are several tutorials to help you get started quickly. You can watch these as a supplement to this book.

To do so, select **Help**, **Learning Center Tutorials** from the menu bar. Click a category on the left, or select any of the links to jump-start your use of QuickBooks. When you are finished viewing the tutorials, click Go to QuickBooks to close the Learning Center.

Preferences

> **tip**
>
> Click any icon on the Home page (other than the Home icon), and see the Open Windows list on the left grow with each transaction or task that is opened. Would you like to close all open windows quickly? From the menu bar, select **Window, Close All**.
>
> After closing all open windows, if you want to return to the Home page, from the menu bar, select **Company, Home Page**.

Preferences come in two types: Company Preferences, which are global settings that all users are assigned, and Personal Preferences, which are those preferences each user can select individually. You can customize QuickBooks to suit your specific business needs while maintaining individual preferences.

You are required to save your changes as you work with each preference. Some preferences might have you close all open windows to effect the change. Simply return to the Preferences dialog box until you are finished specifying all your preferences by selecting **Edit**, **Preferences** from the menu bar.

To return to the original preference setting, select a preference on the left side of the Preferences dialog box and click the Default button. Be aware that the Default button is not available for all preferences. Click OK to close the Preferences dialog box.

Preferences come in two important types:

- **Company Preferences**—Affect all users of the currently opened QuickBooks file. Only the QuickBooks Admin and External Accountant user have full rights to set these preferences. Learn more about different types of users and user permissions in Chapter 1, p. 36.

- **My Preferences**—Specific to the currently logged-in user; do not affect the settings for other users of the same file or other QuickBooks files.

This section provides a review of the most common, general-use preferences. Most of the preference settings are self-explanatory and do not need to be discussed here. However, most chapters in this book include specific details about important preferences relevant to the specific topic in the chapter.

Accounting—Company Preferences

These are global preferences—when modified, they affect all users of the opened QuickBooks file:

- **Date Warnings**—A new file defaults to Warn If Transactions Are 90 day(s) in the Past and Warn If Transactions Are 30 day(s) in the Future (see Figure 2.12). At times, you might want to edit these date ranges, such as when you are just starting to use QuickBooks and need to enter data for a period in the past.

DATE WARNINGS

☐ Warn if transactions are `90` day(s) in the past

☐ Warn if transactions are `30` day(s) in the future

Figure 2.12
QuickBooks can warn when transaction dates do not fall within a specific date range.

Desktop View—My Preferences

These are personal preferences; when modified, they affect only the currently logged-in user (see Figure 2.13):

- **View**—One Window or Multiple Windows per user preference. This preference also can be selected from the View menu on the menu bar.

- **Desktop**—Includes the following options:

  - **Save When Closing Company**—Default setting that saves every open window when a QuickBooks session is closed. When QuickBooks is reopened, each report and transaction left open in the last session is restored. This preference is not recommended for a file that has multiple users logging in to the file simultaneously. Restoring multiple windows, transactions, or reports at startup can slow the time it takes for the QuickBooks file to open.

  - **Don't Save the Desktop**—Closes each open window automatically when the QuickBooks program is closed. This is the most efficient choice; if a transaction has not been completed, QuickBooks notifies you before closing the transaction and gives you the option to save any changes to custom report settings.

  - **Save Current Desktop**—When you reopen QuickBooks, displays any previously opened nontransaction window.

  - **Keep Previously Saved Desktop**—Selected for you automatically when you choose the Save Current Desktop option.

  - **Show Home Page When Opening a Company File**—When you launch QuickBooks, displays the Home page automatically.

  - **Switch to Colored Icons/Light Background on the Top Icon Bar**—Preference available after updating to Release 4 or newer. Many prefer this new colored icon bar to the default dark blue with white text icon bar.

- **Windows Settings**—Manages the Windows computer display and sound settings.

 note

QuickBooks delivers enhancements to the software through maintenance release patches. To view the release you are using, from an open QuickBooks file, press F2 on your keyboard. The release displays at the top of the Production Information Window. For more information, see "Installing a QuickBooks Maintenance Release," p. 652. This book was written with the beta version of Release 3.

tip

To simplify your daily QuickBooks use, from the menu bar, select both the **One Window** and **Open Window List** view.

- **Company File Color Scheme**—Assigns a default color to a file to help visually identify a data file. Useful if you have multiple QuickBooks data files. Figure 2.1 shows the default dark blue color assigned. Choose from 14 other color choices.

Certain preferences override these defaults, particularly if you have selected Show Home Page When Opening a Company File. When this option is selected, the Home page always opens when you launch QuickBooks.

Figure 2.13
My Preferences enables users to customize their view of the QuickBooks file.

General—My Preferences

These are personal preferences—when modified, they affect only the currently logged-in user:

- **Pressing Enter Moves Between Fields**—When this is *not* selected, you use the Tab key to move between fields and the Enter key to save a transaction or activate a highlighted command.

  If you want to use the Enter key to move between fields (perhaps you have grown accustomed to using the Enter key in this way with other software), place a checkmark in this preference. Using the Tab key on your keyboard also moves between fields.

- **Automatically Place Decimal Point**—When selected, .01 (instead of 1.00) displays when you type the number 1 in QuickBooks.

> ⏱ **tip**
>
> If you selected the preference **Pressing Enter Moves Between Fields** and you want to save a transaction or activate a highlighted command, use the combination Ctrl+Enter from your keyboard.

- **Bring Back All One Time Messages**—If data entry mistakes have been ignored in the past, turning on this warning can call attention to possible mistakes in the future.

- **Keep QuickBooks Running for Quick Startups**—When selected, the QuickBooks software might open faster. This is the only preference that also affects other data files.

Spelling—My Preferences

These are personal preferences—when modified, they affect only the currently logged-in user. Options include:

- Always Check Spelling

- Ignore Specific Words Or Word With Numbers, Internet Address, And So On

When enabled, the Description, Memo, Notes, and Message fields of the following transactions are spell-checked:

- Invoices

- Estimates

- Sales receipts

- Credit memos

- Purchase orders

If you do not select the option to always check spelling, on certain transactions, you will be able to manually run spell-check.

Help Options

As a business owner or accounting professional new to QuickBooks, you will find many resources for getting the help you need. To access Help in QuickBooks, you can press the F1 key on your keyboard or select **Help**, **QuickBooks Help** from the menu bar.

Also, QuickBooks 2014 has a search tool on the right side of the Top Icon Bar (or at the top of the Left Icon Bar). From the drop-down list on the icon bar search field, select **Search Company File** if you want to search through your lists or transactions, or select **Help** if you want to search technical resources. If you are using the Top Icon Bar, you can select Set Search Preferences to default what type of search you normally perform.

QuickBooks provides help in several distinct ways and enables you to search each with a single dialog box, as Figure 2.14 shows.

Search results can include how-to instructions from the in-product help content, as well as related content shared in the Ask Community forums.

If the displayed search results do not answer your question, click the Ask Community and pose the question to other QuickBooks users.

Would you prefer to have a local QuickBooks experienced professional come to your place of business to help you get started quickly? If so, from the menu bar, choose Help, Find a Local QuickBooks Expert. You are asked for your zip code to help locate a list of QuickBooks Certified ProAdvisors in your area, and fees might apply.

Figure 2.14
Search multiple help resources all at once.

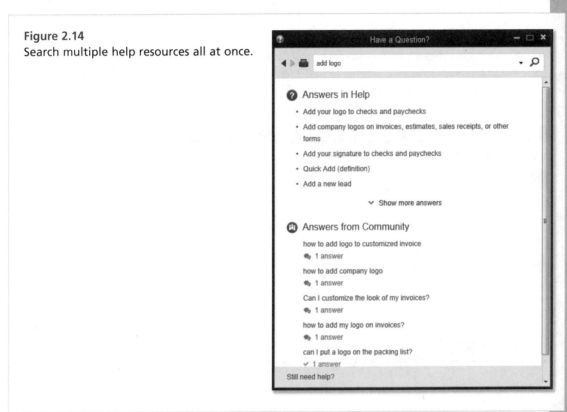

Selecting a Company File to Open

In general, you should not have any trouble opening your QuickBooks file because the software automatically opens your data file each time you launch QuickBooks. However, you can open your QuickBooks data file in several ways. Listed here are the most common.

Opening Your Data File for the First Time

After creating your new file, QuickBooks opens your data file each time you launch the software. However, if you are opening your data for the first time on a new computer, you need to follow these steps:

1. Launch your QuickBooks software by clicking the QuickBooks icon on your desktop.

2. From the menu bar, select **File**, **Open or Restore Company**.

3. In the Open or Restore Company dialog box, select the **Open a Company File** option button, in Figure 2.15.

➡ *For more information about the other file actions in Figure 2.15, see. "QuickBooks File Types," p. 599.*

4. Click Next.

5. QuickBooks defaults to the last known folder that a QuickBooks file was opened within, or you can browse to locate where you stored the file. Select the file and click Open. If required, enter your username and password to open the file.

Figure 2.15
If you have moved your file to a new computer, select the Open a Company file option and browse to the location of the stored file.

Choosing from a List of Multiple Data Files

Chapter 1 introduced you to working with the QuickBooks sample data that installs automatically with your QuickBooks software. Using sample data can give you the freedom to practice what you learn and gain confidence in working with your software.

You also learned in Chapter 1, p. 36, how to create your company's QuickBooks file using a variety of methods.

In this section, you learn how to open a QuickBooks file from a list, which is especially useful if you have multiple data files or want to open the sample data again after working in your own file.

> ⓦ **tip**
> Chapter 16, "Sharing QuickBooks Data with Your Accountant," discusses in more detail different file types and their purposes. The QuickBooks instruction of selecting **File**, **Open** opens only a file with the extension of .QBW.

To choose from a list of multiple data files, follow these steps:

1. From the menu bar, select **File**, **Open Previous Company**. A list of previously opened files (up to a maximum of 20) displays, as Figure 2.16 shows.

Figure 2.16
Access previously opened QuickBooks files easily.

File Edit View Lists Favorites Accountant Company Customers Vendors Employees Banking Reports Window Help

New Company...
New Company from Existing Company File...
Open or Restore Company...
Open Previous Company ▶ C:\Client Data Folders\Best Builders\Best Builders, Inc..qbw
Open Second Company   C:\Client Data Folders\ABES Diner\ABE's Diner.QBW
Back Up Company ▶   C:\Client Data Folders\Anthony's Pizza Parlor\Anthony's Pizza Parlor.QBW
Create Copy...   C:\Client Data Folders\The Photo Gallery\The Photo Gallery.QBW
Close Company   C:\Client Data Folders\Angelas Decorating Services\Angela's Decorating Services.QBW

Switch to Multi-user Mode   Set number of previous companies...

2. Select a file in the list to open it.

3. Enter your username and password, if required.

If you need to increase the number of files shown, open any QuickBooks file, and then from the menu bar, select **File**, **Open Previous Company**, **Set Number of Previous Companies**. QuickBooks can display up to 20 data files in this list. Enter the number you want to include in your list and click OK when finished.

In Chapter 1, p. 36, you learned how to open and test with sample data and create your own file. In this chapter, you learned how to navigate the many features and tools in QuickBooks. Let's take a quick break from QuickBooks and discuss some basic accounting in the next chapter, Chapter 3, "Accounting 101." I promise, it will be worth your time and help you make better use of your QuickBooks file.

ACCOUNTING 101

In this chapter, you find a brief discussion of fundamental accounting principles for the non-accountant business owner. If you used another method or software for tracking your financials prior to QuickBooks, you can follow step-by-step instructions in this chapter for entering these beginning balances.

Basic Principles of Accounting

This chapter provides a quick review of some of the more important accounting concepts, written especially for the non-accountant business owner. Although there is much more to learn about accounting principles than this chapter covers, you learn enough to help you manage the financials of your business.

You made an important choice when you selected QuickBooks software to help you track the day-to-day financial transactions of your business. QuickBooks completes most of the accounting behind-the-scenes so you can focus on what you do best.

The Matching Principle

The *matching principle of accounting* refers to recognizing revenue and associated expenses in the same period. Matching income and costs in this manner gives you a much more accurate representation of your financial situation and performance.

Most businesses offer products or services that have related costs, such as the following:

- **Asset purchases**—Examples are inventory for sale and fixed assets (equipment) used in the production of your product.

- **Cost of Goods Sold expenses**—Direct expenses incurred when making your product or providing a service. Examples are cost of materials and labor expenses.

- **Expenses**—Overhead that has fixed costs and variable expenses, such as rent, office supplies, advertising, and so on.

- **Other expenses**—Expenses of the business not related to the product or service you provide, such as interest expense or depreciation expense.

It is important to understand the different account types when recording costs so that you categorize your bills or expenses correctly when entering them into QuickBooks.

 note

This book does not offer tax or accounting advice. Be sure to consult your accounting professional when necessary.

note

Inventory that you purchase is an asset purchase; it later becomes a cost of goods sold expense when you sell it.

➡ *For more information, see "Account Types," found in Chapter 4, "Understanding QuickBooks Lists," p. 108.*

No discussion of the matching principle is complete without defining revenue. *Revenue* (income) is the funds received from customers. Income is typically one of the following:

- **Operating income**—Income derived from selling your business's product or service.

- **Other income**—Income derived from sources other than selling your product or service. An example of other income might be interest earned on balances in your checking account.

You probably already understand the general concept of revenue versus expense. So what does the matching principle have to do with accounting? A retail bike store might keep parts such as wheels, pedals, and chains on hand in its inventory so it can assemble bicycles for its customers. The matching principle requires this store to record the costs of the bike at the time of sale. The initial purchase of inventory is not an expense; it is simply trading one asset, cash, for another asset, inventory. When the asset is sold, the initial purchase cost becomes an expense, which reduces the resulting revenue.

Inventory management, as discussed in this example, is pretty straightforward. QuickBooks tracks your initial purchase as an asset and then records the average cost of each part as an expense when you create an invoice to record the sale to a customer. If you are using QuickBooks Enterprise Solutions, you can opt to use First-In, First-Out inventory costing. Appendix C, "QuickBooks Enterprise Solutions Features," has more information.

➡ *For more information, see Chapters 5 and 6 "Setting Up Inventory," p. 151, and "Managing Inventory," p. 205.*

However, let's tackle something a bit more difficult. In this same business, you are required to pre-pay six months of general liability insurance. Recording this entire balance as an expense in a single month would make that month's net income appear artificially lower, along with making net income for the next five months artificially higher. To match the expense, you would assign the initial payment to a prepaid expenses account on your balance sheet. You would then use a journal entry each month to record an increase in insurance expense and a decrease in the prepaid expenses account. Each month would then have the cost for insurance that belonged in a single month.

➡ *For more information, see "Recording Vendor Prepayments," p. 295.*

QuickBooks accrual basis reporting can help you view your financials in a format that matches revenue with expense. The next section discusses accrual basis reporting.

Accrual Versus Cash Basis Reporting

Although the purpose of this book is not to give specific accounting or tax advice on any of the topics covered, it is worth discussing the nature of accrual versus cash basis reporting as it pertains to creating a new data file.

Cash basis accounting follows these rules:

- **Revenue**—Recognized when the customer payment is received, not necessarily the same day or month the service or product was provided.

- **Expenses**—Recognized when the payment is made to the vendor or employee, not necessarily the same day or month the expense relates to.

Accrual basis accounting follows these rules:

- **Revenue**—Recognized as income on the date of the customer invoice transaction, regardless of when the customer pays the invoice.

- **Expenses**—Recognized as a cost on the date of the vendor bill, check, or credit card charge, regardless of when you make the payment.

Understanding the basics of these two types of reporting is important. When filing a tax return, businesses must specify cash or accrual as their accounting method. However, for management purposes, business owners can view one or both types of reports when making internal decisions. The capability to view reports in either accrual or cash basis is one of the features that sets the QuickBooks software apart from other accounting solutions.

Cash basis reporting can give you a sense of how cash flows through your business, whereas accrual basis reporting uses the matching principle to give you a much more accurate representation of how revenue and expenses are related.

The difference between the two methods is in the timing of when income and expenses are recognized in your financials. Table 3.1 shows how QuickBooks treats the different types of transactions in both reporting methods on the Profit & Loss statement.

Table 3.1 Accrual Versus Cash Accounting

Transaction Type	Profit & Loss Accrual Basis	Profit & Loss Cash Basis
Customer Invoice	Revenue is recognized as of the date of the invoice.	Revenue is recognized as of the date entered on the customer's payment transaction.
Customer Credit Memo	Revenue is decreased as of the date of the credit memo.	No impact.
Vendor Bill	Cost is recognized on the date entered on the vendor's bill.	Cost is recognized on the date of the bill payment check.
Vendor Credit Memo	Cost is decreased as of the date of the vendor credit memo.	No impact.
Check	Cost is recognized as of the date entered on the check transaction.	Cost is recognized as of the date entered on the check transaction.
Credit Card	Cost is recognized as of the date entered on the credit card transaction.	Cost is recognized as of the date entered on the credit card transaction.
General Journal	Cost or revenue is recognized using the date entered on the general journal transaction.	Cost or revenue is recorded using the date entered on the general journal transaction.
Inventory Adjustment	Date of inventory adjustment is the date the financials are affected.	Date of inventory adjustment is the date the financials are affected.

In QuickBooks preferences, you can set a global default basis for all reports which means that when you run reports, they will use the basis you set in the QuickBooks preferences. To do this, follow these steps:

1. Log in to the file as the Admin or External Accountant user type.

2. From the menu bar, select **Edit**, **Preferences**, **Reports & Graphs**.

3. Click the Company Preferences tab and choose Accrual or Cash from the Summary Reports Basis section.

You can also modify the basis of many reports individually. From a displayed report, select **Customize Report** and, in the Summary Report Basis section, choose Accrual or Cash.

For management analysis, I encourage all business owners to view their financials often using accrual basis reporting. When you review accrual basis reports, you can see trends from one period to the next. Management decisions based on accrual basis reports might be different from decisions made when based on cash basis reports.

Basic Financial Reports

This section describes financial reports that are important to managing the finances of your business.

➡ *For more details on working with reports, see "Reviewing Your Data," p. 575.*

Balance Sheet

The balance sheet represents the overall financial health of the business. Of the financial statements detailed here, the balance sheet is the only statement that applies to a single date in the business's calendar year.

A standard company balance sheet has three sections and is represented by this equation: Assets = Liabilities + Equity. The categories include the following:

- **Assets**—Cash, along with economic resources that can be converted to cash. Assets include:
  - **Current Assets**—Cash, accounts receivable, inventory, and prepaid expenses, to name a few.
  - **Fixed Assets and Depreciation**—Buildings and equipment and their depreciation.
  - **Other Assets**—Goodwill (typically the value of an asset that is intangible but has a quantifiable value), trademarks, and copyrights.
- **Liabilities**—A debt the business is obligated to pay. Liabilities include:
  - **Current Liabilities**—Debt that typically is paid back within one year.
  - **Long-term Liabilities**—Debt that is expected to take longer than one year to pay back.
- **Equity**—Owner's investments, draws, and residual net income or loss in the business over time.

Business owners should review the balance sheet as often as they review the income statement. Most business owners who review the balance sheet have a pretty good idea of whether the information is accurate just by looking at the balances.

Income Statement

The income statement also is referred to as a Profit & Loss statement in QuickBooks. My experience over the years is that business owners review this report often. In QuickBooks, a simple income statement includes these basic sections or totals:

- **Income**—Monies received from the sale of products and services.
- **Cost of Goods Sold**—Direct costs of producing your product or service.
- **Gross Profit**—Income minus cost of goods sold.
- **Expense**—Costs associated with your business that are not directly related to producing goods or services, often referred to as overhead.
- **Net Ordinary Income (Loss)**—Income or loss from operations.

- **Other Income/Expense**—Income or expense not related to operations, such as interest income or interest expense.

- **Net Income (Loss)**—Income or loss from operations minus other income/loss.

QuickBooks offers you the flexibility to review your Profit & Loss Standard report in either accrual or cash basis. Creating an income statement that shows 12-month periods on the accrual basis makes it easy to spot changes and trends from period to period.

Statement of Cash Flows

The primary purpose of this report is to show the sources and uses of cash in the business. The statement of cash flows includes the following groups:

- **Operating Activities**—These include the production of the product, sales, and the delivery of the product. They also include activities related to payment from the customer.

- **Investing Activities**—These activities include the purchase or sale of assets or loans. Assets and loans involve both suppliers and customers.

- **Financing Activities**—These activities are related to the inflow and outflow of cash. Investors and shareholders are participants in these activities.

Additionally, the following information is included in the statement of cash flows report:

- Net cash increase for the period

- Cash at the beginning of the period

- Cash at the end of the period

QuickBooks automatically assigns a specific chart of accounts to cash flow report categories, based on the account type assigned.

You also can manually assign a chart of accounts to a specific section of the statement. To do this, follow these steps:

1. Log in to the file as the Admin or External Accountant user to set this preference.

2. From the menu bar, select **Edit**, **Preferences**, **Reports & Graphs**, and select the Company Preferences tab.

3. Click the Classify Cash button and follow the instructions on the screen.

 note

The reports referenced in this section are the basic reports used to analyze the financial health of a business. Many chapters in this book include sections that detail specific reports relevant to the topic of that chapter.

Accounting Checklist to Help You Manage Your Financials

This checklist is provided to help the business owner or accounting professional take an organized approach to periodically reviewing a QuickBooks file. This book includes several chapters that help you learn how to accurately and efficiently manage your data, using this checklist.

Client Name: _____

Date Due: _____

Data for Year Ended: _____ 201____

QuickBooks Version: _____ QuickBooks Release: _____

Method of Accessing Client Data (circle one):

On-site   .QBB Backup Data

.QBM Portable Co. File   .QBX Accountant's Copy

Remote Access   Send Journal Entry

External Accountant Username and Password: _____

Or Client Admin Password: _____

___ Backup of Data Made Before Correcting Transactions

___ Review of Working Trial Balance Ending Balances from Prior Year

___ Prior-Year Balances Changed? Print Audit Trail, Voided/Deleted, Retained Earnings QuickReport

___ Review Chart of Accounts for Any Newly Created Accounts

___ Proper Account Type Selected?   ___ Duplicated Accounts?

___ Assign as Subaccount?

___ Item List Review—Print Reports—For the Item List Including Account and COGS Account

___ Proper Accounts Assigned?   ___ Duplicated Items?

___ Assign as Subitem?

___ Review Accounts Receivable

___ Small Open Balances   ___ Unapplied Credits

___ Undeposited Funds   ___ Old Outstanding A/R

___ Review Accounts Payable

___ Paid Open Vendor Bills   ___ 1099-MISC. Income Form Setup

___ Unapplied Vendor Credits   ___ Old Outstanding A/P

___ Review Payroll

___ Nonpayroll Transactions   ___ Employee Defaults

___ Payroll Item Mapping

___ Run Payroll Checkup

___ Review Completed Bank Reconciliations

___ Account(s) Reconciled   ___ Agrees With Balance Sheet?

___ Review Uncleared Bank Transactions

___ Review Inventory Setup

    ___ Inv Valuation Summary Asset Total Agrees With Balance Sheet

    ___ Old Outdated Item Receipts

    ___ Journal Entries Posted To Inventory Asset Account

Setting Up a QuickBooks Data File for Accrual or Cash Basis Reporting

This section is provided for the owner who was tracking business finances in other software or on paper prior to using QuickBooks. In this section, you learn about properly entering the startup balances from your previous records.

However, if you have recently started a new business and QuickBooks is the first financial tracking software you have used, rest easy: You can skip this section because QuickBooks does not require any complex entries to start using the software. Instead, you simply begin the daily tasks of paying vendors or employees and invoicing customers.

If instead you are converting to QuickBooks from a software application other than those currently supported with the QuickBooks conversion tool, you might have to manually enter open customers, vendors, bank account balances, and additional startup information. That is where this section comes in handy.

➥ *For more information, see "Converting from Other Accounting Software," p. 50, in Chapter 1.*

When you begin using QuickBooks, you need to define a start date—the date you first want QuickBooks to track your financial accounting. If the business had expenses or sold products and services before this start date, you most likely have open transactions. For example, if your start date is January 1, 2017, your beginning balances then are dated as of December 31, 2016.

The following is recommended information to collect when creating a new QuickBooks data file. The dollar totals of the information collected should represent their respective value as of the day before your QuickBooks start date:

- **Accounts Receivable**—List by customer of amounts owed you on the day before your start date, including any invoices for which the payment was received but not deposited by the start date, the date you select to begin tracking your financials using QuickBooks.

- **Accounts Payable**—List by vendor of bills you had not paid as of your start date.

- **Bank Ending Balance**—Ending balance from your bank statement on the day before your start date.

- **Uncleared Checks and Deposits**—List of all checks and deposits that have not yet cleared your bank account as of your start date.

- **Other Balances**—List of all other assets, liabilities, and equity you have in the business.

- **Payroll**—Year-to-date totals for each employee (if using payroll in QuickBooks and you issued payroll checks before using QuickBooks).

To get your QuickBooks data ready for entering current transactions, you need to record these open balances. However, before doing so, you need to have a few things already set up in QuickBooks.

Before You Begin Entering Opening Balances

If you are converting your financials from information tracked in other software or on paper, you need to enter beginning balances. Before you begin entering these startup balances, make sure you have the following lists created in your QuickBooks data file. Each item in this list has its own chapter in this book to help you with this task:

- Chart of Accounts (see Chapter 4)
- Items List (see Chapters 4 and 5)
- Customer and Job Names (see Chapter 9)
- Vendor Names (see Chapter 7)
- Employee Names (see Chapter 11)
- Payroll Items (see Chapter 11)

The following sections detail these important startup balances that you need to enter when you convert to QuickBooks from some other accounting software or paper records.

Cash or Accrual Basis Startup Transactions: Accounts Receivable

When you have finished creating your new data file, you need to take some additional steps that are important to the successful setup of your new QuickBooks file. One of these steps is to create a list of customers or jobs that currently owe you money. You might want to review Chapter 9, "Setting Up Customers," before completing the activities in this section.

Creating a customer or job is easy in QuickBooks; follow these instructions:

1. From the menu bar, select **Customers**, **Customer Center**.

2. Select **New Customer & Jobs** (top left of the Customer Center), or select the menu to **Add Multiple Customer:Jobs**.

3. Type a Customer Name. By default, QuickBooks sorts the list numerically and alphabetically by this name.

4. QuickBooks enables you to enter an amount in the Opening Balance field on a new Customer or Job record, see Figure 3.1. If you do that, QuickBooks creates a *single* invoice for the entire amount owed. This method can present a problem when your customer owes you for multiple invoices. Also note the caution above about using this field to record the opening balances.

> **caution**
>
> Recording open customer invoices in the New Customer or New Job dialog box is generally not recommended. Instead, create individual invoices to match the open balance records from your previous accounting software for each customer.

> **tip**
>
> Pressing Ctrl+I on your keyboard opens a customer invoice form or accesses it directly from the opening screen in QuickBooks, known as the Home page.

Instead create an invoice(s) for the opening balance(s)

Figure 3.1
Best practice
is to not use
the Opening
Balance field
in a New
Customer
dialog box.

- **Accrual basis reporting**—For this type of reporting, the Opening Balance field increases Accounts Receivable (debit) and increases Uncategorized Income (credit) assigned the date in the As Of field on the New Customer or New Job dialog box.

- **Cash basis reporting**—For this type of reporting, the field has no effect until the date of customer payment. When the customer payment is received, it increases (debit) the account you assign to customer payments (either the QuickBooks Undeposited Funds or the bank account) and increases Uncategorized Income (credit).

5. To create an individual customer invoice, from the menu bar, select **Customers**, **Create Invoices** (see Figure 3.2).

6. In the Customer: Job drop-down list, select the customer or job.

7. In the Date field (it should be before your start date), enter the original invoice date.

8. Enter the originally assigned invoice number.

9. In the Item column, enter the item(s)—the products or services that were sold—if you want to accurately track your revenue from this item. It should be the same item(s) that appeared on the original invoice to the customer.

10. Enter a value in the Quantity column.

Figure 3.2
Record individual invoices for your customers' starting balances.

11. If the rate did not prefill (because it was not included with a list item record), enter a value in the Rate column.

12. The correct tax status on the line should prefill if the list item was set to the proper sales tax status. If some customers pay sales tax and others do not, you must first indicate the taxable status of an item by selecting from the menu bar **Lists**, **Item List**. Highlight the item in question, click the Item button, and select Edit Item. The Edit Item dialog box opens, and you can mark the item with the appropriate sales tax code.

QuickBooks first determines whether an item is taxable, and then it checks whether the customer is a sales-tax-paying customer before assessing sales tax on a customer balance.

13. Check your Balance Due to make sure it agrees with the list item total from which you are working.

14. Click Save & Close if you are finished, or click Save & New if you have more invoice transactions to record.

QuickBooks offers useful Sales by Item reports that provide more granular detail about the items being sold. If you record a partially paid customer invoice only for the balance due, your item sales reports will not offer complete sales information for the item. Instead, you can choose to follow the instructions in the next section. However, this process involves more steps, so proceed only if you find the Sales by Item reports important for these partially paid customer invoices.

> **note**
>
> Entering invoices with partial payment detail provides you with sales reports by item. If this level of detail is not needed on past transactions, you can simply enter a net amount due on the invoice.

Partially Paid Open Customer Invoices on Cash Basis Reporting

To properly prepare reports with cash basis reporting, and to properly report on sales by item, you should perform additional steps for those open invoices that had partially paid balances as of your startup date. These steps are required only if you want to accurately track sales by item:

1. From the menu bar, select **Lists, Chart of Accounts**.

2. In the Chart of Accounts dialog box, from the Account drop-down list, select **New**. The Add New Account: Choose Account Type dialog box opens.

3. Select the **Bank** account type and click Continue.

4. In the Account Name field, type the name **Prior Year Payments Account**. If account numbering is enabled, enter an account number. Select **No** to the Set Up Bank Feed message. This is a temporary account that will later have the balances moved to the Opening Balance Equity account in step 15. Click Save & Close.

5. From the menu bar, select **Lists, Item List**.

6. In the Item drop-down list, select **New**. The New Item dialog box opens.

7. In the Type drop-down list, select **Payment**, and then in the Item Name/Number field, type the name **Prior Year Payments**.

8. Assign the Prior Year Payments account created in step 1 as the account to Deposit To (see Figure 3.3). Click OK.

9. To create a partially paid invoice with an open balance, from the menu bar, select **Customers, Create Invoices**.

10. In the drop-down list, choose the appropriate Customer:Job.

11. Enter the original invoice date (it should be before your QuickBooks start date), and enter the invoice number originally presented to the customer for payment.

Figure 3.3
Create a payment item type to use on partially paid startup customer invoices.

12. On line 1 (or more, if needed) of the customer invoice, enter your normal service or product item you sold to the customer. On the next available line, use the new Prior Year Payments item you created, and enter the total of the customer's prior payments as a negative amount (see Figure 3.4). Click Save & Close if you are finished, or click Save & New to create additional open customer invoices.

Figure 3.4
This example illustrates creating an invoice that was partially paid before the date you started using QuickBooks.

13. Verify that the Balance Due amount on the invoice accurately matches the open invoice total from your prior accounting list or report.

14. Compare your QuickBooks A/R Aging Summary report to your open invoices startup list total. If the balances agree, go to step 15. If they do not agree, review either the Summary or the Detail A/R Aging report, and identify which customer(s) balances are incorrect.

15. When your totals agree, click Banking, Use Register, and select the **Prior Year Payments Account**.

16. To close the fictitious bank account balance to the Open Balance Equity account, enter the following on the next available line of the register.

   ■ For the date, enter the day before your startup date. Optionally, for the number, use the term Closing.

- In the payment column, enter the same dollar amount as the register total displayed prior to this transaction.

- In the Account field, select the QuickBooks-created equity account named **Opening Balance Equity**.

17. Click Record to save the transaction.

Your Prior Year Payments bank register should now have a zero balance.

➡️ *For more information, see "Closing Opening Balance Equity into Retained Earnings," p. 593.*

Cash or Accrual Basis Startup Transactions: Accounts Payable

Accounts Payable startup refers to vendor bills that were not paid as of your start date. These are the vendor bills you will be paying in your first month of using QuickBooks. Correctly setting up the starting Accounts Payable balance is just as important to your financials as setting up Accounts Receivable.

1. From the menu bar, select **Vendors**, **Enter Bills**. In the Vendor drop-down list, choose the appropriate vendor (see Figure 3.5).

2. Enter the bill date. This date should be on or before your QuickBooks start date, and it is often the date on the vendor's bill you received.

3. In the Ref. No. field, enter the vendor's bill number. This serves two important purposes: One is to optionally print the reference number on the bill payment stub that is sent to the vendor, and the other is to allow QuickBooks to warn you if a duplicate bill is later entered with the same Ref. No.

4. Enter a number in the Amount Due field. If you previously paid part of the bill, the amount should equal the balance remaining to be paid. (See the sidebar "Partially Paid Open Vendor Bills on Cash Basis Reporting.")

5. QuickBooks defaults the Bill Due date to the terms specified on the Payment Settings tab in the New Vendor or Edit Vendor dialog box; however, you also can override the Bill Due date on this screen, if necessary.

6. Click the Expenses tab and assign the appropriate expense account. If you are tracking costs by items, use the appropriate item on the Items tab. For accrual basis, the account or item selected is not as important because the expense was recorded on the vendor's bill date in your previous software or accounting method. For cash basis, it is most important because the cost is recorded to the expense account or item not when the bill is dated, but on the date of the bill payment check transaction, which should occur after the start date.

7. Click Save & Close, or click Save & New to add more transactions.

Figure 3.5
Enter a vendor bill that
was unpaid at your
startup date.

Bill

VENDOR	Cal Gas & Electric	DATE	12/28/2016
ADDRESS	Cal Gas & Electric P.O. Box 5037 Middlefield CA 94482	REF. NO.	55868976
		AMOUNT DUE	102.60
		BILL DUE	01/12/2017
TERMS	Net 15	DISCOUNT DATE	CLASS
MEMO			

| Expenses | $102.60 | Items | $0.00 |

ACCOUNT	AMOUNT	MEMO	CUSTOME...	BILL...	CLASS
65100 · Utilities:65110 · Gas an...	102.60	Unpaid as of 12/31/16			

8. From the menu bar, select **Reports**, **Vendors & Payables**, **A/P Aging Summary** (or **A/P Aging Detail**), and compare the totals with your previous accounting software or manual records.

9. If the open bills you are entering are for inventory, make sure you read the details in Chapter 5, "Setting Up Inventory," p. 152.

note

QuickBooks offers useful Purchase by Item reports that provide more granular detail about the items being purchased. If you record a partially paid vendor bill only for the balance due, your item purchase reports will not offer complete purchase information for the item. Instead, you can choose to follow the instructions in the next section. However, this process involves more steps, so proceed only if you find the Purchases by Item reports important for these partially paid vendor bills.

Partially Paid Open Vendor Bills on Cash Basis Reporting

To properly prepare reports on cash basis, you should perform additional steps for open vendor bills that have partial payments as of your startup date. These steps are required if you want to accurately track your costs by item, including in reports such as the Purchases by Item.

Use the Prior Year Payments bank account that you created in the previous set of steps. This is a temporary account; you will move the balances to the Opening Balance Equity account in step 9.

1. From the menu bar, select **Lists**, **Item List**. The Item List dialog box opens.

2. In the Item drop-down list, select **New**.

3. In the New Item dialog box, select the **Other Charge** item type. In the Item Name/ Number field, type **Prior Year Vendor Payments** (see Figure 3.6). Assign it to the Prior Year Payments bank account by selecting it from the Account drop-down list.

(You created this account in the previous set of steps. See the sidebar "Partially Paid Open Customer Invoices on Cash Basis Reporting.") Click OK to save.

Figure 3.6
Create an Other Charge type item to record prior-year vendor payments on startup vendor bills.

4. Follow steps 1–6 in the preceding section titled "Cash or Accrual Basis Startup Transactions: Accounts Payable," with the exception that you need to record the full amount of the original bill. You can use the Expenses tab and assign the appropriate expense account, or if you are tracking costs by item, you can use the Items tab and assign the correct item.

5. On the Items tab of the Enter Bills dialog box, add the Other Charge type item, called Prior Year Vendor Payments. Enter a negative amount equal to the total of all previous bill payments (see Figure 3.7).

Figure 3.7
Create an open vendor bill, including any prior-year vendor payment line detail.

6. Verify that the Amount Due amount on the Enter Bills dialog box accurately matches the open vendor invoice total from your previous software (or accounting method) report.

7. Compare your QuickBooks A/P Aging Summary report to the open vendor bill startup list total from your previous software. If the balances agree with each other, go to the next step. If they do not agree, review either the Summary or Detail A/P Aging report, and identify which vendor(s) balances are incorrect; then make the needed changes.

8. When the totals of your prior accounting Payables agree with the new QuickBooks A/P Summary report, from the menu bar, click Banking, Use Register. In the Use Register dialog box, select the Prior Year Payments fictitious bank account. Click OK.

9. On the next available register line, enter the day before your startup date and the word Closing for the number. In the Deposit column, enter the total amount you see in the balance column of this register. In the Account field, select the QuickBooks-created equity account named **Opening Balance Equity**.

10. Click Record to save your transaction.

When completed, your Prior Year Payments account will have a zero balance.

 For more information, see "Closing Opening Balance Equity into Retained Earnings," p. 593.

Cash or Accrual Basis Startup Transactions: Bank Account Statement Balance

In addition to setting up the Accounts Receivable and Payable startup transactions, you must record the balance the bank had on record as of the start date. Having accurate information is necessary when you are ready to reconcile the bank account in QuickBooks to the bank's monthly statement.

To create your beginning bank balance, follow these steps:

1. From the menu bar, select **Banking, Make Deposits** to record your bank statement beginning balance (if a positive balance). However, if you have been using QuickBooks for recording payments before you entered your beginning bank balance, you might need to close the displayed Payments to Deposit dialog box.

2. In the Deposit To field, enter your bank account from your chart of accounts list. The date should be the same as your bank statement ending date, usually the day before your QuickBooks start date.

> **tip**
>
> To check whether your QuickBooks recorded bank balance is correct, from the menu bar, select **Banking, Use Register**, and then select your bank account to open the register.
>
> If the amount is correct and agrees with your bank's statement ending balance, no further action is required. Otherwise, double-click the transaction and edit the amount. If the QuickBooks register does not yet have a beginning balance, follow the steps listed in this section.

3. In the From Account drop-down list (see Figure 3.8), select **Opening Balance Equity**. The balance belongs in Retained Earnings, but posting it here first gives you a chance to make sure the opening entries for your cash account are correct.

➡️ *For more information, see Chapter 15, "Closing Opening Balance Equity to Retained Earnings," p. 593.*

> **tip**
> If your bank account has a negative balance as of your start date, you can use a check to record that amount.

Figure 3.8 Enter the ending balance from the bank's statement.

4. Enter an optional Memo.

5. Enter the Amount. The amount recorded here is the ending balance from the bank statement the day before your QuickBooks start date. This amount should not include any uncleared checks or deposits; these are added later individually.

6. Click Save & Close to record the transaction.

If you have outstanding deposits that did not clear your bank funds, the way you enter them depends on the basis of accounting used:

- Accrual basis users create the deposit(s) using the same steps as outlined for entering the beginning bank balance and date the transactions before the start date.

- Cash basis users select Customers, Receive Payment from the menu bar, and apply the deposit to an open invoice, which you created earlier in this chapter. Date this transaction *on* or *after* your start date.

Cash or Accrual Basis Startup Transactions: Recording Uncleared Bank Checks

You are almost finished with the startup entries. The last thing to do is to record the checking account's uncleared checks and debits, as in Figure 3.9. To complete the startup process for your banking transactions, follow these instructions to create your uncleared checks:

1. From the menu bar, select **Banking**, **Write Checks**.

2. In the Write Checks dialog box, enter the actual check number that was issued in the No. field.

3. In the Date field, enter the date of the original check, which should be before the start date.

4. In the Pay to the Order Of drop-down list, select the payee.

5. Enter the amount of the check.

6. On the Expenses tab (see Figure 3.9), select the **Opening Bal Equity** account. (This account is used because, in both accrual and cash basis reporting, the check expense amount was included in our prior software or accounting method profit and loss totals.)

Figure 3.9 These details illustrate entering a check that was not cashed by the bank as of the start date.

7. Click Save & Close (or Save & New) until you have completed this task.

To verify the accuracy of the information, from the menu bar, select **Reports**, **Company & Financial**, **Balance Sheet Standard**, and set the date to be one day before your start date. Your bank account balance(s) should be equal to Bank Statement Ending Balance plus Outstanding (uncleared) Deposits minus Outstanding (uncleared) Checks.

QuickStart

Step 1. Add or Edit the Chart of Accounts   **110**

Step 2. Create an Item to Use on a Customer
Invoice   **116**

4

UNDERSTANDING QUICKBOOKS LISTS

QuickBooks offers several methods for tracking and reporting on your accounting data so you can review how your business is doing financially.

With QuickBooks, you can use the following lists to analyze your business:

- **Chart of Accounts**—For organizing your daily transactions

- **Items List**—For tracking the profitability of individual services and products sold

- **Class List**—For tracking different corporate profit centers (divisions)

- **Customer Type List**—For viewing your gross profit by user-defined customer types

The QuickBooks chart of accounts is easy to set up. It might already exist if you created your file with the Express Start discussed in Chapter 1, "Getting Started with QuickBooks," p. 36. What becomes problematic for some is how to efficiently use each of the available list types when you want to segment the business reporting activity in QuickBooks. We start first with the chart of accounts.

> ⊙ **tip**
>
> A well-defined QuickBooks data file most likely includes the use of items, classes, and customer types, in addition to the chart of accounts.

Chart of Accounts

The chart of accounts is a list of asset, liability, equity, income, and expense accounts to which you assign your daily transactions. This list is one of the most important lists you will use in QuickBooks; it helps you keep your financial information organized. When this list is created with summary accounts and you use the other list types for detail, you can capture information in a timely manner, which helps you make good financial and management decisions for the business.

Account Types

Understanding the chart of accounts isn't complicated. Six standard account categories track the financial activity of your business: assets, liabilities, equity, income, cost of goods sold, and expense.

Assets

Assets include something you have purchased in the past that you will use in the future to generate economic benefit. QuickBooks offers these categories in the order of how liquid the asset is—or, in simple terms, how quickly you can turn the asset into cash:

- **Bank**—This account type tracks your cash in and out of the business. This account type and the credit card account type are the only account types you can select as the payment account in the Pay Bills or Write Checks dialog box.

- **Accounts Receivable**—This account type requires a Customer or Customer and Job name with each entry. You use this account type when generating an invoice or credit memo transaction or when receiving a customer payment. You can create more than one Accounts Receivable account, if needed. (This is not recommended, however, because it adds the extra work of recording customer payments.)

- **Other Current Asset**—This general account includes the QuickBooks Inventory Asset and the Undeposited Funds account. The Undeposited Funds account is used like a "desk drawer," in that it holds customer payments to be totaled on a single deposit ticket.

- **Fixed Asset**—This account tracks purchases of tangible property that will have a useful life of longer than one year. Accumulated Depreciation totals are also held in this account as a negative fixed asset.

- **Other Assets**—This account includes intangible assets that have a life of more than one year; it also includes any asset that is not a Fixed Asset or Current Asset.

Liabilities

Liabilities are the debts the company has yet to pay. QuickBooks includes these subgroups:

- **Accounts Payable**—This account type is reserved for the QuickBooks Accounts Payable account where vendor bills and bill payments reside.

- **Credit Cards**—Optionally, users can use this grouping to track the charges and payments made against a company credit card. One benefit is that you can reconcile this account as you do your bank account and download your credit card transactions directly into QuickBooks.

- **Other Current Liability**—This is debt that is expected to be paid within one year. This grouping includes the QuickBooks-created Payroll Liabilities account and Sales Tax Payable account, in addition to other user-defined liability accounts.

- **Long-Term Liability**—This is debt that will not be paid within one year.

Equity

The Equity account category holds the owner's (or owners') residual interest in the business after the liabilities are paid. Accounts in this category include Common Stock, Owner's Investments and Draws, Retained Earnings, and Opening Balance Equity (an account created by QuickBooks.

➡️ *To learn more, see "Closing Opening Balance Equity into Retained Earnings," p. 593.*

Income

Money earned from the sale of your products or services is recorded as income. Your company might have one Income account or several, depending on the detail needed for your financial analysis. Another category of income is Other Income, or income generated from the sale of a product or service not normal to your operations. Interest Income is an example of an Other Income account type.

Cost of Goods Sold

The Cost of Goods Sold account is for costs directly related to producing a service or good for sale. A direct relationship exists between these costs and your revenue. If your company sells a product, your cost of goods sold (COGS) expenses are the material, labor, and other costs incurred to make and sell the product. By contrast, your office expenses for rent or advertising are considered indirect and should not be posted to the Cost of Goods Sold account type.

 tip

When you are creating your Cost of Goods Sold accounts, consider using summary accounts, such as material, labor, and subcontract, and letting your Item List track more detail. For example, if you are a construction company and you have expenses for site work, concrete, framing, painting, and so on, instead of having a Cost of Goods Sold account for each trade, use the Item List for these. See the section "Adding an Item" in this chapter for more details. Reports by item are available to break down the total of the Cost of Goods Sold account into more detail.

Expense

An expense is recorded when an asset is used or there is an outflow of cash. The expense accounts were created during the Express Start or Advanced Setup and provide you with the basic classifications needed for properly tracking your expenses.

Although QuickBooks does not automatically create other groupings within the expenses category, a recommendation is to group your expenses by fixed (or uncontrollable) and variable (or controllable) costs. When you review your costs, these additional groupings make easy work of determining which costs you have more control over.

You can also categorize an expense as an Other Expense, which is an expense that is not normal to your operations. Contact your accountant for advice on what expenses are appropriate to record to an Other Expense category type.

Adding a New Account

If you created your own new data file using one of the methods taught in Chapter 1, p. 36, you might already have the basics of your chart of accounts created for you. Let's think positively and use the example that your business is doing so well that you have opened a new money market account with your bank. You know you need to create a new bank account in QuickBooks so that you can reconcile your banking activity with your financial institution's records.

Creating a New Account

To practice adding a new account record, open the sample data file as instructed in Chapter 1, p. 37. If you are working in your own file, use these instructions to create a new bank account (or other type of account) in your chart of accounts:

1. From the menu bar, select **Lists**, **Chart of Accounts**, or use the keyboard shortcut Ctrl+A.

2. In the Chart of Accounts dialog box, from the Account drop-down list, select **New**. Optionally, use the keyboard shortcut Ctrl+N.

3. In the Add New Account dialog box (see Figure 4.1), click the Bank option button; and then click Continue.

4. In the Account Name field, type **Money Market**. In the Number field (if account numbering is enabled) type **10600** (see Figure 4.2).

5. Optionally, select the **Subaccount Of** checkbox and select the account you want to associate this account with. (Typically, you do not make a bank account a subaccount of another account.)

6. Enter an optional description; this description displays in certain reports.

7. Accept the default Tax-Line Mapping, which comes from your sample data file or the choices you made when creating your own new file using the Express or Advanced Setup option in Chapter 1, p. 36. You can also select the drop-down list and choose a different tax line assignment, or click the "How do I choose the right tax line?" link for more information. If opened, close the Help dialog box to continue.

Figure 4.1
When creating a new account, you see useful information about the account type displayed on the right.

Add New Account: Choose Account Type

Choose **one** account type and click Continue.

Categorize money your business earns or spends

○ I_ncome

○ E_xpense

Or, track the value of your assets and liabilities

○ Fixed A_sset (major purchases)

⦿ Bank

○ Loa_n

○ Credit Car_d

○ E_quity

○ Other Account Types   <select> ▾

Help me choose the right account type.

Bank Account

Create one for each cash account, such as:

• Petty cash
• Checking
• Savings
• Money market

More...

[Continue]   [Cancel]

Figure 4.2
Here you add a new account when account numbering is enabled.

Add New Account

Account Type   Bank ▾   Number   10600

Account Na_me   Money Market

☐ S_ubaccount of _____ ▾

OPTIONAL

_Description   Money Market

Bank Acct. No. _____

Routing Number _____

Ta_x-Line Mapping   B/S-Assets: Cash ▾   How do I choose the right tax line?

[Enter Opening Balance...]   Should I enter an opening balance?

Remind me to order checks when I reach check number _____

☐ Order checks I can print from QuickBooks   Learn more

[Sa_ve & Close]   [Save & N_ew]   [Cancel]

The tax line is necessary only if you or your accountant prepares the business's tax return using software that integrates with QuickBooks.

8. Click No if the Set Up Online Services dialog box displays. If you're working in your own data file, you might want to click Yes. More details are available in Chapter 13, "Working with Bank and Credit Card Accounts," p. 519.

9. Click Save & Close.

The Add New Account dialog box also includes several other important fields:

- **Bank Acct No.**—This information is used if you set up your QuickBooks bank account for online banking downloads. For more information, see Chapter 13.

- **Routing Number**—This information is used if you set up your QuickBooks bank account for online banking downloads (see Chapter 13).

- **Enter Opening Balance**—This button opens the Enter Opening Balance dialog box, where you can enter your Statement Ending Balance and Statement Ending Date. Click the "Should I enter an opening balance?" link for help in entering these important starting numbers.

> ➡️ *For more information about beginning balances, see "Setting Up a QuickBooks Data File for Accrual or Cash Basis Reporting," p. 94.*

This dialog box also enables you to request a reminder to order checks when you reach a specific check number or order checks directly from Intuit.

The specific details required when creating a new account vary depending on the type of account you are adding to the chart of accounts.

Creating a new account in the chart of accounts is simple. However, if after reviewing the content in this chapter you find the need to make corrections, read the section "Modifying an Account in the Chart of Accounts" in this chapter.

Items

Items are what you sell or buy and are used on all customer transactions and, optionally, on purchase transactions. Items provide a quick means for data entry. However, a more important role for items is to handle the behind-the-scenes accounting while tracking product- or service-specific costs and revenue detail.

Understanding Items

Using a construction business as an example, you can create an item for Site Work, Electrical, and Plumbing Subcontractor, and assign each item to your single Cost of Goods Sold—Subcontractors account in the chart of accounts.

Using items enables you to capture cost detail by trade instead of by creating an account for each type of expense. When you view your Profit & Loss statement, you can easily see what your total Cost of Goods Sold—Subcontractors is for all trade labor expenses. See Figure 4.3.

Figure 4.3
Item reports provide detail while keeping the Profit & Loss statement easy to read.

Use the Items List for detailed reporting

Use the Profit & Loss report for summary reporting

From the menu bar, select **Reports, Jobs, Time & Mileage** for reports that provide detailed information about transactions assigned to items, including:

- Job Profitability Summary or Detail

- Job Estimates vs. Actuals Summary or Detail

- Item Profitability

- Time by Item

tip

Use the Items tab on expense transactions such as Write Checks or Enter Bills to ensure that you have the detailed reporting you need to review customer or job profitability.

These reports are useful for business owners who want to know the profitability of individual customers or jobs.

Item Types

QuickBooks has 11 item types to choose from (not including the Fixed Asset Item), although your data file might not list some of the items if the related feature is not enabled. You can choose the type to assign to a list item; however, each type has certain unique characteristics. Here are some general guidelines about the proper use for item types:

- **Service**—Create this type for services you or your subcontractors offer.

■ **Inventory Part**—This type displays only if you select the **Inventory and Purchase Orders Are Active** checkbox on the Items & Inventory—Company Preferences tab of the Preferences dialog box. (Access the menu bar by selecting **Edit, Preferences**.) Inventory is used to track products you make or buy, place in a warehouse location, and later sell to a customer. Inventory is increased with a received purchase order or bill and is decreased on a customer invoice.

> ➡ *For more information, see Chapter 5, "Setting Up Inventory," p. 151 and Chapter 6, "Managing Inventory," p. 205.*

■ **Inventory Assembly**—This item type is an assembling of multiple inventory components, as in a Bill of Materials. When an inventory assembly is built, the individual items (components of the assembly) are deducted from inventory and the quantity of the finished assembly product is increased. The assembly functionality is available only in QuickBooks Premier, Accountant, or Enterprise.

■ **Non-inventory Part**—This type is used for products you purchase but do not track as inventory. Correct use of this type includes products you purchase that are ordered for a specific customer and directly shipped to the customer, or materials and supplies you purchase but do not sell to the customer.

■ **Other Charge**—This is a multipurpose item type. Freight, handling, and other miscellaneous types of charges are examples of the proper use of the Other Charge item type. Using this type makes it possible to segregate sales of your service or product from other types of revenue and expenses in reports.

■ **Subtotal**—This type is used to add subtotal line items on sales and purchase transactions. This item is especially useful if you want to calculate a specific discount on a group of items on a customer invoice.

■ **Group**—This type is used to quickly assign a grouping of individual items on sales and purchase transactions. Unlike assemblies, groups are not tracked as a separate finished unit. Groups can save you data entry time and enable you to display or hide details on a customer's printed invoice.

■ **Discount**—This type facilitates dollar or percent deductions off what your customers owe. You cannot use this item type on purchase transactions.

■ **Payment**—This item type is not always necessary to set up. You create this item type if you record the payment directly on an invoice as a line item, such as with a Daily Sales Summary (see the QuickBooks Help for more details). On typical customer invoices, you should not record payments in this manner because no tracking of the customer's check or credit card number is done.

■ **Sales Tax Item**—This type is available only if you enabled sales tax on the Sales Tax—Company Preferences tab of the Preferences dialog box. (Access it from the menu bar by selecting **Edit, Preferences**.) In most cases, QuickBooks automatically assigns this item to an invoice. In some states or industries where multiple sales tax rates can apply for a given sale, you can also add this item to an invoice as a separate line item.

■ **Sales Tax Group**—This type is used to group multiple tax district flat-rate sales tax items that are combined and charged as one sales tax rate.

> ## 🛜 caution
>
> Carefully determine the correct item type to use when creating items. After they are created, you cannot change the following item types to any other item type: Service, Inventory Assembly, Subtotal, Discount, Payment, Sales Tax Item, and Sales Tax Group.
>
> If you find you have set up the wrong item type, correcting it might require making an accounting adjustment. To avoid using the incorrect item on future transactions, mark the item as inactive by selecting **Lists**, **Item List** from the menu bar to open the Item List dialog box. From the Item drop-down list, select **Edit Item**, and then select the **Item Is Inactive** checkbox. When this box is selected, as Figure 4.4 shows, the item is not included in any drop-down lists on transactions, but is included in reports if used during the period being reported.
>
> However, do not make an inventory type inactive if QuickBooks still shows available inventory quantity.

Figure 4.4
Marking a list item inactive removes it only from drop-down lists, not from reports.

Adding an Item

Adding items to your QuickBooks file takes some planning, but the effort will pay off with improved reporting on the different services or products your company provides.

Later in this chapter, you learn how to add multiple items at a time using the Add/Edit Multiple List Entries. In this example, you add a single new Service Item type to the sample data file.

Adding a New Service Item

To practice adding a new Service Item, open the sample data file as Chapter 1 instructed. If you are working in your own file, use these instructions to begin creating your own service items.

1. From the menu bar, select **Lists**, **Item List** to open the Item List dialog box.
2. From the Item drop-down list, select **New**. Optionally, use the keyboard shortcut Ctrl+N.
3. From the Type drop-down list, select **Service**.
4. In the Item Name/Number field, type **Inspection**.
5. Select the **This Service Is Used in Assemblies or Is Performed by a Subcontractor or Partner** checkbox, shown in Figure 4.5. This makes the item "two-sided," assigning both an expense account when used with a purchase transaction and an income account when used with a sales transaction.

Select this box to use this item on both purchase and sales transactions

Figure 4.5
Items are used on customer sales transactions and purchase transactions.

6. In the Purchase Information text box, type **Inspection**.
7. Enter a default Cost. This amount defaults on a purchase transaction, but you can also change it at the time of entry. If you do not want a default cost for the item, leave the box blank.

8. In the Expense Account field, select the appropriate account. For this example, we use the Cost of Goods Sold account because the item is directly related to our Customers or Jobs.

9. In the Preferred Vendor field, assign a vendor or leave it blank. When a preferred vendor is assigned, QuickBooks prefills that vendor name on a purchase order transaction when the item is selected.

10. Accept the default description in the Sales Information text box or type a unique description. This description defaults on your sales transactions for this item. Optionally, enter a default Sales Price. This amount defaults on sales transactions, but you can change it at the time of entry.

11. From the Tax Code drop-down list, select **Non**. In your own file, select the tax code, choosing Tax if the item is subject to sales tax or Non for nontaxable services. Check with your state's taxing authority if you have any questions about whether an item or service is taxable.

12. From the Income Account drop-down list, for this practice example, select the **Subcontracted Labor Income** account.

13. If you are finished adding items, click OK to save and exit the New Item dialog box. If you want to continue adding items, click Next to add another item.

➡️ *For more information about tracking product inventory, see "Inventory Item Type Descriptions," p. 159.*

➡️ *For more information about other uses of the items list, see "Unique Customer Transactions," p. 431.*

Class

Another method for segmenting your QuickBooks financial information is to use classes. The use of classes is a preference setting and must first be enabled by logging in to the data file as the Admin or External Accountant user.

To enable classes, follow these steps:

1. From the menu bar, select **Edit, Preferences**.

2. In the Preferences dialog box, select the **Accounting** preference on the left.

3. Select the **Company Preferences** tab.

4. Select the **Use Class Tracking for Transactions** checkbox, as Figure 4.6 shows.

5. Click OK to save your changes and close the dialog box.

Figure 4.6
Class tracking provides another method for financial reporting for management purposes.

Classes are typically used when a company has multiple revenue-generating business types or multiple profit centers. These class list items are then assigned to each transaction, as in Figure 4.7. Examples of classes are a construction company that offers either new construction or remodeling services, or a restaurant with multiple locations. In both examples, using classes that are assigned to each transaction line for both revenue and costs enables you to report profit and loss by class.

Figure 4.7
Assigning a class list item to a check transaction line provides additional management-reporting capabilities.

When deciding to use classes, it is important to have only one primary purpose for the class structure. If you try to track more than one "type" of class, the value in the reporting is diminished. For example, suppose your company has both an East Coast and a West Coast division. These represent a single use of the QuickBooks class feature. However, using classes to also track the source of the business—for example, Yellow Pages, email

tip

When using class tracking, be sure to enable the preference to be prompted to assign a class. You can find this preference by selecting **Edit, Preferences, Accounting,** and the **Company Preferences** tab.

marketing, and so on—would diminish the success of class reporting because you would be tracking two unrelated groupings. Instead, you can use classes for one purpose and customer types for another.

With QuickBooks Enterprise Solutions 14.0, you can set a global preference allowing users to assign default classes to one of the following lists:

- Accounts
- Items
- Names

For example, if you selected to assign classes to items, when setting up an item, you can identify the default class to use on the transaction, as Figure 4.8 shows. This saves users time in data entry and improves the accuracy of assigning the desired default class.

Figure 4.8
With QuickBooks Enterprise, you can choose to default classes to accounts, items, or names.

Customer Type

You can use customer types to categorize your customers in ways that are meaningful to your business. A retailer might use customer types to track retail versus wholesale, a medical office might track types of services, and a service company might track what marketing event brought in customers. You can filter certain reports by these customer types, giving you critical information for making business management decisions. These customer types can also be useful for marketing purposes when you want to direct a letter to a specific customer group.

To create or edit a customer record and assign a customer type, follow these steps:

1. On the Home page, click the Customers button. Optionally, use the shortcut Ctrl+J.

2. Double-click to select a customer name in the list that displays.

3. In the Edit Customer dialog box, click the Additional Info tab and select a type from the Type drop-down list. Optionally, from the drop-down list, select **<Add New>** to add a new type, as in Figure 4.9.

Figure 4.9
Assign a customer type for additional segmented reporting.

4. Click OK to save your changes.

You can filter many of the customer reports by customer type, making it another useful list for management reporting.

Managing Lists

You have learned about some of the more important lists to set up in your QuickBooks file. This section shares details about managing these lists, including preference settings that can help make you more efficient and accurate with your daily data entry.

This section also provides you with multiple options for importing your lists (but not transactions) into your new QuickBooks file and managing these lists when they are in QuickBooks. When importing your lists, you can select from multiple methods, including the following:

- Adding or modifying the list directly in QuickBooks, one item at a time

- Adding or modifying your lists using Add/Edit Multiple List Entries, or adding or modifying multiple records at a time in a single list

- Using the Advanced Import tool in QuickBooks

- Importing a list from another QuickBooks file using the IIF (Intuit Interchange File) format

If you are starting with a new QuickBooks file, you might first want to review the preference settings that affect the chart of accounts.

Chart of Account Preferences

Setting preferences in QuickBooks can help you be more accurate and efficient with your data entry. In Chapter 2, p. 67, "Getting Around QuickBooks," you learned about Company Preferences, which are global for all users, and My Preferences, which affect only the settings for the currently logged-in user.

Using specific preferences, you can modify how many of the QuickBooks features work. To do so, from the menu bar, select **Edit, Preferences** and select the **Accounting—Company Preferences** tab, as Figure 4.6 previously showed.

These preferences in the Accounting—Company Preferences tab affect the chart of accounts:

- **Use Account Numbers**—Selecting this option turns on the data field that holds a numeric assignment for each chart of accounts. By default, this feature is not selected in a newly created QuickBooks file.

- **Show Lowest Subaccount Only**—You can select this preference only if you selected the **Use Account Numbers** checkbox and if each account has been assigned an account number. If you have created a subaccount listing under a main (parent) listing, when you type the subaccount name, only the subaccount name and account number display in transactions. Without the feature selected, when you type a subaccount name on an expense transaction, you see both the main account name and subaccount name.

> ⬤ **tip**
>
> For accounts that have an account number assigned, deselecting the Use Account Numbers option does not remove the account number—it simply hides the field. For accountants, turn on the feature and assign your desired account numbers; then turn off the feature when the file is returned to your client. When you review the file again, any accounts created since your last review will not have an account number, which makes locating them easy.
>
> Alternatively, accountants who use the QuickBooks Accountant 2014 software can track changes made to the chart of accounts, including additions, renames, deletions, or merges made using the Client Data Review tools. Appendix A, "Client Data Review," has more information.

> 🔍 **note**
>
> On a report, if you see an amount reporting to an Other subaccount row title under a main account, it is the result of posting to the main (or parent) account instead of to the appropriate subaccount.

■ **Require Accounts**—By default, this feature is selected in a newly created QuickBooks file. If this feature is not selected, any transactions saved without selecting an account are posted to an automatically created uncategorized income or uncategorized expense account. This process follows the rule that there must always be a debit and credit side to each transaction. Fortunately, you do not have to know how to post a debit or credit because QuickBooks does this thinking for you with each transaction.

Add/Edit Multiple List Entries

Adding or modifying several entries in a single QuickBooks list can be a daunting task when you have to work with one list entry at a time. In Chapter 1, p. 36, you might have created your lists using the QuickBooks Setup to add the people you do business with, the products or services you sell, and your bank accounts.

With the Add/Edit Multiple List Entries feature (see Figure 4.10), you can add to or modify Customer or Vendor records. You can also add or modify your Service, Inventory Parts, Non-Inventory Parts, and Inventory Assemblies. Using this feature can save you precious time, particularly when you want to add or make changes to multiple entries on a list all at once.

Practice Using the Add/Edit Multiple List Entries Feature

Learn how to use the Add/Edit Multiple List Entries feature by adding a customer record and customizing the columns of data displayed. To complete this task, open the sample data as instructed in Chapter 1, p. 36.

Figure 4.10
Use the Add/Edit Multiple Lists Entries to add or modify your lists efficiently.

1. From the menu bar, select **File**, **Open Previous Company** and select the sample data file you previewed in Chapter 1, p. 37.

2. From the menu bar, select **Lists**, **Add/Edit Multiple List Entries**. In the Add/Edit Multiple List Entries dialog box that displays, the Customers list should default in the List drop-down. (If you are adding or modifying one of the other supported lists, your data fields will vary from the figures shown here.)

3. On the right side, click the Customize Columns button. The Customize Columns dialog box displays.

4. From the Available Columns panel on the left, select the **Terms** field and click Add. The Terms data field is now added to the Chosen Columns panel.

5. With the Terms field selected, click the Move Up or Move Down button to reposition the location of that data column. Adding, removing, or repositioning columns can be useful if you are copying data from an existing Excel worksheet.

6. With your cursor, in the Chosen Columns panel, select the **M.I.** (middle initial) field. Click the Remove button.

7. Click OK to close the Customize Columns dialog box.

8. Optionally, select the **View** drop-down list to filter the list results, or type in the Find box a specific search term to add as a filter to the resulting list.

9. For practice in this sample data, right-click and select **Insert Line**. Complete the data entry fields as displayed for this practice example for adding a customer record. Or if your own business's customer list is already in an Excel spreadsheet, you can also use Excel's cut-and-paste functionality to add the customer details from an existing Excel spreadsheet.

10. Click Save Changes. QuickBooks indicates the number of customer record(s) that have been saved. Click OK. If you are modifying several records, you might want to save your work often.

11. Click Close to close the Add/Edit Multiple List Entries dialog box when you have completed your additions or modifications.

 tip

If a sample file is not listed, select **File, Close Company or File, Close Company/Logoff**. In the No Company Open dialog box, select a file to practice with from the Open a Sample File drop-down list.

tip

Using the Add/Edit Multiple List Entries dialog box for importing via Excel's cut and paste can be an efficient way to get started and to update existing lists.

caution

On the Customers list, the Name field is the "look-up" (or internal) name you give a customer. It can be the same as the Company Name field or a different name. The customer invoice displays the name you type in the Company Name field, so be sure you do not leave it blank.

If you type a name in the Name column that already exists, QuickBooks highlights the duplicate name and requires you to amend the name. You cannot have the same Name field duplicated on a single list or other lists. For example, a customer named ABC Services cannot exist more than once on the customer list and cannot also be a vendor with the same spelling. If you have a customer that is also a vendor, modify the vendor listing to ABC Services—V and put the actual name of the vendor in the Company Name field and the Print on Check As field in the vendor record.

From the grid, you can right-click with your cursor for other functionality. From this menu, you can use Copy Down, Duplicate Row, Clear Column, and other useful features.

Add Your Excel Data to QuickBooks Utility

You can also add lists to QuickBooks for Vendors, Customers, and Products You Sell (Items) directly from a ready-made Excel spreadsheet using the Add Your Excel Data to QuickBooks utility.

> ### ⚡ caution
> When working in your own data, make sure your columns of data in Excel match the Add/Edit Multiple List Entries columns when cutting and pasting from Excel.

If you choose to use the Advanced (Excel) Import feature of this utility, you can also import a chart of accounts list, something you cannot do using the Add/Edit Multiple Lists Entries feature. This functionality is supported using Microsoft Excel 2003 or newer.

Enter Data into Preformatted Spreadsheets

Follow these steps to import lists using the preformatted Excel spreadsheets included with this utility:

1. From the menu bar, select **File**, **Utilities**, **Import**, **Excel Files**.

2. An information message might display regarding the Add/Edit Multiple List Entries feature discussed in the prior section. Optionally, place a checkmark in the Do Not Display This Message in the Future box.

3. Click No to continue using the Add Your Excel Data utility. The Add Your Excel Data to QuickBooks Wizard displays, as in Figure 4.11.

Figure 4.11
Choose the type of list to which you want to add information using this utility.

4. Click to select the type of data you want to add to QuickBooks. You can choose from these options:

- Customers
- Vendors
- Products I Sell

5. In this example, click Customers. QuickBooks might display an information message about not being able to undo this import. It is prudent to make a backup of your data file before proceeding. Click Yes.

 - *For more information, see "Creating a QuickBooks Backup," p. 653.*

 tip

If you choose, you can save this spreadsheet as you work. It will have an Excel file extension of .xlsm, a Macro-Enabled Workbook. When you are ready to return to finish adding to the data, return to step 1 of this section, click the Find It Now button, and then browse to the stored workbook.

6. Optionally, click the Show or Hide Coach Tips and Show or Hide Detailed Instructions. Both provide onscreen details about working with this preformatted spreadsheet. See Figure 4.12.

Figure 4.12 Preformatted spreadsheets make entering data with this utility easy.

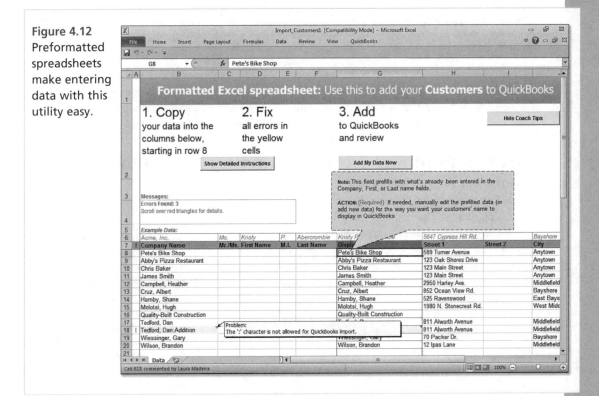

7. Begin adding data to the spreadsheet using one of these two methods:

   - Copy and paste from an existing Excel worksheet.

   - Manually type your data into the spreadsheet.

8. When your work is complete, you have the following options:

   - Save the workbook and later open it by returning to step 1, selecting the option to Find It Now, and browsing to the stored file.

   - Click the Add My Data Now button.

9. If you selected **Add My Data Now**, you are prompted with Save & Add My Data Now or I'll Add My Data Later.

10. If you selected **Save & Add My Data Now**, you are prompted to select a location to store the file. Click Save. QuickBooks provides confirmation listing the number of records that were imported successfully.

11. Select the **View Customer List** button to view the data that was imported.

12. Click Close to leave the Add Your Excel Data to QuickBooks.

> **note**
>
> Although manually adding and copying data from Excel are both options using this utility, you might find that working with the Add/Edit Multiple List Entries (from the prior section) is a more efficient method for this type of entry.

This utility has been available for many years but was greatly improved in QuickBooks 2014, offering access to more fields. Using this feature helps you get your lists quickly into a new QuickBooks file. I personally prefer working with the Add/Edit Multiple List Entries dialog box because I can arrange the columns of data to match my existing spreadsheet I might be copying from.

Advanced Import from an Existing Excel Worksheet

The advantage to using the Advanced Import is the capability to import a chart of accounts list into a new QuickBooks file from an existing Excel worksheet. This is a common practice among accounting professionals. The other methods of importing discussed in this chapter so far do not offer the capability to import one of the most important lists, the chart of accounts.

However, most users do not necessarily need to import this list. When you use the Express Start feature for creating a new QuickBooks file, QuickBooks automatically creates a chart of accounts list based on the industry type you selected during that process.

 For more information, see "Express Start," p. 39.

Follow these instructions to import the chart of accounts from an Excel spreadsheet:

> **tip**
>
> Accounting professionals have another method for creating a new file using a chart of accounts that was previously set up. Create a template QuickBooks file with the chart of accounts and other settings as desired. If you're using a version of QuickBooks Accountant, from the menu bar, select **File, New Company From Existing Company File**; then follow the onscreen prompts.

1. From the menu bar, select **File**, **Utilities**, **Import**, **Excel Files**. On the right, click the Advanced Import button. The Import a File dialog box displays, with the Set Up Import tab selected.

2. In the Select a File pane, browse to the location of your saved Excel spreadsheet that contains the chart of accounts.

3. If the workbook has multiple sheets, select the appropriate sheet to use from Choose a Sheet in This Excel Workbook, as in Figure 4.13.

Figure 4.13
Advanced Import is a useful utility if you already have your lists in an Excel worksheet. This utility does not require that you copy and paste the details.

4. If this is your first time using this utility, in the Data Mapping pane, select **Add New** in the Choose a Mapping drop-down. The Mappings dialog box displays.

5. Type a name into the Mapping Name field. This enables you to select this mapping for use again.

6. For the Import Type, in this example, select **Account**.

7. The left column lists the fields available in QuickBooks (see Figure 4.14). The fields in your selected spreadsheet appear in the Import Data pane on the right. From the drop-down list, select the matching field.

8. Click Save to store this mapping for future use. You then return to the Import a File dialog box.

tip
When creating the Excel worksheet, use text in your column headers that will be easy to match to the QuickBooks fields.

Figure 4.14
When using Advanced Import, map the columns of an existing spreadsheet to the fields in QuickBooks.

9. Click Preview to see the results of what the import will be prior to completing this step. Any errors in the import file show the word *Error* displayed in red text. Click any row with an error, and QuickBooks details the reason so you can fix it before importing.

10. Select how to handle errors by choosing from the following:

   ■ Import Rows with Errors and Leave Error Fields Blank

   ■ Do Not Import Rows with Errors

11. Click Import to complete the process—or click OK to close the Preview dialog box, or click Cancel to not make any changes. See Figure 4.15.

12. If you selected Import, QuickBooks displays an information dialog box recommending that you back up your data prior to the import. You cannot undo the import process. Click Yes to continue the import, or No to make a data backup first.

13. If QuickBooks detects duplicate records, a message displays and you can choose from options listed below. When making a selection you will be able to Click Apply, Apply to All, or Help to complete the selected action.

   ■ Keep existing data and discard import data

   ■ Replace existing data with import data, ignoring blank fields

   ■ Replace existing data with import data, including blank fields

Figure 4.15
Preview the import and view
any rows with errors.

	Preview	✕

File to be imported: C:\Users\Owner\Documents\Chart of Accounts.xlsx

Mapping definition used: Chart of Accounts

DATA PREVIEW:

In data preview show: [all data ▼]

✓ all data
only errors

OK	5	
OK	6	
OK	7	Accounts Payable
ERROR	8	Payroll Liabilities

19 rows processed with 1 errors (5 % of the file)

DETAILS FOR:

QUICKBOOKS FIELD	FILE COLUMN	DATA	ERROR
Type	Type	Current Liability	Invalid Account ...
Number	Number	25000	
Name	Name	Payroll Liabilities	
Description	Description	Payroll Liabilities	
Bank Acct. No./Car...	Bank Accnt #		

ERROR HANDLING:

When errors are detected during import:
- ⦿ Import rows with errors and leave error fields blank
- ○ Do not import rows with errors

[Import] [OK] [Cancel] [Help]

14. If you selected Yes to the Import message, QuickBooks confirms the records that were imported. Select **Save** to save the Error Log (browse to a location to store the file) or **Don't Save**.

15. To view the chart of accounts that was imported, from the menu bar, select **Lists, Chart of Accounts**.

With QuickBooks 2014, you have several options for importing your lists. Getting started using QuickBooks is fast and easy. The next section details another method you can choose to use, especially if you are choosing to copy lists from one QuickBooks file to another.

Importing an Intuit Interchange Format File (IIF)

The term *Intuit Interchange Format (IIF)* refers to data exchange functionality that has been around for some time. It is a method for exporting lists from one QuickBooks file and importing these lists into a new QuickBooks file. The process creates a tab-delimited value format file with the extension of .iif. You can view and edit this file using Excel.

The most common use for this tool is to export lists from one QuickBooks data file to a new QuickBooks data file. The process is easy and relatively error free. Other uses for the tool include transaction imports. This book does not cover the topic of transaction imports using IIF-formatted files; however, you can find more information about this utility by typing **IIF** into the search field at www.quickbooks.com/support.

The IIF format is a preferred and easy method to use if you already have a QuickBooks file with a chart of accounts (or other lists) that you want to replicate in another file.

The only disadvantage to working with an IIF format file is all the extra information that is in the text file, making it awkward to edit or add to the existing information.

To export an IIF-formatted chart of accounts file from an existing QuickBooks file, follow these steps:

1. From the menu bar, select **File**, **Open** or **Restore Company** to open the QuickBooks file that has the chart of accounts (or other lists) you want to export and duplicate in another file.

2. From the open QuickBooks file, on the menu bar, select **File**, **Utilities**, **Export**, **Lists to IIF Files**.

3. In the Export dialog box, select the **Chart of Accounts** checkbox (or other type of list you want to export), shown in Figure 4.16.

tip

Creating individual IIF files for each of the master lists you want to export is preferable to creating one combined file. In other words, create one file for your chart of accounts, separate from a file for vendors or customers. This way, if one list has trouble importing, it won't prevent the other lists from importing.

Figure 4.16
The Export dialog box shows choices of lists available for export.

4. Click OK. You are prompted to provide a filename and to save the file. Remember the location where you store the file; you need to browse to the file to import into another QuickBooks file.

Figure 4.17 shows the exported QuickBooks chart of accounts in the IIF format in an Excel workbook. You can see that it is not as user friendly as the Add/Edit Multiple List Entries dialog box discussed previously.

note

The Add/Edit Multiple List Entries feature does not include modifying the chart of accounts list. To import the chart of accounts, see the section "Advanced Import from an Existing Excel Worksheet" in this chapter.

Figure 4.17
This chart of accounts IIF format file can be imported into another QuickBooks file.

To import the saved IIF file into a new QuickBooks file, follow these steps:

1. From the menu bar, select **File**, **Open or Restore Company**, and select the QuickBooks file you want to import the previously exported list into.

   If you have not already created your new file, select **File, New** and follow the prompts. (See Chapter 1 for more information.)

2. From the menu bar, select **File, Utilities, Import, IIF Files**.

3. In the Import dialog box, browse to the location of the stored IIF-formatted file.

4. With your cursor, select the file and click Open.

5. QuickBooks then imports the IIF-formatted file into the QuickBooks data file. Click OK to close the Your Data Has Been Imported message box.

Now that you have your new data file with new lists from another file, you are ready to begin entering transactions. Think of all the time you saved by not having to manually create each list item in the new file.

> **⚠ caution**
>
> The IIF file format is a tab-delimited text file with an extension of .iif. Be sure to keep this format when saving your changes; do not save as an .xls or .xlsx Excel file type.

Reporting on Lists

With a QuickBooks file created and lists entered, you can now review the efforts of your work.

Let's start with a simple listing of your vendors.

1. From the menu bar, select **Reports**, **List**. Take a moment to review the many lists available for reporting on in this menu. Some lists display only if the associated preference in QuickBooks is enabled.

2. Select the **Vendor Contact List**. Optionally, click the Customize Report button.

3. The Modify Report dialog box opens, with the Display tab selected. From the Columns listing, add or remove checkmarks to include or exclude information from the list report.

4. Click OK when finished.

You learn more about modifying these and other reports in Chapter 14, "Reporting in QuickBooks," p. 554.

Reviewing your lists before you begin entering transactions can ensure that the information provided in reports is correct.

Finding and Fixing Chart of Account Errors

When searching for reasons why your financial statements do not appear correctly, the first place to look is often the chart of accounts. It is also important to carefully consider the impact of the change on your financials and make sure you choose the right method for correction.

You can resolve errors found on the chart of accounts in many ways. However, before attempting any of the suggested methods here, you should consider the following:

- The effect the change could have on prior-period financials

- The effect the change could have on previously recorded transactions

- The impact the changes would have on the records your accountant has kept for the company

A quick review of the chart of accounts should include the following:

- Duplicated accounts

- Unnecessary accounts (too much detail)

- Accounts placed in the wrong account type category

- Misplaced subaccounts

QuickBooks Required Accounts

The accounts listed here are required for specific functionality of a transaction. If you have previously removed the account, QuickBooks re-creates it when you use a transaction that depends on that specific account. Additionally, these accounts are automatically created when a related transaction is opened for the first time:

- Accounts Receivable
- Inventory Asset
- Undeposited Funds
- Accounts Payable
- Payroll Liabilities
- Sales Tax Payable

- Opening Balance Equity
- Retained Earnings
- Cost of Goods Sold
- Payroll Expenses
- Estimates (nonposting)
- Purchase Orders (nonposting)

Making an Account Inactive

Marking an account inactive is usually the best choice when you have duplicate or extra list entries on your chart of accounts. Making an account inactive removes it from any drop-down list where the item can be selected. However, for reporting periods where the account has a value, any reports generated will include the inactive account balance.

Do you need to mark several accounts as inactive? Select the **Include Inactive** checkbox at the bottom of the chart of accounts list, shown in Figure 4.18. You can mark any list items you want to become inactive by clicking in front of the list item name. If Include Inactive is grayed out, right-click an account and choose Make Account Inactive. You now have the option to place a checkmark in the Include Inactive box.

In the future, if you try to use an inactive account, QuickBooks will prompt you to choose Use It Once or Make It Active.

note

In earlier versions of QuickBooks, you might have accounts that have an asterisk (*) in front of the name to indicate a duplicate account name. This situation usually happens only when you did not select to use one of the sample charts of accounts. QuickBooks has certain accounts that it creates automatically.

For example, if you did not select a sample default chart of accounts and you created your own Accounts Receivable account, QuickBooks automatically adds another Accounts Receivable account when an invoice transaction is opened. Because QuickBooks recognizes that you already have an Accounts Receivable account (the one you created), QuickBooks appends the name with an asterisk. You should merge your created account (the one without the *) into the QuickBooks-created account. See the later section titled "Merging Duplicated Accounts" for instructions on how to merge two like accounts.

Click with your cursor in front of the item

Select the "Include inactive"

Merging Duplicated Accounts

Another method to remove duplicated accounts is to merge the similar accounts. To perform a chart of accounts merge, both accounts must be in the same chart of accounts category; in other words, you cannot merge an Asset-type account with a Liability-type account.

Before merging accounts, perform a backup of your data, just in case the result is not what you expected. To create a backup of your file, from the menu bar, select **File**, **Backup Company** and follow the prompts. When the accounts are merged, all transactions previously assigned to the removed account now appear as if they were always assigned to the remaining account.

To merge two accounts, follow these steps:

1. From the menu bar, select **Lists**, **Chart of Accounts**, and highlight the account you want to remove with the merge. With the account highlighted, press Ctrl+E on your keyboard to open the Edit Account dialog box.

2. If you are using account numbering, replace the account number with the account number for the account you want to retain. Optionally, you can type the exact spelling of the name of the other account you are merging with this one into the Account Name field.

QuickBooks cautions you that the name is already being used and asks whether you want to continue (see Figure 4.19). If you do not get this message, you didn't accurately type the name or account number. You need to try again.

3. Click Yes to merge the accounts.

> **caution**
>
> This method potentially changes your financials. Cautiously perform it only after you have discussed the effect with the company's accountant and have made a backup of the data file.

> **caution**
>
> Chart of accounts, customers, jobs, vendors, and other names lists can all be merged within their own type or category. Be careful—there is no undo function, making the action irreversible.

Figure 4.19
QuickBooks offers a word of caution when you are merging two charts of accounts list entries.

> Merge
>
> ⚠ This name is already being used. Would you like to merge them?
>
> Yes   No

📡 **caution**

Exercise caution before changing an account type. The change affects any prior-period financials. If this consequence is a limitation for your company, a simple solution is to create a general journal entry to remove the amount from one account and assign it to another, dating the transaction in the current period. This method preserves the integrity of prior-period financials.

The Audit Trail report in QuickBooks does not track that a change was made to an account type. However, if your accountant views your data with QuickBooks Accountant 2014 software, the accountant can view the changes you or your employees made to an account type.

Modifying an Account in the Chart of Accounts

The mistake most often made when creating your own chart of accounts is assigning the wrong account type. QuickBooks provides additional subcategories under the six standard accounting categories, as identified in the "Account Types" section at the beginning of this chapter.

The Add New Account dialog box, previously shown in Figure 4.1, can help you reduce errors that occur when creating a new account. When you select an account type, QuickBooks provides a general description of the proper use of the selected account.

Changing an account type can also be advantageous when you want to fix future transactions and prior-period transactions. For example, suppose you created a Current Asset account type instead of the correct Expense account type. Simply changing the account type via the Edit Account dialog box (see following steps) corrects all prior-period and future transactions to be assigned to the new account type.

However, you cannot change an account type or merge a chart of an account if subaccounts are associated with that chart of account list item. For more information, refer to the note on page 137.

To change an account type, follow these steps:

1. From the menu bar, select **Lists, Chart of Accounts** (or press Ctrl+A). The Chart of Accounts dialog box displays.

2. Select the account for which you want to change the type.

3. From the Account drop-down list, select **Edit Account** (or press Ctrl+E to open the account for editing). The Edit Account dialog box displays.

4. Click the drop-down arrow next to Account Type (see Figure 4.20) and choose a new account type from the list.

5. Click Save & Close.

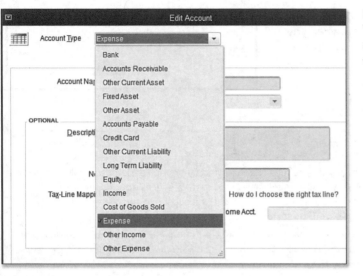

Figure 4.20
You can usually, but not always, change an account type.

note

Not all account types can be changed. Accounts Receivable, Accounts Payable, Credit Cards (with online access configured), and any of the default accounts QuickBooks creates cannot be changed to a different type. In addition, for any Balance Sheet account whose account type is changed to a non–Balance Sheet account type, QuickBooks warns that you can no longer use a register for this account or enter transactions directly into this account.

Assigning or Removing a Subaccount Relationship

Often in accounting reports, you have specific accounts for which you want to see a more detailed breakdown of the costs. You can get this breakdown easily by creating the main account and associating subaccounts with the main account.

Figure 4.21 shows Utilities as a main account, with an indented subaccount for each type of utility expense.

To edit an existing account to be a subaccount of another main account, follow these steps:

1. From the menu bar, select **Lists**, **Chart of Accounts** (or press Ctrl+A). The Chart of Accounts dialog box displays.

2. Select the account that you want to be a subaccount of another account.

3. From the Account drop-down list, select **Edit Account** (or press Ctrl+E to open the account for editing). The Edit Account dialog box displays.

4. Select the **Subaccount Of** checkbox and, from the drop-down box, choose the account you want it to be associated with. (It must be of the same account type.)

Figure 4.21
The chart of accounts shows a subaccount relationship to the parent account.

NAME	⚡ TYPE	BALANCE TOTAL
◦ Tools and Machinery	Expense	
◦ Union Dues	Expense	
◦ Utilities	Expense	
◦ Gas and Electric	Expense	
◦ Telephone	Expense	
◦ Water	Expense	
◦ Interest Income	Other Income	
◦ Other Income	Other Income	

5. Click Save & Close.

Users can assign a subaccount that is only in the same general account type. For example, an Expense type cannot be a subaccount of a Current Asset type account (see Figure 4.22).

Figure 4.22
Assigning a subaccount to a parent account.

Add New Account

Account Type: Expense

Account Name: Gas and Electric
☑ Subaccount of: Utilities

OPTIONAL
Description: Gas and Electric
Note:
Tax-Line Mapping: <Unassigned>   How do I choose the right tax line?
☐ Track reimbursed expenses in Income Acct.

🔍 **note**

If you need to change the subaccount to another General Ledger account type, first deselect the Subaccount Of checkbox. Click Save & Close to save the change. Then edit the account and change the type. You cannot change subaccount types when they are associated with a main account. You also cannot change the account type when that account has subaccounts associated with it.

Another method for changing the assignment of a subaccount to a main account is easily done directly from the list view. To remove or add a subaccount directly from the list, follow these steps:

1. In the Chart of Accounts dialog box, click with your cursor over the diamond in front of the list item (see Figure 4.23).

Figure 4.23
Dragging the diamond in front of an account is an easy way to change the subaccount relationship within the same category type.

2. Drag the diamond so the selected account is immediately below the main account grouping.

3. Drag the diamond to the right to create a subaccount–account relationship to the main account. Or optionally, drag the diamond to the left to remove the subaccount relationship.

   The chart of accounts list shows the corrected relationship (see Figure 4.24).

Financial reporting is more accurate when you take the time to review and correct your chart of accounts setup. Often you can manage the information better when you group similar income or expense accounts using the subaccount feature.

Figure 4.24
The chart of accounts looks like this after changing the subaccount relationship.

Finding and Fixing Item List Errors

Do you want to quickly fix some of the most common errors in QuickBooks? Reviewing and correcting items in QuickBooks can be an efficient way to repair a company's data file accounting errors. Often the reason for misstatement on a company's financials can be traced to incorrect setup of items. Some indicators of this might be understated revenue, negative costs, or just an overall lack of confidence in the financials. This is because QuickBooks items are "mapped" to the chart of accounts; if an item is improperly assigned to the wrong type of an account, this could create errors in accurate financial reporting.

To help you when incorrectly set-up items might not be so apparent, the following sections offer a few methods for reviewing the item list.

Reviewing the Item List on the Computer Screen

Adding and removing columns you view in the Item List can help you notice any setup errors that exist.

Customizing the View of the Item List

To modify the columns that display on the Item List, follow these instructions:

1. In the Item List dialog box (select **Lists, Item List** from the menu bar), right-click and select **Customize Columns**.

2. In the Customize Columns dialog box, shown in Figure 4.25, add the COGS Account by highlighting it in the Available Columns pane and clicking Add to include the account in the Chosen Columns pane on the right. Add to (or remove from) the Chosen Columns pane those fields that you want (or don't want) to see when viewing the Item List dialog box.

3. Click the Move Up or Move Down buttons in the center of the dialog box to customize the order in which you want to view the columns. Then click OK.

4. Optionally, to widen columns of displayed data on your computer screen, place your mouse on the right edge of a column header and drag to make the column wider or smaller.

5. Optionally, click a header column to sort the displayed data by the selected column.

6. Click the X in the top-right corner to close the Item List.

Figure 4.25
Right-click the Item List to customize the columns to display.

Now you can conveniently review the list on the computer screen for items that do not have a cost of goods sold or expense account assigned, or that might have the wrong account assigned. Not having an expense account assigned becomes problematic when the item is both purchased and sold; both types of transactions report only to the single account selected as the Income Account.

See the "Correcting One-Sided Items" section of this chapter for a more detailed discussion of how to properly fix this issue. Refer back to Figure 4.3 for details on creating a two-sided item in QuickBooks.

Item Listing Report

Another method for reviewing the Item List setup is to use the Item Listing report (by choosing Reports, List, Item Listing from the menu bar). Click Customize Report from the top left of the displayed report. In the dialog box that displays, click the Display tab to select the columns to view. Useful columns include Item, Description, Type, Account, Asset Account (for inventory items only), COGS Account, and Sales Tax Code, as in Figure 4.26. Whenever the item is used on a purchase or sales transaction (such as an invoice, a sales receipt, a bill, a check, and so on), these columns show where QuickBooks posts the transaction on the chart of accounts.

Figure 4.26
Modify the Item Listing report to provide just the details you need.

What exactly are you looking for on the list item report? First, look for items that you use on both purchase and sales transactions but that are missing the COGS Account, as shown in Figure 4.27. Alternatively, you might look for items with the incorrect account assigned. If you collect sales tax, be sure the correct sales tax code is selected.

➡ *For a more detailed discussion of sales tax in QuickBooks, see "Setting Up Sales Tax,"*
p. 327.

Figure 4.27
Review the Item Listing report for item setup errors or missing information.

These items do not have an expense account assigned

Rock Castle Construction
Item Listing
December 15, 2017

Item	Description	Type	COGS Account	Sales Tax Code
Blueprint changes		Service		Non
Blueprints	Blueprints	Service		Non
Concrete Slab	Foundation slab – prep and pouring	Service		Non
Floor Plans	Floor plans	Service		Non
Framing	Framing labor	Service		Non
Installation	Installation labor	Service		Non
Labor		Service		Non
Removal	Removal labor	Service		Non
Repairs	Repair work	Service		Non
Subs	Subcontracted services	Service	Job Expenses:Subcontractors	Non
Subs:Carpet	Install carpeting	Service	Job Expenses:Subcontractors	Non
Subs:Drywall	Install drywall	Service	Job Expenses:Subcontractors	Non
Subs:Duct Work	Heating & Air Conditioning Duct Work	Service	Job Expenses:Subcontractors	Non
Subs:Electrical	Electrical work	Service	Job Expenses:Subcontractors	Non

Profit & Loss Standard Report

If you suspect errors with your financials, drilling down (double-clicking with your cursor) on the Total Income, Cost of Goods Sold, or Expense totals on a Profit & Loss Standard report might provide clues to the mistakes. To generate this report for your data, follow these steps:

1. From the menu bar, select **Reports, Company & Financial, Profit & Loss Standard**.

2. On the Profit & Loss Standard report, double-click the Total Income subtotal, shown in Figure 4.28. A Transaction Detail by Account report displays, showing each line of detail that makes up the amount you viewed on the original Profit & Loss Standard report.

Figure 4.28
Drill down to review the details of your business Total Income dollars.

3. On the Transaction Detail by Account report, click Customize Report. In the dialog box that displays, click the Filters tab. In the Choose Filter pane, scroll down to select **Transaction Type**.

4. In the Transaction Type drop-down list, select **Multiple Transaction Types**, as shown in Figure 4.29. The Select Transaction Type dialog box displays. Click to place a check next to each transaction type that normally would *not* be reported to an income account, such as a check, bill, credit card, and so on; then click OK.

The resulting report now shows all purchase type transactions (or whatever transaction types you selected) that were recorded to income accounts. In the example in Figure 4.30, a vendor bill transaction type displays in the totals for income. This is because, on the vendor bill, an item was used that had only an income account assigned. After you determine that you have these types of errors in posting, you should review your Item List for any one-sided items. The next section discusses this topic.

Figure 4.29
Filter the report to include transaction types that should not be reporting to income accounts.

Figure 4.30
The Transaction Detail by Account report shows a purchase-type transaction reporting to an income account in error.

As with any data correction in QuickBooks, you should make a backup of the data before attempting these methods. The preferred backup method is a QuickBooks backup (a file with the extension of .QBB). You can create a data backup by selecting **File**, **Back Up Company** from the menu bar. If the result after fixing items is not what you expected, you can easily restore the backup file.

This section showed some effective ways to determine whether your items are incorrectly set up. In the next section, you learn the methods of fixing these item setup errors in QuickBooks.

If you are an accounting professional, you will want to review your client's item setup and possible errors using the Client Data Review features and tools available exclusively with QuickBooks Accountant 2014. Appendix A, "Client Data Review," has more information.

Correcting One-Sided Items

A one-sided item is an item that has only one account assigned. See Figure 4.31, which shows the Framing item setup. Notice the only account assigned to this item is Labor Income. When this item is used on a customer invoice, it increases the Labor Income amount. However, if the same item is used on a check or bill, the amount of the expense records directly to the Labor Income account as a negative number. This would cause both income and cost of goods sold to be understated.

You should not have one-sided items if you plan to use the same item on both purchase transactions and sales transactions.

You might have several items on your list that can qualify to be one sided because they are used only on sales transactions and never on purchase transactions, or always on purchase transactions and never on sales transactions. What can become problematic is that, at some time, a user might mistakenly use the item on the other transaction type.

tip

These methods might affect your financials for prior accounting periods. Take care when selecting a method that will impact financial periods that have already been used to prepare your tax documents. Discuss these choices with your accountant before making the changes.

If you would like to be warned when making changes to prior periods, consider entering a Closing Date into your file. For more information, see Chapter 16, "Sharing QuickBooks Data With Your Accountant."

When this is not selected, you cannot assign both an income and expense account

Figure 4.31
Items with only one account assigned can misstate financials if used on both purchase and sales transactions.

Inventory items default as two sided. For the other item types, I recommend that you create them all as two-sided items (see Figure 4.32). You do so by selecting the checkbox labeled **This Service Is Used in Assemblies or...** (the rest of the label depends on what item type is selected) in the New or Edit Item dialog box.

Figure 4.32
The corrected one-sided item now has both an expense and an income account assigned.

The results are new Purchase Information and Sales Information panes. Now the "Account" has become an "Income Account" and you have a new Expense Account field to assign your proper expense account. This way, if you use the item on both a vendor bill or check and a customer sales transaction, your financials show the transaction in the proper account.

> 📡 **caution**
>
> Before making these suggested changes, have you made a backup of your data? Remember, some of the recommended changes are not reversible.
>
> You might even consider printing reports before and after changes, to compare and verify that you achieved the desired end result.
>
> To learn more about properly creating a backup of your QuickBooks data, see Chapter 17, "Managing Your QuickBooks Database."

When you make the change and click OK, QuickBooks might open a dialog box (if this item has been used in a transaction) prompting you to update existing transactions or apply the change only for future transactions. The decision made at this time to change the account assignment is critical to your financials. Clicking Yes to updating existing transactions causes all previous transactions to now report to the new account assigned. If you are attempting to fix historical transactions, this can be a time-saving feature because you do not have to change each individual transaction manually.

Click No if you do not want to update prior-period transactions. This option might be recommended if you have already prepared your tax data with QuickBooks financial information. The change then takes effect only for future transactions.

Additional Warnings for One-Sided Items

You aren't completely on your own when it comes to locating one-sided item errors in item assignments. QuickBooks helps you recognize the potential error by displaying a warning message when you are using an item on a purchase transaction that is assigned only to an income account. Figure 4.33 shows the warning message you see when a check is being written to a vendor but the item used is assigned only to an Income Account. Be aware that this warning displays only if you have not checked the Do Not Display This Message in the Future checkbox.

Figure 4.33
This warning message displays when you use an item on a purchase transaction that is mapped only to an Income Account.

If you ignore the message, in this example, QuickBooks posts the expense to the revenue account selected in the New or Edit Item dialog box. The effect of this is to understate revenue (an expense is a negative amount in the revenue account) and to understate your costs (because no cost was recorded to an expense account). Both of these messages distort your financial details, so be sure you don't disregard this important message.

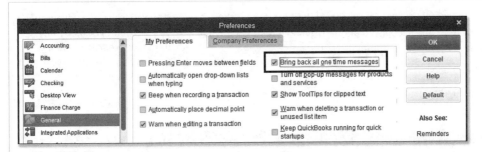

Figure 4.34
To be notified of transaction errors previously disregarded, select the Bring Back All One Time Messages checkbox.

Making an Item Inactive

If you have found errors in your Item List, a safe method for avoiding future mistakes by using the incorrect items is to make them inactive. An inactive item still displays in reports but is not included in any drop-down lists on sales or purchase transactions.

To mark an item as inactive, follow these steps:

1. From the menu bar, select **Lists**, **Item List**.

2. Select the item you want to make inactive by clicking it once.

3. Right-click the selected item.

4. Select **Make Item Inactive**.

5. If a warning message displays (for example, stating that the item is part of a group), click Yes to make the item inactive or click No to cancel your change.

Making an item inactive does not have any impact on the company's financials. If you want to correct your financials, you need to choose one of two options:

- Edit the account assignment on each item. This gives you the option to fix all previous transactions that used this item retroactively. (Use this cautiously because it changes prior-period financials.) The effect of changing an account assignment on an item is the same as the one discussed in the section "Correcting One-Sided Items" in this chapter.

- Create a General Journal Entry transaction to reassign the amounts from one account to another. This method is typically completed by your accountant.

Before making changes, make a backup of your data, and always discuss the method you choose with your accountant.

> **tip**
>
> Open the Item List by selecting **Lists, Item List** from the menu bar. Select the **Include Inactive** checkbox (in the lower center of the dialog box). Click once to the left of any list item to make the item inactive, as in Figure 4.35.
>
> If the checkbox is grayed out, you have not yet made any item inactive. After making the first item inactive, you can select the checkbox.

Figure 4.35
Marking Item List elements as inactive causes the item not to show on dropdown lists.

Except for inventory items, generally no ramifications apply when marking a list item inactive. Only inventory items with a zero quantity on hand should be made inactive. See Chapter 6 for more details on handling inventory errors.

Merging Items

If you have duplicated items, one easy method for fixing the problem is to merge items of the same type. When merging two items, you first need to decide which item is going to be merged into the other item. The item merged will no longer exist on your Item List.

To merge two items, follow these steps:

1. From the menu bar, select **Lists, Item List**.

2. Review the list for duplicate items; note the name of the item you want to remain.

3. Double-click the item you want to merge into another item. The Edit Item dialog box displays.

4. In the Item Name/Number field, type the name exactly as you noted it in step 2. You can also use the Copy And Paste command to avoid typing lengthy names or long numbers.

5. Click OK to save your change. QuickBooks provides a warning message that you are merging items (see Figure 4.36).

Figure 4.36
A warning displays when you merge two items.

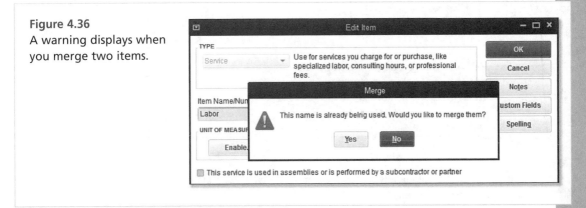

Carefully consider the consequences of merging before you do it (and be sure you have a backup of your QuickBooks file). All the historical transactions merge into the remaining list item.

Creating Items As Subitems

Creating an item as a subitem of another item is one way to easily organize reports for a group of similar items. Your accounting data is not affected by having or not having items as subitems.

To make an item a subitem of another item, follow these steps:

1. From the menu bar, select **Lists**, **Item List**.

2. Double-click the item you want to assign as a subitem. The Edit Item dialog box opens.

3. Select the **Subitem Of** checkbox, in Figure 4.37.

4. From the drop-down list, select the item you want to relate this subitem to.

> 🔊 **caution**
> You can merge only items of the same type. Duplicate service item types can be merged, but a service item type cannot be merged with a non-inventory item type. Merging inventory items is not recommended; see Chapter 6 for more detail.

Figure 4.37
The Sitework Sub service item is being made a subitem of Subs (short for Subcontracted).

You can create a subitem only within the same item type. For example, service items cannot be subitems of inventory items.

You can also rearrange the list by assigning a subitem to another item by using your mouse pointer on the Item List to move the item up or down and to the right or left. This functionality is the same as the example discussed in the section "Assigning or Removing a Subaccount Relationship" in this chapter.

You have now completed the important steps in getting your file ready to work with. In the next few chapters, you learn about inventory, vendors, customer activities, and much more.

QuickStart

Step 1. Enable Inventory **156**

Step 2. Add Inventory Parts **161**

Step 3. Purchasing Inventory with a Vendor Bill **189**

Step 4. Selling Inventory **193**

5

SETTING UP INVENTORY

Inventory can be described as a company's merchandise, raw materials, and finished and unfinished products that have not yet been sold.

QuickBooks can track the products you purchase, stock, and then later sell to customers. QuickBooks can also track the products you assemble (a component) and use to create a product for sale (finished good). QuickBooks has a perpetual inventory system, meaning each time you record a purchase transaction, inventory is increased, and when you record a sales transaction, inventory is decreased. (See the "Proper Inventory Processes" section later in this chapter.)

QuickBooks Pro, Premier, and Enterprise Solutions record the cost of inventory using the Average Cost method, in contrast to LIFO (Last In, First Out) or FIFO (First In, First Out). This means that the cost recorded at the time a product is sold is equal to the number of inventory units purchased divided by the total cost of the units. QuickBooks automates this process for you. As long as you record your documents correctly and date them appropriately, QuickBooks assigns the correct average cost.

If you are using QuickBooks Enterprise Solutions 14.0, you also have the *option* to use FIFO costing, or the First-In, First-Out method. The upcoming section "Inventory Features by QuickBooks Edition with Advanced Inventory" highlights the main differences among the editions of QuickBooks.

➥ *If you are using QuickBooks Enterprise for inventory management, refer to Appendix C, "QuickBooks Enterprise Solutions Features," p. 783.*

Ask yourself these important questions to differentiate between using inventory and non-inventory items in QuickBooks:

- **Will you be selling what you buy, and do you not know the customer at the time of purchase?**—An example is a furniture store that purchases furniture for resale to customers, or a retail store that purchases medical supplies that are sold to customers. These qualify as the proper use of inventory items.

- **Are you manufacturing what you sell?**—In other words, you buy components (raw materials) and later assemble the components into a finished product that is sold to a customer. An example is a bike store that purchases wheels, steering columns, chains, and so on, and then assembles the components into a completed bike for sale to the customer. This qualifies as the proper use of inventory items.

- **Are you purchasing materials that you use, but do not sell?**—For example, a car detailing business purchases buffing pads and paint supplies. These items are stored in inventory but are not sold directly to a customer. This example is a more appropriate use of non-inventory items.

- **Is the dollar value of your inventory not significant?**—Often companies carry a small amount of inventory, but the majority of their vendor product purchases are drop-shipped directly to the customer's address. For example, a construction company can order appliances for a new home but generally does not stock them. Instead, it has the appliances shipped directly from the vendor to the new home. This example is a more appropriate use of a non-inventory item.

Making the decision to track inventory takes commitment on your part. QuickBooks can help you efficiently and accurately track your inventory with features unique to each edition of QuickBooks.

Inventory Features by QuickBooks Edition

The release of QuickBooks 2014 has again dramatically changed the features available when your business tracks inventory. Now, more than ever, you need to review those features you need the most and make sure you are working in the right QuickBooks edition for your business inventory tracking needs.

If you are using the QuickBooks Pro or Premier editions and later decide your business would benefit from the features available only with QuickBooks Enterprise Solutions, you can expect the transition to be seamless. When you are ready to upgrade, you open your company file in Enterprise Solutions, and your lists, data, report templates, and user permissions automatically transfer.

QuickBooks Pro 2014

QuickBooks Pro 2014 is easy to set up and learn to use. With QuickBooks Pro, you can have up to three simultaneous users working in the same data file. QuickBooks Pro *does not* come in industry-specific editions.

QuickBooks Pro has the most basic of inventory features, including the following:

- **Inventory Items**—Included are Inventory Part and Non-inventory Part.

- **Purchase Orders**—Commitment to purchase from a vendor.

- **Change Item Prices in Batch**—Feature to change more than one item price at a time by a fixed amount or percentage.

- **Warn If Not Enough Inventory to Sell**—Preference that enables a warning when attempting to sell inventory without enough quantity on hand.

- **Integrate Your FedEx, UPS, and USPS Software**—Simplify the management of tracking your shipping documents from within QuickBooks.

After reviewing the inventory features in this chapter, you might decide there are inventory features that you could use in the other editions of QuickBooks. You can easily convert a QuickBooks Pro file to QuickBooks Premier or Enterprise. Chapter 17, "Managing Your QuickBooks Database," has more information on upgrading your file

QuickBooks Premier 2014

QuickBooks Premier 2014 offers several industry-specific editions. The inventory features include everything offered with QuickBooks Pro 2014 and, in addition, the following:

- **Inventory Center**—Central location for inventory activities and reporting.

- **Inventory Assembly**—Creates a finished good from a bill of materials.

- **Sales Orders**—Handles customer preorders.

- **Quantity Available**—Preference settings for handling how quantity available is calculated.

- **Multiple Unit of Measure**—You purchase in one unit and sell in another. (Available only in selected Premier or Enterprise editions.)

If you have purchased the QuickBooks Premier Manufacturing & Wholesale 2014 edition, you have all the preceding features plus the following:

- **Sales Order Fulfillment Worksheet**—Provides ease in filling orders.

- **Create Customer Return Materials Authorization Form**—Creates a Word template for you to enter information into.

- **Report on Nonconforming Material Report**—Creates a Word template for you to enter information into.

- **Damaged Goods Log**—Creates a Word template for you to enter information into.

- **Several Industry-Specific Reports**—Includes Inventory Reorder Report by Vendor.

QuickBooks Enterprise Solutions Editions

QuickBooks Enterprise Solutions 14.0 offers specific features for companies that track inventory. This chapter lists the features for the following versions of QuickBooks. Many of the features are more detailed in Appendix C.

- QuickBooks Enterprise Solutions 14.0

- QuickBooks Enterprise Solutions Manufacturing & Wholesale 14.0

- Either of the preceding two versions with an Advanced Inventory subscription

- Either of the preceding two versions with an Advanced Pricing subscription

QuickBooks Enterprise Solutions 14.0

QuickBooks Enterprise Solutions 14.0 includes all the features mentioned previously, as well as the following:

- **Auto Create POs**—From the inventory stock status reports (and others), you have the option to create multiple purchase orders at one time. New functionality in Enterprise 14.0 includes the Auto Create POs suggesting a quantity needed to order.

- **Default Class Assignment**—You can set a preference to default class (departments) assignment to Accounts, Items, or Names.

- **Enhanced Inventory Receiving**—Optional workflow improves how you receive and pay for inventory. Item receipts increase inventory and inventory offset (current liability) accounts until the vendor bill is received and entered.

- **Automatic Cost and Price Updates**—You can set a preference for automatically handling changes to an item's default cost, sales price, and markup as recorded with the item record.

- **Edit Markup**—You can define how markup is calculated from cost.

- **Inventory Center Add Image**—You can attach an image to an item record. (Currently, you cannot attach an image to a transaction.)

- **Custom Fields**—These track additional specific detail for your inventory items. Custom fields can be required upon entry and can be defined by type of data, numbers, date, phone, and so on.

- **Job WIP Summary Report**—Used by construction companies or any type of industry that needs to adjust revenue recognized by percentage of completion. Appendix C has more details.

- **Committed Costs by Job Report**—Construction companies and other types of industry that review project budgets and want to also factor in open purchase order balances and unpaid wages use this. Appendix C has more details.

QuickBooks Enterprise Solutions Manufacturing & Wholesale 14.0

If you purchased the QuickBooks Enterprise Solutions Manufacturing & Wholesale 14.0 edition, you will have the same industry-specific tools available with QuickBooks Premier Manufacturing & Wholesale 2014, including the following:

- **Sales Order Fulfillment Worksheet**—Creates an easy form for filling orders.

- **Create Customer Return Materials Authorization Form**—Creates a Word template for you to enter return information into.

- **Report on Nonconforming Material Report**—Creates a Word template for you to enter non-conforming information (or materials that did not meet required specifications) into.

- **Damaged Goods Log**—Creates a Word template for you to enter inventory damage information into.

- **Inventory Reorder Report by Vendor**—Ease in viewing your inventory part reorder needs grouped by vendor.

Advanced Inventory Subscription

Both QuickBooks Enterprise Solutions 14.0 and QuickBooks Enterprise Solutions Manufacturing & Wholesale 14.0 with an Advanced Inventory subscription include these additional features:

- **Bin/Shelf/Row Location Tracking**—Tracks specific items to bin/shelf/row location within one or more inventory locations. Sorts pick lists and item receipts by location.

- **Barcode Scanning**—Increases efficiency and reliability of data entry by scanning items and serial numbers without a keyboard. Helps you create your own barcodes. (Requires any simple USB barcode scanner.)

- **Multiple Inventory Sites**—Reports and tracks inventory in multiple locations.

- **Lot or Serial Number Tracking**—Tracks one or the other and a variety of related preference settings.

- **FIFO**—First-In, First-Out Inventory costing. This means that the oldest inventory items are recorded as sold first, but it does not necessarily mean that the exact oldest physical object has been tracked and sold.

The optional Advanced Inventory functionality is built into QuickBooks Enterprise Solutions, has an annual fee, and requires a current Full Support Plan (annual fee).

 For more information see the section in Appendix C titled, "QuickBooks Enterprise with Advanced Inventory" p. 806.

Advanced Pricing Subscription

Available exclusively with QuickBooks Enterprise Solutions, Advanced Pricing is an add-on with functionality built into the software. With Advanced Pricing, users can automate sales price changes due to:

- Quantity discounts

- Manufacturer markdowns

- Scheduled promotions

- Regional price changes (using Class or Customer Type list)

- Specific item price specials

Advanced Pricing includes two features:

- **Price Rules**—You can implement special promotions with user- created sophisticated price rules. You can create thousands of price rules based on any combination of factors, including customers, items, classes, custom fields, and more.

- **Quantity Discounts**—Let QuickBooks automate pricing discounts, rewarding your customers for buying a specified quantity of your product or service.

➡ *For more information on using Advanced Pricing, see Appendix C.*

QuickBooks has a version right for your business inventory tracking needs. If you need more personalized help in finding the right solution, you can request the help of a QuickBooks certified professional in your area. From the menu bar, select Help, Find a Local QuickBooks Expert. A web page opens in QuickBooks, and you are prompted for a zip code and a preferred distance for the results of the search.

With the help of a qualified consultant, you can be certain you are using QuickBooks correctly for your business.

Enabling Inventory Preferences

To begin using QuickBooks to track inventory, you must first turn on the feature found in the Items & Inventory preference in QuickBooks. By default, when you create a new company data file, inventory management is not enabled.

To turn on the inventory feature, follow these steps:

1. Log in to the data file as the Admin or External Accountant user.

2. From the menu bar, select **Edit**, **Preferences** to open the Preferences dialog box.

3. On the Items & Inventory—Company Preferences tab, select the **Inventory and Purchase Orders Are Active** checkbox.

4. Click OK to save the preference.

The preferences Figure 5.1 shows do not affect the accounting for inventory; instead, they enable specific features and preferences within inventory management. The preferences available in your QuickBooks data might differ, depending on the year and edition of QuickBooks you are using.

Your QuickBooks Home page now shows the inventory workflow (see Figure 5.2). To have the Home page display automatically when you open your QuickBooks file, from the menu bar, select **Edit**, **Preferences**. Click the My Preferences tab and select Desktop View on the left, click the Show Home Page When Opening a Company File checkbox.

Figure 5.1
Preferences that enable QuickBooks inventory vary by the version of QuickBooks being used.

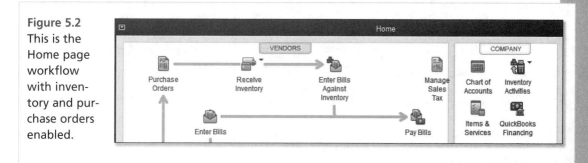

Figure 5.2
This is the Home page workflow with inventory and purchase orders enabled.

One additional preference that can affect your setup of inventory is found in the Time & Expenses—Company Preferences tab (accessed as you did previously for the Items & Inventory preference). When you enter a percentage in the Default Markup Percentage field, QuickBooks automatically makes the default Sales Price the cost multiplied by the markup on a new item when the cost is first recorded (see Figure 5.3). As part of the setup, you are required to select an account for the Markup amount; usually this is an income account type.

For example, when you create a new inventory list item and enter a cost of $3.00, QuickBooks defaults the sales price of $3.90, or $3.00 + 30% markup, as Figure 5.4 shows.

Figure 5.3
Including a Default Markup Percentage makes the sales price of a newly created inventory item cost multiplied by the markup.

Figure 5.4
QuickBooks automatically calculates the sales price when you set the preference for default markup in the Time & Expenses preference.

QuickBooks Enterprise Solutions offers many more features, which Appendix C explores.

➥ *For more information, see "QuickBooks Enterprise Solutions Features," p. 783.*

Another feature for inventory management is the Unit of Measure (on the Items & Inventory—Company Preferences tab). When selecting this preference (see Figure 5.5), you can define the following for inventory items or non-inventory items in QuickBooks:

> **🔍 note**
> QuickBooks Enterprise 14.0 includes more robust preferences for automatically handling markups when item costs change on purchase documents.

- **Single Unit of Measure**—Choose this if you buy, stock, and sell each item by the same unit of measure. For example, if you buy by the pound, sell by the pound, and track your inventory by the pound, this option is the best choice.

Figure 5.5 Both QuickBooks Premier and Enterprise include the Multiple Unit of Measure (U/M) preference.

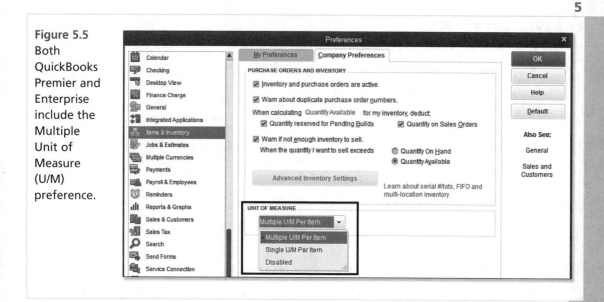

- **Multiple Unit of Measure**—If you buy in one measurement—for example, you purchase by the skid (multiple cases of soda)—and sell to the customer in single units (a can of soda), but ship by the case (multiple cans of soda), the Multiple Unit of Measure option is the best choice.

When you select Multiple Unit of Measure and assign it to an inventory or non-inventory item, you can also define your default units of measure for purchase, sales, and shipping transactions.

➡ *For more information, see "Setting Up Multiple Unit of Measure," p. 177.*

Unit of Measure settings indirectly affect your accounting by defaulting the unit and the associated cost and sales price. Using this feature can improve your buying and selling accuracy on your documents and can help ensure that proper inventory quantities are recorded.

Inventory Item Type Descriptions

QuickBooks provides several item types for use in managing inventory and non-inventory. You can use these items on purchase and sales transactions. This section details the purpose of these QuickBooks item types used primarily with inventory management.

➡ *For details on additional types of QuickBooks items, see Chapter 4, "Understanding QuickBooks Lists," and Chapter 9, "Setting Up Customers."*

Inventory Part

Create an inventory part if any of the following applies to your business:

- Items are purchased and sold.

- Items are stored in stock and later sold.

- Items are purchased and used as components of a finished product (assembled).

The capability to create an assembled good and track the quantity on hand of the finished product is available only in QuickBooks Premier (all editions) and QuickBooks Enterprise (all editions).

Non-inventory Part

Create a non-inventory part if any of the following applies to the specific part:

- Purchased but not sold

- Sold but not purchased

- Purchased and resold, but not tracked as stock (drop-shipped directly to the customer or immaterial in dollar amount)

> *For more information, see "Adding or Editing Inventory Items," p. 161.*

Group Items and Inventory Assemblies

The group item types and inventory assembly types are similar; in that they both let you record multiple items with a single entry on purchase or sales transactions. The group item type is included with QuickBooks Pro, Premier (all editions), and Enterprise (all editions). Inventory assemblies are included only with QuickBooks Premier (all editions), Accountant, or QuickBooks Enterprise (all editions).

You might want to use assemblies in QuickBooks for a few reasons:

- Track finished goods separately from individual inventory items.

- Customize the price of assembled items. You can specify a price for an assembly, which is different than the sum of the default prices of its component items.

- Get detailed information about your finished goods, including date they were assembled, quantity and cost, and list of component items.

- Set reminders for future builds.

If you are using QuickBooks Pro, Premier (all editions), or QuickBooks Enterprise Solutions (all editions), you might benefit from creating group items.

What are some reasons you would work with a group item? They might include the following:

- Get detailed sales, cost, and budget reporting for multiple items

- Use the option to show a single line of detail when invoicing the customer

You can add inventory assemblies to both purchase and sales transactions. You can add Group Items only to sales transactions. Both help automate the process of entering multiple items on transactions.

Table 5.1 compares the details of using the Group Item or Inventory Assembly Item. This should help you determine the proper type to use for your business.

Table 5.1 Comparing Group and Inventory Assembly Items

Group Item	Inventory Assembly Item
Can include any item type except other groups.	Can include any of the following item types: service, inventory part, inventory assembly (subassemblies), non-inventory part, and other charge.
Capability to print on sales transactions the individual items in the group item or a single line summary.	Prints only the assembly name, not the component part names on sales transactions.
No reports specific for group items.	On standard inventory reports, including pending builds report.
Quantity on hand of each individual item is adjusted at the time of sale.	Quantity on hand of each individual item is adjusted at the time of build.
Sales tax calculated by individual items.	One sales tax code (rate) applies to the entire assembled (finished) good.
Cannot be included in another group item.	Can be included (nested) in other assemblies and in group items.
Does not track the finished item; only the individual parts are tracked.	Tracks the quantity of the finished product and depletes the quantity of components.
Price of the group item is the sum of the parts (you can include another item to adjust the sales price).	Sales price of an assembly item defaults to the sales price of the sum of the parts but can be manually adjusted.
Can include both taxable and nontaxable items.	Must be entirely designated as either taxable or nontaxable.

Included in the next section are details on creating both the group item and the inventory assembly. Both save data entry time and improve accuracy when recording purchase and sales transactions with the same multiple items.

Adding or Editing Inventory Items

With inventory and purchase order tracking enabled in your QuickBooks file, you can add your inventory or non-inventory products to the item list. You have several options for adding or modifying your list of products. Choose the method that best meets your needs.

Before you begin tracking inventory, you should know the commitment you are making to additional accounting responsibilities. When choosing to track inventory in the normal course of your business, you need to use purchase transactions to increase inventory, and use sales transactions to decrease inventory. You also need to commit to periodic inventory counts because your inventory can often get out of sync with your accounting information.

Adding or Editing Individual Items

Efficiently add or modify individual inventory or non-inventory items in your QuickBooks data, or use one of several tools detailed in this chapter for working with multiple items at a time.

With QuickBooks Enterprise, you have the added convenience of editing the inventory item's stored cost and sales price, as well managing the markup and margin with the Inventory Center, without having to open and edit each item record.

➡ *For more information, see the "Inventory Center" section in Appendix C, p. 789.*

Inventory Part

When you purchase or build your product and then stock it in your warehouse for future sale to your customer, you should create an inventory part (see Figure 5.6).

Figure 5.6
Adding a new inventory part item.

When inventory is used, an Inventory Asset account is increased when you purchase and stock the product. The income and related cost are not recorded until you include the inventory item on your customer's invoice.

Adding an Inventory Part

To practice adding a new inventory part item, open the sample data file as instructed in Chapter 1, "Getting Started with QuickBooks," p. 37:

1. On the Home page, click the Items & Services icon. The Item List displays.

2. In the lower-left corner, click the Item button and select **New,** or use the keyboard shortcut Ctrl+N. The New Item dialog box displays.

3. In the Type drop-down list, select **Inventory Part**.

4. In the Item Name/Number field, type **Natural Oak Cabinet**.

5. Check the Subitem Of checkbox and then, from the drop-down list, select **Cabinets**.

6. Leave the boxes for Manufacturer's Part Number and U/M Set (for Unit of Measurement) blank.

7. In the Description on Purchase Transactions box, select the newly created **Natural Oak Cabinet**.

8. In the Cost field, type **100.00**.

9. From the Account drop-down list, select the **Cost of Goods Sold** account if QuickBooks usually defaults this account for you.

10. In the Preferred Vendor field, select or begin typing **Thomas Kitchen & Bath**; the existing vendor name populates the field.

11. In the Sales Price field, type **200.00**.

12. Leave the default of Tax assigned in the Tax Code field.

13. In the Income Account drop-down list, select the **Construction Income:Materials Income** account. You can also select the account by typing **40100** (the account number in this example).

14. In the Asset Account drop-down list, leave the Inventory Asset account that displays by default. (Optional) Enter a quantity for Reorder Point reporting.

15. Leave the On Hand field blank. See the Caution that follows about entering your quantity on hand in this manner. If you choose to enter an On Hand quantity, QuickBooks enters a financial transaction that increases the inventory asset account and increases the Opening Balance Equity account.

16. If you entered an On Hand quantity (not recommended), QuickBooks automatically calculates the Total Value field by multiplying the On Hand quantity by the amount recorded in the Cost field. You can override this calculated Total Amount field, but you should do so only if the resulting value is the proper amount to record for this asset. (See the Caution following this sidebar.)

17. If you entered an On Hand quantity, select the As Of date you want to record the increase in your inventory asset value.

18. Click OK to save your changes and close the New Item dialog box.

> **⚡ caution**
>
> Converting to QuickBooks after having used other software to track inventory? It is recommended that you use an Inventory Adjustment transaction to enter your opening quantity on hand instead of entering a quantity in the On Hand field of a new inventory item record. For more information, see "Adjusting Inventory," p. 205.
>
> Offering a new product for sale to your customers? Do not enter an amount in the On Hand field; instead, use the Items tab of the Enter Bills, Credit Card Charges, or Write Checks transactions to record the purchase of this new inventory item.
>
> After you save a new item record, you cannot edit many fields, including the On Hand and Total Value fields.

Following are optional fields or actions in an item record (depending on the version of QuickBooks you are using) that are useful:

- **U/M Set**—Assigns default units of measure for purchases, sales, and shipping of the selected item.

- **Notes**—Provides internal notes for the currently selected item.

- **Custom Fields**—Give you the flexibility to add information that QuickBooks does not already track. Review the section in this chapter titled "Inventory Features by QuickBooks Edition" to see if the custom field you need is already tracked in a different edition of QuickBooks.

- **Spelling**—Click Spelling, and QuickBooks spell-checks the description fields of the individual item being added or edited.

- **Item Is Inactive**—Use only when the item inventory count for the selected item is zero and you no longer want the item to be included in drop-down lists. The section "Making an Item Inactive" in Chapter 4, p. 147, has more information on efficiently managing your items.

> **⚙ tip**
>
> The Cost field in a new (or edited) inventory part record is optional. Entering a default cost can be useful for automating entry on purchase transactions and, in some instances, can help with properly reporting a change in value when an inventory adjustment record is recorded.

Non-inventory Part

Your company might want to create non-inventory items. For example, a construction company that orders appliances for the new homeowner but does not stock the appliances would create non-inventory items.

When non-inventory is used, the expense account on the non-inventory item record is used to record the cost at the time of purchase. These items never increase your inventory asset balances.

Adding a Non-inventory Part

To practice adding a new non-inventory item, open the sample data file as instructed in Chapter 1, p. 37:

1. On the Home page, click the Items & Services icon. The Item List displays.

2. In the lower-left corner, click the Item button, and select **New**, or use the keyboard shortcut Ctrl+N. The New Item dialog box displays.

3. From the Type drop-down list that displays, select **Non-inventory Part**.

4. In the Item Name/Number field, type **Stain**.

5. Select the **Subitem Of** checkbox; from the drop-down list, select **Lumber**.

6. Leave the boxes for Manufacturer's Part Number and U/M Set (for Unit of Measurement) blank.

7. Check the This Item Is Used in Assemblies or Is Purchased for a Specific Customer checkbox as in Figure 5.7. See more details about the importance of this in the Caution that follows these instructions.

Selecting this box will allow you to assign both an income and an expense account

Figure 5.7
Use Non-inventory part type for items you stock but do not sell.

8. In the Description on Purchase Transactions box, type **Stain**.

9. In the Cost field, type **25**.

10. In the Expense Account drop-down list, select the **Cost of Goods Sold** or, if you prefer, the expense account of your choice.

11. In the Preferred Vendor field, select or type **Timberloft Lumber**.

12. In the Sales Price field, type **100.00**.

13. Leave the default of Tax assigned in the Tax Code field.

14. From the Income Account drop-down list, select the **Construction Income:Materials Income** account. You can also select the account by typing **40140** (the account number in this example).

15. Click OK to close the New Item dialog box.

Whether or not you are tracking inventory in your business, non-inventory parts are a great way to track items you consume as part of your business operations.

Entering or editing each inventory item can be time-consuming and takes you away from more important tasks. The next few sections provide alternatives for adding or editing multiple inventory items at one time.

> ## 🛜 caution
>
> Non-inventory parts require only one account by default. This is okay if you do not purchase and sell the item. To ensure proper accounting, I recommend that, when you create a non-inventory item type, you place a checkmark in the This Item Is Used in Assemblies or Is Purchased for a Specific Customer:Job box, as in Figure 5.7. This enables you to assign both an expense and an income account if you purchase and sell the item.

Using Add/Edit Multiple List Entries

Adding or modifying several list items in a single QuickBooks list can be a daunting task when you have to work with one list item at a time. In Chapter 1, p. 42, you might have created your lists using QuickBooks Setup to add the people you do business with, the products or services you sell, and your bank accounts.

With the Add/Edit Multiple List Entries feature (see Figure 5.8), you can add to or modify service items or inventory and non-inventory parts. Using this feature can save you precious time, particularly when you want to add or make changes to multiple items on a list all at once.

With QuickBooks 2014, you can also access the Markup and Margin fields in the Add/Edit Multiple Lists feature when using QuickBooks Enterprise.

Figure 5.8
Use the Add/
Edit Multiple
Lists Entries to
add or modify
multiple inven-
tory parts
efficiently.

ITEM NAME	SUBITEM OF	COST	SALES PRICE	COGS ACCOUNT	PREFERREC
Cabinets		0.00	0.00	50100 · Cost of Goods Sold	Thomas
Natural Oak	Cabinets	100.00	200.00	50100 · Cost of Goods Sold	
Cabinet Pulls	Cabinets	3.00	0.00	50100 · Cost of Goods Sold	Patton H:
Light Pine	Cabinets	1,500.00	1,799.00	50100 · Cost of Goods Sold	Patton H:
Door Frame		12.00	0.00	50100 · Cost of Goods Sold	Patton H:
Hardware		0.00	0.00	50100 · Cost of Goods Sold	Patton H:
Brass hinges	Hardware	3.00	0.00	50100 · Cost of Goods Sold	Perry Wir
Doorknobs Std	Hardware	15.00	30.00	50100 · Cost of Goods Sold	Perry Wir
Lk Doorknobs	Hardware	34.95	38.00	50100 · Cost of Goods Sold	Perry Wir
Wood Door		0.00	0.00	50100 · Cost of Goods Sold	Patton H:
Exterior	Wood Door	590.39	120.00	50100 · Cost of Goods Sold	Perry Wir
Interior	Wood Door	35.00	72.00	50100 · Cost of Goods Sold	Perry Wir
Custom Door	Wood Door	1,850.00	2,200.00	50100 · Cost of Goods Sold	Perry Wir
		0.00	0.00	50100 · Cost of Goods Sold	

Add/Edit Multiple List Entries
① Select a list. ② Customize columns to display. ③ Paste from Excel or type to add to or modify your list. [Customize Columns]
List: Inventory Parts   View: Active Inventory Items   Find: [ ] ☐ Search within results
Currently Editing: Wood Door:Custom Door

tip

When using the Add/Edit Multiple List Entries tool, use the Tab key on your keyboard to move efficiently
from one field to the next.

From the grid, you can right-click for other functionality. From the right-click menu, you can choose from
Copy Down, Duplicate Row, Clear Column, and other useful features.

Add/Edit Multiple Items at Once

Practice using the Add/Edit Multiple List Entries feature by adding a Custom Door
inventory item and customizing the columns of data displayed for editing.

Open the sample data as instructed in Chapter 1, p. 37:

1. From the menu bar, select **Lists**, **Add/Edit Multiple List Entries**.

2. In the List drop-down list, select **Inventory Parts**.

3. In the View drop-down list, select **Active Inventory Items**.

4. On the right, click the Customize Columns button to open the Customize Columns
   dialog box.

5. View the fields in the Chosen Columns pane. These fields are currently displayed
   in the Add/Edit Multiple List Entries grid.

6. To add a column to the grid, select **Purchase Description** and click the Add> button in the center.

7. To rearrange the order of the columns, in the Chosen Columns pane, select the newly added Purchase Description and click the Move Up button several times until the Purchase Description field is immediately below the Subitem Of field.

8. Click OK to close the Customize Columns dialog box.

9. At the bottom of the Add/Edit Multiple List Entries dialog box, use the scrollbar to view the fields available.

10. In the Item Name field, click in the next available blank row. Optionally, with your cursor, right-click to insert a line and access other features for using this tool.

11. In the Item Name field, type **Custom Door**.

12. In the Subitem Of drop-down list, select **Wood Door**.

13. In the Purchase Description field, type **Custom Wood Door**.

14. In the Cost field, type **1,850.00**.

15. In the Sales Price field, type **2,200.00**.

16. Accept the default account: Cost of Goods Sold. (Optional) Select Perry Windows & Doors in the Preferred Vendor field.

17. In the Income drop-down list, select **Construction Income** account.

18. Accept the default Asset Account: Inventory Asset.

19. In the Reorder Pt (Min) field, type **5**; and in the Reorder Point Max field, type **10**.

20. Leave the default Total Value column blank.

21. Accept the default Tax in the Sales Tax Code column.

22. Skip the Manufacturer's Part Number field.

23. Skip the Qty on Hand field.

24. Click Save Changes.

25. QuickBooks displays the number of record(s) saved. Click OK, and then click Close.

To view your newly added inventory item, in the Look For field at the top of the Item List, select **Lists**, **Item List**; then type **Wood Door** and press the Enter key on your keyboard. Do you see the newly created Custom Door listed? Click the Reset button to return to the original list.

You can also enter your inventory data into an Excel spreadsheet and then copy and paste it into the Add/Edit Multiple List Entries dialog box.

⚠ caution
When cutting and pasting from Excel, make sure your columns of data in Excel match the order of the Add/Edit Multiple List Entries columns in QuickBooks.

Importing an Intuit Interchange Format File (IIF)

The term *Intuit Interchange Format (IIF)* refers to data exchange functionality that has been around for some time. It is a method for exporting lists from one QuickBooks file into a new QuickBooks file. The process creates a tab-delimited text file with the extension of .iif. You can view and edit this file using Excel.

The IIF format is a preferred and easy method to use if you already have a QuickBooks file with an items list you want to replicate in another QuickBooks file. To export an IIF-formatted items file from an existing QuickBooks file, follow these steps:

1. Open the QuickBooks file that has the items list you want to export and duplicate for another file.

2. From the menu bar, select **File**, **Utilities**, **Export**, **Lists to IIF Files**.

3. Select the **Item List** checkbox.

4. Click OK. You are prompted to provide a filename and to save the exported file. Remember the location where you store the file; you will need to browse to the .iif file to import it into another QuickBooks file.

5. Click OK to the message that your data was exported successfully.

Figure 5.9 shows the exported items list in the IIF format in an Excel workbook. You can see that it is not as user friendly as the Add/Edit Multiple List Entries previously discussed.

Figure 5.9
An exported items list in IIF format can be imported into another QuickBooks file.

To import the saved IIF file into a new QuickBooks file, follow these steps:

1. Open the QuickBooks file you want to import the previously exported list into. If you have not already created your new file, select **File**, **New** from the menu bar and follow the prompts. (For more information, see Chapter 1.)

2. From the menu bar, select **File**, **Utilities**, **Import**, **IIF Files**.

3. When the Import dialog box opens, browse to the location of the stored IIF-formatted file.

> **⚠ caution**
> The IIF file format is a tab-delimited text file format with an extension of .iif. If you edit the details of the file, be sure to keep this format when saving your changes; do not save as an .xls or .xlsx Excel file type.

4. Select the file and click Open.

5. QuickBooks then imports the IIF-formatted file into the QuickBooks data file. Click OK to the Your Data Has Been Imported message.

Now that you have your new data file with new lists from another file, you are ready to begin entering transactions. Just think of all the time you saved by not having to manually create each list item in the new file.

Changing Item Prices

Your business might have a variety of items, including Service, Inventory, Non-inventory Parts, and even Other Charge items. During the course of doing business, your costs of supplying these products or services will change, and you might want to update the Sales Price or Rate field stored with your items. Included with QuickBooks Pro, Premier, or Enterprise is the Change Item Prices tool (see Figure 5.10).

Figure 5.10
You can efficiently manage multiple inventory part sales price changes with Change Item Prices.

With this feature, you can change the price of the following:

- One item at a time

- More than one item at a time

- Several items by a fixed amount based on Current Price or Unit Cost

- Several items by a percentage based on Current Price or Unit Cost

🔍 note

Do you want QuickBooks to automatically generate a sales price change based on some criteria, such as Class, Customer Type, or a specific time period for the new sales price?

QuickBooks Enterprise Solutions has this functionality with an Advanced Pricing subscription. See Appendix C for more details.

Practice Using the Change Item Prices

To practice using the Change Item Prices feature, open the sample data as previously instructed in Chapter 1, p. 36:

1. From the menu bar, select **Customers, Change Item Prices**.
2. In this example, in the Item Type drop-down list, select **Inventory Part**.
3. Place a checkmark next to the Cabinets:Light Pine item.
4. In the Adjust Price of Marked Items by (Amount or %) field, type **10%**. See the Caution that follows for including the % symbol.
5. Leave the default of Based On Current Price selected. The other option available is to base the change on the Unit Cost.
6. Click Adjust. Notice that the New Price is calculated based on your specifications in step 4.
7. In the Round Up to Nearest drop-down list, leave the No Rounding option selected. Other options include the capability to round up or down by a specific increment.
8. Click OK to close the Change Item Prices dialog box.

📡 caution

When using the Change Item Prices, if you want to increase the Current Price by a percentage, be sure to type the amount with the percentage symbol. For example, if you want to increase the New Price by 15 percent, you type **15%**—without the % symbol, QuickBooks assumes that you want to raise the price by a fixed amount of $15.

📡 caution

In Chapter 9, p. 358, you learn about working with memorized transactions and groups. Note that changes made to item prices *do not* automatically change the prices you have previously recorded on a memorized customer invoice.

Using the Change Item Prices dialog box can be an efficient way of updating your pricing for multiple items at one time. QuickBooks Enterprise Solutions 14.0 provides more control over changes to the default part cost, sales price, and markup when an item's cost changes. When entering a cost on a purchase transaction that differs from the cost in the item record, QuickBooks prompts the user to set a preference for updating the item record and sales price. See Figures 5.11 and 5.12.

Figure 5.11
Available only in QuickBooks Enterprise is the option to update the default cost and sales price when recording a purchase transaction.

Figure 5.12
With QuickBooks Enterprise, you can define specific settings for handling markup percent or amount.

Creating Inventory Assemblies

The inventory assembly (see Figure 5.13) can include the following item types:

- Other Assemblies (Subassemblies)
- Inventory Parts
- Non-inventory Parts
- Service Items
- Other Charge Items

Figure 5.13
Inventory Assembly items are available in QuickBooks Premier, Accountant, or Enterprise.

Practice Using Inventory Assemblies

To practice adding a new inventory assembly (only if you have QuickBooks Premier or Enterprise), open the sample data file as instructed in Chapter 1, p. 37, and follow these steps:

1. On the Home page, click the Items & Services icon. The Item List displays.

2. In the lower-left corner, click the Item button, and then select **New** or use the keyboard shortcut Ctrl+N.

   → *For more information, see "Using Add/Edit Multiple List Entries," p. 166.*

3. In the Type drop-down list, select **Inventory Assembly**.

4. In the Item Name/Number field, type **Deck**.

5. Leave the I Purchase This Assembly Item from a Vendor checkbox and the Unit of Measure (U/M) Set field blank.

6. Leave the Cost field blank.

7. Accept the default COGS Account.

8. In the Description field, type **Decking**.

9. Leave the Sales Price blank.

10. Leave the default Tax Code of Tax.

11. In the Income Account drop-down list, select account number **40140** or **Construction Income:Materials Income**.

12. In the Item drop-down list, enter the Bill of Materials by selecting the following items:

    - In the Lumber item group, select **Trim**. In the Qty column, type **5**.
    - In the next row, select the new item you created in an earlier exercise in this chapter, **Stain**. Type a Qty of **8**.

    Notice how QuickBooks calculates the Total Bill of Materials Cost, which is the sum total of the individual default costs recorded with each item record. Knowing the cost of the items can help you assign a proper Sales Price.

13. In the Sales Price field, type **1,125.00**.

14. Leave the default Asset Account.

15. In the Build Point (Min) field, type **3**; in the Build Point (Max) field, type **5**.

16. Leave the On Hand and Total Value fields blank. Leave the default date value in the As Of field.

17. Click OK to close the New Item dialog box.

caution

Working with assemblies requires some care and attention on your part. A couple items are worth noting:

- Future changes to the Item default cost will update the costs of all assemblies that use that item.

- An assembly with items included that have zero for quantity cannot be built until the QTY has a number greater than zero. Using QuickBooks Enterprise can help with this, by building the subassemblies first. Appendix C has more details.

- QuickBooks Enterprise makes it possible to substitute parts in multiple assemblies at one time.

Carefully review the details of your assemblies by selecting Full View in the Add or Edit Assembly dialog box.

Creating the assembly is only part of the process. You also need to "build" the assembly.

Using inventory assemblies can help your business track whether you have enough components in inventory to build the finished product for your customers. You can edit inventory assemblies, but QuickBooks does not track the revision history for an item. If you are no longer selling a particular assembled item, you can make the item inactive so that it cannot be used on future purchase or sales transactions.

note

You can include up to 50 different items in a Group Item. In versions earlier than QuickBooks 2013, you could have only up to 20 individual items in a Group Item.

Creating Group Items

Previously, Table 5.1 listed the differences between working with Group items (see Figure 5.14) and working with an Inventory Assembly. In this section, you learn how to work with Group items.

Unlike working with assemblies, when creating or editing a group item, you do not assign a cost for each item or a sales price for the group item. The cost and sales price are calculated for you from the respective totals for each of the included items.

➥ *To practice using this Group item on an invoice, see the section "Working with Group Items," p. 194.*

Figure 5.14
Creating Group items can save you time when you need to enter multiple items.

When not selected, the customer's invoice will only display the detail in the Description box.

Practice Using Group Items

In this exercise, you edit an existing Group item. Open the sample data as previously instructed in Chapter 1, p. 36:

1. On the Home page, click the Items & Services icon. The Item List displays.

2. Scroll down the list and select the **Door Set** group (near the bottom of the list in the Group section). (Optional) You can also begin selecting Door Set in the Look For box at the top of the Item List and click the Search button.

3. Double-click to select the Door Set group. The Edit Item dialog box displays.

4. When working with your own data, enter a Group Name/Number of your choosing that will serve as reminder of what items are included in this Group.

5. In the Description box is the desired detail that will display on a customer's invoice. You can modify the description on the invoice, if needed.

6. Don't select the Print Items in Group checkbox. This is one unique feature of working with the Group item type. When the Print Items in Group checkbox is *not selected*, the customer's invoice shows only the Description from step 5.

7. Currently, the Group includes two items: Doorknobs Std and Exterior Wood Door. In the Item column, click the next available row and select the Service item named **Repairs** from the drop-down list.

8. In the Qty. column, type **2**, assigning two hours of repair labor when installing this door.

9. Click OK to close the Edit Item dialog box. You return to the Item List and your new group is highlighted (selected).

Setting Up Multiple Unit of Measurement

If you are using QuickBooks Premier or Enterprise, you have the option to set up Multiple Unit of Measure. A benefit of this feature is the capability to assign a specific unit default for purchases, shipping, and sales transactions.

To begin using Multiple Unit of Measure in your Premier or Enterprise file, you need to enable the preference setting. To do so, follow these steps:

1. Log in to the file as the Admin or External Accountant user.

2. From the menu bar, select **Edit**, **Preferences**.

3. Select the **Items & Inventory—Company Preferences** tab.

4. In the Unit of Measure box, click the Enable button. This button is not present if the feature is already enabled.

5. Select either **Single U/M Per Item** or **Multiple U/M Per Item** (see Figure 5.15). For more information, see "Enabling Inventory Preferences," p. 156.

6. Click Finish. Click OK to close the Preferences dialog box.

Now that the preference is enabled, create the different unit measurements you will be tracking.

Figure 5.15
To begin using Multiple Unit of Measure, first enable the preference.

With Multiple Unit of Measure defined for this item, entering inventory on transactions will be easier and more accurate.

Using Multiple Unit of Measure

After enabling the Unit of Measure preference, you can create Multiple Unit of Measure for the Stain Non-inventory part. You created this part in the section of this chapter titled "Non-inventory Part":

1. From the menu bar, select **Lists, Item List**.

2. Select the **Stain** non-inventory part you created earlier. Double-click the stain item to open the Edit Item dialog box.

3. From the Unit of Measure drop-down list on an existing item, select **Add New** to open the Unit of Measure dialog box.

4. The Unit of Measure dialog box displays. Select **Count** (each, box, case, dozen, and so on). When working in your own file, if you do not see the desired unit displayed, select the **Other** option, as in Figure 5.16, and follow the instructions after you click Next to create a new base unit.

Figure 5.16
QuickBooks provides multiple units of measure types, or you can select Other to create your own.

5. Click Next and select **Each** (ea) as the Base Unit of Measure for this practice example (not shown).

6. Click Next to display the Add Related Units screen (see Figure 5.17).

Figure 5.17
For the unit of measure created, you define the number of base units (in this example, # of ea).

7. Place a checkmark next to the individual units of measurement you want to add to the selected item (see Figure 5.17 for the quantities used in this practice example). Click Next when complete.

8. The Select Default Units of Measure screen displays. In the drop-down list, select the default units for Purchase, Sales, and Shipping transactions, as in Figure 5.18.

Figure 5.18
The benefit of working with Multiple Unit of Measurement is the capability to define the default units for specific transaction types.

9. Click Next.

10. The Name the Unit of Measure Set screen displays. Type a name for the unit of measure set, or accept the default name displayed.

11. Click Finish. The U/M Set now shows the configured Multiple Unit of Measurement assigned to the selected item.

12. Click OK to close the New Item dialog box or Edit Item dialog box.

> 📡 **caution**
>
> When working with Multiple Unit of Measure, if you edit an existing unit of measure assigned to an item, you are warned, "Any changes you make to this unit of measure set will affect all items that use this set."

Proper Inventory Processes

Understanding the recommended inventory process and the associated transactions can help you properly use the inventory feature. If you are new to inventory management, QuickBooks makes getting started with it easy, via the workflow outlined on the Home page, as shown previously in Figure 5.2.

Use a Purchase Order if you want to compare the bill the vendor sends with the original agreed-upon quantity and cost. With purchase orders, you can also keep track of what items have been ordered and have not yet been received.

You can receive inventory in one of two ways. With one method, you receive inventory with the vendor's final bill. If you record full receipt of the quantity, QuickBooks marks the purchase order as closed. You can also choose to receive inventory without a bill. QuickBooks creates an Item Receipt document that is included in the accounts payable reports but cannot yet be paid in the Pay Bills dialog box.

Rest assured that, as you create the vendor's final bill, QuickBooks recognizes whether you have outstanding purchase orders or item receipts that you want to associate with the vendor's bill.

Table 5.2 shows a listing of all transaction types you should use when working with inventory and their related effects on the company's accounting.

Table 5.2 Inventory Transaction Types

Transaction Type	Purpose of Transaction	Effect with Accounting
Purchase Order	Records order placed with vendor	No effect
Item Receipt without Bill	Records receipt of inventory items	Increases inventory, increases accounts payable (bill cannot be selected in the Pay Bills dialog box)

Transaction Type	Purpose of Transaction	Effect with Accounting
Item Receipt with Bill	Records receipt of inventory items	Increases inventory, increases accounts payable (bill can be selected in the Pay Bills dialog box)
Bill	Records bill (optionally, assigns purchase order or item receipt)	Increases inventory, increases accounts payable
Check	Items tab selected (optionally, assigns purchase order or item receipt)	Increases inventory, decreases cash
Credit Card	Items tab selected (optionally, assigns purchase order or item receipt)	Increases inventory, increases credit card liability
Estimates	Records quote for sales of items to a customer	No effect
Sales Order	Manages sales of inventory by committing it for sale (used to manage back orders of inventory)	No effect, except to show the items in inventory as committed
Invoice	Records sale of inventory to customer	Decreases inventory, increases accounts receivable, increases cost of goods sold, and increases income
Sales Receipt	Records sale of inventory to customer	Decreases inventory, increases cash, increases cost of goods sold, and increases income
Inventory Adjustment—Quantity	Records a change to the quantity of stock on hand	Decreases or increases inventory quantity, and decreases or increases Inventory Adjustment account (Cost of Goods Sold type or Expense account type)
Inventory Adjustment—Value	Records a change to the value of the stock on hand	Decreases or increases inventory value, and decreases or increases Inventory Adjustment account (Cost of Goods Sold type or Expense account type)

tip

QuickBooks Enterprise Solutions 14.0 (all industry versions) includes the option to use Enhanced Inventory Receiving. When this feature is enabled as detailed in Appendix C, QuickBooks records an item receipt as an increase to Inventory and an increase to an Inventory Offset account (other current liability account created automatically by QuickBooks). Later when the vendor bill is entered, Accounts Payable is increased and the Inventory Offset account is decreased.

As a business owner, you do not need to worry about the details; QuickBooks Enterprise does all the behind-the-scenes accounting for you.

➡ *To learn more, see Appendix C, section titled "Enhanced Inventory Receiving," p. 800.*

Purchasing, Receiving, and Entering the Vendor Bill

An important reason to purchase accounting software is to have the capability to track the expenses incurred in providing products or services to your customers. In fact, you can improve the business's profitability by effectively managing your purchasing costs. In this section, you learn a recommended purchasing process specifically for inventory items and non-inventory items. This process is similar to the steps outlined in Chapter 7, "Setting Up Vendors," p. 232.

Review Table 5.2 in the previous section for how QuickBooks handles the accounting for inventory. To manage your inventory purchasing with the greatest level of control, follow these three steps:

1. Create a Purchase Order recording a commitment to purchase.

2. Receive inventory without a vendor bill to create an Item Receipt.

3. Enter Bills upon receipt and associate it with the open Item Receipt.

> ## 📶 caution
>
> You can use other transaction types to pay for your inventory purchase: Write Checks or Credit Card Charges. If you use these transaction types to record your inventory purchases, you must use the Items tab to enter the items being purchased. However, these transactions do not track the vendor's bill reference number.

Creating the Purchase Order

If you are practicing in your own data file, make sure you have read the section in this chapter titled "Enabling Inventory Preferences."

Practice Creating a Purchase Order

Using the sample company referred to in Chapter 1, p. 36, let's practice creating a purchase order and receiving the inventory:

1. On the Home page, shown in Figure 5.2, click the Purchase Orders icon to open the Create Purchase Order transaction.

2. In the Vendor drop-down list, begin typing the letters **Th**. QuickBooks automatically prefills with the vendor **Thomas Kitchen & Bath**. Alternatively, you can scroll through the drop-down list and click to select a vendor for the purchase order.

3. Use the Tab key to move to the Class field, and select **New Construction**. If you have not enabled class tracking in your file, you will not have this field.

4. In this example, leave the Drop Ship To field blank. Accept the default Template, Date, P.O. No., Vendor, and Ship To details.

5. From the Item drop-down list, select the **Light Pine** item, a subitem of Cabinets.

6. Accept the default description.

7. In the Qty field, click the icon (see Figures 5.19 and 5.20) to view the Current Availability of the item. This useful feature is available only with QuickBooks Premier or Enterprise. Click Show Details for. From the Show Details for drop-down list, select **Sales Orders**.

Click the icon to view Current Availability details for this part

Figure 5.19
Creating a purchase order helps you manage your expected costs.

Figure 5.20
Current Availability information for inventory items is conveniently included on purchasing and sales transactions in Premier or Enterprise editions only.

8. Click Close to close the Current Availability dialog box.

9. In the Qty field, type **2**.

10. Accept the default Rate.

11. Leave the Customer field blank. For inventory items, the cost is assigned to the customer when the inventory item is included on a customer's invoice. Select the customer only if you are using an item type other than inventory, and only if you know the customer at the time of purchase.

12. For this exercise, if U/M (Unit of Measure) is enabled, leave the field blank.

13. Accept the default Amount.

14. (Optional) In the lower-left Vendor Message field, type a message to the vendor.

15. (Optional) Enter a Memo. This field displays on reports and can be useful when you have multiple open purchase orders for one vendor at a time.

16. (Optional) Select the Print Later or Email Later box at the top of the transaction. Emailing transactions and reports requires the Send preference be enabled. You can access this preference from the Send Forms—My Preferences tab of the Preferences dialog box (from the menu bar, select **Edit, Preferences**).

17. For this practice example, click Save & New. If the Check Spelling on Form warning displays, select the **Ignore All** option.

18. Let's preview the purchase order just created. From the Create Purchase Orders transaction, click the arrow (top left) pointing to the left. The purchase order just created displays.

19. Click Preview from the drop-down menu under the Print icon found on the Main tab of the transaction ribbon.

20. Your newly created purchase order displays using the default purchase order template.

➥ *For more information, see "Customizing QuickBooks Forms," p. 339.*

21. Click Close to close the preview, and click Save & Close to close the Create Purchase Orders transaction.

tip

Did you know that, by default, QuickBooks would have you use the Tab key on your keyboard to advance from one field to another with certain transactions?

If you inadvertently used the Enter key on your keyboard, QuickBooks might store the incomplete transaction. If this happens to you, use the arrows at the top left of the open transaction to find the transaction you did not fully complete.

If you prefer to use the Enter key on your keyboard to advance between fields, you can set that preference on the General—My Preferences tab of the Preferences dialog box (select **Edit, Preferences, General** from the menu bar). Select the **Pressing Enter Moves Between Fields** checkbox, and click OK to save your preference setting. Later, when recording transactions, you can press Ctrl+Enter on your keyboard to save a transaction.

To simplify creating purchase orders, you can access useful tasks from the ribbon toolbar on the top of the Create Purchase Orders transaction. The ribbon toolbar includes the following tabs, shown in Figure 5.21.

tip

If you want to minimize the ribbon toolbar at the top of a displayed transaction, click the arrow on the top right that is pointing up. Clicking expands or collapses the ribbon toolbar, depending on its present state.

- **Main**—Central location for common tasks related to working with purchase orders. From this tab, you can use the Find, Save, Print, and Email functions and access other purchase order functions.

- **Formatting**—Preview, manage, download, and customize the purchase order form. Chapter 9 has more information.

- **Reports**—Get quick access to common reports for the displayed purchase order, and get useful purchase order reporting on all purchase orders.

Figure 5.21
Use the transaction ribbon toolbar to access commonly used tasks and reports.

To the right of a displayed purchase order, you might see the following tabs, which Figure 5.19 showed earlier. If you do not see these tabs, click the small arrow pointing to the right next to the Template to view them:

- **Vendor**—Review summary and recent transaction information for the vendor selected on the purchase order. Also includes links to edit the vendor record, create a QuickReport, and enter notes for the current transaction.

- **Transaction**—View summary information, related transactions, and notes for the currently displayed purchase order.

If you are using QuickBooks Enterprise software, you have the added feature of automatically creating purchase orders from your inventory stock status reports. New for QuickBooks 2014, the Auto Create Purchase Orders now suggests a quantity to purchase. The suggested Quantity factors in the Quantity Available and Quantity on Purchase Orders and then compares this to the Reorder Point, Max value for the item.

To use QuickBooks Enterprise to automatically create multiple purchase orders, follow these steps:

1. From the menu bar, select **Reports, Inventory, Inventory Stock Status by Item or Vendor**.

2. On the top of the displayed stock status report, click the Create Auto PO's button, shown in Figure 5.22.

Figure 5.22 With QuickBooks Enterprise, review your stock status reports and prepare replenishing purchase orders easily.

3. The Create Auto PO's dialog box displays (see Figure 5.22).

4. Items with Preferred Vendors stored on the part record display with that vendor's name. In the vendor column, change the vendor as needed.

5. Place a checkmark next to the parts you want to include on the purchase orders. QuickBooks creates one purchase order per vendor.

6. QuickBooks suggests a quantity to order based on the Max reorder point value stored with the inventory item. You can change the Qty to Order as appropriate.

> *For more information on how easy it is to upgrade your Pro or Premier file to QuickBooks Enterprise, see "Upgrading Your QuickBooks Version," p. 651.*

Congratulations on taking the first step toward successfully managing your inventory!

Receiving Item(s) into Inventory

Next, you work with receiving your items into inventory. You will find many of the same ribbons on top and tabs to the right that were available on the purchase order transaction.

Practice Receiving Items

Continuing with your practice using QuickBooks sample data and building on the previous exercise, let's record the receipt of the inventory:

1. From the Home page, from the drop-down list next to the Receive Inventory icon, select **Receive Inventory Without Bill**. The Create Item Receipts transaction opens.

2. In the Vendor field, begin typing the letters **Th** and press the Tab key on your computer keyboard. QuickBooks automatically prefills the rest of the vendor's name.

3. The Open POs Exist dialog box displays. Click the default Yes.

4. Click to place a checkmark in the first column to assign the purchase order to this Item Receipt (see Figure 5.23).

Figure 5.23
When creating an item receipt, QuickBooks lists open purchase orders for that vendor.

5. Click OK. The Create Item Receipts transaction prefills with the information from the original purchase order.

6. In this exercise, accept the default date. In the Ref. No. field, type **1234**.

7. To continue with the practice example here, record only a partial receipt of the inventory items, and replace the 2 in the Qty field by typing **1** (see Figure 5.24).

8. Leave the Customer:Job and Billable? fields blank. Accept the default Class and PO No. assigned.

Figure 5.24
When receiving inventory without the final vendor bill, QuickBooks creates an Item Receipt.

9. Notice other useful buttons on the Create Item Receipts transaction:

- **Clear Qtys**—Click this if you want to clear all quantity fields and enter them manually.

- **Show PO**—Click this to open the selected purchase order. It is useful if you need to make changes to the purchase order details.

10. To continue with the practice, click Save on the Main tab of the ribbon toolbar on the Create Item Receipts transaction. This saves the details but leaves the current transaction displayed for this exercise. (Normally, you will be selecting Save & New or Save & Close at the bottom of the transaction.)

11. Click the Transaction tab to the right to view Related Transactions, including a link to the Purchase Order used to create this item receipt. Another option is to select Transaction History on the Report tab of the ribbon toolbar.

12. Click the Purchase Order link in the Related Transactions section of the Transaction tab to view the Purchase Order that the Item Receipt is linked to.

13. The Create Purchase Orders transaction now includes a column with the Backordered quantity.

14. Click Save & Close to close the Create Purchase Orders transaction.

15. Click Save & Close to close the Create Item Receipts transaction.

Notice other useful features or reports found on the Create Item Receipts ribbon toolbar:

- **Main**—Central location for common tasks related to working with item receipts. From this tab, you can find, save, create new item receipts, enter time (from time sheets), and clear splits (remove the line detail), to name just a few of the additional functions available.

- **Reports**—Quick access to common reports for the displayed item receipt. New for QuickBooks 2014, the Report tab of the ribbon toolbar includes access to more reports.

---

 tip

Did your vendor not supply you with a vendor bill number (same as Ref. No.)? You might want to use the same date as the vendor bill in the Ref. No. field. The primary purpose of the Ref. No. field is to warn you if you enter a bill with the same reference number more than once.

Now might be a good time to advance to the section titled "Inventory Reporting," p. 211 in Chapter 6. Specifically, look for reports in the Report Center, Vendors and Payable section. You can review several excellent purchasing reports.

Entering the Vendor Bill

When it comes to inventory, the more controls you have in place surrounding your purchasing process, the more accurate your accounting data will be. In the next step, you learn how to enter a vendor bill and assign it to the previously recorded item receipt.

tip

Do you have freight, shipping, or handling charges to add from the vendor's item receipt? To track them as an added expense but not as part of the average cost of this inventory item, click the Expenses tab on the vendor bill, or write a check transaction and add the additional charges.

Practice Entering a Vendor Bill and Assigning the Item Receipt

Continuing with your practice using QuickBooks sample data (as discussed in Chapter 1, p. 36), let's record the vendor bill and assign it to the open item receipt from the previous exercise:

1. On the Home page, click the Enter Bills Against Inventory icon. The Select Item Receipt transaction opens.

2. In the Vendor field, select **Thomas Kitchen & Bath** as the vendor from the drop-down list.

3. (Optional) Select the Use Item Receipt Date for the Bill Date checkbox. Because QuickBooks removes the item receipt and replaces it with a bill, you want to be sure to use the date you want your financials affected. You can also set a Default Date to Use for New Transactions by selecting **Edit, Preferences, General—My Preferences** tab from the menu bar.

4. Select the appropriate item receipt to associate with this bill, as in Figure 5.25.

Figure 5.25
Be certain your item receipt is highlighted before clicking OK.

5. Click OK to close the Select Item Receipt transaction. The Enter Bills transaction displays and the item receipt no longer exists as an item receipt transaction.

6. In this exercise, accept the vendor's Ref. No., Qty, and Cost. When you are creating your own vendor bill transactions, you should carefully inspect that the vendor's bill details for Ref. No., Qty, and Cost agree with your records generated by the original purchase order.

7. Click Save & Close. If the message stating you have changed the transaction displays, click Yes.

Your business will benefit from the added cost controls put in place when you use a purchase order and receive item transactions. This process is particularly useful when the vendor sends the final bill separately from the original shipment. When you do get the vendor bill in the mail, you can review the details to make sure they agree with your records.

Paying for Inventory

You have now learned how to efficiently manage your inventory, beginning with the purchase order that tracks the quantity ordered and the agreed-to cost. Next, when the product is delivered to your warehouse, you enter an item receipt with or without the vendor bill.

After creating a vendor bill in the previous section, you are ready to process a payment by check, credit card, or electronic funds transfer (ACH) to your vendor.

Practice Paying for Inventory

Using the sample company referred to in Chapter 1, p. 36, you will now create a payment to the vendor for the bill created in the earlier exercise:

1. On the Home page, click the Pay Bills icon. The Pay Bills dialog box displays.

2. Leave the Show All Bills option selected.

3. In the Filter By drop-down list, select **Thomas Kitchen & Bath**. When you are ready to pay your bills in your own QuickBooks file, you will probably not need to filter for a specific vendor because you will process multiple checks for many vendors at once.

4. In the Sort By drop-down list, view the other options for sorting the bills in the Pay Bills dialog box.

5. Place a checkmark next to both of the bills in the first column on the left. Notice that, after you place a checkmark, the Amt. to Pay column for each bill equals the Amt. Due column (see Figure 5.26).

6. With a bill selected, click the Go to Bill button. Notice how easy it is to get to the original transaction. Press the Esc key on your keyboard to close the Enter Bills transaction and return to the Pay Bills dialog box.

Figure 5.26
You can filter the Pay Bills dialog box for a single vendor.

7. For this exercise, leave the default Payment Date. When working in your own data, enter the date you want to print on the vendor checks.

8. Accept the default of Check for Payment Method.

9. In the Account field, accept the default of Checking account. (When working with your own data, you will select the account you are recording the payment from.) Notice that QuickBooks displays your projected Ending Balance for your bank account.

10. Click Pay Selected Bills. QuickBooks opens the Payment Summary dialog box.

11. Review the details displayed, including payment date, account, and method.

12. Choose from Print Checks, Pay More Bills, or in this exercise click Done if you do not want to practice printing (using plain paper).

13. If you selected the option to Print Checks, the Select Checks to Print dialog box displays. Accept the defaults for Bank Account and First Check Number.

14. Review the list of checks to be printed. Each will have a checkmark in the column to the left. Remove the checkmarks from any checks you do not want to print at this time.

15. Click OK to open the Print Checks dialog box. Select your printer from the Printer Name drop-down list, and then choose the proper Check Style from Voucher, Standard, or Wallet. Chapter 13, "Working with Bank and Credit Card Accounts," has more detailed instructions on setting check printing preferences

16. Click Print. For this exercise, make sure you have plain paper in your printer. A check printed to plain paper is not a negotiable document.

17. The Print Checks—Confirmation dialog box displays. In this exercise, click OK to close the confirmation.

See how easy it is to print checks paying your vendors? You can order checks from most reputable check suppliers or order directly from Intuit. To order checks from Intuit, select the Print Checks icon on the lower right of the Home page, or click the Order Checks button at the bottom of the left icon bar. An Internet connection is required.

In the next section, you learn how to handle selling inventory on a customer invoice.

tip

When selecting vendor bills to pay, you can override the Amt. to Pay and type an amount of your choice. QuickBooks keeps track of the remaining balance due to the vendor.

tip

Did you know that you can pay your vendors by a number of methods? These methods include printing a check, recording a manually written check, using credit card, and even making an online bank payment. To learn more about preferences for printing checks or making online payments directly from your QuickBooks file, see Chapter 13.

Selling Inventory

For your business to survive, you need to sell your products (or services) to customers. The next important task discussed in this chapter shows just how easy it is to prepare invoices for your customers in QuickBooks.

First, it might be helpful to review the proper accounting for inventory at the time of sale. Recall that Table 5.2 detailed the impact an invoice or sales receipt has on accounting—namely, to decrease inventory, increase accounts receivable or cash, increase cost of goods sold, or increase income.

Your inventory item setup does all this complicated work for you behind the scenes. First, each inventory item in QuickBooks is assigned an inventory asset account, COGS (cost of goods sold account), and an income account. Second, QuickBooks uses the average cost method to calculate the cost of your product at the time of the invoice.

➡ *For more information, see "Reviewing the Recorded Average Cost Valuation," p. 217.*

Practice Selling Inventory

Follow these steps to practice creating an invoice for a customer using the sample data installed with QuickBooks and discussed in Chapter 1, p. 36:

1. On the Home page, click the Create Invoices or Invoices icon. The icon name differs, depending on whether you have enabled specific Time and Expenses preferences. If another menu drop-down list displays, select Create Invoices.

2. In the Customer:Job drop-down list, select **Garage Repair** for the customer Baker, Chris.

3. In the Class drop-down list, select **New Construction**.

4. Accept the default Template, Date, Invoice #, Bill To, Ship To, Terms, and Due Date fields.

5. In the Item column drop-down list, select the **Doorknobs Std** inventory part from the Hardware parent inventory part.

6. In the Quantity field, type **1**. If you are using the QuickBooks-supplied sample data for this practice example, you will have an invoice for 1 doorknob inventory part with tax.

7. For this practice example, click Save on the top of the form. This saves the invoice and assigns the invoice number, but keeps the invoice open for viewing. See the tip that follows this exercise.

8. From the top of the open invoice, select **Preview** from the Print drop-down list. Click Close when you're done with the Print Preview dialog box.

9. Click Save & Close (or Save & New) to practice creating another invoice.

QuickBooks truly makes it easy to create invoices for your customers. Getting your customers to pay them is another task! Join me later in Chapter 10, "Managing Customers," in the sections "Income Tracker," p. 388 and "Enable the Collections Center," p. 391.

🎯 tip

When recording customer invoices in your own data, you have the option to click the Save button at the top. Typically, you do not need to do this each time. Instead, you can choose between the Save & Close button and the Save & New button on the lower right.

Working with Group Items

Using Group items can save time when you need to enter several items on a purchase or sales transaction.

Practice Using Group Items

Using the sample company referred to in Chapter 1, p. 36, let's practice creating an invoice with the Group item modified in an earlier exercise:

1. On the Home page, click the Create Invoices or Invoices icon. The icon name differs, depending on whether you have enabled specific Time and Expenses preferences. If another menu drop-down list displays, select Create Invoices.

2. In the Customer:Job drop-down list, select the **Barley, Renee:Repairs** job. Select **Remodel** for the Class field. Accept the default Template, Date, Invoice #, Bill To, Ship To, Terms, and Due Date fields.

3. In the Item column, select **Door Set**.

4. QuickBooks adds multiple rows to the invoice. For this exercise, click the Save button at the top of the invoice so that you can easily preview the invoice. When working with your own data, you can ignore this step and choose one of the save options in the lower right of the transaction.

5. In the Print drop-down list at the top of the invoice, select **Preview**.

6. Click Zoom In at the top to enlarge the detail displayed. Notice that the QuickBooks customer invoice includes one line of detail for the customer, but your internal reports and transaction screens show multiple lines of detail.

7. Click Close to close the preview. Click Save & Close to close the Create Invoices transaction.

Using Group items makes data entry more efficient when you need to enter multiple items at one time. An added benefit is that using Group items also provides the option to hide individual line details on the invoice provided to the customer.

Next, continue your practice by working with assembly items.

Working with Assemblies

Assemblies are used when you want to enter multiple items at one time and track the on-hand quantity for the finished good. Inventory assemblies are available only with QuickBooks Premier (all editions), Accountant, and Enterprise (all editions).

Working with assemblies is a two or three-step process:

1. Create the assembly.

2. Build the assembly.

3. If the assembly contains other assemblies as a component, build the "nested" assembly first.

New for QuickBooks Enterprise 14.0 are many improvements for working with assemblies.

➡ *For more information, see "Working with Assemblies" in Appendix C, p. 195.*

Practice Using Assemblies

Using the sample company referred to in Chapter 1, p. 36, let's practice building an assembly and creating an invoice with an assembly item in your sample data:

1. From your Home page, from the drop-down list next to the Inventory Activities icon, select **Build Assemblies**. The Build Assemblies dialog box opens (see Figure 5.27).

Figure 5.27 You must first build the assembly to track the quantity of manufactured products.

Build Assemblies

Previous Next Attach

ASSEMBLY ITEM: Interior Door kit

Date: 12/15/2017   Build Ref. No.: 9003

Build Assembly

QUANTITY ON HAND	20 Build Point: 5
QUANTITY ON SALES ORDER	0
QUANTITY RESERVED FOR OTHER ASSEMBLIES	0
QUANTITY AVAILABLE	20

Components Needed to Build Interior Door kit

ITEM	DESCRIPTION	TYPE	U/M	QTY ON HAND	QTY NEEDED
Hardware:Doorknobs Std	Standard Doorknobs	Inv Part		124	5
Wood Door:Interior	Interior wood door	Inv Part		47	5
Hardware:Brass hinges	standard interior brass hinge	Inv Part	ea	246	15
Door Frame	standard interior door frame	Inv Part		21	5

Maximum number you can build from the quantity on hand: 21

QUANTITY TO BUILD   5

MEMO

Build & Close   Build & New   Clear

2. In the Assembly Item drop-down list, select **Interior Door Kit**.

3. Accept the default Date and Build Ref. No.

4. Review the individual items and note the reported maximum number of items that can be built with the stock on hand (lower right).

5. In the Quantity to Build box, type **5**. Enter an optional memo for your own reporting.

6. Click Build & Close.

With the assembly now built, you are ready to add the assembly to a customer's invoice. To do so, follow these steps:

1. On the Home page, click the Create Invoices or Invoices icon. The icon name differs, depending on whether you have enabled specific Time and Expenses preferences. If another menu drop-down list displays, select Create Invoices.

2. In the Customer:Job drop-down list, select the **Baker, Chris:Family Room** job. Select **Remodel** for the Class field. Accept the default Template, Date, Invoice #, Bill To, Ship To, Terms, and Due Date fields.

3. In the Item column, select **Interior Door Kit**.

4. In the Quantity field, type **1**.

5. In the Rate field, type **125.00**. This rate would have been prefilled if a sales price were associated with the inventory assembly.

6. Click Save & Close to close the Create Invoices transaction.

How do you handle your accounting when you do not have enough inventories on hand to ship to a customer? Join me in the next section for details on working with sales orders to track these backorders.

tip

The sales order transaction type is available only in QuickBooks Premier (all editions), QuickBooks Accountant, and QuickBooks Enterprise Solutions (all editions). If you need this functionality, consider upgrading your file to Premier or Enterprise. For more information, see "Upgrading Your QuickBooks Version," p. 651.

Additionally, working with sales orders is a preference that is enabled by logging in to the file as the Admin or External Accountant. From the menu bar, select **Edit**, **Preferences**, **Sales & Customers—Company Preferences**, and click the Enable Sales Orders checkbox.

Handling Inventory Backorders

Do you want to "commit" inventory to a customer ahead of purchasing the inventory? Handling backorders for your customers is best tracked using the Create Sales Order transaction available with QuickBooks Premier (all editions), QuickBooks Accountant, and QuickBooks Enterprise Solutions (all editions).

Using sales order transactions, you can record that you have committed inventory (backordered) for sale to the customer, provide the customer details of the sale for prepayment, and later create the customer invoice directly from the sales order details. If you do take a prepayment from a customer, you will want to review the instructions included in Chapter 9, in the section "Recording the Customer Payment," p. 370.

Sales orders are considered a nonposting document, meaning that when they are created, they do not affect inventory, revenue, or costs until the sales order is converted to an invoice; on the other hand, if you use a sales receipt, you affect your inventory, revenue, and costs when the sales receipt is recorded.

Using this sales order transaction type is the best solution if you must provide a sales document to a customer before the customer receives the merchandise.

Practice Working with Sales Orders

Using the same sample data discussed in Chapter 1, p. 36, let's create a sales order after enabling this in preferences:

1. On the Home page, click the Sales Orders icon. If you do not have this icon, make sure sales orders are enabled in the Sales & Customers—Company Preferences.

2. In the Customer:Job drop-down list, select the **Home Remodel** job for the customer **Bauman, Mark**, as in Figure 5.28.

Figure 5.28
Use a sales order to commit inventory for a future sale.

3. For the Class field, select **Remodel**.

4. Leave the default template, date, S.O. No., Ship To, and P.O. details.

5. In the Item column drop-down list, select the **Wood Door:Exterior** inventory part. Accept the default description.

6. In the Ordered column, type **2**. Leave the other fields on the row as the default. If you are using the QuickBooks-supplied sample data for this practice, you will have a Sales Order for 2 Exterior Wood Doors with tax.

7. For this exercise, click Save at the top of the transaction. This saves the sales order and assigns the sales order number, but it keeps the sales order open for viewing. We do this just for the purposes of this practice example. In your own data, you would want to select **Save & Close** or **Save & New** at the bottom of the transaction.

8. In the Print drop-down list, at the top of the open sales order, select **Preview**. Click Close when you are done with the Print Preview dialog box.

9. Click Save & Close (or Save & New) to practice creating another sales order.

10. Next, create an invoice for the open sales order. On the Home page, click the Create Invoices or Invoices icon. (Optional) From an open sales order, you can click the Create Invoice icon at the top of the transaction to create the invoice.

11. In the Customer:Job drop-down list, on the Create Invoices transaction, select **Bauman, Mark:Home Remodel** job. The Available Sales Orders dialog box shown in Figure 5.29 displays.

Figure 5.29
Don't forget to place a checkmark next to each available sales order you want to invoice.

12. Click in the first column to place a checkmark next to the listed open sales order(s) you want to include on the invoice to the customer.

13. Click OK. The Create Invoice Based on Sales Order(s) dialog box displays. For this exercise, select the **Create Invoice for Selected Items** option button, shown in Figure 5.30.

Figure 5.30
Invoicing a partial sales order.

14. Click OK. QuickBooks displays the Specify Invoice Quantities for Items on Sales Order(s) dialog box, as in Figure 5.31.

Specify Invoice Quantities for Items on Sales Order(s)							×

Invoice for: Bauman, Mark:Home Remodel

For each item below, specify the quantity you will ship on this invoice.

☐ Show quantity available instead of quantity on hand

ITEM	DATE	S.O. ...	ON HAND	ORDERED	PREV. INVO...	TO INVOICE	U/M
Wood Door:Exterior	12/15/2017	7004	16	2	0	1	

Figure 5.31
Use this dialog box to specify the quantity of the sales order items you want to invoice.

15. (Optional) Select the **Show Quantity Available Instead of Quantity on Hand** checkbox. How quantity available and quantity on hand differ is determined by your settings in Inventory preferences (see Figure 5.1).

16. In the To Invoice column, type **1** (to record a partial invoice).

17. Click OK to return to the Create Invoices transaction.

18. Review the details on the invoice (see Figure 5.32) for the Wood Door:Exterior with details for Ordered, Prev. Invoiced, and Invoiced. If you selected multiple sales orders to invoice, you will also have a column for Backordered on the invoice template. Click Save on the top of the transaction.

Figure 5.32
The invoice now shows separate columns for Ordered, Prev. Invoiced, and Invoiced.

19. In the Recent Transactions section on the Customer tab (on the right side of the dialog box), click the link to the Sales Order you created in this exercise. (Optional) From a displayed transaction, select Transaction History from the Report tab on the ribbon toolbar.

20. The Create Sales Order transaction displays with the details of the original sales order. Notice the new columns of detail for Backordered and Invoiced on the sales order.

If your customer orders inventory before you have made or ordered the part, using the sales order transaction can keep track of these committed sales. Reviewing your open sales orders is important for effective inventory management.

Handling Customer Inventory Returns

When your company offers an inventory product for sale, you will probably also have customers returning product. In QuickBooks, you use a credit memo transaction to record the return.

Processing your customer returns correctly can be important to your company's financials. A returned inventory product from your customer affects the following:

- Inventory physical count and inventory valuation on the balance sheet
- Accounts receivable balance on the balance sheet

■ Income and cost of goods sold

■ Sales tax payable (if applicable to your business and product)

To help you be more efficient with this process, you can create a credit memo directly from the original customer invoice. This functionality can help QuickBooks users be more accurate when recording customer returns.

Practice Recording Customer Returns

Using the same sample data discussed in Chapter 1, p. 36, you can continue with the practice exercise you completed earlier when creating an invoice:

1. On the Home page, click the Customers icon to open the Customer Center (see Figure 5.33).

Figure 5.33
The Customer Center can be the easiest place to find specific transactions.

2. On the Customers & Jobs tab, select the **Garage Repair** job for the customer **Baker, Chris**.

3. On the right side of the Customer Center, you should see the invoice you created in the earlier practice example. Double-click it to open the selected invoice.

4. With the customer invoice open, from the Main tab of the ribbon toolbar (at the top of the Create Invoices transaction), select **Refund/Credit**.

5. The Create Credit Memos/Refunds transaction displays with the same item(s) that was included on the original invoice. Review and leave the default information. In your own data, you might need to add or remove items from the Create Credit Memos/Refunds transaction.

6. Click Save & Close. The Available Credit dialog box displays, as shown in Figure 5.34, with these options:
   - Retain as an Available Credit
   - Give a Refund
   - Apply to an Invoice

Figure 5.34
Multiple options are available for handling customer credits.

7. For this practice, select the **Apply to an Invoice** option button. Click OK. The Apply Credit to Invoices dialog box displays (see Figure 5.35). In this practice example, QuickBooks has automatically selected the invoice you created in the previous practice.

Figure 5.35
You can manually override the amount or invoice selection in how a customer credit is applied.

8. Click Done. You return to the Create Invoices transaction that, for this exercise, shows a Balance Due of 0.00 in the lower-right corner with a Paid stamp on the invoice.

9. Click Save & Close.

QuickBooks makes it easy to create and track customer returns.

Handling Vendor Inventory Returns

Perhaps after receiving the returned inventory from your customer, you find that the product was not manufactured to your specifications and needs to be returned to the vendor.

Handling these types of returns properly is important and can affect these financial balances:

- Inventory physical count and inventory valuation on the balance sheet

- Accounts payable balance on the balance sheet

To create a vendor return in your QuickBooks data file, follow these steps:

1. On the Home page, click the Enter Bills icon.

2. Select the **Credit** radial button at the top of the Enter Bills transaction to create a vendor credit.

3. From the Vendor drop-down list, select the vendor you are returning the product(s) to.

4. For the Date field, enter the date you want to record for the return of the inventory.

5. In the Ref. No. field, enter your vendor's credit authorization number, if supplied.

6. Click the Items tab and select the inventory item(s) being returned.

7. In the Qty field, type the number of units being returned.

8. Review the default Cost, and adjust as needed to agree with your vendor's credit authorization.

9. Click Save & Close (or Save & New) to enter another vendor credit.

 tip

When applying a credit memo to an invoice in the Apply Credit to Invoices dialog box, shown in Figure 5.35, QuickBooks matches the credit to an invoice of the same amount if there are multiple invoices with open balances by default. If no match is found, QuickBooks applies the credit to the oldest invoice(s) first.

Entering a vendor credit is the first step in the process. When you know which bill your vendor applied the credit to, you can assign the credit to the same bill. For more detail, see "Applying Vendor Credits," p. 259.

6

MANAGING INVENTORY

Inventory management requires adherence to a strict process to monitor
the items being purchased into stock and later being sold. Failure to have
these processes in place can wreak havoc on the company's financials
by misstating the value of the inventory or the associated costs for that
inventory. This chapter provides details on how to use QuickBooks to
properly manage your inventory activities.

Adjusting Inventory

For companies that track inventory, I find that inventory balances receive
less attention than the company's receivables and payables. You review
your accounts receivable because you have customers that need to pay
you. You keep up with your accounts payable because you have vendors
that won't supply you without first getting paid. Why exactly is it that
inventory "reconciling" is often at the bottom of the list, yet it can have
the greatest impact on a company's financials?

Experience has taught me that most companies are unaware that
QuickBooks can be used to properly review and audit their inventory bal-
ances. This section outlines specific reports and methods you can use in
QuickBooks to make sure inventory balances are correct.

If you are using inventory in your QuickBooks data, it is recommended
that you view your financial reports in accrual basis. Most companies
that have inventory also report their tax financials on an accrual basis.
However, a more important reason is that, with accrual basis reporting,
QuickBooks matches the cost with the related sale. The exception is when
using non-inventory items. These items, when purchased, do not increase
an Inventory Asset account. Instead, they are recorded directly to the Cost
of Goods Sold account or the Expense account that was assigned when
the item was created.

Any company that manages inventory needs to minimize inventory errors. Business owners list any of the following reasons for having to correct their accounting inventory errors:

- Errors in the physical counted results

- Damaged goods

- Theft of inventory

- Open vendor item receipts or bills that are not due to the vendor

- Incorrect valuation given to the inventory at the startup of a data file

This section discusses the methods for correcting inventory errors you might find in your QuickBooks data.

Performing a Physical Inventory Count

If you have a good inventory count commitment from your team and manage the resulting information from the QuickBooks Inventory Valuation Summary report, you should see little to no data entry errors; instead, you probably will be adjusting inventory only for damage or theft.

All too often, here is where I find a complacent attitude about inventory management. I agree that performing a physical inventory count is a time-consuming task. However, if effort is put to this task, your overall financials will be more accurate.

To make recording the count easier, on the menu bar, click Reports, Inventory, Physical Inventory Worksheet. You cannot modify the report or filter it for specific dates (see Figure 6.1), so you should run the report at the moment you start to do your physical count and be certain that you have entered all your inventory-related transactions. If you want to keep a record of the original worksheet, you can export it to Excel or email it as a PDF attachment.

After completing a physical inventory count, you can confidently create an inventory adjustment so the accounting records match your actual physical inventory.

Figure 6.1
Create a physical inventory worksheet to record the actual inventory counts.

tip

When printing the Physical Inventory Worksheet, you might want to remove the Quantity on Hand Column, to make sure the staff actually counts the inventory and does not just assume that the on-hand quantity is what the warehouse stock level is.

Quantity Adjustments

If you discovered quantity differences between your accounting records and your physical inventory account, you should record an inventory quantity adjustment to correct your accounting records.

To create an inventory quantity adjustment in your data, follow these steps:

1. On the Home page, in the Company section, click the Inventory Activities icon and then, from the menu, select **Adjust Quantity/Value on Hand**. From the Adjust Quantity/Value on Hand dialog box that displays, use the Find & Select Items button to add items to adjust (see Figure 6.2).

caution

Before creating the accounting adjustment, make sure you have created an account in the chart of accounts to hold the value of the inventory adjustment. The account type can be either a Cost of Goods Sold type or an Expense type. Business owners should consult their accountant when making this decision.

Figure 6.2
Use the Find & Select Items button to efficiently select multiple inventory items to adjust quantity.

2. From the Adjustment Type drop-down list, select **Quantity**.

3. Select an **Adjustment Date** and type an optional **Ref. No.**

4. Select the appropriate **Adjustment Account**. This account is usually a Cost of Goods Sold account or an Expense account named Inventory Overage/Shortage.

5. (Optional) Assign a Customer:Job and/or specify a Class if it's being tracked. However, Job Profitability reports do not include inventory adjustment transactions; only the Profit & Loss by Job reports include the value of these adjustments.

6. To efficiently select multiple items at once, click the Find & Select Items button. Click with your cursor to place a checkmark (see Figure 6.2) next to the items you want to create a quantity adjustment for.

7. Click Add Selected Items to return to the Adjust Quantity/Value on Hand dialog box.

8. In the New Quantity column, enter your count from the completed physical inventory or, optionally, enter the change in the Qty Difference column.

9. Click Save & Close when finished.

> **⚠ caution**
>
> Inventory Quantity (and Value) adjustments assigned to a customer or job are included in the Profit & Loss by Job reports but not in any of the other reports offered when you select **Reports, Jobs, Time & Mileage** from the menu bar.

QuickBooks provides details on the Item Info After Adjustment and summarizes the Total Value of the Adjustment and the Number of Item Adjustments.

The accounting effect of the transaction in Figure 6.3 is to adjust the quantity on hand for each of the items shown. The net effect of this adjustment is to increase the Inventory value on the books with the offset to the assigned Adjustment Account.

Figure 6.3
Use Inventory Adjustments to properly adjust your inventory in your accounting to match your physical counts.

Value Adjustments

Timing is important when doing a valuation adjustment. You want to carefully consider value adjustments, if appropriate, for their impact on the company's resulting financials.

Value adjustments differ from quantity adjustments because they do not adjust the quantity—instead, they adjust the recorded value of the specific items in inventory.

To create a value-only inventory adjustment in your data, follow these steps:

1. From the menu bar, select **Vendors**, **Inventory Activities**, **Adjust Quantity/Value on Hand**. A dialog box with the same name (Adjust Quantity/Value on Hand) opens (see Figure 6.4).

2. In the Adjustment Type drop-down list, select **Total Value**.

3. Select an **Adjustment Date** and type an optional **Ref. No**.

4. Select the appropriate **Adjustment Account**. This account is usually an Expense account named Inventory Overage/Shortage.

> **⚠ caution**
> Generally, value adjustments are not done as often as quantity adjustments. The purpose of this book is not to explore or offer tax advice, but certain guidelines determine when an inventory valuation adjustment is appropriate. Ask your tax accountant to provide guidelines for you.

Figure 6.4
Value adjustments are not used often; be sure to ask your accountant first if they are appropriate for your needs.

5. (Optional) Assign a Customer:Job and/or specify a Class if it's being tracked. However, Job Profitability reports do not include inventory adjustment transactions; only the Profit & Loss by Job reports include the value of these adjustments.

6. To efficiently select multiple items at once, click the Find & Select Items button. Click with your cursor to place a checkmark next to the items you want to create a quantity adjustment for.

7. Click Add Selected Items. You return to the Adjust Quantity/ Value on Hand dialog box.

8. In the New Value column, enter the new calculated total value you want assigned to the item.

9. Click Save & Close when finished.

The accounting result of this inventory value adjustment, shown in Figure 6.4, is no net change to inventory quantities, a decrease (credit) to your Inventory Asset account, and an increase (debit) to your Inventory Adjustments account (either a Cost of Goods Sold type or an Expense type). A new average cost will be computed

> **⚡ caution**
> Did you know how important the date is when assigning the inventory adjustment? If you backdate your inventory adjustment, QuickBooks recalculates your Cost of Goods Sold from that date forward, using the new average cost as of the date of the sales transaction. Take care not to date an inventory adjustment in a prior year for which tax returns have already been filed.

based on the (Original Asset Value + or − the Value Difference)/Quantity on Hand, as recorded on the inventory value adjustment. You can view the newly assigned average cost in the lower left of the inventory adjustment.

> ## ⚙ tip
>
> Two preferences help control dating transactions. To access them, log in as the Admin or External Accountant user in single-user mode. From the menu bar, select **Company, Set Closing Date** to open the Preferences dialog box with the Accounting—Company Preferences tab selected (see Figure 6.5).
>
> Setting Date Warnings ensures that users are warned when a transaction is dated so many days either in the past or in the future. Set Date/Password is another option to "close" QuickBooks to prevent adding, modifying, voiding, or deleting transactions prior to a selected closing date. Chapter 16, "Sharing QuickBooks Data with Your Accountant," more fully discusses setting a closing date and related features.

Figure 6.5
Choices for controlling past- or future-dated transactions.

The new average cost is recorded when a sales transaction uses this item *on or after* the date of the inventory adjustment.

Inventory Reporting

You have learned just how easy it is to buy, sell, and adjust your inventory. Good inventory management also includes frequent reviews of inventory-specific reports available in QuickBooks.

This section introduces you to some of the more common reports. However, take the time to review all available reports—you might have a specific reporting need in addition to those mentioned here.

Inventory Center

To access the Inventory Center, from the Home page, in the Company section, click the Inventory Activities icon; from the drop-down menu, select the Inventory Center (see Figure 6.6). Similar to the other "centers" in QuickBooks, the Inventory Center offers one convenient location to manage your inventory reporting and activities, including the following:

- **New Inventory Item**—Quick access to creating an individual new inventory item or to the Add/ Edit Multiple List Entries functionality.

- **New Transactions**—Quick access to all inventory-related transactions.

- **Print**—Quick access to printing the item list, information, or transaction list.

- **Excel**—Exports to Excel the item or transaction list. Import the item list from Excel. In addition, you can add new items from Excel via import or by pasting.

Figure 6.6 Access the most common transactions and reports for your inventory from the Inventory Center.

Click with your cursor on a specific inventory item, and to the right you will see detailed information, transactions, and links to some of the more common reports for managing your inventory.

You can also attach a document to the inventory item using the free QuickBooks attachments feature. Click the Paperclip icon in the Inventory Center with a specific item selected, or from the menu bar, select **Company, Documents**.

Click the Edit button after you select an item in the Inventory Center to make changes, as Chapter 5, "Setting Up Inventory," discussed previously in the section titled "Adding or Editing Inventory Items."

---

tip

The Inventory Center enables you to filter your inventory list by ready-made filters or custom filters of your choosing. One important selection is the capability to filter for inventory with a negative inventory quantity on hand (QOH <= zero). You learn later in this chapter how important it is to accurate financials to not let your inventory get negative (when you have the appearance of having sold more than what you have on hand).

Report Center

Use the Report Center to find the right report for your inventory management needs. See Figure 6.7.

To open the Report Center, follow these steps:

1. From the menu bar, select **Reports**, **Report Center**.

2. On the Report Center's Standard tab, select **Sales**.

3. Scroll down to the bottom of the page to find the Open Sales Orders—by Customer or by Item report, which is useful when managing inventory. This report is available only if you are using QuickBooks Premier, Accountant, or Enterprise Solutions.

Figure 6.7
The Report Center makes finding the right inventory management report simple.

4. On the Standard tab of the Report Center, select **Purchases** to view these inventory management reports:

- **Purchases by Vendor**—Summary or Detail

- **Purchases by Item**—Summary or Detail

- **Open Purchase Orders**—Summary, Detail or by Job

The Report Center provides a thumbnail image of how the data would look in the report.

5. Below each report, you can change the dates, click Run to prepare the report with your data, click Info to preview a larger thumbnail image, click Fave to include the report in the Favorites section of the Reports Center, or click Help for more details.

6. On the Standard tab of the Report Center, select Inventory to view these inventory management reports:

- **Inventory Valuation**—Summary or Detail. The next section has more details.

- **Inventory Stock Status**—By Item or Vendor.

- **Physical Inventory Worksheet**—Used for recording your physical inventory count totals.

- **Pending Builds**—For QuickBooks Premier, Accountant, or Enterprise users who have assembly inventory items.

7. If you are using the Manufacturing & Wholesale edition of QuickBooks Premier or Enterprise Solutions, click Mfg & Wholesale on the Standard tab of the Report Center for additional useful inventory management reports.

Inventory Valuation and Your Financials

Another equally important task in inventory management is to compare your Inventory Valuation Summary report to your Inventory Asset balance on your accrual basis Balance Sheet report.

---

tip

Because you might want to compare the following reference reports side by side, from the menu bar, select **View, Multiple Windows**. Next, from the menu bar, select **Window, Tile Vertically**. Both reports display side by side, as in Figure 6.8. This works if these reports are the only open windows in QuickBooks.

Comparing Inventory Reports to Financials

Using the sample company referred to in Chapter 1, "Getting Started with QuickBooks," p. 36, use this exercise to practice how to compare the Inventory Valuation Summary report to the Balance Sheet Inventory Asset balance. Your sample data may have different default dates than are discussed in this section.

1. From the menu bar, select **Reports, Report Center**. From the Standard tab, select **Inventory**. Find the Inventory Valuation Summary report and click the Run icon to display the report. Accept the default report date; "As of December 15, 2017" data is displayed (see Figure 6.8). The default date in your sample file may differ.

2. Take note of the Asset Value column Total. In Figure 6.8, the total Asset Value is $30,683.38. Your sample data total may differ.

3. From the Report Center, on the Standard tab, select Company & Financial; then, under the Balance Sheet Standard report (scroll down to find this report), click Run. Accept the default report date.

4. Compare the balance in the Inventory Asset account (in the Other Current Assets group) to the total from step 2.

Figure 6.8
Compare your total Asset Value with your Balance Sheet Inventory Asset balance.

What if the two balances do not match? The most common cause is entering a transaction that affects the Inventory Asset account but does not affect inventory items. The Inventory Summary report shows only the results of transactions that use inventory items. For example, if a General Journal has been used to adjust the Balance Sheet balance, those transactions do not affect the Inventory Valuation Summary report.

⚠ caution

When working with inventory adjustments, never use a General Journal transaction. The specific reason is that a General Journal transaction does not use Items, and any adjustments using this transaction affect only the Balance Sheet balance, not the Inventory Valuation Summary reports.

Using the Inventory Asset account on the Expense tab of a Vendor Bill, Vendor Credit, Credit Card Charge or Credit, or Write Checks transaction is also not appropriate. To properly use these transactions, use the Items tab with the appropriate inventory item.

If you need to adjust inventory, from the menu bar, select **Vendors, Inventory Activities, Adjust Quantity/ Value on Hand**, as discussed earlier in this chapter.

To find General Journal entries in your own data that might be causing the out-of-balance amount, follow these steps:

1. On your Balance Sheet report, double-click the Inventory Asset balance. QuickBooks creates the Transactions by Account report.

2. From the Dates drop-down list, scroll to the top and select **All**.

3. To locate the General Journal entries, from the Sort By drop-down list (in the upper-right corner of the report), select **Type**, as in Figure 6.9. QuickBooks now organizes the data by transaction type. Look for General Journal type transactions.

Figure 6.9 General Journal transactions should not be used to adjust inventory balances.

Do not modify, delete, or void these transactions, especially if they were used in accounting periods that have already had tax returns prepared using the current financial information. Continue with the remaining methods in the sections that follow before making any corrections.

Reviewing the Recorded Average Cost Valuation

As mentioned earlier in this chapter, QuickBooks uses the Average Cost method for valuing inventory. From the menu bar, select **Reports**, **Inventory**, **Inventory Valuation Summary**. Figure 6.10 shows the value assigned to your costs when you sell an inventory item.

Figure 6.10
Use the Inventory Valuation Summary report to verify the cost being recorded when an inventory item is sold.

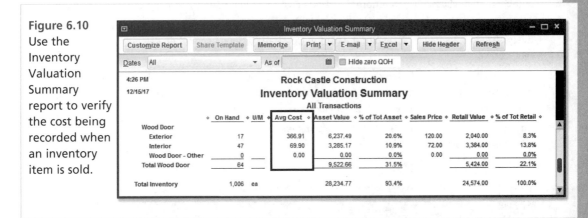

If you are using QuickBooks Enterprise Solutions 14.0 with FIFO (First-In, First-Out) costing enabled, it might not be necessary to review this section because FIFO costing replaces average costing. Beginning with QuickBooks Enterprise 13.0, you can review your inventory valuation reports using either the Average Cost method discussed here or the First-In, First-Out (FIFO) method. FIFO costing in QuickBooks Enterprise is a preference setting that you can enable or disable.

General Journal transactions should not be used to adjust inventory balances.

> **note**
> The Inventory Valuation Summary report and others include the option to hide (exclude from the report) inventory items when the quantity on hand is zero.

➡ *To learn more about this and other inventory features, see Appendix C, "QuickBooks Enterprise Solutions Features," p. 783.*

For example, assume you are selling an inventory product with the transactions shown in Table 6.1.

Table 6.1 Calculating Average Cost

Date	Quantity Purchased	Actual Cost per Unit	Total Cost	QuickBooks Cumulative Average Cost per Unit
12/15/17	100	$10.00	$1,000.00	$10.00
12/25/17	50	$8.50	$425.00	$9.50
TOTAL	150		$1,425.00	(1425/150)

Sales transactions that are dated on or between 12/15/17 and 12/24/17 for this item will record cost of goods sold at $10.00 per unit (assuming that no other replenishing purchases are made during that time).

The average cost of the 150 units will be $9.50 each if none are sold prior to 12/26. However, any quantity sold from the first order, prior to the purchase on 12/25, will change the weighting of the unit cost. This will result in a different average cost recorded when the second order is received.

To further explain how important it is to enter your inventory transactions daily (and not retroactively), Table 6.2 shows the resulting Average Cost calculations used when selling more inventory than is available.

In Table 6.2, the cost recorded on 12/20/17 is $10.00 per unit. However, after the replenishing transaction, the actual average cost is $8.50 per unit. The costs in 2017 will be overstated by $1.50 per unit, with the correcting entry to Cost of Goods Sold reported in the 2018 financials.

These details assume that no other transactions were recorded for this item, except as noted in the following transactions.

Table 6.2 Calculating Average Cost When Selling Negative Inventory

Date	Quantity Purchased	Quantity Sold	Actual Cost per Unit	Resulting Inventory Value	Resulting Average Cost
12/15/17	100		$10.00	$1,000.00	$10.00
12/20/17		−125	$10.00	$(250.00)	$10.00
01/05/18	50		$8.50	$425.00	$8.50
Remaining Quantity	25		Remaining Value	$212.50	$8.50

Average costing is a perfect fit for a business that sells a product that does not fluctuate significantly in cost from one period to the next. However, this is not always the case, so it becomes important that you verify the relative accuracy of the average cost QuickBooks has recorded on the Inventory Valuation Summary report.

In Figure 6.10, shown previously, the average cost for the Interior Wood Door is listed as $69.90. Compare this amount to a recent vendor bill. If the amount is significantly different, you should review the purchase details for the item.

From the menu bar, select **Reports**, **Inventory**, **Inventory Valuation Detail**. You might want to customize and filter the report for specific dates or items. Chapter 14, "Reporting in QuickBooks," has more on working with reports.

In Figure 6.11, the Inventory Valuation Detail is shown for the Interior Wood Door. Reviewing the individual lines in the Average

> ## 📡 caution
> In Table 6.2, a business that reviews profitability by customer would see inventory costs attributed to that customer overstated. Why? The replenishing purchase that resulted in a different average cost was dated after the sales document. Proper data entry should have the replenishing document dated before the sales transactions that resulted in negative inventory.

Cost column can help you determine whether an issue exists with the average cost. If the average cost changes dramatically, you might want to review the specific bill or check details recorded when the product was purchased.

Figure 6.11
Create an
Inventory
Valuation
Detail report
to research
changes in
average cost.

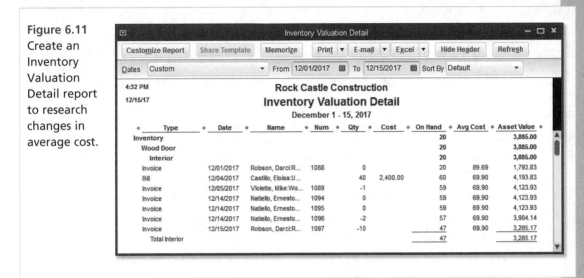

Reviewing and correcting the average cost of items is just as important as adjusting the quantity on hand.

Reviewing Aged Item Receipts

The "Purchasing, Receiving, and Entering the Vendor Bill" section of Chapter 5 provides details about the inventory process. One of the methods of receiving inventory is without the vendor's bill.

The effect of receiving inventory without a bill is to increase your inventory asset (debit) and increase your accounts payable (credit). The unique feature of this method is that QuickBooks creates an item receipt transaction that *will not* show in the Pay Bills window. QuickBooks recognizes that because you did not receive the bill, you will not likely be paying it without the final bill details.

Often goods will arrive at your business without a bill. A vendor might ship the goods to your place of business without a final bill for a couple reasons:

- Shipping charges need to be added to the bill. Often the vendor does not know the shipping charges when the goods are initially shipped.

- Vendors do not want to disclose the value of the inventory so that those who handle the inventory during shipping will not know the value of the goods being shipped.

Item receipts age just like an outstanding accounts payable bill. To see whether you have open, outdated item receipts, go to the Vendor Center and click the Transactions tab (see Figure 6.12). Select the Item Receipts transaction type. Filter by All Dates and click the Date column to sort the transactions by date.

Figure 6.12
Use the Transactions tab of the Vendor Center to see all open item receipts.

If you find you have aged item receipts and you know you have paid the vendor, use the following steps to assign the check to the open item receipt. If you have paid your vendor with a credit card, you might also want to use these same instructions, substituting the credit card transaction for the check transaction:

1. From the Vendor Center, select the **Item Receipts** transaction type on the Transactions tab.

2. Unapplied item receipts display on the right. Click the header for the Date column to sort by date. You are looking for any old, outdated item receipts.

3. If you find an aged item receipt that you know was paid to the vendor, double-click the item receipt to open the Create Item Receipts transaction.

4. Select the Bill Received checkbox (top right), shown in Figure 6.13. The item receipt now becomes a vendor bill transaction type.

Click here if you are ready to record the final bill

Figure 6.13
Item receipts do not show up with bills to be paid.

5. Click Save & Close, and then click Yes to acknowledge that you want to record the change.

6. Locate the check that was written to the vendor. From the Vendors tab on the Vendor Center, select the same vendor the item receipt was created for.

7. On the right, in the Show drop-down list, select **Checks**. (Optional) Select a **Filter By** and **Date** range.

8. After locating the check in the Vendor Center, double-click the check to open the Write Checks transaction. Modify the Account on the Expenses tab to be Accounts Payable, as in Figure 6.14.

Figure 6.14
Changing the Expenses account to Accounts Payable and adding the vendor name on the same line creates a vendor credit from the check.

9. Assign the Vendor name in the Customer:Job column. The effect of this updated transaction is to decrease (debit) Accounts Payable and decrease (credit) Cash.

10. Click Save & Close.

11. From the Home page, click the Pay Bills icon. The Pay Bills dialog box opens.

12. In the Filter By drop-down list, select the vendor you are correcting the records for.

13. Place a checkmark next to the bill (see Figure 6.15).

Figure 6.15
After the bill is selected, the Set Credits option is available.

14. Click the Set Credits button to assign the modified check transaction from step 7 to the open vendor bill (see Figure 6.16).

Figure 6.16
QuickBooks automatically matches a credit with a bill of the same amount, or you can select the credit and modify the amount assigned.

15. Click Done to return to the Pay Bills dialog box. If your credit is the same amount as the open vendor bill the Amt. To Pay column will be zero.

16. Click Pay Selected Bills. Click Done to close the Payment Summary dialog box.

Reviewing Aged Accounts Payable

At the same time you review your open item receipts, you should review your accounts payable unpaid bills that have aged more than 60 days.

To review your accounts payable, from the menu bar, select **Reports**, **Vendors & Payables**, **Unpaid Bills Detail**. If you see open vendor bills you are sure you have paid, it might be because you used the Write Checks transaction to pay your vendor bills instead of using the Pay Bills dialog box (accessed from the Vendors, Pay Bills menu). Having both an open vendor bill and a check paying for the same purchase overstates your costs or inventory.

QuickBooks tries to prevent you from doing this by providing a warning message when you try to write a check to a vendor for which you have an unpaid bill (see Figure 6.17).

Figure 6.17
A warning displays if you try to use the Write Checks transaction to pay a vendor instead of creating a bill payment from the Pay Bills dialog box.

If you did use the Write Checks transaction to issue a vendor payment for a currently open vendor bill, you can resolve this problem by reassigning it. To do so, follow the steps outlined in the "Reviewing Aged Item Receipts," section, starting with step 7.

After completing the steps, you have successfully assigned the check you wrote using the Write Checks transaction to the open vendor bill that should have been paid by a check in the Pay Bills dialog box. This correction has now removed the expected overstatement in your costs and removed the bill from being included in your open accounts payable balances.

tip
If you are an accounting professional using the QuickBooks Accountant 2014 software, you will find a tool in Client Data Review that simplifies the steps outlined in this section. For more information, refer to Appendix A, "Client Data Review."

How QuickBooks Handles Negative Inventory

QuickBooks enables you to oversell your inventory, which results in negative inventory. This means that you can include an inventory item on a customer invoice or sales receipt before you have recorded the item receipt or bill for the purchase of the item into your inventory.

When a transaction will cause you to have a negative inventory balance, you will see the warning message in Figure 6.18. The warning does not prevent the user from completing the intended transaction, but it should be an indication that the user should research why QuickBooks does not have enough stock of that item in inventory to record the sale.

Figure 6.18
Not enough quantity warning indicates an issue with not following the recommended processes for proper inventory management.

Although ignoring the warning message can be useful for getting the invoice to the customer, it can create issues with your company's financials. The following sections detail how QuickBooks handles the costing of the inventory behind the scenes when you sell negative inventory and provide information on how to avoid or minimize the negative effect it can have on your company's financials.

When Inventory Has an Average Cost from Prior Purchase Transactions

If you review the Inventory Valuation Detail report (select **Reports**, **Inventory**, **Inventory Valuation Detail** from the menu bar) for the item(s) that have negative values, and there are previously recorded average cost amounts, QuickBooks assigns the most recent average cost dated on or before the invoice date that created negative inventory. When the purchase transaction is later recorded, QuickBooks adjusts the Cost of Goods Sold or Expense type for any difference.

➥ *For more information, see how to work with the Client Data Review tool in Appendix A, p. 695.*

> **⚡ caution**
>
> On the Items & Inventory—Company Preferences tab of the Preferences dialog box (select **Edit**, **Preferences** from the menu bar), you can enable a warning if not enough inventory quantity is on hand (QOH) to sell (see Figure 6.18). Your preferences may differ, depending on the version of QuickBooks you are using.

> **tip**
>
> With the QuickBooks Accountant 2014 Client Data Review feature, you can troubleshoot inventory discrepancies between the Inventory Valuation Summary report and the inventory balance on the Balance Sheet report. This troubleshooting tool automatically compares the balances from the two reports and details which transactions are potentially causing the discrepancy.
>
> Additionally, this tool identifies which items are negative (you have sold more than you have purchased) for the specific accounting period being reviewed, as well as for a current date. You learn in this chapter just how important it is to not let your inventory go negative.

Figure 6.19 shows that the average cost on the date of the invoice as $150.00 per unit. QuickBooks records a decrease (credit) to inventory for the two units of $300.00 total and an increase (debit) to Cost of Goods Sold of $300.00 for the two units sold.

Figure 6.19
QuickBooks records the cost of goods sold for negative inventory items at the last known average cost.

To show how important the date of the replenishing purchase transaction is, review the details provided next. This example assumes that no additional transactions were recorded except as noted.

The new inventory asset value is calculated as follows:

($150.00)	Inventory asset value as of 12/15/17 due to selling "negative inventory."
$600.00	12/25/17 replenishing purchase of 3 units @ $200.00/unit.
$450.00	Asset value before the QuickBooks automatic adjustment to COGS.
	Actual inventory value is 2 remaining units at $200 each, or $400.00 total.
$(50.00)	On the date of the replenishing vendor bill, QuickBooks automatically creates a transaction that decreases (credits) Inventory Asset and increases (debits) COGS. See Figure 6.20. This increase in cost adjustment is not associated with the recorded per-unit cost to the customer.
$400.00	Resulting Inventory Asset value on 12/25/17, as shown in Figure 6.21.

Figure 6.20
When you replenish inventory shortages, QuickBooks automatically makes an adjustment to agree with what the average cost would have been.

Figure 6.21
The Inventory Valuation Detail report shows the actual inventory value after recording the replenishment transaction.

When QuickBooks creates an adjustment to reflect what the average cost should have been, the adjustment is *not* assigned to customers or jobs—making it even more important to not sell negative inventory.

tip

QuickBooks does not retroactively record the additional cost back to the customer's negative inventory invoice date. In fact, QuickBooks records the adjustment as of the date of the purchase transaction and does not associate the adjustment with the original customer at all, thereby overstating gross profit on a Profit & Loss by Job report.

The date of the replenishing purchase transaction becomes increasingly important to manage when you let inventory go negative in your data at the end of a fiscal or tax year.

When Inventory Does Not Have a Prior Average Cost

Sometimes when you stock a new item, you add it to a customer invoice before recording any purchase activity for the item. If this happens, you should at least record a default cost on the New or Edit Item dialog box.

When an Inventory Item Has a Default Cost

If you have assigned an inventory item that you have not yet purchased (that is, the quantity on hand is zero) to a customer invoice, and if you *did* define a default cost when you first created the inventory item, QuickBooks uses this default cost as the suggested per-unit cost when the invoice is recorded.

Suppose you stock a new inventory item for a Wood Door with Glass. When creating the item, you record a default cost of $150.00, as shown in Figure 6.22.

Before any purchase is recorded for this item, it is sold on a customer invoice. When you create an invoice for which not enough quantity is on hand, QuickBooks provides a warning, as Figure 6.18 showed earlier.

QuickBooks has to estimate the cost of the item and, in this example, uses the cost assigned to the item in the New or Edit Item dialog box (see Figure 6.23). When you save this invoice, QuickBooks creates the entry in Table 6.3.

Figure 6.22
This new stock item was created in QuickBooks with a default cost of $150.00.

Figure 6.23
QuickBooks uses the cost assigned in the New or Edit Item dialog box when you sell inventory that you have not recorded any purchase transactions for.

Table 6.3 Accounting When Inventory Is Sold

Debit	Credit
Accounts Receivable (increase)	Income (increase)
Cost of Goods Sold (increase)	Inventory Asset (decrease)
	Sales Tax Payable (if applicable) (increase)

To view this report, with the transaction displayed, on the Reports tab of the transaction ribbon, choose Transaction Journal.

This impact to your financials (positive or negative) can be significant if the actual purchase price differs from the recorded default cost on the New or Edit Item dialog box.

When an Inventory Item Does Not Have a Default Cost

If you have assigned an inventory item you have not yet purchased (that is, the quantity on hand is zero) to a customer invoice, and *did not* define a default cost when you first created the inventory item, QuickBooks uses -0- as the default cost per unit when the invoice is recorded, showing a 100% profit margin for your financials and for that customer.

Now, using the same previous example, only *not* recording a default cost when setting up the item, as in Figure 6.24, QuickBooks does not calculate any cost or inventory reduction with the sale of the inventory (see Figure 6.25).

Imagine the impact this can have on your financials and the profitability reports you might review for your business or clients. Simply heeding the warnings QuickBooks provides about the errors of selling negative inventory can prevent this from happening in your data file.

Figure 6.24
Setting up an item without including a default cost is not recommended.

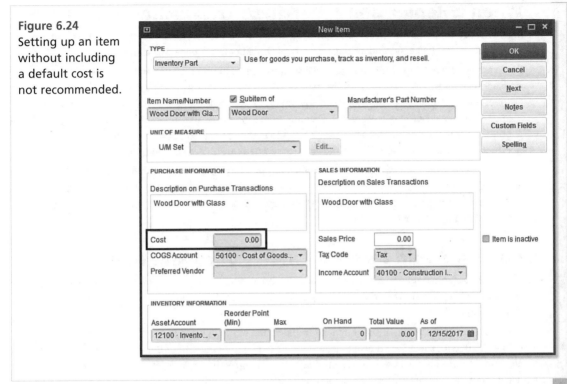

Figure 6.25
No inventory decrease or cost is recorded when selling an item you do not have in inventory, have not purchased, and did not record a default cost for.

When a Replenishing Purchase Transaction Is Created

Exactly what happens when you do record purchase transactions? The date recorded on the purchase transaction has a significant impact on how QuickBooks handles this transaction.

For example, if a sale resulting in negative inventory was dated in October and the replenishing transaction (vendor bill) was dated in November, QuickBooks records the revenue in the month of October and records cost in the month of November. From month to month, it might not be noticeable, but if the transactions cross years, revenue would be overstated in one year and costs in another. Additionally, the revenue is tracked by the customer assigned to the invoice, but the cost *is not* tracked by the customer because the cost is recorded on the date of the purchase transactions.

To limit the negative impact, date your replenishing purchase transactions *before* the date of the customer invoice that caused the negative inventory. QuickBooks recalculates the average cost of all sales transactions dated after this "replenishing" purchase transaction. Of course, it is simply best not to sell negative inventory at all.

How to Avoid Incorrect Inventory Valuation

Troubleshooting negative inventory can be an eye opener to show how important proper inventory management is. To help with this task, rely on the Inventory Valuation Detail report, shown previously in Figure 6.21.

You can avoid these issues if the purchase transactions or inventory adjustments are dated on or before the date of the sales transactions creating the negative inventory. Backdating inventory adjustment transactions can be a powerful solution for correcting months of misstated financials, so use it where appropriate after discussing it with your accountant.

Using solid inventory management processes and being current with your data entry can avoid recording negative inventory. If you do have negative inventory, be sure to correct it at the end of your tax year, or your tax return information will potentially be incorrect.

QuickStart

Step 1. Add a Vendor **242**

Step 2. Record a Vendor Bill **251**

Step 3. Pay the Vendor **256**

7

SETTING UP VENDORS

Your business is off to a great start using the QuickBooks software. Tracking the expenses your company incurs is important to the overall financial health of the business. This chapter helps you work more efficiently with the vendors who are the suppliers of your products or services.

Customizing Your Home Page for Vendor Activities

QuickBooks makes performing vendor activities easy with a customizable list of tasks on the Home page (see Figure 7.1).

When working with accounts payable, you can customize the Home page to include or exclude the following:

- The option to enter bills and pay bills

- Inventory-related activities

- Time tracking, which is useful if you pay vendors for time worked on jobs

➡️ *For more information on customizing the Home page, refer to Chapter 2, "Getting Around QuickBooks."*

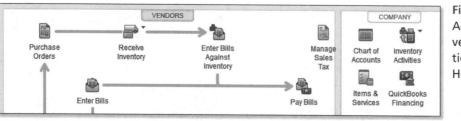

Figure 7.1
Access common vendor activities from the Home page.

Preferences That Affect Accounts Payable

Did you know that you can streamline accounts payable processes by setting certain QuickBooks preferences? Setting preferences saves keystrokes, which, in turn, can save data entry time.

Not every preference that affects accounts payable impacts your financials; some preferences enable specific features. To view and modify these QuickBooks settings, from the menu bar, select **Edit**, **Preferences**.

Preferences in QuickBooks come in two forms:

- **My Preferences**—Settings that are unique to the current user logged in to the data file and that other users do not share. Click the My Preferences tab to modify the user-specific settings for the logged-in user.

- **Company Preferences**—Settings that are common to all users. Click the Company Preferences tab to modify settings globally for all users.

The following sections detail the preferences that can affect your use of the accounts payable functionality.

Accounting

The Accounting preferences are important to review when you first create your data file. These choices affect much of how your accounting information is recorded in accounts payable.

> **note**
>
> To set Company Preferences, you need to open the file as the Admin or External Accountant user and switch to single-user mode (if you are using the data file in a multiuser environment). The Admin user is the default user created when you begin using QuickBooks for the first time.
>
> Proper data entry security includes limiting which employees have access to logging in as the Admin and setting Company Preferences that are global for all users.

Company Preferences

Company Preferences are shared globally by all users. The Accounting preferences include the following:

- **Accounts**—These settings are important for proper management of recording revenue and expenses. The following are the preferences settings for Accounts:

  - **Use Account Numbers**—If enabled, this setting requires the use of an account number in addition to the account name when creating a new chart of account list item. Users can type either the number or the name when referencing an account on a transaction line.

- **Show Lowest Subaccount Only**—You can choose this option if account numbering is enabled and all the chart of account items have a number assigned. This setting changes how the account name is displayed. If you see an "other" named account on your financials, users recorded a transaction using the parent account and not one of the available subaccounts.

- **Require Accounts**—Use this option to determine whether QuickBooks displays a prompt when you forget to choose an account on a transaction line. If you leave the option turned off, QuickBooks assigns the transaction to Uncategorized Income or Uncategorized Expense. When you create a new data file, this default is automatically selected.

- **Use Class Tracking for Transactions**—Classes in QuickBooks provide a secondary means of grouping transactions, such as into profit centers. The optional Prompt to Assign Classes selection enables you to enforce class tracking in a similar way as the Require Accounts option. See the QuickBooks Help menu for more information on how you can use class tracking to track multiple profit centers on your income statement and for some balance sheet accounts.

- **Automatically Assign General Journal Entry Number**—This preference automatically sequentially numbers any general journal entries. You can modify each entry number at the time of input.

- **Warn When Posting a Transaction to Retained Earnings**—You can post to the Retained Earnings account, but you don't want to because QuickBooks uses this account at year's end to close out the year's Profit or Loss totals. Note that, when creating a new data file, this option is enabled by default.

- **Date Warnings**—When you create a new data file, the default date range set is from 90 days in the past to 30 days in the future, calculated from your current computer system date. Users can modify these date ranges, and QuickBooks warns users when they enter or modify a transaction outside these dates.

- **Closing Date**—The Admin or External Accountant user login can set a date so that transactions cannot be modified, added, or deleted prior to that date without having permission and entering the closing date password (if one was created).

My Preferences

My Preferences are unique to the username currently logged in to the data file. These settings are not shared globally.

- **Autofill Memo in General Journal Entry**—When this is selected, QuickBooks repeats the memo detail from the first line in the journal entry to all other lines in the same journal entry.

Bills

Review your Bills preferences to determine whether the defaults QuickBooks set are appropriate for your company's needs.

Company Preferences

All users share Company Preferences. The following are the Bills preferences:

- **Entering Bills, Bills Are Due**—Specifies the default number of days vendor bills should be paid within. You can change this global default on each vendor's record information or on a specific transaction. By default, QuickBooks sets the default due date for bills (when a vendor record does not have payment terms set) to 10 days. Users can modify this for their company's specific bill-paying terms.

- **Warn About Duplicate Bill Numbers from Same Vendor**—Ensures that you don't enter the same bill twice. This safeguard is an important reason for entering bills first instead of skipping a step and instead using the Write Checks transaction type when you pay vendors.

- **Paying Bills, Automatically Use Credits and Discounts**—Enables QuickBooks to apply any unapplied credits or discounts to your vendor bill payments automatically if your vendor is set up with discount terms and the bill is being paid within the discount date defined. Be sure to select your preferred chart of account for recording these credits.

My Preferences

You cannot set any My Preferences in the Bills section.

Calendar

Review and set preferences for the Calendar view for upcoming transactions.

Company Preferences

You cannot set any Company Preferences in the Calendar preferences.

My Preferences

My Preferences are unique to the username currently logged in to the data file. These settings are not shared globally. For Upcoming and Past Due Settings, you have these options:

- **Display**—Choose from Hide, Show, Show Only if Data Exists, and Remember Last.

- **Upcoming Events & Past Due Settings**—Set the default to show upcoming and past-due data.

Checking

The Checking preferences improve the accuracy of your day-to-day data entry. Be sure to review them when setting up a new data file.

Company Preferences

All users share the Company Preferences. The following are the Checking preferences:

- **Print Account Names on Voucher**—The default is to print the General Ledger account when using the Write Checks transaction. General Ledger accounts do not appear on checks printed via the Pay Bills transaction.

- **Change Check Date When a Noncleared Check Is Printed**—If you choose to have a check or bill payment printed later, this setting changes the check date to the current system date when you print the checks.

- **Start with Payee Field on Check**—This time-saving option places your curser in the Payee field when you use the Write Checks transaction type.

- **Warn About Duplicate Check Numbers**—QuickBooks warns you if the user is using a check number that the system has already recorded.

- **Autofill Payee Account Number in Check Memo**—You can assign the account number your vendor has assigned to you and have this number print on the memo field of the bill payment check.

- **Select Default Accounts to Use**—You can assign the default bank accounts QuickBooks uses when creating paychecks or payroll liability checks.

- **Bank Feeds**—Users can select from two data-viewing options and methods for creating renaming rules when downloading transactions.

My Preferences

My Preferences are unique to the username logged in to the data file. These settings are not shared globally:

- **Select Default Accounts to Use**—Assign what bank account you want to use for the following:
  - Open the Write Checks transaction
  - Open the Pay Bills transaction
  - Open the Pay Sales Tax transaction
  - Open the Make Deposits transaction

General

Everyone using QuickBooks should review the settings in General Preferences. Although I have named a couple here, many are worth selecting and customizing for your company's specific needs.

Company Preferences

All users share Company Preferences. The following General Preferences might affect your use of accounts payable functions:

- **Time Format**—If you track your vendors' time with QuickBooks timesheets, you can set a default for how portions of an hour display.

- **Never Update Name Information When Saving Transactions**—When this option is not selected and you change the payee name or address, QuickBooks asks whether you want to update the payee's information. By default, this preference is not selected in a newly created QuickBooks file.

- **Save Transactions Before Printing**—By default, this preference is selected in a newly created QuickBooks file.

My Preferences

My Preferences are unique to the user currently logged in to the data file. These settings are not shared globally:

- **Pressing Enter Moves Between Fields**—When this setting is not selected, the Tab key advances through fields in a transaction; using the Enter key saves a completed transaction. If this option is selected, both the Tab and Enter keys advance through fields on a transaction. The keyboard combination of Ctrl+Enter saves a completed transaction.

- **Automatically Open Drop-Down Lists When Typing**—This time-saving feature is selected by default. It is useful if the chart of accounts has subaccounts.

- **Warn When Editing a Transaction**—By default, this option is selected. It helps you avoid unintentional changes to a transaction being reviewed.

- **Warn When Deleting a Transaction or Unused List Item**—By default, this setting is selected. It helps you avoid unintentionally deleting a transaction being reviewed.

- **Automatically Recall Information**—Check this option to recall both the previously assigned account and the amount, when creating a new vendor transaction.

- **Default Date to Use for New Transactions**—Exercise caution to ensure that you select the appropriate choice. If you are entering transactions from the past, you might want to choose the last entered date. Otherwise, I recommend setting the default to use today's date.

Reminders

When setting the Company Preferences for reminders, do not forget to also set the My Preferences for this section.

Company Preferences

On the Reminders preference page, you set the default for QuickBooks reminders to show a summary or a list, or you opt not to be reminded of all checks to print, bills to pay, or purchase orders to print.

My Preferences

If you want reminders to display when you open the QuickBooks data file, select the My Preferences tab of the Reminders preference and choose Show Reminders List as an option when opening a Company file.

Reports and Graphs

The person responsible for how QuickBooks reports your accounts payable aging should review these preferences choices.

Company Preferences

All users share Company Preferences. The Reports and Graphs preferences include the following:

- **Summary Reports Basis**—This feature is important because it tells QuickBooks the default basis you want to use when viewing your Balance Sheet, Profit & Loss statement, and other reports. You can always override the default when you prepare the report. Chapter 3, "Accounting 101," has more details on the differences between accrual and cash report basis.

- **Aging Reports**—You can choose to age your reports from the due date or from the transaction date.

- **Reports Show Items By**—This setting affects how reports listing items display.

The remaining preferences affect the appearance of your reports.

My Preferences

My Preferences are unique to the username logged in to the data file. These settings are not shared globally:

- **Prompt Me to Modify Report Options Before Opening a Report**—By default, this preference is not selected. If it's selected, each time you open a report, the Modify Report dialog box displays.

- **Report and Graphs**—These settings determine how a report is refreshed when the data used in the report changes. The default in a newly created QuickBooks file is Prompt Me to Refresh. I recommend selecting the refresh automatically. You can make this decision for yourself, depending on the size of your QuickBooks data file and the speed of your computer's processor.

- **Graphs Only**—Specify whether to draw graphs in 2D (faster) and whether to use patterns.

Tax:1099

Setting up your vendors for proper 1099 status is important. However, be assured that if, after reviewing this information, you determine that the original setup was incorrect, any changes made to this preference will correct prior- and future-dated reports and transactions.

The Internal Revenue Service requires a business to provide a Form 1099-MISC at the end of the tax year to any person or unincorporated business paid $600 or more for services in a given calendar year. Most incorporated businesses are not required to get a Form 1099-MISC. Contact your accountant for the most current IRS guidelines.

Company Preferences

Select the Do You File 1099-MISC Forms? option to let QuickBooks know that you will be providing 1099 forms to your vendors at the end of the year.

The dialog box in Figure 7.2 is the first step in getting ready to track your Form 1099-MISC payments.

Figure 7.2
Choose Yes if you are required to submit 1099-MISC forms to the Internal Revenue Service.

➡️ *For more information, see "Tracking and Reporting Vendor 1099-MISC Payments," p. 275.*

My Preferences

You cannot set any My Preferences in the Tax:1099 section.

Time & Expenses

If you track time or your vendor's supply services, or if you add time and costs to your customers' invoices, commonly known as Time & Expense billing, you should review these preferences.

Company Preferences

All users share Company Preferences. The Time & Expenses preferences in Figure 7.3 include the following:

- **Time Tracking**—This preference enables the use of timesheets (for both vendor and employee time tracking) and the First Day of Work Week assignment. With this preference selected, you can include employees' or vendors' time details on your customer's invoices, and you can change this status on individual time entries.

- **Invoicing Options**—Here you can take advantage of the improved functionality of creating invoices from a list of time and expenses. Additionally, when using the Time & Expense method of billing your customers, these options offer added functionality:

  - **Create Invoices from a List of Time and Expenses**—This setting enables the use of a single dialog box displaying all unbilled time and expenses for batch invoicing to customers.

> **note**
>
> When Track Reimbursed Expenses as Income is selected, you can define unique income accounts on the Expense chart of account, as Figure 7.4 shows. When setting Time & Expenses preferences for Invoicing Options, if Track Reimbursed Expenses as Income is not selected, then when the cost is included on a customer's invoice, the original expense account is decreased (credited).

  - **Track Reimbursed Expenses as Income**—When selected, the billable expense is treated as income when invoiced. This is the preferred method for billing in the legal profession, as well as other industries.

  - **Mark All Expenses as Billable**—Do you provide your customers with details of your expenses? If you do, you should select this preference.

  - **Default Markup Percentage**—Enter a percentage, and each time you add a cost to a customer's invoice, QuickBooks adds this amount as a default markup embedded in the invoice line amount (not displayed separately).

  - **Default Markup Account**—Select a preferred default account (usually an Income category type).

My Preferences

Time & Expenses has no My Preferences.

Figure 7.3 Review the Time & Expenses preferences if your invoices to your customer include detailed line-item time and costs.

Figure 7.4 Optionally, you can choose to have invoiced reimbursed expenses post to an income account.

Working with the Vendor Center

QuickBooks makes adding, modifying, and researching vendor activity easy using the Vendor Center. Vendors are individuals or companies that you purchase services or products from, and they are managed in the Vendor Center (see Figure 7.5).

Figure 7.5
Complete common vendor tasks from the Vendor Center.

Click here to edit the selected vendor

From the Vendor Center, you view contact details for your vendors and can access many tasks, including the following:

- Create a new vendor or edit an existing one.

- Add multiple vendors (using the Add/Edit Multiple List Entries feature discussed in Chapter 4, "Understanding QuickBooks Lists," p. 108).

- Record commonly used vendor transactions.

- Print the vendor list, information, or transactions.

- Export the vendor list or transactions; import or paste vendors from Excel.

- Prepare vendor letters and customize the vendor letter templates.

- Filter your list of vendors to include All Vendors, Active Vendors, Vendors with Open Balances, or a custom filter of your choice.

- Attach documents to vendor records, such as attaching a copy of the signed subcontractor agreement.

- Access a map and driving directions to a vendor's location.

- Order checks from Intuit.

- Add and edit vendor contact names, to-do reminders, and notes, and track sent emails.

- View and filter a list of transactions by vendor or by transaction type.

- Prepare a QuickReport or Open Balance Report for a given vendor.

Use the Vendor Center to access many of the common vendor transactions and reports you learn about in this chapter and in Chapter 8, "Managing Vendors," p. 265.

The following sections provide more detail about creating a vendor and using the Vendor Center for researching transactions.

Adding or Modifying Vendors

When you are ready to purchase materials or services for your business, you need to create a vendor. You might already have a head start on adding vendors to your file if you used the Adding Contacts feature available with the Express Start QuickBooks setup discussed in Chapter 1, "Getting Started with QuickBooks," p. 36.

However, another less frequently used list in QuickBooks is worth mentioning here: the Other Names list. One occasion when you might choose to add a payee to the Other Names list is when you are recording a one-time purchase. Later, if you begin using the vendor regularly, you have a one-time option to remove the payee from the Other Names list and add it to your Vendor list.

This section offers instructions specific to setting up vendors. If your company will be using the Enter Bills process, you have to use a payee from the vendor list; the vendor bill transaction does not allow you to use an Other Names list item in the payee field.

---

tip

Would you like to efficiently create new vendor records? Start by entering data in the Company Name field. When you move your cursor out of the Company Name field, QuickBooks also automatically populates the Vendor Name, Billed From, and Print on Check As fields (found on the Payment Settings tab).

The Vendor Name field in QuickBooks is a "look-up" name; this field also controls how your vendors are automatically sorted in the Vendor Center.

If you prefer to use a different vendor look-up name, be sure to enter the proper vendor name in the Print On Check As field on the Payment Settings tab.

Adding a New Vendor

To practice adding a new vendor record, open the sample data file as instructed in Chapter 1. If you are working in your own file, use these instructions to begin entering the vendors you purchase goods and services from:

1. On the Home page, click the Vendors button. Alternatively, from the menu bar, select **Vendors, Vendor Center**.

2. If the New Feature highlights display, read the information provided. To dismiss these messages in the future, click the X in the What's New dialog box. You can enable help from the menu bar by selecting **Help, What's New**.

3. In the New Vendor drop-down list, in the upper-left corner of the Vendor Center, select **New Vendor**.

4. The New Vendor dialog box displays (see Figure 7.6). In the Vendor Name field, type **ABC Subcontractor**. Note that no two names from any of the lists in QuickBooks can be the same.

Figure 7.6
Completing the contact information for your vendor is good practice for your record keeping.

5. Leave the Opening Balance field blank. Chapter 3 discusses entering beginning balances in a new QuickBooks file (when previous accounting transactions already were recorded in some other accounting software or by another method). If you are a new business, you will later enter a vendor bill to increase the balance owed to the vendor instead of entering an Opening Balance amount in the New Vendor record.

   The As Of (date) field does not have any effect in your QuickBooks file if a dollar value was not entered in the Opening Balance field.

6. On the Address Info tab, consider completing the Salutation, First Name, and Last Name fields so you have the option to send letters to your vendors in the future.

7. Complete any remaining fields you deem applicable, such as contact information and address.

8. Click the Payment Settings tab in Figure 7.7. In the Account No. field, enter the account number your vendor has assigned to you, if applicable. This account number can optionally be printed on the memo line of a vendor bill payment check.

Figure 7.7
QuickBooks can add the Account No. field to the memo line of voucher-style checks.

9. Select the appropriate payment terms, such as net 30 days, your vendor has assigned to your account. If you don't see the specific term you need, select **Add New** to add more payment terms to the list.

10. (Optional) Complete the Print Name on Check As field. This field is necessary only if the printed name on the check differs from the Vendor Name field.

11. If you are using certain versions of QuickBooks Premier, Accountant, or any version of Enterprise, you have the option to select a Billing Rate Level for your vendor. Billing rates enable you to assign an hourly rate to billable time you will later add to a customer invoice.

12. Click the Tax Settings tab to enter the vendor's tax ID and assign the vendor as eligible for 1099 reporting. Note that if you do not have this information handy when you first create the vendor, you can add this information later and still track all the details. Click No to Entering The Tax ID Now message.

13. Click the Account Settings. Select the **Repairs:Building Repairs** expense account. You can begin typing the account name, or if you know the account number, you can type the account number. QuickBooks vendors can have up to three different accounts assigned that display automatically when you create a new transaction. If you also download transactions from your bank or credit card, click the link to review the information provided about how Account Prefill works with Online Banking now titled Bank Feeds.

14. Click the Additional Info tab. From the drop-down Vendor Type menu, select from the provided types or select **Add New** to create a new vendor type. Use the Vendor Type field to categorize your vendors, which you can then use to filter your vendor and transaction reports.

15. If you have created a Custom Field, complete the value for that field. Custom Fields enable you to track supplemental information about your vendors. Click the Define Fields button to add or remove custom fields.

16. At any time, you can select or deselect the Vendor Is Inactive checkbox. In such cases, the vendor still appears on reports but does not appear in most drop-down lists you use for creating new transactions. Do not make a vendor inactive if there is a balance in Accounts Payable.

17. Click OK to save your changes and close the New Vendor dialog box, or click Cancel to discard your work.

tip

Are you using QuickBooks Enterprise? With this edition, you can choose from more robust settings when you use Custom Fields. Custom fields are assigned to customers, vendors, employees, or items. For example, you might use custom fields when your inventory items have multiple sizes or colors. With Enterprise, you can have up to 15 custom fields for items. These custom fields are then assigned to items; they can be selected on transactions and can be reported on.

QuickBooks Enterprise adds more robust custom field functionality by permitting you to assign the custom field to use for specific transaction types. With each custom field, you can specify the characteristics of the data, such as a text, date, or number field with or without decimals, or offer a multichoice list for the user to select when entering an item. These are just a few of the available data field types that you can assign. For more information on working with custom fields, see Appendix C, "QuickBooks Enterprise Solutions Features," p. 783.

Now that you have created a new vendor in the sample file, you are prepared to create a list of your own vendors. Return to the Vendor Center anytime you need to update a vendor's information.

caution

QuickBooks does not keep a time stamp on revisions made to your vendors' contact information. After you make a change, all previous records reflect the change to the address or contact information.

However, changes to the Account Prefill selection affect only the newly created transactions.

Finding Vendor Transactions

The Vendor Center not only provides access for adding to or modifying your vendor records in QuickBooks, but also includes convenient access to finding vendor transactions.

With the Vendor Center open, select a vendor to display a list of that vendor's transactions on the right. Earlier in Figure 7.5, you can see that vendor A Cheung Limited is selected, and to the right are the individual transactions.

You can filter the resulting transactions by selecting options in the Show, Filter By, and Date drop-down lists. The options in the Filter By list change as you make a selection from the Show list.

Figure 7.8 shows representative vendor transaction types. Your transaction types might differ from the displayed types if you do not have the related feature enabled in Preferences. The only transaction type that can have a vendor record assigned that is not included in these options is Make Journal Entry.

The Transactions tab in the Vendor Center enables you to review transactions by type rather than by vendor.

Figure 7.8
Filter the displayed vendor transactions based on multiple criteria.

Researching Vendor Transactions

To practice finding vendor transactions by type, open the sample data file as instructed in Chapter 1, p. 37. If you are working in your own file, use these instructions to easily locate vendor transactions:

1. On the Home page, click the Vendors button to open the Vendor Center. On the left, click the Transactions tab.

2. Select the **Purchase Orders** transaction type (see Figure 7.9).

Figure 7.9
Use the Transactions tab of the Vendor Center to find like transaction types.

3. (Optional) From the Filter By drop-down list, select **Open Purchase Orders**.

4. (Optional) Filter for a specific date range. This is useful if you are looking specifically for older-dated open purchase orders.

5. (Optional) Click any column header to sort that column.

6. To view a transaction, double-click or right-click and select **Edit Transaction**.

7. Click the Print icon to print the listed transactions.

8. (Optional) Click the View Vendor Info button and click OK if the New Feature message displays. QuickBooks opens the Edit Vendor dialog box for the currently selected vendor. Click OK to close and return to the Vendor Center:Purchase Orders listing.

9. Click the Export icon to export the list of transactions to an Excel worksheet or to a comma-separated value file.

The Vendor Center provides one location to create or modify your vendor records and even research vendor transactions.

Next, you learn about the proper accounts payable process so you can successfully track your vendor business expenses.

The Accounts Payable Process

QuickBooks includes a flexible payable process. Your company can choose to use the purchase order and receive item transactions for controlling and monitoring costs and delivery, or you can skip these steps and create a bill to be paid later.

An important reason for using a vendor bill to record your business expenses is the ability to track the vendor's bill reference number. If your vendor invoices you more than once for the same services or items, QuickBooks preferences for Bills includes the option to be warned about duplicate bill numbers from the same vendor.

If you created your data file using the Express Start option, you might need to enable the features discussed in the earlier section "Preferences That Affect Accounts Payable." If you are ready to work in your own data file, make sure you have created your new file as Chapter 1 instructed.

Accounts Payable Transactions

Many of the accounts payable transactions use QuickBooks items. If you are considering using the accounts payable process for the first time, be sure to review Chapter 4, which discusses the use of items and how to set them up properly.

If you choose to use purchase order transactions, you need to create items. Items are a list of the products or services you sell to customers or purchase from vendors. The primary purpose of items is to perform the accounting behind the scenes and to automate the data entry process by prefilling descriptions, costs, and sales price on purchase and sales transactions.

Should you use items even if you do not plan to use purchase order or item receipt transactions? I recommend that you do, especially if you follow the instructions in the nearby tip. A powerful feature of items is that each time the item is purchased or sold, QuickBooks records the amount to the specific account(s) defined in the Add New or Edit Item dialog box. This reduces or eliminates potential errors created from recording the transaction to the wrong account when using the Expense tab of a purchase transaction.

How can items help you track your customer's profitability? Many of the QuickBooks reports that provide profitability information are based on transactions recorded using items on the Items tab and do not provide the same information if the transaction is recorded using the Expenses tab.

For example, imagine that a home builder creates a budget for the project (using an estimate transaction) and wants to track actual versus budgeted expense. To take advantage of the many customer and job profitability reports, you must enter your expenses using the Items tab on an accounts payable bill (and use the same process for the Write Checks transaction), as Figure 7.11 shows.

> **tip**
>
> Many users inadvertently post revenue and expenses to the same account for Services, Non-inventory Parts, Other Charges, and Discounts when selecting a single chart of account. The New or Edit Item dialog box includes a checkbox (see Figure 7.10) that enables you to avoid this problem and provides separate revenue and expense account fields. Choosing to set up items correctly can be one of the most important decisions you make in using accounts payable.

Table 7.1 lists the transaction types available in accounts payable and the purpose each type serves. Also review Table 8.1 on page 273 in Chapter 8, which outlines the accounting that goes on behind the scenes with these same transactions.

Figure 7.10
Set up items with both an income account and an expense account.

Figure 7.11
Use the Items tab to record expenses you want to track in customer or job profitability reports.

Table 7.1   Accounts Payable Transactions

Accounts Payable Transaction Name	Primary Purpose of Transaction
Purchase Order	Document a buyer issues to a seller indicating the products or services, quantity, and amounts the buyer has agreed to pay
Item Receipt (receiving inventory, non-inventory, or other item recorded on a purchase order)	Records receipt of inventory, non-inventory items, or other item types when the goods arrive before the vendor's final bill
Enter Bills	Records an increase to accounts payable and the associated expense
Vendor Credit Memo	Records a decrease of what is owed to a vendor
Bill Payment Check	Pays the vendor bill and decreases accounts payable and cash account balances

Accounts Payable Workflow

In this section, you learn about the importance of using the accounts payable process in place of using the write check transaction type for recording business expenses. The QuickBooks Home page and Vendor Center, shown in Figures 7.1 and 7.5, respectively, make managing all your purchasing activities easy.

Your Home page workflow might vary, depending on the version of QuickBooks you are using and the preferences you have enabled.

To perform typical vendor-related activities from the QuickBooks Home page (see Figure 7.1), follow these steps:

1. Access the Vendor Center.

2. (Optional) Create a purchase order to the vendor.

3. (Optional) Receive inventory with or without the final vendor bill.

4. Enter bills against inventory (does not create an item receipt).

5. Enter a bill to the vendor.

6. Pay the bill (typically within the agreed-upon payment terms for that vendor—for example, 30 days from the bill date).

Some companies choose not to use accounts payable transactions, but instead pay their vendors via the check transaction (from the menu bar, selecting **Banking, Write Checks**). Often this choice is made because the process of paying a vendor with a check is quick and easy and takes fewer steps than creating and paying a vendor bill.

However, by choosing not to use accounts payable transactions, you ignore several important controls for managing the purchases your company makes. These purchasing controls include the following:

- **Associating the bill with the purchase order (or item receipt) to automatically calculate quantity and cost**—When you enter the vendor's name on a bill or write a check, QuickBooks prompts you with an open purchase order (or item receipt) dialog box (see Figure 7.12) and prefills the bill for you.

- **Receiving a warning when entering a vendor invoice number twice**—It can happen—or, more likely, the user might inadvertently enter it twice. However, when you use a vendor bill (versus the Write Checks transaction) and you enter the vendor's invoice number in the Ref No. field, QuickBooks warns you if the vendor's reference number appeared on a previous bill (see Figure 7.13).

Figure 7.12
This warning displays when you enter a bill for a vendor that has an open purchase order.

- **Not recognizing costs in the month they were incurred**—When you opt to use the Write Checks transaction instead of a vendor bill, QuickBooks uses the date of the check as the date the expense is recorded (recognized). How often do you pay the vendor's bill the same day or month you receive it? You might be overstating or understating the expenses incurred in a specific month if you use the check instead of the bill transaction type.

Figure 7.13
QuickBooks
provides a
warning mes-
sage when you
enter a bill
with the same
reference (ven-
dor invoice)
number.

■ **Taking advantage of discounts offered by your vendor**—Only if you use vendor bills can you set a preference to have QuickBooks automatically calculate and record the discount if you are paying the bill within the vendor's discount terms.

The purchasing controls and warnings in QuickBooks make using the accounts payable process a smart choice for your company. Additionally, your company benefits from having financial statements that can be viewed in both cash and accrual basis.

Entering a Purchase Order

Your business might choose to record purchase orders to track the expected product or service cost. Purchase orders are nonposting, which, in accounting vernacular, means that when you record a purchase order, you are not recording an expense or liability. Instead, a purchase order serves as a reminder that you expect to receive a bill from the vendor at a later date.

➡ *To learn more about working with purchase orders, see "Creating the Purchase Order," p. 182, and also "Auto Create Purchase Orders," p. 791.*

Recording Vendor Bills

You are on your way to properly using accounts payable transactions to help track and report on your business expenses. You learn how to enter your vendor bills in this section.

Practice Entering a Vendor Bill

To practice adding a new vendor bill, open the sample data file as instructed in Chapter 1, p. 37. If you are working in your own file, use these instructions to begin entering bills for the products and services you have purchased:

1. On the Home page, click the Enter Bills icon to open the Enter Bills transaction (see Figure 7.14).

2. From the Vendor drop-down list, type the first few letters of the vendor name **ABC Subcontractor** (created earlier in this chapter). You can also select the vendor from the drop-down list by scrolling through the list and selecting a specific vendor.

3. Use the Tab key on your keyboard to advance to the Date field. If you are practicing, accept the default date; otherwise, enter the actual date for your transaction. In your file, you can use the (+) or (-) key on your keyboard to change the date by a single day forward or backward. Appendix C details other shortcuts. You use this date to record the expense when viewing your financial reports in accrual basis.

➡ *See more information on the accounting for transactions in Table 8.1 in Chapter 8, p. 273.*

4. Type **1234** in the Ref. No. field. This represents the invoice number your vendor supplied on his bill. If your vendor did not provide an invoice number, I often recommend using the digits of the bill date. For example, I might use 121517 as the Ref. No. if I am also dating the bill 12/15/2017.

5. Using the Tab key again, advance to the Amount Due field and type **100**. QuickBooks automatically formats the amount as 100.00. In your own file, you can manage this preference from the menu bar by selecting **Edit**, **Preferences**, **General**, **My Preferences** tab. If you enabled the Automatically Place Decimal Point option, QuickBooks would have formatted your input of 100 as 1.00 instead.

Figure 7.14

Entering a Bill enables you to record the expense when it is incurred but pay the vendor at a later date.

6. The Bill Due, Terms, and Discount Date fields prefill from the vendor's record. You can override these inputs on the specific vendor bill you are entering. If no defaults are included in the vendor record, QuickBooks uses the default due date calculation on the Bills—Company Preferences tab of the Preferences dialog box (see Figure 7.15). You must be logged in to the file as the Admin user or External Accountant to change the Company Preferences settings for bills.

Figure 7.15
QuickBooks uses the Company Preferences term when a vendor record doesn't specify terms.

7. (Optional) Enter a memo. This memo prints on the bill payment check. If your vendor record has a stored Account No. as detailed in the section on Adding or Modifying Vendors, leave the memo field blank; QuickBooks includes the Account No. on the printed bill payment check automatically.

   In this exercise, QuickBooks automatically prefilled the Account column on the Expenses tab with Repairs:Building Repairs. This account was set as a default for this vendor.

8. (Optional) Enter a memo for your reporting needs. This memo does not print on the final check. Although its name is similar to the Memo field on the check, this field enables you to describe the transaction line for your reporting.

9. Select a customer or job name from the list, when applicable.

10. Use the Billable? field when you specify a customer or job and you want to include this expense on a future customer invoice that lists expenses and then a markup amount. If you do not invoice your customers in this manner, you can ignore this field and leave it checked or unchecked. To set a preference for this, from the menu bar, select **Edit**, **Preferences**, **Time & Expenses**. On the Company Preferences tab, select or deselect Mark All Expenses as Billable.

11. If you are using Class tracking, enter the appropriate class.

12. Click Save & Close.

The ribbon toolbar at the top of the transaction window includes access to commonly used transaction features that were hidden or hard to find in previous editions of QuickBooks. The ribbon toolbar on an Enter Bill transaction includes the following tabs:

- **Main**—Use this tab to access the following:
    - Browse or search saved vendor bills or credits using the arrows.
    - Create, save, delete, copy, or memorize vendor bills. The Save option on the ribbon toolbar keeps the transaction open. You'll still use Save & Close or Save & New at the bottom of the dialog box after you complete your transaction.
    - Print the vendor bill. You might do this to provide details to a sister company that is paying the bill or when you need management's approval before paying.
    - Attach source documents. This is a free service and offers local document storage on your computer.
    - Select PO or Enter Time to autofill the vendor bill with stored information from these transaction types.
    - Clear Splits removes the line detail on the Expenses or Items tab but retains the vendor name, date, and other information on the header portion of the vendor bill.
    - Recalculate updates the Amount Due field, which is helpful when you have additional line items.
    - Pay Bills opens the Pay Bills dialog box with Filter By selected for the same vendor displayed in the transaction and the bill marked ready to be paid.
- **Reports**—From this tab on the ribbon toolbar, access a variety of reports specific to this type of transaction.

🔘 **tip**

By default, QuickBooks requires you to use the Tab key on your keyboard to advance from one field to another on certain transactions.

If you inadvertently use the Enter key on your keyboard, QuickBooks might save and close the transaction. If this happens to you, from an open transaction dialog box, click the arrows on the Main tab of the ribbon toolbar in the top-left corner.

If you prefer to use the Enter key on your keyboard to advance between fields, you can set that preference from the menu by selecting **Edit, Preferences, General Preferences**. On the My Preferences tab, select the **Pressing Enter Moves Between Fields** checkbox. You can save a transaction using the Ctrl+Enter keyboard shortcut. Click OK to save and close your preference setting.

Recording Vendor Credits

Now that you are recording your business expenses with vendor bills, what about returning a product to the vendor or receiving a credit for a service that was not performed to your specifications? The next section shows you how easy it is to create a vendor credit.

Practice Entering a Vendor Credit

To practice entering a vendor credit, open the sample data file as instructed in Chapter 1, p. 37. If you are working in your own file, use these instructions to begin entering credits you receive from your vendors:

1. On the Home page, click the Enter Bills icon.

2. Select the Credit option at the top of the Enter Bills dialog box (see Figure 7.16). The dialog box now displays a credit, decreasing accounts payable and decreasing the account(s) assigned on the Expenses tab or, if you are using the Items tab, the account assigned to the item(s) being used.

Select to create a vendor credit

Figure 7.16
Credits reduce both what you owe your vendor and the account assigned on the credit or associated with the item.

3. To continue with the earlier practice example, begin typing the vendor name **ABC Subcontractor**. Press the Tab key on your keyboard to advance to the Date field.

4. If you are practicing, accept the prefilled date. In your own file, you can select the date from the calendar.

5. In the Ref. No. field, type **1223**. This is the credit memo number your vendor has assigned this record.

6. In the Credit Amount field, type **100.00**.

7. Enter an optional memo. If you want the memo to display in reports based on your expense lines, be sure to use the Memo field in the Expenses tab or the Description field on the Items tab.

8. In this exercise, QuickBooks used the Repairs:Building Repairs expense account assigned to the vendor record and the amount entered in the Credit Amount field. If needed, you can change the account or add lines.

9. Click Save & Close.

This vendor credit is currently unapplied and available to be applied when you record a bill payment. If you know that a vendor has an unpaid bill pending, you can either apply the credit against that bill now or wait until the next time you need to pay the vendor.

If you want to view this unpaid bill on a report, select **Reports**, **Vendors & Payables**, **Unpaid Bills Detail** report from the menu bar. An unapplied credit then is listed in this report, as Figure 7.17 shows.

🔍 **note**

For ease in typing, QuickBooks formats the date for you. For example, if your current computer system year is 2017, you need to type only **1220** in a date field, and QuickBooks formats the date as 12/20/17.

Figure 7.17
The Unpaid Bills Detail report makes it easy to see open vendor credits.

Paying Vendor Bills

One of the benefits of entering vendor bills is that you can record the expense during the month you incur it but pay the balance at a later date.

If you are ready to pay your bills, make sure you have a vendor bill or some record of the expense being incurred. Develop a process at your business for accurately reviewing your unpaid bills.

Practice Paying Vendor Bills

To practice paying a vendor bill, open the sample data file as instructed in Chapter 1, p. 36. If you are working in your own file, use these instructions to begin paying the bills you owe your vendors:

1. On the Home page, click the Pay Bills icon.

2. For this exercise, leave the Show All Bills option button selected. When working with your own data, you can filter the bills that display in the Pay Bills dialog box by selecting the Due On or Before option button and entering a date (see Figure 7.18).

3. In the Filter By drop-down list, select **C.U. Electric** or begin typing the name as you learned in an earlier exercise.

4. Review the choices available in the Sort By drop-down list, but leave Vendor selected.

5. Place a checkmark next to each of the bills for C.U. Electric, or optionally click the Select All Bills button. If you are printing checks, QuickBooks creates one check for the two selected bills (see Figure 7.18).

6. When working with your own data, if you did not want to pay the full balance, you can manually type an amount in the Amt. to Pay column on a specific bill's row. Later when you are prepared to pay the balance, QuickBooks includes the remaining balance due in the Amt. to Pay column.

7. With a bill selected, click the Go to Bill button. QuickBooks opens the Enter Bills dialog box, where, if necessary, you can make changes. Click Save & Close to return to the Pay Bills dialog box.

8. (Optional) View the discount terms or credits available. The next section has more details on working with discounts and credits.

Figure 7.18
Use the Pay Bills dialog box to record payment by check, credit card, or online payment to your vendor.

9. When working with your own data, you can specify payment options in the Payment section of the Pay Bills dialog box, including the following fields (for this exercise, leave the choices as in Figure 7.18):

   - **Date**—This is the date that will print on your checks or will be assigned to the transactions in your accounting.

   - **Method**—Select Check if you will be printing a check or recording a manually written check. Select Credit Card if you are paying the bill with the company's corporate credit card. Select Online Bank Pmt if you are using online banking.

   - **To Be Printed or Assign Check Number**—If you selected Check as your method of payment, you can select the To Be Printed option button. If you manually wrote the check, you can select Assign Check Number.

   - **Account**—Depending on your Method selection, you can assign either the bank account or the credit card account used to make the payment.

   - **Ending Balance**—QuickBooks displays the ending balance for the bank or credit card account selected.

10. Click Pay Selected Bills. QuickBooks opens the Payment Summary dialog box.

11. Review the details in the Payment Summary dialog box, including payment date, account, and method.

12. Click the Print Checks button on the Payment Summary dialog box. (Optional) You can click the Pay More Bills button to return to the Pay Bills dialog box, or click Done if you do not want to practice printing (using plain paper).

13. If you selected the Print Checks button, the Select Checks to Print dialog box displays (see Figure 7.19). Leave selected the default bank account and the prefilled first check number.

Figure 7.19
When printing checks, specify the first check number to print.

14. Review the list of checks to be printed. Each has a checkmark in the column to the left. Remove the checkmarks from any checks you do not want to print at this time.

15. Click OK to open the Print Checks dialog box. Select your printer from the Printer Name drop-down list in Figure 7.20, and then choose the proper Check Style from Voucher, Standard, or Wallet.

Figure 7.20
Select the printer name, check style, and other printer settings for preparing checks from QuickBooks.

16. Click Print. For this exercise, make sure you have plain paper in your printer. A check printed on plain paper is not a negotiable document.

17. The Print Checks—Confirmation dialog box displays. In this exercise, click OK to close the confirmation.

➡ To learn more about printer settings for checks, see "Printing Checks," p. 526.

You have now learned how to complete basic accounts payable tasks, including using bills to record your expenses and preparing the payment for the vendor. In the next sections, you learn how to work with vendor discounts and credits.

Applying Vendor Credits

Your vendor might offer discounts for timely payment or issue a credit for products or services that did not meet your expectations.

Continue your QuickBooks practice by applying the vendor credit created in an earlier practice section "Recording Vendor Credits" of this chapter.

tip

Using QuickBooks, you can efficiently prepare a bill payment check for a single vendor.

To do so, open a previously saved vendor bill; on the Main tab on the transaction ribbon toolbar at the top, click the Pay Bill icon. The Pay Bills dialog box opens, with the Filter By field already selected for the same vendor as the open vendor bill.

Practice Applying Vendor Credits

To practice applying a credit, open the sample data file as instructed in Chapter 1, p. 37. If you are working in your own file, use these instructions to apply vendor discounts or credits to your vendor's open balances:

1. Review your preference for applying credits. From the menu bar, select **Edit**, **Preferences**, and go to the Bills—Company Preferences tab on the Preferences dialog box. (You must log in to the file as the Admin or External Accountant user type.) See the previous Figure 7.15. These settings determine whether QuickBooks automatically applies any open credits for you. If you don't select the Automatically Use Credits checkbox, you must manually apply the credits. Pick the selection that best meets your business needs.

2. Click OK to close the Preferences dialog box.

3. On the Home page, click the Pay Bills icon. The Pay Bills dialog box opens.

4. For this practice example, select the **ABC Subcontractor** vendor in the Filter By drop-down list. Filtering can be useful if you have many open invoices for multiple vendors, but it is not required.

5. Place a checkmark next to the open bill you want to apply the vendor credit to. If you didn't select to apply credits automatically in step 1, QuickBooks shows the total number of available credits and their total value in the Discount & Credit Information for Highlighted Bill section (see Figure 7.21).

6. To apply the credit, or if you want to modify the amount or change which credits are selected, click the Set Credits button. The Discount and Credits dialog box displays (see Figure 7.22). You can modify which credit is selected by changing the checkmark from one credit to another or by manually overriding the Amt. to Use.

7. Click Done to close the Discount and Credits dialog box.

8. Click Pay Selected Bills to exit the Pay Bills dialog box. If the AMT. TO PAY column is 0.00, you have associated a credit memo with a vendor bill, and no additional check transaction is created.

9. Click Done in the Payment Summary dialog box, or click Pay More Bills if you want to return to the Pay Bills dialog box.

> **tip**
>
> New for QuickBooks 2014, if the open balance of a vendor's bill is paid completely by a bill credit, QuickBooks includes the details of the invoice and bill credit on a bill payment stub.

Figure 7.21
When paying vendor bills, QuickBooks shows the number of available credits for the selected vendor.

Figure 7.22
The Discount and Credits dialog box enables you to manage how the credits are applied to open vendor bills.

If you are an accounting professional using QuickBooks Accountant or QuickBooks Enterprise Accountant, you might want to use the Client Data Review feature. From one convenient window, you can assign the vendor unapplied credit memo to the open accounts payable bill, replacing the previous steps numbered 3–8.

➡ *To learn more about time-saving features for accounting professionals, see "Client Data Review," p. 695.*

🔍 **note**

When you need to change a prior year's open balance for a vendor, credit memos can be the safest way to not inadvertently affect prior year financials. With a credit memo, you can date the correcting transaction in the current year, which is important if you have already used the prior year's data to prepare and file a tax return.

Taking Discounts on Vendor Bills

Your company might be able to save money by paying vendors within their allowed discount terms. Some vendors offer discounts to encourage quick payment of their invoices.

If you are going to assign discounts to your vendor bills, record your bills at the "gross" amount, or total amount before any discount. Then, over time, you can watch the amount you have saved grow.

Practice Taking Discounts on Vendor Bills

To practice applying a vendor discount, open the sample data file as instructed in Chapter 1, p. 35. For this practice, you complete all the steps necessary for QuickBooks to automatically calculate the discount when paying a vendor bill. If you are working in your own file, you need to log in as the Admin or External Accountant user type to set the preference mentioned. You can then use these instructions to apply discounts to your vendors' open balances:

1. From the menu bar, click **Edit**, **Preferences**, and in the Preferences dialog box, click the Bills—Company Preferences tab. Check the Automatically Use Discounts checkbox, as Figure 7.15 showed earlier.

2. Select **Job Expenses:Less Discounts Taken** as the Default Discount Account.

3. Click OK to save your selection and close the Preferences dialog box.

4. Assign discount terms to a vendor. From the menu bar, select **Vendors, Vendor Center**.

5. In the QuickBooks sample data, select **Bayshore CalOil Service**. To the right, click the Edit icon (looks like a pencil).

6. In the Edit Vendor dialog box for Bayshore CalOil Service, click the Payment Settings tab.

7. If not already assigned, select the **2% 10 Net 30** terms in the Terms drop-down list. When this option is selected, QuickBooks calculates a 2% discount if the payment is dated within 10 days of the invoice date. Otherwise, the full amount is payable within 30 days.

8. Click OK to save your changes and close the Edit Vendor dialog box.

9. From the Vendor Center, with Bayshore CalOil Service, select **Enter Bills** from the New Transactions drop-down list.

10. Using the Tab key, advance to the Ref. No. field. Type **567**.

11. In the Amount Due field, type **1,000.00**. QuickBooks assigns the Terms and Discount Date and adds the amount to the Expenses tab, using the account used on previous transactions (or you can choose another account).

12. Assign Overhead to the Class column on the Expenses tab.

13. Click Save & Close.

14. From the Home page, select **Pay Bills**.

15. The Pay Bills dialog box displays. Place a checkmark next to the Bayshore CalOil Service bill you just created. Notice that, as a result of selecting Automatically Use Discounts in step 1, QuickBooks displays the terms and the Sugg. Discount (see Figure 7.23).

Figure 7.23
Set QuickBooks preferences to automatically calculate early payment discounts.

16. (Optional) You can click the Set Discount button to change the amount of the discount, assign a different discount account, and assign a discount class. Click Done to close the Discounts and Credits dialog box.

17. For this practice example, click Cancel to close the Pay Bills dialog box. If you are assigning discounts to your own vendor bills, continue with the check printing process.

caution

If you decide to add discount terms to your vendor's record after creating vendor bills, you need to edit any unpaid vendor bills and manually change the terms or discount date.

MANAGING VENDORS

In Chapter 7, p. 231, "Setting Up Vendors," you learned the particulars for adding, editing, and creating transactions for vendors. In this chapter, you learn how to best manage the vendor details in your QuickBooks file. Additionally, you learn how to handle unique vendor transactions.

Accounts Payable Reporting

Accounts payable mistakes can be one of the primary causes of misstated company financials. Knowing which reports are best to review will make you much more efficient at keeping your accounts payable "clean," meaning with correct and up-to-date data. What makes troubleshooting data errors most difficult is often not knowing exactly what you should be looking for. The next section addresses this problem by explaining some of the more common reports you use to identify whether your accounts payable information is correct.

Reconciling Balance Sheet Accounts Payable Balance to A/P Aging Summary Report Total

With QuickBooks, you don't have to worry that the Balance Sheet Accounts Payable balance does not match the A/P Aging Summary report total because any transaction posting to the Accounts Payable account must have a vendor assigned. When providing year-end documentation to your accountant, be sure to include the A/P Aging Summary or Detail report and compare the total amount from these reports to the Balance Sheet balance for Accounts Payable.

To compare the Balance Sheet Standard report balance for Accounts Payable with the A/P Aging Summary report total, follow these steps:

1. From the menu bar, select **Reports, Company & Financial, Balance Sheet Standard**. On the Balance Sheet report that opens, select the As of Date you want to compare to. To accurately compare the Balance Sheet report Accounts Payable balance and the A/P Aging Summary report total, you must create your Balance Sheet on the accrual basis. If your reporting preference default is for cash basis, you can temporarily change the reporting basis by clicking the Customize Report button on the active report window and selecting Accrual as the report basis. Click OK to return to the report.

2. Note the balance of your Accounts Payable account(s) on the Balance Sheet (see Figure 8.1).

Figure 8.1
Use an accrual basis Balance Sheet report when reconciling your Accounts Payable Aging report.

3. From the menu bar, select **Reports, Vendors & Payables, A/P Aging Summary** (see Figure 8.2). Make sure the date is the same as the date you selected in step 1.

Your Accounts Payable balance on the Balance Sheet Standard report should match the total on the A/P Aging Summary report. If it does not, it might be a data integrity issue. If the two balances do not match, first make sure your Balance Sheet Standard report is created in the accrual basis. Then verify your data by selecting **File, Utilities, Verify Data** from the menu bar. Chapter 17, "Managing Your QuickBooks Database," discusses this in more detail.

Figure 8.2
Your A/P Aging
Summary report
should always
reconcile with
the Accounts
Payable total on
an accrual basis
Balance Sheet
report.

A/P Aging Summary						
Customize Report	Share Template	Memorize	Print ▼	E-mail ▼	Excel ▼	Hide Header	Colla

Dates Today ▼ 12/15/2017 Interval (days) 30 Through (days past due) 90

4:19 PM
12/15/17

Rock Castle Construction

A/P Aging Summary

As of December 15, 2017

	Current	1 - 30	31 - 60	61 - 90	> 90	TOTAL
C.U. Electric	750.00	0.00	0.00	0.00	0.00	750.00
Cal Gas & Electric	122.68	0.00	0.00	0.00	0.00	122.68
Cal Telephone	91.94	0.00	0.00	0.00	0.00	91.94
Daigle Lighting	52.00	1,539.00	0.00	0.00	0.00	1,591.00
Hamlin Metal	670.00	0.00	0.00	0.00	0.00	670.00
Hopkins Construction Rentals	700.00	0.00	0.00	0.00	0.00	700.00
Lew Plumbing	1,330.00	0.00	0.00	0.00	0.00	1,330.00
Middlefield Drywall	1,200.00	0.00	0.00	0.00	0.00	1,200.00
Patton Hardware Supplies	1,020.00	3,459.20	0.00	0.00	0.00	4,479.20
Perry Windows & Doors	4,905.00	1,800.00	0.00	0.00	0.00	6,705.00
Sergeant Insurance	4,050.00	0.00	0.00	0.00	0.00	4,050.00
Sloan Roofing	1,047.00	0.00	0.00	0.00	0.00	1,047.00
Thomas Kitchen & Bath	585.00	0.00	0.00	0.00	0.00	585.00
Timberloft Lumber	215.10	0.00	0.00	0.00	0.00	215.10
Vu Contracting	1,250.00	0.00	0.00	0.00	0.00	1,250.00
Washuta & Son Painting	600.00	0.00	0.00	0.00	0.00	600.00
Wheeler's Tile Etc.	1,250.00	0.00	0.00	0.00	0.00	1,250.00
TOTAL	19,838.72	6,798.20	0.00	0.00	0.00	26,636.92

Should agree with your Balance Sheet report

Reviewing the Unpaid Bills Detail Report

If you need more detail than the A/P Aging Summary report offers, consider the Unpaid Bills Detail report. This report is helpful because it displays individual vendor bill and credit memo lines for each open vendor transaction instead of summarizing amounts by aging interval.

By default, this report is perpetual, which means that even if you create it using a date in the past, QuickBooks shows those open vendor bills, or unapplied credit memos, as of *today's* computer system date, including all payments recorded before and after the report date. You can override this default and then properly reconcile the Unpaid Bills Detail report to your Balance Sheet and your A/P Aging Summary report for a date prior to today's date. To do so, follow these steps:

1. From the menu bar, select **Reports**, **Vendors & Payables**, **Unpaid Bills Detail**. As mentioned previously, this report includes all payments made before and after the report date you have chosen.

2. If you are creating this report for a date other than today, you will likely want to have the report match your Balance Sheet totals as of that same date. To do so, click Customize Report. The Modify Report dialog box opens, with the Display tab selected.

3. Click the Advanced button to open the Advanced Options dialog box.

4. Under Open Balance/Aging, select the **Report Date** option, as in Figure 8.3, and click OK to close the Advanced Options dialog box.

5. Click OK to return to the report.

Figure 8.3
Modify the Unpaid
Bills Detail report so
that it agrees with
the Balance Sheet for
a date in the past.

Modifying this report enables you to see each open vendor bill or unapplied credit detail as of some date in the past. This report becomes useful for reconciling your Accounts Payable unpaid bills or open credit detail to your Balance Sheet Accounts Payable total. You might want to send a copy of this modified report to your accountant after verifying that it agrees with the Balance Sheet for the same date.

If an amount is listed on this report, it is presumed that you owe the money; in the event of a credit, your vendor owes you.

Reviewing Aged Open Item Receipts

When goods are purchased for inventory, non-inventory, or other item types, vendors often ship the product with a packing slip and then send the final vendor bill later. One reason for doing this is that receiving departments in a warehouse should not necessarily know the value of the goods being delivered. Another reason is that the vendor might need to add freight and handling to the final bill before sending it to your company.

The QuickBooks Create Item Receipts transaction records the receipt of the stock into your place of business, increases the quantity on hand for this item (if it is an inventory item), and increases your accounts payable due to that vendor.

However, because you have not yet received the final bill from the vendor, QuickBooks does not include these item receipts in the Pay Bills dialog box. This is because QuickBooks recognizes an item receipt transaction as not yet having received the final bill to be paid.

An error in your accounting can result if you entered a bill, ignored the warning message that outstanding item receipts existed for that vendor, and created another bill. Or perhaps you used the

Write Checks transaction to pay for the same charge as recorded on the original item receipt. Both of these types of mistakes overstate your expenses or inventory value.

> ## 🔍 note
>
> QuickBooks Enterprise Solutions 14.0 offers an Enhanced Inventory Receiving feature that enables you to specify a different method of accounting for item receipts.
>
> With Enhanced Inventory Receiving enabled, when an item receipt is recorded without the final bill, QuickBooks increases (debits) the Inventory Asset and increases (credits) the Inventory Offset account, a current liability account that QuickBooks creates automatically when you enable the feature.
>
> Later when you enter the final vendor's bill, QuickBooks decreases (debits) the Inventory Offset account and increases (credits) Accounts Payable. For more information, in Appendix C see "Enhanced Inventory Receiving," p. 800.

First, to see if this issue is a problem for your data file, from the menu bar, select **Reports**, **Vendors & Payables**, **Unpaid Bills Detail**. On the report, do you have line items with a transaction type of Item Receipt? (See Figure 8.4.) If you do, these are from receiving inventory, non-inventory, or other types of items without receiving (or recording) the final vendor bill.

Figure 8.4
Aged item receipts are acceptable only when you have not yet received the vendor's final bill.

After reviewing your Unpaid Bills Detail report, if you find outdated item receipts that you do not owe the vendor, determine whether they have been paid by requesting an open payables statement from your vendor. To see if the bill was paid with a Write Checks transaction instead of the proper Pay Bills transaction, follow these steps:

1. On the Home page, click the Vendors button.

2. Click the Vendor name on the left. If you don't initially see the vendor you want, click any vendor on the list, and then type the first letter of the name to advance to the first list entry with that letter.

3. On the Transaction tab, on the right, click the Show drop-down list to select the **Checks** transaction type (see Figure 8.5).

Figure 8.5
Use the Vendor Center to easily review checks written to a vendor, as opposed to bill payment checks.

You can optionally print the vendor transaction list via the Print drop-down list at the top of the Vendor Center dialog box.

In Figure 8.4, shown previously, Perry Windows has an open item receipt dated 06/05/17. To see whether this vendor was paid by check, follow the previous steps to see any Write Checks (not Pay Bills) transaction type that was written to the vendor.

➡ *For more information, see "Correcting Accounts Payable Errors," p. 285.*

Reviewing Item Setup

Items play an important part in the accounts payable process if you use purchase orders, item receipts, or the Items tab on a vendor bill, credit, credit card charge, credit card credit, or check.

Figure 7.10 (in the previous chapter) pictured a service type item with a checkmark in the box titled This Service Is Used. Be sure

⚠ caution

How exactly does QuickBooks manage the use of Item Receipt transactions?

- Item receipts age like other open payables on the A/P Aging Summary report.
- The Unpaid Bills Detail report does not show any days in the aged column, yet item receipts are aging.
- QuickBooks does not let you pay an item receipt in the Pay Bills dialog box.

to select this option if you buy and sell the same item. If you do not choose this option and you use the same item on a purchase and a sales transaction, QuickBooks records both the revenue and the expense to the single account selected on the New Item dialog box or Edit Item dialog box. In this case, total revenues and total expenses will both be understated because QuickBooks nets the two amounts together into a single general ledger account.

It is acceptable to create an item with only one account if you know that you will never buy and sell the same item. However, I usually recommend setting up each item as two-sided, with the item record requiring both an expense and an income account.

Chapter 4, "Understanding QuickBooks Lists," discusses properly setting up lists in more detail. This section focuses on how you can determine whether your items are the cause of errors on your financials for a company data file with transactions. If your data file does not yet have transactions in it, use this report to check your item setup.

Imagine that an item was created with only an income account assigned. The item was used on a vendor bill, and the user has to decide whether to ignore the warning shown in Figure 8.6.

Figure 8.6
You receive this warning on an expense transaction when using an item that has only an income account assigned.

> **Warning** ✕
>
> ⚠ This item is associated with an income account. Do you want to continue?
>
> ☐ Do not display this message in the future
>
> [OK]   [Cancel]

To see whether this type of error affects your data, create the following report:

1. From the menu bar, select **Reports**, **Company & Financial**, **Profit & Loss Standard**.

2. Double-click the Total Income account (see Figure 8.7). QuickBooks creates a Transaction Detail by Account report, as in Figure 8.8.

3. At the top right of the resulting Transaction Detail by Account report, select **Type** from the Sort By drop-down list. QuickBooks groups all transactions by type within each income account or subaccount. Notice in Figure 8.8 that the Labor Income account has a vendor bill transaction posting to an income account.

Figure 8.7
Double-click the Total Income amount to create a Transaction Detail by Account report.

Figure 8.8
A Bill transaction type should not post to an income account unless the item does not have an expense account assigned.

Accounts Payable Balance on Cash Basis Balance Sheet

The nature of accounts payable suggests that when you review your financials in cash basis, you do not see an Accounts Payable balance. See Table 8.1 for a listing of the transactions you can use in accounts payable and the effect the transaction has on both accrual and cash basis reporting.

Table 8.1   Accounts Payable on Accrual or Cash Basis Balance Sheet

Transaction Name	Accrual Basis	Cash Basis
Create Purchase Orders	No effect.	No effect.
Create Item Receipt (Receiving inventory *without* the vendor's bill)	Date of Item Receipt—increase (debit) account assigned to the item (normally a Cost of Goods Sold type account or may also be an Expense type account); increase (credit) Accounts Payable. (Note that Item Receipts *do not* display in the Pay Bills dialog box.)	No effect.
Create Item Receipt (Receiving inventory *with* the vendor's bill)	Date of Item Receipt—increase (debit) account cost of goods sold (or expense account); increase (credit) Accounts Payable. (Note that Item Receipt has now become a Bill and *does* display in the Pay Bills dialog box.)	No effect.
Enter Vendor Bill for Non-inventory, Other Item Types, or General Expenses	Date of Bill—increase (debit) account assigned to item, or account used on the Expenses tab; increase (credit) Accounts Payable.	No effect until date of bill payment check.
Enter Bills (Credit)	Date of Credit—decrease (debit) Accounts Payable; decrease (credit) inventory, account assigned to item, or account used on the Expenses tab of the credit.	No effect until date credit is applied against a bill payment.

What can cause an Accounts Payable balance to appear on a cash basis Balance Sheet report? Any of the following:

- A/P transactions that have expenses or items posting to other balance sheet accounts.

- Inventory items on an invoice or credit memo (typically, inventory management should be done using accrual basis reporting).

- Transfers between balance sheet accounts.

- Unapplied accounts payable vendor payments.

- Payments applied to future-dated vendor bills.

- Preferences that contradict each other. (This can happen if you select cash basis on your summary reports and accrual basis as your sales tax preference.)

- Data corruption. To confirm (and hopefully resolve) this problem, from the menu bar, select **File**, **Utilities**, **Verify Data**. Chapter 17 has more details.

What can you do if you do have an Accounts Payable balance on your cash basis Balance Sheet? The following steps help you locate the transactions making up this balance:

1. From the menu bar, select **Reports, Company & Financial, Balance Sheet Standard**.

2. Click the Customize Report button to open the Modify Report dialog box with the Display tab selected.

3. Select **Cash** for the report basis.

4. Click OK.

5. Double-click the Accounts Payable amount in question (see Figure 8.9). The Transactions by Account report is created.

6. Click the Customize Report button to open the Modify Report dialog box with the Display tab selected.

7. For the Report Date Range, remove the From date and leave the To date.

8. Click the Advanced button and, from the Open Balance/Aging box, select **Report Date**, shown in Figure 8.10. Click OK to close the Advanced Options dialog box.

9. Click the Filters tab.

10. In the Choose Filter box, scroll down to select **Paid Status**.

11. Select **Open** for Paid Status.

12. Click OK to return to the report and look for transactions that fall into any of the categories described earlier. The Transaction Detail report in Figure 8.11 shows several inventory transactions and a prepaid insurance transaction. All these transactions post to other balance sheet accounts, one of the common causes of having an Accounts Payable balance on a cash basis Balance Sheet report.

> **tip**
>
> Many schools of thought address how to handle transaction corrections when preparing cash basis financials with accrual basis results, but my experience has been to let the tax accountant make the needed adjustments on the tax return and let QuickBooks continue to include the accrual basis results.

7:26 PM 12/15/17 **Cash Basis**	**Rock Castle Construction** **Balance Sheet** As of December 15, 2017	
		◇ _____ Dec 15, 17 _____ ◇
▼ LIABILITIES & EQUITY		
▼ Liabilities		
▼ Current Liabilities		
▼ Accounts Payable		
20000 · Accounts Payable		13,534.20
Total Accounts Payable		13,534.20
▼ Credit Cards		
20500 · QuickBooks Credit Card		94.20
20600 · CalOil Credit Card		382.62
Total Credit Cards		476.82

Figure 8.9
Cash basis Balance Sheet report with an Accounts Payable balance.

Figure 8.10
Use the Advanced button on the Modify Report dialog box to filter a report for transaction status as of a specific date in the past.

Figure 8.11
Filter for transactions that make up the Accounts Payable amount on a cash basis prepared Balance Sheet report.

Tracking and Reporting Vendor 1099-MISC Payments

If your company pays individuals and certain types of businesses, you might need to file a Form 1099-MISC at the end of each calendar year. Currently, only vendors paid $600 or more in a given year must be reported to the IRS.

When submitting 1099 forms to the IRS, you must also include Form 1096. This transmittal document summarizes the individual 1099 forms. QuickBooks prints both the 1096 summary and individual 1099 forms, using preprinted tax forms available through Intuit or most office supply stores.

Intuit also offers the option to use its E-File Service for filing your 1099 and 1096 tax forms.

Before you begin using the QuickBooks 1099 Wizard, review your vendor settings using the following reports. To access these, from the menu bar, select **Vendors, Print/E-file 1099s**.

- **Review 1099 Vendors**—Lists each vendor's Tax ID, Address, and other useful information. Sort by Eligible for 1099 at the top of the report to help verify that you have all the vendors selected for whom you need to issue a Form 1099-MISC.

- **1099 Summary Report**—Lists Box 7: Nonemployee Compensation details by vendor and other 1099 applicable reporting boxes.

- **1099 Detail Report**—Lists individual transactions used to calculate the amount reported for the vendor's Form 1099-MISC earnings.

Properly setting up your 1099 tax form preferences in QuickBooks ensures compliance with federal tax reporting guidelines. If you have specific questions about what type of vendor should receive this document, refer to the www.irs.gov website or contact your company's accountant or tax advisor. Next, let's get your file ready to track and report your Form 1099-MISC payments to vendors using the six steps in the QuickBooks 1099 Wizard.

Step 1—Select Your 1099 Vendors

Not all vendors are required to receive a Form 1099-MISC at the end of the year. Make sure you have reviewed the reporting requirements on the IRS website or have asked for advice from your company's accountant or tax advisor.

To select your 1099 vendors, follow these steps:

1. Log in to your file as the Admin or External Accountant user.

2. From the menu bar, select **Edit, Preferences** to open the Preferences dialog box, as Figure 7.2 on page 238 in Chapter 7.

3. Select the **Tax:1099—Company Preferences** tab. Select the **Yes** option for Do You File 1099-MISC Forms?

4. Next to If You're Ready to Prepare Your 1099s, Including Mapping Accounts, click the **Click Here** link.

5. Click Yes to the Save Changes message, if displayed. QuickBooks opens the 1099 Wizard, in Figure 8.12.

6. Review the steps and click Get Started.

> **note**
> Did you just start using QuickBooks during the calendar year? Did you previously pay your 1099-MISC eligible vendors using some other software? If yes, review the section titled "Entering Midyear 1099 Balances," later in this chapter, for help with reporting the proper amount of calendar year payments.

> **caution**
> The QuickBooks 1099 Wizard helps you comply with ever-changing IRS regulations. Be sure to check for QuickBooks software updates before you issue 1099s or other tax documents. Chapter 17 has instructions on updating your data file.
>
> Press Ctrl+1 on your keyboard to view the Product Information dialog box. The Product field lists the QuickBooks version, year, and release you are currently using.

7. Place a checkmark in front of the vendors for which you want to track Form 1099-MISC earnings. (Optional) Click the Select All button. See Figure 8.13.

Figure 8.12
In a few simple steps, you can use the 1099 Wizard to review eligible payments and generate 1099 forms.

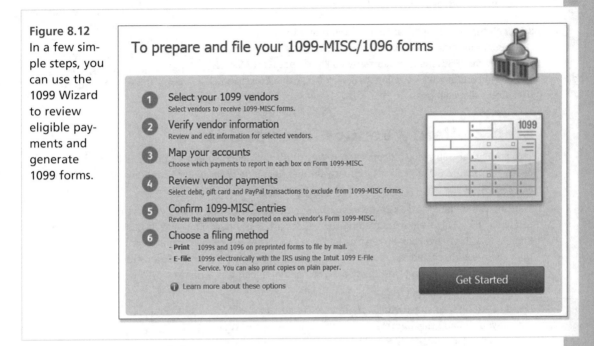

Figure 8.13
Select the vendors that will receive a Form 1099-MISC.

8. Click Save & Close if you are not ready to complete the remaining steps in the 1099 Wizard, or click Continue to advance to the next step.

Select all the vendors that should get the required tax form. QuickBooks automatically excludes any vendors whose payments fall below the IRS threshold (currently $600). Do not worry here if you are uncertain which vendors to select. You can always come back and make changes.

 tip

If you do not complete the 1099 settings in one sitting, you can easily return to the 1099 Wizard. On the menu bar, select **Vendors, Print/ E-File 1099s, 1099 Wizard.**

Step 2—Verify Vendor Information

This step in the 1099-MISC Income Setup Wizard displays each vendor you have assigned that needs the 1099-MISC income tax form at year end. If you do not see a vendor that should be on this list, click Back and place a checkmark next to vendors who qualify for the form.

You can also update the Tax Settings tab within the vendor record for any vendors that should receive a 1099. This includes recording the vendor's Tax ID number, as well as clicking the "Vendor Eligible for 1099" checkbox on the Tax Settings tab of a New or Edit Vendor record. You can request the vendor's address and tax identification number using IRS form W-9, "Request for Taxpayer Identification Number and Certification." You can download this form from the www.irs.gov website.

If you omitted these steps when you initially created your vendor record, you can add this information at any time during the year, and QuickBooks will include the vendor payments in your 1099 reporting.

To verify vendor information, follow these steps:

1. If you selected Continue after step 7 (select your 1099 vendors) in the previous section, you should now verify your 1099 vendors' information.

2. The list shows only the vendors you selected. Confirm that the Tax ID, Company Name, Address, and other fields are all completed correctly for each vendor. See Figure 8.14.

3. If information is missing or inaccurate, click in the field and enter the appropriate information.

4. Click Save & Close if you are not ready to complete the remaining steps in the 1099 Wizard, or click Continue to advance to the next step.

 tip

The end of any calendar year is a busy time. Consider reviewing your vendors' 1099 information throughout the year so that you have time to collect the missing information before the tax forms are due.

Businesses must provide eligible vendors with their Form 1099-MISC by the end of January following a calendar year. Some vendors want their forms as early as possible in January, so prepare in advance.

Figure 8.14
Changes
made in the
1099 Wizard
automatically
update the
corresponding
vendor record
in QuickBooks.

Click to add or modify the information

Verify your 1099 vendors' information

Edit each vendor's information as needed. Changes you make are saved in QuickBooks.

Vendor Name	Tax ID*	Company Name	First Name	M.I.	Last Name	Address*	Phone
A Cheung Limited	555-11-8899	A Cheung Limited	Angela		Cheung	381B Bear Rd. West	510 555 5723
Chris Holly	123-45-6789	Chris Holly	Chris		Holly	201 S. Cherry Blvd	415-555-4300
Craig Carlson	111-22-3333					P.O. Box 76	415-555-0046
Mark Hamlin	666-55-2224	Mark Hamlin	Mark		Hamlin	270 Old Bayshore Rd	415-555-8965
Shannon Keswick	222-33-4444	Shannon Keswick				P.O. Box 620	415-555-0305
Vu Contracting	333-22-1111	Vu Contracting	Don		Vu	89304 Freedom Dr.	829-555-9019

*Required if e-filing

Need more information?   Back   Save & Close   Continue

Step 3—Map Your Accounts

QuickBooks provides the option of including or excluding specific general ledger accounts from being used when reporting your vendor's payments. For example, you might pay your vendor for services and record it to a specific Subcontractors expense account. You might also reimburse that same vendor for material purchases and record that portion of the expense to a different expense account.

To map your accounts, follow these steps:

1. After verifying your 1099 vendors' information, click Continue.

2. For the vendors you have selected, the 1099 Wizard displays the accounts that were assigned on the vendor payments. For each account displayed, you can choose to omit these payments from Form 1099-MISC income reporting or select from several 1099 box reporting options. See Figure 8.15.

3. (Optional) Click the Show 1099 Accounts drop-down list, and select **Show All Accounts** if you want to omit or map your 1099 reporting for all your accounts on your chart of accounts.

4. (Optional) Select the **Report All Payments in Box 7** checkbox. When you do so, all the displayed accounts are assigned to Box 7:Nonemployee Compensation.

> ## caution
>
> It is not the intent of this book to provide tax filing advice, so check with the IRS website for more details or ask your company's accountant or tax advisor.

caution

The only 1099 form that QuickBooks prints or that Intuit 1099 E-File Service can print is the Form 1099-MISC. However, you can assign the general ledger in QuickBooks to any of the 14 boxes on the Form 1099-MISC.

You can assign (map) multiple cost of sales, ordinary expense, and other expense accounts to a single box on the Form 1099-MISC. However, you cannot assign a single account to more than one reporting box on the form.

If a Balance Sheet account (such as a vendor prepayment) is used when recording a payment to a 1099 eligible vendor, that account does not display by default in the Map Vendor Payment Accounts dialog box. However, if you select **Show All Accounts**, you have the option to omit the payments recorded to Balance Sheet accounts from 1099 or assign them to the appropriate Form 1099-MISC box.

5. If you see the warning message "Your Settings Do Not Match the Current IRS Thresholds," click the Show IRS 1099-MISC Filing Thresholds link.

6. Read the information displayed in the 1099-MISC IRS Thresholds dialog box. Click the Reset to IRS Thresholds button. QuickBooks updates the thresholds with current tax information.

7. Click Save & Close to return to the 1099 Wizard.

8. Click Save & Close if you are not going to complete the remaining steps in the 1099 Wizard, or click Continue to advance to the next step.

Step 4—Review Vendor Payments

Do you pay your vendor bills by credit card? Beginning with the 2011 reporting tax year, the IRS established new rules to exclude from Form 1099-MISC any payments you made by credit card, debit card, gift card, or third-party payment network such as PayPal. (The IRS now requires that card issuers and third-party payment networks report these transactions on Form 1099-K.) You should review both included and excluded payments on the Review Payments for Exclusions screen in the 1099 Wizard, in Figure 8.16.

Payments to vendors that are made by credit card should always be recorded in QuickBooks via the Enter Credit Card Charges form. If instead you use the Pay Bills or Write Checks transaction forms, you need to take special guidelines into account. To record a vendor payment made with a credit card, debit card, or gift card, or using a third-party payment network such as PayPal but recorded in QuickBooks with a Bill Payment Check or Write Check, you should note the payment method in the No. field of a Bill Payment Check or Write Checks dialog box. QuickBooks recognizes, and automatically excludes from Form 1099-MISC, these payments if the following notations in the check number field (limited to eight characters) are used:

- Debit
- Diners
- Chase
- MC

- DBT card
- Debitcar
- Paypal
- Discover

- Visa
- DCard
- DBT

- MCard
- Masterc
- Debit cd

Figure 8.16
The 1099 Wizard enables you to verify whether payments should be included or excluded in the year's 1099 reporting.

Review payments for exclusions

Select Vendors — Verify Vendors — Map Accounts — Review Payments — Confirm Entries — Choose Filing

The IRS requires you to exclude from Form 1099-MISC any payments you make by credit card, debit card, gift card, or PayPal.

If you made payments to vendors by debit card, gift card, or PayPal, click **View Included Payments**, and edit the check number field to include an appropriate notation so QuickBooks can exclude these payments from Form 1099-MISC.

Click **View Excluded Payments** to verify these payments have been excluded from Form 1099-MISC. (This list does not show credit card transactions, which QuickBooks automatically excludes.)

View Included Payments

View Excluded Payments

Need more information?   Back   Save & Close   Continue

To view the transactions included in your 1099 reporting, follow these steps:

1. Click View Included Payments. QuickBooks creates a report titled "Check Payments Included on Forms 1099-MISC" (see Figure 8.17).

2. If any of these payments were made by credit card, debit card, gift card, or third-party payment network such as PayPal, you need to edit the check number, which displays in the Num column on this report.

3. Double-click to open a single transaction that was paid by debit card. The associated check displays. Modify the information in the No. field using one of the accepted notations listed previously.

4. Click Save & Close to save your changes. QuickBooks no longer includes this payment in your 1099-MISC Income reporting.

5. Click the View Excluded Payments button. QuickBooks creates a report titled Check Payments Excluded from Forms 1099-MISC. Verify that the transactions listed on this report qualify to be excluded from 1099-MISC income reporting.

6. Click the X in the top-right corner to close the report(s).

7. Click Save & Close if you are not going to complete the remaining steps in the 1099 Wizard, or click Continue to advance to the next step.

> **tip**
>
> Save yourself from having to modify the check number assigned to bill payment checks or other checks when recording vendor 1099 payments made by credit card using these transaction types. Instead, when paying a vendor bill, assign the payment to a credit card account or use the Enter Credit Card Charges dialog box to record the expense (from the menu bar, select **Banking, Enter Credit Card Charges**).
>
> QuickBooks automatically excludes from Form 1099-MISC reporting any bill payment made using the credit card payment method.

If payments were by debit card, modify the Num to agree with the acceptable notations.

Figure 8.17
Review checks recorded as payments to vendors that might have been paid by debit card.

Step 5—Confirm 1099-MISC Entries

The 1099 Wizard displays a list of the Vendors that will receive a Form 1099-MISC (see Figure 8.18).

To confirm 1099-MISC entries, follow these steps:

1. Click the Summary Report link to see a summary for all vendors included in your Form 1099-MISC income reporting. Modify the dates and filters as needed.

2. In the top right, click the X to close the 1099 Summary Report.

3. Click the Detail Report to see a list of all transactions grouped by vendor. Modify the dates and filters as needed.

4. In the top right, click the X to close the 1099 Detail Report.

5. Click Save & Close if you are not going to complete the remaining step in the 1099 Wizard, or click Continue to advance to the next step.

Figure 8.18 Preview vendor payments to include or not include in your Form 1099-MISC income reporting.

Confirm your 1099 entries

Review this summary of vendors for whom you are creating Form 1099-MISC and the amounts being reported for the calendar year shown. Double-click any amount to review transaction details.

See Other Years: Summary Report | Detail Report

Form 1099-MISC for 2016

Vendor Name	Tax ID	Box 7: Nonemployee compensation	Total Included on 1099	Total Unmapped Payments	Total
Chris Holly	123-45-6789	625.00	625.00	0.00	625.00
Craig Carlson	111-22-3333	2,125.00	2,125.00	0.00	2,125.00
Shannon Keswick	222-33-4444	1,500.00	1,500.00	0.00	1,500.00
Vu Contracting	333-22-1111	45,925.00	45,925.00	0.00	45,925.00
TOTAL		50,175.00	50,175.00	0.00	50,175.00

Need more information?   Back   Save & Close   Continue

Select Vendors — Verify Vendors — Map Accounts — Review Payments — Confirm Entries — Choose Filing

Step 6—Choose a Filing Method

The QuickBooks 1099 Wizard provides information to help you choose a filing method, either printing or electronically filing the forms (see Figure 8.19).

To print your 1099-MISC Income forms, follow these steps:

1. Click the Order Forms link to order your tax forms from Intuit. You can also purchase tax forms from your local office supply store.

Figure 8.19
The 1099
Wizard
makes it easy
to print 1099
forms or file
electronically.

Choose a filing method

① Select Vendors — ② Verify Vendors — ③ Map Accounts — ④ Review Payments — ⑤ Confirm Entries — ⑥ Choose Filing

✅ **You're ready to choose a filing method!**

Print

Print 1099s and the 1096 on preprinted forms and mail to the IRS. (The IRS doesn't accept forms on plain paper.)

Need to order preprinted forms?

Our forms are designed specifically for QuickBooks and print your data directly from QuickBooks on to the correct section of each form

Get forms in as little as 3 days

Order forms   Print 1099s

E-file

File electronically with the IRS using the Intuit 1099 E-File Service. Fees apply.

Is e-filing right for you?

• The IRS requires you to e-file if you submit over 250 forms.

• You can print copies for vendors or yourself on plain paper.

• When you e-file, the IRS doesn't require a 1096 summary form.

• If your state participates in the combined federal/state e-filing program, e-filing, your federal 1099s can simplify your state filings. Does my state participate?

Go to Intuit 1099 E-File Service

ⓘ Need more information?

Back   Save & Close

2. Click Print 1099s to print the documents on the preprinted forms you have purchased.

3. QuickBooks displays the 1099-MISC and 1096 Forms dialog box. Select the year you are printing your forms for. Typically, you select **Last Calendar Year**.

4. The Select 1099s to Print dialog box displays, with each vendor selected. (Optional) Click Select All or Select None.

5. QuickBooks displays the number of vendors selected and the total dollar amount for the selected vendors.

6. If you will be e-Filing your 1099s, skip to the instructions that follow step 11. If you are printing, continue with step 7.

7. Click Print 1099. The Print 1099s settings display. Place the tax forms in your printer and select **Print**. You need to print on preprinted forms; unlike W-2s, the IRS does not accept 1099 forms on plain paper.

8. View the documents that printed. When you have finished printing 1099s, click Print 1096 and insert the preprinted form into your printer.

9. Enter the Contact Name in the 1096 Information dialog box. If circumstances warrant, select **This Is My Final Return**.

10. Choose your printer and click Print. QuickBooks returns to Select 1099s to Print.

11. When printing finishes, click the X in the top-right corner to close the Select 1099s to Print dialog box.

If you will be e-Filing, click the Go to Intuit 1099 E-File Service. Follow the instructions for filing. You will complete three steps:

1. **Sign up for the Service**—Use your Intuit Account username and password.

2. **Set up Intuit Sync Manager**—Enable QuickBooks to send your information to the Intuit E-File 1099 Service.

3. **Purchase, Print, and E-File**—Print and E-File your returns with a click of a button.

The information window provides a toll-free number to call if you have any questions. 1099 forms for a given tax year cannot be filed until January of the following year.

You have successfully completed the steps to properly track and report your vendors' Form 1099-MISC income payments.

Correcting Accounts Payable Errors

Chapter 7 provided a recommended workflow and preference settings that help you avoid making mistakes with your accounts payable transactions. This chapter provides specific details about methods you can use to correct existing accounts payable errors.

The purpose of this book is not to give business-specific accounting or tax advice, but rather to introduce you to ways you can fix specific mistakes you have found.

> **⚡ caution**
> Before making any of the suggested changes, be sure you have made a backup of your data, in case the change does not give you the desired result. Additionally, obtaining your accountant's advice regarding the changes you are contemplating is always prudent.

When Vendor Bills Are Paid Without Using the Proper Process

Earlier in this chapter, in the section "Reviewing the Unpaid Bills Detail Report," you learned a way to reconcile your A/P Aging Summary report total to your Balance Sheet Accounts Payable total (refer to Figures 8.1 and 8.2). As important as this task is, it is also necessary for you to review those items listed as unpaid to your vendor. If you notice an open vendor bill that you know is no longer due, it might be because you paid the vendor with a Write Checks transaction instead of the proper Pay Bills transaction type.

You should experience fewer of these types of mistakes in recent years because QuickBooks directs you to the Pay Bills dialog box, in Figure 8.20, when you attempt to write a check to a vendor with open bills.

If you choose to modify the original vendor check, carefully consider the accounting effect this type of correction will have on your financials:

- Is the change a significant dollar amount? Both cash and accrual basis reports will be affected.

- Consider the date of the check and the date of the bill—are they in different tax years?

- Will the correction affect a year in which the data has already been used to prepare a tax return?

Figure 8.20
You see this warning if you attempt to create a Write Check transaction when paying a vendor with open bills.

If you answered yes to any of these questions, be sure to discuss with your accountant the impact this change could have on your financials.

You can modify this check, making it become a vendor credit. In other words, it will decrease (debit) Accounts Payable and maintain the original decrease (credit) to your cash account. To do so, follow these steps:

1. Locate the Write Checks transaction used to pay the vendor. One easy way is to click the Vendors button on the Home page to open the Vendor Center. Choose your vendor from the list on the left, and select **Checks** from the Show drop-down list, as Figure 8.5 showed earlier.

2. Double-click the check to open the Write Checks transaction.

3. On the Expenses tab, in the account column, replace the currently listed account with the Accounts Payable account in Figure 8.21. This creates a decrease (debit) to the Accounts Payable account.

4. In the drop-down list in the Customer:Job column, select the vendor name. If you previously listed a Customer:Job in this field, you are warned to choose a Vendor name instead. This assigns the accounts payable decrease to a specific vendor. You cannot save the transaction without assigning a vendor name.

5. Click Save & Close, and then click Yes to record your changes.

Figure 8.21
Using a check to record a vendor pre-payment (debit to Accounts Payable).

			Write Checks - Checking

Main   Reports

BANK ACCOUNT   10100 · Checking   ENDING BALANCE   **43,439.10**

NO.   517
DATE   12/15/2017

PAY TO THE ORDER OF   Wheeler's Tile Etc. $ 1,250.00

One thousand two hundred fifty and 00/100 * DOLLARS

ADDRESS

Wheeler's Tile Etc.
650 Old Bayshore Rd
Bayshore CA 94326

MEMO

Expenses   **$1,250.00**   Items $0.00

ACCOUNT	AMOUNT	MEMO	CUSTOMER:JOB	BILLABLE?	CLASS
20000 · Accounts Payable	1,250.00		Wheeler's Tile Etc.		

Add the vendor name in this column

6. From the menu bar, select **Vendors**, **Pay Bills**, and use the arrow key on your keyboard to move up and down through the list of vendors in the Pay Bills dialog box. Optionally, you can select the vendor name from the Filter By drop-down list. Before placing a checkmark in the box next to the vendor's specific invoice, QuickBooks shows the total number of credits and their total value in the Discount & Credit Information for Highlighted Bill section. (See Figure 7.21 on page 261 in Chapter 7.)

7. When you have located the correct bill, place a checkmark in the box to the left of the Date Due column. When a bill is selected, QuickBooks automatically applies the available credits to the selected vendor invoice (if the preference was set). If not, and you want to modify the amount or which credits are selected, click the Set Credits button. The Discount and Credits dialog box displays (previously shown in Figure 7.22 on page 261 in Chapter 7). Users can modify which credit is selected by changing the checkmark from one credit to another or by manually overriding the amount of the credit.

8. Click the Done button when the credit is assigned.

9. QuickBooks shows in the Pay Bills dialog box that the bill is paid by a credit (if the entire bill is being paid by the credit, QuickBooks does not create a check). Click Pay Selected Bills when you finish.

10. QuickBooks offers you Pay More Bills or Done choices. Click Done if you do not have any other transactions to correct using this method.

Misapplied Vendor Credit

Have you ever been given a credit from a vendor, only to find out later that your vendor applied the credit to a different open bill than you did in your accounting records?

QuickBooks makes it easy to reassign a vendor credit from one accounts payable bill to another bill. You temporarily assign the credit to another vendor and then reapply it to the correct vendor. To do so, follow these steps:

1. On the Home page, click the Vendors button to open the Vendor Center.

2. Select the vendor with the misapplied credit.

3. In the Show drop-down list, select **Bills** (this also lists vendor credits).

4. From the transactions listed, select the misapplied credit memo by double-clicking it. The Enter Bills dialog box, with the word *Credit* displayed, opens for the selected transaction.

5. On the vendor line of the credit, select a different vendor. (Remember who you assign it to.)

6. Click Save & Close. QuickBooks removes the credit transaction from the vendor bill it was previously associated with.

7. QuickBooks also warns that the transaction you edit will no longer be connected. Click Yes to continue (see Figure 8.22).

Recording Transaction

This transaction is connected to other transactions. You have changed it so that it will no longer be connected to all or some of them. Do you want to change it anyway?

[Yes]   [No]   [Cancel]

Figure 8.22
You see this warning when you unapply a previously applied vendor credit.

8. From the same Vendor Center, select the other vendor to which you assigned the credit. From the Show drop-down list, select **Bills** and double-click the credit you just assigned in step 5. The Enter Bills dialog box, with the word Credit displayed, opens for the selected transaction.

9. On the vendor line, select the original vendor.

10. Click Save & Close, and click Yes to making the change.

QuickBooks now shows the credit as unapplied to your original vendor, and you can follow the steps outlined previously for applying the credit to the correct open vendor bill.

Removing Aged Open Item Receipts or Vendor Bills

One of the most important tasks you can do to maintain correct accounting records is to remove old, aged item receipts or payables you do not owe or will not collect.

You have three options when you want to remove these aged (old) transactions:

- Create a credit memo and apply it.

- Void the item receipt or bill.

- Delete the item receipt or bill.

To create and apply a credit memo to a vendor bill, follow the same steps as listed in the earlier section titled "Applying Vendor Discounts or Credits."

You must give special consideration to applying a credit memo to an open item receipt. First, convert the item receipt to a bill. To do so, follow these steps:

1. Locate the open item receipt using any of the methods suggested in Chapter 7, p. 231.

2. When you select the open item receipt, QuickBooks opens the Create Item Receipts dialog box. Place a checkmark in the Bill Received box at the top right, as in Figure 8.23.

Figure 8.23
Converting an unapplied Item Receipt to a bill is necessary before applying a vendor credit memo.

Clicking here will include this in the Pay Bills dialog

You can now apply your credit memo to the item receipt, which has been converted to a bill.

When considering whether to void it or delete it, I always prefer the void option because it leaves a record of the original transaction. Before voiding or deleting, you need to verify that the aged open item receipts or bills do not have any other transactions associated with them. To verify this, follow these steps:

1. Open the item receipt or bill using any one of the many methods in Chapter 7, p. 231.

2. Open a previously recorded bill or create an Item Receipt transaction. The Transaction tab to the right includes information about linked transactions. QuickBooks displays in the Summary box information about when the transaction was created and edited (if applicable). The Related Transactions box provides links to the original transactions (if any).

If you had voided or deleted the vendor bill in Figure 8.24, you would have created an unapplied vendor payment (the Bill Pmt-Check listed in the Related Transactions section). In effect, you would have traded one correction for another problem. So be careful when making corrections to your accounts payable transactions.

Figure 8.24
Before voiding, deleting, or modifying a bill, click the Transaction tab to the right to see whether any transactions are associated with this bill.

Making General Journal Adjustments to Accounts Payable

All too often, I find that accounting professionals are quick to make adjustments to accounts payable using the Make General Journal Entries transaction, also referred to as a journal entry. The following are some of the issues surrounding the use of a journal entry for accounts payable adjustments:

- Only a single vendor or customer name can be in the Make General Journal Entries transaction, not both a vendor and a customer in the same transaction. This minimizes the usefulness of the transaction for large volume corrections.

- General journal entries do not include the option to assign an item, including service, non-inventory, inventory, and so on. The adjustment would affect the Profit & Loss reports but not specific QuickBooks reports that use item information, such as the Job Profitability reports or Inventory Valuation reports.

- You still need to go to the Pay Bills dialog box to assign the balance the general journal generates to the other related vendor transactions.

This type of error is more apparent when a multiple-line general journal entry form includes a Customer:Job Name on the first line. When preparing a Profit & Loss by Job report, QuickBooks would include all lines of the general journal entry as belonging to that job!

A quick fix is to add a blank line at the beginning of each general journal entry. Another recommendation is to create a fictitious bank account and call it Adjusting Entries, but then leave the debit and credit fields blank. If you assign the first line of the entry to this account, QuickBooks provides a "register" for you to locate these types of transactions and, at the same time, avoid the issue addressed in this section. See Figures 8.27 and 8.28 to see how adding the line at the beginning of the transaction solves the problem in reporting.

> **⚑ caution**
>
> Use of the general journal entries often does not provide the desired results in your reporting. Did you know that the first line of any general journal entry is considered a "source" line? Specifically, this means that if the first line of a multiple-line general journal entry includes a vendor, customer, or any list item name in the Name column, as in Figure 8.25, that name element displays in reports on the lines below the first line, even if there is no relationship (see Figure 8.26).

Figure 8.25

When the first line of a multiple-line general journal includes a list name in the Name column, QuickBooks associates the name entry with all lines of the transaction.

Figure 8.26
QuickBooks associated the vendor's name with all lines of the journal entry because the vendor list name was on the first line of the general journal.

Leave details for row one blank

Create a bank account type of account

Figure 8.27
Including the fictitious bank account on the first line of a general journal entry prevents the source line (line 1) from being associated with each additional unrelated line.

These simple tips often can help make your QuickBooks reporting much more accurate.

If you have journal entries recorded to your Accounts Payable account, your Unpaid Bills Detail report might resemble Figure 8.29.

 If your Unpaid Bills Detail report includes journal entries, see "Applying Vendor Credits," p. 259.

Figure 8.28
QuickBooks no longer associates the vendor's name with the unrelated general journal lines.

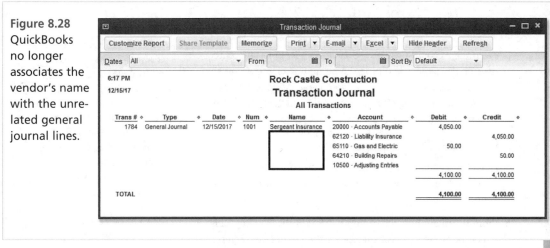

Figure 8.29
Your Unpaid Bills Detail report might show the general journal entry as unapplied.

Handling Unique Accounts Payable Transactions

So far, you have learned about the accounts payable transactions and workflow, preferences you can set to improve your data entry, reports to review when troubleshooting errors, and methods of correcting accounts payable errors. This section offers specific solutions to some of those unique transactions you might need to record.

Bartering Services with Your Vendors

Exchanging goods or services on a noncash basis with a vendor that is also a customer is commonly referred to as bartering. A common scenario is that your vendor also purchases your goods or services, and you plan to "swap" and not pay each other for the items purchased from each other.

To track the exchange of goods, follow these steps:

1. From the menu bar, select **Lists**, **Chart of Accounts**.

2. From the Account drop-down list, select **New** to create a new bank account, and type the name **Bartering**. If you have account numbering turned on, you also need to assign an account number. This bank account will always have a net zero balance if you record the transactions properly.

3. Click Save & Close.

4. From the menu bar, select **Vendor**, **Enter Bills** to record your vendor bill as if you were going to make the purchase from the vendor.

5. From the menu bar, select **Vendor**, **Pay Bills**. The Pay Bills dialog box opens. Select the bill for the vendor you will barter with.

> **note**
>
> QuickBooks does not allow the same name to reside on multiple lists. To get around this limitation, when creating the customer name for your vendor, follow this convention: Johns Plumbing–C. I have added a –C after the "vendor name" on my customer list. This is helpful when you are picking the name from a list and you need to be certain to select the customer list item.

6. In the Pay Bills dialog box, select the **Bartering Account** as the payment account (as in Figure 8.30). You can then choose to assign a fictitious check number and record only the amount that is to be traded. Any balance remaining can be paid as it normally would to the vendor.

7. On the Home page, click the Customers button to open the Customers Center.

8. From the New Customer & Job drop-down list, select **New Customer** and complete the contact information for the new customer; otherwise, click to select the customer or job you will be bartering with to select it.

9. From the Customers Center, in the New Transactions drop-down list, select **Invoices**. Prepare the invoice to the new customer (also your vendor) using the same items on the invoice as if you were selling them to a customer. Click Save & Close.

10. From the Customers Center, in the New Transactions drop-down list, select **Receive Payments**. Record the fictitious payment from the customer (your vendor) for the same amount you are bartering. Click Save & Close.

11. Depending on how your preferences are set up for customer payments, deposit the fictitious customer payment into the same Bartering bank account you created earlier.

12. If you properly recorded the value of what you purchased as equal to the value of what you sold, your Bartering bank account will have a net zero ending balance. If not, return and review your entries. The amount shown as paid on the vendor bill and the customer invoice should be the same.

13. Any remaining balances on the vendor bills or customer invoices are handled as they normally are for those transactions.

Figure 8.30
When you
are bartering
goods with
your vendor,
choose the
fictitious bank
account when
recording the
"payment"
of the vendor
bill.

Recording Vendor Prepayments

If your business is required to prepay a vendor for purchases, you can choose from a couple methods:

- Assign expenses to the other current asset type account, typically named Prepaid Expenses.

- Record a decrease (debit) transaction to the Accounts Payable account.

Often you have expenses that you must pay before you enjoy the benefit of the service or product being purchased. An example is a business's general liability insurance. Typically, you pay several months in advance for this type of insurance. Recording this annual or semiannual expense all in one month would make that month unfairly take on the total expense.

A preferred method is to record the expense in equal monthly increments. The following steps show you how to record the original prepaid expense and record the expense to the individual months.

To accomplish this task, when you pay the insurance vendor, assign the expense to other current asset type account, and then create a recurring entry that QuickBooks uses to remind you to enter the expense. Or QuickBooks can automatically enter the expense each month, depending on how you set up the reminder. This example shows how you would prepay a general liability insurance bill of $12,000 for 12 months of coverage.

To record vendor prepayments, follow these steps:

1. Complete an Enter Bills or Write Checks transaction payable to your insurance provider. On the Expense tab of the transaction, assign the prepaid account, which is an other current asset type. In this example, the account is Prepaid Insurance.

2. Pay the bill to the vendor as normal.

3. Set up a recurring transaction to charge [1/12] of the total to each month. If the amount remains the same from month to month, set up the recurring entry to automatically post to QuickBooks. To do so, from the menu bar, select **Company**, **Make General Journal Entries**. Create a journal entry with a debit to your expense account and a credit to the prepaid other current asset type account.

The next step is to memorize the transaction so that QuickBooks can automatically record it each month, or remind you to do so. Follow these steps:

1. Create the transaction you want to memorize. You can also use this process to memorize any of the QuickBooks transaction types, checks, bills, invoices, and so on.

2. From the ribbon toolbar, Main tab (on most transactions), click Memorize to display the Memorize Transaction dialog box. You can memorize a transaction in other ways, too. With the transaction displayed, press Ctrl+M on your keyboard, or from the menu bar, select **Edit**, **Memorize** to open the Memorize Transaction dialog box.

3. Choose to have QuickBooks remind you of a specific frequency, or to have QuickBooks automatically enter the transaction (see Figure 8.31).

Figure 8.31
Memorized transactions can automate repetitive transactions or serve as a reminder to enter the transaction.

The other method discussed here is to record a debit balance to the vendor's accounts payable account. This is appropriate if you will be using the prepayment soon as payment toward the final vendor bill. To do so, follow these steps:

1. From the menu bar, select **Banking**, **Write Checks**.

2. In the Pay to the Order Of field, select the vendor's name.

3. Enter the amount of the prepayment.

4. On the Expenses tab, in the account detail area, select the **Accounts Payable** account (see Figure 8.32).

5. In the Customer:Job column, enter the vendor's name (must be a vendor type for this method to work).

6. Click Save & Close.

QuickBooks now records a vendor credit (debit to Accounts Payable), as Figure 8.33 shows.

---

tip

QuickBooks displays memorized transactions on the Memorized Transaction List, which is available by pressing Ctrl+T on your keyboard. You can also select **Lists**, **Memorized Transaction List** from the menu bar.

You might want to check your company reminders to be sure you enable a reminder for showing your memorized transactions. To do so, from the menu bar, select **Edit**, **Preferences** and then, on the Preferences dialog box, select the **Reminders** tab.

Figure 8.32 Assign the Accounts Payable account and the vendor name to a check when recording a vendor prepayment.

At a later date, you record a bill for the full purchase price and apply this credit, as Chapter 7 previously detailed.

Figure 8.33
QuickBooks records the vendor prepayment as a negative entry to Accounts Payable (or a debit to Accounts Payable).

Entering Midyear 1099 Balances

If you start your QuickBooks data file midyear (or at some other time than the first of a new calendar year), you might have amounts paid previously to vendors who are eligible to receive the Form 1099-MISC.

To properly record the amounts paid to vendors in your prior accounting software, and to make sure that QuickBooks reports all amounts paid to the vendor on the Form 1099-MISC, follow these steps:

1. From the menu bar, select **Company**, **Make General Journal Entries**. If you use any of the job profitability reports, leave the first line (source line) of the journal entry blank.

2. On the following lines (one line per vendor), in the Account column, enter the cost of goods sold account or expense account assigned in the preferences for Tax:1099.

3. For each Debit line amount, in the Name column, be sure to select the vendor's list name (this must be a vendor type).

4. On the last line, enter one line total assigning the same account as the other lines so that the Debit column is equal to the Credit column (see Figure 8.34).

Your overall financials will not change because the same account was used for both the debit and credit sides of the transaction. Including the vendor name on the debit side of the transaction lines causes QuickBooks to include the amount in the reported Form 1099-MISC income amount.

Figure 8.34
When starting a QuickBooks file midyear, create a general journal entry to record year-to-date vendor Form 1099-MISC income tax payments.

Memorizing Recurring Transactions

QuickBooks can also help you not forget a recurring accounts payable bill. Memorized bills work best if the amount being paid is the same from month to month (or whatever frequency you set). An example is your rent payment.

To memorize a recurring accounts payable transaction, follow these steps:

1. Create a vendor bill as normal, assigning the amount and expense account that you want it to be associated with.

2. With the Enter Bills dialog box open, press Ctrl+M to open the Memorize Transaction dialog box (see the previous Figure 8.31).

3. Enter a name that identifies this transaction in the memorized transaction list.

4. Choose one of the available options and then click OK to close the Schedule Memorized Transaction dialog box:

    - **Add to My Reminders List**—If you select this option, you need to choose how often and the next date you want to be reminded.

    - **Do Not Remind Me**—Use this option if you want to stop permanently, or even temporarily, your reminders for this transaction.

    - **Automate Transaction Entry**—Use this option if you want QuickBooks to create the entry automatically.

    - **Add to Group**—You can assign multiple transactions to a group and then process them with one keystroke. First, create a group by choosing Lists, Memorized Transaction List from the menu bar. From the Memorized Transaction drop-down list, select New Group. Give the group a name and choose options for the group from the following options: Remind Me, Do Not Remind Me, or Automatically Enter.

> **note**
>
> If you assign the Automate Transaction Entry option for memorizing a transaction, QuickBooks provides a reminder dialog box that displays when you log in to the QuickBooks file.
>
> From the Enter Memorized Transactions dialog box, you can enter all the selected transactions, select those you want to enter, or enter them all later (see Figure 8.35).

5. Click Save & Close on your bill only if you want to create the vendor bill now and also add it to your memorized transaction list. If not, select **Clear** to remove the bill details, knowing that QuickBooks will prompt you to enter it on the frequency and date you selected.

To manually enter the transactions (if they're not set to Automate Transaction Entry), from the menu bar, select **Lists**, **Memorized Transaction List**, or press Ctrl+T on your keyboard to quickly call up the list. Select the group or individual transactions you want to post by double-clicking the group or individual item from the memorized transaction list.

Figure 8.35
QuickBooks reminds you to process Memorized repeating transactions.

If you clicked a memorized group, QuickBooks creates each of the transactions in the group, asking you to assign a transaction date globally to all the transactions in the group. Use the memorized transaction tool to save time and to remind yourself to pay those important recurring bills.

Depositing a Vendor Refund

Occasionally, you might receive a refund from a vendor you previously paid. To add a vendor refund check to your bank deposit, follow these steps:

1. Create your deposit (normally done with customer invoice payments) as usual.

2. On the next available deposit line, enter the vendor name in the Received From column, and then choose one of these two options:

   ■ If you do not have an open vendor credit in your Accounts Payable, select the expense account you want to reduce in the From Account column.

   ■ If you do have an open vendor credit that you want to associate this refund with, select the **Accounts Payable** account in the From Account column. Then apply the deposit to the open credit.

3. Enter an optional memo.

4. Enter the amount.

5. Click Save & Close when the total of the deposit agrees with the bank deposit total.

Although this method is quite easy to use, it does not allow you to assign an item, so any refund recorded this way is not included in certain job cost reports that are prepared from the use of items.

Instead, you create a vendor credit to record the reduction in a job cost and then follow the preceding instructions for applying the deposit to the open vendor credit.

Paying and Recording a Credit Card Bill

You have flexibility in how you choose to record and pay your credit card bills. The decision is based on your own circumstances because several ways can be appropriate.

Options for recording credit card expenses include the following:

- Enter a bill to the credit card vendor, summarizing the total charges on one bill and entering a separate line for each expense account amount.

- Enter individual credit card charges. From the menu bar, select **Banking, Enter Credit Card Charges**. You might be prompted to add a credit card account to QuickBooks.

- Use the QuickBooks Online Banking feature, and automatically download your credit card charges and payments directly into your QuickBooks data file. Not all credit card providers offer this functionality. To see whether your card offers this option, select **Banking, Online Banking, Participating Financial Institutions** from the menu bar.

> *For more information, see "Bank Feeds," p. 532.*

Options for paying your credit card bill include the following:

- If you selected to enter a bill to your credit card vendor, pay the bill as you do other bills, paying it partially or in full.

- If you selected one of the other two options, you need to create a vendor bill or check and, in the Account column of the transaction, assign the Credit Card type account you previously recorded the transactions to. The vendor bill simply decreases the balance owed on the credit card liability account.

The cash basis Balance Sheet might show this credit card payment amount if it is not paid by the date you prepare your financials.

> *For more information about how QuickBooks handles certain accounts on a cash basis, see "Accounts Payable Balance on Cash Basis Balance Sheet," p. 272.*

QuickBooks offers two choices with the Automatically Recall Information preference (select **Edit**, **Preferences** from the menu bar and then select the **General—My Preferences** tab):

- **Automatically Recall Last Transaction for This Name**— Recalls both the account and the previous amount.

- **Prefill Accounts for Vendor Based on Past Entries**—Recalls only the account(s) used, not the amounts.

A more efficient process is to assign up to three default charts of accounts to each vendor record. To add these accounts, follow these steps:

1. From the Home page, click Vendors to open the Vendor Center.

2. Select the vendor to which you want to assign accounts, and click Edit Vendor to open the Edit Vendor dialog box.

3. Click OK to close the New Feature message, if it displays.

4. Click the Account Settings tab. In the fields provided, select the desired account(s) from the drop-down list.

If you rarely use the additional accounts, you might want to consider adding them only when needed. All newly created transactions include up to the three lines assigned. If you do not remove these lines, they result in blank lines of data in many reports.

The selected accounts override any preference setting for Recall or Prefill and instead insert these accounts automatically on a Write Checks or Enter Bills transaction. This is just another method to help you keep your accounting accurate.

> **⟳ tip**
>
> Have you ever found that QuickBooks users assign a different expense account each time they create a check or bill to pay for costs of the business? This can make reviewing your specific expenses for the business less accurate. You can default this behavior by setting preferences detailed in this section.

QuickStart

Step 1. Create a Customer Record   **320**

Step 2. Invoice the Customer   **352**

Step 3. Collect Payment   **371**

Step 4. Make the Deposit to Your Bank
Account   **373**

9

SETTING UP CUSTOMERS

It is not surprising to me—and perhaps not to you, either—that the accounts receivable process is the most organized and "cared for" task in QuickBooks. The process of producing a customer invoice needs to be completed quickly because you have to provide a document to a customer to get paid.

In this chapter, you will find useful information to help you do the following:

- Customize and set important preferences

- Work with prospecting activities

- Set up customers, jobs, and supporting lists

Whether you are a first-time QuickBooks user or you have been using the software for years, the details in this chapter will help you set up your customers in QuickBooks correctly.

Customizing Home Page Customer Activities

QuickBooks makes performing customer activities easy with a customizable list of tasks on the Home page (see Figure 9.1).

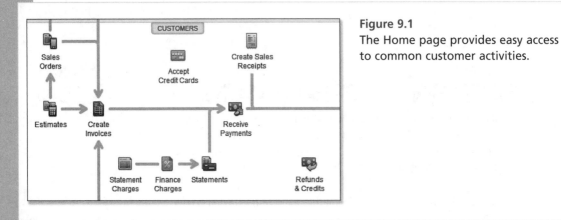

Figure 9.1
The Home page provides easy access to common customer activities.

Depending on your version of QuickBooks, you can add or remove the following transaction types or tasks from your Home page:

- **Sales Orders**—Use this transaction to commit a sale to a customer (QuickBooks Premier, Accountant, or Enterprise).

- **Estimates**—Use this transaction type to provide customers with quotes for your product or service and, most important, provide the basis for Customer or Job budgets.

- **Sales Tax Tracking**—Use this task to collect sales tax from your customers and remit to the taxing authority.

> *For more information on customizing the Home page, refer to Chapter 2, "Getting Around QuickBooks," p. 67.*

The next section details the selected features that can be enabled or disabled on the Home page.

Preferences That Affect Accounts Receivable

You can simplify your Accounts Receivable tasks by setting certain QuickBooks preferences. Some of these preferences save you keystrokes, which can save data entry time.

Not every preference that affects Accounts Receivable impacts your financials. Some preferences enable specific features such as those shown in Figure 9.2. To set preferences in QuickBooks, from the menu bar, select **Edit**, **Preferences**, and then choose the type of preference on the left side of the Preferences dialog box.

Figure 9.2
Preferences enable features and specific types of customer transactions.

Preferences in QuickBooks come in two forms:

- My Preferences are settings that are unique to the user logging in to the data file and are not shared by other users.

- Company Preferences are settings that are common for all users. When a preference is modified on the Company Preferences tab of the Preferences dialog box, the change affects all users.

To set Company Preferences, open the file as the Admin or External Accountant user and switch to single-user mode (if you are using the data file in a multiuser environment).

The sections that follow outline the preference settings that improve your QuickBooks accounts receivable workflow. Many preferences can help you work more efficiently in QuickBooks. Be sure to have each user log in to QuickBooks with his or her username and review all the available preferences on the My Preferences tab.

> **⚡ caution**
> The Admin user is the default user that is created when you first start using QuickBooks. Proper controls should be in place to allow only certain individuals to log in to the data file as the Admin user. For more information, see "Setting Up Users and Permissions," p. 55.

Payments

Payments preferences help you with customer payment processing and improve your overall process for receiving money from customers. From the menu bar, select **Edit**, **Preferences**; then on the left side of the Preferences dialog box, select **Payments**.

Company Preferences

These specific preferences are set for all users:

- **Receive Payments**—These settings make it easier for you to assign customer payments to the customers' invoices:

  - **Automatically Apply Payments**—When you select this option and record the receive payment transaction, QuickBooks applies the payment to an invoice of the same amount. If no invoice amount matches the exact dollar amount, the payment is applied to the oldest invoice first. See Figure 9.3.

Set defaults for online payment method

Figure 9.3
Payment preferences are important to review and set before sending invoices to your customers.

- **Automatically Calculate Payments**—When selected, you do not need to put a total in the Amount box on the Receive Payments dialog box. QuickBooks calculates and prefills the amount as the sum total of each of the invoices marked as received.

- **Use Undeposited Funds as a Default Deposit to Account**—When selected, this preference causes QuickBooks to place all customer payments into a current asset account that is created by QuickBooks. Undeposited Funds is like a safe that holds your customer payments before they are taken to the bank for deposit. When you record a Make Deposit transaction, QuickBooks removes the funds from the Undeposited Funds account and places them in your bank account.

- **Invoice Payments**—After signing up for Intuit PaymentNetwork, your customers can pay your invoices online via bank-to-bank transfer, Electronic Funds Transfer (EFT) similar to paying with a company check, or a credit card. Following are the invoice payments options:

  - **Allow Customers to Pay Each Invoice Online**—Click Learn More to sign up for the Intuit PaymentNetwork service.

  - **Include Online Payment Link on Invoices**—Adds a payment web address to all invoices you email from QuickBooks. You can choose to allow payments to be made by bank account only or by bank account and credit card. Select the Explain link to learn more. You can modify this file preference for selected customers or even on an invoice-by-invoice basis.

  - **Also Include on Printed Invoices**—Adds a payment web address on invoices printed or emailed.

  - **Intuit PaymentNetwork Email**—Enter the email address you use (or plan to use) to sign in to Intuit PaymentNetwork.

- **Turn Off Online Payments**—This action turns off links for all invoices and all customers. If you resend a past invoice that includes the link, the newly sent invoice will not include the online payment link.

My Preferences

The Payments settings do not have My Preferences.

Sales & Customers

The Sales & Customers preference settings enable you to customize QuickBooks for the tasks you use to manage customer activities. You can also make it easier for your employees to do their daily tasks by customizing the Home page so that the needed transaction types are available. From the menu bar, select **Edit**, **Preferences**; then on the left side of the Preferences dialog box, select the **Sales & Customers** preference.

Company Preferences

These specific preferences are available for all users:

- **Sales Forms**—These settings enable you to set a default shipping method that displays on customer forms. You can also choose to be warned when duplicate invoice numbers are detected.

- **Miscellaneous**—A drop-down list enables you to select the default packing slip form.

- **Collections Center**—This option enables the Collections Center, which has now been replaced with the Income Tracker.

- **Custom Pricing**—With this option, you can disable or enable Price Levels. Price Levels are assigned to your customers and automate unique customer pricing. For example, you might use the price level feature to offer wholesale pricing to certain customers and charge retail pricing to others.

  ➡ *For more information on using Advanced Pricing in QuickBooks Enterprise, refer to Chapter 9, "Using Advanced Pricing in QuickBooks Enterprise," p. 334.*

- **Sales Orders**—Available with QuickBooks Premier, Accountant, or QuickBooks Enterprise Solutions, the Sales Order transaction type enables you to commit sales to customers and track backorders. Preferences include warning about duplicate sales order numbers, printing options for items with zero amounts, and choosing templates for Packing Slips and Pick Lists.

My Preferences

These settings affect the currently logged-in user:

- **Add Available Time/Costs to Invoices for the Selected Job**—This setting determines how QuickBooks prompts the logged-in user when unbilled costs exist for a Customer or Job. Options include the following:

  - Prompt for Time/Costs to Add

  - Don't Add Any

  - Ask What to Do

Checking

The Checking Preferences are for defining specific bank accounts for sales-related activities, such as depositing a customer's payment into a predefined bank account. From the menu bar, select **Edit**, **Preferences**; and then on the left side of the Preferences dialog box, select the **Checking** preference.

Company Preferences

No Checking Company Preferences affect your workflow for accounts receivable tasks.

My Preferences

The Open the Make Deposits default account preference is optional. Use this preference to specify the default bank account selected for making deposits. If you have multiple bank accounts you make deposits to, you might not want to set a default on this tab. When no preference is set, the first bank account listed on the Chart of Accounts is the default.

Finance Charge

Does your company charge your late-paying customers a finance charge on open balances? If so, you will want to set these preferences. From the menu bar, select **Edit**, **Preferences**; then on the left side of the Preferences dialog box, select the **Finance Charge** preference.

Company Preferences

These preferences set your company's annual interest rate, minimum finance charge, grace period, and income account you want to credit.

These settings affect your financial reports and determine how QuickBooks calculates and reports on finance charges (see Figure 9.4):

- **Annual Interest Rate (%)**—Enter the interest rate you want to use when calculating finance charges on late payments.

- **Minimum Finance Charge**—Enter a dollar amount to use as the minimum finance charge.

- **Grace Period (days)**—Use this setting to calculate a grace period before finance charges apply.

- **Finance Charge Account**—Enter the account you will use to track the finance charges you collect from your customers. Typically, you would select an income account type.

- **Assess Finance Charges on Overdue Finance Charges**—When selected, this option includes unpaid finance charge amounts previously invoiced in the new amount used to calculate additional late fees. In my experience, when you do this, you become the "squeaky wheel" that gets paid.

- **Calculate Charges From**—The choices are Due Date and Invoice/Billed Date. If you create an invoice for a customer for $1,000 that is due in 30 days and you select the Calculate Charges from Due Date option, the amount is not considered overdue until 30 days from the invoice due date.

- **Mark Finance Charge Invoices "To Be Printed"**—If this option is not selected, you can send a statement to the customer at the end of your billing cycle to communicate the amounts that are owed instead of sending an invoice for the finance charges assessed.

Figure 9.4
Assess finance charges, and remember that the "squeaky wheel" is the one that gets paid!

My Preferences

Finance Charge settings do not have My Preferences.

Jobs & Estimates

The preference settings found in this section enable certain accounts receivable transaction types in QuickBooks. From the menu bar, select **Edit**, **Preferences**; then on the left side of the Preferences dialog box, select the **Jobs & Estimates** preference.

Company Preferences

These choices have to do with enabling specific estimating and invoicing features in QuickBooks, as well as defining custom job status descriptions (see Figure 9.5):

- **Job Status Descriptions**—Selecting this option enables you to modify the job status descriptions, such as changing Not Awarded to Lost.

- **Do You Create Estimates?**—Selecting Yes adds an icon to the Home page for Estimates.

- **Do You Do Progress Invoicing?**—Selecting Yes brings up a dialog box when creating an invoice from an estimate. The dialog box includes the options to create an invoice for all items, a percentage, or selected items from a multiline estimate.

- **Warn About Duplicate Estimate Numbers**—Selecting this option provides good internal controls over your documents.

- **Don't Print Items That Have Zero Amount**—Selecting this option is useful when creating a progress invoice with many lines. This selection is available if you selected Yes with the Progress Invoicing option.

Figure 9.5
Jobs &
Estimates
preferences
enable spe-
cific transac-
tion types for
you to use.

My Preferences

Jobs & Estimates do not have My Preferences.

Reminders

The Reminders Preferences can be useful if you want QuickBooks to prompt you when certain accounts receivable tasks are due. From the menu bar, select **Edit**, **Preferences**; then on the left side of the Preferences dialog box, select the **Reminders** preference.

Company Preferences

The Company Preferences for Reminders, shown in Figure 9.6, determines how QuickBooks shows reminders. Options include Summary, List, and Don't Remind Me. Accounts Receivable reminders include Invoices/Credit Memos to Print, Overdue Invoices, Almost Due Invoices, and other customer activity–related reminders.

Figure 9.6 The selections on the Company Preferences tab determine how QuickBooks reminds all users.

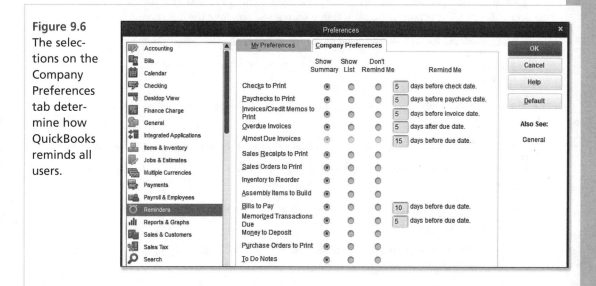

My Preferences

Users can specify whether they want to see the reminders when they open the QuickBooks data file. Regardless of this setting, users can select **Company**, **Reminders** from the menu bar or by selecting the **Reminders** icon located to the far right of the icon bar at any time to review the reminder list contents.

Reports & Graphs

Review the My Preferences and Company Preferences for working with reports and graphs. You can override the defaults set here at the time a particular report is prepared. From the menu bar, select **Edit**, **Preferences**; and then on the left side of the Preferences dialog box, select the **Reports & Graphs** preference.

Company Preferences

Review each of the listed preferences; they often affect how certain Accounts Receivable reports calculate:

- **Summary Report Basis**—Choose to have the default basis for reports selected for you. Although this setting affects many reports in QuickBooks, selected reports can be prepared only on the accrual basis (for example, this affects Accounts Receivable or Accounts Payable reports).

- **Aging Reports**—This option sets the default for calculating overdue invoices. You can choose to age from the due date or from the transaction date. Typically, aging from the transaction date causes invoices to show as overdue earlier than if you age from the due date.

- **Reports—Show Items By**—This item reports setting has the following options:

  - **Name Only**—Item Reports display the Item Name/Number associated with the product or service you sell.

  - **Description Only**—Item Reports display the description typed in the New or Edit Item dialog box.

  - **Name and Description**—Item reports display both the Name/Number and the Description field.

- **Reports—Show Accounts By**—This setting offers you the following options for displaying reports:

  - **Name Only**—Reports display the name and account number (if the preference to enable account numbers is selected).

  - **Description Only**—Reports display the description typed in the New or Edit Account dialog box (see Figure 9.7). No account numbers display on the reports.

  - **Name and Description**—Reports display the account number (if enabled in preferences), the name, and the description as typed in the New Account or Edit Account dialog box in parentheses (see Figure 9.8).

- **Classify Cash**—If you need to prepare a cash flow statement, QuickBooks uses these settings to determine which accounts are considered Operating, Investing, or Financing. This preference does not specifically relate to accounts receivable.

- **Format**—This option enables you to override the default header, footer, and font for all QuickBooks reports. Do not override the Report Title, Subtitle, or Date Prepared because QuickBooks will accurately fill in this information for you each time you prepare a report.

Figure 9.7
Enter an optional description in the New or Edit Account dialog box; reports can display this description.

Figure 9.8
Reports show the additional description when you select the Name and Description reporting preference.

My Preferences

The My Preferences selections include the following:

- **Prompt Me to Modify Report**—This opens the Modify Report dialog box with each created report. (This action is the same as selecting Customize Report from a displayed report.)

- **Reports & Graphs**—These are refresh options for reports and graphs when data changes. These prompt the user to refresh or to not refresh.

- **Graphs Only**—These are specific display settings for preparing graphs.

Sales Tax

The Sales Tax preference shown in Figure 9.9 is important if your business is required to collect sales tax on sales made to your customers. Be sure to research each state's sales tax regulations so you can comply with the laws and avoid penalties. From the menu bar, on the left side of the Preferences dialog box, select **Edit**, **Preferences**; then select the **Sales Tax** preference.

Company Preferences

To enable sales tax tracking, next to the Do You Charge Sales Tax? Field, select **Yes**. Additionally, complete the following selections:

- **Set Up Sales Tax Item**—When you click the Add Sales Tax Item button, QuickBooks opens the New Item dialog box with the Sales Tax item type selected. Here you define a name for the sales tax item, type a description and a rate, and assign the tax agency you will be remitting the collected tax to. A separate drop-down list enables you to select your most common sales tax item.

Figure 9.9
Use these Company Preferences to configure Sales Tax defaults in QuickBooks.

- **Assign Sales Tax Codes**—This is the name of the code that will be assigned to your product or service items. Usually the defaults of Tax and Non are considered appropriate. You can select to have a *T* print on your customer invoices for items that are taxable. This option is useful if on one invoice you sell both taxable and nontaxable items.

- **When Do You Owe Sales Tax?**—If you are not sure what each state department of revenue requires, review the websites or call to get the correct information.

- **When Do You Pay Sales Tax?**—This setting tells QuickBooks what date range to select automatically when paying your sales tax. For example, if you select **Monthly**, QuickBooks computes the amount owed for the previous month in the Pay Sales Tax Liability dialog box. This setting also defaults the reporting period for Sales Tax Liability reports.

My Preferences

There are no My Preferences for Sales Tax.

Send Forms

For sending forms, users have the option to use Web Mail, Outlook, or QuickBooks Email. From the menu bar, select **Edit**, **Preferences**; then on the left side of the Preferences dialog box, select the **Send Forms** preference.

Company Preferences

This preference enables you to set email defaults, including a default message when sending supported forms or reports. Select the different forms from the Change Default For drop-down list. Click the Spelling button to check your template content for spelling errors.

Create multiple email templates with merged data from the QuickBooks file. You can select from these templates when emailing by selecting from the menu bar **File, Send Forms**.

Figure 9.10 QuickBooks provides the option to create multiple email templates.

My Preferences

These settings affect the currently logged-in user:

- **Auto-Check the "Email Later"**—If enabled, QuickBooks automatically selects the To Be Emailed checkbox on newly created invoices where the customer's Preferred Delivery Method is email.

- **Send Email Using**—You can select your preferred method for sending transactions and reports:

  - Web Mail

  - Outlook

  - QuickBooks Email (Using Billing Solutions)

QuickBooks users can use Outlook, Outlook Express, other web-based email (such as Gmail or Hotmail), or the QuickBooks email server as the preferred method for sending reports and transactions from within QuickBooks. If you select **Outlook**, however, your preference can affect certain Billing Solutions features. From the menu bar, select **Help** and, in the search box, type **billing solutions.**

Spelling

This preference determines how QuickBooks assists you with spelling on accounts receivable transactions. From the menu bar, select **Edit**, **Preferences**; then on the left side of the Preferences dialog box, select the **Spelling** preference.

Company Preferences

There are no Company Preferences for the Spelling preference.

My Preferences

Users can set QuickBooks spelling preferences for sales and purchase transactions and can include custom-added spelling words.

Time & Expenses

Time & Expenses is a specific method of invoicing that is common to the professional services industry. With this method, customers' sales are invoiced based on hours or costs of the project plus an agreed-to markup and/or overhead fee. Select **Edit**, **Preferences** from the menu bar; then on the left side of the Preferences dialog box, select the **Time & Expenses** preference.

Company Preferences

If your company needs to provide customers with an invoice showing employee or vendor time and/ or individual costs plus an added markup, enable this preference (see Figure 9.11) by selecting from the following:

- **Time Tracking**—The Time Tracking options include the following:

  - **Yes**—With this feature, selecting Yes enables time recording on timesheets, which can be transferred to vendor and employee payment transactions and customer invoices.

  - **First Day of Work Week**—This feature lets you define the first day of the work week.

  - **Mark All Time Entries as Billable**—This feature is useful if you list vendor or employee time on the invoices to your customers.

Figure 9.11
Enable these
preferences if
your company
tracks time or
bills customers
for reimburse-
ment of costs.

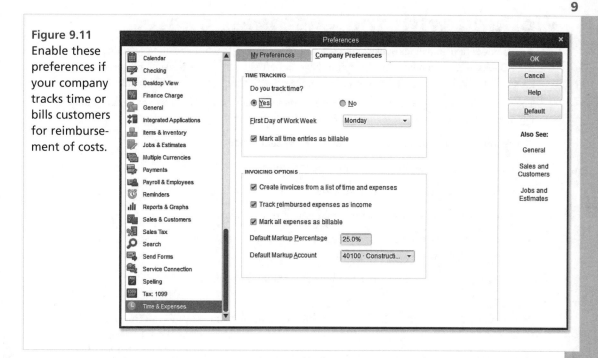

■ **Invoicing Options**—The Invoicing options include the following:

■ **Create Invoices from a List of Time and Expenses**—Select Yes for Do You Track Time to
enable time recording on timesheets, which can be transferred to customer invoices. This is
useful when your company will be detailing on a customer's invoice specific amounts associated with hours paid to vendors, employees, or payees on the Other Names list.

■ **Track Reimbursed Expenses as Income**—Select this checkbox if you want to track costs
invoiced to customers as income. An example might be a law firm that charges the customer
for costs incurred for shipping charges and wants to show the amount as income. The income
would be offset by the expense, usually in an overhead expense account.

■ **Mark All Expenses as Billable**—Select this option to mark all expense line transactions as
billable if a customer is assigned to the line. This feature is useful if you list detailed costs on
the invoices to your customers.

■ **Default Markup Percentage**—Select this option to define a percentage to add to the customer's invoice when billing for time and costs. An example is including a 10% markup, adding
$10.00 to a $100.00 cost reimbursement invoice.

■ **Default Markup Account**—Use this option to select a default account (typically an Income category) for tracking all amounts charged to the customer as markup.

My Preferences

There are no My Preferences for the Time & Expenses settings.

Working with the Customer Center

Are you new to using QuickBooks? I expect one of the first lists you have already added to in QuickBooks is the customer list. You might have imported your customers while creating your new file using the Express Start as discussed in Chapter 1, "Getting Started with QuickBooks," p. 36.

The Customer Center (see Figure 9.12) provides one location for viewing contact details and accessing many customer tasks and reports, including the following:

- Creating a new Customer or Job, or editing an existing one

- Accessing the Add Multiple Customers:Jobs feature

- Recording commonly used customer transactions

- Printing the Customer & Job list, information, or transactions

- Exporting the Customer list or transactions as an Excel or CSV file; importing or pasting customers from Excel

- Preparing customer letters and customizing the built-in letter templates

- Accessing the Collections Center (replaced by the new Income Tracker)

- Filtering your list of customers to include All Customers; Active Customers; Customers with Open, Overdue, or Almost Due Balances; or a custom filter of your choice

- Attaching documents to the customer record, such as a copy of a signed agreement

- Accessing a map and driving directions to the Customer or Job location

- Adding or editing customer notes and to-do reminders and tracking emails sent

- Viewing and filtering transactions by customer or by transaction type

- Preparing a QuickReport, Open Balance Report for the currently selected customer

- Showing Estimates and a Customer Snapshot for the currently selected customer

The following sections provide more details about creating a customer or job and using the Customer Center for researching transactions.

> **◉ tip**
>
> You can customize the information displayed on the Customers & Jobs tab (left side of the Customer Center.)
>
> 1. On the displayed list of customers, right-click with your cursor and select **Customize Columns**.
>
> 2. The Customize Columns dialog box displays. Click a data field listed in the Available Columns box; then in the center of the dialog box, click the Add button. Your selected field is now added to the Chosen Columns.
>
> 3. To reposition the placement of the columns of data, highlight a field in the Chosen Columns box and click either Remove, Move Up, or Move Down.

Figure 9.12
From the
Customer
Center, you
can access
most customer
activities and
useful reports.

Adding or Modifying Customers and Jobs

Customers are the individuals or businesses you sell your product or service to. QuickBooks can also track a job for a customer, if you want to track the profitability for different projects for the same customer. For example, if you're renovating a house, you might create a job for each room. Similarly, an attorney might track the revenue and costs for individual legal matters for the same customer.

Creating jobs is not required in QuickBooks, but it is helpful when you have multiple projects for a single customer. This section offers instruction specifically for setting up customers and jobs of customers.

With a customer listing on the left selected in Customer Center, you can access the following:

- **Transactions**—View and filter the transactions assigned to the currently selected customer or job record.

- **Contacts**—Store multiple contact names for each customer or job record.

- **To Dos**—Keep track of important To Dos by assigning the event an action, such as a call, meeting, task, and so on. Associate the To Do with a lead, customer, vendor, or employee. Assign the task a due date and time with details that will display on your QuickBooks calendar (from the menu bar, select **Company**, **Calendar**).

> **tip**
>
> You can efficiently enter multiple customers or jobs at one time using an Excel-like data entry grid. Do you have a ready-made list of customers in an Excel file? To learn more about adding multiple customer records, see "Add/Edit Multiple List Entries," p. 122.
>
> If you are just setting up your QuickBooks file, review the information in Chapter 1, "Getting Started with QuickBooks," in the section titled "Adding People You Do Business With," p. 36. In this referenced section, you learn how to import your contacts from Outlook, Gmail, or another email provider.

- **Notes**—Add, edit, and filter notes assigned to customer or job records.

- **Sent Email**—Track emails sent to customers or jobs from within QuickBooks. List can be filtered for a specific date range.

> ## tip
>
> If you begin typing the name of your customer or job in the Company Name field, QuickBooks populates the Customer Name and Bill To Name field in a new Customer or Job record.

Creating a Customer and Job Record

To practice adding a new customer record and assigning a job to that customer, open the sample data file as described in Chapter 1, p. 36. If you are working in your own file, use these instructions to begin entering the customers you sell your product or service to:

1. On the Home page, or from the menu bar, click the Customers button and select **Customers, Customer Center**.

2. In the New Customer & Job drop-down list, select **New Customer**.

3. The New Customer dialog box displays with the Address Info tab selected (see Figure 9.13). In the Customer Name field, type **Angela's Decorating**. It is important to mention that no two names from any of the lists in QuickBooks can be the same.

Figure 9.13
Completing the contact information for your customer is good practice for your record keeping.

➡ *For more information, see "When a Customer is Also a Vendor," p. 432.*

4. Leave the Opening Balance field blank. To learn more about entering opening balances in QuickBooks, see Chapter 3. If you are a new business, the amounts your customer owes you will be recorded using the accounts receivable transactions detailed in this chapter.

5. The As Of (date) field supports the Opening Balance field and has no effect when no dollar value is entered in the Opening Balance field.

6. Complete the remaining fields for this practice by adding the contact information and address. Consider completing the Salutation, First Name, and Last Name fields. Doing so enables you to send professional-looking letters to your customers in the future.

7. For this exercise, on the Payment Settings tab, for Payment Terms, select **Net 30** from the drop-down list. This instructs QuickBooks to calculate due dates that are 30 days from your invoice dates. In your own data, use the Add New choice to create terms that suit your specific needs. Leave the remaining Payment Settings as defaults for this exercise.

When you are working with your file, you can define these additional fields:

- **Account No**—This is the account number you assign to your customer; it can optionally be printed on customer transactions.

- **Preferred Delivery Method**—Select this if you will be using the Create Batch Invoices feature available with QuickBooks Premier, Accountant, and Enterprise.

- **Preferred Payment Method**—Prefill the customer payment transaction with this default.

- **Credit Card Information**—Safely and securely store your customer's credit card numbers for ease in processing payments. However, be sure to review the instructions for setting up user rights in the file, to limit who can modify or view this information. See more information in Chapter 1, p. 236.

- **Credit Limit**—Setting this limit enables QuickBooks to warn you when a transaction will exceed the allowed credit.

- **Price Level**—Available with QuickBooks Premier, Accountant, or Enterprise, this offers the capability to default to a specified rate for the items or services you sell. For example, you might offer a 10% discount on all purchases made by this customer. You can have only one price level assigned per customer, and it cannot be based on volume pricing. Refer to Figure 9.25 for the information used to create a Price Level.

  ➡ *For more flexibility with pricing, see "QuickBooks Enterprise with Advanced Pricing," p. 826.*

- **Add Online Payment Link to Invoices**—Choices include using the company default set in preferences, using the bank only, using bank or credit card payment links, and turning off the links on invoices for this customer.

8. Click the Sales Tax Settings tab. The information in this dialog box defaults from the Sales Tax preferences discussed earlier in this chapter. If necessary, you can change them at the time the transaction is created.

9. Click the Additional Info tab. If you're working in the practice file, select **Commercial** from the Customer Type field, or select **Add New** to create your own customer type. Many sales reports can be filtered by customer type.

10. Leave the Rep field blank for this exercise. In your own data, you can select the Rep field if you will be tracking sales by Rep.

11. For this exercise, leave the custom fields blank. When working with your data, you can click the Define Fields button and add custom fields that you assign to your Customer, Vendor, or Employee records. You can also add these custom fields to your sales transactions and include them in many reports.

12. Select the **Job Info** tab. For this exercise, leave the Job Status information blank. In your own file, if you are tracking project activity at the customer level, complete the fields as needed. Some of the job profitability reports can be filtered by these fields.

13. Click OK to close the New Customer dialog box. You return to the Customer Center, and Angela's Decorating is selected.

14. From the New Customer & Job drop-down list, select **Add Job**.

15. Type **Office Remodel** for the Job Name. Complete any other fields as desired on each of the New Job tabs.

16. Click OK to add this job record to the Angela's Decorating customer record. You return to the Customer Center, and Office Remodel displays beneath Angela's Decorating, as Figure 9.14 shows.

Right-click to customize the columns displayed here

Figure 9.14
Create jobs to track costs and revenue for multiple projects for the same customer.

> **⚡ caution**
>
> Specifying terms is part of the process for managing your Accounts Receivable balances. You should also review the Reporting—Company Preferences tab on the Preferences dialog box for settings that affect A/R Aging reports. You can select to have the A/R Aging or Detail reports age from the invoice due date or age from the invoice transaction date.

Now that you have created a new customer in the sample file, you are prepared to create a list of your own customers. When your customer's address or contact information changes, you can return to the Customer Center to edit the same information.

Finding Customer Transactions

The Customer Center provides access for adding to or modifying your customer or job records in QuickBooks, but it also includes convenient access to finding customer transactions.

With the Customer Center open, select a customer or job with your cursor. Then click the Transactions tab on the right, and the individual transactions assigned to that customer or job display. In the previously displayed Figure 9.12, the job Remodel Bathroom for customer Abercrombie, Kristy is selected, and to the right are individual transactions for that job.

You can filter the resulting transactions by selecting options in the Show, Filter By, and Date drop-down lists. The options available differ depending on the type of transaction being filtered for.

In Figure 9.15, the options available for filtering include customer transactions. Your transaction types might differ from the displayed types if you do not have the related feature enabled in preferences. The only transaction type that can have a customer or job record assigned that is not included in these options is the Make Journal Entry.

Another useful feature of working with the Customer Center is available on the Transactions tab. On the Transactions tab, you can locate similar transaction types for all customers.

To do so, follow these steps:

1. From the Customer Center, click the Transactions tab.

2. Select the **Estimates** type, as in Figure 9.16.

3. From the Filter By drop-down list, select **Open Estimates**.

4. (Optional) Filter for a specific date range.

5. Click any column header to sort the data by that column.

6. Double-click any transaction to open the selected transaction. Click Save & Close to return to the Transactions tab details.

7. Click the Print button to print the listed transactions. Click OK to close the Transaction Report message. Click Print to print the list of transactions, or click Cancel to return to the Customer Center's Transactions tab.

Figure 9.15
Conveniently filter for specific transaction types and dates for the selected customer or job.

Figure 9.16
Use the Transactions tab of the Customer Center to find like transaction types.

8. Click the Customer & Job Info tab. QuickBooks displays the Edit Customer or Job dialog box for the selected customer or job, edit as needed. Click OK to close and be returned to the Customer Center:Estimates listing.

9. Click the Excel button to export the list of transactions to an Excel worksheet or CSV file format.

10. (Optional) Click the Manage Transactions or Run Reports drop-down choices at the bottom of the Customer Center.

The Customer Center provides a single location from which you can create or modify your customer records or research customer transactions.

In the next section, you learn about managing your prospects using the Lead Center.

Working with Prospects in the Lead Center

The Lead Center helps you keep track of your business prospecting activities. From the menu bar, select **Customers**, **Lead Center** to open the Lead Center (see Figure 9.17).

From the Lead Center, you can click the following options, which perform various functions:

- **New Lead**—Enter a single new lead.

- **Import Multiple Leads**—Using a preformatted grid, you can enter multiple leads row by row, or copy and paste from an existing Excel worksheet.

- **Excel**—Export a Lead Contact List, a Lead Status List, or a list of Converted Leads (leads that became customers).

Figure 9.17
Keep track of prospect contacts and activities in the Lead Center.

Use the new Lead Center to track important business prospecting activities and save time when creating customer records from your lead base.

Creating a New Lead

To practice creating a new lead record, open the sample data file as instructed in Chapter 1, p. 37. You might also use these instructions if you are getting started with lead management in your own data file:

1. In the Lead Center, click New Lead.

2. In the Name field, type your own name.

3. Complete the remaining fields on the Company and Contacts tab.

4. (Optional) Add other locations or contacts for this new lead.

5. Click OK to complete adding the lead.

6. With the lead selected on the left, click the To Do button on the To Do List to add a new reminder activity. See Figure 9.18. These To Do activities are included in your calendar reminders. See Chapter 18, "Using Other Planning and Management Tools."

Figure 9.18
Stay organized with your prospecting activities by adding To Dos to the lead record.

7. Click any header column to sort the data by that column.

8. Click the Contacts, Locations, or Notes tab to view additional information about your lead.

9. Continue adding a few more leads using any of the mentioned methods.

10. In this exercise, select a lead from the list and click the icon in the top right to Convert to Customer. QuickBooks creates a new customer record from the details in the Lead Center. Select **Yes** to the Convert Lead message, confirming that that action cannot be undone.

11. The lead is no longer listed in the Lead Center. Open the Customer Center to view the new customer record, contacts, and notes that transferred with the lead.

Setting Up Sales Tax

In QuickBooks, you can collect and remit sales tax on behalf of governmental authorities. To do so, you need to establish sales tax items and codes. You might also need to create sales tax groups.

Do not forget to register with the department of taxation for the state(s) you will be selling in. Each state has specific rules and guidelines and also provides you with a unique filing identification number for your business. Not all states require sales tax to be charged to your customers on specific items sold. To see if the taxing authority has special guidelines to follow, call the sales tax department; my experience is that staff members are quite helpful and can direct you to the needed documentation.

> ⌁ **tip**
>
> Each state has different requirements and rates for reporting sales tax. It is critical that you research the applicable regulations and set up QuickBooks correctly. Otherwise, your business can be subjected to expensive— and avoidable—penalties.

Creating Sales Tax Items

Sales tax items identify specific rates charged to your customers and the tax authority vendor to which you remit the sales tax. You might have one sales tax item or several on your item list.

After enabling Sales Tax in preferences, to create a sales tax item in your data file, follow these steps:

1. From the menu bar, select **Lists, Item List**.

2. In the Item drop-down list, select **New** to open the New Item dialog box.

3. In the Type drop-down list, select **Sales Tax Item,** as in Figure 9.19.

4. Enter a sales tax name for the sales tax item; the name should identify the applicable jurisdiction (see Figure 9.20).

5. Enter a Description you want printed on the customer's invoice.

6. In the Tax Rate (%) box, enter the rate the taxing authority charges.

7. In the Tax Agency (vendor you collect for) drop-down list, select the vendor to which you remit your sales tax payments. If your vendor is not set up in QuickBooks, select **Add New** at the top of the list to create a sales tax vendor record.

8. Click OK to save the sales tax item.

Figure 9.19
Sales tax is properly calculated and tracked in QuickBooks when you use the Sales Tax Item type.

Figure 9.20
Setting up your Sales Tax Item with the proper rate and vendor ensures that you collect and remit sales taxes correctly.

With sales tax items created, you can group them into sales tax groups if the state requires collection and reporting on multiple tax entities.

Creating Sales Tax Group Items

Sales Tax Groups are optional in QuickBooks. In many states, you are required to report the collection of sales tax for a combination of city, county, and state, but you want to show the customer a single tax rate. In QuickBooks, you can accomplish this by first creating your individual city, county, and state sales tax items, and then assigning them to a Sales Tax Group item type. The Sales Tax Group item is then assigned to the customer.

To create a Sales Tax Group item in your data file, follow these steps:

1. From the menu bar, select **Lists**, **Item List**.

2. From the Item drop-down list, select **New** to open the New Item dialog box. If necessary, click OK to close the New Feature message.

3. In the Type drop-down list, select the **Sales Tax Group** item.

4. Enter a Group Name or Number that identifies the group.

5. In the Description box, enter the description you want printed on the customer's invoice.

6. In the Tax Item column, from the drop-down list, select the appropriate city, county, or state sales tax items previously created (refer to Figure 9.20).

7. Click OK to save the new Sales Tax Group item.

In the example in Figure 9.21, you are going to collect and remit the sales tax at a rate of 8.05%. In this example, part of the payment will be made to the State Board of Equalization, and the other portion will be paid to the City of East Bayshore. However, when this tax group is assigned to a customer, the invoice shows a single rate of 8.05%.

Figure 9.21
Use Sales Tax Groups to track multiple taxes but show one tax rate on a customer's invoice.

Creating Sales Tax Codes

The primary purpose of sales tax codes in QuickBooks is to identify a product or service as taxable or nontaxable and identify a customer as taxable or nontaxable. If you track sales tax, you must have at least one taxable code, but you might have multiple nontaxable tax codes.

A sales tax code list also is useful when the state has reporting requirements on the types of non-taxable sales you make. Creating a unique nontaxable sales code for each of these nontaxable sales types enables you to report the total sales by nontaxable sales tax type.

Examples of nontaxable tax codes might include some or all of the following:

- Nontaxable reseller

- Out-of-state sales

- Sale to a nonprofit organization

- Government entity

To see a list of suggested nontaxable tax codes, from your keyboard, press F1 to open the Help content. From the Have a Question window, type **Sales Tax Code** and select the **Nontaxable Sales Tax Codes Examples** topic. QuickBooks provides a list of commonly used sales tax codes. See Figure 9.22 for a sample Sales Tax Code List.

When creating a customer invoice, QuickBooks determines whether the item being sold is taxable and whether the customer is assigned a taxable or nontaxable sales tax code before computing any sales tax charge on an invoice.

Figure 9.22
Sales tax codes are assigned to your customers and help with reporting requirements by your taxing authority.

To create a list of Sales Tax Codes or edit the existing Sales Tax Codes in your data file, follow these steps:

1. Make sure you have enabled the sales tax preference, as discussed earlier in this chapter.

2. From the menu bar, select **Lists**, **Sales Tax Code List**.

3. In the Sales Tax Code drop-down list, select **New** to create a new code. Alternatively, select a sales tax code from the list and then, in the Sales Tax Code drop-down list, select **Edit Sales Tax Code**. (Note that a new QuickBooks data file defaults with one taxable tax code and one nontaxable tax code.)

> **note**
> Items are typically assigned a generic taxable or nontaxable sales tax code. You might create other Sales Tax Codes for resellers or out-of-state sales, which you assign to customers but not items.

4. In the New Sales Tax dialog box (or Edit Sales Tax dialog box), Type a three-character code in the Sales Tax Code field. Make the three-character code something meaningful. You will see this code on the dialog boxes New Item, Edit Item, New Customer, and Edit Customer, and optionally on the lines of the customer's invoice.

In the next section, you complete the process and assign the appropriate code to your customer record.

Assigning Sales Tax Codes to Products or Services

Items are created in QuickBooks for use with sales and purchase transactions. The primary purpose of creating items is to handle the behind-the-scenes accounting and to assign the taxable status for an item on a customer invoice.

The following items in QuickBooks enable you to assign a taxable code, as Figure 9.23 shows:

- **Service Item**—created for selling or buying service items

- **Inventory Part**—created for selling or buying inventory items

- **Inventory Assembly**—created for simplifying the build of a finished good

- **Non-inventory Part**—created for selling or buying items you do not stock in inventory

- **Other Charge**—created for selling or buying other items, like freight or miscellaneous charges

- **Discount**—created for use on sales forms to auto calculate discounts

Figure 9.23
When an item is set up with a Non-Tax Code, no tax is calculated, even if the customer is taxable.

Select the proper tax status for this item

If you expect to charge sales tax on an item, it should be marked as taxable even if it is sold to a nontaxable customer. QuickBooks validates whether an item is taxable and then verifies that the customer is taxable before it charges sales tax.

If the item is always nontaxable, even if it is sold to a taxable customer (for example, labor), it should be assigned a nontaxable sales tax code so that it will never have sales tax calculated on the sale of that item.

Some states require the sale of labor services to be taxed if they are invoiced with products and not taxed if they are invoiced separately. Although this might not be the requirement for the state jurisdictions you sell in, to handle this situation, create two Labor Service type items—one named Taxable Labor and assigned a taxable tax code, and another named Nontaxable Labor and assigned a nontaxable tax code. You can then select the appropriate item when you invoice your customers.

Assigning Sales Tax Codes and Sales Tax Items to Customers

Enabling the sales tax preference and creating sales tax items, groups, and codes are part of the sales tax setup. You also need to assign a tax code and a tax item to each customer.

To assign or edit an existing customer's tax code (as well as tax item), as in Figure 9.24, follow these steps:

Figure 9.24
Assign the proper sales tax code and sales tax item to each of your customers.

1. On the Home page, click the Customers button to open the Customer Center.

2. Select the customer for whom you want to assign or edit a tax code.

3. Click the Edit Customer button.

4. In the New or Edit Customer dialog box, click the Sales Tax Settings tab.

5. In the drop-down lists in the Sales Tax Information box, select the appropriate Tax Code and Tax Item. If the customer is a reseller of your product, for best recordkeeping practices, record the Resale No. you might be required to provide, in case of a sales tax audit.

Creating Price Level Lists

Each time you sell a product or service to a customer with an assigned price level, QuickBooks defaults the sales price to match the price level. (This feature is available in specific editions of QuickBooks Premier, Accountant, or all Enterprise Solutions editions.) The price level assigned to a customer affects all sales to the customer for the selected item(s). Price levels cannot be based on discounts earned from buying a product in bulk. However, the following section in this chapter details using a feature that permits offering price discounts based on volume purchasing.

To create a price level, follow these steps:

🔍 **note**
Using the price level feature is truly a time saver! However, I also make the case for showing the customer the full price and then manually adding a discount line on the invoice. Doing this helps the customer see the financial benefit of doing business with your company.

1. Enable the use of Price Levels. From the menu bar, select **Edit**, **Preferences**, **Sales & Customers**. On the Company Preferences tab, place a checkmark in the Enable Price Levels setting. Click OK to save your selection.

2. From the menu bar, select **Lists**, **Price Level List**. After creating the price level, assign the price level to the appropriate customers.

3. Calculate the price level using one of two methods (see Figure 9.25):

   - **Fixed Percentage Price Levels**—An example is creating a Price Level that awards a customer a 10% discount on all purchases.

   - **Per Item Price Levels**—You might have preferred customers who get a specific rate for a particular item.

4. To assign a price level to a customer, from the Customer Center, select a customer on the left.

5. Click the Edit Customer button and choose the Payment Settings tab.

6. From the Price Level drop-down list, select the proper Price Level to assign to this customer. You can assign one Price Level per customer.

Figure 9.25
Price levels automate custom sales prices and can be assigned to specific customers.

It is important to note that Price Levels do not work with the batch invoicing method, discussed later in this chapter. Join me in the following section to learn about a unique pricing tool offered only in QuickBooks Enterprise with Advanced Pricing.

Using Advanced Pricing in QuickBooks Enterprise

New for 2014 is Advanced Pricing, a feature exclusively available with QuickBooks Enterprise Solutions. Advanced Pricing is a subscription-based feature, charged annually. The feature replaces the free Price Levels, discussed in the previous topic, with much more sophisticated automated price settings.

Advanced Pricing provides the capability to have QuickBooks automatically apply:

- Quantity discounts

- Manufacturer discounts

- Scheduled promotions with future start dates

- Thousands of price rules or combinations of rules

With Advanced Pricing, QuickBooks automatically changes the prices of items on sales forms according to the rules you create. Each price rule can contain multiple conditions that must be met before QuickBooks changes the sales price.

Price Rules

After purchasing Advanced Pricing, follow these steps to set up a Price Rule:

1. Enable Advanced Pricing. From the menu bar, select **Edit**, **Preferences**, **Sales & Customers**. From the Company Preferences tab, select **Enable Advanced Pricing** and choose your option for handling price rounding.

2. If your file previously had Price Levels, you will see a message about QuickBooks converting these to Price Rules. Click to dismiss the message. It is prudent at this time to review the details of the former Price Levels that are now Price Rules.

3. To create a new Price Rule, from the menu bar, select **Lists**, **Price Rules**. The New Price Rule window displays.

4. From the Price Rule drop-down list at the bottom of the Price Rule List, select **New**.

5. Type a Price Rule Name and Description (see Figure 9.26).

Multiple conditions can be assigned to one Price Rule

Figure 9.26
With Price Rules, QuickBooks automates pricing when conditions are met.

6. Provide conditions for the newly created Price Rule. These conditions can be any combination of the following:

   - Customer Name, Type, Job Type or Custom Fields

   - Item Name, Item Type, Preferred Vendor

   - Class

   - Sales Rep

7. Select a **Date Range** if this promotion is for a specific period of time.

8. Specify the price to be a percentage or amount decrease or increase over the item's current base price. The base price is determined by the item's Sales Price or Rate, depending on which item type you are assigning. Or you can choose to calculate the decrease or increase from the cost recorded on the item's record.

9. In the Options section, select whether there are to be any Price Overrides. When selected, you can specify a price for selected items that will be used instead of the Price Rule decrease or increase.

10. Select **Exclusive Rule** when you want this rule to not be combined with any other rules used in calculating the price for items on sales forms.

11. Click OK when finished.

Quantity Discount

Also included with your Advanced Pricing subscription is Quantity Discounts. As detailed previously, with Quantity Discounts, you can reward your customers for making bulk purchases. For example, QuickBooks can charge different prices when a customer buys 10 to 19 items, or 20 to 29 items, or 30 or more items.

After purchasing Advanced Pricing, follow these steps to set up a Quantity Discount and assign it to a specific item (product or service):

1. Enable Advanced Pricing. From the menu bar, select **Edit**, **Preferences**, **Sales & Customers**. From the Company Preferences tab, select **Enable Advanced Pricing** and choose your option for handling price rounding.

2. If your file previously had Price Levels, you will see a message about QuickBooks converting these to Price Rules. Click to dismiss the message.

3. To assign Quantity Pricing to an item from the menu bar, select **Lists**, **Item List**; with an item selected, on the right, click the Qty Discount button to open the Quantity Discount window for the selected item (see Figure 9.27).

Figure 9.27
Quantity
Pricing is new
to Enterprise
2014; reward
your customers
for bulk
purchases.

4. In the Qty From column, type an amount. Note that, for this feature to work properly, your item should have an amount recorded in the Rate (or Cost) field of an Item record.

5. Enter a discount %. The New Rate column calculates automatically.

6. Optionally, enter the New Rate amount. The Discount % calculates automatically.

7. Select a Discounts effective date.

8. Click OK when completed.

🔊 caution

Multiple price rules and quantity rules can both apply on a single customer invoice. Test the use of the Price Rule and the Quantity Rule, to make sure you achieve your desired results.

QuickBooks provides details when price rules are used on an invoice, but not when Quantity Discounts are used. See Figure 9.28.

You can now create invoices to customers, and QuickBooks will automatically calculate Price Rules and Quantity Discounts where the conditions are met.

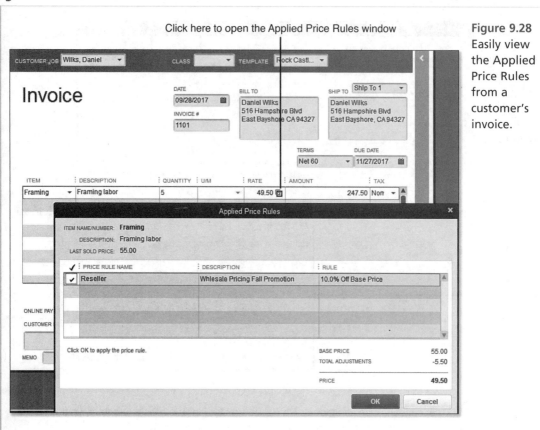

Click here to open the Applied Price Rules window

Figure 9.28 Easily view the Applied Price Rules from a customer's invoice.

Creating Payment Terms

QuickBooks terms offer a shortened description and calculate on an invoice when you expect to receive payment from a customer or when a vendor expects to receive payment from you. For example, 1% 10 Net 30 is an expression for payment due in 30 days, with a 1% discount if paid within 10 days.

If you want the due date to be a specific date, use the Date Driven terms and complete the necessary fields.

Creating a Payment Term

To practice creating a payment term, open the sample data file as instructed in Chapter 1, p. 37. You might also use these instructions if you are creating a new payment term in your own data file:

1. From the menu bar, select **Lists, Customer & Vendor Profile Lists, Terms List**. A list of terms displays (see Figure 9.29).

	Terms List	– □ ×

TERMS

1% 10 Net 30

2% 10 Net 30

Due on receipt

Net 15

Net 30

Net 60

Terms ▼ Reports ▼ ☐ Include inactive

Figure 9.29
Terms lists calculate due dates on customer and vendor transactions.

> 2. In the Terms drop-down list, select **New**. The New Terms dialog box displays (see Figure 9.30).

	New Terms	– □ ×

Terms [45 Days]   [OK]

◉ Standard   [Cancel]

Net due in [45] days.   [Next]

Discount percentage is [0.0%]. ☐ Term is inactive

Discount if paid within [0] days.

Figure 9.30
Complete all the fields when creating a new payment term.

> 3. In the Terms field, type **45 Days**.
>
> 4. Select the **Standard** option and type **45** in the Net Due In field.
>
> 5. Click OK. You return to the Terms List.
>
> 6. (Optional) Click the Reports button, and then select **QuickReport** to prepare a report of transactions using the selected term.
>
> 7. You can now assign this term to the customer and vendor record or transactions.

Customizing QuickBooks Forms

You can customize most forms in QuickBooks, such as sales orders and customer invoices. You can access these powerful features from the ribbon toolbar tabs displayed at the top of most transactions.

 To learn more about working with the Create Invoices ribbon, see "Using the Ribbon Toolbar," p. 350.

When customizing the QuickBooks invoice form, you can use these options:

- **Overall Design**—Includes how the form looks, whether the form has a design imprint, and whether field titles are shaded, as well as other format options.

- **Data Fields**—Customizes the data layout on a form.

Let's first tackle customizing the overall design of the invoice using the Customize My Forms Wizard.

Using the Customize My Forms Wizard

To create a consistent look and feel for your printed forms, consider using the Intuit—Customize My Forms Wizard. This feature is free for the first 30 days for each QuickBooks data file. After 30 days, if you need to make changes to a design, the fee is $4.99 per design. Any changes you pay for come with a 60-day satisfaction guarantee.

In just a few simple steps, you can add a professional look to all the QuickBooks forms. To customize QuickBooks forms, follow these steps:

1. From the menu bar, select **Customers**, **Create Invoices**.

2. To customize your forms, select the **Customize Design** icon on the Formatting tab of the ribbon toolbar at the top of the transaction and select **Customize Design**.

3. The QuickBooks Forms Customization dialog box opens (see Figure 9.31). An Internet connection is required. Choose a background that is specific to your business from the Industry drop-down list. As you select a background, the resulting design displays on the right for you to view.

4. Click the Add button under Company Logo to browse for your logo file. If you do not have a company logo, click the Need a Logo? Get Started button. Intuit has partnered with 99designs to offer affordable custom design services.

> **note**
>
> If you want to "practice" using this tool before committing the changes to your own forms, use the Rock Castle Construction file as instructed in Chapter 1, p. 36.
>
> When using the sample data for this exercise, you cannot save the design or apply it to your own data's QuickBooks forms.

> **note**
>
> Our firm uses this same Intuit design service partnered with 99designs to create the logo displayed on our website, www.quick-training.com.

5. Click Next to display Step 2—Colors and Fonts, shown in Figure 9.32. Select your font and grid colors overall or for specific fields by clicking the appropriate drop-down list. A grayed-out field indicates that the data for that field does not exist in your QuickBooks data file. (Optional) Place a checkmark in the box to indicate that you mail your invoices in window envelopes. Click Next.

6. Step 3—Select a Grid Style displays. Click to select a shaded style grid of your choice. Click Next at the top of the dialog box.

7. Step 4—Review Design displays. Click the Back button to make changes. Click Continue to select the forms to assign the design to. Click No Thanks to cancel your changes. You are redirected to a website that displays matching business forms.

Figure 9.31
Add a professional look to your business forms.

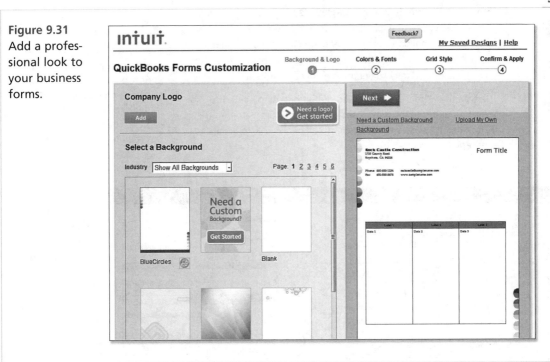

Figure 9.32
Select font and grid colors and other design options for your customized forms.

8. The Apply Design dialog box displays (see Figure 9.33). Place a checkmark next to each of the forms to which you want to apply the customized design. You can select from the many QuickBooks forms (Invoice, Sales Receipt, Purchase Order, and so on), making it easy to customize several forms at once.

9. Click Apply. The Design Applied dialog box displays with instructions for identifying your customized templates on the Templates list. After reading the details, click OK to close the message.

> 🔍 **note**
>
> If you are prompted for payment to apply the designs to your forms, this indicates that you have previously used the initial free service. After a period of time, the service is available but requires a minimal fee.

Figure 9.33
Apply the design customization to multiple forms at once.

10. The Save Design Online (Recommended) dialog box displays with these options:

   - **Save**—The design is available for future editing; you are prompted to define a name for the design and to create a secure login for future editing. A message displays showing the date the form was customized and the last day to make changes without an additional fee. Click OK to close.

   - **No Thanks**—Select this if you do not want to save the design. A warning message displays; click OK to close, and you are redirected to a website showing other business items that match your customized style. Close the open web pages when completed reviewing the information.

11. The Intuit Business Forms web page displays. Click the X in the top-right corner to close the web page when you're finished with your review of the information.

Now that you have customized the overall design of your invoice form, let's look at managing the data that is both displayed on the screen during input and printed on the customer's invoice.

Using the Customize Data Layout Tool

Use the Customize Data Layout tool to create a new template or edit the layout and design of an existing invoice, purchase order, or other template. One distinct difference from the method taught previously is that the changes you make now are only for the currently selected form. If you want to make changes to the format for multiple forms at one time, use the method discussed in the previous section.

Customizing the Data Layout on an Invoice Template

In this exercise, you create a new invoice template using the sample data as instructed in Chapter 1, p. 37. Your selection options might differ, depending on the version of QuickBooks you are using and whether you are using a different sample data file.

To customize the QuickBooks data layout on forms, follow these steps:

1. From the menu bar, select **Customers, Create Invoices**.

2. Select the **Manage Templates** icon on the Formatting tab of the ribbon toolbar at the top of the Create Invoices transaction.

3. The Manage Templates dialog displays. Scroll through the list of templates to select the template you want to modify. As each template is selected, a preview of the finished template displays to the right. For the instructions that follow, I have selected the Intuit Product Invoice. Click OK when you have selected the template you want to modify.

4. The Basic Customization dialog box displays. Review the information that you can modify from this dialog box, including the following:

    - **Use Logo**—Browse for your logo image file to attach to the form. QuickBooks copies the logo to a folder that resides in the same location as your QuickBooks data file.

    - **Select Color Scheme and Apply Color Scheme**—Alter the color of borders and header fonts.

    - **Change Font For and Change Font**—Select a data field and choose Change Font to change the font for that specific field.

    - **Company & Transaction Information and Update Information**—Click to select the fields you want to display on your form, and then click the Update Information button.

5. Click the Additional Customization button at the bottom of the screen.

6. If prompted with the Locked Template message, click the Make a Copy button. Intuit protects the original templates and does not allow you to edit them without making a copy first. The Additional Customization dialog box displays with the Selected Template name in the top left.

7. Click the following tabs to modify the respective information:

    - **Header**—Each field selection offers the option to view onscreen, print on the invoice, and add a title. See Figure 9.34.

- **Columns**—Each field offers the option to select which columns appear onscreen and in print, and in what order. Accept the default title or assign a new title to each field. See Figure 9.35.

Figure 9.34
Customize your forms for which fields to display onscreen and print on the invoice.

Figure 9.35
For your customized forms, define the label and order of the displayed and printed fields.

- **Prog Cols**—If you have enabled Estimates or Sales Orders, these fields allow you to select which columns appear onscreen or in print, and in what order. Accept the default title or type a new title in the field.

- **Footer**—These fields enable you to manage the data that displays at the bottom of forms onscreen and in print. Accept the default title or assign a new title to the field. Optionally, select to include a long text disclaimer on your invoice and to include the Intuit PaymentNetwork link (allowing your customers to pay online by check) on printed invoices.

- **Print**—Here you find settings for managing the printing of the invoice, adding page numbers, and printing trailing zeros.

8. If you added any fields to your form, you might be prompted with a Layout Designer message. For this exercise, click OK to dismiss the message.

9. Click Print Preview to take a closer look at the changes.

10. At the bottom of the Additional Customization dialog box, click the Layout Designer button. Use the layout designer in Figure 9.36 to do the following:

Figure 9.36
Use the layout designer to rearrange the fields or modify the attributes of the field.

- Modify the properties for the selected field's font, text, border, and background.

- Add a text box, data field, or image.

- Copy or remove a field.
- Use the Copy Format button to apply formatting from one field to others. Click End Format to turn off this feature.
- Make multiple fields the same height, width, or size by holding down the Ctrl key on your keyboard while selecting the desired fields.
- Click Center to place a selected field in the center of the form.

11. Click Undo or Redo as needed.

12. Use the Zoom In or Out buttons to see the detail more closely.

13. Click the Margins button to set the margins for the form. Click OK to close.

14. Click the Grid button to see various options related to the grid. Click OK to close.

15. If you use window envelopes, click Show Envelope Window to determine whether the business address is positioned correctly.

16. Click OK to save your changes, or select **Cancel** or **Help**. Select **Yes** to the Layout Designer message to return to the Additional Customization dialog box.

17. Click OK to close the Additional Customization window. Click OK to close the Basic Customization dialog box. You return to the Create Invoices dialog box (in this example).

You can use the newly created or modified invoice format when preparing an invoice for your customers.

🌑 tip

QuickBooks can help you put on a professional look for your communications with suppliers and customers. To download ready-made customized forms, from the ribbon toolbar at the top of a displayed Create Invoices transaction, click the Formatting tab and choose Download Templates. An Internet connection is required.

The Forms Intuit Community site displays. Scroll through the list of forms that you can download and use with your QuickBooks data.

Forms include Credit Memos, Estimates, Invoices, Purchase Orders, Sales Orders, Sales Receipts, Statements, and, specifically for nonprofit entities, Donation forms.

Accounts Receivable Processes

Within QuickBooks, you have some flexibility in how you handle your company's receivables workflow. Your company might use some or all of the transaction types listed in this chapter, depending on the product or service that you sell.

In the section "Preferences That Affect Accounts Receivable" in this chapter, I discuss the preferences you can define after you determine what sales transaction type or feature you need.

Table 9.1 details the transactions used in the Accounts Receivable module and their primary purposes.

Table 9.1 Accounts Receivable Transactions

Transaction Types	Primary Purpose
Estimates	Create a job budget and proposal
Sales Orders	Record a committed sale
Invoices	Record the sale of services or products on account
Sales Receipt	Record the sale of services or products COD (cash at the time of delivery)
Receive Payment	Record customer payment of invoices
Online Payments	Download online customer payments (requires a monthly subscription)
Record Deposits	Record the bank account deposit
Statement Charges	Assess customers' recurring charges
Finance Charges	Assessed to customers with a past-due balance
Statements	Periodic statement provided to the customer of account activity
Refunds & Credits	Returns or credits given to customers

Whether you start with an estimate or sales order or you prepare an invoice for a customer, the proper workflow for recording a sale has some or all of these steps:

1. (Optional) Create a quote using an estimate transaction type. Estimates are useful if you will be providing a quote or multiple quotes for a prospect. Estimates not won can be marked as inactive.

2. (Optional) Create a sales order. Sales orders are best when you have a commitment for a sale to a customer, but you cannot fulfill it at the time the order comes in. Sales orders can be created directly from an estimate.

3. Prepare an invoice, sales receipt, or statement charge. The invoice transaction can be created directly from the estimate or sales order.

4. Receive the customer payment in an Undeposited Funds account.

5. Record the deposit in your bank account.

Performing these related tasks in QuickBooks is easy from the Home page, as Figure 9.1 shows. Whether you are new to QuickBooks or are an experienced user, you will find the Home page useful in getting around QuickBooks and in determining what the next transaction process should be.

Over my years of consulting with clients, I have noticed that many do not know the proper accounts receivable process. Following a recommended workflow helps you avoid some of the more common errors instead of having to fix them at a later date.

Using QuickBooks Estimates

Use a QuickBooks estimate to give prospects a quote for your products or services. The estimate helps you keep track of the sales price you have quoted and keep track of your estimated costs. In accounting terms, the estimate is considered "nonposting," which means that when you record an estimate, you are not yet recording revenue.

Estimates also provide the means for QuickBooks to prepare a budget (expected costs and revenue) for a customer or job. Many job costing reports use the estimate details. You can view these reports using the sample data referred to in Chapter 1, p. 37. From the Reports menu, select **Jobs**, **Time & Mileage**, and view the Job Estimates vs. Actuals Summary or Detail (to name just a couple).

> ### ⟋ tip
>
> Do you need to track Active versus Inactive Estimates? From the ribbon toolbar on the Create Estimates dialog box, select the **Main** tab and toggle the checkmark on or off for Mark as Active or Mark as Inactive.
>
> When an estimate is inactive, it does not display on drop-down lists or reports that are filtered only for active estimates.

Creating an Estimate

To practice creating a new estimate, open the sample data file as instructed in Chapter 1, p. 37. If you are using your own data file, make sure you have enabled estimates as discussed in the preferences section of this chapter:

1. On the Home page, click the Estimates icon. The Create Estimates transaction displays (see Figure 9.37).

Figure 9.37

Use estimates to track your projected job costs and to save time creating invoices when the quote becomes a sale.

2. In the Customer:Job drop-down list, select the customer **Allard, Robert:Remodel** job.

3. For this exercise, leave the prefilled values in the Template, Date, Estimate #, and Name/Address fields.

4. Click the first field in the Item column and use Installation. Accept the prefilled description of Installation Labor.

5. In the Qty field, type **10**.

6. Leave the U/M (Unit of Measure) field blank.

7. Accept the Cost field default of $35.00.

8. In the Markup field, type 30%. (See the caution that follows this sidebar.) Accept the default Tax line assignment.

9. In the Item column on the next available row, select the non-inventory part, **Flooring**.

10. In the Qty field, type **1**. Leave the U/M (Unit of Measure) field blank.

11. In the Cost field, type **2,500.00**.

12. In the Markup field, type **30%**. Accept the default Tax line assignment.

13. Click Save & Close to complete the estimate, or click Save & New to practice creating another estimate.

You now have an estimate and can track quotes you provide to your prospects. When your prospect becomes a customer, create the invoice from the estimate.

You can also use estimates to create sales orders, which the next section covers.

📡 caution

When working with estimates, if you want the markup to be a percentage over cost, you must also type the percent (%) character. To charge a fixed dollar amount over cost, type the dollar amount.

If you do not include anything in the Markup column, QuickBooks job budget vs. cost reports considers the amount in the Cost column the same as the Total, which is essentially the Sales Price. Best practice is to include a markup percentage or dollar amount.

Using QuickBooks Sales Orders

Sales orders are used to record the sale of products you do not have in stock or services you have scheduled to provide at some future date. Sales orders are perfect for tracking backorders. Sales orders are not available with QuickBooks Pro, but are included with all other editions of the QuickBooks for Windows desktop products.

You can start with a blank sales order, or if you created an estimate, you can create the sales order from the estimate.

The Sales & Customers—Company Preferences tab on the Edit Preferences dialog box offers settings you can adjust, which makes working with sales orders more efficient for your business.

➡ *For instructions on creating sales orders, see "Handling Inventory Backorders," p. 196.*

Creating Customer Invoices

If my guess is correct, this is one of the first sections of the book you have turned to. My clients typically are quick to get an invoice to a customer for payment for the product or service being sold.

This section provides some basic instruction for using multiple methods of invoicing in QuickBooks. You might even learn some new techniques.

Using the Ribbon Toolbar

The ribbon toolbar is accessible from the top of the Create Invoices dialog box and on other transaction types. The selections on the toolbar differ depending on the particular transaction type that is displayed.

When working with the Create Invoices transaction, on the ribbon toolbar at the top of the transaction, you have the following available:

- **Main**—On this tab, access these commonly used transaction tools and features:

  - **Find**—Search for a specific invoice, or use the arrows to move backward or forward one record at a time.

  - **New, Save or Delete**—Create a new transaction, save a transaction, or delete the currently displayed transaction.

  - **Create a Copy**—Duplicate the currently displayed invoice.

  - **Memorize**—Assign the displayed transaction to a list of memorized transactions. More information follows in this section.

  - **Mark as Pending or Mark as Final**—When an invoice is marked as pending, it is considered nonposting and does not affect your Accounts Receivable balance or the accounts assigned to the items used. I recommend not using this method and instead using sales orders when you need to record a committed sale that you cannot fulfill at the time of the commitment.

  - **Print or Email (with option for Later)**—Here you have options for providing the invoice to your customers. When you select the box for Print Later or Email Later, you can efficiently process these multiple transactions at one time.

  - **Attach File**—This option gives you free document storage (local on your server or computer hard drive) of scanned documents, emails, and so on.

  - **Add Time/Costs**—This is useful if you do Time and Expense Invoicing, discussed later in this section.

  - **Apply Credits**—Click to apply open credits for the selected Customer or Job.

  - **Receive Payments**—Record money in from your customer for this specific invoice.

  - **Create a Batch**—Create a batch of invoices when the customers being invoiced all share the same invoice template, date, items, and rates. The section "Batch Invoicing," later in this chapter, covers this more.

  - **Refund/Credit**—Selecting this icon opens the Create Credit Memos/Refunds dialog box. If you click the icon when a saved invoice is displayed, QuickBooks creates a new Credit Memo with the same lines as on your original invoice.

- **Online Pay**—Learn about how you can sign up (no monthly fee) for taking online payments from your customers. Our company wouldn't be without this service. If you are not presently accepting credit cards from your customers, let the author's company provide you with a quote and any current giveaways for signing up for a merchant services account. Email the author at info@quick-training.com.

- **Formatting**—On this tab, you can access the following:

  - **Preview**—View the invoice format as your customer would see it.

  - **Manage Templates**—See a list of all the templates available with the currently opened QuickBooks file.

  - **Download Templates**—Intuit offers many customized forms already; be sure to check this out! An Internet connection is required.

  - **Customize Data Layout**—Settings here include ways to control what data displays and what data prints, along with many other useful settings.

  - **Spelling**—Spell-check the currently displayed transaction. Customize your spell checker list by selecting **Edit**, **Preferences**, **Spelling**, and choosing the My Preferences tab.

  - **Insert Line**—Insert a line directly above where your cursor is placed on the displayed transaction. A shortcut to this same task is available by pressing Ctrl+Insert on your keyboard.

  - **Delete Line**—Delete the currently selected line. A shortcut to this same task is available by pressing Ctrl+Delete on your keyboard.

  - **Copy Line**—Copy the selected line to the windows clipboard.

  - **Paste Line**—Duplicate the line details in the clipboard to the currently selected line.

  - **Customize Design**—You can customize multiple forms in just a few steps with self-service and paid-for service. Use this to create a new customized design or apply a saved design.

- **Send/Ship**—QuickBooks offers several options for managing distribution of your invoice to your customers, including the following:

  - **Email**—Email a single invoice or a batch of invoices at one time.

  - **FedEx, UPS, USPS**—Include options when working with these shipping vendors to send, find, schedule, track, and print postage on shipping labels or directly on envelopes (fees might apply).

  - **Mail Invoice**—Use your own web mail account to send invoices by email. Sign up for Intuit QuickBooks Billing Solutions and send your customer an invoice with a tear-off remittance slip, as in Figure 9.38.

  - **Prepare Letter**—Efficiently communicate with your customers by preparing letters directly from your QuickBooks file. Customize the letter templates to meet your business's specific needs.

- **Reports**—Access these reports detailing the currently displayed transaction:

  - **Quick Report**—Displays only if a Create Invoices transaction is open.

Figure 9.38
Using Intuit's QuickBooks Billing Solutions; provide your customers with an invoice with a tear-off remittance slip.

- **Transaction History**—Displays related transactions (if any). This information is also available on the Transaction tab to the right of the invoice details.

- **Transaction Journal**—Detailed report showing the behind-the-scenes transaction accounting.

- **View Open Invoices**—Listing by Customer and Job of all open invoices.

- **Sales by Customer Detail**—Detailed sales information by customer.

- **Average Days to Pay Summary**—Useful details about the length of time it takes for your customers to pay their balances.

You are now ready to create a basic invoice to provide to your customers.

Creating a Basic Invoice

QuickBooks makes it easy to prepare and send invoices to your customers. A basic invoice might contain a single line or many lines, depending on the nature of the products and services you provide.

tip

When entering data, you can use common keyboard shortcuts to complete transactions. For this exercise, start typing **Rice** into the Customer:Job field—the customer Rice, Linda displays.

Without leaving the field, press the Alt key while you tap the down arrow key to navigate through the list from that point forward.

When you have the proper job selected, use the Tab key to advance to the next field.

Creating an Invoice

To practice creating an invoice, open the sample data file as instructed in Chapter 1, p. 37. You might also use these instructions if you are creating an invoice for your own customers:

1. On the Home page, click the Create Invoices icon. Depending on the sales and customer preferences you have enabled, you might have to select Create Invoices from the drop-down list next to the Invoices icon.

2. The Create Invoices transaction displays, as in Figure 9.39. Select the **Rice, Linda:Repairs** job.

Figure 9.39
Creating a basic invoice is simple using QuickBooks.

3. In the Class field, select **Remodel**.

4. Leave the prefilled Template, Date, Invoice #, Bill To, Ship To, Terms, and Due Date details. If you are working in your own data, optionally choose a different template.

5. Select the **Floor Plans** item in the Item column.

6. Accept the prefilled description.

7. In the Quantity field, type **2** and leave the U/M (Unit of Measure) field blank.

8. In the Rate field, type **100.00**. QuickBooks did not include a rate because the item record did not have a value recorded in the Sales Price field of the stored item record. QuickBooks automatically calculates the row total. The item used, Floor Plans, is a nontaxable item (per the original setup of this item), even though the customer is taxable.

9. (Optional) Select to include a link on the invoice for your customer to pay online. Links include options for your customer to pay by Electronic Funds Transfer (EFT) only or to choose between paying by EFT or credit card.

10. (Optional) Select or create a new Customer Message that will display on the invoice for your customer.

11. (Optional) Type a Memo. This detail will be included in your reports and will not be included on the customer's invoice.

12. Leave the **Sales Tax** item selected. This location is assigned to the original setup of your customer on the Sales Tax Settings tab of the customer (not job) record.

13. Leave the assigned Customer Tax Code; this is also set up with the customer's record.

14. In the Print drop-down list, select **Preview**. (Optional) Click the Zoom In button to see more details.

15. Click Close to return to the Create Invoices dialog box.

16. Click Save & Close if you have completed this task, or click Save & New to practice creating another invoice.

🌐 **tip**

New for QuickBooks 2014: conveniently add multiple attachments to your emails generated from within QuickBooks. From the ribbon toolbar or a displayed customer invoice select **Email, Invoice and Attached Files**. You can then browse to select the items you wish to attach.

Do you routinely add multiple items to your invoices? QuickBooks Enterprise Solutions 14.0 (all editions) includes the capability to select multiple items (see Figure 9.40) in one easy, searchable window.

Figure 9.40
QuickBooks
Enterprise
includes the
capability to
quickly add
multiple items
to an invoice.

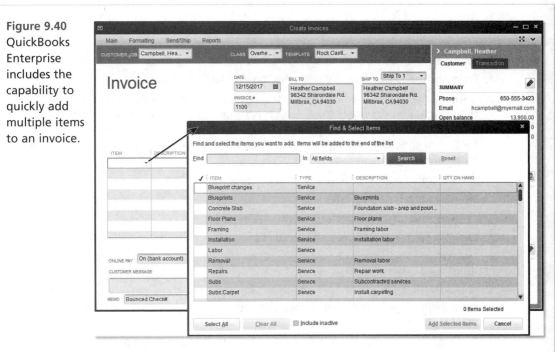

Batch Invoicing

Do you issue recurring invoices to a group of customers for the following?

- Same service or product item?

- Same price?

- Same billing frequency?

- Same invoice template?

If you answered Yes to each of the above, you will save time invoicing using the QuickBooks Batch Invoicing feature.

Batch Invoicing involves three basic steps:

1. Creating your billing group involves naming the group and then assigning customers and/or jobs

2. Selecting the line items and rates for the batch invoices

3. Reviewing the list of invoices to be prepared

You might be asking, what if customers have different items or rates, but on a recurring basis? The next section details how to use Memorized Invoice transactions when Batch Invoicing doesn't meet your specific needs.

> 🔍 **note**
>
> To successfully use Batch Invoicing, make sure that each customer or job has important information in your records, including Terms, Send Method, and Tax Status. These items are more difficult to change after processing a batch of invoices.

Using Batch Invoicing

To practice using Batch Invoicing, open the sample data file as instructed in Chapter 1, p. 37. You might also use these instructions if you are creating Batch Invoicing with your own data:

1. From the menu bar select, **Customers, Create Batch Invoices**.

2. If the warning message "Is Your Customer Info Set Up Correctly?" displays, read the information provided. Your success with using Batch Invoicing depends on how well your customer records are set up. The message refers to the following fields that should be defined for each customer before creating invoices using the Batch Invoicing feature:
   - Customer payment terms
   - Customer sales tax rates
   - Customer and Job preferred send method

3. Click OK to dismiss the message for this practice.

4. The Batch Invoice dialog box displays. Click the Billing Group drop-down list (top right), and select **Add New**.

5. In the Group Name field, type **Monthly** and then click Save. Or, if you are creating a Billing Group in your own data, provide a name that is meaningful to your business. Click Save.

6. In the Search Results box, which displays all active jobs, select a few jobs of your choice. In this example, three jobs were selected, as Figure 9.41 shows. Notice you can search for a specific list of customers or choose **Select All** or **Clear All** for ease in setting up your Billing Group.

Figure 9.41
When creating a Billing Group, select the Customers or Customer:Jobs you want to issue a recurring invoice for.

7. Click Save Group. You can return to this dialog box at any time to modify the list of customers or jobs included.

8. Click Next. "Step 2 of 3" displays, as in Figure 9.42. Leave the Rock Castle invoice template selected. If you are working in your own data, select the invoice template you want to use.

				Batch Invoice			✕

Step 2 of 3: Choose the line items for the batch invoice and click **Next**.   How do I enter the terms, sales tax rate, and send method?

Date 12/15/2017 📅   Template Rock Castle Invoice ▾

ITEM	DESCRIPTION	QUANTITY	U/M	RATE	AMOUNT	TAX
Installation	Installation labor	5		35.00	175.00	Non

Figure 9.42
Batch invoices share the same item, description, quantity, rate, and tax status.

9. In the Item column, select **Installation**.

10. In the Quantity column, type **5**.

11. Leave the U/M (Unit of Measure) blank.

12. Leave the prefilled rate of $35.00 that was originally stored with the item record. QuickBooks calculates the Amount field and assigns the Tax status recorded with the item record.

13. (Optional) Select or add a new Customer Message (not shown).

14. Click Next. "Step 3 of 3" displays, as in Figure 9.43. Unclick any customers or jobs you don't want to invoice at this time.

			Batch Invoice						✕

Step 3 of 3: Review the list of invoices to be created for this batch and click **Create Invoices**.

Invoice Date: 12/15/2017

SELECT	CUSTOMER	TERMS	SEND METHOD	AMOUNT	TAX CO...	TAX RATE	TAX	TOTAL	STATUS
✔	Baker, Chris:Family Room	Net 30	Email	175.00	Tax	7.75%	0.00	175.00	OK
✔	Balak, Mike:Utility Shed	Net 30	Email	175.00	Tax	7.75%	0.00	175.00	OK
✔	Bristol, Sonya:Repairs	Net 30	Email	175.00	Tax	7.75%	0.00	175.00	OK

Figure 9.43
Review the listed terms, the send method, and the tax settings before creating the invoices.

15. Click Create Invoices when you are ready. If any of the fields displayed are blank or show incorrect information, click Cancel. Update the corresponding customer records, and then return to the Batch Invoicing menu to complete the steps listed here.

16. After you click Create Invoices, the Batch Summary dialog box displays. Here you can print or email the newly created invoices. If you did not indicate a Preferred Send method in the Customer or Job record, the invoice is included in the unmarked total.

Memorized Transaction Group

Memorized transactions offer a recurring invoice alternative to Batch Invoicing. With memorized transactions, you can assign different items or prices to each customer, yet still create a group of invoices all at once.

When working with a memorized group, you need to do the following:

1. Create a memorized group.

2. Define the frequency of the recurring transactions.

3. Assign memorized transactions to the group.

Creating Memorized Transactions

To practice using a Memorized Transaction Group of customer invoices, open the sample data file as instructed in Chapter 1, p. 37. This practice builds on the exercise completed in the section titled "Basic Invoicing":

1. From the menu bar, select **Lists, Memorized Transaction List**.

2. In the Memorized Transaction drop-down list, select **New Group**.

3. Type a group name. In this practice, type **Monthly**. See Figure 9.44.

Figure 9.44
Create the Memorized Transaction Group first.

4. In the How Often drop-down list, choose Monthly.

5. For this exercise, you can accept the date that QuickBooks prefills in the Next Date field, or assign a different date if you are using your own data.

6. Click OK to close the New Memorized Transaction Group message. You return to the Memorized Transaction List, and your newly created Group name is in bold text. Next, you add a previously recorded invoice to your memorized group.

7. On the Home page, click the Create Invoices icon. Depending on the sales and customer preferences you have enabled, you might have to select Create Invoices from the drop-down list next to the Invoices icon.

8. At the top left, on the Main tab of the ribbon toolbar, click the arrow pointing to the left. A previously recorded invoice displays. Alternatively, create a new invoice from scratch.

9. From the Main tab of the ribbon toolbar, select **Memorize Transaction**.

10. In the Name field, type a descriptive name, such as the customer or job name on the invoice. When creating a memorized transaction (see Figure 9.45) in your own data file, type a name that will be helpful for you to identify the transaction in a group.

11. Click to select **Add to Group**, and then select your newly created group from the Group Name drop-down list.

12. Click OK.

13. Return to the Memorized Transaction List (see Figure 9.46) to see your memorized transaction now part of the memorized transaction group.

Figure 9.45
Click the Memorize icon on the Main tab of the ribbon toolbar to store a transaction for future recurring use.

Figure 9.46
The Memorized Transaction Group name displays in bold text, with the transactions assigned to that group indented to the right.

14. To process this recurring Memorized Transaction Group, double-click the group name, Monthly.

15. The Using Group dialog box displays, QuickBooks prefills the Date that will be assigned to each of the transactions in the group. Alternatively, choose another date.

16. Click OK. QuickBooks creates the transactions in the group. Click OK again to close the message indicating that the transactions in the group were entered. Review the tip on emailing these forms that follows these steps.

You have learned several easy techniques for invoicing your customers: how to create and send a basic invoice, use the batch invoicing feature, and memorize recurring invoices. Let's get a little more complex with the next invoice method, named Progress Invoicing. This type of invoice is often used in the construction industry or any industry that invoices customers based on % (or $) completion of the work contracted.

 tip

Do you need to print or email your newly created forms? Select **File**, **Print Forms**, or **Send Forms** and follow the instructions.

Progress Invoicing

The progress invoicing feature enables you to generate multiple invoices from a single estimate. To use progress invoicing, you must first enable the preference on the Jobs & Estimates—Company Preferences tab of the Preferences dialog box. (You must log in to the file as the Admin or External Accountant User type.)

Certain industries you do business with might require the work performed or products being made to be invoiced in stages of completion. This method of invoicing is often referred to as *percentage of completion*. Conversely, you would not need to use progress invoicing when you present a single invoice at the point of delivery or project completion.

note

Use your mouse cursor on the sides or corners of the Memorized Transaction list to expand the information, or click the top-right box (next to the X) to expand the list contents.

Creating a Progress Invoice

To practice creating a progress invoice for a customer, open the sample data file as instructed in Chapter 1, p. 37. If you are working in your own data, the Company Preferences for progress invoicing must be enabled on the Jobs & Estimates—Company Preferences tab of the Preferences dialog box.

This practice exercise continues with the estimate created earlier:

1. On the Home page, click the Create Invoices icon. Depending on the sales and customer preferences you have enabled, you might have to select from the drop-down list next to the Invoices, Create Invoices icon. The name of the icon may differ if you have not enabled Time and Expense invoicing as discussed on p. 363.

2. In the Customer:Job drop-down list, select the **Allard, Robert:Remodel** customer.

3. In the Available Estimates dialog box, select the estimate. The selected row is shaded, as in Figure 9.47.

4. Click OK, and QuickBooks displays a Create Progress Invoice Based on Estimate message.

5. For this exercise, select **Create Invoice for Selected Items or for Different Percentages of Each Item**, and then click OK. You might also want to familiarize yourself with the other options. See Figure 9.48. Click OK.

Figure 9.47
Select the Estimate you want to use for creating the progress invoice.

Figure 9.48
When Progress Invoicing is enabled, you can choose from these options when creating an invoice.

6. QuickBooks opens the Specify Invoice Amounts for Items on Estimate dialog box.

7. Toggle the Show Quantity and Rate and Show Percentage options to see how the displayed view changes.

8. In the Qty column for Installation, type **7**. In the same column for Flooring, type **.50** (invoicing for 50% of the materials). Figure 9.49 displays the result of entering these values.

9. Review the dollar total by row displayed in the Amount column.

10. When you click OK, QuickBooks adds the items to your invoice.

11. From the top-right corner of the invoice, in the Template drop-down list (see Figure 9.50), select the **Progress Invoice** template.

ITEM	EST QTY	EST RATE	EST AMT	PRIOR ...	PRIOR A...	PRIO...	QTY	U/M	RATE	AMOUNT	CURR %	TOT %	TAX
Installation	10	45.50	455.00	0		0.0%	7		45.50	318.50	70.0%	70.0%	Non
Flooring	1	3,250.00	3,250.00	0		0.0%	0.5		3,250.00	1,625.00	50.0%	50.0%	Tax

Specify Invoice Amounts for Items on Estimate

Progress Invoice for: Allard, Robert:Remodel

For each item below, specify the quantity, rate, amount or % of the estimate amount to have on the invoice.

☑ Show Quantity and Rate   ☑ Show Percentage

OK
Cancel
Help

Total (w/ taxes)   2,069.44

Note: All items will transfer to the invoice. The quantities and amount will be as you indicated. Although items with a zero amount display on screen, they can be set not to print from the Jobs and Estimates Preferences.

Figure 9.49
Enter either a Qty or a percentage in the Curr % column to add line items to the customer's progress invoice.

Select the Progress Invoice template

Invoice

CUSTOMER:JOB Allard, Robert...   CLASS Remo...   TEMPLATE Progress I...

DATE 12/15/2017

INVOICE # 1100

BILL TO
Robert Allard
92834 Chandler St.
Millbrae, CA 94030

P.O. NO.   TERMS Net 15   DUE DATE 12/30/2017   CONTRACT #

ITEM	DESCRIPTION	EST AMT	PRIOR %	QTY	U/M	RATE	CURR %	AMOUNT	TAX
Installation	Installation labor	455.00	0.0%	7		45.50	70.0%	318.50	Non
Flooring	Flooring	3,250.00	0.0%	0.5		3,250.00	50.0%	1,625.00	Tax

ONLINE PAY On (bank account)

CUSTOMER MESSAGE
Thank you for your business.

MEMO

TAX San Tomas (7.75%)   125.94
TOTAL   2,069.44
PAYMENTS APPLIED   0.00
BALANCE DUE   **2,069.44**

CUSTOMER TAX CODE Tax

Save & Close   Save & New   Clear

Figure 9.50
The Progress Invoice template includes columns for Estimate Amount and Prior Percentage invoiced.

12. For this exercise, click Save & New to practice creating a second invoice. A blank Create Invoice dialog box displays.

13. Repeat the preceding steps 2–4.

14. On the Create Progress Invoice Based on Estimate dialog box, select **Create an Invoice for Selected Items or for Different Percentages of Each Item** (see Figure 9.48). Click OK.

15. QuickBooks prepares the transaction. Click Save on the Main tab of the ribbon. The transaction remains displayed.

16. In the Main tab on the ribbon toolbar, click the Print, Preview option to see the completed invoice.

17. Click Close to return to the Create Invoices dialog box. Click Save & Close.

🕮 caution

Are you tracking inventory in your QuickBooks data file? Be careful to progressively bill only whole increments of inventory part items, such as 3 wheels, instead of 2.5 wheels.

If instead you are trying to create a printable document to record a customer's deposit or prepayment, use the instructions in Chapter 10, "Managing Customers" in the section "Unique Customer Transactions," p. 431.

With progress invoicing, your customers can see the percentage of the quoted contract that they are being invoiced for. The next method, time and expense invoicing, often referred to as cost plus invoicing, meets the needs of customers for whom you quote a fixed markup over your costs.

Time and Expense Invoicing

Time and expense invoicing enables you to charge your customers the costs you incur on their behalf plus an agreed-upon markup (to cover overhead costs and profit).

The time and expenses feature is available in QuickBooks Pro, Premier (all editions), Accountant, and QuickBooks Enterprise Solutions (all editions). You can enable this feature on the Time & Expenses—Company Preferences tab of the Preferences dialog box.

> ## 🔍 note
> It is not necessary to remove (or add) the checkmark in the Billable column if you are not providing your customers a Time and Expense type of invoice.

Before you begin creating a time and expense invoice, you must have billable charges for your customer. The Write Checks, Enter Bills, Credit Card Charges and Make General Journal Entries transactions can all have costs selected as billable, as in Figure 9.51.

Optionally, you can set a preference that defaults all time or all expense entries as billable to your customers when a customer or job is assigned to the transaction line. On the menu bar, select **Edit, Preferences, Time & Expenses** and select the **Company Preferences** tab.

You can review the costs marked as billable by selecting **Reports, Jobs, Time & Mileage, Unbilled Costs by Job** from the menu bar.

Figure 9.51
When creating a customer- or job-related expense, place a checkmark in the Billable column if you need to add the charge to a future customer invoice.

The memo field will print on the customer's invoice

The description from the Items tab will print on the customer's invoice

Creating a Time and Expense Invoice

To practice creating a time and expense invoice, open the sample data file as instructed in Chapter 1, p. 37. You might also use these instructions if you are creating a time and expense invoice for your own customers:

1. Review the preference setting for working with Time and Expense invoicing. On the menu bar, select **Edit**, **Preferences**, **Time & Expenses** (at the end of the list) and select the **Company Preferences** tab. You must be logged in to the file as the Admin or External Accountant user type.

   ➡️ *For more information on selecting the proper preference setting, see "Time & Expenses," p. 316.*

2. Click OK to close the Time & Expenses Preferences dialog box.

3. On the Home page, in the drop-down list next to the Invoices icon, select **Invoice for Time & Expenses**. A message about this improved feature might display. Read and optionally select the **Do Not Display This Message in the Future** checkbox. Click OK to close the message.

4. The Invoice for Time & Expenses dialog box displays. Select a **Date Range**. For this practice exercise, accept the prefilled To Date of 12/15/201x. Figure 9.52 shows the date of 12/15/17.

Click on any header to sort

Figure 9.52
Invoice multiple customers more efficiently after enabling the preference to create invoices from a list of time and expenses.

5. In the sample company, select the **Rock Castle Invoice** template, or select a template from your data that suits your needs.

6. (Optional) Click any header column to sort the list by the selected column. For example, clicking the Total column sorts the list in ascending or descending order of the amount to be invoiced.

7. For this exercise, place a checkmark next to Abercrombie, Kristy:Family Room. In your own file, you could select multiple customers at once, if desired.

8. Select the **Let Me Select Specific Billables for This Customer:Job** checkbox at the bottom of the dialog box.

9. Click Create Invoice. QuickBooks displays the Choose Billable Time and Costs dialog box. From here, you can view expenses marked as billable from the following tabs:

   ■ **Time**—This is employees' time from paychecks; click the Options button to see choices for transferring employee time to the customer's invoice. Click OK to return to the Choose Billable Time and Costs dialog box.

   ■ **Expenses**—These are costs from the Expense tab of a write check, vendor bill, credit card charge, or journal entry.

- **Mileage**—These costs are recorded using the menu Company, Enter Vehicle Mileage.

- **Items**—These are costs from the Items tab of a write check, credit card charge or vendor bill.

10. From the Time tab, place a checkmark in the first column next to the time entry for Gregg O. Schneider. Or optionally, click Select All for this practice. In your own data, you can choose which costs you want to include on the customer's invoice. If you will not be invoicing the client for any of the displayed costs, review the caution that follows these instructions.

11. When you click OK, QuickBooks transfers the charges you selected to the invoice. The Description on the invoice defaults from the item record or the memo field included in most expense transactions (see Figure 9.51, earlier).

12. Click Save & Close. QuickBooks replaces the Billable checkmark on the originating expenses transactions with an invoice icon. This indicates that the cost has been included on a customer invoice.

note

The Choose Billable Time and Costs dialog box enables you to review the expenses invoiced to your customer. You can click any column header to sort by that field. When sorted, the invoice lines will be in the same order as the sort. You can also click the Hide column at the right of a charge to indicate that you won't be invoicing the customer for certain charges.

Choosing to Hide an expense does not remove the expense from your own records; instead, it excludes the expense from this or future Time and Expense invoices.

Do you invoice your customers for the services of vendors or employees? If necessary, you can create billing rate levels (see Figure 9.53) that you associate with your vendors and/or employees. In turn, QuickBooks applies the proper billing rate when you add expenses marked as billable (refer to Figure 9.51) to an invoice. The billing rate feature is available only in QuickBooks Premier and QuickBooks Enterprise editions.

To use billing rates, follow these steps:

1. Create your service items. See Chapter 4 for more details.

2. Create your billing rate levels. From the menu bar, select **Lists, Billing Rate Level List** and follow the prompts.

3. Assign each billing rate level to vendors, employees, or other names, as needed.

4. Invoice your customers using Add Time/Costs. QuickBooks uses the corresponding billing rate you have assigned.

Use time and expense invoicing when you are permitted to add a markup to job expenses.

Figure 9.53
Billing Rate Levels are assigned to vendors, customers, and other name lists. They default the sales price for a person when time is tracked to specific service items.

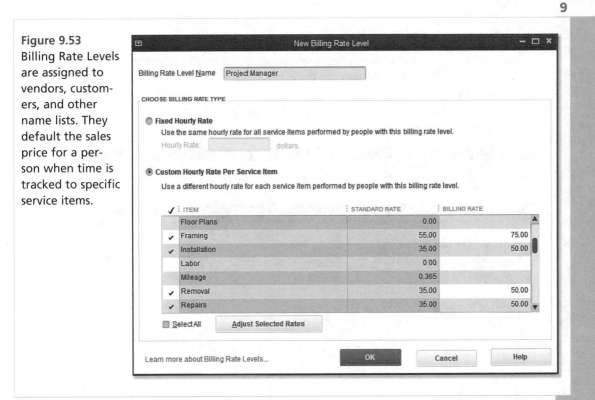

Recording a Sales Receipt

Use a QuickBooks Sales Receipt when you are recording a sale and taking payment at the time of sale, commonly referred to as Cash on Delivery, or COD. Recording a sales receipt does not increase Accounts Receivable because you are receiving payment at the time of sale.

You can add QuickBooks Sales Receipts or remove them from the Home page in the Desktop View—Company Preferences tab of the Preferences dialog box. To change this preference, you need to log in to the file as the Admin or External Accountant User.

Sales receipts are a perfect choice for a company that does not offer terms to its customers. Some retail establishments might summarize the day's cash register tally into a sales receipt for a generic customer named Daily Sales.

You might be asking, where did the money that you just recorded go in your accounting records? First, review your Payments preference, as discussed earlier in this chapter; then learn how to add these payments to a bank deposit in the section "Making the Bank Deposit."

Creating a Sales Receipt

To practice creating a sales receipt, open the sample data file as instructed in Chapter 1, p. 37. You might also use these instructions if you are creating a sales receipt in your own data:

1. On the Home page, click the Create Sales Receipts icon. The Enter Sales Receipts dialog box displays, as in Figure 9.54.

Figure 9.54

Enter sales receipts when payment is collected at the time of sale.

2. In the Customer:Job drop-down list, select **Sage, Robert:Remodel** job.

3. In the Class field, select **Remodel**.

4. For this exercise, leave the Template, Date, and Sale No. as prefilled by QuickBooks.

5. Select the **Check** icon as the payment type. Type **1234** in the Check No. box.

6. In the Item column, select **Repairs**.

7. Using the Tab key on your keyboard, advance to the Qty field and type **5**. QuickBooks prefills the Amount column. Accept the defaulted Tax column data. This tax assignment is assigned to the Repairs item setup.

8. (Optional) Select a **Customer Message**.

9. For this exercise, click Save on the Main tab of the transaction ribbon. In the Print drop-down list on the Main tab of the ribbon, you can preview, print, or choose from other useful commands.

10. Click Save & Close to complete the Sales Receipt, or click Save & New to practice creating another sales receipt transaction.

Recording a Statement Charge

Statement charges are useful if you want to accumulate charges before requesting payment, or if you assess a regular monthly charge to your customer. Use statement charges when you are not going to be providing the customer with an invoice, but instead will provide the customer with a periodic statement.

Recording statement charges one customer at a time can be time-consuming. If this charge is recurring, consider adding the transactions to a Memorized Transaction Group discussed previously.

Recording a Statement Charge

To practice recording a statement charge, open the sample data file as instructed in Chapter 1, p. 37:

1. On the Home page, click the Statement Charges icon.

2. In the Customer:Job drop-down list, select the **Babcock's Music Shop:Remodel** job. See Figure 9.55.

3. For this exercise, place your cursor in the next available row and accept the pre-filled date. The selected customer's Accounts Receivable register displays.

4. Leave the Number field blank. In the Item field, type **Repairs**.

5. In the Qty field, type **5**.

6. In the Class field, type **Remodel**.

Select the Customer and Job here

Figure 9.55
Use statement charges for a customer or job when you are not providing an invoice for the charges.

7. Click Record to save the charge on the customer's register. Repeat steps 2–7 as needed to add more statement charges.

Recording the Customer Payment

Sales Receipts record your customer's payment at the time of the sale. However, many businesses issue invoices or statement charges and expect the customer to remit payment within an agreed-upon number of days.

> ### note
>
> Does your company accept credit card payments from your customers? Although a discount fee is charged, the benefit of possibly getting paid more quickly might outweigh the costs.
>
> Intuit offers a Merchant Service that permits your customers to pay online by check or credit card. You can learn more by clicking the Add Credit Card Processing on the Main tab of the ribbon toolbar on certain transactions. If you would like to receive our discounted rates and receive our current credit card processing promotions, contact the author at info@quick-training.com.

When your customer pays an amount that is due in full or in part, you record a receive payment transaction.

When a customer payment is posted to your bank account depends on your payment preference settings.

Access information about the many online customer payment methods that work with your QuickBooks file at http://payments.intuit.com/products/quickbooks-payment-solutions/quickbooks-online-billing.jsp.

To review your current payment settings, choose **Edit**, **Preferences** from the menu bar and select the **Payments** preference, **Company Preferences** tab. You need to be logged in to the file as the Admin or External Accountant User type. See Figure 9.56.

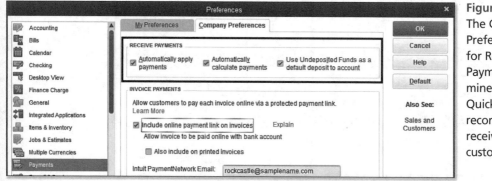

Figure 9.56
The Company Preferences for Receive Payments determines how QuickBooks records money received from customers.

Access these additional features from the following tabs on the ribbon toolbar located at the top of the Receive Payments transaction.

- **Main**—Access common payment actions from the following tabs:

  - **Find**—Click Find to open the Simple and Advanced find dialog box. Or click the arrows to move forward and backward through previously recorded transactions.

  - **New, Delete**—Complete the selected task for the currently displayed transaction.

  - **Print/Email**—Print or email a payment receipt.

  - **Attach File**—Take advantage of free document storage (local on your server or computer hard drive) of scanned documents, emails, and so on.

  - **Look Up Customer/Invoice**—Find a customer or specific invoice.

  - **Un-Apply/Auto Apply Payment**—Clear the payment details in the grid or automatically apply the payment.

  - **Discounts and Credits**—Open the Discount and Credit dialog box. The next section has more details.

  - **Record Bounced Check**—Assists when you need to record a check that is returned for insufficient funds.

  - **Process Payment**—When selected and the transaction is saved, automatically begins the process to approve the payment by credit card or ACH.

  - **Add Credit Card Processing**—Select this to learn about Intuit Merchant Service for QuickBooks.

- **Reports**—Access commonly used reports, including a Processed Payment Receipt and an Open Invoices report.

- **Payments**—Link to adding credit card processing or accepting eCheck processing. Get paid faster!

> **tip**
>
> Often a customer will send in a payment but will not indicate on the payment what invoice he or she is paying for.
>
> On the Main tab of the ribbon toolbar for searching selected fields, click the Look Up Customer/Invoice icon.
>
> From the displayed results, select any of the matches and click the Use Selected Customer or Transaction.

This Receive Payments transaction reduces the balance your customer owes you and increases the balance in your Undeposited Funds account. In the next section, you learn how to add this and other monies received to complete the deposit transaction in QuickBooks.

Recording a Customer Payment

To practice recording a customer payment, open the sample data file as instructed in Chapter 1, p. 37:

1. On the Home page (see Figure 9.1), click the Receive Payments icon.
2. The Receive Payments dialog box displays.

3. From the Received From drop-down list, select **Melton Johnny:Dental office**.

4. In the Amount field, type **5,000.00**.

5. Select the **Credit Debit** icon. See Figure 9.57. The Save Credit & Debit Card Information dialog box displays.

6. Select the proper payment type, and enter the credit card number and expiration date if you will be processing the payment using one of Intuit's Merchant Payment solutions. Click **Done** to return to the Receive Payments window.

Figure 9.57
Record a Receive Payments transaction when a customer remits funds to you.

7. If you selected the preference Automatically Apply Payments, QuickBooks first tries to match the payment with an invoice for the same amount. If a match is not found, the oldest invoice is marked as paid, moving then to each succeeding invoice until the payment is fully applied.

8. For this practice, QuickBooks displays an underpayment message, as well as a link to View Customer Contact Information. Accept the default choice of Leave This as an Underpayment.

9. Click Save & Close to complete this exercise, or click Save & New to practice adding more customer payments.

Making the Bank Deposit

When receiving payments from your customers, you record the payments and then physically store the checks or cash received in a safe place until you can go to the bank.

Depending on the preferences you set, QuickBooks uses an account titled Undeposited Funds to hold payments received but not yet included on a bank deposit ticket.

The Undeposited Funds account also plays an important role in making the bank reconciliation process easier and more accurate. If you list multiple customer payments on one deposit ticket taken to the bank, you need to match this deposit ticket total to the deposit transaction recorded in QuickBooks. By setting the preference to have QuickBooks forward all your customer payments into a temporary Undeposited Funds account (see Figure 9.56), you can group these individual payments in QuickBooks using the Make Deposits transaction. The deposits in your bank account register will now match the deposit amounts on your bank statement.

Check and Cash Payment Deposits

Creating a bank deposit for your cash and check payments correctly is one of the important tasks necessary to properly track the balance of funds you have in your bank account.

Recording a Bank Deposit

To practice making a deposit, open the sample data file as instructed in Chapter 1, p. 37:

1. On the Home page, click the Record Deposits icon.

2. Using the sample data for practice, the Payments to Deposit dialog box displays a listing of payments received that have not yet been recorded as a deposit into the bank account. When you are working in your data, if this message does not display, you do not have any payments that were recorded to the Undeposited Funds account.

3. From the View Payment Method Type drop-down list, select **Cash and Check**. This step is optional, but it helps to group the payments by the type of deposit.

4. Click the Select All button to place a checkmark next to each of the amounts listed. See Figure 9.58. Your total might differ if you did not complete the exercise in the previous section.

5. Compare your deposit ticket total to the payments subtotal on the Payments to Deposit dialog box. See Figure 9.59.

6. When you click OK, QuickBooks adds the selected payments to the Make Deposits dialog box.

7. Confirm that the Deposit To account is correct, and select the Date your bank will credit your account with the funds. Details in the Memo field will display in reports.

8. From the Print drop-down list, select to print a deposit slip (preprinted forms are necessary) or print a deposit summary for your file. See Figure 9.60.

9. Click Save & Close to complete the task, or click Save & New to record another bank deposit.

Figure 9.58
You can filter the Payments to Deposit for specific payment types, helping you group the payments to agree with your bank's deposit records.

This subtotal should match your bank deposit ticket

Figure 9.59
Place a checkmark next to each payment item on your deposit ticket.

Figure 9.60
Using the Make Deposits dialog box is the final step in recording customer payments.

It's really that simple! Create an invoice, receive the customer's payment, and make the deposit into your bank account records. Next, we look at another kind of deposit: when your customer pays you by credit card.

Recording Credit Card Deposits Less a Discount Fee

If you collect credit card payments from your customers, consistently following the process of receiving payments and making deposits is important. Because you don't physically hold the payment from your customer as you do with cash or check payments, tracking these credit card payments accurately and reconciling with the bank's monthly statement helps you avoid some common mistakes.

When your business accepts credit card payments from your customers, your merchant account vendor charges you, the seller, a discount fee. Your credit card processor might charge the fee at the time of the deposit, at the end of the billing cycle, or a combination of both.

If you are charged a fee at the end of the month, you can enter the fee into your checkbook register in QuickBooks or create a journal entry with a debit to your credit card expense account and a credit to your bank account.

What if your merchant vendor reduces the amount of your customer's payment credited to your bank account? To help you keep accurate records, follow these steps:

1. Follow the instructions in the section titled "Recording the Customer Payment," p. 370.

2. Confirm the amount of the deposit made to your bank from your credit card merchant. If you have online access to your bank institution, you can find this information without having to wait for the monthly bank statement.

> **tip**
>
> I teach my clients to leave credit card deposits in the QuickBooks Undeposited Funds account until they know the exact amount and date that money was deposited to their bank.

3. On the Payments to Deposit dialog box, select the credit card payments that were included in the batch transmitted to your bank account. Does your business receive many payments by credit card? Having a printout of the batch details from your merchant vendor can be helpful.

4. Click OK. QuickBooks includes these credit card payments on a Make Deposits transaction.

5. On the next available line, in the From Account column, enter your credit card discount fees expense account. See Figure 9.61.

Figure 9.61
Record discount fees as part of your credit card deposit.

6. In the Amount column, enter a negative amount equal to the fee charged.

7. Confirm that the deposit total on the Make Deposits transaction agrees with the exact amount credited to your bank account by the merchant. Click Save & Close if you are done. Click Save & New to record another deposit.

Timely recording of credit card deposits in agreement with your bank's deposit records will help your business better manage the monies received in your bank account.

Recording and Applying a Customer Credit Memo

Use the Create Credit Memos/Refund transaction when a customer returns a product or you want to reduce the amount a customer owes you and then either give a refund or maintain the credit toward a future purchase.

Creating a Customer Refund Check

To practice refunding an overpayment with a check, open the sample data file as instructed in Chapter 1, p. 37:

1. On the Home page, click the Customers button to open the Customer Center.

2. For this exercise, scroll through the Customers & Jobs list and select the **Hendro Riyadi:Remodel Kitchen** job.

3. Double-click the invoice listed on the right.

4. From Main tab on the ribbon toolbar, select **Refund/Credit** (see Figure 9.62). QuickBooks duplicates the details from the original invoice to a new Create Credit Memos/Refunds transaction.

Figure 9.62
QuickBooks duplicates the invoice lines and creates a credit memo.

5. Review the lines included on the newly created credit memo. When working in your own data, remove individual lines as needed to agree with the products returned or services to be credited.

6. Click Save & Close. QuickBooks displays the Available Credit message.

7. Select the option to **Apply to an Invoice**, as in Figure 9.63.

8. QuickBooks displays the Apply Credit to Invoices dialog box. From here, you can change which invoice or how much of the credit is applied. For this exercise, leave the transaction as shown in Figure 9.64.

9. Click Done.

10. QuickBooks returns to the Create Invoices dialog box. In this practice exercise, a paid stamp displays on the invoice. Click Save & Close to complete the activity, or click Save & New to create another credit memo.

Figure 9.63
Choose how you will record the available credit in QuickBooks.

Figure 9.64
Make sure your records for applying the credit agree with your customer's records.

tip

To efficiently remove lines on a newly created transaction, with your cursor, select a row and press Ctrl+Delete on your keyboard to remove an entire line one at a time.

Refunding a Customer's Overpayment

Has your company received an overpayment from a customer? Although it is rare during difficult economic times, knowing how to handle the transaction can help keep your financial records correct and your customer happy.

When you receive an overpayment, you can leave the overpayment in your books and apply it to future invoices, similar to the process for applying credit memos to open invoices.

However, your customer might request that you refund the overpayment.

Refunding a Customer's Overpayment

To practice refunding an overpayment with a check, open the sample data file as instructed in Chapter 1, p. 37:

1. Record an overpayment in this sample file you are using. On the Home page, click the Receive Payments icon.

2. In the Received From drop-down list, select the **Robson, Darci:Robson Clinic** job.

3. The customer balance displays on the Receive Payments dialog box. In the Amount field, type **12,500.00**. Leave the other fields as they default.

4. QuickBooks displays a message in the lower left about the overpayment. Select **Refund the Amount to the Customer**.

5. (Optional) Click the View Customer Contact Information to edit the customer's address that will print on the check. Click OK to return to the Customer Payment transaction.

6. Click Save & Close.

7. QuickBooks opens the Issue a Refund dialog box, shown in Figure 9.65. In the Issue This Refund Via drop-down list, select **Check**.

Figure 9.65
Be sure to specify a method when you issue a customer refund.

8. Leave the prefilled bank account as is.

9. (Optional) Enter a Class and Memo.

10. Check or remove the checkmark from the To Be Printed checkbox.

11. Click OK.

12. To print the check, from the menu bar, select **File**, **Print Forms**, **Print Checks**, and enter the check number you are placing in your printer.

13. You can also modify the To Be Printed status of a transaction in the Number/Type field in the bank register by selecting **Banking**, **Use Register** from the menu bar.

If you did not apply the credit when you first created it, you can later process the credit as a refund or apply it to an open invoice by selecting the **Credit To** drop-down list from the Create Credit Memos/Refunds dialog box.

Congratulations on reviewing one of the most important chapters, properly working with customer transactions in QuickBooks. Make sure you also review the next chapter, to learn how to manage these transactions.

MANAGING CUSTOMERS

As a business owner, you do your best to take care of those that keep you in business, your customers. Customers are one of the most valuable assets you have and are necessary to stay in business.

This chapter focuses on managing the accounting that goes on in the back office for customer-related transactions. You learn what reports to review, how to handle sales tax, and how to work with unique customer transactions, as well as other pertinent information.

Accounts Receivable Reporting

You have already learned how to use some of the most common customer-related transactions and carry out important customer-oriented activities in your QuickBooks data file.

If your business sends invoices to customers for payment, you have offered the customer terms of payment. Those terms might be net 30 or net 60 and might include discounts if you receive early payment.

Using the A/R Aging Summary, Detail, or Open Invoices reports helps you identify customers who are late in paying. These other useful reports included in the Reports, Customers & Receivables menu assist with collections analysis:

- Customer Balance Summary

- Customer Balance Detail

- Collections Report

- Average Days to Pay Summary

- Average Days to Pay

QuickBooks provides a wide variety of reports for documenting sales, customer balances, and other useful management reporting. Chapter 14, "Reporting in QuickBooks," has details on working with QuickBooks reports, including accessing a variety of customer-related reports from the following menus:

- From the menu bar, select **Reports**, **Report Center**; select the **Customers & Receivables** or **Sales** reports from the Standard tab.

- From the menu bar, select **Company**, **Company Snapshot**; select the **Payments** or **Customer** tab.

The next several sections in this chapter help you review and troubleshoot your own data for accuracy. Following are some of the more common reports to identify whether your accounts receivable information is correct.

Reviewing A/R Aging Summary and Detail Reports

Preparing your customer invoices and recording payments from customers is important to the accuracy of your financials. Several reports summarize the status of unpaid or unapplied customer transactions included in your Accounts Receivable balance on the Balance Sheet report. You can prepare these reports with your own data or review the report details using the sample data in Chapter 1, "Getting Started with QuickBooks," p. 37.

From the menu bar, select **Reports**, **Customers & Receivables**, and then select one of the following from the submenu:

- **A/R Aging Summary**—Report groups open customer transactions by job into a series of aged date ranges (see Figure 10.1). Use this report for a quick view of customers who have older unpaid balances.

- **A/R Aging Detail**—The report in Figure 10.2 provides detail for all open customer transactions, grouped by aging status.

| Dates | Today | | 12/15/2017 | Interval (days) 30 | Through (days past due) 90 | Sort By Default |

Rock Castle Construction
A/R Aging Summary
As of December 15, 2017

	Current	1 - 30	31 - 60	61 - 90	> 90	TOTAL
Allard, Robert						
Remodel	0.00	0.00	0.00	14,510.00	0.00	14,510.00
Total Allard, Robert	0.00	0.00	0.00	14,510.00	0.00	14,510.00
Burch, Jason						
Room Addition	1,005.00	0.00	0.00	0.00	0.00	1,005.00
Total Burch, Jason	1,005.00	0.00	0.00	0.00	0.00	1,005.00
Campbell, Heather						
Remodel	13,900.00	0.00	0.00	0.00	0.00	13,900.00
Total Campbell, Heather	13,900.00	0.00	0.00	0.00	0.00	13,900.00
Cook, Brian						
2nd story addition	5,418.00	0.00	0.00	0.00	0.00	5,418.00
Kitchen	3,279.33	0.00	700.00	0.00	0.00	3,979.33
Total Cook, Brian	8,697.33	0.00	700.00	0.00	0.00	9,397.33

Figure 10.1
Use the A/R Aging Summary report to identify which customers have overdue balances.

Click to collapse detail for selected customer

Use these reports to identify customers who are in need of collection efforts, and use the tools discussed in the sections, "Income Tracker" and "Enable the Collections Center" in this chapter.

Figure 10.2
The A/R Aging
Detail report
groups aged
customer
transactions
by aging
status.

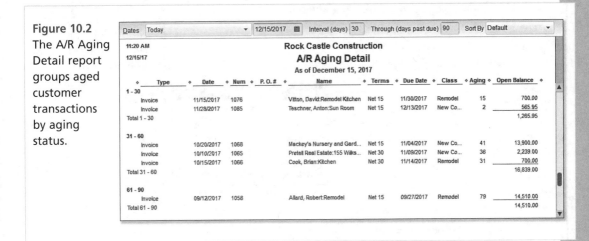

Reviewing the Open Invoices Report

Different from the A/R Aging Summary report, the Open Invoices report is particularly useful because it shows individual lines for each open (unapplied) transaction grouped by customer and job. This report is a perpetual report, meaning it shows open invoices as of today's date, not some fixed time in the past, unless you modify the reports as detailed here.

To modify the Open Invoices report so you can compare it to your Balance Sheet report for some specific date in the past, follow these steps:

1. From the menu bar, select **Reports**, **Customers & Receivables**, **Open Invoices**. By default, this report includes all payments your customer made as of today's computer system date.

2. If you are changing the date of this report to a date in the past, click the Customize Report button and then click the Advanced button on the Display tab of the Modify Report dialog box.

3. In the Open Balance/Aging box of the Advanced Options dialog box, select the **Report Date** option (see Figure 10.3). This modification to the report enables you to see each invoice balance detail as of the previous report date. If you do not modify this report, QuickBooks displays the earlier date on the report and also reduces the balances owed for payments made after the report date.

4. On the Open Invoices report (see Figure 10.4), you can view details of all open balances and any unapplied credits, grouped by customer and job.

> **note**
>
> Changing the date on the Open Invoices report does not change the detail displayed. This Open Invoices report is perpetual. If you need to document your balances for a date in the past, use the Accounts Receivable Aging reports.

Figure 10.3
You can compare the Open Invoices report, when modified, to the totals on your Balance Sheet report for a previous date.

Figure 10.4
Unlike the Aging Summary report, the Open Invoices report subtotals open or unapplied transactions by customer or job instead of by aging date.

Reconciling Accounts Receivable Totals

With QuickBooks, you don't have to worry that the Balance Sheet report and Accounts Receivable Aging Summary report match because any transaction posting to the Accounts Receivable account must have a customer assigned. You want to make sure you always create your Balance Sheet with the accrual basis because you can prepare the A/R Aging Summary report only on accrual basis.

To prepare the reports needed for this comparison, follow these steps:

1. From the menu bar, select **Reports**, **Company & Financial**, **Balance Sheet Standard**. The selected report displays. For the date, select the **As of Date** you want to compare to.

2. In the Balance Sheet report that displays, note the balance in the Accounts Receivable account (see Figure 10.5).

> **tip**
>
> To compare your Balance Sheet report with the A/R Aging Summary report, you must create your Balance Sheet on an accrual basis. If your reporting preference default is for cash basis, you can still run most reports using accrual basis. Just click the Customize Report button at the top of the report and select **Accrual** as the reporting basis.

Figure 10.5
Use your Balance Sheet report (accrual basis) to reconcile your Accounts Receivable report.

| Dates | This Fiscal Year-to-date | As of 12/15/2017 | Columns | Total only | Sort By | Default |

11:27 AM
12/15/17
Accrual Basis

Rock Castle Construction
Balance Sheet
As of December 15, 2017

	Dec 15, 17
ASSETS	
Current Assets	
Checking/Savings	
10100 · Checking (Cash)	46,969.10
10300 · Savings (Savings)	17,910.19
10400 · Petty Cash (Petty Cash)	500.00
Total Checking/Savings	65,379.29
Accounts Receivable	
11000 · Accounts Receivable (Accounts Receivable)	93,007.93
Total Accounts Receivable	93,007.93
Other Current Assets	
12000 · Undeposited Funds (Undeposited Funds)	2,440.00
12100 · Inventory Asset (Inventory Asset)	30,683.38
12800 · Employee Advances (Employee Advances)	832.00

3. From the menu bar, select **Reports**, **Customers & Receivables**, **A/R Aging Summary**, making sure the field shows the same date as the date selected in step 1. The image in Figure 10.6 has been collapsed to make viewing the information easier. To expand to see more detail, click the Expand button at the top of the report.

Dates	Today	▼	12/15/2017 📅	Interval (days) 30	Through (days past due) 90	Sort By Default

11:29 AM
12/15/17

Rock Castle Construction
A/R Aging Summary
As of December 15, 2017

	Current	1 - 30	31 - 60	61 - 90	> 90	TOTAL
▶ Allard, Robert	0.00	0.00	0.00	14,510.00	0.00	14,510.00
▶ Burch, Jason	1,005.00	0.00	0.00	0.00	0.00	1,005.00
▶ Campbell, Heather	13,900.00	0.00	0.00	0.00	0.00	13,900.00
▶ Cook, Brian	8,697.33	0.00	700.00	0.00	0.00	9,397.33
▶ Ecker Designs	1,468.30	0.00	0.00	0.00	0.00	1,468.30
▶ Hendro Riyadi	4,223.00	0.00	0.00	0.00	0.00	4,223.00
▶ Jacobsen, Doug	2,320.00	0.00	0.00	0.00	0.00	2,320.00
▶ Lew Plumbing - C	220.00	0.00	0.00	0.00	0.00	220.00
▶ Mackey's Nursery and Garden Supply	0.00	0.00	13,900.00	0.00	0.00	13,900.00
▶ Melton, Johnny	8,618.64	0.00	0.00	0.00	0.00	8,618.64
▶ Pretell Real Estate	2,787.50	0.00	2,239.00	0.00	0.00	5,026.50
▶ Robson, Darci	12,420.98	0.00	0.00	0.00	0.00	12,420.98
▶ Teschner, Anton	0.00	565.95	0.00	0.00	0.00	565.95
▶ Violette, Mike	4,732.23	0.00	0.00	0.00	0.00	4,732.23
▶ Vitton, David	0.00	700.00	0.00	0.00	0.00	700.00
TOTAL	60,392.98	1,265.95	16,839.00	14,510.00	0.00	93,007.93

Figure 10.6
A/R Aging Summary report is collapsed here for reviewing report totals.

The balance from the Balance Sheet report should match the total on the A/R Aging Summary. If it does not, the cause might be a broken transaction link. You can detect these types of issues by selecting **File**, **Utilities**, **Verify Data** from the menu bar; Chapter 17, "Managing Your QuickBooks Database," has additional details.

Viewing the Accounts Receivable Balance on a Cash Basis Balance Sheet

The nature of cash basis reporting implies that you do not see an Accounts Receivable balance on your Balance Sheet. In short, cash basis accounting doesn't recognize revenue until you deposit the funds.

What should you do if you see an Accounts Receivable balance on a cash basis Balance Sheet? Any of the following can be the cause:

- A/R transactions with items posting to other Balance Sheet accounts

- Inventory items on an invoice or credit memo (inventory management should be reported in accrual basis reporting)

- Transfers between Balance Sheet accounts

- Unapplied Accounts Receivable customer payments

- Customer payments applied to future-dated Accounts Receivable invoices

- Preferences that contradict each other (which can happen if you select Cash Basis on your Summary Reports but Accrual Basis as your Sales Tax preference)

- Data corruption (from the menu bar, select **File**, **Utilities**, **Verify Data** to check for data corruption)

Preparing reports detailing accounts receivable balances is easy with the QuickBooks software. However, if you review a cash basis Balance Sheet, you might have an Accounts Receivable balance. Use the next section to learn more about discovering what makes this happen.

Accounts Receivable Balances on Cash Basis Balance Sheet

To determine why an Accounts Receivable balance displays on a cash basis Balance Sheet, follow these steps:

1. From the menu bar, select **Reports, Company & Financial, Balance Sheet Standard**, as in Figure 10.7.

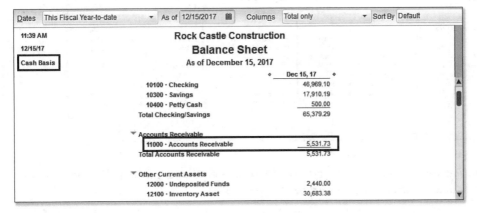

Figure 10.7
Use these instructions, when there is an Accounts Receivable balance on a cash basis Balance Sheet.

2. Click the Customize Report button.

3. The Modify Report dialog box opens with the Display tab selected. Select **Cash** for the report basis.

4. Click OK.

5. Double-click the Accounts Receivable amount in question. The Transaction by Account report is created.

6. Click the Customize Report button. The Modify Report dialog box opens, with the Display tab selected.

7. For the Report Date Range, remove the From date and leave the To date.

8. Click the Advanced button and, from the Open Balance/Aging box, select **Report Date**.

9. Click the Filters tab.

10. In the Choose Filters box, scroll down to select **Paid Status** and select the **Open** option.

11. Click OK.

Look for transactions that fall into any of the categories described previously. Figure 10.8 shows transactions that affected other Balance Sheet accounts. Any item used on a customer invoice that is mapped to another Balance Sheet account (including inventory) displays on a cash basis Balance Sheet report.

Figure 10.8
This modified report identifies the individual transactions that are included in the Accounts Receivable amount showing on a cash basis Balance Sheet.

Now that you have reviewed your customers' open and aged balances, you will appreciate the tools available in your QuickBooks software to help you with critical customer-related tasks.

Income Tracker

New for QuickBooks 2014 is the Income Tracker. The Income Tracker makes it easy to review and work with your unbilled sales (estimates and sales orders), unpaid sales (open and overdue invoices), and paid sales (payments and sales receipts).

The Income Tracker replaces the need for the Collections Center, although as the next section shows, you can choose to enable the Collections Center. You can choose to have both the Income Tracker and the Collections Center working in your file. This is useful for those companies that are accustomed to using the Collections Center.

> **note**
> The default Admin user QuickBooks creates has access to the Income Tracker. All other users created must be granted Full access to Sales and Accounts Receivable tasks.

The Income Tracker provides a single window for viewing and managing customer transactions. Business owners can see at a glance the progression of the estimates, sales orders, open and overdue invoices, and payments made in the last 30 days. The transaction types displayed vary depending on the version of QuickBooks you are using and whether you have enabled that feature.

From the Income Tracker, you can do the following:

- Filter the displayed list of customer-related transactions

- Select and work with transactions individually

- Select transactions in batch

- Print a batch of same-type transactions

- Email a batch of transactions

- Review important information about the selected transaction, including the last date an email was sent

To use the Income Tracker, from the menu bar, select **Customers, Income Tracker**. The Income Tracker displays summary information at the top in colored blocks and detailed transactions below. See Figure 10.9.

Figure 10.9
Use the Income Tracker to manage customer-related transactions.

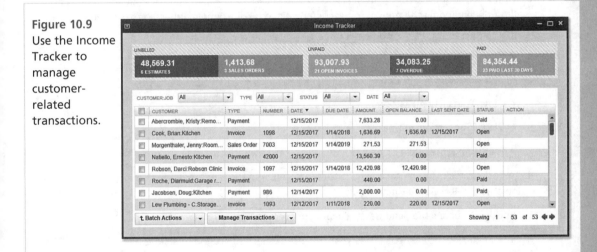

With the Income Tracker displayed, click any of the colored bars at the top to filter for that specific transaction type. Figure 10.10 shows the results filtered for sales orders. Sales orders are available if you are using QuickBooks Premier or Enterprise.

Do you need to email or print a batch of invoices? Follow these instructions:

1. Click the respective color block at the top to filter the results displayed.

2. Place a checkmark next to each transaction you want to email (or print).

Figure 10.10
Take action on the selected transaction.

3. (Optional) Right-click with your mouse cursor to access transaction-specific actions. The actions differ depending on the type of transaction displayed. For example, when you right-click an Invoice listing, you have these options:

- Print Row

- Edit Customer & Job Info

- View Transaction History

- View Transaction Journal

- Edit Highlighted Row

4. To perform tasks for multiple invoice transactions, from the Batch Actions drop-down in the lower left, select **Batch Email** (or **Print**).

5. QuickBooks opens the Send Batch Email window (see Figure 10.11).

6. Click Send Now. QuickBooks uses your preferred email application to send the forms attached as a PDF.

The Income Tracker also permits a user to open a specific transaction and make edits as needed. Use the Income Tracker to keep a close eye on the status of your customer activities.

Enable the Collections Center

QuickBooks 2014 replaced the Collections Center with the Income Tracker that the previous section discussed. However, many users are accustomed to using the features of the Collections Center, so I have chosen to leave these instructions. In QuickBooks 2014, you can choose to use the Income Tracker, the Collections Center, or both. As you become proficient at using the Income Tracker, you will not need to use the Collections Center.

To enable the Collections Center in QuickBooks 2014, follow these instructions:

1. Log in to the file as the Admin user.

2. From the menu bar, select **Edit**, **Preferences**, **Sales & Customers**.

3. Select the **Company Preferences** tab.

4. In the Collections Center, place a checkmark beside Enable Collections Center.

5. Click OK to close the Preferences dialog box.

To work with the QuickBooks Collections Center, in Figure 10.12, use these instructions:

1. On the Home page, click the Customers button.

2. The Customer Center opens with the Customers & Jobs tab selected. From the top of the Customer Center, click the Collections Center icon.

3. The Collections Center opens, with the Overdue tab selected. Click any column header to sort by that column.

4. Click the Notes/Warnings icon next to any open item; QuickBooks populates the date and time, and you can add your collection notes. Click Save. These notes become part of the customer or job notes record, and you can view them from the Customer Center. After the note is saved, hover your mouse over the Notes/Warnings icon; QuickBooks displays the contents without opening the note.

5. Click the Select and Send Email link, as in Figure 10.13.

6. Place a checkmark next to each overdue invoice you want to send a collection notice for. Select all or deselect all using the checkmark in front of the Customer Name column header.

7. To the right, modify the boilerplate text to include in the email communication. Add the From, Cc:, and Bcc: email addresses. You can set your default text for these communications on the Send Forms—Company Preferences tab of the Preferences dialog box.

8. QuickBooks uses the email provider you designated on the Send Forms—My Preferences tab of the Preferences dialog box.

9. Repeat steps 4–7 for customers with open invoices listed on the Almost Due tab.

10. Click the X in the top right to close the Collections Center.

Click the Notes icon to add details
of your collection activities

Figure 10.12
Managing collection activities using the Collections Center.

Figure 10.13
Manage email communications in batch for past-due customers.

The notes assigned to the overdue invoice can also track the day and time an email was sent.

Even with your best efforts, sometimes you are not able to collect the money owed to you. For these instances, you want to accurately write off the balance to your Bad Debt expense account. Review the "Removing an Open Balance from a Customer Invoice" section for details.

Generating the Missing Customer Invoices Report

Most companies establish some control over the process of creating customer invoices. If invoices are created manually in the field and later entered into QuickBooks, one control is to maintain a numeric invoicing pattern. Usually each invoice is one number larger than the previous invoice. This method of invoice record keeping can be an important process to have if your company is ever audited and you are required to provide a list of all invoices.

To see whether your data has any missing numbers in the invoicing sequence, follow these steps:

1. From the menu bar, select **Reports**, **Banking**, **Missing Checks**.

2. In the Missing Checks dialog box, in the Specify Account drop-down list, select **Accounts Receivable** and click OK to generate the report (see Figure 10.14).

Figure 10.14
Create a report that lists all your customer invoices by invoice number.

Missing Checks		✕
Specify Account	11000 · Accounts Receivable ▾	
OK	< Add New >	

10100 · Checking	Bank	
10300 · Savings	Bank	
10400 · Petty Cash	Bank	
11000 · Accounts Receivable	Accounts Receivable	
12000 · Undeposited Funds	Other Current Asset	
12100 · Inventory Asset	Other Current Asset	
12800 · Employee Advances	Other Current Asset	
13100 · Pre-paid Insurance	Other Current Asset	
13400 · Retainage Receivable	Other Current Asset	
15000 · Furniture and Equipment	Fixed Asset	
15100 · Vehicles	Fixed Asset	
15200 · Buildings and Improvements	Fixed Asset	
15300 · Construction Equipment	Fixed Asset	
16900 · Land	Fixed Asset	
17000 · Accumulated Depreciation	Fixed Asset	
18700 · Security Deposits	Other Asset	

3. Rename the report by choosing Customize Report, clicking the Header/Footer tab, and typing a new title for the Report Title field, such as Invoice List.

4. Click OK to display the newly renamed report.

This customized report makes the process of identifying missing or duplicated invoice numbers easy (see Figure 10.15). Use this information to determine whether you need better company practices to avoid this situation.

Figure 10.15
This modified report shows a list of all missing or duplicated invoice numbers.

Sales Tax Payable Reports

When your company is required to collect sales tax from your customers, you become an agent for the state. As an agent, you have an obligation to maintain proper records of your sales and taxes collected. This section provides you with easy-to-follow instructions on properly reporting on sales tax and correcting common sales tax data entry errors.

I recommend that you review these reports each time you prepare to pay your sales and use tax to the taxing authority. Properly "reconciling" these reports to each other helps minimize any chance that your QuickBooks data will not support what you filed on your sales tax return.

Reviewing Customer Lists for Tax Code and Tax Item Assigned

Check your customers' taxable status often. This task is quite easy to do and helps prevent the costly mistakes caused by not charging sales tax or charging the incorrect rate.

1. From the menu bar, select **Reports**, **List**, **Customer Phone List**.

2. On the top left of the report, click the Customize Report button.

3. In the Modify Report dialog box that opens, place a checkmark in the Columns box next to items you want to review for the list, including Sales Tax Code and Tax Item. Not shown in the image is the Resale Num field; you might want to include this on your report.

4. From the drop-down list, select **Sales Tax Code**.

5. To give the report a unique title, select the **Header/Footer** tab and type a name for the report in the Report Title field. Click OK.

From this list, which Figure 10.16 shows, double-click any line item detail to open the Edit Customer dialog box and make needed changes.

Figure 10.16
Prepare this report often to review the accuracy of the sales tax codes and items assigned to your customers.

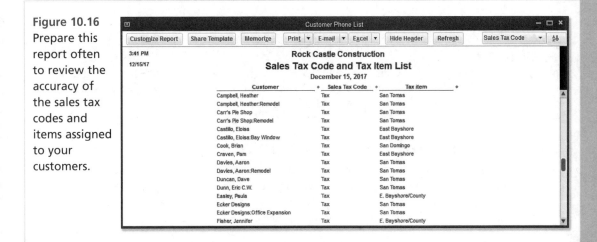

Reviewing the Item List for Tax Code Assigned

Another review that I recommend you do periodically is to look at the list of services and products you sell and determine whether the proper tax code has been assigned (see Figure 10.17).

Follow these steps to customize the Item Price List report:

1. From the menu bar, select **Reports**, **List**, **Item Price List**.

2. At the top left of the report, click the Customize Report button.

3. In the Columns box of the Modify Report dialog box, remove checkmarks from the data fields you do not want to display on this report. Place a checkmark next to the data fields you want to review for the list, including Sales Tax Code.

4. In the drop-down list, select **Sales Tax Code**.

5. If desired, click the Header/Footer tab to change the report title. Click OK.

Figure 10.17
Prepare a
report of
the sales
tax codes
assigned to
your items.

> 🔊 **caution**
>
> When you make a change to a customer's assigned tax code or tax item or to the tax code assigned to a product or service you sell on your item list, QuickBooks does *not* correct or modify previously saved transactions. Only new transactions show the change in the sales tax status or rate.

Reconciling Total Sales to Total Income

The term *reconciling* (also known as proofing) refers to the act of comparing two related numbers from two different reports. The importance of this task cannot be overstated. If your company is selected to have a sales tax audit, one of the first numbers the auditor will want to determine is the total sales you reported on your tax returns for the time period being audited.

> ➡️ *For more information, see "Setting Up Sales Tax," p. 327.*

When comparing these two reports, you must know the reporting basis you have selected for your sales tax. To compare your total sales on the Sales Tax Liability report to your total income on the Profit & Loss report using the same basis as your Sales Tax Preference, follow these steps:

1. From the menu bar, Select **Reports**, **Vendors & Payables**, **Sales Tax Liability**. This report is not listed if you have not yet enabled your Sales Tax preference (see the section "Sales Tax Setup" in Chapter 9, "Setting Up Customers").

2. Make a note of the date range and total sales on this report.

3. From the menu bar, select **Reports**, **Company & Financial**, **Profit & Loss Standard**.

4. Select the same date range you used for your Sales Tax Liability report in step 1.

5. Verify that this report uses the same reporting basis as the Sales Tax Liability report. If necessary, click Customize Report and then select **Cash** or **Accrual** from the Report Basis section of the Display tab.

6. Compare total income on the Profit & Loss report (see Figure 10.18) to the total sales from the Sales Tax Liability report. *Note:* You might have to deduct any non-sales income on your Profit & Loss Total Income amounts. Also make sure you prepare the reports using the same reporting basis.

Figure 10.18 Compare the total income on the Profit & Loss report to the total sales on the Sales Tax Liability report.

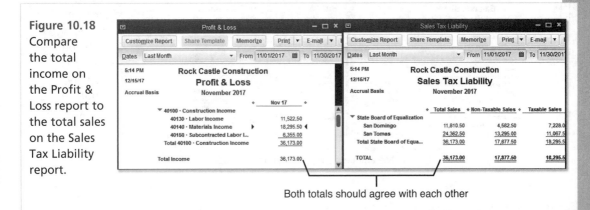

Both totals should agree with each other

If your totals on these two reports do not match, review the instructions in the "Correcting Sales Tax Errors" section of this chapter.

Reconciling Sales Tax Liability to Balance Sheet Sales Tax Payable

Another important comparison to make is between the amount reported for Sales Tax Payable on the Balance Sheet report and the Sales Tax Payable total on the Sales Tax Liability report. Carefully check that you are using the same cash or accrual basis for each report when completing this review.

If you created your own Sales Tax Payable account, you might not be able to accurately compare the two reports. QuickBooks creates a Sales Tax Payable account automatically.

To compare the Balance Sheet Sales Tax Payable account balance with the Sales Tax Payable total on the Sales Tax Liability report, follow these steps:

1. From the menu bar, select **Reports**, **Company & Financial**, **Balance Sheet Standard** (see Figure 10.19).

2. On the report, select the **As of Date** you are comparing to (this date must be the same ending date you use when you prepare your Sales Tax Liability report in the next step).

3. From the menu bar, select **Reports**, **Vendors & Payables**, **Sales Tax Liability**. See Figure 10.19. QuickBooks defaults the date range, depending on your sales tax preference setting.

Each month before you prepare your sales tax return, compare the total of these two reports. Later in this chapter, you learn about methods you can use to troubleshoot these totals when they do not match.

Figure 10.19 The Balance Sheet Sales Tax Payable amount should agree with your Sales Tax Liability report.

These amounts should agree on both reports.

When a Check or Bill Is Used to Pay Sales Tax

A common mistake when recording payment of the sales tax payable is to use a Write Checks or Enter Bills transaction. If you use these types of transactions and the Sales Tax Payable account is assigned on the form, QuickBooks reduces the Sales Tax Payable amount on the Balance Sheet but does not make the same adjustment in the Pay Sales Tax dialog box. Instead, this type of transaction is included in the Pay Sales Tax dialog box as a negative Amt. Due.

To find the transaction(s) that might be the cause of differences between the Balance Sheet Sales Tax Payable amounts to your Sales Tax Liability report amount to be paid, follow these steps:

1. On the Home page, click the Vendors button to open the Vendor Center.

2. Select your sales tax vendor from the Vendors list.

3. From the Show drop-down list, select **Checks** (or Bills), making sure you are looking in the appropriate date range.

Any checks or bills that appear here could be the reason your two reports do not agree. The correct sales tax payment transaction is named TAXPMT when viewing transactions in your bank register. The following section details how to properly record the payment of the collected sales tax in your QuickBooks data.

Paying Sales Tax

Now that you have your sales tax correctly set up and you have reviewed your sales tax payable reports, you need to know how to properly pay your sales tax.

Paying Sales Tax Without an Adjustment

As mentioned earlier, when you collect sales tax, you are acting as an agent for the state. Most often, you pay the state or city taxing authority the same amount that you collected from your customers. Sometimes the state allows you to discount the sales tax due for prompt payment or charges a penalty for paying late. This section discusses each of these situations.

Paying Sales Tax Without an Adjustment

To practice paying sales tax without an adjustment, open the sample data file as instructed in Chapter 1, p. 37. Use these instructions when creating your own sales tax payments—selecting accounts and dates that are correct for your needs:

1. From the menu bar, select **Vendors**, **Sales Tax**, **Pay Sales Tax**. The Pay Sales Tax dialog box displays (see Figure 10.20).

Figure 10.20
Use this transaction type to properly remit your sales tax payable amount.

2. For this exercise, in the Pay from Account field, leave the Checking account selected.

3. In the Check Date field, select **January 15, 2018** or whatever date you are assigning on the check.

4. In the Show Sales Tax Due field, select **December 31, 2017**. This date should default to your preference setting. You can change this date, if necessary.

5. Leave the Starting Check No. unchanged. We assume here that a manual check was written and that this was the check number. If instead you are printing your check, place a checkmark in the To Be Printed box in the lower left. Alternatively, if you are paying online, enter EFT in the Starting Check No. field.

6. Place a checkmark in the Pay column on the left for the individual items you want to pay. QuickBooks creates or prints a separate check transaction for each line item with a different vendor.

7. Verify that the Amt. Paid column agrees with your Sales Tax Liability report for the same period.

8. Click OK. QuickBooks creates a transaction with the TAXPMT type viewable from your checkbook register (see Figure 10.21).

DATE	NUMBER	PAYEE		PAYMENT	✔	DEPOSIT	BALANCE
	TYPE	ACCOUNT	MEMO				
01/15/2018	517	City of East Bayshore		0.29			46,968.81
	TAXPMT	25500 · Sales Tax					
01/15/2018	518	State Board of Equalization		957.34			46,011.47
	TAXPMT	-split-	ABCD 11-234567				
2/15/2017	Number	Payee		Payment		Deposit	
		Account	Memo				

Splits   ENDING BALANCE   **46,011.47**

1-Line

Sort by   Date, Type, Number/Ref

Record   Restore

Figure 10.21
Sales Tax Payment transactions displayed in a checkbook register.

tip
You can set a user-specific default account for paying the sales tax liability. From the menu bar, select **Edit**, **Preferences**, **Checking** and choose the My Preferences tab.

Paying Sales Tax with an Adjustment

Sales Tax Payable might not agree with the actual amount you need to pay for many reasons (the agency can't know in advance what it expects you to pay):

- Discount offered for early payment

- Penalty or fee assessed for late payment

- Credit received for overpayment on an earlier period's sales tax return

- State sales tax holiday or rate reduction

- Rounding errors

- Rounding to whole dollars

note
If you select the items to be paid *first* and then click the Adjust button recording the discount or increase, QuickBooks provides a warning that your previously selected checkmarks will be removed and you will need to select the line items again, including the new adjustment to include with the payment.

If any of these apply to your business, follow these steps:

1. Perform steps 1–5 in the preceding section ("Paying Sales Tax Without an Adjustment"), making sure to select the proper accounts and dates for your specific needs.

2. In the Pay Sales Tax dialog box, click Adjust to open the Sales Tax Adjustment dialog box (see Figure 10.22).

Figure 10.22
Use the Sales Tax Adjustment dialog box to increase or decrease your sales tax payment.

3. Select the appropriate Adjustment Date. This date should be on or before the Show Sales Tax Through date.

4. Enter an Entry No., or QuickBooks defaults a number if that preference is set.

5. Choose the Sales Tax Vendor for which you are decreasing or increasing your payment.

6. Select the appropriate adjustment account from your chart of accounts. Ask your accountant what is preferred—the account might be either of the following:

   ▪ Other Income, if you are recording a discount for early payment

   ▪ Expense, if you are recording a penalty or fine

7. Select the option **Increase Sales Tax By** or **Reduce Sales Tax By,** and enter the appropriate dollar amount.

8. In the Memo section, enter a description for your reports or accept the default description.

9. Click OK to record the sales tax adjustment.

10. Click OK to close the warning message when recording a sales tax adjustment.

11. QuickBooks now shows the Pay Sales Tax dialog box, with an additional line showing the adjustment. This example shows a reduction in sales tax due (see Figure 10.23).

Figure 10.23
When preparing your sales tax payment, select the sales tax lines and the adjustment line.

QuickBooks creates a general journal entry when the sales tax adjustment is recorded.

Correcting Accounts Receivable Errors

After reviewing your Accounts Receivable reports, you might have identified some data entry errors. Before you can fix these, you need to determine the best method to correct the errors. When deciding which method is best, ask yourself the following questions:

- **Are the errors in an accounting year that I have already filed a tax return for?**—If yes, then adjusting these transactions by dating the modifying entry in the current tax year and not modifying the original transaction is best. Some methods in this section do not enable you to select a date different from the original transaction date.

- **Are the errors significant in the dollar amount, collectively or individually?**—If yes, obtain the advice of your accountant before you make any adjustments so that changes that affect your tax status are carefully considered.

- **Am I going to fix detail or summary information?**—In other words, are you going to fix individual invoices or correct a group of customer invoices with one adjusting transaction?

- **Am I modifying an invoice with sales tax recorded on the invoice?**—If yes, refer to the "Correcting Sales Tax Errors" section in this chapter for a detailed discussion on adjusting invoices with sales tax. Make these corrections only with transactions dated in the current accounting month.

Removing an Open Balance from a Customer Invoice

You might have open balances on your Accounts Receivable invoices for several reasons. You can also correct overstated or understated balances through several methods, each with its own effect on your company's financials.

If you are an accounting professional and you are using QuickBooks Accountant 2014 or QuickBooks Enterprise Solutions Accountant 14.0 software, you should review Appendix A, "Client Data Review."

Included in the Client Data Review (CDR) are useful tools that accounting professionals can use to streamline the process of applying open customer payments and credits to open customer invoices and simplify writing off small open balances in batch.

The following sections detail methods you can use to remove open customer balances with your QuickBooks Pro, Premier, or Enterprise software.

> **🔔 caution**
>
> Writing off amounts on the Receive Payments transaction affects your financials as of the date recorded on the Receive Payments transaction. Ask your accountant first about making these types of changes for years for which you have already filed your company's income tax returns.

Writing Off a Customer Balance by Modifying the Original Customer Receive Payments Transaction

This method of modifying the original customer payment to write off a customer balance records the change as of the date of the Receive Payments transaction and permits a write-off amount equal to the underpayment amount. You can write off the amount at the time you first record the payment or at a later date.

Follow these steps to write off a balance due from a customer directly from the Receive Payments transaction:

1. On the Home page, click the Customers button to open the Customer Center.

2. From the list on the left, select the appropriate customer.

3. In the Show drop-down list, select **Payments and Credits** or just **Received Payments** and any other date criteria you want to use (see Figure 9.15 on page 324 in Chapter 9).

4. Double-click the selected customer payment to open it. In the example in Figure 10.24, the customer paid $10.00 less than the amount due. Write off this amount by selecting the **Write Off the Extra Amount** option in the lower left of the Receive Payments dialog box.

5. Select **Save & Close**. QuickBooks prompts you for an account to assign for the write-off amount.

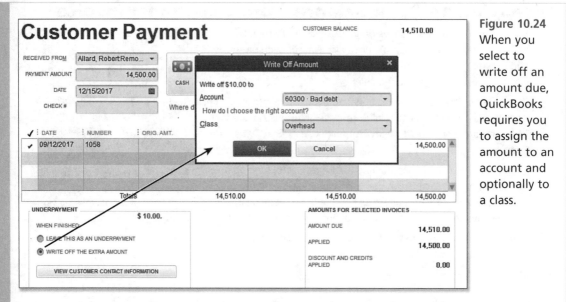

Figure 10.24
When you select to write off an amount due, QuickBooks requires you to assign the amount to an account and optionally to a class.

Recording a Discount to Remove a Customer Balance

Another way to remove an open customer balance is to record a discount. This method records the change as of the date of the Receive Payments transaction. You can record a discount initially when the customer's short payment is recorded, or later by creating a new payment without placing any dollars in the Amount field and choosing the Discounts & Credits option. However, the discount amount cannot be more than the amount due.

If the amount due is an insignificant amount, you might not want to take the time to collect it. The easiest method of dealing with it is to write off the remaining amount on the date the payment is recorded. If you do not write off the remaining amount, QuickBooks warns you of the underpayment.

The difference between a write-off and a discount is the placement on the Profit & Loss statement. A write-off is used when the debt has gone bad and cannot be collected; it is often an expense type. In contrast, the discount is used when you decide to reduce the sale price; this account is typically an income type.

To record a discount, click the Discount & Credits button on the Receive Payments dialog box. Similar to the Write Off Amount dialog box, you are asked to identify an account to post the amount to (see Figure 10.25).

Figure 10.25
For small unpaid balances, recording a discount can be an easy method to remove the balance.

Recording a Credit Memo to Remove a Balance Due

The most accurate method for removing a balance due is to record a credit memo because it creates a good audit trail. You can date the credit in a period for which you want to reduce the appropriate income account and, if applicable, sales tax due.

➡️ *For more detailed instructions on working with customer credit memos, see "Recording and Applying a Customer Credit Memo," p. 376.*

Recording a Journal Entry to Remove (or Increase) a Customer Balance

Another way to remove or increase a customer balance is to record a journal entry. The company accountant often creates this type of transaction when adjusting Accounts Receivable.

If you are going to record a journal entry adjustment, you need to keep in mind the following:

- Only one customer is allowed per journal entry.

- If the general journal entry has other non-customer-related adjustments, the first line of the journal entry should remain blank. For more information, read the caution in this section.

- The date of the general journal entry is the date the transaction will impact your financials for accrual or cash basis.

- If you print cash basis reports, make sure the income account is not recorded on the first line of the journal entry.

- You can enter and apply one lump sum to multiple open customer invoices.

⚠ caution

If you use a customer on the first line of a journal entry, every other adjustment made—even noncustomer adjustments—displays on the Profit & Loss by Job report for that customer. The first line of any journal entry is a source line and causes a relationship with transactions below the first line.

To avoid this problem, always leave the first account line of a journal entry blank, as in Figure 10.26. Including a memo on the first line is acceptable.

Leave row 1 blank

Figure 10.26
Journal entries that adjust Accounts Receivable balances should then be applied against a customer's open invoice(s).

To record a journal entry adjustment to a customer balance, follow these steps:

1. From the menu bar, select **Company, Make General Journal Entries**.

2. In the Make General Journal Entries dialog box, record a debit to increase Accounts Receivable or credit to reduce Accounts Receivable (refer to Figure 10.26). Be sure to assign the customer name to each line (except the first line—see the previous caution) so that a Profit & Loss by Job report shows the adjustment.

3. Assign the General Journal Entry to the appropriate customer invoice. From the menu bar, select **Customers, Customer Center**.

4. Select the correct customer from the list on the left, and in the Show drop-down list, select **Invoices**. Double-click the appropriate invoice with the open balance.

5. The Create Invoices dialog box opens. From the Main tab on the ribbon toolbar at the top, select **Apply Credits**. QuickBooks then provides a list of available credits to choose from (see Figure 10.27).

6. On the Apply Credits dialog box that opens, select the appropriate credits by placing a check-mark next to the credit. Click Done to assign the credit(s) to the customer invoice.

7. Click Save & Close.

Figure 10.27
Accept the defaults for applying open credits, or manually assign them.

Correcting Customer Payments

Applying the customer's payments exactly as the customer intended is important. If you apply the customer's payment to an invoice of your own choosing, communicating any discrepancies with open invoice balances can be more confusing than necessary.

However, many times your customer does not give you the correct invoice number, and you might apply his payment to an incorrect invoice. QuickBooks makes changing how you applied the payment to an invoice easy.

Fixing Unapplied Customer Payments and Credits

You might notice that your Open Invoices report includes unapplied payments (see Figure 10.28). This happens when the payment is recorded by a QuickBooks user who does not assign the payment to an open invoice.

To correct this, double-click the payment transaction listed on the report, and add the checkmarks to the invoice(s) being paid. This transaction change affects earlier-year financials in cash basis reporting, so be sure to notify your accounting professional of the change.

| Dates | Today | ▼ | 12/15/2017 📅 Sort By | Default | ▼ |

7:12 AM			**Rock Castle Construction**			
12/15/17			**Open Invoices**			
			As of December 15, 2017			

◦ Type ◦	Date ◦	Num ◦	Terms ◦	Due Date ◦	Class ◦	Aging ◦	Open Balance ◦
Pretell Real Estate							
155 Wilks Blvd.							
Payment	12/15/2017						-5,026.50
Invoice	10/10/2017	1065	Net 30	11/09/2017	New Co...	36	2,239.00
Invoice	11/15/2017	1074	Net 30	12/15/2017	New Co...		1,072.50
Invoice	12/10/2017	1090	Net 30	01/09/2018	New Co...		1,715.00
Total 155 Wilks Blvd.							0.00
Total Pretell Real Estate							0.00

Figure 10.28
Unapplied Receive Payments transactions show on the Open Invoices report as a credit for that customer.

Fixing a Payment Applied to the Wrong Invoice Number

After you compare your customer's records with yours, if you find you have applied the payment to the wrong invoice, follow these steps to unapply the payment and then reapply it to the correct invoice:

1. From the menu bar, select **Customers, Customer Center**.

2. On the list on the left, select the appropriate customer or job.

3. In the pane to the right of the customer list, in the Show drop-down list, select **Payments and Credits**.

4. Optionally, select all or just unapplied payments and credits, and/or select a specific date range from the appropriate drop-down list. QuickBooks lists all received payment transactions for this customer.

5. Double-click the payment that was misapplied.

6. The Receive Payments dialog box opens. Remove the checkmark from one invoice and place it next to the correct invoice. Ensure that the amount of the payment total does not change. Click Save & Close.

Fixing a Payment Applied to the Wrong Customer or Job

From the Customer Center, find the appropriate customer, filter for Received Payments, and locate the payment in question, as previous sections instructed.

Determine whether the payment has already been included on a deposit by clicking Transaction History on the Reports tab of the transaction ribbon. If it has been deposited and you attempt to change the customer name on the payment screen, QuickBooks warns you that you first need to delete the payment from the deposit.

If the payment has been included on a deposit, follow these steps to correct the customer or job assigned. You will temporarily remove the amount from a deposit and then add back the corrected payment.

To reassign a payment received to another customer or job, follow these steps:

1. From the Receive Payments dialog box for the payment assigned to the incorrect customer or job, on the Reports tab of the ribbon toolbar, click Transaction History (see Figure 10.29).

Figure 10.29
To reassign a recorded payment to a different customer or job, you first have to remove the payment from the deposit.

2. From the Transaction History—Payment dialog box, select the deposit and click Go To. The Make Deposits dialog box opens.

3. Record on paper the total deposit amount and date. You will need this information later in step 8.

4. If multiple payments are on the deposit, go to step 5. If the payment amount being corrected is the only deposit line item, go to step 9.

5. Highlight the line item to be removed, as in Figure 10.30, and press Ctrl+Delete on your keyboard. Click OK to close the Delete warning message. Then click Save & Close. This step removes the line item from the deposit. QuickBooks also warns you if the item has previously been cleared.

> **tip**
> If you follow these steps carefully, you restore your deposit to the correct amount and avoid any reconciliation differences.

Figure 10.30
Use
Ctrl+Delete
on your
keyboard to
remove an
entire trans-
action line.

6. Locate the customer payment that was in error and change the Customer or Job assigned.

7. Return to the bank register and locate the deposit. Double-click the deposit. With the deposit open, select **Payments** at the top and place a checkmark next to the payment with the corrected Customer or Job (see Figure 10.31). Click OK to add the payment to the deposit.

Figure 10.31
With the orig-
inal deposit
open, click
the Payments
icon to add
back the
corrected
payment.

8. Verify that the total of the deposit agrees with the original amount you recorded on paper. When this transaction is saved with the same original amount, your bank reconciliation will not show a discrepancy. The process is now complete (see Figure 10.32).

9. If the payment you are correcting is the only deposit line item, from the menu bar, select **Customers**, **Receive Payments** and record the information for the correct customer or job. Then follow steps 7 and 8 to assign your newly created payment to the existing deposit. Next, delete the incorrect line item and save the deposit.

10. From the Customer Center, locate the incorrect payment and void or delete it.

Figure 10.32
The corrected payment has been added to the original deposit, preserving the cleared bank status of the original deposit.

	Make Deposits							— □ ×
◆ Previous ◆ Next ■ Save ⬛ Print ▾	⬛ Payments ⬛ History ⬛ Journal	⬛ Attach						

Deposit To 10100 · Chec.. ▾   Date 07/25/2017 📅   Memo Deposit

Click Payments to select customer payments that you have received. List any other amounts to deposit below.

RECEIVED FROM	FROM ACCOUNT	MEMO	CHK NO.	PMT ME...	CLASS	AMOUNT
Rahn, Jennifer:Remodel	12000 · Undeposited Funds		24234	Check		20,300.00
Fomin, Slava:Utility Shed	12000 · Undeposited Funds		5693	Check		5,000.00

Deposit Subtotal 25,300.00

To get cash back from this deposit, enter the amount below. Indicate the account where you want this money to go, such as your Petty Cash account.

Cash back goes to   Cash back memo   Cash back amount

Deposit Total 25,300.00

When a Credit Memo Is Applied to the Wrong Customer Invoice

Often you create a credit memo and apply it to a specific invoice. Then when you communicate with the customer, you find out he or she applied it to a different invoice. When you are making those credit and collections calls, the discrepancy can end up costing you critical time in outstanding invoices paid. If in the end the total due from the customer remains the same, I find it easier to defer to the customer's records when applying credit memos.

Without agreeing with the customer, your collections process would be delayed as both parties sort out what remains unpaid. This process temporarily has you reassign the credit memo to another customer. The following steps help you reassign the credit memo to the correct invoice, or at least the same invoice your customer assigned it to:

1. From the Customer Center, locate the customer who had the credit memo applied to the wrong invoice. If you are not sure, click the Customer Center's Transactions tab and select **Credit Memos** from the list of available transaction types. You can filter for Open or All Credit Memos, as well as filter by transaction dates to narrow your search.

2. To reassign the incorrectly assigned credit memo to another invoice, open the credit memo and temporarily change the Customer or Job name to any other customer or job name.

3. Make a note of the new customer assigned to the changed credit memo. From the Main tab of the ribbon toolbar at that top, select **Save**.

4. Click Yes to close the message that you want to record the change.

5. Click OK to the Available Credit message, leaving the Retain as an Available Credit option selected.

6. With the open credit displayed and showing a Remaining Credit balance assigned to the temporary customer, click the Customer:Job drop-down list and choose the correct Customer or Customer:Job.

7. Click Save & Close.

8. Click Yes to close the message that you want to record the change.

9. The Available Credit message displays. Click the Apply to Invoice option.

10. The Apply Credit dialog box opens. Place a checkmark next to the appropriate credit amounts. By default, QuickBooks selects the invoice with an exact match. You can override this selection by unchecking the default and applying the credit as needed.

11. Select **Done**. Click Save & Close.

When Deposits Were Made Incorrectly

Many users follow these four steps to properly manage most Accounts Receivable tasks:

1. Create a quote using an estimate or sales order (optional).

2. Prepare an invoice, sales receipt, or statement charge.

3. Receive the customer payment into an Undeposited Funds account.

4. Record the deposit into your bank account.

This section details how to correct your QuickBooks data when the receive payments step was skipped in recording deposits to the bank account.

How can you know when this situation happens? You need to do a little troubleshooting first to identify the problem:

- Do you have open invoices for customers you know have paid you?

- Is your bank account balance reconciled and correct?

- Does Income on your Profit & Loss report appear to be too high?

If you answered yes to these questions, you need to determine just how the deposits in the bank account register were recorded.

Viewing Deposits in the Bank Register

To determine how deposits were made to the bank account, view the deposits in your bank register. To open a bank register, select **Banking**, **Use Register** from the menu bar and select the appropriate bank account.

The two deposits dated 12/15/17 (see Figure 10.33) were each individually recorded to the account by assigning the checking account directly on the Receive Payments transaction. This would be acceptable if the individual checks were on different deposit tickets taken to your bank and if the date of the receive payment was also the same date as the deposit. Often these are not the normal conditions, and having the payment recorded to the Undeposited Funds is the best process.

Figure 10.33
The checkbook register indicates the record type for each deposit.

DATE	NUMBER	PAYEE		PAYMENT	✔	DEPOSIT	BALANCE
	TYPE	ACCOUNT	MEMO				
12/15/2017		Abercrombie, Kristy:Remodel Bathroc				7,633.28	34,537.98
	PMT	11000 · Accounts I					
12/15/2017		Natiello, Ernesto:Kitchen				13,560.39	48,098.37
	PMT	11000 · Accounts I					
12/15/2017	516	State Board of Equalization		1,629.27			46,469.10
	TAXPMT	-split-	ABCD 11-234567				
12/15/2017	SEND					500.00	46,969.10
	TRANSFI	10300 · Savings					
12/16/2...	Number					2,000.00	48,969.10
	DEP	12000 · Undeposi	Deposit				

Different types of
deposit transactions

In the checkbook register view, the account shown represents the account from which the transaction originated. You might see Accounts Receivable, an income account, or you might see -Split-, which indicates several lines of detail for this single transaction. To view the -Split- detail, double-click the transaction itself to open the originating QuickBooks transaction.

By contrast, look at the deposit dated 12/16/2017 for $2,000.00 in Figure 10.33. The account shown is Undeposited Funds, which is the account where the transaction originated.

To summarize, look for a "pattern" of how deposits were made to your QuickBooks data. The examples here show two types of deposits: one that was recorded to the checking account and others that first went through the Undeposited Funds account. You might have others in your data where the account shown is your income account. The next section, "Viewing the Deposit Detail Report," discusses this type of transaction.

You also need to look to see which transactions have been cleared in the bank reconciliation and which deposits remain uncleared. Chapter 13, "Working with Bank and Credit Card Accounts," discusses bank reconciliation. In fact, it is best to complete the reconciliation task before you begin fixing your deposit details. Why? If you see an uncleared deposit, it helps you identify your potential errors in the Undeposited Funds account.

Viewing the Deposit Detail Report

Use this report to review how deposits were recorded to the bank account in QuickBooks and identify deposits that followed the recommended process of being recorded first to the Undeposited Funds account.

To open the Deposit Detail report, follow these steps:

1. From the menu bar, select **Reports, Banking, Deposit Detail**.

2. Click the Customize Report button at the top of the report.

3. Click the Filters tab. In the Choose Filter box, the Account filter is already selected. In the drop-down list, select your bank account or use the default of all bank accounts. Click OK to prepare the report.

In Figure 10.34, the deposit for $2,000.00 on 12/16/17 was recorded using the recommended process of automatically assigning the payment to the Undeposited Funds account. The other payments did not follow this same process; the next sections provide details for correcting these.

Figure 10.34
The Deposit Detail report also indicates the record type of each deposit.

Creating a Payment Transaction List Detail Report

Do you find the Deposit Detail report too lengthy and difficult to read? You can create a report that shows the detail in list form and provides a total of the column detail using these steps:

1. From the menu bar, select **Reports**, **Custom Reports**, **Transaction Detail**. The Modify Report dialog box opens, with the Display tab selected.

2. Select the Report Date Range you want to view, as well as the columns you want to see on the report.

3. From the Filters tab, in the Choose Filter box, select **Account** and choose a specific bank account.

4. Set an additional filter for Multiple Transaction Types, including the deposit, payment, and journal (although it's less likely a journal was used).

5. Click OK to close the Transaction Type filter, and optionally select the **Header/Footer** tab to modify the Report Title.

6. Click OK to display the report with the selected filters.

Now you can view in list format all payments that were recorded to the Checking account (see Figure 10.35).

Figure 10.35
Use a filtered Custom Transaction Detail report for a simple view of all deposits into the bank account.

Assigning the Make Deposits Transaction to the Open Customer Invoice

Did your research reveal Make Deposits transactions recorded directly to an income account instead of using the Receive Payments transaction? For the business owner, assigning the deposits to the customer invoice is a two-step process. If you have the time to correct individual transactions, this method retains your bank reconciliation status and identifies the payment with the customer's open invoice. Be prepared for a bit of tedious work. You need to have a good record of which deposit was paying for which customer invoice. Remember, these steps are to correct transactions that have been recorded incorrectly.

To manually correct recorded Make Deposits and apply them to the correct open invoice, follow these steps:

1. From the menu bar, select **Banking, Use Register**.

2. The Use Register dialog box opens. Select the bank account to which the deposit was made.

3. Locate the deposit in the checkbook register and double-click it to open the Make Deposits transaction. Change the account assigned in the From Account column from Income to Accounts Receivable. The effect of this step is to credit, or decrease, Accounts Receivable (see Figure 10.36). Click Save & Close.

> **tip**
>
> I like using the Reports, Customers & Receivable, Open Invoices report because I can see both the unapplied credits and open invoices grouped by customer or job.

Figure 10.36
Changing the From Account column on a deposit to Accounts Receivable creates a credit for the customer listed in the Received From column.

4. From the menu bar, select **Reports, Customers & Receivables, Open Invoices**, and double-click the unpaid invoice.

5. From the Main tab of the ribbon toolbar, click the Apply Credits icon and select the credit that pertains to this invoice.

6. Click Done to close the Apply Credits dialog box. Click Save & Close.

You have now corrected the deposit and assigned the amount to the open customer invoice, all without changing your bank reconciliation status of the item. This process works well, but it can be tedious if you have many transactions with this type of error.

Grouping Deposited Items to Agree with Bank Deposit

Unless you take every check or cash payment from your customers to the bank on a separate bank deposit ticket, your customer payments should be grouped, with the total matching your bank deposit slip.

If you group your customer payments on the same deposit transaction and match the total deposited to your bank deposit ticket, your bank reconciliation will be much easier to complete each month.

Do not attempt this correcting method if you have reconciled your bank account in QuickBooks. Also, if you are correcting years of unreconciled transactions, this method might just be too tedious.

The easiest place to see the problem is in your bank account register. From the menu bar, select **Banking**, **Use Register**, and choose the appropriate bank account.

As in Figure 10.33, assume that the deposit total per the bank records on 12/15/17 was $21,193.67 but that, in the QuickBooks checkbook register, you recorded two individual deposits.

This situation was caused by choosing Checking as the Deposit To account when receiving the customer's payment (see Figure 10.37). The preferred method would have been to select Undeposited Funds and group them on one deposit transaction.

Figure 10.37
This customer payment won't be grouped with other customer funds on the same bank deposit ticket.

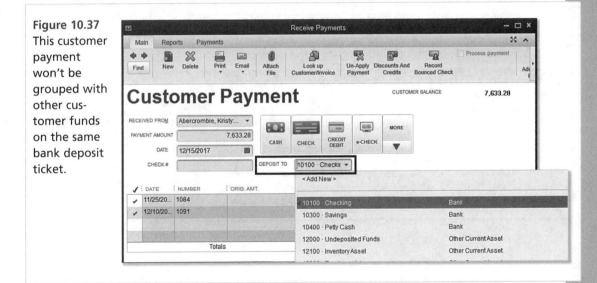

To correct these errors (be aware that it is a time-intensive process if you have many months or years of transactions), follow these steps:

1. From the displayed Receive Payments transaction that was originally deposited directly to the bank account, select the **Deposit To** drop-down list and select **Undeposited Funds**.

2. From the menu bar, select **Banking, Make Deposits**. QuickBooks displays a list of all the payments received but not yet included in a deposit (included in the Undeposited Funds balance sheet account balance).

3. Click to place a checkmark next to the grouped payments, and verify that the total deposit agrees with each individual bank deposit.

4. Click OK. The Make Deposit transaction now agrees with the actual bank deposit recorded by the bank.

Eliminating the Print Queue for Customer Invoices Marked to Print

On the Main tab of the ribbon toolbar on each customer invoice is the option to select **Print Later**. QuickBooks remembers the setting from the last stored invoice, which can sometimes hinder your own company process.

If you find that you have many invoices selected to print and you don't intend to print them, try this easy solution:

1. Place one or two sheets of paper in your printer. From the menu bar, select **File, Print Forms, Invoices**. The Select Invoices to Print dialog box displays the invoices that are marked to be printed (see Figure 10.38).

Figure 10.38 View the invoices selected to print.

2. The checkmark next to the invoice tells QuickBooks you want to print the invoice on paper. Click OK to send the forms to the printer.

3. After a couple invoices print, a message displays showing a list of the forms that did not print. Because you don't want to print them, click OK; each transaction is marked in QuickBooks as if it were printed. You might also need to cancel the print job at your printer. Another option is to print the invoices to a PDF printer (file).

Correcting Sales Tax Errors

Sales tax errors can be a bit tricky to fix, so make sure you can answer the following questions:

- Have you made a backup of your data?

- Have taxes or financials been prepared using the current data? If yes, you need to be concerned about the dates and types of the corrections you make.

- If the QuickBooks sales tax due is incorrect, have you determined outside QuickBooks how much was or is due?

Print your sales tax reports before you begin to make corrections to your data file. Then when your corrections are complete, print the same reports to be sure you achieved the desired end result. Of course, keep good paper documentation of why you did what you did, in case you are subject to a sales tax audit.

When a Check or Bill Is Used to Pay the Sales Tax

In newer versions of QuickBooks, the error of using a check or bill to pay sales tax should happen less often. QuickBooks provides messages to users attempting to pay their sales tax vendors incorrectly.

When you pay a vendor and assign the Sales Tax Payable account (created by QuickBooks) on a check or bill, QuickBooks provides the warning in Figure 10.39.

Figure 10.39
Warning when using a check to record a sales tax payment.

Paying Sales Tax by Check

The account you chose could be a sales tax liability account. If you're trying to pay sales tax, you should use the Pay Sales Tax window instead. Recording this check transaction will not be considered a payment against any sales tax owed. To pay sales tax, go to the Vendors menu, choose Sales Tax, and then click Pay Sales Tax.

☐ Do not display this message in the future

OK

When you locate a sales tax payment made by check (or bill), first determine whether the check has been included in the bank reconciliation. If it has not, void the check and re-create the check per the instructions in the section titled "Paying Sales Tax."

If the check has already been included in the bank reconciliation, use the following method to assign the check or bill to the line items in the Pay Sales Tax dialog box:

1. From the menu bar, select **Vendors**, **Vendor Center**. Select the vendor to which sales tax payments were made using the incorrect transaction type.

2. From the Show drop-down list to the right, click All Payments Issued. Click a selected transaction to open it to view.

3. Assign the Sales Tax Payable liability account in the Account column of the Expenses tab.

4. In the Customer:Job column, select the Sales Tax Vendor from the list of vendors (make sure it is a vendor and not an Other Name list item).

5. Click Save & Close to close the check (or bill).

6. From the menu bar, select **Vendors**, **Sales Tax**, **Pay Sales Tax**. The corrected transaction displays in the Pay Sales Tax dialog box if it is dated on or before the Show Sales Tax Due Through date.

7. When you are ready to pay your next period's sales tax, place a checkmark next to each sales tax line item, including the line item with the correction to associate the check or bill payment with the sales tax due (see Figure 10.40). If the net total amount is zero, wait and select each of the items for the next period you pay your sales tax.

> **note**
>
> If you are an accounting professional working with QuickBooks Accountant 2014 software, review Appendix A, "Client Data Review." CDR includes a tool that helps you efficiently correct sales tax payments that were recording using the incorrect payment transaction type.

Figure 10.40
Include the corrected check (or bill) with your next period sales tax payment.

If the net Amt. Due is zero, place a checkmark next to each item; QuickBooks associates your check or bill payment with the related sales tax due. When you return to the Pay Sales Tax dialog box, the amount previously showing as unpaid no longer is displayed. If the Amt. Due does not agree with your records, you might need to create a sales tax adjustment before making your next sales tax payment.

When the Sales Tax Liability Report Shows Past Sales Tax Due

If your collected sales tax amount and the amount showing payable on the Sales Tax Liability report do not match, as in Figure 10.41, it is because sales taxes collected before the current report's Show Sales Tax Through date remain unpaid. Perhaps the payments were incorrectly paid using a check or bill; if so, you should correct these errors following the instructions in the previous section.

These two amounts should match.

Figure 10.41
When the tax collected and the sales tax payable do not match, previous sales taxes have not been properly recorded or remitted.

To verify the totals and make the needed corrections, follow these steps:

1. From the menu bar, select **Vendors**, **Sales Tax**, **Sales Tax Liability**.

2. From the Dates drop-down list, select **This Month-to-Date**.

3. If the Tax Collected and Sales Tax Payable totals agree for today's date, your sales tax payment made previously was given the wrong Show Sales Tax Through date. To fix this error, you can void and reissue the payment or know that the QuickBooks report prepared for a future date should reflect the payment accurately.

4. If the two totals do not match, verify that the tax collected for the current period is correct. You can verify this amount by reviewing the invoices you have issued for the month.

5. Verify that the tax collected for the earlier period was correct.

6. Determine to what account(s) your sales tax payments were incorrectly recorded. The previously made payments would cause these accounts to be overstated.

   In the correcting entry example in Figure 10.42, your research found that a Sales Tax Expense type account was used when recording a sales tax payment in error.

7. From the menu bar, select **Company**, **Make General Journal Entries** to create a correcting entry.

8. Date the entry in the period you are correcting.

9. Give the entry a number, or let QuickBooks automatically number it if you've set that preference.

10. Leave the first line of the general journal blank.

11. On the second line in the Account column, select the **Sales Tax Payable** liability account.

12. Enter a debit amount if you are decreasing your sales tax payable amount. Enter a credit amount if you are increasing your sales tax payable amount.

Figure 10.42
Journal entries can correct sales tax payable errors.

13. On the third line, select the account that you discovered to be overstated or understated in your review (see step 6).

14. Enter the same amount from line 2 in the opposite column (debit or credit) from the previous line. Verify that your debits are equal to your credits.

15. Click Save & Close to close the general journal.

You now can select this line item with other sales tax lines for future tax payments, similar to what Figure 10.40 showed.

You might opt for this method to fix many months' errors with one journal entry and then put in place better controls for future sales tax management.

When Total Sales Does Not Equal Total Income

One of the important comparisons to make is to compare the Sales Tax Liability total sales with the Profit & Loss Standard total income. The section "Reconciling Total Sales to Total Income" discussed both reports. Before comparing the reports, be sure to create both using the same accounting basis: accrual or cash. The default basis for the sales tax report comes from the Sales Tax Preference discussed earlier in this chapter. With the report displayed, you can click the Customize Report button to change the basis being used for that report.

What can cause your total sales on your Sales Tax Liability report not to match your total income on your Profit & Loss report? Some of the reasons might be the following:

- **Different accounting basis between reports**—Your Sales Tax Liability report basis conflicts with your Profit & Loss reporting basis. By default, the basis of the report is printed on the top left of the report. Both reports must be either accrual basis or cash basis before comparing.

- **Non-sales-type transactions recorded to income accounts**—Locate these transactions by double-clicking the total income amount on your Profit & Loss report. Doing so opens the Transaction Detail by Account report. At the top right of the report, select **Sort By** and choose Type. Within each income account group, QuickBooks sorts the transactions by transaction type. Review the report for nonsales transaction types, such as General Journal or Bill (to name a couple). If you find an expense transaction in this report, often the cause is using items on expense transactions, when the item record has only an assigned income account. Chapter 4, "Understanding QuickBooks Lists," has more details on properly setting up items.

 tip

Because you want to compare the totals, try this: From the menu bar, select **Window, Tile Vertically**. Both reports display side by side, as in Figure 10.43, if these reports are the only currently open windows.

- **Using items on sales forms that are assigned to a non-income account**—For example, a company that collects customer deposits might be using an item that is assigned to a current liability account. Total sales on the Sales Tax Liability report would include this amount, but the Profit & Loss would not.

- **Income recorded as a result of vendor discounts**—If you have set up an income account for your vendor discounts in your bills preferences setting, you need to deduct this amount from your total revenue when you compare the two totals. If you are using an income account, create a separate income account for these discounts so that you can easily identify them.

You can correct the first two bullet points in the previous list by changing the reporting basis or correcting the original item record (from the menu bar, select **Lists, Item List**) to include both an income and an expense account.

The last two points are less likely to be changed in your process. Instead, you might need to prepare specific reports to proof your totals, making sure that you are using the correct information when you file your sales tax return.

Now that you have identified the difference, what exactly does it mean? If your state requires you to report total sales as income earned on your sales tax reports, in this example, the proper amount to report would come from your Profit & Loss report. Your company's results might differ and might be more difficult to identify.

In the following exercise, use the sample data to see how these reports can help you reconcile the differences.

Reconciling Financials and Sales Tax Reports

To practice reconciling (proofing) the Profit & Loss total income to the sales tax payable on the Sales Tax Liability report, open the sample data file as Chapter 1 instructed. Your totals might differ from those shown in the figures here, but the process remains the same:

1. From the Reports menu, open these two reports:

    - **Company & Financial, Profit & Loss Standard**—In the Dates drop-down list, select Last Month.

    - **Vendors & Payables, Sales Tax Liability**—By default, Last Month is selected in the Dates field.

2. Notice in this exercise that Total Sales from the Sales Tax Liability report and Total Income from the Profit & Loss report (on the right in Figure 10.43) do not match. The difference between the two amounts in this example is $2,174.50.

These two totals should agree.

Figure 10.43
When comparing two reports, select **Window, Tile Vertically**.

3. From the menu bar, select **Reports, Sales, Sales by Item Summary**. In the Dates drop-down list, select Last Month. See Figure 10.44.

4. Click Customize Report, and remove the checkmarks for COGS, Ave. COGS, Gross Margin, and Gross Margin % because you do not need this information for your analysis. Click OK.

5. To make this report easier to read, consider clicking the Collapse button at the top right of the open report.

6. What exactly are you looking for? Because this report shows all items sold on customer sales forms during the same month being reconciled, you are looking for items that do not map to ordinary income accounts. In Figure 10.44, the difference is easy to spot: The Retainage 1 item was used on sales transactions during the month. A review of the item record shows that the account assigned is a Balance Sheet account (see Figure 10.45).

    Optionally, you might want to try customizing the Sales Tax Liability report. Click the Customize Report button, select the Filters tab in the Modify Report dialog box, and select **All Ordinary Income Accounts** from the Accounts drop-down list, as in Figure 10.46. From here, review the amount displayed in the Total Sales Column. If this amount now agrees with your Profit & Loss report, you can be sure there are items on invoices that are mapped to accounts other than ordinary income accounts.

Figure 10.44
Report differences might arise when items with non-income accounts assigned are included on sales transactions.

Figure 10.45
When reviewing differences, review the account assigned to items sold during the period.

Figure 10.46
Modify the Sales Tax Liability report to troubleshoot discrepancies.

Correcting Undeposited Funds Account Errors

Did you make it through the review of each of the referenced reports in the earlier sections of this chapter? You don't want to jump into fixing transactions that affect your Accounts Receivable balances without due diligence in researching what the correct balance should be. Without the review and troubleshooting time, you might hastily delete, void, or modify a transaction, only to compound the problem.

This section details specific steps for correcting the errors you might find. It is important to first discover why the error was made and then fix it so you can avoid the same error on future transactions.

Reviewing the Balance in the Undeposited Funds Account

Before you can begin to agree or disagree with your Undeposited Funds account balance, it is best to review your QuickBooks data, concentrating on certain reports that help you simplify the review process.

This section provides instructions on creating specific reports you can use for this task.

> **⚡ caution**
>
> Before you troubleshoot your Undeposited Funds Detail, reconcile your bank account. Identify what transactions have cleared your bank and which transactions have been recorded in QuickBooks but did not clear your bank in a timely manner.
>
> ➡️ *For more information, see "Reconciling the Bank or Credit Card Account," p. 538.*

Creating an Undeposited Funds Detail Report

The first report I create for a client is a custom report titled Undeposited Funds Detail. This is not a prebuilt report in QuickBooks, but it is easy to create.

This report is fundamental because you cannot troubleshoot a total balance for the undeposited funds you see on a balance sheet report without knowing the detail behind the numbers. If you print the register for the account, too much data displays, making it difficult to identify what is not deposited.

How do transactions get to this account? When you select the Undeposited Funds account as the deposit-to account (or you set the preference to have QuickBooks automatically do this), QuickBooks increases the balance in the Undeposited Funds account. Then when you complete a Make Deposit, QuickBooks reduces the Undeposited Funds account balance and, behind the scenes, marks the original increase and the new decrease as cleared. Table 10.1 shows the relationship of these transactions to your accounting.

Table 10.1 Transaction Effect on Undeposited Funds Account

Transaction Type	Accounts Receivable	Undeposited Funds	Bank Account
Customer Receive Payments with Undeposited Funds Account Selected as the Deposit To Account	Decreases (credit)	Increases (debit)	No effect
Make Deposits	No effect	Decreases (credit)	Increases (debit)

Before we dig too deeply, let's see if you agree with the detail of the Undeposited Funds balance in your QuickBooks data. You also might want to memorize this report for the convenience of reviewing the detail often, avoiding any data entry errors this section might help you uncover.

> **⚐ caution**
>
> The modified custom report you named Undeposited Funds Detail always shows the present state of the transaction, which means that when a payment is received and is included on a Make Deposits transaction, the report for a prior date will no longer show that item as undeposited. Behind the scenes, QuickBooks marks the transaction as cleared as of the transaction date; therefore, you cannot get a historical snapshot with this report.

To create this Undeposited Funds Detail report, follow these easy steps:

1. From the menu bar, select **Reports**, **Custom Reports**, **Transaction Detail**. The Modify Report dialog box opens.

2. Display the date range as All.

3. For Total By, from the bottom of the list, select **Payment Method**.

4. For Columns, select the ones you want to view on the report.

5. Click the Filters tab. In the Choose Filter box, select **Account**, and choose the account named **Undeposited Funds** from the drop-down list.

6. Also from the Filters tab, select **Cleared** and click the No button.

> **◉ tip**
>
> For the date range field, type the letter **a** to make the date range default to All.

7. Click the Header/Footer tab. Type **Undeposited Funds Detail** as the report title. Click OK.

This report provides the details of the amounts that are included in the Undeposited Funds account balance. You might want to include preparing this report at the end of each month for your records. Following are other reports you might find useful when reviewing the balance in your Undeposited Funds account.

Creating a General Ledger Report of the Undeposited Funds Account

You can review a General Ledger report of the Undeposited Funds account balance that agrees with the ending balance on your Balance Sheet report, but without quite a bit of manual work, you cannot identify each individual transaction that makes up the Undeposited Funds account for a specific prior period. Why? Because each time you deposit a receive payment, QuickBooks marks the original dated line item as cleared. This is why you must first create a custom report to see if the current (today's date) detail is correct.

If you review your balances monthly, you need to print the Undeposited Funds Detail report you created earlier in this chapter, on the last day of your accounting month. Save this report in your paper file for future reference because you cannot go back to a historical date and get the same information.

If you take credit cards as payments from your customers, I recommend that you not complete the Make Deposits task until you view a bank statement showing the funds deposited into your bank account. This does not mean waiting a month for the statement to arrive, because most financial institutions now offer online account access to your account statements.

For those clients, particularly retail businesses, where there is often a large volume of customer receipts in any day, I recommend reviewing the modified report as part of the month, quarter, or year-end process. Notice whether any old dated transactions are on the list. If you find none, you can assume that the Balance Sheet balance in Undeposited Funds as of the earlier period date is probably correct.

To generate a General Ledger report, follow these steps:

1. From the menu bar, select **Reports**, **Accountant & Taxes**, **General Ledger**.

2. Select **Customize Report** from the report screen.

3. In the Modify dialog box that opens, enter an appropriate Report Date Range.

4. From the Columns box, select the columns you want to see. (You might want to include Clr to see the cleared status of transactions.)

5. Click the Advanced button and, from the Include box, select **In Use**. This streamlines the data that results on the report.

6. Click the Filters tab, choose to filter for Account, and select the **Undeposited Funds** account from the drop-down list.

7. Click OK.

You can use this General Ledger report to see details for the Undeposited Funds account and to see if the running balance in this report agrees with your Balance Sheet report. However, you still cannot use this report to identify which Receive Payments transaction was not deposited as of the report date because QuickBooks does not capture the information with an "as of" date.

Removing Old Dated Payments in the Undeposited Funds Account

Did your review of the data uncover old dated payment transactions still in the Undeposited Funds account? If yes, use the following method to remove these payments without editing or modifying each transaction.

This method of correcting makes the following assumptions:

- Your bank account is reconciled before making these changes.

- You have reviewed your Accounts Receivable Aging reports and made any necessary corrections.

- You have identified which payment amounts are still showing in the Undeposited Funds account, and these are the same amounts that have already been deposited to your bank register by some other method.

- You have identified the specific chart of accounts (typically income accounts) to which the deposits were originally incorrectly recorded.

🛜 caution

The date you assign the Make Deposits transaction is the date the impact will be recorded in your financials. You have several important considerations to take into account when selecting the appropriate date:

- Are the corrections for an earlier year?

- Has the tax return been prepared using current financial information from QuickBooks for that earlier period?

- Has another adjustment to the books been done to correct the issue?

If you answered yes to any of these, you should contact your accountant and ask advice about the date this transaction should have.

This method enables you to remove the unwanted balance in your Undeposited Funds account with just a few keystrokes. To remove old payments in the Undeposited Funds account, follow these steps:

1. If the funds that remain in your Undeposited Funds account are from more than one year ago, you first should identify the total amount that was incorrectly deposited for each year. See the sidebar "Creating a Payment Transaction List Detail Report" in this chapter. Filter the report for the specific date range.

2. Now start the process of removing these identified Undeposited Funds items by selecting **Banking**, **Make Deposits** from the menu bar. The Payments to Deposits dialog box displays. From the Sort Payments By drop-down list, select **Date**. See Figure 10.47.

Figure 10.47
The older payments in Undeposited Funds were posted to the checking account by some other method.

3. In the Payments to Deposit dialog box, select all the payments for deposit with dates in the date range you are correcting by placing a checkmark next to the payment items. Click OK.

The Make Deposits dialog box opens, with each of the previously selected payments included on a new Make Deposit.

4. On the next available line, enter the account to which the incorrect deposits were originally recorded. In this example, you discovered that the Construction Income account was overstated by the incorrectly recorded deposits. The effect of this new transaction is to decrease (debit) the Construction Income account and decrease (credit) the Undeposited Funds account without any effect on the checking account, as in Figure 10.48.

Figure 10.48
Enter a line with a negative amount recorded to the account that was previously overstated.

RECEIVED FROM	FROM ACCOUNT	MEMO	CHK NO.	PMT ME...	CLASS	AMOUNT
Pretell Real Estate:75 Sunset Rd.	12000 · Undeposited Funds		588009...	Check		23,583.14
Smallson, Fran:Office remodeling	12000 · Undeposited Funds		485096	Check		1,665.00
Vasquez, Anabel:Basement Re...	12000 · Undeposited Funds		19482	Check		25,471.56
Bauman, Mark:Home Remodel	12000 · Undeposited Funds		39923	Check		16,500.00
Fisher, Jennifer:Home Remodel	12000 · Undeposited Funds		29304	Check		16,500.00
Prentice, Adelaide:Guest Villa	12000 · Undeposited Funds		83984	Check		36,575.00
	40100 · Construction Income	Correcting				-143,030.66

Make Deposits — Deposit To: 10100 · Chec... Date: 12/31/2016 Memo: Deposit

Click Payments to select customer payments that you have received. List any other amounts to deposit below.

Deposit Subtotal   0.00

To get cash back from this deposit, enter the amount below. Indicate the account where you want this money to go, such as your Petty Cash account.

Cash back goes to   Cash back memo   Cash back amount

Deposit Total   0.00

5. Make sure to mark as cleared this net -0- deposit in your next bank reconciliation.

You should now be able to review the Undeposited Funds Detail report and agree that the items listed on this report as of today's date are those you have not yet physically taken to your bank to be deposited or that the credit card vendors have not yet credited to your bank.

Unique Customer Transactions

This chapter details ways you can review and troubleshoot your data, and provides instructions on how to fix many of the common Accounts Receivable errors. This section of the chapter shares some ways to handle unique transactions—the type of transaction you might come across but are not sure how to enter.

Recording Your Accountant's Year-End Adjusting Journal Entry to Accounts Receivable

Adjustments at tax time often include adjustments to your Accounts Receivable account. Your accountant typically creates this transaction using a Make General Journal Entries transaction. What can make the entry more difficult for you is when no customer(s) are identified with the adjustment.

You can request a breakdown by customer of the adjustments made to the Accounts Receivable account. If that is not available and you need to enter the adjustment, you might want to consider using the following method:

1. From the Customer Center, enter a fictitious customer name—something such as **Accountant YE Adj**.

2. Use this customer to apply the line item to in the Make Journal Entry. Remember that this is a temporary fix, and the balance for the fictitious customer will display on your Open Invoices report.

Later, when you are able to collect from the actual customer(s) who make up the adjustment, you can enter a reversing entry for the fictitious customer and create new entries for the correct customers.

> **caution**
>
> You can add new customers by selecting the Customer Center from the QuickBooks Home page.
>
> However, QuickBooks does not let you use the same name on the customer list as the vendor list. A little trick can help with this; when naming the new fictitious customer, enter a - **C** after the name. This naming convention will not display on invoices, but when selecting this name from lists, it will bring to your attention that you are using the "customer" list item.

When a Customer Is Also a Vendor

Often I am asked how to handle a transaction when you are selling your company's product or service, but instead of getting paid, you are trading it for the products or services of your customer.

To keep track of the both the revenue and costs in this bartering arrangement, follow these steps:

1. From the menu bar, select **Lists**, **Chart of Accounts** to open the Chart of Accounts dialog box.

2. Click the Account button. Select **New** and create an account named Barter Account as a bank account type following the instructions on the screen. Click Save & Close.

3. Create a new customer record for your vendor (or a new vendor record for your customer) using instructions found in previous chapters and using the naming tip provided in the caution in this section. The following instructions assume that you are selling your product or services to your vendor in a bartering agreement.

4. From the menu bar, select **Customers**, **Create Invoices**. Select the new customer you created (your vendor that was added to the customer list). Enter the information as if you were selling your products or services to this customer. Click Save & Close.

> **caution**
>
> If your default preference is set to assign the specific bank account when you receive the payment, select the **Barter Account** for this type of transaction.

5. From the menu bar, select **Customers**, **Receive Payments**. Select the new customer you created and record the amount of the payment, placing a checkmark next to the appropriate fictitious invoice.

6. From the menu bar, select **Banking**, **Make Deposits** to open the Payments to Deposit dialog box. Place a checkmark next to the fictitious transaction, and click OK to advance to the Make Deposits dialog box.

7. In the Make Deposits dialog box, select the **Barter Account** as the Deposit To account and select the date you want this transaction recorded. Click Save & Close when done. See Figure 10.49.

Figure 10.49
Deposit the fictitious payment into the Barter Account.

You have recorded the potential revenue side as well as the fictitious payment of the invoice of the barter agreement. Now you need to record the expense side of the transaction.

I recommend keeping the transactions going into and out of the barter account equal in value; if not, you will need to make an adjustment in the register. Select **Banking**, **User Register** from the menu bar. Select the **Barter Account**, and increase or decrease the amount to an income or expense account as determined by the amount left in the account.

To continue with the example presented previously, let's record the fictitious payment to your vendor you are bartering with. When working with your own data, you might instead be bartering with your customer:

1. Enter your expense transaction as you normally would, as if you were going to pay your vendor for the products or services being purchased.

2. If you are using a Write Check transaction, select the **Barter Account** as the checking account. If you are using the Enter Bill transaction, complete the bill entry as you normally would.

3. For the check or reference number, use any number or alphanumeric characters you want.

4. For the payee, select the vendor you are bartering with. This should be the same vendor you entered the Write Check or Enter Bill transaction for in step 2.

5. Record to the normal expense account an amount as if you were purchasing the goods or services with a check.

6. Click Save & Close. If you are paying by check, the process is complete. If you recorded a vendor bill, continue with the following steps.

7. To pay the bill, select **Vendors**, **Pay Bills** from the menu bar. Optionally, filter the Pay Bills dialog box with the vendor's name.

8. Place a checkmark next to the appropriate bill that has been paid by providing the vendor with your product or services.

9. In the Payment Method box, select the choice to assign a check number because you don't expect to print a check to give to the vendor.

10. In the Payment Account box, select the newly created **Barter Account** as the payment account.

11. Click **Pay Selected Bills** to open the Assign Check Numbers dialog box. Assign a fictitious check number of your choosing. You can even use the term Barter for the check number. Click OK, and QuickBooks displays a payment summary. Click Done.

When this process is finished, your Barter Account should have a zero balance (see Figure 10.50), as indicated earlier in this section. You might even want to perform a bank reconciliation of the Barter Account to clear both equal sides of the transaction.

Figure 10.50
The Barter Account will have a net -0- balance when all transactions are recorded properly.

Recording a Customer's Bounced Check

QuickBooks 2014 now automates the entry of the transactions needed to properly record the effects of a customer's bounced check. Banks refer to this as insufficient funds, or NSF.

Typically, banks charge the QuickBooks user's account a fee when this occurs, in addition to reducing the QuickBooks user's bank account by the amount of the deposit.

Failure to keep the accounting correct for these transactions leads to misstated bank account balances, as well as understated customer receivables.

Before recording a payment in your QuickBooks file as NSF, the following conditions must be met:

- Only Check payment types can be reversed using the Bounced Check feature.

- The Receive Payments check transaction must already be included in a Make Deposit transaction.

> 🔍 **note**
>
> Receive Payments transaction type not yet deposited (included in the Undeposited Funds balance) cannot be recorded as bounced until they have been included in a Make Deposit transaction. You can determine this quickly because the Record Bounced Check icon is grayed out.

➡️ *For more information about working with the Undeposited Funds account preference, see "Payments," p. 306.*

Follow these steps to use the new QuickBooks 2014 feature for recording bounced checks:

1. Locate the Receive Payments transaction that has been returned by your bank. You can do this in several ways, including the following:

   - From the menu bar, select **Customer**, **Customer Center**; with the customer selected on the left, you can filter and browse the transactions on the right.

   - From the menu bar, select **Customer**, **Receive Payment**. At the top right of the Main tab on the transaction ribbon toolbar, click the arrow to scroll through recent receive payments, or click the Find button to filter for the transaction.

2. On the Main tab of the transaction ribbon toolbar, click the Record Bounced Check icon. The Manage Bounced Check dialog box displays (see Figure 10.51).

3. In the Manage Bounced Check dialog box, enter any fee your bank charges, the date of the charge, and the expense account you want this charge recorded to.

4. Optionally, if you want to charge your customer a fee, enter the fee in the Customer Fee box.

5. Click Next. QuickBooks displays the Bounced Check Summary details (see Figure 10.52).

6. Click Finish. QuickBooks returns you to the original Receive Payments transaction and adds a Bounced Check stamp (see Figure 10.53).

> 🔍 **note**
>
> The original invoices are marked as unpaid, and the new journal entry created for the NSF is now marked as paid by the original Receive Payments transaction.

If you selected to charge the customer a fee, QuickBooks automatically creates the following, to create a new invoice for payment by the customer:

- **Income Account**—Titled Returned Check Charges

- **Other Charge Item**—Titled Bounce Check Charge, assigned to the newly created Income account

Figure 10.51
QuickBooks 2014 includes a new feature named Record Bounced Check.

Figure 10.52
QuickBooks displays a summary of the transactions automatically created.

Figure 10.53
A Bounced
Check stamp
identifies this
original trans-
action as NSF.

For accounting professionals, Table 10.2 details the individual accounting effect of the transactions:

Table 10.2 Bounced Check Transactions

Type	Date	Debit	Credit	Notes
Journal Entry	User selects	Accounts Receivable	Bank Account	Records NSF for the original deposit and re-assigns the original payment to this transaction
Journal Entry	User selects	Account/Class user assigns	Bank Account	NSF fee charged by the bank
Invoice	User selects	Accounts Receivable	Income	NSF fee charged to client using an item QuickBooks creates
Original invoice(s) are removed from the original Receive Payments assignment and are unpaid on an aged receivable report.				

You have successfully created the transactions needed to properly record the effects of the customer's bounced check.

Tracking Customer Deposits in QuickBooks

Do you require your customers to pay a deposit before shipping the product or providing the service? You might want to track these in one of two ways:

- As a credit to the Accounts Receivable balance for the specific customer

- As a credit to an Other Current Liability account

You might want to ask your company accountant which method is preferred. The first method is often easier and takes fewer steps. The second method of using a current liability account reports the prepayment in the proper category on the business's balance sheet.

If you are choosing the first method, you create a receive payment when your customer pays and do not assign the payment to an invoice. In effect, this debits (increases) your Undeposited Funds account or bank account and credits (reduces) Accounts Receivable balances.

If you choose to use the second method, follow these steps:

1. If needed, start the process to create a Customer Deposits account by selecting **Lists**, **Chart of Accounts** from the menu bar.

2. Click the Account button at the bottom of the screen and select **New**.

3. In the Add New Account dialog box that opens, from the Other Account Types drop-down list, select the **Other Current Liability** type account and follow the remaining steps on the screen.

4. Create an item to be used on invoices for this prepayment. From the menu bar, select **Lists**, **Item Lists**.

5. Click the Item button on the bottom of the list and select **New**.

6. In the New Item type drop-down list, select **Other Charge**.

7. In the Item Name/Number field, type a name such as **Customer Deposits**. Enter an optional description and select the **Customer Deposits** other current liability account from the Account drop-down list.

8. Prepare your invoice to the customer for the amount of the prepayment you are requiring. When the customer pays, record the Receive Payments transaction.

9. When the project is completed and you are ready to recognize the revenue associated with the sale, create your invoice using the item(s) that were sold to the customer. On the next available line of your invoice use the Customer Deposit item—but this time, enter a negative amount. See Figure 10.54.

QuickBooks records the revenue in the period the sale was completed, and the final invoice is reduced by the amount of the deposit previously paid.

Using the method described here does have a trade-off. If you are a cash basis taxpayer, you would not expect to see a balance in your Accounts Receivable account when the Balance Sheet report is prepared on a cash basis. However, when you use this method, you will see an Accounts Receivable balance on a cash basis Balance Sheet report. One cause of this is that QuickBooks reports an Accounts Receivable balance on a cash basis Balance Sheet report when items are used that map to other Balance Sheet accounts.

Figure 10.54
Proper accounting for customer deposits paid on the final invoice when you track the original payment as a liability.

Invoice

DATE	BILL TO	SHIP TO	Ship To 1 ▼
12/15/2017 📅	Pam Craven	Pam Craven	
INVOICE #	7105 N. Landon	7105 N. Landon	
1102	E. Bayshore, CA 94327	E. Bayshore, CA 94327	

TERMS	DUE DATE
Due on receipt ▼	12/15/2017 📅

ITEM	DESCRIPTION	QUANTITY	U/M	RATE	AMOUNT	TAX
Subs:Electrical	Electrical work	1		5,000.00	5,000.00	Non
Subs:Insulating	Install insulation	1		2,500.00	2,500.00	Non
Subs:Painting	Painting	1		750.00	750.00	Non
Customer Deposits	Customer Deposits			-3,000.00	-3,000.00	Non

	East Bayshore ▼ (0.3%)	0.00
ONLINE PAY Off ▼	Total	5,250.00
Customer Message	PAYMENTS APPLIED	0.00
We appreciate your prompt payment. ▼	BALANCE DUE	**5,250.00**

Unique Sales Tax Transactions

Over the years, I have come across some unique sales tax transaction tracking needs. This section addresses several that you might find useful if your state has similar guidelines.

As always, because you are acting as the agent for the state in collecting sales tax from your customers, you should take the time to research the sales tax regulations for each state where you do business.

The state you sell in might require you to collect and track multiple sales tax rates, depending on where the customer is located. If you have a customer with different tax rate locations, you need to create a customer for each tax location if you want QuickBooks to automatically calculate the correct tax amount, because QuickBooks tracks the sales tax rate by customer, not by job.

When Your State Imposes a Maximum Sales Tax

I have encountered having to track a state-imposed maximum sales tax a few times. If your state imposes a maximum sales tax for a certain type of sale, I recommend the following method:

1. From the menu bar, select **Lists**, **Item List**. The Item List displays.

2. If you do not have a subtotal item on your list, select the Item drop-down list in the lower left and select **New**.

3. From the Type drop-down list, select **Subtotal**. Type **Subtotal** for the both Item Name/Number and Description. Click OK and click the X in the top-right corner to close the Item List.

4. To create the invoice to your customer, select **Customers**, **Create Invoices** from the menu bar.

5. Enter the taxable items on the invoice, making sure the Tax column has Tax listed.

6. Enter a subtotal item—you might even want to type in the description that this amount is subject to sales tax.

7. Enter the next sale item that is normally taxed. If you have met a threshold defined by your state, select **Non** in the Tax column. See Figure 10.55.

QuickBooks now records the total sales (in this example) of $6,000.00, but it shows only $5,000 in the Taxable Sales column of the Sales Tax Liability report (see Figure 10.56).

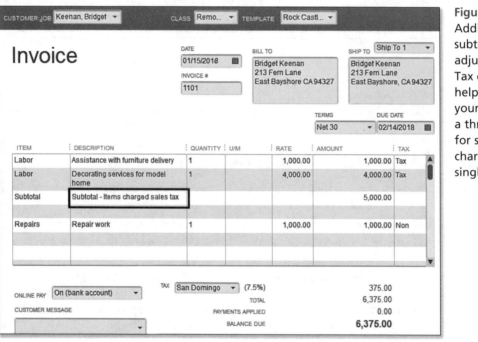

Figure 10.55 Adding a subtotal and adjusting the Tax column helps when your state has a threshold for sales tax charges on a single invoice.

Figure 10.56 QuickBooks properly separates the taxable revenue amount from the nontaxable sale amount.

Multiple Sales Tax Rates on One Invoice

In particular, if your business sells retail items, liquor, and food all on one sales form, chances are good that each item type is subject to a unique sales tax rate. Follow these steps for creating the subtotal item and 0% sales tax item. Assign this newly created 0% sales tax item to your customer's record on the Sales Tax Settings tab.

Next, create your customer's invoice as detailed in the previous section, following these additional steps:

1. Create these items:

   - **Subtotal Item**—Follow the steps outlined in the previous section.

   - **Sales Tax Item**—Type **See Above** for both the name and the description. Tax Rate is 0.0%. Tax Agency should be your most common Tax Agency vendor.

   - **Sales Tax Items**—Represent the tax jurisdictions you are required to collect and report on. Name them clearly so your customer can identify them.

2. Enter the line item(s) subject to one tax rate.

3. Enter a subtotal line.

4. Enter the appropriate sales tax item.

5. Enter additional invoice lines, each with a subtotal and appropriate sales tax items.

QuickBooks calculates and reports on the correct amount of sales tax charged for the different item types being sold.

To further clarify this point, the example in Figure 10.57 does not track sales by customer, but just provides a retail summary for the day's sales. The example also shows how to charge multiple sales tax rates on a single invoice by placing a subtotal after each group of sales and then placing the correct sales tax rate after the subtotal.

> **tip**
>
> If you want more information on this, press the F1 key on your keyboard to open QuickBooks Help. Click the Search tab and, on the top search bar, type **sales summaries**; then follow the link for more information on this topic.

Add subtotals before using multiple sales tax rates on the same invoice

Figure 10.57
Creating a
Daily Sales
Summary is a
perfect choice
for a retail
establishment
that does not
track individual customer
activity.

Issuing Credit Memos When Sales Tax Should Not Have Been Charged

Issuing customer credit memos is necessary for correct reporting when you file your sales tax on accrual basis (sales tax payment liability accrued as of the date of the customer invoice) and is not required when you report sales tax liability on cash basis (sales tax payment liability not accrued until the date of customer's payment). However, I still recommend having controls in place that limit the ability to modify an invoice from an earlier month.

After you have filed your sales tax return with your state, you should not adjust any invoices or sales tax payments recorded on or before your file-through date. If you do, QuickBooks recalculates the taxable sales, nontaxable sales, and amount owed, and your return as filed with the state will no longer agree with your QuickBooks data.

> **note**
>
> In Chapter 16, "Sharing QuickBooks Data with Your Accountant," p. 626, I discuss setting a closing date for your data. I recommend using this same control with your file after preparing your monthly or quarterly sales tax returns for your state.

Instead of adjusting a customer's invoice, consider using the QuickBooks customer credit memos/ refund. For example, suppose you charged sales tax to a nontaxable customer by mistake. Let's also assume you have filed your accrual basis sales tax return for the month of that invoice, overstating taxable sales.

Follow these steps to create a credit memo that simply adjusts the sales tax payable amount:

1. From the menu bar, select **Customers**, **Create Credit Memos/Refunds**.

2. Date the credit memo in the current period so that your next sales tax payment will include the credit.

3. Enter the taxable line item(s) that the original invoice included.

4. On the following row(s), enter the same line items as negative amounts and change the Tax status to Non (see Figure 10.58). The result is that the credit memo will be for the sales tax portion only.

5. Follow the same steps outlined in the section "Recording and Applying a Customer Credit Memo" in Chapter 9, p. 376, to complete the process of applying this credit to the customer's open invoice.

Figure 10.58 Create a credit memo that reduces the sales tax liability paid in a previous month.

You want to be sure to date the credit memo in the current month for which you have not yet filed your state sales tax reports. The credit memo then reduces the sales tax you owe for the current period.

I hope after reading this chapter you feel more empowered to efficiently manage your customer related tasks in QuickBooks.

QuickStart

Step 1. Sign Up for a Payroll Service **447**

Step 2. Complete the Payroll Setup **458**

Step 3. Pay Employees **482**

Step 4. Pay Liabilities **487**

11

SETTING UP PAYROLL

When your business hires employees, one of your most important tasks is making sure your QuickBooks data is set up correctly to handle this responsibility. This chapter details for you the proper way to set up your payroll. In Chapter 12, "Managing Payroll," p. 492, you learn how to efficiently review your payroll data and handle some of those unique payroll transactions.

Getting Started

For the new business owner, here is a common definition of an employee: "a person in the service of another under any contract of hire, express or implied, oral or written. The employer also has the power or right to control and direct the employee in the material details of how the work is to be performed." If your company hires individuals who meet this criteria, your company is responsible for paying wages, collecting and paying certain federal and state payroll taxes, and filing quarterly and annual forms.

Your company becomes an agent of the federal and state governments because the company must collect certain payroll-related taxes and pay these on predetermined payment schedules.

Payroll Process Overview

QuickBooks is designed to help you set up and manage your company's payroll. Payroll tasks are easily completed using the Employee Center and Payroll Center. Scheduling your payrolls and related liability payments practically eliminates the chance of making errors.

The recommended payroll workflow detailed here, when combined with the frequent review of reports, can help you manage your company's payroll efficiently and accurately:

note

Are you already using QuickBooks for your payroll processing? Start with the QuickBooks Run Payroll Checkup on p. 466.

1. Sign up for an Intuit QuickBooks payroll subscription.

2. Set Payroll and Employee preferences for your company.

3. Complete (if your data is new) the Payroll Setup process or use the Run Payroll Checkup diagnostic tool included with your QuickBooks software.

4. Set up scheduled payrolls to pay your employees.

5. Pay your scheduled payroll liabilities.

6. Reconcile your bank account each month, verifying that the paychecks distributed were cleared for the proper amounts.

7. Review and compare your business financials and payroll reports.

8. Prepare your quarterly and annual state and federal payroll forms directly in QuickBooks (depending on which payroll subscription you have purchased).

When managing payroll in QuickBooks, you use these transactions:

- **Paycheck**—Record payment to an employee and automatically calculate all additions and deductions. You can identify these in your bank register as the transactions with a PAY CHK transaction type, as in Figure 11.1.

Figure 11.1
Properly created employee paychecks have PAY CHK as the transaction type.

- **Pay Liabilities**—Record the payment of the accrued payroll taxes to the state and federal government.

- **Liability Adjustment**—Modify the payroll liability amounts computed from actual paychecks. You can identify these transactions in your bank register as transactions with a LIAB CHK transaction type.

- **Refund Deposit for Taxes and Liabilities**—Record any refund received from overpaying your payroll liabilities. You learn more about this transaction type in Chapter 12, p. 514.

You can access each of these transactions from the Payroll Center or by selecting submenus from Employees on the menu bar.

When you use the proper payroll transactions, QuickBooks includes the amounts in preparing payments of payroll liabilities due or when preparing state and federal payroll reports in QuickBooks.

Selecting and Activating a Payroll Service Subscription

For QuickBooks to automatically calculate your payroll, you need to purchase a payroll service subscription from Intuit (in addition to purchasing your QuickBooks financial software).

QuickBooks financial software partnered with an Intuit-provided payroll service makes setting up payroll, collecting taxes, remitting timely payments of the collected taxes, and filing the required payroll reports trouble free.

Purchase your payroll service subscription at www.payroll.com, or click the Turn On Payroll icon on the Home page and select a plan that works for your company. You can choose from several payroll subscriptions that start at these levels:

- **Do My Own Payroll**—Stay in control with just a few steps.

- **Intuit Provided Payroll Services**—Opt for worry-free payroll; you enter the hours and Intuit does the rest.

As of this writing, Intuit offers four payroll service options, one of which is sure to meet the needs of your company.

Preparing and Printing Paychecks Only

On the Home page, select **Turn On Payroll**. Choose the **I Want My Accountant** option. Click See My Plan. This option is the Intuit Basic Payroll subscription and includes the following:

- The capability to enter employee hours and let QuickBooks automatically calculate payroll taxes, additions, and other deductions

> **tip**
>
> The payroll offerings are detailed in this chapter, or you can visit http://payroll.intuit.com/compare/compare-quickbooks-payroll.jsp for a graphical comparison.

> **note**
>
> You can enable manual payroll in QuickBooks without purchasing a subscription. With manual payroll, QuickBooks does not calculate the payroll taxes or prepare the payroll forms. I do not recommend this method unless you have only a few payroll checks that are always the same amounts each pay period.
>
> From the menu bar, select **Help, QuickBooks Help**. In the search box, type **process payroll manually** and select the link with the same name. Read the information and follow the provided instructions.

- The option to print checks, or you can use free direct deposit of earnings into your employees' bank accounts

- Expert help via online knowledgebase or live assistance during business hours

- A variety of reports your accountant can use to complete payroll tax forms

Preparing and Printing Paychecks and Filing Tax Forms

On the Home page, select **Turn On Payroll**. Choose the **I Want To Pay & File** option and click See My Plan. This service is the Intuit Enhanced Payroll subscription and includes the following:

- Capability to enter employee hours and let QuickBooks automatically calculate payroll taxes, additions, and other deductions

- Option to print checks, or you can use free direct deposit of earnings into your employees' bank accounts

- Automatic completion of federal and most state tax forms for you to E-pay, print, or E-file

If you are an accounting professional, you can select the **Intuit Enhanced Payroll for Accountant's** subscription. With this subscription, you can do all the preceding tasks named plus the following:

- Create after-the-fact payroll

- Calculate net-to-gross paychecks

- Support up to 50 Federal Employer Identification Numbers (FEINs) with your paid payroll subscription

- Prepare Client Ready Payroll Reports (using Excel)

 note

If you currently use an outsourced payroll solution that does not integrate with QuickBooks, consider the Full Service payroll subscription. Entering payroll into QuickBooks can save time and improve accuracy.

For more details about the ProAdvisor program, visit http://proadvisor.intuit.com.

Allowing Intuit Payroll Experts to Prepare Your Payroll

On the Home page, select **Turn On Payroll**. Choose the **I Want Intuit Payroll Experts** option. Click See My Plan. This is the Assisted Payroll, and it gives you capabilities to do the following:

- Participate in one-on-one guidance with Intuit payroll experts to set up or transfer all your employee data.

- Enter hours into QuickBooks to create paychecks. Intuit reviews the payroll for accuracy. All your taxes, additions, and deductions are calculated automatically.

- Print checks or offer direct deposit into your employees' bank accounts.

- Allow Intuit to process tax payments and forms for you, guaranteed to be accurate and on time.

Using Intuit Online Payroll

With an Intuit Online Payroll subscription, you can prepare payroll anytime, anywhere, as long as you have an Internet connection. To learn more about this payroll offering, visit http://payroll.intuit.com/payroll_services/online_payroll.jsp

With Intuit Online Payroll, you can do the following:

- Enter employee hours online and make paycheck additions—deductions automatically calculate.

- Receive email reminders when it's payday or for tax filing deadlines.

- Print paychecks or direct-deposit employees' paychecks into their bank accounts.

- Process electronic payments and tax filings.

- Allow employees to view their pay stub information online.

- Process payroll using your mobile device.

- Prepare many detailed payroll reports.

- Process an unlimited number of payrolls each month.

- Import the transactions into QuickBooks (as a Write Checks transaction).

> ### 🔍 note
> Are you an accounting professional? Would you like to share responsibility with your client for payroll processing?
>
> With an Intuit Online Payroll for Accounting Professionals subscription, your client can enter the payroll hours and leave the responsibility for tax filings to you. Visit http://accountants.intuit.com/payroll-payments/.

Updating Payroll Tax Tables

Your purchase of an Intuit payroll subscription includes periodic tax table updates. When the federal or state government makes changes to payroll taxes or forms, you will be notified that a new tax table is available.

To update your tax tables, make sure you are connected to the Internet and have a current payroll subscription. To update payroll tax tables, follow these steps:

1. From the menu bar, select **Employees**, **Payroll Center**. Your payroll subscription status is detailed to the left. See Figure 11.2.

Figure 11.2
Check the status and manage your payroll subscription from the Payroll Center.

2. From the menu bar, select **Employees, Get Payroll Updates**.

3. (Optional) Click the Payroll Update Info button for details about the currently installed tax table version.

4. (Optional) Click the Account Info button. You need to sign into your account to view the QuickBooks Payroll Account Maintenance information about your subscription, including type of service, payroll company FEIN information, billing details, and direct deposit details. Click the X in the top-right corner to close the QuickBooks Payroll Account Maintenance dialog box.

5. Select the option to download only changes and additions to the installed payroll files, or download the entire payroll update. Click the Update button.

6. Click OK to close the Payroll Update message that tells you a new tax table or updates were installed. Click Troubleshooting Payroll Updates if the update does not install successfully.

7. QuickBooks opens the Payroll Update News dialog box. Click through the tabs of information to learn more about changes made with the installed update. Press the Esc key on your keyboard to close.

8. From the menu bar, select **Employees, Payroll Center**.

9. On the left side of the Payroll Center, view information about your payroll subscription status.

> **tip**
>
> Because payroll requirements are changing all the time, make sure you have an accounting professional who can review your payroll setup or who can file the returns for you.

Employer Resources

Getting started with payroll can seem like a daunting task. This section discusses the many resources that can help you successfully get started with payroll.

Classifying Workers as Employees

Your business might hire employees and independent contractors (see Chapter 7, "Setting Up Vendors," for more). Use these IRS guidelines when classifying a worker as an employee:

- **Behavioral**—Does the company control or have the right to control what the worker does and how the worker does his or her job?

- **Financial**—Are the business aspects of the worker's job controlled by the payer? (These include factors such as how the worker is paid, whether expenses are reimbursed, and whether the business owner provides tools and supplies.)

- **Type of Relationship**—Are written contracts or employee-type benefits (pension plan, insurance, vacation pay, and so on) in use? Will the relationship continue, and is the work performed a key aspect of the business?

The IRS provides additional comments on this topic on its website, www.irs.gov. Type **contractor or employee** into the help search box, and click the links provided for more details.

Federal and State Required Identification

Your business likely has identification numbers assigned by federal, state, and local governments. The identification numbers detailed here represent the basic identification numbers you need to properly report and pay payroll liabilities.

As mentioned earlier, your company becomes an agent of the state and federal government when it collects from employees certain taxes that governments require you to report and pay to the respective legal entity. Your company needs the following identification numbers for properly reporting and remitting your payroll taxes:

- **Federal Employer Identification Number**—Commonly referred to as FEIN. You can obtain this number from the Internal Revenue Service. Visit www.irs.gov for instructions.

- **State Withholding Tax ID**—Issued by the states you do business in. You use this ID to file and pay state income tax you withhold from your employees' paychecks. Some jurisdictions also require IDs by city, county, or both. Call your state tax department or search your state's website for more details.

- **State Unemployment ID**—Issued by the states you do business in. You use this ID to pay and file state unemployment reports. Call your state tax department or search your state's website for more details.

- **Other identification numbers**—Possibly required by the state, county, or city jurisdictions you do business in.

You might process your first payrolls before you have your assigned identification numbers. Check with your state taxing authority for instructions on paying these liabilities while you wait for your proper identification number to be assigned.

 tip

The reporting regulations for federal and state governments can be time consuming to learn about. Hiring legal and accounting professionals to guide you through the process can save you time and allow you to concentrate on building your business.

IRS and Other Forms

Your business is required to have on file for each employee a Form W-4: Employee's Withholding Allowance Certificate. You can access this form and other useful forms for your business in the Your Taxes section of the http://payroll.intuit.com/support/forms website. If the forms this site provides are not the most current, you can also go to www.irs.gov.

tip

Business owners face many other requirements when paying employees, including displaying the most current federal and state labor law posters at the place of business. Find more information at www.freeposteraudit.com.

State Reporting

Each state where you have employees working has specific filing requirements. You are even required to report new hires and, in some states, independent contractors. Your state might also require city and county reporting. You can access information from each state's website, or Intuit provides useful information on the following websites:

- http://payroll.intuit.com/support/compliance

- http://payroll.intuit.com/support/PTS/statelocaltax.jsp

Properly tracking and reporting your payroll activity to the state helps you avoid costly penalties for not filing timely.

Creating Payroll Accounts in the Chart of Accounts

Proper payroll tracking includes having the necessary payroll liability and expense accounts in the chart of accounts.

Review your data to make sure you have these accounts, or create them as needed. Adding subaccounts (see Figure 11.3) to the default accounts QuickBooks creates can help you track the financial details of payroll more efficiently.

Figure 11.3
Create subaccounts for payroll liability and expenses for more detailed reporting.

➡ See "Chart of Accounts," p. 108, for more information on creating these subaccounts.

Typical accounts to create for recording payroll transactions include the following:

- **Bank Account**—QuickBooks does not require that you have a separate bank account for payroll transactions. Companies with large amounts of funds from operations might choose to have another bank account for payroll transactions. Having a separate bank account for payroll can limit the business's financial exposure from fraud.

- **Payroll Liabilities**—Other Current Liability. QuickBooks uses this account type to track the amount owed to federal or state governments, health insurance providers, and the like. QuickBooks creates this account for you automatically. Include the following as subaccounts to this account, and add other subaccounts as needed:

  - FICA/Medicare Payable (also referred to as 941 taxes). For simplicity, I recommend using a single account that combines the employee deductions and employer contributions.

  - State Unemployment Payable (also referred to as SUTA).

- Federal Unemployment Payable (also referred to as FUTA).

- Health Insurance Payable.

- Wage Garnishments.

- **Job Costs**—Cost of Goods Sold. Many industries track the costs associated with providing a service or product to their customers or jobs. To track these properly on your Income Statement, use the Cost of Goods Sold account category. Do not overuse this category by adding too many to the chart of accounts; instead, use QuickBooks items for greater detail.

> ➡ *For more information, see "Understanding Items," p. 112.*

- **Overhead Costs**—Expense. When you create a company-paid payroll item, you assign an account for the expense. Payroll items are used on paycheck transactions and have account(s) assigned to them. QuickBooks automatically creates a Payroll Expenses account. Typically, you want to add the following as subaccounts:

<table>
<tr><td>

tip

Have you been recording QuickBooks payroll transactions without using these recommended subaccounts? Create the desired subaccounts and then edit the payroll items, assigning the newly created subaccount.

QuickBooks reassigns all previous transactions to the newly created subaccounts. Always make a backup of your data before you attempt a procedure such as this.

</td></tr>
</table>

- **Salaries & Wages**—Assign these to payroll compensation items.

- **Payroll Taxes**—Assign these to the employer Social Security and Medicare payroll items.

- **State Unemployment**—Assign this to your state(s) unemployment payroll item.

- **Federal Unemployment**—Assign this to the Federal Unemployment payroll item.

- **Employee Benefits**—Assign these to company-paid benefits, including health, dental, life insurance, and other types of benefits.

A comprehensive chart of accounts that includes subaccounts for liabilities and expenses makes it easy for you to review your payroll and fix any errors.

⚡ caution

Do you have employees who work in the office doing administrative tasks and other employees who perform work related to customers and jobs? If you do, properly recording payroll costs assigns the costs of administrative payroll to an overhead expense account and assigns customer or job payroll expenses to a Cost of Goods Sold account.

However, QuickBooks has a limitation with this process. Company-paid payroll tax items allow only a single-expense account. As a result, each specific company-paid payroll tax expense is reported to a single account. Keep this in mind when you are reviewing your financials.

Setting Up Payroll Tax Vendors

You can improve tracking, paying, and reporting payroll liabilities balances if you identify the vendors by the tax or benefit being paid. This is important for states or other agencies that have the same payee name for multiple state tax liabilities.

Creating separate vendor records is recommended. When processing the payroll liability payments from the Payroll Center, QuickBooks prepares a separate liability check for each:

- Unique liability payroll item assigned to a specific payee. For example, 941 payroll taxes will be paid together, but not on the same check with 940 payroll taxes.

- Liability payments with different due dates.

When preparing the Federal 941/944 and Federal 940 payments, QuickBooks creates a separate check for each type of liability or for same payroll item types but with different due dates. See the Pay Scheduled Liabilities section in Figure 11.4. This is necessary so that the reporting and payment for these liabilities follow strict due date guidelines dictated by the state, federal government, or other entity being paid.

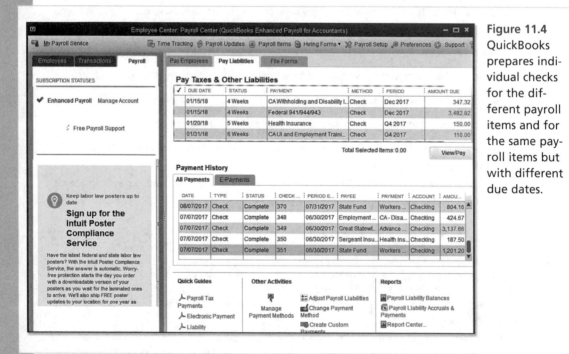

Figure 11.4
QuickBooks prepares individual checks for the different payroll items and for the same payroll items but with different due dates.

➡ *To learn more about creating your vendor records, see "Adding or Modifying Vendors," p. 242.*

The following is a list of some of the more common payroll vendors you should create when you are managing payroll:

- United States Treasury—941

- United States Treasury—940

- State income tax department

- State unemployment tax department

- Health insurance vendor

Payroll Preferences

After you sign up for one of the Intuit Payroll Service subscriptions, you need to enable payroll and set some payroll- and employee-specific preferences. QuickBooks offers two types of preferences:

- **My Preferences**—Settings that are unique to the user logged in to the data file and that other users do not share.

- **Company Preferences**—Settings that are common for all users. When a preference is modified on the Company Preferences tab, the change affects all users.

For this section, reference is made only to preferences on the Company Preferences tab. The My Preferences settings do not directly affect the payroll process. Log in to the file as the Admin or External Accountant user in single-user mode to set the following preferences.

Payroll and Employee Preferences—Company Preferences

These specific preferences are set for all users. To set up payroll and employee preferences, follow these steps:

1. From the menu bar, select **Edit**, **Preferences** to open the Preferences dialog box. Select the **Payroll & Employees—Company Preferences** tab (see Figure 11.5).

2. Select the **Full Payroll** option in the QuickBooks Payroll Features box. This enables the remaining features in the Preferences dialog box.

3. Select the checkbox next to the features that are appropriate to your business:

    - **Enable ViewMyPaycheck**—Gives your employees online access to their pay stubs, W-2s, and other payroll info—free with your QuickBooks Payroll subscription. For more information, see section "ViewMyPaycheck," later in this chapter.

    - **Copy Earnings Details from Previous Check**—Copies hours, rates, and Customer:Job from the previous paycheck.

    - **Recall Quantity Field on Paychecks**—Recalls line 1 of a previous paycheck, payroll item, and rate only; no Customer:Job is recalled.

Figure 11.5 Setting defaults improves accuracy and efficiency when working with payroll activities.

Preferences

| My Preferences | Company Preferences |

QUICKBOOKS PAYROLL FEATURES

- ● Full payroll
- ○ No payroll
- ○ Online payroll

SET PREFERENCES FOR

- Pay Stub & Voucher Printing
- Workers Compensation
- Sick and Vacation

OK
Cancel
Help
Default

Also See:
General
Tax:1099

☐ Copy earnings details from previous paycheck
☑ Recall quantity field on paychecks   ☑ Recall hour field on paychecks
☑ Job Costing, Class and Item tracking for paycheck expenses
   Assign one class per   ● Entire paycheck   ○ Earnings item

Changing the employee name display preferences will cause all QuickBooks windows to close. Please finish paying your employees before you do this.
DISPLAY EMPLOYEE LIST BY:
● First Name   ○ Last Name   Employee Defaults...
☐ Mark new employees as sales reps
☐ Display employee social security numbers in headers on reports

Left sidebar list:
Accounting
Bills
Calendar
Checking
Desktop View
Finance Charge
General
Integrated Applications
Items & Inventory
Jobs & Estimates
Multiple Currencies
Payments
Payroll & Employees
Reminders
Reports & Graphs
Sales & Customers
Sales Tax
Search
Send Forms
Service Connection
Spelling

- **Recall Hour Field on Paychecks**—Recalls total hours only and places the total number of hours on a single line even if the previous paycheck had several lines.

- **Job Costing, Class, and Item Tracking for Paycheck Expenses**—Enables QuickBooks to add the cost of company-paid taxes to the burdened cost for time that is assigned to a Customer:Job. QuickBooks also offers the Class Tracking by Paycheck or Earnings Item option if you have the Class Tracking preference enabled.

> **tip**
>
> Setting these payroll defaults ensures consistency and saves time when setting up employees in QuickBooks.

4. Choose the default for displaying employee names on reports, either First Name or Last Name.

5. Select the **Mark New Employees as Sales Reps** checkbox if you want new employees automatically added to the sales rep list. An employee who is also a sales rep can be listed on a customer invoice transaction so you can report on sales by rep.

6. Select the **Display Employee Social Security Numbers in Headers on Reports** checkbox if you want to display this sensitive information on reports.

7. Click the Employee Defaults button to set the following defaults for new employees:

   - Earnings items and rate

   - Time data to create paychecks

- Additions, deductions, or company contributions payroll items

- Employee coverage by qualified pension plan

- Payroll schedule or pay frequency

- Class (if the QuickBooks Class preference is enabled)

- Taxes for federal and state tax settings

- Sick days and vacation settings

8. Click OK to close the Employee Defaults dialog box.

9. Click the Set Preferences for Pay Stub and Voucher Printing button to open the Payroll Printing Preferences dialog box in Figure 11.6. In this dialog box, you can customize what detail prints on employees' paycheck stubs.

Figure 11.6
Customize the information that prints on the employee's paychecks or paystubs.

10. Click the Workers Compensation button to set the preference to track worker's comp, to be warned when worker's comp code is not assigned, and to exclude overtime hours from worker's compensation calculations. Workers Compensation tracking is not included with the Basic payroll subscription.

11. Click the Sick and Vacation button to set the default accrual period, hours accrued, and maximum number of hours, and to specify whether the hours should be reset each new year.

Checking—Company Preferences

The Checking-specific preferences are set for all users. From the menu bar, select **Edit**, **Preferences** to open the Preferences dialog box. Select the **Checking** preference from the left side, and click the Company Preferences tab.

In the Select Default Accounts to Use box, select the **Open the Create Paychecks** checkbox or the **Open Pay Payroll Liabilities** checkbox, and specify a bank account from the drop-down list.

Time and Expense—Company Preferences

The Time and Expense preferences are set for all users. To set up time and expense preferences, follow these steps:

1. From the menu bar, select **Edit**, **Preferences** to open the Preferences dialog box, and select the **Time & Expenses—Company Preferences** tab.

2. Select **Yes** in the Time Tracking box if you plan to use timesheets to record employee work hours.

3. If necessary, change the First Day of Work Week from the drop-down list.

4. Placing a checkmark in the Mark All Time Entries as Billable is helpful if you create invoices for your customers that include the employees' time on the invoice. This type of billing is often referred to as Cost Plus or Time and Expense billing.

> **note**
>
> Do you invoice customers for time, expense, and a markup percentage? If yes, the Invoicing Options can help you with this task. For more information, see "Time and Expense Invoicing," p. 363.

Using the Payroll Setup Interview

The Payroll Setup Interview is helpful for new and existing QuickBooks payroll users. New users will appreciate how it walks you through setting up your first payroll.

For existing QuickBooks payroll users, the Payroll Setup feature helps you by identifying missing information necessary for properly preparing, reporting, and paying payroll. If you do not have all the information needed at the time of setup, select **Finish Later** to exit the Payroll Setup. You can return later to update the information.

Information Needed to Set Up Payroll

Before you begin to set up your payroll, you should collect the following information, where possible:

- **Compensation types**—Compile a list of the types of pay you offer, such as hourly, salary, overtime, vacation, and so on. You will establish a QuickBooks payroll item for each of these.

- **Other additions or deductions to payroll**—Some examples are dental insurance, uniforms, and union dues.

- **Employee names, addresses, and Social Security numbers**—Included in the employee provided Form W-4: Employees Withholding Allowance Certificate.

- **Payroll tax payment schedules and rates**—This refers to the frequency with which your business is required to pay payroll taxes, including the rate you pay for your state unemployment tax and other taxes.

- **A year-to-date payroll register from your previous payroll system**—If you're transferring your payroll process to QuickBooks at any other time than the first of a calendar year, request a year-to-date payroll register and filed forms from your previous payroll system.

  ➡ *For more information, see "Midyear Payroll Setup,"* *p. 463.*

- **Any year-to-date payroll tax and other liability payments made before using QuickBooks**—These help you prepare your startup payroll records in QuickBooks.

> **🔍 note**
>
> If you have been using QuickBooks to prepare payroll, consider using the Run Payroll Checkup diagnostics. From the menu bar, select **Employees, My Payroll Services, Run Payroll Checkup**. To learn more about working with this feature, see "Using the Run Payroll Checkup Diagnostic Tool," p. 466.

With this information collected, you are ready to begin using the Payroll Setup Interview. This handy tool uses a question-and-answer format to walk you through customizing your payroll settings. When it's completed, you can begin preparing payroll checks for your employees.

Introduction

The Payroll Setup Interview guides you through adding the necessary payroll items so you can begin processing payroll.

After purchasing a payroll service subscription, launch Payroll Setup (see Figure 11.7) by selecting **Employees, Payroll Setup** from the menu bar. Optionally, click the link Payroll Item Checklist (not shown in Figure 11.7). Click Continue.

Choose one of the following that best describes your business payroll setup needs:

- **The Company Has Never Issued Paychecks**—You have not done so manually or through an accountant, or using another payroll service.

- **The Company Is Changing to QuickBooks Payroll**. Select this option if you have been using another method for preparing payroll during the current year.

The following instructions assume that no paychecks have ever been issued. Your menu options will differ if you selected Company Is Changing to QuickBooks Payroll.

QuickBooks Payroll Setup

QuickBooks
Payroll Setup

☞ 1 Introduction
☐ 2 Company Setup
☐ 3 Employee Setup
☐ 4 Taxes
☐ 5 Year-to-Date Payrolls
☐ 6 Data Review
☐ 7 Finishing Up

Welcome to QuickBooks Payroll Setup

We'll get you set up with the payroll settings that are right for you. To help us please choose the payroll situation that applies to your company.

○ The company has never issued paychecks

We have never issued paychecks manually, through an accountant, or using another payroll service.

○ The company is changing to QuickBooks Payroll

We have issued paychecks or paid payroll taxes before.

⌇ Free Payroll Support
New Employer Guide
Payroll Setup Checklist

[Finish Later]   UPS1.2262   [Continue >]

Figure 11.7
Selecting the right option for setting up payroll affects the menus provided in the QuickBooks Payroll Setup dialog box.

Company Setup

The Company Setup introduction provides two methods for creating pay types and benefits:

- **Typical New Employer Setup**—QuickBooks automatically creates common payroll items, and then you can later add items. I recommend selecting this option.

- **Custom Setup**—Selecting this option enables you to create custom payroll items. If you are familiar with setting up payroll, you can use this method. You can make changes to your setup later in your QuickBooks file, if needed.

> ➡ *To learn more about adding custom payroll items, see "Adding or Editing Payroll Items," p. 475.*

The following instructions assume that you selected **Typical New Employer Setup**. Click Continue to begin setting up your employees (see Figure 11.8).

Figure 11.8
Be sure to have your employees' information ready when you run the Payroll Setup Interview so you can complete each of the required fields.

Employee John Smith   ✕

Enter employee's name and address

Legal name

First name   John   M.I.

* Last name   Smith

Print on check as   John Smith

Employee status   Active   ▾   Explain

Contact information

* Home Address   400 Oak Shores Road

* City   Anytown

* State   CA - California   ▾

* Zip Code   ⚠ Enter employee home zip code for printing on W-2.

* required field

Cancel   Next >

Employee Setup

You can work most efficiently with entering your employees if you have all the required information listed here. Complete the following information:

- Legal name.

- Contact information.

- Employee type—Regular, Officer, Statutory, or Owner—and other hiring information.

- Payroll schedule, pay type, and rate (see Figure 11.9).

- Additions or deductions to employees' payroll.

- Method of payment to use for the payroll—check, direct deposit to an Intuit Pay Card, bank account, or multiple direct-deposit bank accounts that split the amount.

- The employee's state where worked and state subject to withholding taxes.

- Federal tax information from the employee's Form W-4 and the proper withholdings and credits. Most employees' wages are subject to Medicare, Social Security, and Federal Unemployment.

- State tax information and whether the employee is subject to any special local taxes.

Information required differs from state to state.

> **tip**
> After completing some of the information, you have the option of Finish Later (lower left). When you choose Finish Later, QuickBooks retains the information you have entered, and you can return later to the Payroll Setup Interview to complete the missing information.

Figure 11.9
Assign the pay frequency and rate to improve the accuracy of the prepared paycheck.

Click Finish (not shown in Figure 11.9) to complete the setup for employees. If you have not completed all the information, you might get a Missing Information error message, as in Figure 11.10. Read the information, and click OK to close the message or Cancel to return to the setup. Choose Add New to continue with the next employee setup, or select an employee from the list and click Edit, Delete, or Summary.

Figure 11.10
The QuickBooks Payroll Setup detects any setup errors or missing information.

First Paychecks

With the few steps you have completed, you can immediately create paychecks. If you are in a hurry to prepare paychecks, click First Paychecks, step 4 on the QuickBooks Payroll Setup dialog box. You have the following choices; however, I recommend completing the setup by selecting the second option listed next:

- Click the Create Paychecks button to return to the Payroll Center, where you can immediately pay your employees.

- Click the Continue button to Continue to Tax Setup, providing agency information (recommended).

Taxes

Continuing with the payroll setup, select the **Taxes** menu item in the Payroll Setup, review the tax items created automatically for you, and enter the rates your business pays for federal and state taxes:

- **941/944 Form**—Identify which tax form you file.

- **Federal Taxes**—Review the federal payroll tax items created for you (you will add to or edit them later).

- **State Tax**—Click Add New to create a specific local/custom tax and define the state you are creating a payroll tax item for. Click Finish. Click Add New, Edit, or Delete. Click Continue when you have finished setting up state tax payroll items.

- **Schedule Payments**—Assign the tax item deposit method of check or E-pay, the payee, and the payment frequency. If you are uncertain what payment schedule your business should follow, contact your tax accountant; you also can click How Often Should I Pay These Taxes? for additional resources.

> **⚠ caution**
> When a Fix This Error Now icon displays during Payroll Setup, heed the warning. If you don't, your payroll transactions or reporting might be incorrect. See Figure 11.10 earlier.

> **⚠ caution**
> If you are creating midyear payroll records, you need to complete each of the following: paychecks, tax payments, and nontax payments. Failure to complete each of these can result in misleading information in the QuickBooks payroll module.

Midyear Payroll Setup

In the accounting community, the term *midyear* refers to setting up payroll at any time other than at the beginning of the current calendar year.

This method is needed only for companies converting to QuickBooks payroll in a calendar year that had prior payroll produced using software or through a payroll service provider.

When you make the decision to begin using QuickBooks payroll in a year in which you already had payroll transactions, you can do the following:

- Manually re-create in detail all your previous payroll transactions. You do not need to follow the steps in this section.

- Record year-to-date totals for previously issued payroll checks and liability payments, following the steps in this section.

> ### 🔍 note
>
> The Enter Paychecks by Employee option *will not* create any accounting entries (it has no effect on the Balance Sheet or Profit & Loss). However, the entries *will* affect payroll reports and forms you file for your state and the federal government. The transactions entered here are used to enter year-to-date totals so that certain taxes on future paychecks calculate correctly and for completing quarterly and annual payroll forms using QuickBooks.
>
> You will separately record the payroll liability balances for the Balance Sheet and payroll expenses for the Profit & Loss reports with a beginning trial balance entry provided by the company accountant.

Before you begin this process, make sure you have accurate records of the prior-period payrolls, preferably subtotaled by calendar quarter. To set up midyear payroll totals using Payroll Setup, follow these steps:

1. On step 1 of Payroll Setup (select **Employees, Payroll Setup** from the menu bar), select **The Company Is Changing to QuickBooks Payroll**. QuickBooks adds menus to the Payroll Setup that are necessary for completing YTD entries.

2. Complete steps 2–4, entering the required information for Company, Employee, and Taxes setup as detailed previously.

3. On step 5 (Year-to-Date Payrolls), select **Determine if Needed**.

4. Click Yes to answer the question Has Your Company Issued Paychecks This Year?

5. Click Continue. QuickBooks opens the Enter Paychecks by Employee dialog box, shown in Figure 11.11. This dialog box, with functionality similar to Microsoft Excel, streamlines the task of entering year-to-date payroll totals for your employees.

Figure 11.11
Use this worksheet in QuickBooks Payroll Setup to record prior-period paychecks from the same year.

6. Click the Show Steps button to have QuickBooks provide a pop-up dialog box of the steps for entering the information to be typed in each cell.

7. Click the Customize Columns button to arrange the columns of data to match the reports from your prior software or payroll provider, which simplifies the data entry process.

8. To begin entering data for your employees, click the drop-down list for You're Entering Paychecks For and select the employee name.

9. Right-click to conveniently copy, paste, delete, or insert rows. This functionality is especially useful when entering repeating information, such as for salaried employees.

10. Conveniently check your monthly and annual totals as you type directly from the Enter Paychecks by Employee dialog box, to make sure your data entered agrees with your earlier payroll records.

11. Click View Reports. QuickBooks includes the following two reports to help report on the accuracy of the setup details:

- **Historical Paycheck Report—Basic**—The report details the gross pay and any deductions or company expenses. Carefully review this report to make sure the totals match your earlier payroll records.

- **Historical Paycheck Report—Advanced**—Click Switch to Advanced Report. The Advanced report compares the combination of historical paycheck detail with any employee or company payroll liability adjustments. If you correctly entered your historical payroll and adjustments (if needed), QuickBooks-Calculated amount column should equal your totals for those payroll tax items as reported to your federal and state governments.

  After the reports display, you can print the report, export the report to Excel, or compress the report to fit on the printed page. See Figure 11.12.

 note

If you previously started using the Payroll Setup, step 5 instead displays the Payroll Summary. Click Edit next to the desired information you need to complete, including paychecks, tax payments, or nontax payments.

caution

The Enter Paychecks by Employee dialog box allows you to enter only payroll check dates in the current calendar year (determined by the year on your computer).

note

After you click View Reports, if your computer has Internet security settings enabled, you might see a yellow bar near the top of your Internet browser. Click the yellow bar, select **Allow Blocked Content**, and click Yes if prompted.

Figure 11.12
The Historical Paycheck Report—Basic is useful to review and compare to the payroll records you have before using QuickBooks.

Check Date		Gross Pay	Federal Withholding (Tax)	Social Security Company (Tax)	Social Security Employee (Tax)	Medicare Company (Tax)	Medicare Employee (Tax)	Federal Unemployment (Tax)	CA-Withholding (Tax)	Net Pay
2017 Paychecks		4,500.00	-250.00	279.00	-189.00	65.25	-54.00	27.00	-100.00	3,907.00
Q1 Jan-Mar		4,500.00	-250.00	279.00	-189.00	65.25	-54.00	27.00	-100.00	3,907.00
January		4,500.00	-250.00	279.00	-189.00	65.25	-54.00	27.00	-100.00	3,907.00
1/31/17										
	John Smith	4,500.00	-250.00	279.00	-189.00	65.25	-54.00	27.00	-100.00	3,907.00
	1/31 Total	4,500.00	-250.00	279.00	-189.00	65.25	-54.00	27.00	-100.00	3,907.00
February										
March										

12. Click the X in the top-right corner to return to the Enter Paychecks by Employee dialog box.

13. Click the Done Entering Paychecks button to return to the QuickBooks Payroll Setup dialog box. As you enter each paycheck, tax payment, and nontax payment, the boxes will be shaded green progressively until each task is complete, making it easy to return where you left off.

Congratulations! You have completed the tasks necessary to set up your year-to-date payroll; you can now process new payroll transactions. This is a good time to complete the Run Payroll Checkup diagnostics the next section discusses.

Using the Run Payroll Checkup Diagnostic Tool

After you complete the payroll setup and you have created payroll checks or year-to-date entries in QuickBooks, you are ready to review your data using the Run Payroll Checkup diagnostic tool. This feature is similar to the previously listed Payroll Setup feature. In fact, when you open the Run Payroll Checkup diagnostic tool, it also opens the Payroll Setup feature, but some of the menu choices are different.

What makes the Run Payroll Checkup tool different from the Payroll Setup tool? After you have set up your payroll, you will most likely use the Run Payroll Checkup tool to diagnose errors with setup and transactions.

The QuickBooks Run Payroll Checkup gives you an option called Finish Later so you can return where you left off. Before you begin the Run Payroll Checkup dialog box, make sure you have the following information available, in case any of it is missing or incorrect:

- Employees' names, addresses, and Social Security numbers.

- Compensation, benefits, and other additions or deductions your company offers.

- Missing or incomplete information when you originally set up the employees. Figure 11.10, earlier, showed an example.

- Compensation items, other additions, and deductions for missing or incomplete information.

For existing data, review of actual wage and tax amounts provides an alert if any discrepancy arises. See Figure 11.13.

John Smith

Problem:	The accrued amount of one or more payroll taxes was less than the amount indicated by the rate and wage information in QuickBooks.
Solution:	Review all of the problems listed on the page. Though some messages are considered warnings, review them to ensure that they don't indicate problems in your payroll data. If you're not sure, consult with your accountant, a tax advisor, or the payroll service. To learn about entering and editing year-to-date amounts for your employees, go the Help index and enter "employees, year-to-date amounts for".

Payroll Item	Wage Base	Rate	Should Be	QB Amount	Discrepancy
CA - Disability	$4500.00	1.00%	$45.00	$43.00	$2.00

Print...

Figure 11.13
QuickBooks Payroll Setup detects certain payroll tax computation errors.

To have the payroll diagnostic tool in QuickBooks review your payroll setup for missing information and paycheck data discrepancies, do the following:

1. From the menu bar, select **Employees**, **My Payroll Service**, **Run Payroll Checkup**. Follow each of the dialog boxes, clicking Continue through each step.

2. In the Data Review dialog box, click Yes. QuickBooks reviews the wages and taxes in the payroll records.

3. If errors are detected, click the View Errors button. QuickBooks opens the error detail, as in Figure 11.13.

4. Click the Print button in the Payroll Item Discrepancies dialog box.

5. If you click the Continue button, you will need to fix some errors before you can proceed.

6. Click the Finish Later button to close the Run Payroll Checkup diagnostic tool so you can create correcting entries.

> **tip**
>
> The Run Payroll Checkup diagnostic tool is optional for Intuit's Basic or Enhanced Payroll subscribers. However, I recommend that you process the Run Payroll Checkup regardless of the payroll subscription you select. Using the tool as often as once a quarter before you prepare quarterly payroll tax returns can help ensure that your data is correct.
>
> Be prepared to take the time to fix the errors detected. The QuickBooks Run Payroll Checkup diagnostic tool allows you to ignore warnings, but doing so might result in additional payroll calculation errors.

Using the errors displayed earlier in Figure 11.13 as an example, the following are the typical steps for correcting them. (Your errors will be different and might require adjustments to other types of payroll items than the ones detailed here.)

1. From the menu bar, select **Reports**, **Employees & Payroll**, **Payroll Summary**. Review this report for either earlier or current payroll quarters (depending on where the error was detected). In Figure 11.14, compare the Payroll Summary report to the Payroll Item Discrepancies report shown earlier in Figure 11.13. The Should Be amount should equal what your Payroll Summary report shows when prepared today.

> **caution**
>
> Carefully consider the adjustments that need to be made if they affect an earlier calendar quarter you have already filed with the state or federal government.
>
> Be prepared to promptly file a correcting return with the appropriate agency when you adjust your QuickBooks payroll data from what you previously reported.
>
> Correcting earlier quarters can often be the best choice, especially if your data is ever audited.

2. From the menu bar, select **Employees**, **Payroll Taxes and Liabilities**, **Adjust Payroll Liabilities**, as in Figure 11.15.

3. Enter the Date and Effective Date. Both should be dated in the quarter for which you want to make the change.

Figure 11.14
The amounts included in the Payroll Summary report should match the Should Be amounts in the Payroll Item Discrepancies report.

The Payroll Checkup calculated this amount to be $45.00.

4. Select either **Company** or **Employee** for the adjustment. Company indicates it is a company-paid adjustment. Employee indicates an employee-paid adjustment and affects W-2 reported amounts.

5. (Optional) Assign a class if your business tracks different profit centers.

Figure 11.15
Create a liability adjustment to correct any errors found in the Payroll Item Discrepancies report.

6. Click Accounts Affected only if you do not want the adjustment to affect liability and expense account balances. This would be necessary if your Balance Sheet is correct but the Pay Scheduled Liabilities balances in the Payroll Center are incorrect. Click OK to close the Accounts Affected dialog box (if displayed).

7. Click OK to save the transaction.

8. Return to the Run Payroll Checkup menu to review your payroll data again after the correction. If your adjustments were successful, QuickBooks displays a Congratulations message showing that all adjustments have corrected the discrepancies.

Do You Need to Run Payroll Checkup for an Earlier Year?

If you need to complete a Run Payroll Checkup diagnostic for an earlier year, follow these instructions. If you are working in a multiuser environment, ask everyone to log out of the QuickBooks file and close the data file.

Next, change your computer system date to a date in the earlier year. When selecting the date, keep in mind how QuickBooks will review and report on "prior quarters" dependent on this new system date.

Run the Payroll Checkup diagnostic; QuickBooks now checks the payroll data that corresponds to the year of your computer's system date.

Don't forget to close the file and then reset your computer date to the current date before you open the file again and allow other users into the system.

You might want to contact your computer hardware professional before you change the system date in a networked environment because it might impact other running programs.

Setting Up Employees

If you are a new QuickBooks payroll user, I recommended using the Payroll Setup for adding payroll items and employees. You can return to the Payroll Setup to add employees or use the following instructions to add or edit employee information.

Using the Employee Center

QuickBooks makes adding, modifying, and researching employee activity easy from the Employee Center (see Figure 11.16).

On the Home page, click the Employees button to open the Employee Center. Alternatively, you can click the Employees icon on the icon bar.

From the Employee Center, you can view contact details for your employees and access many payroll-related tasks to do the following:

- Add a new employee or edit an existing employee's information

- Manage employee sales rep information and new employee defaults

- Print paychecks, paystubs, and other useful list information

- Enter time for employees

- Export to Excel employee lists and transactions

- Export to Excel Client-Ready Payroll Reports (requires a payroll service subscription for accounting professionals)

Figure 11.16
The Employee Center provides one place to access common employee tasks and reports.

- Prepare employee letters and customize vendor letter templates using Word

- Filter the list of employees to include All Employees, Active Vendors, or Released Employees

- Attach documents to the employee record

- Access a map and driving directions to the employee's address

- Add and edit employee notes and to-do reminders

- *New for QuickBooks 2014!* Track emails sent

- View and filter the list of transactions by employee or by transaction type

- Schedule To Do's reminding you of important employee-related tasks

- Record miscellaneous Notes in the employee's record

- Prepare a QuickReport, Payroll Summary, Paid Time Off report, or Payroll Transaction Detail report for the selected employee

Use the Employee Center to access many of the common employee transactions and reports you learn about in this chapter.

Adding or Editing Employee Information

Have you completed the steps outlined in the Payroll Setup? You can now easily add a new employee or modify the information for an existing employee in the Employee Center.

> 🔺 **caution**
>
> Is this your first time setting up employees in QuickBooks? You might want to start by using Payroll Setup. For more information, see "Using the Payroll Setup Interview," p. 458.

Adding an Employee

To practice adding a new employee record, open the sample data file as instructed in Chapter 1, "Getting Started with QuickBooks," p. 37. If you are working in your own file, follow these instructions to add a new employee:

1. From the menu bar, select **Employees, Employee Center**. Click New Employee.

2. Complete the fields in the Personal, Address and Contact, and Additional Info tabs. For this exercise, enter fictitious information into each of the fields. On the Additional Info tab, your QuickBooks version might offer a Billing Rate Level field. For more information, see p. 366.

3. Select the **Payroll Info** tab. Select **Biweekly** for the payroll schedule, as in Figure 11.17. In your own file, click Add New to create a payroll schedule. Payroll schedules help you keep track of the next payroll processing date. Payroll schedules also facilitate grouping employees into different pay frequencies. For example, you might pay your field labor every week and your administrative staff biweekly. This is an example of setting up two different payroll schedules.

Figure 11.17
The Payroll Info tab should include each pay period's earnings and deduction items.

4. In the Class field, select **New Construction**. The option to assign a single class (department) to the entire paycheck or assign multiple classes to a single paycheck is defined in the Payroll & Employee preferences section. From the menu bar, select **Edit, Preferences, Payroll & Employees, Company Preferences**.

5. The Regular Pay wage item defaults in the Item Name column of the Earnings box. Type **15.00** into the Hourly/Annual column. To view other compensation items, click the down arrow next to Regular Pay.

6. For this exercise, do not select either of these options: Use Time and Expense Data to Create Paychecks, or Employee Is Covered by a Qualified Pension Plan.

7. Record other Additions, Deductions, and Company Contributions for this employee. In the Item Name drop-down list for this exercise, select **Health Insurance**. Type **25.00** into the amount column and accept the defaulted Limit—QuickBooks deducts this amount from each paycheck. The Limit allows you to set an upper limit and specify whether the limit is reset annually. You can define the Limit amount globally for all employees when setting up the deduction, or you can make the Limit a specific amount for each employee.

8. The Direct Deposit button is inactive in the sample data for this exercise. If this button is enabled in your own file, clicking it displays a QuickBooks dialog box to verify your company information, enter bank information, and select check security limits.

9. Click the Taxes button to see the information in Figure 11.18. The information selected in the fields on the Federal, State, and Other tabs determines how the respective taxes are calculated. Use the information on the employee's completed Form W-4 when selecting Filing Status, Allowances, and Extra Withholding settings. Click OK to close. If you did not select a State Worked, you might be prompted to complete the setup.

Figure 11.18
Assign the employee's federal, state, and other tax status.

10. Click the Sick/Vacation button. Use these settings to accrue and track employees' sick and vacation time. Click OK to close.

11. (Optional) Click the Employment Info tab to record Employment Dates and Employment Details.

12. (Optional) Click the Worker's Comp tab to assign the Worker's Comp Code available with selected Intuit payroll subscriptions.

13. Click OK to close the New Employee dialog box.

Managing your employees' information from the Employee Center is easy. To edit an employee's information, select an employee on the left side of the dialog box and click the Edit Employee icon above and to the right of the employee's contact information.

Finding Payroll Transactions

The Employee Center provides a central location for maintaining employee records and reviewing payroll transactions in QuickBooks.

On the Home page, click the Employees button to open the Employee Center. Select an employee on the left side of the dialog box to display individual transactions assigned to that employee on the right. For example, with the employee Dan T. Miller selected in the Employee Center, QuickBooks displays individual transactions for that employee. See Figure 11.19.

tip

Working in your own file, if you select **Use Time and Expense Data to Create Paychecks**, QuickBooks uses that time data from time cards to prefill the hours on a paycheck. This can save you time, making your payroll processing more efficient.

To learn more about using the QuickBooks Timer, see p. 690.

Figure 11.19
Filter for specific transaction types and dates for the selected employee.

Another useful feature of working with the Payroll Center is on the Transactions tab. From the Transactions tab in the Employee Center, you can easily locate payroll and nonpayroll transactions for all employees. When reviewing payroll, it can be helpful to see what payments, if any, were paid to the employees using payroll transactions or payments made with other transaction types. Payments made to an employee not through a payroll transaction type are not included in state and federal payroll reporting.

You are now proficient in adding or editing an employee's information. In the next section, you learn about managing your payroll items.

Researching Payroll and Nonpayroll Transactions

To practice finding employee transactions by type, open the sample data file as instructed in Chapter 1, p. 37. If you are working in your own file, use these instructions to locate your own employee's transactions.

1. From the Employee Center, click the Transactions tab.

2. Select the **Liability Checks** type, as in Figure 11.20.

Figure 11.20
Use the Transactions tab of the Employee Center to research by transaction type.

3. From the Date drop-down list, select **This Calendar Quarter**. (If you are using the QuickBooks-supplied sample data, the date selected might be sometime in the future.)

4. Click any column header to sort the data by that column.

5. Double-click any transaction to open it. Click Save & Close to return to the Transactions tab details.

6. Click the Print button to print the listed transactions.

7. Click the Enter Time drop-down list to enter a Weekly Timesheet or Time/Enter Single Activity.

8. Click the Excel drop-down list to choose from the following:

   - **Export Transactions**—Exports the displayed transactions to an Excel worksheet.

   - **Client-Ready Payroll Reports**—Available if you are using QuickBooks Accountant 2014 or QuickBooks Enterprise Accountant 14.0. A robust set of payroll reports is created for you using Excel.

   - **Summarize Payroll Data in Excel**—A collection of useful payroll reports.

   ➥ *For more details, see "Excel Reports," p. 492.*

🌀 **tip**

To customize the information displayed, right-click in the column area of the transaction display and select **Customize Columns**. You can then choose to add or remove available columns of data and change the order in which the information is displayed.

Setting Up Payroll Items

QuickBooks uses payroll items to calculate and track compensation, additions, deductions, and company expenses that result from paying employees. You need to set up your payroll items only once, which makes processing payroll as easy as reporting the time an employee works.

Adding or Editing Payroll Items

If you are new to QuickBooks payroll, I recommend that you begin by using the Payroll Setup. During the Payroll Setup, you were provided with two options for creating your list of payroll items:

- **Typical New Employer Setup**—QuickBooks adds the most common payroll items for you.

- **Custom Setup**—Select this option if you need to set up sick time, vacation time, or insurance benefits.

If you have been using QuickBooks for payroll, you will no longer see these two options. The fields required to be completed will differ depending on the type of payroll item.

To add or edit a deduction payroll item, follow these steps:

1. From the menu bar, select **Lists**, **Payroll Item List**.

2. Select **New** from the Payroll Item menu (or use the Ctrl+N keyboard shortcut). You can also right-click a payroll item and choose Edit Payroll Item if you need to make changes.

3. Select one of the following methods:

   - **EZ Setup**—Opens the Payroll Setup using standard settings, recommended for most users. To learn more about using this option, see "Using the Payroll Setup Interview," p. 458.

   - **Custom Setup**—Offers a more traditional approach to setting up payroll items, recommended for expert users.

4. If you selected Custom Setup in step 3, the Add New Payroll Item dialog box displays.

5. Select a payroll item type, such as **Deduction** (see Figure 11.21), and then click Next.

Figure 11.21
Select the appropriate payroll item type to create.

Add new payroll item

Payroll item type

Select the type of payroll item you want to create.

- ○ _W_age (Hourly Wages, Annual Salary, Commission, Bonus)
- ○ _A_ddition (Employee Loan, Mileage Reimbursement)
- ● _D_eduction (Union Dues, 401(k) deferral, Simple IRA, HSA)
- ○ Co_m_pany Contribution (Employer 401(k) matching contribution, HSA contribution)
- ○ _F_ederal Tax (FUTA, Social Security, Medicare)
- ○ _S_tate Tax (State Withholding, SDI, SUI)
- ○ _O_ther Tax (Local Tax, Misc. State Tax)

6. Type a name for the payroll item. This name will display on paychecks and in reports. Selecting Track Expenses by Job might be suitable for most company contribution and addition items and would include costs to this payroll item in Job Profitability reports. Click Next.

7. On the Agency for Employee-Paid Liability screen, enter the following:

   ▪ From your vendor list, select the agency or vendor to which you pay the liability. If necessary, click Add New to create a new vendor record. Skip this field if the deduction is not being paid to anyone. For instance, Figure 11.22 shows how to establish a cell phone reimbursement item.

Figure 11.22
Payroll deductions can recover a portion of a business-paid expense.

   ▪ If your liability vendor assigns an account number to your business, enter it into the account number field.

   ▪ Make a selection from your chart of accounts. In this example, the Telephone Expense account is selected. If the deduction payroll item is used to recover a business-paid expense from employees, select the corresponding expense account. Normally, you accept the default account of Payroll Liabilities. If you followed the previously recommended process for creating detailed payroll accounts on your chart of accounts, select the appropriate subaccount. Click Next.

8. Select the appropriate Tax Tracking Type, or select **None** if none of the types applies, as in Figure 11.23. This choice is important to properly set up your payroll items. If you are unsure, ask your accountant for advice. Click Next.

9. The Taxes screen displays. In most cases, you do not need to modify the settings in this screen. Click Default to return to the original settings. Click Next.

10. The Calculate Based on Quantity screen offers the following choices:

    ▪ Calculate This Item Based on Quantity

    ▪ Calculate This Item Based on Hours

    ▪ Neither

> **note**
>
> You can always edit the settings for a specific payroll item. However, some changes affect only future payroll checks, not those recorded before you make the change.

11. After making a selection, click Next.

Figure 11.23
Carefully reviewing the Tax Tracking Types can help with accurately setting up payroll.

12. Select an option for calculating the deduction: either Gross Pay or Net Pay. If you are unsure, ask your accountant; the correct selection depends on the item being set up. Click Next.

13. Enter a Default Rate and an optional Default Upper Limit, and specify whether the limit is annually reset, is monthly reset, or is a one-time limit. If the rate or upper limit differs for each employee, do not enter amounts here; you can add the rate and limit individually to each employee's record. Click Finish.

14. Click OK after reading the Schedule Payments message. For more information, see "Creating or Editing a Payroll Schedule," p. 482.

Now that you have properly set up your payroll items, let's learn about reporting on them. In the early stages of your payroll use, you should carefully inspect your setup to avoid any mistakes with payroll payments.

Reporting About Payroll Items

Reviewing your Payroll Item List after adding to or modifying it is prudent to make sure the changes are correct. Follow these steps for reviewing the payroll item list:

1. From the menu bar, select **Lists**, **Payroll Item List** (see Figure 11.24). QuickBooks displays the Payroll Item List dialog box.

2. To expand the report for better viewing, double-click the words *Payroll Item List* in the title bar of the dialog box.

3. To add or remove columns, right-click and select **Customize Columns**.

Figure 11.24
View the Payroll Item List for information about the setup and accounts assigned to the payroll items.

The following information displays by default when viewing the Payroll Item List:

- **Item Name**—This name appears on paychecks and reports.

- **Type**—This comes from a predefined list in QuickBooks. The types are more wide ranging than that because they describe pay types and tax types, as well as additions and deductions.

- **Amount**—This figure is often determined by the QuickBooks-provided payroll tax tables, with the exception of addition and deduction calculations, which include amounts that the user can set as well.

- **Annual Limit**—This figure is often determined by the QuickBooks-provided tax tables, and the user cannot modify it. Incorrect limits for standard tax calculations could be the result of a payroll tax table that is not current.

- **Tax Tracking**—When you create a new payroll item and select a payroll item type, QuickBooks provides a predetermined list of tax tracking types associated with that item type. Tax tracking determines how QuickBooks treats the item on payroll returns and on the W-2 year-end employee tax form.

- **Payable To**—Checks are payable to the named entity.

- **Account ID**—This is the identification number your tax payment agency or payroll item vendor has assigned to your company.

- **Expense Account**—If the payroll item type is considered an expense, users can define the default expense account from the chart of accounts list in the payroll setup. QuickBooks defaults this account to a generic Payroll Expense account, which is created automatically by QuickBooks when payroll is enabled.

- **Liability Account**—This account is used for payroll items that are accrued with payroll and paid to the state or federal government. QuickBooks defaults these items to a generic liability account created when payroll is enabled. You can define what liability account is assigned. If you are creating a new account, it should be a subaccount of the one QuickBooks provides if you want to see certain warnings when you try to create a transaction incorrectly.

> 🌐 **tip**
>
> On the displayed Payroll Item List, to add or remove specific columns of data, right-click and select **Customize Columns**.

Additionally, from this screen view of the payroll item list, you can access the following:

- **Payroll Item**—Add, edit, delete, make an item inactive, find an item in transactions, and print a list.

- **Activities**—Access Payroll Setup and other common payroll item tasks.

- **Reports**—Access a summary or detail reports of payroll item transactions.

Congratulations! You have the needed items set up for preparing payroll for your employees. In the next section, you learn how to prepare and process your payroll. Take your time with the details; accuracy is everything when it comes to payroll processing.

Paying Employees

Having completed your Payroll Setup and Run Payroll Checkup, you are ready to begin paying your employees. If you previously paid your employees' payroll with other software or by a payroll agency, record the year-to-date payroll totals for each employee.

➥ *For more information, see "Midyear Payroll Setup," p. 463.*

The next sections provide details on preparing payroll for your employees.

Payroll Home Page Workflow

With a paid payroll subscription, you might have all or some of the following icons on your Home page, providing easy access to the typical payroll workflow. Your icons might differ from Figure 11.25, depending on the payroll subscription purchased and the preferences you have set in QuickBooks.

Figure 11.25
The Home page provides access to the proper payroll workflow.

Entering Employee Time

QuickBooks includes weekly or single-activity timekeeping you can use to record employee work time and create paychecks. You can access timesheets by clicking the Enter Time icon on the Home page.

Using timesheets simplifies the process of creating payroll records if you track employees' time by customers, jobs, or service items. Timesheets are not necessary if your employees are paid a fixed amount (salary) or work the same hours each pay period. Features of using timesheets in QuickBooks include the following:

- Using a stopwatch to time an activity as it is performed.

- Entering the time manually using a weekly timesheet or individually by the activity (see Figures 11.26 and 11.27).

- Adding the time to a customer's invoice. For more information, see "Time and Expense Invoicing," p. 363.

To record payroll timesheet activity, follow these steps:

1. On the Home page, click the drop-down arrow next to the Enter Time icon and select **Use Weekly Timesheet** or **Time/Enter Single Activity**. The following instructions presume you selected the Weekly Timesheet.

2. From the Name drop-down list, select the employee whose time you want to enter. If you want to enter multiple names, select **Multiple Names (Payroll)** from the top of the list. Adding multiple names to a timesheet can be useful if you have crew labor that works the same hours, on the same service items for the same customers or jobs.

> **note**
>
> Time tracking is enabled in the Preferences dialog box. From the menu bar, select **Edit**, **Preferences** to open this dialog box and then select the **Time & Expenses— Company Preferences** tab.
>
> Timesheet entries can help you efficiently create payroll records each pay period. On the Payroll Info tab for each employee (refer to Figure 11.17), select the **Use Time Data to Create Paychecks** checkbox.

Figure 11.26
Weekly timesheets can help you create payroll transactions.

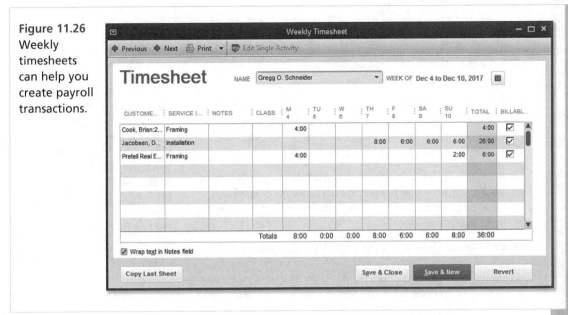

Figure 11.27
The Time/Enter Single Activity dialog box includes a stopwatch.

➡️ *For more detailed information and instructions, see "Using the QuickBooks Timer," p. 690.*

3. Click Copy Last Sheet if you would like to repeat the detail from a previously recorded timesheet.

4. Enter data as needed (the user might not have time for each day, for instance) in each of the columns. Your columns might differ, depending on your purchased payroll subscription and the payroll preferences you enabled.

5. (Optional) Click the Print button to print the current timesheet with a signature line. If you want to print a blank timesheet, click the down arrow to the right of the Print button and select **Print Blank Timesheet**.

6. Click Save & Close when completed with the timesheet entry.

Using timesheets can help you enter payroll more efficiently, and you can print them for the employees to sign, approving the hours they will be paid.

> **tip**
>
> Do you want to have employees track their own time on jobs at their computer, even if they do not have access to the QuickBooks file? Enter **QuickBooks Timer** in the search box in the upper-right corner of the menu bar, select **Help** from the drop-down list, and click the Search icon to the right. Follow the links for installing and working with the QuickBooks Timer.

Preparing Employee Paychecks

You are now ready to create paychecks for your employees. Following the instructions provided in this chapter can help make this process efficient and accurate.

Creating or Editing a Payroll Schedule

A payroll schedule defines the payroll frequency, the pay period end date, and the date that should print on the employee's paycheck. If you create at least one payroll schedule, the Payroll Center displays the next scheduled payroll. Another use for payroll schedules is to separate your employees into different groups. If your business pays the administrative staff biweekly but your operations employees weekly, you would set up two payroll schedules.

To create or edit a payroll schedule, from the menu bar, select **Employees, Add or Edit Payroll Schedules**. Complete the information required and click OK to save the schedule. Press the Esc key on your keyboard to close the Payroll Schedule List.

Next, assign your employees to the newly created scheduled payroll.

➡️ *For more information, see "Adding or Editing Employee Information," p. 470.*

Paying Employees

To prepare your QuickBooks payroll paychecks, follow these steps. To help you along, when you prepare your first payroll, QuickBooks displays a "Welcome to Your First Payroll" message. After you review the details, click OK, I'm Ready!

1. On the Home page, click the Pay Employees icon. The Payroll Center opens (refer to Figure 11.2).

2. Select a **Payroll Schedule** and click Start Scheduled Payroll.

3. From the Enter Payroll Information dialog box, do the following:

   ■ Accept the default Pay Period Ends and Check Date selections, or change as necessary.

   ■ Place a checkmark next to each employee you want to pay. Optionally, click the Check All or Uncheck All button, in Figure 11.28.

   ■ Optionally, use Sort By and Show/Hide Columns to customize how the information displays.

   ■ If time entered on a QuickBooks timesheet doesn't appear for a given employee, verify that the employee record has the Use Time Data to Create Paychecks option selected (refer to Figure 11.17).

Figure 11.28
The payroll information defaults from the scheduled payroll setup and employee's salary or timesheet details.

   ■ Optionally, enter your employee's hours in the Enter Payroll Information dialog box.

   ■ Optionally, click the Open Paycheck Detail, to review or edit information not displayed on the Enter Payroll Information dialog box. Click Save & Next or Save & Close to return to the Enter Payroll Information dialog box.

4. Click Continue. The Review and Create Paychecks dialog box displays (see Figure 11.29).

5. Change the Bank Account selection, if necessary.

6. Choose either Print Paychecks from QuickBooks or Assign Check Numbers to Handwritten Checks.

7. Click Create Paychecks.

The following section details printing of paychecks or paystubs.

Figure 11.29
Select paycheck printing options and review paycheck details.

Printing Paychecks or Paystubs

The last step in preparing payroll for your employees is printing the checks. You have two options:

- **Print Paychecks**—Prints on check stock for employees to deposit or cash.

- **Print Paystubs**—Creates a nonnegotiable document detailing the employee's earnings. Use this dialog box when an employee is paid by direct deposit.

When you click Create Paychecks, the Confirmation and Next Steps dialog box displays (see Figure 11.30).

After successfully printing your employees' paychecks, you should promptly pay the payroll liabilities, to avoid costly penalties and late fees.

➥ *To learn more about printer settings in QuickBooks, see "Setting Form Defaults and Making Printing Adjustments," p. 526.*

Do your employees ask for information about previously paid payroll? Check out the next section for details on using the free service ViewMyPaycheck.

Figure 11.30
You can print paychecks now or print later by selecting **File**, **Print Forms**, **Print Paychecks**, or **Print Paystubs** from the menu bar.

ViewMyPaycheck

With ViewMyPaycheck, a free service included with your QuickBooks payroll subscription, you can give your employees online access to their pay stubs, W-2s, and other payroll info. Access the information from any Internet connection or on your mobile device.

How does the ViewMyPaycheck service work? Following are the steps:

1. After subscribing to one of the QuickBooks integrated payroll subscriptions, from the menu bar, select **Employees**, **Send To ViewMyPaycheck.com**. This is a free service for companies that have a paid QuickBooks payroll subscription.

2. The ViewMyPaycheck dialog box displays. Click Connect.

3. The Intuit App Center displays. Here you create an Intuit Account or sign in to an existing account. Complete the fields as required.

4. You might get an If You're Almost Ready message, indicating you have more than one Intuit Account and need to associate this service with the correct account. Click Continue.

5. A message displays with details about how the application ViewMyPaycheck will access your Intuit company data. Click Authorize.

6. A message displays that you are securely connected to ViewMyPaycheck. Click Return to ViewMyPaycheck.

7. If this is your first time signing up for this service, you will see a ViewMyPaycheck message. Select **Send** to send the latest paystubs to the service so employees can view and print them.

8. If prompted, click the Invite My Employees button or the I'll Do This Later button. The ViewMyPaycheck dialog box displays in the administrator view (see Figure 11.31).

Logging in to ViewMyPaycheck as the Administrator (the original user who signed up for the service), you can access the following:

- Paychecks tab

  - Choose either Print Pay Stub or Download/Save PDF.

  - Filter paychecks listed for a specific date range.

  - View paystub information, including Used and Available Paid Time Off.

- Taxes tab

  - Enables W-2 Access. If you are an employee of the company as well as the ViewMyPaycheck administrator, you need to set yourself up as an employee and sign into the service.

  - Provides a link for sending your QuickBooks W-2 data to ViewMyPaycheck.

Figure 11.31
Invite employees to access their payroll information using the free ViewMyPaycheck service on the Internet or mobile device.

- Manage Employees tab

    - Manage administrators by adding new administrators or removing access.

    - Enter employees' email addresses and send invitations to set up access to view their own payroll information.

- Preferences tab

    - Offers the option to send email notification to employees when pay stubs are uploaded.

    - Shows all paychecks dated through today's date or the latest paycheck date.

If you would like more information about this service, go to http://viewmypaycheck.intuit.com/.

Preparing Payroll Liability Payments

When your business pays employees, you also become responsible for paying the liabilities associated with the payroll to governmental and other entities.

Paying Scheduled Liabilities

To pay scheduled payroll liabilities, follow these steps:

1. On the Home page, click the Pay Liabilities icon. QuickBooks opens the Pay Liabilities tab in the Payroll Center. The Pay Scheduled Liabilities lists each payroll liability (amount you owe), with the Due Date, Status, Payment Description, Method, Period, and Amount fields (refer to Figure 11.4).

2. To process a payment, place a checkmark next to the payroll item you want to pay. (Optional) Double-click Amount to view a listing of the transactions that are included in the amount due.

3. Click View/Pay. QuickBooks prepares a Liability Payment for your review (see Figure 11.32).

4. Change the Bank Account, if needed. The payroll items and amount included on the liability payment are calculated from payroll transactions. Check E-Payment to process your payment electronically, or for more information, click the How Do I E-Pay link.

5. Print the checks from the top-right Print icon, or print later by selecting **File**, **Print Forms**, **Print Checks** from the menu bar.

6. Click Save & Close when you are finished. The Payroll Liability Summary window displays. Click Print Checks, Print Summary, or Close.

7. Click the X in the top-right corner to return to the Payroll Center.

> **⚡ caution**
>
> If you do not see all the payroll liabilities you accrue each pay period, you might not have the correct payroll liability due date assigned. From the Payroll Center, click Manage Payment Methods in the Other Activities at the bottom of the Pay Liabilities tab of the Payroll Center.
>
> QuickBooks Payroll Setup displays. You can review and edit the Schedule Tax Payments and Benefits & Other Payment lists.

Figure 11.32
QuickBooks payroll calculates the tax payments automatically.

Do not adjust amounts here; instead use a liability adjustment transaction

Adjusting Payroll Liabilities

QuickBooks automatically calculates payroll liabilities as you process paychecks. If you determine that an amount is not calculating correctly, review the settings for that payroll item.

Your accounting professional might choose to create a journal entry to correct the business financials. However, this type of transaction will not affect the amounts included in Pay Scheduled Liabilities in the Payroll Center or the payroll reporting forms. Instead, use the Liability Adjustment dialog box for changes to the amounts that are reported as liabilities and to affect federal and state reporting forms.

After reviewing your payroll reports detailed in Chapter 12, p. 492, you can adjust payroll liabilities. To do so, follow these steps:

1. From the menu bar, select **Employees**, **Payroll Taxes and Liabilities**, **Adjust Payroll Liabilities** (refer to Figure 11.15).

2. Select the **Date** and **Effective Date**. These dates might affect your payroll reporting forms, so specify the date carefully.

3. Select **Company** if the adjustment is for a company-only payroll item, such as a company-paid health insurance benefit.

4. Select **Employee** if the adjustment is for an employee-reported liability or if you need to change the employee's W2 amounts. Select **Class** if you are using this feature in QuickBooks.

5. From the Item Name drop-down list, select the payroll item or items to be adjusted.

6. Enter an Amount (positive or negative).

7. Enter the Wage Base (positive or negative) if the payroll item being adjusted is subject to a wage threshold similar to federal or state unemployment.

8. Enter the Income Subject to Tax (positive or negative) to adjust the amount reported on tax forms.

9. (Optional) Enter a Memo.

10. (Optional) Click Accounts Affected. The default is to affect liability and expense accounts. If your financials are correct but the payroll reporting and liabilities are incorrect, select **Do Not Affect Accounts**. Click OK to close the message.

11. Click Next Adjustment to add a record, or click OK to close the Adjust Payroll Liabilities dialog box.

It's a good practice to review your payroll reports again after making the adjustments, to be certain they display the expected results.

This chapter has prepared you well for working with payroll processes. Join me in the next chapter for details on managing your payroll, including what reports to review and how to verify that your payroll data is correct.

MANAGING PAYROLL

Many areas in QuickBooks deserve a thorough review. One, in particular, is payroll. Managing your payroll includes verifying that you are paying your employees properly and that you remain in compliance with state and federal regulations regarding your company's payroll obligations.

If your company processes payroll for employees, this chapter can help you better manage the many facets of providing payroll.

Report Center Payroll Reports

Reporting on payroll activity is necessary to properly manage your business payroll activity. QuickBooks offers several payroll reports that you can customize to suit your needs. For more details on customizing reports, see Chapter 14, "Reporting in QuickBooks." Whether you are new to QuickBooks or an expert, you will benefit from the payroll reports in the Report Center. To open the Report Center, from the menu bar, select **Reports**, **Report Center**. Select any of the icons on the top right to change the viewing method for the Report Center:

- Carousel View

- List View

- Grid View

By default, the Report Center opens with the Standard tab selected and displays several report categories. Click Employees & Payroll. To the right, you see sample payroll reports (see Figure 12.1) using Grid View.

Underneath each sample report, you can click the corresponding icons to prepare the report using your data and a date you select, get more information about the report, mark the report as a favorite, or access help information for the report. Icon descriptions display when you hover your cursor over a report.

Figure 12.1
Preview and
prepare pay-
roll reports
in the Report
Center.

The Report Center also offers these tabs:

- **Memorized**—From any displayed report, click Memorize to add the report to this tab in the Report Center.

- **Favorites**—Mark a report as a Favorite (or Fave) to include the report in this tab group.

- **Recent**—QuickBooks lists reports you have recently prepared here.

- **Contributed**—You can download custom reports created by Intuit or other QuickBooks users and use them with your data. You can also share reports you create with the community-at-large. When sharing a report, you are not sharing sensitive information—you share just the format of the report.

You can also type a descriptive search term into the search box in the Report Center to display a list of relevant reports. Additional payroll reports are available in QuickBooks using pivot tables in Microsoft Excel. The next section details these reports.

Excel Reports

If you did not find the report you needed in the Report Center, check out the many reports that use pivot tables in Microsoft Excel. Your QuickBooks software includes these reports.

To access these reports, follow these steps:

1. From the menu bar, select **Reports**, **Employees & Payroll**, **Summarize Payroll Data in Excel**. QuickBooks launches Excel and provides a dialog box that enables you to do the following:

   - Select Date ranges for collecting payroll data.

   - Select Options/Settings that include updating worksheet headers, changing column widths, and enabling drill-down on data and other useful settings.

   - Select optional reports, including 8846 Worksheet, Effective Rates by Item, YTD Recap, and Deferred Compensation report.

2. Click Get QuickBooks Data. Excel collects data for the selected date range and creates a workbook with several worksheets (see Figure 12.2), including the following:

   - Employee Journal

   - YTD Summary (two versions)

   - Hours

   - Rates & Hours by Job

   - State Wage Listing

   - Deferred Comp

   - Quarterly details

   - 8846 Worksheet

   - Calculated % By Payroll Item and Employee

You can save this report as an Excel worksheet for future reference. However, this report cannot be updated with more current data, unlike many other exported Excel reports.

In addition to these reports, there are other reports that QuickBooks creates using Excel.

From the menu bar, select **Reports**, **Employees & Payroll**, **More Payroll Reports in Excel**. Choose which specific report you want from the following:

- Payroll Summary by Tax Tracking Type

- Employee Time & Costs

- Employee Sick & Vacation History

- Employee Direct Deposit Listing

- Tax Form Worksheets

- New! Certified Payroll Report

As you can see, QuickBooks provides plenty of options for finding the right payroll report for your needs, either within QuickBooks or using the automatically generated Microsoft Excel reports.

Figure 12.2 You can prepare this and many other payroll reports with your data using Excel spreadsheets.

Tax Forms and Filings

Up to this point, you have set up payroll, managed employees and payroll items, paid your employees and the state and federal liabilities, and prepared payroll reports. You now see how QuickBooks helps you comply with the required payroll reporting.

In Chapter 11, "Setting Up Payroll," p. 447, you learned about the many payroll subscription offerings you can choose from. If you want your QuickBooks software to automatically calculate your payroll transactions and prepare federal and state forms, you need to have the Intuit QuickBooks Payroll Enhanced subscription. For accounting professionals who prepare payroll for multiple clients, Intuit QuickBooks Payroll Enhanced for Accountants is the subscription most suitable.

QuickBooks can print required federal and state payroll forms or E-File them for you; completing your payroll reporting tasks is so easy.

Preparing and Printing Tax Forms

Before preparing your first payroll tax form, complete the Payroll Contact information in the Company Information window. To do so, from the menu bar, select **Company**, **My Company**. In the top-right corner, click the Edit icon. Select the **Payroll Tax Form Information** and confirm the Contact Name, Title, and Phone No. that will be included on the prepared payroll tax forms (see Figure 12.3).

To prepare your federal or state forms, follow these steps:

1. On the Home page, click the Process Payroll Forms icon.

2. QuickBooks opens the File Forms tab of the Payroll Center.

3. If a Payroll Subscription Alert message displays, informing you to update your tax tables, go to step 4; otherwise, go to step 6.

Figure 12.3
QuickBooks
prefills payroll
tax forms with
specified
contact
information.

4. Click Get Updates or Skip. I recommend that you select Get Updates to ensure that you have the latest tax tables and forms.

5. Click OK to close the Payroll Update message.

6. After you update the payroll taxes, if the Payroll Center does not display, on the Home page, click the Process Payroll Forms icon.

7. Select the appropriate form. Click the File Form button (see Figure 12.4).

Figure 12.4
With the
Enhanced
Payroll
Subscription,
QuickBooks
can prepare
all your fed-
eral forms
and many
state forms.

8. (Optional) Click Auto-Fill Contact Info and complete.

9. Select Filing Period, Quarter, and Quarter Ending date. Click OK.

10. Complete any required fields on the displayed form. If you have questions about the form details, click the provided links. When you have completed the form, click the Check for Errors button (see Figure 12.5). If any errors display, click the error; QuickBooks advances to that section of the form for you to complete or correct.

Figure 12.5
Save time and prepare accurate payroll tax forms using the Enhanced Payroll subscription.

Click here before printing or filing

11. Click Next to advance to the next form page.

12. Click Save & Close if you need to return later to your saved work.

13. Click Save as PDF to save a PDF for your records, click Print for Your Records to prepare a paper copy, or click Submit Form if you have signed up for E-File of your payroll forms (discussed in the next section).

E-Filing Tax Payments and Forms

If you selected the Intuit QuickBooks Payroll Enhanced subscription or the Intuit QuickBooks Payroll Enhanced for Accountant's subscription for your business, you can sign up for the E-File and E-Pay service.

With E-File and E-Pay, you prepare your payroll liability payments in QuickBooks and select E-Pay. Intuit debits your bank account for the funds and remits them directly to the IRS or appropriate state(s) on your behalf.

With E-File of your payroll forms, you can select Submit Form and have QuickBooks process your payroll form and send it to the IRS. You will receive email notification that the form was accepted (or rejected) by the IRS or state(s). To take advantage of the E-File and E-Pay service, you need the following:

- An active Enhanced Payroll subscription.

- A supported version of QuickBooks (typically not older than three years from the current calendar year).

- An Internet connection.

- The most recent payroll tax update.

- Enrollment with the Electronic Federal Tax Payment System (EFTPS), which the IRS uses for employer or individual payments. For more information, visit www.eftps.gov.

You can get more detailed information by clicking the Electronic Payment link at the bottom of the Pay Liabilities tab of the Payroll Center. As your business E-Pays and E-Files, you can click the E-Payments tab, which displays documentation that the payments and forms were successfully transmitted to the IRS.

Troubleshooting Payroll

Using the QuickBooks Run Payroll Checkup diagnostic tool is a recommended way to review and validate the accuracy of your payroll data. You can also review your data setup and accuracy manually by reviewing the reports detailed in this section.

Reviewing the Payroll Item Listing can also be helpful when you need to troubleshoot payroll issues.

➡️ *For more information, see "Reporting About Payroll Items," p. 478.*

Comparing Payroll Liability Balances to the Balance Sheet

Periodically comparing your Balance Sheet payroll liabilities account balance to the amount on the Payroll Liabilities Balances report is important. To do so, follow these steps:

1. From the menu bar, select **Reports**, **Company & Financial**, **Balance Sheet Standard**.

2. Select the As Of date for the period you are reviewing.

3. From the menu bar, select **Reports**, **Employees & Payroll**, **Payroll Liability Balances**.

4. From the Dates drop-down list, select **All** from the top of the list. Leave the From date box empty. In the To date box, enter the same date that was used on the Balance Sheet Standard report. Doing so ensures that you are picking up all transactions for this account, including any unpaid balances from prior years. Click Print if you want to have a copy of this report to compare to your Balance Sheet payroll liabilities balance.

These two reports should have matching totals. In the examples in Figure 12.6, the Balance Sheet and Payroll Liabilities reports do not match.

The totals might not match because nonpayroll transactions are used to record adjustments or payments to payroll liabilities using nonpayroll transactions, including the Make Journal Entry, Enter Bill, or Write Check transaction types.

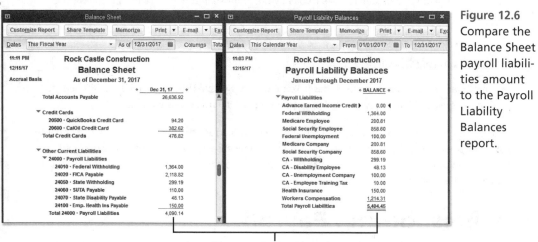

Figure 12.6
Compare the Balance Sheet payroll liabilities amount to the Payroll Liability Balances report.

These totals should match.

To troubleshoot payroll liabilities differences, you can use the Custom Transaction Detail report. To access the report, follow these steps:

1. From the menu bar, select **Reports**, **Custom Reports**, **Transaction Detail**. The Modify Report dialog box opens.

2. In the From date box, leave the field blank; in the To date box, enter the date you used on the Balance Sheet Standard report.

3. Select the same Report Basis as the Balance Sheet report.

4. In the Columns box, remove or add a checkmark for the information you want to display on the report. Be sure to include Type.

5. In the Sort By drop-down list, select **Type**.

6. Click the Filters tab; in the Choose Filters box, the Accounts filter is already selected. From the Accounts drop-down list to the right, select the **Payroll Liabilities** account.

7. Click OK to create the report.

QuickBooks creates a useful and telling report (see Figure 12.7). When this report is sorted by type of transaction, you can easily see what non-payroll-related transactions are affecting your Balance Sheet Standard report Payroll Liability balance and are not affecting your Payroll Liability Balances report.

Figure 12.7
Use the Custom Transaction Detail report to easily identify nonpayroll transactions that are recorded to the Payroll Liabilities account.

If you are an accounting professional working with the Client Data Review feature, you can also select the Find Incorrectly Paid Payroll Liabilities custom report from the menu bar by selecting **Accountant**, **Client Data Review**, **Find Incorrectly Paid Payroll Liabilities**.

➡️ *For more information, see "Find Incorrectly Paid Payroll Liabilities," p. 739.*

You can double-click any of the listed transactions to see more detail about the transaction that was used to create the adjustment to the Balance Sheet. If the Balance Sheet is correct and the Payroll Liability Balances report is not, you can choose between the following options:

- If there are only a few nonpayroll transactions, you might consider voiding them and re-creating them with the correct payroll liability payment transaction. However, if the transactions have been included in bank reconciliations, you have other factors to consider and should consider the next option.

- Create an Adjust Payroll Liabilities transaction.

➡️ *For more information see, "Preparing Payroll Liability Payments," p. 487.*

Comparing the Payroll Summary Report to Filed Payroll Returns

Has your company ever received a notice from the IRS indicating that your year-end payroll documents do not agree with your quarterly payroll return totals, or have you received a similar notice from your state payroll tax agency?

Listed in this section are some basic comparisons you should do both before filing a payroll return and afterward, if you allow users to make changes to transactions from previous payroll quarters.

> ➡️ *For more information about preventing these changes, see "Set a Closing Date,"*
> *p. 613.*

Compare the following items routinely while doing payroll in QuickBooks and ensure that all apply:

- Each calendar quarter QuickBooks payroll totals agree with your filed payroll return totals. Look at these specific totals when reviewing the Payroll Summary:

    - Total Adjusted Gross Pay in QuickBooks agrees with the Federal 941 Form, Wages, Tips, and Other Compensation.

    - Federal Withholding in QuickBooks agrees with the Federal 941 Form, Total Income Tax Withheld from Wages, and so on.

    - Employee and Company Social Security and Medicare in QuickBooks agrees with the computed Total Taxable Social Security and Medicare on the Federal 941 Form.

- Total payroll tax deposits for the quarter in QuickBooks agrees with your paper trail. Whether you pay online or use a coupon that you take to the bank, make sure you recorded the correct calendar quarter with the IRS for your payments.

- Total Adjusted Gross Pay for the calendar year in QuickBooks agrees with the reported Gross Wage total on the annual Federal Form W-3, Transmittal of Wage, and Tax Statements.

- Total Adjusted Gross Pay for the calendar quarter in QuickBooks agrees with the Total Gross Wage reported to your state payroll agency.

- Total Payroll expense from the Profit & Loss report agrees with total Adjusted Gross Pay on the Payroll Summary report. This will be possible if you have set up a separate chart of accounts for the payroll taxes expense of payroll.

Comparing these critical reports with your federal and state tax filings ensures that your data agrees with the payroll tax agency records.

Reconciling Payroll Reports to Business Financials

When applying for a business loan from your bank, your company might be required to produce compiled, reviewed, or audited financials. One of the many items that will be reviewed is the comparison of payroll costs included in the business financials to those in the payroll returns filed with federal or state governments.

If you are uncertain about which accounts within your chart of accounts to review, refer to the account you assigned to the payroll item. Here are a few selected comparisons you can do yourself as a business owner:

- Compare Federal Form 941 Wages, Tips, and Other Compensation (Box 2) to the expense accounts used to report salaries and wages. You might need to add multiple accounts to match the total in Box 2.

- Compare the company portion of the payroll taxes reported to federal or state governments. If you are uncertain about the amount, ask your accountant or view information about payroll taxes on the www.irs.gov website.

This section has given you several critical comparisons to make and reports to review. No matter how proficient you are with QuickBooks, review these reports often. The next section of this chapter provides instructions on handling unique payroll transactions.

Recording Unique Payroll Transactions

The following sections detail several common payroll transactions you might need in your business.

Employee Loan Payment and Repayment

Your business might offer a loan to an employee in advance of payroll earnings. This amount should not be taxed at the time of payment if you expect the loan to be paid back to the company.

Paying an Employee Paycheck Advance

When you offer to pay employees an advance on their earnings, you are creating a loan payment check. If this is a loan to be paid back to the company, follow these steps:

1. From the menu bar, select **Employees**, **Pay Employees**, **Unscheduled Payroll**. The Enter Payroll Information dialog box opens.

2. Place a checkmark next to the employee you are creating the loan check for.

3. QuickBooks might warn that a paycheck for that period already exists. Click Continue if you want to create the loan payment check. You return to the Enter Payroll Information dialog box.

4. To modify the check to be an employee loan check, click the Open Paycheck Detail button.

5. In the Preview Paycheck dialog box, remove any amounts from the Earnings box (if you expect to be repaid this amount, the amount is not considered taxable earnings).

6. In the Other Payroll Items drop-down list, select the Employee Advances (in this example, it was an Addition type payroll item), as in Figure 12.8, and skip to step 15.

   If you do not have an employee advance payroll item, you can easily create one right from the Preview Paycheck dialog box. In the Other Payroll Items box drop-down list, click Add New.

7. In the Add New Payroll Item dialog box, select the button for the Addition type and click Next.

8. The Add New Payroll Item (Addition) dialog box opens. Name the item Employee Advances (if displayed, do not select the Track Expenses by Job box). Click Next.

Figure 12.8
Use an Addition type payroll item when preparing a nontaxable loan (advance) to an employee.

9. In the Expense Account drop-down list, select Employee Advances, Other Current Asset account. You can also scroll to the top of this list and click Add New in this dialog box to create the Other Current Asset account, if needed. Click Next.

10. On the Tax Tracking Type screen, select None (at the top of the list) and click Next.

🔔 caution

Carefully consider what option you choose when selecting the Tax Tracking type for a new payroll item or editing an existing payroll item. The selection you choose here affects how QuickBooks taxes or doesn't tax the payroll item on paychecks and how QuickBooks handles reporting the payroll item on forms, such as the W-2 form given to employees at the end of a calendar year.

When you select each Tax Tracking type, QuickBooks provides detailed information about how it will be treated for tax calculations and form preparation. Be sure to take the time to read these. If you are unsure of the proper tax tracking type, consult your accounting professional.

11. Do not place a checkmark next to any of the Taxes options. Click Next.

12. The Calculate Based on Quantity screen opens. Leave the default of **Neither** selected and click Next.

13. On the Gross vs. Net screen, leave the default of Gross. This setting has no impact because you are setting it up with a tax tracking type of None. Click Next.

14. The Default Rate and Limit screen opens. Leave it blank because you define the limit amounts individually for each employee. Click Finish to close the Add New Payroll Item (Addition) dialog box.

15. You return to the Preview Paycheck dialog box. From the Other Payroll Items box, in the Item Name column, select the Employee Advance payroll addition item from the drop-down list. Enter the dollar amount of the loan you are providing the employee in the Rate column. QuickBooks creates a payroll advance check without deducting any payroll taxes (see Figure 12.8 shown previously). Note that you do not need to enter anything in the Quantity column.

> **note**
>
> You can also record the employee loan portion using a Write Check transaction type. Make sure the payee listed on the check is the employee's name (not a vendor or other name). Record the loan payment to the Employee Advances other current asset account on the Expense tab.
>
> This type of transaction will not report on the Payroll Summary report, one of the reasons I choose to use a Paycheck and Payroll Items to record the initial payroll loan.

QuickBooks now has on record a loan paid to the employee. If you have defined payment terms with the employee, you need to edit the employee's record so that the agreed-to amount is deducted from future payroll checks. Learn more about this task in the following section.

Automatically Deducting the Employee Loan Repayments

When a company provides an advance to an employee that is to be paid back in installments, you can have QuickBooks automatically calculate this amount and even stop the deductions when the total of the loan has been completely paid back to the company. QuickBooks automatically deducts the loan repayments from future payroll checks. Follow these steps to record a payroll deduction on the employee's setup:

1. From the menu bar, select **Employees**, **Employee Center**.

2. Select the employee who was given a payroll advance or loan. Click the Edit icon in the top right. The Edit Employee dialog box opens.

3. At the right, select the Payroll Info tab.

4. In the Item Name column of the Additions, Deductions, and Company Contributions box, select your Employee Loan Repay deduction item (and skip to step 14), or click Add New to open the Add New Payroll Item dialog box.

5. If you are creating a new item, select type Deduction and click Next.

6. Type a name for the item, such as **Employee Loan Repay**, and click Next.

7. The Add New Payroll Item (Deduction) dialog box opens. Leave the agency name and number fields blank. For the Liability Account, select the drop-down list and select your Employee Advances, Other Current Asset account created when you made the employee advance check. (See Figure 12.9.) Click Next.

Figure 12.9
Assign the Other Current Asset Employee Advances as the liability account for the paycheck deduction.

8. The Tax Tracking type screen displays. Leave the default for Tax Tracking type of None and click Next.

9. The Taxes screen displays. Accept the default of no taxes selected and click Next.

10. The Calculate Based on Quantity screen displays. Leave the default of **Neither** selected and click Next.

11. The Gross vs. Net screen displays. Leave the default of **Gross Pay** selected. This setting has no impact because you are setting it up with a Tax Tracking type of None. Click Next.

12. The Default Rate and Limit screen displays. Leave it blank because you define the limit amounts individually for each employee. Click Finish to return to the New Employee dialog box or Edit Employee dialog box.

13. In the Item Name column of the Additions, Deductions, and Company Contributions box, select the **Employee Loan Repay** deduction item you just created.

14. In the Amount column, enter the per-pay-period amount you want to deduct.

15. In the Limit column, enter the amount of the total loan. QuickBooks stops deducting the loan when it reaches the limit. Click OK to record your changes to the employee setup.

QuickBooks is now properly set up to deduct the stated amount on each paycheck until the employee loan has been fully repaid. If you provide additional employee loans, do not forget to go back to step 15 to add the new amount to the previous loan total.

Reporting Employee Loan Details

Tracking the actual details of the employee loan is equally important. To open a modified version of my favorite report, the Transaction Detail report (in Figure 12.10), follow these steps:

Figure 12.10
Create a report to track your employee loan details.

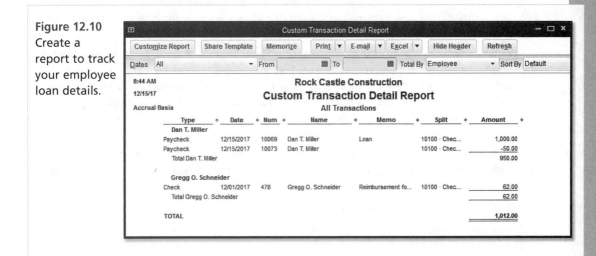

1. From the menu bar, select **Reports**, **Custom Reports**, **Transaction Detail**. The Modify Report dialog box displays.

2. In the Report Date Range drop-down list, select the date range you are reviewing, or choose All to view all dates.

3. In the Columns box, select or deselect the detail you want to see displayed on the report.

4. In the Total By drop-down list, select **Employee**.

5. Click the Filters tab; Account is already selected in the Choose Filters box. In the Account drop-down list to the right, select the **Employee Advances**, **Other Current Asset** account.

6. In the Choose Filters box, select the Amount filter and, optionally, select an amount greater than or equal to .01. Doing so provides a report of only employees with nonzero balances.

7. If you want to change the report title, click the Header/Footer tab and customize the report title.

8. Click OK to view the modified report.

9. If you want to use this report again, click Memorize to save the report for later use.

You are now prepared to advance money to an employee and track the employee's payments against the loan accurately. Don't forget to review the balances and to increase the limit when new loans are paid out.

Reprinting a Lost Paycheck

When any other check in QuickBooks is lost, you typically void the check in QuickBooks and issue a stop payment request to your bank so it cannot be cashed.

With payroll, you need to be a bit more cautious about voiding the transaction because, when you void a payroll transaction and then reissue it, payroll taxes can be calculated differently on the replacement check compared to the original paycheck.

Certain payroll taxes are based on limits; for example, Social Security, Federal Unemployment, and State Unemployment taxes are examples of taxes that are charged to employees or to the company, up to a certain wage limit. When you void a previously issued check, QuickBooks recalculates these taxes for the current replacement check, and these amounts might differ from the original check, potentially affecting the net amount of the check.

Proper control is to issue a stop payment request for the missing check to your bank so it cannot be cashed. In QuickBooks, instead of voiding the payroll check and then re-creating it, print a new payroll check (from the same original payroll check details), record the new check number, and then separately create a voided check for the lost check.

To record these transactions, follow these steps:

1. Locate the lost check in your checking register from the menu bar by selecting **Banking**, **Use Register**.

2. In the Select Account drop-down list, select the bank account that has the missing check and click OK to open the bank register.

3. Find the check in the register that was reported missing. Double-click the specific check to open the Paycheck dialog box (see Figure 12.11). Make a note of the check number, date, and payee.

Figure 12.11
Do not re-create a lost paycheck; instead, select Print Later on the original paycheck.

4. In the open Paycheck dialog box, on the Main tab of the ribbon toolbar at the top of the transaction, select the **Print Later** checkbox.

5. Print the paycheck singly or with others by clicking the Print button at the top of the check on the Main tab of the ribbon toolbar.

6. Enter the Printed Check Number. After printing the check, QuickBooks assigns the new check number and uses the check date and totals assigned to the original check.

7. To keep track of the lost check in your accounting, from the menu bar, select **Banking**, **Write Checks**. Using the original check number, date, and payee, record the check with a zero amount to an account of your choosing. You might get a message warning not to pay employees with a check, but because you are recording a zero transaction, you can ignore this warning.

8. With the lost check created in step 7 still open, from the menu bar, select **Edit**, **Void Check**. QuickBooks prefills with a 0 amount and adds Void to the Memo line of the check. This now shows this check as voided in your register, just in case the employee was able to cash the check. You would notice when reconciling that you marked it as voided.

Using this method for printing a lost payroll check ensures that you do not inadvertently change any prior-period payroll amounts and reported payroll totals; at the same time, recording the lost check helps keep a record of each check issued from your bank account.

Paying a Taxable Bonus

Use an unscheduled payroll to issue bonuses to your employees. This payroll is included in the total taxable wages. To do so, follow these steps:

1. From the menu bar, select **Employees**, **Pay Employees**, **Unscheduled Payroll**. The Enter Payroll Information dialog box displays.

2. Place a checkmark next to the employee(s) receiving a bonus check.

3. If the employee is paid hourly, you can adjust the hours from the regular pay column.

> **note**
>
> When issuing a bonus paycheck, QuickBooks might display a warning that a paycheck already exists for the date you have selected. Click Continue to close the warning. You return to the Enter Payroll Information dialog box.

4. Often you want to edit or remove the default Gross Earnings or Federal Taxes Withheld entries on a bonus check. To adjust this detail, click the Open Paycheck Detail button to modify the default amounts.

5. If you are using the Intuit Enhanced Payroll subscription, you can also select the checkbox for Enter Net/Calculate Gross on the paycheck detail. Selecting this option enables you to specify the net amount; QuickBooks then calculates the gross amount to cover taxes and withholdings.

6. QuickBooks might display a warning dialog box titled Special Calculation Situation to inform you that certain payroll items have reached their limits.

7. In the example in Figure 12.12, the Federal Withholding amount that was automatically calculated was removed. QuickBooks now shows that this paycheck was adjusted.

Figure 12.12
QuickBooks identifies when automatic payroll calculations have been manually adjusted.

> ⚠ **caution**
>
> Adjust paychecks cautiously, making sure you do not adjust items that have a predefined tax table amount, such as Social Security and Medicare. If you do and the adjustment causes the calculated totals to be incorrect for the year, QuickBooks self-corrects the taxes on the next payroll check you create for this employee. You should also obtain the advice of your tax accountant before adjusting taxes withheld on bonus payroll checks.

Adjusting an Employee Paycheck

You should rarely need to adjust a paycheck record in QuickBooks. One example is when you hand-prepare a check and later discover that QuickBooks calculated a different net pay amount.

In this example, the check amount the employee cashed differs from what QuickBooks computed, so adjusting the QuickBooks paycheck is acceptable.

To adjust a prepared employee check before it is printed, or to adjust a paycheck that had the wrong amount in QuickBooks from what was recorded on the actual check, follow these steps:

1. Locate the paycheck in your checking register by clicking the Check Register icon on the QuickBooks Home page.

2. If you have multiple checking accounts, select the account the paycheck was recorded to and click OK to open the bank register.

3. Find the check with the incorrect amount; open the paycheck transaction by double-clicking the check.

4. Click the Paycheck Detail button to display the detail of the check to be modified.

5. Click Unlock Net Pay and review the caution message QuickBooks provides about changing net pay on existing checks. Click OK to close the message (see Figure 12.13).

Figure 12.13
QuickBooks protects inadvertent changes by requiring you to unlock net pay before modifying a paycheck record.

Special Paycheck Situation

Unlocking Net Pay
You are about to enable the capability to change gross and net pay on this paycheck. Changing amounts on an existing paycheck may have consequences for both your company's and the employee's finances.

Caution:
Making changes to an existing paycheck may alter tax amounts due, the wage base for taxes, and the balance of your bank account in QuickBooks. Use caution when unlocking net pay.

If you already issued this paycheck and the employee has not deposited it, you may want to retrieve the paycheck from the employee and issue a new one. If you make changes and have already paid taxes or filed forms for the period that includes this paycheck, you may need to file amended tax forms, and may be liable for additional taxes generated by the changes. See Help for more information.

OK   Cancel   Help

6. Modify the check as needed, being careful not to modify the Social Security or Medicare taxes. Modify the check to reflect the actual check amount that cleared.

7. Click OK to close the dialog box.

8. Click Save & Close to save the changes to the paycheck.

Cautiously consider the effect of changes you make to existing paychecks on previously filed payroll tax returns.

Allocating Indirect Costs to Jobs Through Payroll

This section provides instructions for allocating "indirect" job costs, or costs that your company incurs but that cannot be easily associated with a job. The term *allocating* used here refers to distributing costs to jobs independent of the original cost record. Costs such as cell phones, automobile fuel, training fees, uniforms, and small tools are practically impossible to assign to jobs.

However, don't confuse these costs with the general and administrative costs of the business. These costs are essential to your overall operations and are relatively stable.

Why do I mention this at all? If you review your Profit & Loss report and total the collective value of these costs, it can be significant—and when these costs are not associated with jobs, a job's profitability is overstated.

To begin, make sure that you assign a customer or job to each line on expense transactions. Additionally, using the Items tab (see Figure 12.14) enables you to include these costs in a variety of Job Profitability reports that are item based. To access these reports, from the icon bar, select **Reports**, **Jobs**, **Time & Mileage**.

Figure 12.14
Properly record job costs using the Items tab, and assign a customer or job to the line.

If your company performs much of the labor associated with your service or product (instead of subcontracting the work to a vendor), you can use the payroll records to automatically allocate these costs to customers or jobs. This is easy using just a few steps, as the following sections illustrate.

Identify Costs and Allocation Rate

The first step in this process is to review your Profit & Loss report and identify which expense accounts you post your indirect job expenses to without assigning a customer or job. These costs are easy to identify; they increase when you have more jobs and decrease when you have fewer jobs.

Because this method uses payroll as the tool to automatically allocate the costs, you next need to estimate the number of payroll hours in the period you will be allocating expenses.

Following is an example that you should be able to replicate with your own data. After reviewing my company's Profit & Loss report, I estimate the cost of paying for employee's cellular phones yearly is $15,000.00. I also estimate the yearly labor hours to be 16,000 hours. To arrive at the overhead allocation rate as a per-hour cost, I divide the estimated cost by the estimated hours. In this example, the per-hour cost is rounded to 94 cents per hour.

Create Payroll Items for Allocating

After identifying the indirect expenses and the per-hour allocation rate, you are ready to create list items. You need to create the following:

- **Chart of Accounts Allocation Account**—I recommend that you create a new chart of accounts specifically for the allocation amount (see Figure 12.15). Having a separate account helps you identify over time whether the allocation estimate is closely matched to the like expense being recorded. The normal balance for this type of account is a negative expense balance.

- **Company Contribution Payroll Item**—This item does not affect the employee's gross earnings or net pay. The newly created payroll item provides the means to automatically allocate the cost to a job through the payroll record. When creating this item, follow these guidelines:

  - Select Track Expense by Job checkbox.

  - In the Liability Account (Company-Paid) field, assign the newly created allocated expense account. This account is "credited" during the payroll process.

  - In the Expense Account field, assign the Cost of Goods Sold account, or whatever account you want the allocated costs to record to.

  - Select None for the Tax Tracking Type.

  - Do not select any of the taxes (this is the default for this item).

  - Select Calculate This Item Based on Hours. This is important because your allocation is based on hours.

  - Enter Default Rate (this is your allocation rate). In the current example, the rate is .94.

  ➡️ *To learn more about working with these lists, see "Chart of Accounts," p. 108, and "Setting Up Payroll Items," p. 475.*

Figure 12.15
Creating a unique account for the allocated costs helps identify them when viewing reports.

NAME	⚡	TYPE	BALANCE T...	ATT...
◆65110 · Gas and Electric		Expense		
◆65120 · Telephone		Expense		
◆65130 · Water		Expense		
◆ 65200 · Small Tools		Expense		
◆ 65300 · Allocated Small Tools		Expense		
◆ 69000 · Miscellaneous		Expense		
◆ 70100 · Other Income		Other Income		
◆ 70200 · Interest Income		Other Income		
◆ 80100 · Other Expenses		Other Expense		

Account ▼   Activities ▼   Reports ▼   Attach   ☐ Include inactive

Allocating Through Payroll Records

The method this section details presumes that your company performs the labor instead of hiring vendors to provide the labor for your product. For laborers you included in your estimated hours, add the newly created company contribution calculation to their employee record, on the Payroll Info tab. See Figure 12.16 and the added Allocate Small Tools calculation.

Figure 12.16
Using payroll calculations, you can allocate overhead expenses to jobs.

When you create a paycheck, QuickBooks uses this allocation payroll item in calculating the company's costs. This payroll item had a tax tracking type of None and does not affect the employee's gross or net wages.

Assigning the Calculate This Item Based on Hours option when you set up the payroll item distributes the estimated hourly cost of the small tools to the two jobs reported on the paycheck in Figure 12.17.

Figure 12.17
QuickBooks
automati-
cally uses the
hours on the
paycheck to
allocate the
estimated
costs to the
jobs.

Reporting on Actual and Allocated Costs

When you first begin using this method, you want to verify the payroll item provided for the desired accounting. I find the Transaction Journal report the easiest way to see the accounting that goes on behind the scenes with the payroll items.

From the checkbook register, select a paycheck record that used this newly created allocation item. From the ribbon toolbar at the top of the displayed check, select the **Reports** tab, **Transaction Journal**. The Transaction Journal report for the paycheck shown previously in Figure 12.17 displays in Figure 12.18.

In this example, QuickBooks calculates 80 hours at the .94/hour allocation rate. The total amount is then distributed to the two jobs using a weighted average. The job with the most hours receives the highest allocated cost.

Allocating indirect job expenses takes just a few steps and results in more accurate job profitability reporting.

Figure 12.18 Review the Transaction Journal report, verifying the accuracy of your payroll item setup for allocating overhead costs.

Depositing a Refund of Payroll Liabilities

If you received a refund from an overpayment of payroll taxes, you should not add it to a Make Deposits transaction (as with other deposits you create). If you do, the refunded amount will not correct your overpayment amount showing in the payroll liability reports and in certain payroll forms.

This type of payroll error rarely, if ever, occurs in current versions of QuickBooks, thanks to improved messaging and ease of creating payroll transactions from the Payroll Center.

However, if you were paying your payroll liabilities outside the QuickBooks payroll menus and you had an overpayment that you requested and received a refund for, you can record the deposit to reflect receipt of the overpayment in your payroll reports. To do so, follow these steps:

1. From the menu bar, select **Employees**, **Payroll Taxes and Liabilities**, **Deposit Refund of Liabilities**. The Refund Deposit for Taxes and Liabilities dialog box displays.

2. Select the name of the payroll tax liability vendor.

3. Enter the Refund Date (the date of your deposit).

4. Enter the For Period Beginning date (this should be the payroll month or quarter the overpayment was in).

5. Enter the Deposit Total of the refund.

6. Click the Group with Other Undeposited Funds button if this item is included on a bank deposit ticket with other deposit amounts; alternatively, select the Deposit To button to create a single deposit entry, and select the appropriate bank account from the drop-down list.

7. Select the Payroll Item that needs to be adjusted.

8. (Optional) Add a Memo so that you have a record of why this transaction occurred. Click OK.

See Figure 12.19 for a completed Refund Deposit for Taxes and Liabilities transaction.

Figure 12.19
Use the proper transaction when recording a refund of overpaid payroll liabilities.

	Refund Deposit for Taxes and Liabilities	— □ ×

Vendor	Employment Devel... ▼	Refund Date	12/15/2017 🛗
		For Period Beginning	11/30/2017 🛗

Next Refund
Prev Refund
OK
Cancel
Help

Deposit total: 125.25

● Group with other undeposited funds
○ Deposit To   ▼

Taxes and Liabilities

ITEM NAME	AMOUNT	MEMO
CA- Employee Training Tax	125.25	Refund of Overpayment

Recording Payroll When Using an Outside Payroll Service

In Chapter 11, p. 447, you learned about several Intuit-provided payroll subscription offerings that integrate with your QuickBooks software. If your company uses another payroll provider, you might find these instructions handy for recording the payroll activity in your QuickBooks file.

When using an outside payroll service, I encourage you to request comparative pricing for Intuit's Assisted or Full Service Payroll offerings. One of the primary benefits of using an Intuit-provided payroll service is that you can track your employees' time to jobs in QuickBooks and let Intuit take care of the rest of the payroll responsibility.

The method I recommend for recording this payroll makes the following assumptions:

■ You want to track your employees' time to customers or jobs.

■ You value the customer or job profitability reports found by selecting **Reports**, **Jobs**, **Time & Mileage** from the menu bar including to name just a few:

   ■ Job Profitability Summary or Detail

   ■ Item Profitability

   ■ Profit & Loss by Job

■ You subscribe to one of Intuit's payroll offerings.

■ Your outside payroll vendor consolidates the charges to your bank account, usually two large debits. A typical payroll provider debits your bank account one lump sum for the net amount of the checks and another for payment of taxes to the IRS on your behalf.

If your company does not need or want any of the previously listed items, you can continue recording the payroll using your current method. Be aware that, if you use a journal entry to record these payroll expenses, many of the Job Profitability reports will not reflect the information properly. Instead, use the Items tab on a check or vendor bill (refer to Figure 12.14) so that your Job Profitability reports provide complete details (see Figure 12.20).

The following steps can help you track payroll costs to customers or jobs and record the company's payroll expense. Chapter 11 has detailed instructions for each of these steps.

1. Create a bank account on the chart of accounts list and name it **Payroll Clearing**. The purpose of this account is to record individual net payroll checks. Many payroll vendors debit your bank account for the lump-sum total of the payroll checks, not individually.

Figure 12.20
Using paycheck transactions provides job profitability reports by labor type.

Job Profitability Detail for Abercrombie, Kristy:Kitchen

Customize Report | Share Template | Memorize | Print ▼ | E-mail ▼ | Excel ▼ | Hide Header | Collapse

Dates All ▼ | From [ ] | To [ ] | Columns Total only

12:39 PM
12/15/17

Rock Castle Construction
Job Profitability Detail for Abercrombie, Kristy:Kitchen
All Transactions

	Act. Cost	Act. Revenue	($) Diff.
▼ Parts			
Appliance	695.00	1,030.00	335.00
Custom made counter top	0.00	1,900.00	1,900.00
Plumbing fixtures	250.00	0.00	-250.00
Total Parts	945.00	2,930.00	1,985.00
▼ Service			
Removal labor	0.00	560.00	560.00
▼ Payroll Labor			
Electrical work	100.00	231.00	131.00
Painting	100.00	147.00	47.00
Plumbing	200.00	420.00	220.00
Install tile or counter	300.00	504.00	204.00
Total Payroll Labor	700.00	1,302.00	602.00
Total Service	700.00	1,862.00	1,162.00
No item	1,000.00	0.00	-1,000.00
TOTAL	2,645.00	4,792.00	2,147.00

Use the Items tab on expense transactions to avoid "No Item" detail.

2. Sign up for one of Intuit's payroll subscriptions. If you don't sign up for a subscription, you have to manually type the payroll calculation amounts that your payroll provider details for you. Your time is worth the expense!

3. Complete the payroll setup as detailed in Chapter 11, p. 458. One exception: Because a payroll service is controlling your payroll, use a single Payroll Liabilities account for all taxes due.

4. Prepare timesheets, or record time directly on a paycheck transaction. QuickBooks calculates the expected additions or deductions for you based on your setup.

5. Assign the fictitious bank account named Payroll Clearing to each paycheck.

6. Compare your current payroll totals in QuickBooks to your vendor's payroll reporting by selecting **Reports**, **Employees & Payroll**, **Payroll Summary**. Minor differences due to rounding are expected.

7. To record your vendor's lump-sum debit to your bank account, select **Banking**, **Transfer Funds** from the menu bar.

8. Enter the date the vendor debits (charges) your bank account.

9. In the Transferred Funds From drop-down list, select the bank account that will be charged.

10. In the Transfer Funds To drop-down list, select the **Payroll Clearing** bank account.

11. Review the remaining balance in the Payroll Clearing account. From the menu bar, select **Banking**, **Use Register**, and select the **Payroll Clearing** bank account. Click OK.

12. If the balance is not zero, enter an adjusting entry in the next available row. Enter **ADJ** in the Number column; enter an amount in the Payment column to decrease or in the Deposit column to increase.

13. Assign an expense account of your choice for this small adjustment, and click Record. Your Payroll Clearing account should now have a net zero balance.

14. Record your vendor's payment of the payroll taxes by selecting **Banking**, **Write Checks** from the menu bar.

15. From the Bank Account drop-down list, select the bank account from which your payroll taxes are withdrawn.

16. Enter the word **Debit** in the No. field, and select the date the charge is made to the bank account.

17. Select your payroll service vendor in the Pay to the Order Of drop-down list.

18. Enter the Amount in the field next to the payee name.

19. In the Account column on the Expenses tab, select your payroll liability account. I recommend simplicity here, using a single payroll liability account. You have a payroll service closely monitoring your payments; you might not need the same level of detail on your own balance sheet.

20. Click Save & Close to finish recording the payroll tax payment.

Check your work for accuracy. Your Payroll Clearing account should have a zero balance. The Payroll Liability account on your Balance Sheet should have a zero balance. Your job profitability reports accurately track payroll costs, and your bank register shows the debit transactions your payroll vendor made.

13

WORKING WITH BANK AND CREDIT CARD ACCOUNTS

Incorrect bank account balances are one of the most common problems I find when troubleshooting a client's QuickBooks data. One of the first questions I ask new clients is whether they have reconciled their bank or credit card accounts in QuickBooks. Most tell me they have. I then review any transactions that are not marked as cleared, and I usually find older, dated transactions that have not cleared. For more information, see "Reviewing Uncleared Transactions," in this chapter.

One of the most important reconciliations to do in QuickBooks is to match your bank or credit card transactions recorded in QuickBooks with the same transactions reported by your financial institution in its monthly statement. Just reconciling your account balances can correct many errors on the Profit & Loss statement.

Preferences That Affect Banking and Credit Card Management

You can streamline your banking and credit card processes by setting certain QuickBooks preferences. Setting preferences saves keystrokes, which, in turn, can save data entry time.

Not every preference that affects banking or credit card management impacts your financials; some preferences enable specific features. To set preferences in QuickBooks, from the menu bar, select **Edit**, **Preferences**.

Preferences in QuickBooks come in two forms:

- **My Preferences**—Settings that are unique to the current user logged in to the data file; they are not shared by other users

- **Company Preferences**—Settings that are common to all users

> *For a detailed review of the preferences that affect working with banking and credit card activities, see "Preferences That Affect Accounts Payable," p. 232.*

Working with Write Check Transactions

An important task for any financial management software is the capability to record the expenses that a business has in providing its product or service to its customers.

QuickBooks offers multiple transaction types for recording your business expenses. The Write Checks transaction offers a quick method for entering costs. Another transaction for recording expenses is the Enter Bills transaction.

> *For more information, see "The Accounts Payable Process," p. 247.*

Both the Write Checks transaction and the Enter Bills transaction can record expenses. However, some notable differences exist between the two:

- Using an Enter Vendor Bill transaction enables you to track what is owed until you pay an invoice, whereas using a Write Check transaction simply records the cost as of the date of the check.

- If you use a vendor bill, QuickBooks warns you if you enter the same reference number (vendor's invoice number) that you have already recorded. This warning helps keep you from inadvertently paying a vendor more than once for the same invoice.

> **🔍 note**
>
> To set company preferences, you must log in to the file as the Admin or External Accountant user and switch to single-user mode (if you are using the data file in a multiuser environment). The Admin user is the default user created when you begin using QuickBooks for the first time.
>
> Proper data entry security includes limiting which employees have access to logging in as the Admin and setting company preferences that are global for all users. For more information, see "Setting Up Users and Permissions," p. 55.

You might want to use a vendor bill for selected vendor costs instead of writing a check. This chapter deals only with working with the costs you will be recording using the Write Checks or Enter Credit Card Charges transactions.

Using the Expenses Tab and Items Tab

The QuickBooks Write Checks transaction includes an Expenses and Items tab. The information entered on these tabs provides financial detail about the cost being recorded, as well as other useful information. See Figure 13.1.

Figure 13.1
Use the Expenses tab to record administrative or overhead costs.

The Expenses and Items tabs on a Write Check or Enter Vendor Bill transaction affect QuickBooks reports in different ways. Costs recorded on either tab are included in all the Profit & Loss reports. However, if your business wants to use the many job profitability reports, you must consistently use the Items tab to record job-related expenses, as in Figure 13.2. If you use the Expenses tab, you will see these costs on a Profit & Loss by Job report, but they will not be itemized on the job profitability reports.

Figure 13.2
Use the Items tab to record customer- or job-related expenses to take advantage of the reporting available with job profitability reports.

From the menu bar, select **Reports**, **Jobs**, **Time & Mileage**. These job profitability reports depend on the information entered on the Items tab of the Write Checks transaction.

Tracking job profitability includes setting a budget and tracking costs for the same budgeted items. When you do not use the Items tab on expense transactions (see Figure 13.3); the costs display as a No Item line on job profitability reports (see Figure 13.4). Doing so makes it impossible to track profitability by the budgeted item.

➡ *For more information, see "Items," p. 112.*

Figure 13.3
Using the Expenses tab for job expenses makes job profitability reports less meaningful.

tip

QuickBooks can automatically open drop-down lists when you're typing. From the menu bar, select **Edit**, **Preferences**, and then select the **General—My Preferences** tab on the Preferences dialog box. Place a check-mark in the box. Select the **Automatically Open Drop-Down Lists When Typing**. Click OK to close the dialog box and save your changes.

Another useful purpose of the Items tab is to automate assigning the expense to a specific chart of account. An example is recording telephone expenses. A business that has multiple vendors for telephone, fax, or cellphone services can create an item named Telephone. This item is mapped to the appropriate chart of account. When a bill is received, the cost can be recorded on the Items tab using the Telephone item. QuickBooks automatically assigns the cost to the expense account included in the item setup.

Figure 13.4
Job profit-ability report results when the Expenses tab was used instead of the preferred Items tab for job costing expenses.

Writing a Check

Writing a check is an easy way to record expenses. I recommend using it for one-time purchases from a supplier or service provider, or for recording debit card or ACH payments from your bank account.

Writing a Check

To practice creating a Write Check transaction, open the sample data file as instructed in Chapter 1, "Getting Started with QuickBooks," p. 37. If you are working in your own file, use these instructions:

1. From the menu bar, select **Banking**, **Write Checks**.

2. On the Write Checks transaction that displays, leave the prefilled Bank Account—Checking.

3. In the Pay to the Order Of field, begin typing **Davis Business Associates** until the appropriate vendor displays. QuickBooks prefills the field if it recognizes the name in any of the lists in QuickBooks (see Figure 13.5). To continue with the sample exercise, skip to step 9; if you're working in your own file, continue to step 4.

Figure 13.5
Create a Write Checks transaction to record a business expense.

4. When you are entering checks in your own file and the payee is not included in a list, select **Add New** at the top of the Pay to the Order Of drop-down list.

5. When you're adding a new payee, the Select Name Type message displays where you assign the new payee as a Vendor, Customer, Employee, or Other. After selecting the appropriate list, click OK.

6. Complete the details for the newly created list item.

7. (Optional) Instead of selecting Add New in step 4, if you begin typing the new vendor name in the payee field, QuickBooks offers these choices:

   - **Quick Add**—Creates a new list record with just the name field.

   - **Set Up**—Opens the Select Name Type dialog box. Choose from Vendor, Customer, Employee, or Other Names list. Complete as detailed in step 8.

   - **Cancel**—Select to not add the new payee.

8. Complete the remaining fields for adding the new name to the selected list. This process varies depending on whether you are adding a new vendor, employee, customer, or other name. Click OK to return to the Write Checks transaction.

9. Accept the prefilled date. The cost is recorded in the business financials as of this date.

10. In the amount field, type **100.00**.

11. (Optional) Complete the address details. (When you save the record, QuickBooks prompts you for whether you want to save the changes for future transactions.)

12. Enter an optional Memo (the field below the address box) that prints on the check. If you leave the Memo field blank, QuickBooks can insert the Account Number from the vendor record. For more information, see the section "Adding or Modifying Vendors" in Chapter 7, p. 243.

13. On the first line of the Expenses tab, begin typing the account **Office Supplies**.

14. Use the Tab key on your keyboard to advance to the following fields:

    - **Memo**—Enter an optional memo to include in reports (not on the printed check).

    - **Customer:Job**—Leave this field blank for this exercise. Using the Items tab is recommended when assigning costs to jobs with budgets.

    - **Billable**—Leave this field blank for this exercise. For more information, see "Time and Expense Invoicing," p. 363.

    - **Class**—Select Overhead.

15. Leave the following fields unselected on the Main tab of the ribbon toolbar at the top of the transaction:

    - **Print Later**—When selected, QuickBooks removes any prefilled check number. The check number is assigned when the check is printed.

    - **Pay Online**—Select this if you've established electronic bill payment through your QuickBooks file. For more information, see the section in this chapter titled "Online Banking Center."

16. (Optional) Click any of the following, also found on the Main tab of the ribbon toolbar, to help complete the transaction:

    - **Select PO**—Select this if purchase orders are enabled in inventory preferences. See Chapter 5, "Setting Up Inventory."

- **Enter Time**—Select this if you want to prefill the Write Check with timesheet data. See Chapters 7 and 11.

- **Clear Splits**—This clears the amounts you entered in the detail section of the check and moves the total to the Expenses tab.

- **Recalculate**—This is useful if, after entering an amount at the top of the record, you add lines of detail to the Expenses or Items tab. It then updates the amount of the check to match the total of the newly added detail lines.

- **Batch Transactions**—Here's a useful tool for adding multiple checks in a spreadsheet-like interface. It is available only with QuickBooks Premier Accountant and all versions of QuickBooks Enterprise.

When you are finished with the entry details, you can select from one of the following choices:

- **Clear**—Removes all data entered in fields and starts over

- **Save & Close**—Saves and closes the dialog box

- **Save & New**—Saves and continues with another record

> 🔍 **note**
>
> The Class field does not appear in your data if Class Tracking in the Preferences dialog box is not enabled. To enable Class Tracking, from the menu bar, select **Edit**, **Preferences**, **Accounting**, **Company Preferences** tab.

Printing Checks

Printing checks from QuickBooks can save you time over manually writing checks and later recording them in your software. Printing also helps limit any confusion about the amount the transaction is approved for.

Ordering QuickBooks Checks

Many check-printing suppliers offer QuickBooks-compatible checks. When ordering, confirm with your check supply source that the format supplied works with the QuickBooks software. In QuickBooks, you can make only a few minor adjustments to the placement of data on the printed check.

You can also purchase checks directly from Intuit. For more information, click the Order Checks icon on the Main tab of the Write Checks ribbon toolbar.

Setting Form Defaults and Making Printing Adjustments

Before printing checks from your QuickBooks file, review the printing defaults assigned to checks or paychecks.

To review the printing defaults in your file, follow these steps:

1. From the menu bar, select **File**, **Printer Setup**.

2. From the Form Name drop-down list, select **Check/PayCheck**, as in Figure 13.6.

Figure 13.6
Select the check style you will be printing and other settings.

3. From the Settings tab, you can select the following:

   - **Printer Name and Printer Type**—Choose from available printers in your computer network.

   - **Check Style**—Select from Voucher, Standard, or Wallet.

   - **Print Company Name and Address, Use Logo, or Print Signature Image**—Click the Signature button to the right to locate the electronically stored signature image.

4. Click the Fonts tab to modify the Font used on the check.

5. Click the Partial Page tab if you print standard or wallet format style checks. Use this setting to define how to print a partial page of checks and to specify the position of the check to use with the printer.

6. After printing a check, you might find it necessary to make minor alignment modifications to the printed check. Click the Align button. Select amounts to move the text in 1/100-inch increments (see Figure 13.7).

7. Click Print Sample to check your new settings. Click OK to close Printer Setup when you're finished with this task.

Figure 13.7
From Printer Setup, you can choose to make minor alignment adjustments.

Printing Checks

With QuickBooks, you can print checks individually or in a batch of checks all at once, as in Figure 13.5. To print a check or a group of checks, follow these steps:

1. If the Write Checks transaction isn't already open, select **Banking**, **Write Checks** from the menu bar, and prepare your check for printing.

2. In the Print drop-down list, select from the following:

   - **Print**—Enter the check number you are printing.

   - **Print Batch**—Select the Bank Account. Enter the First Check Number and remove the check-mark for any check you will not be printing in the batch.

3. The Print Checks dialog box displays. Change the defaults as necessary.

4. If you are printing a partial page of checks using the Standard or Wallet check style, click the Partial Page tab. Review the settings specific for how your printer needs you to position the partial page of checks before printing.

5. Click the Print button to print your checks. The Print Checks— Confirmation dialog box displays (see Figure 13.8).

6. Review the checks that just printed. If each check printed successfully, click OK on the Print Checks—Confirmation dialog box. If any check did not print successfully, place a checkmark in the Reprint column. You can return to step 2 and reprint the checks selected.

tip

You can review both printed and to-be-printed check transactions by clicking the Check Register icon on the Home page and selecting the appropriate bank account.

Figure 13.8
Make sure each check prints correctly before clicking OK on the Print Checks—Confirmation dialog box.

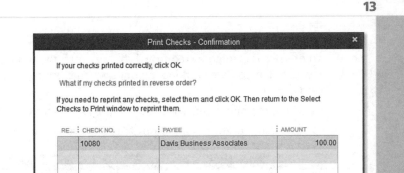

Entering a Bank Debit Charge

If your business uses a debit card for making purchases, you need to record these expenses like any other purchase transaction. A debit card transaction is debited from your bank's available cash balance, unlike a credit card, for which payment for the purchase is made at some later date.

> ➡ *To enter a bank debit charge to your bank account, follow the same steps outlined in the sidebar titled "Writing a Check," p. 523.*

Instead of printing a check, remove the Print Later checkmark and, in the No. field, enter a notation as described in the Caution in this section. Alternatively, you can enter some notation of your own to help you identify the charge as a debit when reconciling the bank account.

> ⚠ **caution**
> If you are recording a debit card payment made to a vendor for whom you issue a year-end Form 1099-MISC, use specific notations in the No. field. For more information, see "Tracking and Reporting Vendor 1099-MISC Payments," p. 275.

Entering Credit Card Charges

QuickBooks uses the Enter Credit Card Charges transaction to record business purchases made on credit. If your business has not been using this transaction type, you might have recorded credit card purchases using a vendor bill payable to the credit card merchant. Listed here are a few reasons to use a credit card receipt to record payments made by credit card:

- Track the vendors paid for the service or product
- Track the date the purchase was made
- Reconcile the credit card activity to the monthly statement from your credit card provider

Recording a Credit Card Charge

To practice recording a credit card charge, open the sample data file as Chapter 1 instructed. If you are working in your own file, use these instructions to enter a credit card charge:

1. From the menu bar, select **Banking, Enter Credit Card Charges**.

2. Leave the prefilled QuickBooks Credit Card account selected (see Figure 13.9).

Figure 13.9
Recording expenses made with the company credit card.

3. For this exercise, leave Purchase/Charge selected. When working in your own data, you can select Refund/Credit when necessary.

4. In the Purchased From drop-down list, start typing **Dianne's Auto Shop**. To add a new payee when necessary, select **Add New** at the top of the list. Select an appropriate type from the Select Name Type dialog box that displays.

5. For this exercise, leave the prefilled date. When working with your own data, use the date the charge was incurred.

6. If you want to record a reference number, enter it into the Ref. No. field.

7. Type the amount of **500.00.**

8. For details in your reporting, enter a Memo.

9. On the Expenses tab, the account column may have prefilled from the default account associated with that vendor, or from past credit card purchases. If no account prefilled, select the appropriate account.

10. For this exercise, leave the Memo and Customer:Job fields blank.

11. For this exercise, leave the Billable column blank and select the Overhead class.

12. (Optional) Click any of the following to help complete the transaction:

   - **Clear Splits**—Clears the amounts you entered in the detail section of the check and moves the total to the Expenses tab

   - **Recalculate**—Recalculates the Amount field from the total of the rows

   - **Clear**—Removes all data entered in fields and starts over

   - **Save & Close**—Saves and closes the dialog box

   - **Save & New**—Saves and continues with another record

Paying the Credit Card Bill

> **tip**
>
> Often credit card purchases are made from one-time suppliers. I recommend that you select the Other name type when adding this type of payee. This limits your vendor list to those you frequently do business with.

As you enter credit card charges, QuickBooks increases the amount you owe your credit card provider. Because the individual charges have already been recorded, when you pay your bill, you need to reduce your bank balance and the amount you owe the credit card company.

If you are using a check to record the payment, from the menu bar, select **Banking**, **Write Checks**. Follow the instructions for writing a check, with one exception. On the Expenses tab, in the Account column, select the other current liability credit card account associated with the bill you are paying (see Figure 13.10).

If you choose to enter a bill, from the menu bar, select **Vendors**, **Enter Bills**.

> ➡ *For more information on working with vendor records, see "Recording Vendor Bills,"* *p. 251.*

On the Expenses tab, in the Account column, select the other current liability credit card account. Process the payment for the vendor bill as with other bills.

Include reconciling your credit card account on your list of monthly accounting tasks; doing so helps you manage your credit card activity.

Figure 13.10
Properly record the payment of your credit card bill by assigning the credit card liability account on the Expenses tab.

Transferring Funds Between Bank Accounts

If your business has more than one bank account, at some time, you will probably need to transfer funds from one account to another account. If you need to physically take a printed check to the bank, use the instructions in the sidebar "Writing a Check," earlier in this chapter. In the Account column, on the Expenses tab, select the bank account you are depositing the funds into.

If you transfer the funds between accounts using your bank's online portal, you can record the transaction using the Transfer Funds Between Accounts transaction type using these steps:

1. From the menu bar, select **Banking**, **Transfer Funds**.

2. Enter the date the transfer is effective.

3. Select the **Transfer Funds From** account and the **Transfer Funds To** account.

4. Enter the Transfer Amount $.

5. (Optional) Enter a memo to display in reports.

6. If you have signed up for Online Banking within QuickBooks and you are transferring funds between two accounts at the same bank, select **Online Funds Transfer**. QuickBooks automatically processes the transfer the next time you synchronize your records with the bank via the Online Banking Center.

Bank Feeds

Manage your banking and credit card balances in QuickBooks by securely downloading transactions from your financial institution directly into your data file. QuickBooks matches the downloaded transactions to existing transactions and marks for review any discrepancies. No need to manually enter the missing transactions!

QuickBooks 2014 has totally redesigned the online banking experience in QuickBooks. You can choose to use an older version of the user interface by selecting the menu bar, **Edit**, **Preferences**, **Checking**, **Company Preferences** tab. You can choose to use the new Express Mode and set preferences for the Renaming Rules, or use the older Classic Mode (Register Mode) for working with Bank Feeds. You also can switch back and forth.

You stay in control, by accepting or ignoring the transactions before adding them to QuickBooks. Downloading transactions is accomplished using one of the following methods:

- **Direct Connect**—Users log in seamlessly to the financial institution within QuickBooks. This chapter discusses this method.

- **Web Connect**—Users download a file from the financial institution's website and then import this file into QuickBooks from the Banking, Bank Feeds menu.

The method used is often determined by your bank's participation in the QuickBooks Bank Feeds feature and might automatically default during setup. The cost (if any) of using Direct Connect with Bank Feeds also depends on your financial institution.

So whether you are up-to-date with your transaction data entry or behind, Bank Feeds helps confirm, reconcile, and add missing transactions. The result is more accurate and timely reporting of your business expenses and account balances.

Set Up Bank Feeds

In just a few steps, you get ready to download bank or credit card transactions into your QuickBooks file:

1. Verify that your financial institution participates. From the menu bar, select **Banking**, **Bank Feeds**, **Participating Financial Institutions**. For participating banks or credit card providers, you must first establish online account access directly with the financial institution. You must enter the user ID and password when completing the remaining setup steps in QuickBooks.

2. From the menu bar, select **Banking**, **Set Up Bank Feeds for an Account**. You can also access setup from the New or Edit Account window, by clicking the Set Up Bank Feeds button at the bottom of the window. The Find Your Bank window displays (see Figure 13.11).

Figure 13.11 Most popular financial institutions participate in Bank Feeds.

3. In the Enter Your Bank's Name field, begin typing the financial institution's name, or select from the list on the right.

4. If your bank or credit card participates, Step 2 in the Bank Feed Setup displays. Enter your User ID and Password. If you are having any troubles with setup, contact information for your bank or credit card provider is listed on each setup window.

5. Next, in Step 3, from the QuickBooks Accounts drop-down list, select an existing QuickBooks account or create a new account. This step specifies which QuickBooks account you want the Bank Feeds transactions to be downloaded into. See Figure 13.12.

Figure 13.12
Associate your online bank or credit card with an account in QuickBooks.

6. Step 4: The "Success!" message displays in the Bank Feed Setup window. Click Close to complete the setup. You are now ready to manage your Bank Feeds in QuickBooks.

If this is your first time downloading data into QuickBooks, do not worry. The Bank Feeds does a great job of matching transactions and avoiding any duplication. Or perhaps you are behind on your data entry and will use the download to automatically create those missing transactions. Bank Feeds easily meets both needs. However, your financial institution controls the period of time that is downloadable your first time with Direct Connect.

Manage Bank Feeds

With each successive download, Bank Feeds knows what has already been downloaded and then adds any new transactions. You can get started with these simple steps:

1. To launch Bank Feeds, from the menu bar, select **Banking**, **Bank Feeds**, **Bank Feeds Center**.

2. The Bank Feeds Account Information displays. At the top right, with your cursor, click the refresh icon, or from the drop-down list, choose Sync All for This Bank or Sync This Account (see Figure 13.13). You choose when to synchronize your file with the financial institution's online data.

3. Type your pin or password recognized by your bank or credit card. (Your user ID was stored when you first created the link between QuickBooks and the institution.) Click OK to proceed.

4. The Bank Feeds Account Information window now displays details about the selected account. One of the many improvements made to the QuickBooks online banking functionality is its at-a-glance summary of the balances per your bank/credit card, compared to the balances in QuickBooks. From this window, you can do the following:

- View the Transaction List of newly downloaded transactions.

- Create new online checks, pay bills, transfer funds, and send your bank or credit card company a message, among other actions. (Your bank might charge a fee for these added online services.)

- Make a credit card payment.

- Contact your bank.

- Disable bank feeds.

Figure 13.13
The new Account Information window helps you manage your online transaction details.

5. From the Bank Feeds Account Information window, select **Transaction List**. Bank Feeds displays a list of downloaded transactions separated into three groupings. Click the colored bar at the top of the window to filter the results for the following:

- **Need Your Review**—Transactions that you have not yet added to your QuickBooks file

- **Chg**—Transactions that have been changed due to a renaming rule

- **Auto**—Transactions that were automatically entered from following a specific renaming rule

- **Add/Approved**—Transactions that you have approved while viewing the Transaction List

6. For each selected transaction, assign a Payee and Account. Choose to manage the transactions individually on the right in the Action column. Options include these:

- **Quick Add**—The transaction will be added to QuickBooks.

- **Add More Details**—You can add a Number, assign a Payee, add a Memo, and break the transaction into multiple lines of detail.

- **Match to Existing Transaction**—This is generally not needed because the Bank Feeds automatically match the transactions. But you can use this option to manually match two like transactions.

- **Ignore**—The transaction will not be added to QuickBooks and will be removed from future download details.

- Choose from other specific actions, depending on the type of transaction selected.

7. Optionally, select Multiple Transactions and choose Add/Approve or Ignore from the Batch Actions drop-down list at the bottom of the window (See Figure 13.14).

Figure 13.14
Manage downloaded transactions with ease in the Transaction List in Bank Feeds.

8. Click any section of the colored bar to filter the results displayed or to open the register.

Success with Bank Feeds occurs when the balance your financial institution reports is the same as the balance in QuickBooks. Now, how easy was that? The QuickBooks user stays in control, viewing each of the transactions before adding them to the file.

Renaming Rules in Bank Feeds

Would you like QuickBooks to "remember" the name and account you previously assigned to a downloaded transaction? QuickBooks does this with Renaming Rules that automate and standardize the names of downloaded banking transactions into QuickBooks. For example, your financial institution might include a transaction number in the downloaded Payee name field. In such cases, QuickBooks might then create a new vendor for each transaction; when you assign a name from one of your QuickBooks lists to this transaction, QuickBooks automatically creates the renaming rule to use for this same transaction in the future.

For example, suppose you purchase mobile phone services from Verizon Wireless. When the transaction is downloaded, the vendor name is "Verizon Wireless—<*transaction code or location*>." You can create a renaming rule that instructs QuickBooks to ignore the transaction code and assign it to the proper vendor.

To create or modify the Renaming Rules; click the Rules icon in the top left of the Bank Feeds window (refer to Figure 13.13).

Figure 13.15 shows the Renaming Rules QuickBooks created. From this window, you can edit or remove the properties of the Renaming Rule or add a new rule manually, as in Figure 13.16.

Figure 13.15
Bank Feeds automatically creates Renaming Rules that you can edit.

Figure 13.16
You can manually add or edit Renaming Rules.

Reconciling the Bank or Credit Card Account

Are you reconciling your bank or credit accounts in QuickBooks? If the answer is no, are you reconciling these accounts on the monthly paper statement your financial institution provides? If you still answered no, you will certainly find value in learning how easy it is to reconcile these accounts in QuickBooks.

Why exactly is it so important? Most businesses record a significant amount of income and expenses through bank or credit card activity. When the reconciliation is not completed in the software, how certain are you that the financial reports are accurate?

A few exceptions arise for income and expenses flowing through a bank account. For example, a restaurant or bar might manage a significant amount of cash during the course of doing business. Do not limit yourself to thinking the task of reconciling is limited to bank or credit card accounts. If you have a cash safe, drawer, or box at the office, you also want to reconcile the ins and outs of the cash in your QuickBooks data.

> **note**
>
> If your work is interrupted while you are reconciling a bank or credit card statement, you can click Leave in the Reconcile—Account dialog box. Clicking Leave keeps the checkmarks you have assigned to transactions and lets you return to finish your work later.

To begin reconciling your bank or credit card accounts, follow these steps:

1. From the menu bar, select **Banking**, **Reconcile** to open the Begin Reconciliation dialog box (see Figure 13.17).

2. From the Account drop-down list, select the appropriate account. (You can reconcile any Balance Sheet type account.)

3. Select the **Statement Date** that matches the ending statement date from your financial institution.

4. Review the Beginning Balance, which should equal the same number your financial institution provided. Later sections in this chapter detail methods of troubleshooting errors in the Beginning Balance.

Figure 13.17
Reconcile your accounting records to your financial institution's monthly statement.

5. Enter the Ending Balance from your financial institution's period statement.

6. (Optional) Enter any Service Charge or Interest Earned; select the appropriate date, account, and Class if you are tracking the use of Classes (departments).

7. Click Continue. The Reconcile—Account Name dialog box opens.

8. Place a checkmark in the box Hide Transactions After the Statement's End Date. This makes the task of reconciling much easier.

9. Place individual checkmarks next to each cleared Check, Payment, Deposit, or Other Credits that are included in the statement from your financial institution.

10. Click Reconcile Now only when the Difference is 0.00. See Figure 13.18. This indicates that your cleared transactions match those the financial institution provided.

    ➡ *For more information, see "Reconciling with an Adjustment," p. 551.*

11. Follow the prompts to print the reconciliation report to attach to your financial institution's statement for safekeeping.

> 🔍 **note**
>
> Where does the Beginning Balance originate from on the Begin Reconciliation dialog box? It is the sum total of all previous transactions, for the selected account that are marked as cleared.

Figure 13.18
Reconcile your QuickBooks transactions to your financial institutions for a specific month.

Other useful features of working with the Reconcile feature in QuickBooks include the following:

- **Highlight Marked**—Makes it easier to differentiate the cleared transactions from the noncleared transactions on the computer screen.

- **Mark All or Unmark All**—Enables you to automatically add or remove checkmarks from transactions during the bank reconciliation process.

- **Go To**—Opens the currently selected transaction. Useful if you need to modify the transaction.

- **Matched**—Matches downloaded transactions to existing transactions in QuickBooks.

- **Columns to Display**—Adds or removes the columns of data displayed.

- **Modify**—Click to change reconcile For Period date or the Ending Balance amount, or to add bank charges or interest earned.

- **Leave**—Click to save your work and close the Begin Reconcile window.

You can also click any column header to sort the data in that column.

Reconciliations are easiest when done each month. However, you might have been using QuickBooks for some time before learning how to complete the reconciliation task. The following section of this chapter helps you learn how to troubleshoot the first reconciliation or fix errors in previous reconciliations.

Troubleshooting Reconciliations

A simple way to determine whether your bank account is correctly reconciled is to compare your bank statement Beginning Balance to the QuickBooks Beginning Balance amount in the Begin Reconciliation dialog box. From the menu bar, select **Banking**, **Reconcile**, and select the appropriate Account. If your QuickBooks Beginning Balance does not agree with your bank statement, you can use one or a combination of several methods in this chapter to figure out why.

🔍 **note**

What makes up the Beginning Balance, as in Figure 13.17? The Beginning Balance is the sum of all previously cleared checks, deposits, and other transactions. A checkmark next to a transaction item in the bank account register indicates it has previously been cleared in the bank reconciliation in QuickBooks. An asterisk indicates that the item is currently being reconciled, as in Figure 13.19. A lightning bolt (not shown) next to a transaction indicates that it has been downloaded and matched, but has not yet been marked as cleared.

Figure 13.19
View the cleared status of transactions in your account register.

Determining Whether the Account Has Been Reconciled

If your business is just starting, now is a good time to modify your regular routine to reconcile your bank account in QuickBooks with the statement you receive each month. However, what if you have been using QuickBooks for years or months and have never reconciled the bank account in the software?

How can you tell whether your bank account has been reconciled? An easy method is to begin the bank reconciliation. From the menu bar, select **Banking**, **Reconcile** and select the desired account.

Review the Last Reconciled On (date) in the Begin Reconciliation window. A month/day/year indicates that the account was previously reconciled (see Figure 13.17). If you have a Beginning Balance amount but no Last Reconciled On (date), no reconciliation has been completed. This Beginning Balance was most likely from entering your bank balance when you first created your QuickBooks file.

➡ *For more information, see "Express Start," p. 39.*

> ### 〽 tip
>
> Are you an accounting professional? Included with QuickBooks Accountant 2014 and QuickBooks Enterprise Accountant 14.0 is the Accountant Center (see Figure 13.20). Open a client's file; the Accountant Center summarizes important information about your client's account reconciliations.

Figure 13.20
The Accountant Center is available with the Accountant editions of QuickBooks.

If no reconciliations have been completed, first determine how many months have gone by. Catching up with a few months of bank statement reconciliations takes much less effort than having to do several years or months of bank statement reconciliations. If you are going to go back to the beginning of the business and reconcile each month, you need to start with the first month of your bank activity and work your way month by month to the current month. Completing your bank reconciliation for each month is the most accurate and thorough process and provides a separate reconciliation report for each month.

However, going back to the start of your business might not be practical when you simply want to get the bank account reconciled in the current month.

> ### 📡 caution
>
> As with any major task or adjustment you plan to make in your QuickBooks data, I recommend that you make a backup copy. You can easily create this backup by selecting **File**, **Create Backup** from the menu bar and then following the instructions on the screen.

Complete the recommendations in the following sections before you attempt to complete a multi-year or multi-month bank reconciliation.

Verifying That All Account Transactions Have Been Entered

Ensuring that all checks, bill payments, payroll checks, customer payments, and any other banking-related transactions have been entered in the QuickBooks data file is critical to accurate reporting in your own or your client's QuickBooks file. You don't want to complete a multi-year or multi-month bank reconciliation if handwritten checks or other bank transactions have not been recorded in the data.

Creating a Missing Checks Report

To help you determine whether any check transactions are missing, create a Missing Checks report. To do so, follow these steps:

1. From the menu bar, select **Reports**, **Banking**, **Missing Checks** report.

2. In the Missing Checks dialog box, select the bank account from the drop-down list.

The resulting Missing Checks report shows all transaction types that reduce your bank account (for example, checks, bill payments, and paychecks sorted by number (see Figure 13.21). Look for any breaks in the detail with a ***Missing* or ***Duplicate* warning.

Figure 13.21
The Missing Checks report can help you determine whether you need to enter any missing transactions before you reconcile.

Creating a Custom Transaction Detail Report

Another method to verify that you have recorded all your transactions requires a bit more effort on your part. Manually add the total of all deductions and additions from the statements your bank provides you, and compare this to the Custom Transaction Detail report.

To do so, follow these steps:

1. From the menu bar, select **Reports**, **Custom Reports**, **Transaction Detail**. The Modify Report dialog box opens.

2. Select the **From** and **To** dates to match the period you are reconciling. If it's from the beginning of the file, you might want to leave the From date blank and enter only the To date.

3. Click the Filters tab.

4. In the Choose Filter box, with the Account filter highlighted, choose the bank account from the drop-down list.

5. Click OK.

This report (see Figure 13.22) totals all debits (money into your bank account) and credits (money out of your bank account). To these totals, you have to add checks and deduct deposits that have not yet cleared the bank. If the resulting totals are exact or close to your manual totals, you can feel confident reconciling multiple years or months at one time.

Figure 13.22
The modified Custom Transaction Detail report shows the total of all money in and out of a bank account for the time period selected.

Identifying All Uncleared Transactions

Make a list of all the uncleared bank transactions as of the month and year you are reconciling. If you have been manually reconciling your bank account, simply find the paper statement for the selected month and look for the list of uncleared transactions.

For example, suppose it is April 2017 and you want to reconcile multiple years or months through December 31, 2016. Collect your bank statements for January through March 2017. Identify any cleared transactions from these 2017 bank statements for which the transaction date was on or before December 31, 2016, but the transaction did not clear your bank until year 2017.

---

tip

If you are choosing to complete a multi-year or multi-month bank reconciliation, consider reconciling through the last month of your previous fiscal year, which for most companies would be your statement ending December 31, 20xx. Choosing a month to reconcile through that is two to three months in the past makes identifying the transactions that have not cleared the bank as of the month you are reconciling much easier.

Completing the Multi-year or Multi-month Bank Reconciliation

To complete the multi-year or multi-month bank reconciliation, follow these steps:

1. From the menu bar, select **Banking**, **Reconcile**. The Begin Reconciliation dialog box displays (refer to Figure 13.17).

2. Select the desired account from the drop-down list, and type the statement date you want to reconcile through. Enter the Ending Balance from the bank statement and click Continue. The Reconcile—Account dialog box displays. Figure 13.18 shows the bank reconciliation in progress for the period ended December 31, 2017.

3. Place a checkmark in the box Hide Transactions After the Statement's End Date, at the top right. Checking this box makes working with the remaining transactions easier.

4. Click the Mark All button. Now each transaction is marked as if it has cleared. Remove the checkmark from any transaction you previously identified as uncleared. Your work is complete when the reconciliation shows a Difference of 0.00 in the lower right of the Reconcile—Account dialog box.

5. Click Reconcile Now. QuickBooks creates a bank reconciliation report you can print.

For added convenience when reconciling, you can sort the uncleared transactions by clicking once on any column header that has a checkmark in the Reconcile—Account dialog box.

Not all bank account reconciliations are this easy to troubleshoot and correct. Often you need to dig deeper into the possible causes of reconciliation errors. QuickBooks makes this task much easier by providing many tools and reports to help with this important process.

---

caution

What if the reconciled difference is not 0.00? First, determine whether the amount is significant. If the answer is yes, the best method for finding errors is to review each item marked cleared in QuickBooks with the transactions listed on your bank statements.

If you choose to record the adjustment, QuickBooks records this amount into an automatically created Expense account called Reconciliation Discrepancies. For more information, see "Reconciling with an Adjustment," p. 551.

Reviewing Uncleared Transactions

If your bank account has previously been reconciled, reviewing your uncleared bank transactions is the best place to start when troubleshooting an incorrectly reconciled bank account.

Creating an Uncleared Transactions Detail Report

This report is one of the most useful to you as you research your bank reconciliation errors. You might want to memorize this report so you can review it again, if needed.

To create an uncleared bank transactions report, follow these steps:

1. From the menu bar, select **Reports**, **Custom Reports**, **Transaction Detail**. The Display tab of the Modify Report dialog box displays. In the Report Date Range box, select **All Dates**. If you have more than one bank account, in the Total By drop-down list, select **Account List** to keep each bank account with separate totals. From the Columns box, select the data you want to appear in the report.

2. Click the Filters tab. In the Choose Filter box, with Account highlighted, select **All Bank Accounts**. Scroll down the Choose Filter list and select **Cleared**, and then click No next to the list, as in Figure 13.23.

3. This report will be useful to you in the future, so go ahead and give it a specific name by clicking the Header/Footer tab and changing Report Title as desired.

4. Click OK to create the report (see Figure 13.24).

5. To store this report for future use, click Memorize. QuickBooks asks you to provide a name for the report. Click OK to close the Memorize Report dialog box.

Figure 13.23
Filter the report to show only uncleared bank transactions.

Memorizing customized reports for later use is easy. First, make sure your Dates selection is appropriate. If your Dates selection is Custom, each time you create this report, it uses the custom dates. Selecting Dates, such as the generic This Month-to-Date or any of the other choices, makes the memorized report more valuable in future months.

Figure 13.24
Create a customized report to easily view uncleared bank transactions.

With the report displayed, click Memorize. QuickBooks offers to save the report with the header name, or you can rename it.

➡️ *For more information, see "Reporting in QuickBooks," p. 553.*

Sorting Transactions

Another method for reviewing uncleared bank transactions is to open your bank register and follow these steps:

1. From the menu bar, select **Banking**, **Use Register**.

2. Select the desired bank account in the Use Register dialog box.

3. At the lower left of the register is a Sort By drop-down list. Select the **Cleared Status** from the drop-down list.

4. Scroll through the register and view those transactions that are either:

   - **Cleared**—Denoted by a checkmark

   - **In process of being cleared**—Denoted by an asterisk (*)

   - **Not cleared**—Shows no checkmark or asterisk (*)

Many times, either a transaction that was erroneously cleared or a transaction that was erroneously uncleared can be the cause of an opening balance not matching.

If you need to unclear a transaction or two, double-click the checkmark next to the item in the bank register. QuickBooks replaces the checkmark with an asterisk. You can also click once more to remove the asterisk, if desired.

If you attempt to make a change to the cleared status of a transaction while in the bank register, QuickBooks provides a warning message.

> 〰️ **tip**
>
> Another useful option is to add this report to your icon bar. With the report displayed, select **View**, **Add** *<name of report>* **to Icon Bar**. If you use the Top Icon Bar, you might need to click the right-facing double arrows to see this icon and others that do not fit on the icon bar.
>
> If you are using the Left Icon Bar placement, scroll down to the bottom of the My Shortcuts list to see the report added.

Using additional reporting tools in QuickBooks can help you find changes made to previously rec-onciled transactions. You will find that using a combination of the following reports when trouble-shooting reconciliation errors is useful.

Reviewing Previous Bank Reconciliation Reports

If you determine that the file has been previously reconciled but no paper copy was kept, no need to worry. This feature is available for QuickBooks Pro, Premier, and Enterprise. From the menu bar, select **Reports, Banking, Previous Reconciliation**. In the Select Previous Reconciliation Report dialog box, choose a Statement Ending Date to view (see Figure 13.25). QuickBooks displays a listing of previous reconciliations for the chosen account (this specific feature is available only in QuickBooks Premier, Accountant, and Enterprise). Choose from the following view options: Summary, Detail, or Both.

Figure 13.25
Select the previous bank reconcili-ation report when troubleshooting errors.

Additionally, you can view the reports in two ways:

- **Transactions Cleared at the Time of Reconciliation**—This stored report shows the bank recon-ciliation details in PDF form as they were completed at the time the account was reconciled.

- **Transactions Cleared Plus Any Changes**—View this report to see how the bank reconciliation would look today.

Compare the stored PDF with the Transactions Cleared Plus Changes report. Any differences between the two should indicate your discrepancies. You might be able to find these discrepancies easily with the Reconciliation Discrepancy report, discussed next.

Locating Bank Account Reconciliation Discrepancies

Finding bank reconciliation discrepancies in QuickBooks is made easier with the Reconciliation Discrepancy report. To prepare this report:

1. From the menu bar, select **Reports, Banking, Reconciliation Discrepancy**. The Reconciliation Discrepancy report displays.

2. Choose the bank account from the drop-down list and select **OK** to create the report.

3. This report identifies any transaction modified after being cleared in the bank reconciliation process. For each transaction on this report, you see the modified date, reconciled amount, type of change (amount added, deleted, or voided), and financial effect of the change (see Figure 13.26).

Figure 13.26
View details of previously cleared transactions that have been modified, deleted, or voided.

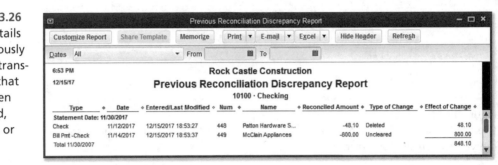

4. You can click Modify Report and add the username that modified the transaction to help identify who made the change to the transaction.

After you have found the reconciliation discrepancy, you can view the Voided/Deleted report (discussed in the next section) to help re-create the transaction(s).

Reviewing the Voided/Deleted Transactions Reports

Other reporting tools that help locate problem transactions are the Voided/Deleted Transactions Summary report and the Voided/Deleted Transactions Detail report.

To create the Voided/Deleted Transactions Summary report (see Figure 13.27), from the menu bar, select **Reports**, **Accountant & Taxes**, **Voided/Deleted Transactions Summary**. Alternatively, you can select **Voided/Deleted Transactions Detail** from the submenu to view the detailed report.

If you are having trouble finding the problem, particularly when the Beginning Balance has changed, this report can help you find the problem transaction(s).

Use this report to re-create the voided or deleted transactions as part of the process of fixing your bank reconciliations.

📡 **caution**

Troubleshoot your bank reconciliation Beginning Balance differences with the previous Reconciliation Discrepancy report before completing the next month's reconciliation. Doing so is important because QuickBooks removes all detail from the discrepancy report when you complete a new reconciliation. This is because QuickBooks determines that you have solved the issue, or you would not have completed the next month's bank reconciliation.

This report does *not* track discrepancies caused by changing the bank account associated with a transaction.

Figure 13.27
Use the Voided/Deleted Transactions Summary report to locate transactions that are possibly causing your reconciliation errors.

If more than a few transactions are in error, restarting or undoing the previous bank reconciliation might be easier than researching each transaction marked as cleared. However, if previously cleared transactions were voided or deleted, you will have to re-create them.

Restarting a Previously Completed Bank Reconciliation

If your review shows a few minor issues with bank reconciliation accuracy, restarting your reconciliation might be the best action to take. To do so, select **Banking**, **Reconcile**, **Locate Discrepancies** from the menu bar. The Locate Discrepancies dialog box displays. From this dialog box, click Restart Reconciliation.

Restarting your bank reconciliation retains your checkmarks on the cleared transactions but enables you to put in a new statement date and ending balance. You can restart only the last month's banking reconciliation.

If you need to restart the reconciliation for more than one banking month, click Undo Last Reconciliation. You can repeat this undo for multiple months in a row—all the way back to the first reconciliation, if desired.

Undoing a Previous Bank Reconciliation

If you have determined that the integrity of one or more completed bank reconciliations is in question, you can easily undo previous reconciliations, one month at a time. From the menu bar, select **Banking**, **Reconcile** and click Undo Last Reconciliation.

QuickBooks opens the Undo Previous Reconciliation dialog box, providing you with ample information about what to expect and recommending that you back up your company data file first. As each month is undone, QuickBooks shows you the Previous Beginning Balance. You should undo bank reconciliations only until you reach a statement where this amount agrees with the same month's bank statement Beginning Balance, so watch it closely.

Click Continue after reviewing the message in Figure 13.28. You can undo the bank reconciliation one month at a time. You know you are back to the first statement when the Undo Previous

Reconciliation dialog box shows the Previous Beginning Balance as 0.00. When you return to the Begin Reconciliation dialog box, you no longer see a Last Reconciled On (date) or a Beginning Balance amount.

Figure 13.28
You can expect to see this message when you complete an Undo Previous Reconciliation transaction.

> **Undo Previous Reconciliation** ✕
>
> Intuit recommends that you back up your company file before undoing a previous reconciliation. Click Cancel on this window, then from the "File" menu choose "Save Copy or Backup...".
>
> What to expect...
>
> When you have finished undoing the previous reconciliation, your beginning balance will revert back to the previous beginning balance shown below:
>
> Current Beginning Balance: 55,689.49
>
> Previous Beginning Balance: 72,300.68
>
> Undoing a previous reconciliation also removes the cleared status of all its transactions, service charges, interest and balance adjustments. You will need to reconcile your previous statement again.

Reconciling with an Adjustment

QuickBooks creates an adjustment to your bank account and financials if you choose to reconcile a bank account that does not have 0.00 in the Difference row of the Reconcile dialog box.

When you decide to reconcile with an adjustment for the difference amount (see Figure 13.29), you need to first consider the following:

- Have you made every attempt to find the difference using the techniques and reports you read about in this chapter?

- Is the difference as reported on the QuickBooks Reconcile dialog box not a significant dollar amount?

If you can answer yes to these two items, let QuickBooks make an adjustment to your financials for the difference.

To reconcile with an adjustment created by QuickBooks, click Reconcile Now in the Reconcile—Account dialog box or the Enter Adjustment in the Reconcile Adjustment dialog box.

tip

Use the Undo a Previous Bank Reconciliation transaction when an incorrect statement date was entered on the bank reconciliation. QuickBooks defaults the next bank statement date to 30 days from the last statement date. Before beginning the bank reconciliation in QuickBooks, verify that the statement date and Beginning Balance are correct.

QuickBooks details the amount of the adjustment and limits your choices to the following:

■ **Return to Reconcile**—Click this option if you want to return to the reconciliation window to look for the difference.

■ **Leave Reconcile**—QuickBooks saves your changes so you can return later and review your work.

■ **Enter Adjustment**—This option forces QuickBooks accounting to match your bank statement.

■ **Help**—This option provides useful links to information about reconciling your accounts.

 tip

One of my favorite tricks for tracking down an unreconciled balance is this: If the amount is evenly divisible by 9, there's a very strong probability that the digits of a transaction amount were transposed when the transaction was entered.

When you choose Enter Adjustment, QuickBooks creates a journal entry and posts the difference to a Reconciliation Discrepancies expense account on the Profit & Loss report.

I don't recommend reconciling with an adjustment. Sooner or later, you will have to identify where the adjustment came from and where it should be posted. However, making an adjustment for a small balance can often save time that you can better spend on activities that grow the business. Always put in place better processes so these types of errors do not occur again.

note

You can reconcile any Balance Sheet type account—not just bank account types. Reconciling credit card accounts provides the same control over the accuracy of your financials. Did you know that any account that transactions flow in and out of can be reconciled? Do you have a car loan? Have you reconciled your car loan account to the lending institution's statement? Do you loan money to employees and then have them pay the loan back? These are all examples of accounts that would benefit from the same reconciliation process used for bank accounts.

REPORTING IN QUICKBOOKS

One reason QuickBooks is so popular is for the ease in which you can get reports of your financial activity. On summary reports, you can "drill down" on a specific number in a report to see the underlying transactions, taking the guesswork out of determining where a number came from.

In this chapter, you learn about the many ways you can access, modify, and memorize often-used reports.

Using the Company Snapshot

The Company Snapshot (see Figure 14.1) is one convenient place to review company information and perform important tasks. The QuickBooks Company Snapshot offers a real-time view of your company's critical information. It provides insight into your business using a variety of analytic and performance indicators.

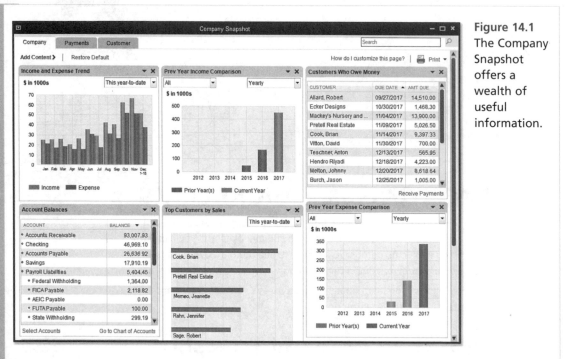

Figure 14.1
The Company
Snapshot
offers a
wealth of
useful
information.

Customizing the Company Snapshot

QuickBooks offers the capability to customize the snapshot information on both a user and company file-specific basis, which can be helpful in multiuser environments. To customize your Company Snapshot, follow these steps:

1. From the menu bar, select **Company**, **Company Snapshot** to view the default graphs and reports.

2. Click Add Content to view and select from additional graphs and reports. See Figure 14.2.

3. Click the + Add button next to a graph or report to add it to your Company Snapshot.

4. Click Restore Default to remove any graphs or reports you added.

5. Click Done to view your modified Company Snapshot.

6. To rearrange the order or placement of a graph and report, click and hold your left mouse button (a four-pointed arrow displays), drag the item to a new location, and release the button.

7. If you want to print the details of the snapshot, select one of the following options from the Print menu in the upper-right corner to print your snapshot or prepare it for printing: select **Print**, **Print Preview**, or **Set Orientation**.

Figure 14.2
Customize
the Company
Snapshot by
adding or
removing
content.

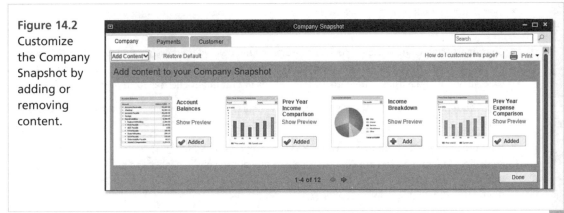

Get an immediate view of the bottom line of your business with these reports available on the QuickBooks Company Snapshot:

- **Account Balances**—By default, View Balance Sheet accounts is shown. You can add any other account type to this view by clicking the Select Accounts link.

- **Previous Year Income Comparison**—View how much money you are making this year, compared to previous years for any or all accounts. You can view monthly, quarterly, weekly, or yearly comparisons.

> 📡 **caution**
>
> If your company has created user restrictions in QuickBooks, users have access only to activities of the Company Snapshot that they have permission to access. If you do not want users to see the Income and Expense of the company, you must set restrictions for both Sensitive Accounting Activities and Sensitive Financial Reporting. To modify a user's security rights, you must be logged in to the data file as the Admin user.
>
> After you have set up the security, log in as that user and verify that the behavior is what you expect. For more comprehensive user security settings, consider using QuickBooks Enterprise Solutions 14.0.

- **Income Breakdown**—View your company's largest sources of income.

- **Previous Year Expense Comparison**—Compare how much money you are spending this year compared to previous years for any or all accounts. You can view monthly, quarterly, weekly, or yearly comparisons.

- **Expense Breakdown**—View your company's biggest expenses.

- **Income and Expense Trend Graph**—In a graph form, view the income and expenses of your business for the selected time period.

- **Top Customers by Sales**—Easily report on your top five customers, based on sales for a given period of time.

- **Best Selling Items**—Know which items and services customers are buying the most during a given period of time. You can view the data by amount or by units.

- **Customers Who Owe Money**—Review customers who owe your company money. Overdue items display in red. To sort any of the columns, click the column header in any of the panes. The Due Date shown is the earliest due date for all invoices or statement charges for that customer.

- **Top Vendors by Expense**—View your top five vendors, based on expenses for a given period of time.

- **Vendors to Pay**—Skip running the aged payables reports by adding this section to your Company Snapshot. Amounts in red are past due. To sort any of the columns, click the column header. The Due Date shown is the earliest due date that the vendor bills are due. The Amt Due column is the total ending balance for that vendor.

- **Reminders**—Never forget important tasks. Include these critical reminders in your Company Snapshot. Click the Set Preferences link in the Reminders box to customize what information you want displayed.

Defaulting the Company Snapshot as Home Page

If you want to have the Company Snapshot display when you first open a company file, follow these steps:

1. Click the Company Snapshot icon on the icon bar to open the Company Snapshot. Alternatively, from the menu bar, select **Company**, **Company Snapshot**.

2. With the Company Snapshot the only window open in QuickBooks, from the menu bar, select **Edit**, **Preferences**; then on the left side of the Preferences dialog box, select **Desktop View**.

3. On the My Preferences tab, click the **Save Current Desktop** option button. See Figure 14.3.

Figure 14.3
The desktop preference settings control what opens automatically when you launch QuickBooks.

4. Uncheck the option Show Home Page When Opening a Company File. When you open your data file, the Company Snapshot automatically displays.

Report Center

Up to this point in the book, you have learned how to get started with QuickBooks and create a variety of transactions. In this chapter, you follow step-by-step instructions to create specific reports to assist you with your QuickBooks setup or review.

If you are new to QuickBooks or you have never reviewed the QuickBooks Report Center, you find out in this section about the many features that help you simplify your reporting needs in QuickBooks.

The Report Center is available in the following editions of QuickBooks: Pro, Premier, Accountant, and Enterprise.

To open the Report Center, on the icon bar, click Reports, or from the menu bar, select **Reports**, **Report Center**. The Report Center displays. Features of the Report Center include the following:

- Option to view the reports or graphs in Carousel view (see Figure 14.4), List view (see Figure 14.5), or Grid view (see Figure 14.6) by selecting one of the icons on the top right of the Report Center.

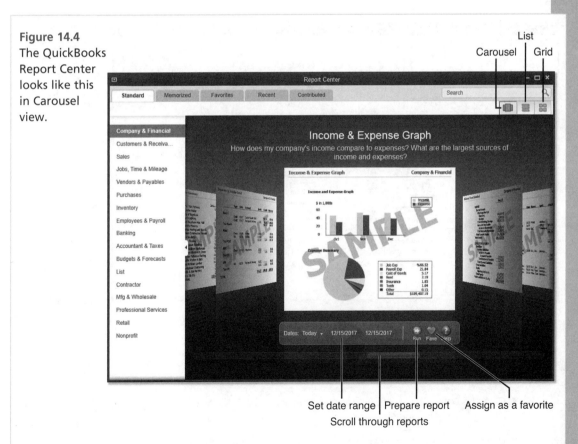

Figure 14.4
The QuickBooks Report Center looks like this in Carousel view.

List

Carousel | Grid

Set date range | Prepare report | Assign as a favorite
Scroll through reports

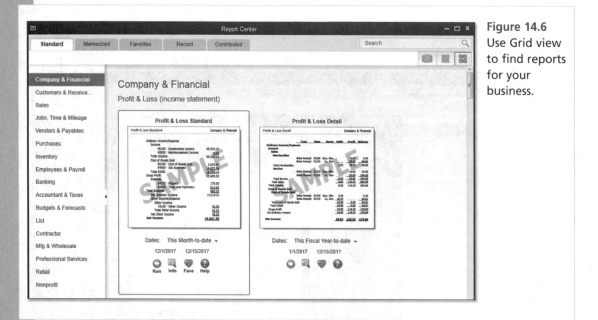

Figure 14.5
Optionally
view your
reports in List
view.

- From the Standard tab, select a grouping of reports. Your displayed report groups might differ from those in Figure 14.4, depending on the version of QuickBooks you are using.

Figure 14.6
Use Grid view
to find reports
for your
business.

- In Carousel view, use the scrollbar at the bottom of the displayed report to move through samples of the reports available in the selected report group. Data displayed is sample data.

- Click the Dates drop-down list to select a specific date, or accept the default date. (You can also click the dates to modify.)

- Click the Run icon to display the report details with your company data.

- Click the Fave icon to mark or unmark a favorite. Marking a report as a favorite places it on the Favorites tab within the Report Center.

- Click the Help icon to open Help information about the specific report.

- Optionally, click the arrow notch on the left of Carousel view to close the menu report group listing.

The Report Center also includes a Contributed tab, which displays reports other QuickBooks users share. QuickBooks does not share any financial data from your company file. When you share a report, you are sharing only the report structure. If the report is filtered for specific chart of accounts or other unique user-defined data, you might not be able to share the report.

To share a report from the Memorize Report dialog box, select **Share This Report Template with Others** and follow the prompts to give the report a title and brief description, as well as other information.

Reports & Graphs Preferences

QuickBooks makes it easy to customize reports globally through Reporting Preferences. Reporting Preferences come in two types: My Preferences, which are unique to a logged-in user, and Company Preferences, which only the Admin or External Accountant user can set and which represent global settings for all users.

My Preferences

The My Preferences setting for reports is user specific. To access user-specific preferences for reports, from the menu bar, select **Edit**, **Preferences**. In the Preferences dialog box, select **Reports & Graphs** and click the My Preferences tab.

You can specify the following settings that are unique for the currently logged-in user (if using QuickBooks in a multiuser mode):

- **Prompt Me to Modify Report Options Before Opening a Report**—When selected, this option causes QuickBooks to open the Modify Report dialog box each time a report is opened.

- **Reports and Graphs**—You have a choice, when report details have changed, to request QuickBooks to select one of the following options: **Prompt Me to Refresh** (this is the default option for a new data file), **Refresh Automatically**, or **Don't Refresh**. I usually choose the Refresh Automatically option. However, if the report is lengthy and you have multiple users entering data, you might want to review a report, make changes, and not have QuickBooks refresh at the time the change is made.

- **Graphs Only**—This option offers settings for drawing in 2D or using patterns.

Company Preferences

Different from the My Preferences setting for Reports and Graphs, Company Preferences can be set only by the Admin or External Accountant user and are global settings for all users.

To access Company Preferences for reports, log in as the Admin or External Accountant user in single-user mode and select **Edit**, **Preferences** from the menu bar. In the Preferences dialog box, select **Reports & Graphs**, click the Company Preferences tab, and set global defaults (for all users) for the following items:

- **Summary Report Basis**—You can choose accrual (default) or cash basis. Business owners should discuss this option with their accountant.

- **Aging Reports**—You can choose to age from the due date (default) or age from the transaction date. This setting determines the aged status of your accounts receivable and accounts payable reports.

- **Reports—Show Items By**—Choose from the following options:

  - **Name Only**—Shows the item name/number on item-based reports.

  - **Description Only**—Shows only the information typed in the Description field on item-based reports.

  - **Name and Description**—Shows both the item name/number and the description on item-based reports. This is the QuickBooks default for a new file or when upgrading to QuickBooks 2014.

- **Reports—Show Accounts By**—Choose from the following options for displaying the account name and description on reports (see Figure 14.7).

  - **Name Only**—Shows the account name and account number, as in Figure 14.8 (if the Use Account Numbers preference is enabled).

  - **Description Only**—Shows only the information typed in the Description field (see Figure 14.9).

  - **Name and Description**—Shows the account number, account name, and description (see Figure 14.10).

Figure 14.7
Optionally, you can include a description in addition to the account name.

Figure 14.8
This is the resulting report when the Name Only report preference is selected in addition to having the account numbering preference enabled.

Figure 14.9
This is the resulting report when the Description Only report preference is selected.

- **Statement of Cash Flows**—View information about uses of Cash for Operating, Investing, and Financing activities. Click the Classify Cash button to open the Classify Cash dialog box and specify which accounts you want included in the Cash Flow analysis.

Figure 14.10
This is the resulting report when the Name and Description report preference is selected in addition to having the account numbering preference enabled.

- **Format**—Click the Format button to set the following options globally for all reports:

  - **Show Header Information**—Leave the default information in place. QuickBooks populates the report with this current information automatically.

  - **Show Footer Information**—Enter an extra footer line, such as **Confidential Information**.

  - **Page Layout**—Adjust the alignment from the default of Standard to left, right, or center justified.

  - **Fonts**—On the Fonts & Numbers tab, you set the fonts for all text or specific text lines. As you select the text line on the left, QuickBooks displays the current font choice and size for that text. Click Change Font.

  - **Show Negative Numbers**—Use this to define how negative numbers are formatted on reports. Format choices include normal, –300.00; in parentheses, (300.00); or with a trailing minus, 300.00–. Optionally, you can select to have these numbers print in red.

  - **Show All Numbers**—Use this to divide all numbers by 1,000, to not show zero amounts, or to show numbers without the cents. Accounting professionals generally use these options when providing a statement to a bank, for example.

Modifying Reports

QuickBooks makes gathering information from your data quick and easy. Many reports already have been created and organized for your use, but you might occasionally want to modify an existing report. This section briefly discusses the options available when you want to modify a report.

Modifying Options Available on the Report Window

A few of the options to modify a report are available directly from any active report dialog box:

- **Hide Header**—Remove the header, or report title section, from the report. Click Show Header when you want it to display.

- **Collapse**—Collapse the information, as shown in Figure 14.11. This enables you to toggle a report between summary and detail views on-the-fly. When you click the Collapse button, QuickBooks removes the subaccount detail from view only.

- **Columns**—For certain reports, enables you to easily control how the data is subtotaled or grouped and to add columns or subcolumns.

- **Sort By**—Groups the detail in useful ways for your review. I use this frequently, especially when looking at reports with many lines of detail. Your Sort By options will vary, based on the type of report you have displayed.

This chapter also discusses other options on the active report window, including customizing, memorizing, and exporting reports to Excel.

> **tip**
>
> Each line on a report can be collapsed or expanded manually. To do this, click the gray arrow in front of any row report detail.

> **note**
>
> *New for QuickBooks 2014,* when printing a report you can define the width and size of a report, including setting a large report to fit on a single page.

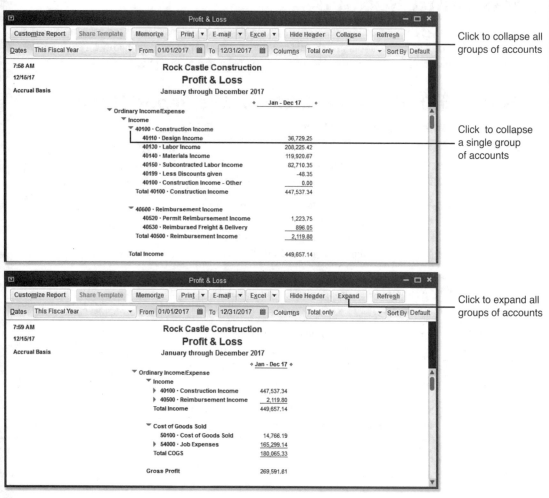

Click to collapse all groups of accounts

Click to collapse a single group of accounts

Click to expand all groups of accounts

Figure 14.11
Click the Collapse button on a report to roll up the subaccounts into the main account.

Customizing Reports

Click the Customize Report button at the top left of the open report dialog box. The options for modifying reports vary by report type. Some reports offer the following choices (others might not offer the same report-modification choices):

- **Display tab**—This tab opens automatically when you choose to customize an existing report. Depending on the report you choose, some or all of the following options are available:

    - **Report Date Range**—Choose from the QuickBooks predefined date ranges, or set a custom date range for your report.

- **Report Basis**—Choose Accrual or Cash. This option is not available on all reports. This enables you to override the default preference you might have set in Reports & Graphs preferences.

- **Columns**—This setting is useful for selecting the information you want to see and specifying whether you want it sorted or totaled by a specific field on the resulting report.

- **Advanced button**—This often-overlooked button enables users to display active, all, or nonzero rows and columns, along with the desired reporting calendar.

- **Revert button**—With this button, you can undo any changes made to the settings.

- **Filters tab**—Use these options to filter for specific accounts, names, or transaction types, as well as many other fields.

- **Header/Footer tab**—Use this tab to modify the report title and the appearance of the information that displays on the report. You can set this information globally for all users; see the section "Company Preferences," earlier in this chapter.

- **Fonts & Numbers tab**—Use this tab to specify fonts for specific line text, as well as determine how numbers appear in your reports. You can set this information globally for all users; see the section "Company Preferences," earlier in this chapter.

tip

Filtering a report is easy and convenient when you want only specific information from a longer report.

If you do filter, you might want to modify your report title so that it identifies what has been filtered. For example, if you are filtering a report to show employee advances detail, you might want to modify the report title on the Header/Footer tab to **Employee Advances Detail** so that anyone who reads the report will know it is pulling out specific information.

tip

From time to time, I encounter mistake-prone clients. In such instances, I advise them on proper procedures and provide a grouping of reports for them to review prior to my appointment.

Report Groups

Users often overlook report groups, which enable you to run two or more reports in QuickBooks at once. This feature can streamline your reporting process. This section highlights how to create, use, and manage report groups.

Creating Report Groups

For accountants, this feature can save precious time each period you work with your client's data. You can create a group of reports that you review each time you work with the client's file.

To create a report group, follow these steps:

1. From the menu bar, select **Reports**, **Memorized Reports**, **Memorized Report List**. The Memorized Report List dialog box displays, showing predefined groups and associated reports.

2. Click the Memorized Report drop-down button at the bottom of the list and select **New Group**.

3. In the New Memorized Report Group dialog box, provide a name for the group. Click OK to return to the Memorized Report List. QuickBooks places your new group alphabetically in the existing list of report groups.

4. Click the X in the upper right to close the Memorized Report List.

> **🔍 note**
>
> If you work in the file with Multiuser access enabled, select **File, Switch to Single User Access** before you attempt to move a group of reports on the list.

If you want to create several reports that are included as part of this report group, move this newly created report group to the top of the list. To move a report group, with your cursor, click the diamond in front of the report group name. You must be logged in to the file in single-user mode. As you memorize reports for this group, QuickBooks defaults the report group in the Memorize Report dialog box to the first report group on the list.

When you are done memorizing the reports to this report group (see the next section), you can move the group list item back alphabetically within the rest of the memorized reports or groups either by dragging the diamond as described shortly or by re-sorting the list under the Memorized Report drop-down menu.

To move a report group up or down the list, place your cursor over the diamond shape in front of the report group name. Keep your left mouse depressed, and drag the item up or down. Figure 14.12 shows the new Monthly Reports group being moved to the top of the list.

Figure 14.12
Create a report group so you can easily display or print multiple reports at one time.

Using Report Groups

The primary purpose of report groups is to simplify displaying or printing multiple reports at one time.

To display a group of reports, follow these steps:

1. From the menu bar, select **Reports, Process Multiple Reports**. The Process Multiple Reports dialog box displays.

2. In the Select Memorized Reports From drop-down list, select the specific report group you want to create, as in Figure 14.13.

Figure 14.13
The Process Multiple Reports dialog box enables you to choose what group of reports to display or print.

3. Remove the checkmark for any report you do not want to process in the group. Figure 14.14 shows a sample of selected reports.

Figure 14.14
The Monthly report group has been selected, and the reports memorized with this group display.

4. In the From and To columns, change the date as needed. Be aware that these changes are not permanent. The next time you create the report group, the original date range stored with the report displays. If you want the new dates to appear next time, you need to memorize the report again and click the Replace button to replace the previously stored report with the new date range.

5. Click Display to view the reports on your computer screen, or click Print to send the selected reports to your printer.

> ### 🔊 caution
>
> When memorizing a report that you want to add to a report group, be aware of the date range selected. If you want to generate a report for the current month-to-date, select This Month-to-Date as the default date range. When the report is generated, QuickBooks uses data from the current month-to-date.
>
> If you select a specific range of dates on a memorized report, QuickBooks considers those dates to be a default setting and always generates the report with those specific dates.

Your report group generates the multiple reports for you to view or print. I often create a report group for my clients named either Monthly or Quarterly Reports. In this group, I put certain reports I want them to review before my appointment. This method helps clients help me in keeping their QuickBooks data reporting organized.

Managing Memorized Report List and Memorized Report Groups

To manage a report group, follow these steps:

1. From the menu bar, select **Reports**, **Memorized Reports**, **Memorized Report List**. The Memorized Report List dialog box displays, showing predefined groups and associated reports.

2. At the bottom of the list, click the Memorized Report button to choose the following memorized report list options:

   - **Edit Memorized Report**—Edit the name of an existing report list item or the group it is associated with (you do not edit the date ranges or filters from this dialog box).

   - **New Group**—Create an association of multiple reports, discussed in the previous section.

   - **Delete a Memorized Report**—Manage the list and changes over time.

   - **Print the List**—Create a printed list of your memorized reports.

   - **Re-sort the List**—Return the list to its original order before making any custom changes to the organization of the list items. You won't need this option often.

   - **Import or Export a Template**—Create and then use reports for multiple client data files.

     ➡ *For more information, see "Exporting and Importing Report Templates," p. 570.*

3. To rearrange your reports, place your cursor on the diamond in front of the report name, and click and drag down and to the right, as in Figure 14.15. Release the mouse button when the report is in the desired position.

From the Memorized Report List, you can also export your reports to Excel without first displaying them in QuickBooks. Use these report groups to streamline your data review. You can use the Memorize feature for many of the special reports discussed in this book and place them in a report group for easy and frequent access.

Figure 14.15
Click and drag the diamond in front of any report or group to rearrange the list manually.

Memorized Reports

After you have created a report group, you can use the report memorize feature to store customized reports for future use. Placing your memorized reports in a group is optional, but using groups helps keep your memorized reports organized.

To memorize a report for use later, click the Memorize button at the top of an open report, as in Figure 14.16. QuickBooks requires you to give the report a name and, optionally, lets you assign it to a report group or share it with others (optional). (You must first create the report group so it displays in the drop-down list in the Memorize Report dialog box.)

Figure 14.16
Click Memorize on any displayed report, give the report a name, and (optionally) assign it to a report group or share the template with others.

If you choose not to assign a report group, your memorized reports are listed individually on the Memorized Report List, as shown previously in Figure 14.15.

Exporting and Importing Report Templates

QuickBooks offers the option to export and import report templates. This feature is useful for accountants who want to save time by having several clients use the same report template.

Only the format and filter settings are stored with report templates. If you create a report template and then have several clients use it, then when the client imports it, the desired report is generated with the current client's data, not the data it was created with.

You can export and import a single report or a group of reports only from the Memorized Report List. Thus, you must first memorize any reports that you want to export.

> ## 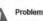 caution
>
> Certain restrictions exist when creating a template for export. For example, if you filter for a specific chart of account or customer name that might not be present in every customer's file, QuickBooks provides the message in Figure 14.17, warning that this report cannot be exported.

Exporting a Report or Report Group Template

To export a report or report group template, follow these steps:

1. From the menu bar, select **Reports**, **Memorized Reports**, **Memorized Report List**.

2. Select the report you want to export, and choose **Export Template**.

3. The Specify File Name dialog box displays, enabling you to select a location to store the template (.QBR extension). Click Save.

4. Attach the stored report template or report group to an email, or copy it to a removable storage device such as a USB drive to share with other QuickBooks data files.

QuickBooks Message

⚠ **Problem**
QuickBooks cannot export this memorized report because it contains filter settings unique to your company file.

Solution
Look for filter settings that would not work for a different company file -- for example, a filter for a particular account, customer, job, vendor, item, employee, currency or inventory site.
Change the filter settings and memorize the report again.

[OK]

Figure 14.17
If your report has specific filters, you might not be able to export and share it with multiple data files.

Importing a Report or Report Group Template

To import a report or report group template, follow these steps:

1. From the menu bar, select **Reports**, **Memorized Reports**. The Memorized Reports List dialog box displays.

2. In the Memorized Reports List drop-down list, select **Import Template**.

3. The Specify File Name dialog box displays, enabling you to select the stored location of the .QBR template.

4. Select the appropriate .QBR report or report group template.

5. Click Open. The Memorize Report dialog box displays for you to assign a name for the report and, optionally, assign it to a group.

6. Click OK to add the report to your memorized report list.

Exporting Reports to a .CSV File or to Excel

Sometimes you want to export your reports to Excel to manipulate them in a more extensive manner than is available within QuickBooks.

To export a report to either .CSV or Excel format, follow these steps:

1. From any report window, click the Excel button at the top of the report.

2. Click Create New Worksheet. (If you are updating a previously exported report, select **Update Existing Worksheet** and follow the prompts to browse to the file location.)

3. The Send Report to Excel dialog box displays with these options:

   - Create New Worksheet

     - In a New Workbook

     - In an Existing Workbook

   - Update An Existing Worksheet

   - Replace An Existing Worksheet

   - Create A Comma-Separated Values (.CSV) File

> ### 🛜 caution
> I generally try to discourage exporting to Excel and do my best with a client to find the appropriate report in QuickBooks, simply because any changes you make to your report in Excel do not "flow" back into your QuickBooks data file. However, you can link exported reports so changes made in your QuickBooks data update your Excel spreadsheet.

4. (Optional) Click the Advanced tab of the Export Report dialog box for options to preserve QuickBooks formatting, enabling certain Excel features and printing options. Try different configurations of these settings to see what best suits your needs. See Figure 14.18. Changes made to the Advanced tab settings affect future exported reports. Click OK.

5. Click Export to create the exported report, shown in Figure 14.19.

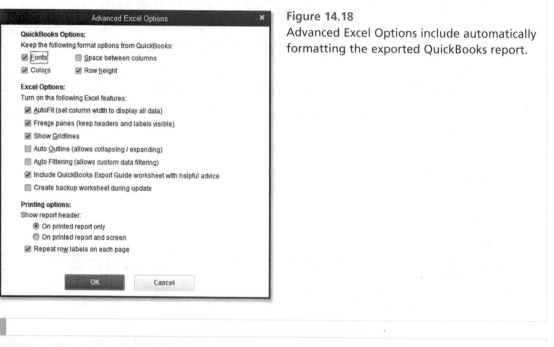

Figure 14.18
Advanced Excel Options include automatically formatting the exported QuickBooks report.

Figure 14.19
Easily convert any QuickBooks report or list to an Excel or .CSV format.

6. Select the **QuickBooks Export Tips** worksheet tab for additional useful hints in working with exported reports. The Advanced button on the Send Report to Excel dialog box includes an option to turn off creating the QuickBooks Export Tips worksheet.

Remember, however, that changes made in Excel to the exported report details are static—their information is fixed in time. Changes made to the Excel report do not transfer back into QuickBooks.

However, you can send changes in QuickBooks to your Excel report by selecting Update an Existing Worksheet. Another method for updating a saved Excel exported report is to click the **QuickBooks tab** in Excel's ribbon interface and select **Update Report**. See Figure 14.20.

Figure 14.20
Update the saved file from the QuickBooks tab in Excel.

Choose company file

`C:\Users\Owner\Documents\My Data\QBA 2012\sample_product-based bus`   Browse

Please select the date range for which you would like to update this report

From `11/ 1/2017` ▾ To `11/30/2017` ▾

Note: QuickBooks must close Excel to update the report. When the update is complete, QuickBooks restarts Excel for you. If your company file is big, this may take a few minutes.

Update   Cancel

Emailing Reports

You can email reports from within QuickBooks. This can be a convenient way to get information to your customers, vendors, management, owners, and even the company accountant. You can email reports as two types of attachments: individual Adobe PDF files or Excel workbooks.

If you want to set Outlook as your default email, from the menu bar, select **Edit**, **Preferences**, **Send Forms**. Select the **My Preferences** tab, where you can set the default email application to be QuickBooks or Outlook. You can also choose from other email providers.

To email a report, follow these steps:

> 🔍 **note**
>
> If you do not use Outlook or other webmail solutions for your email, QuickBooks sends the email through QuickBooks Business Solutions, which has been available for years. Figure 14.22 shows how the email is created within QuickBooks when Outlook is not your default email program.

1. From the open report, click Email and choose either Send Report as Excel or Send Report as PDF. Figure 14.21 shows how the email appears if you are using Outlook 2010 as your default send method. In this example, Send Report as PDF is selected.

2. If a security message displays, indicating that sending information over Internet email is not secure, either click OK to continue or click Cancel.

3. If you are sending the report through Outlook as in Figure 14.22, add your email address and any additional comments to the email. Click Send when you're done. You return to your QuickBooks data file, and the email is stored in your Outlook Sent folder.

   If you are not using Outlook for email, click Send Now (not shown). QuickBooks transmits the email for you though either the QuickBooks servers or your webmail, depending on how you have your Send preferences configured.

Figure 14.21
You can send reports as PDF or Excel attachments using your own email account.

Figure 14.22
Send a report as an attachment through QuickBooks (when you don't use Outlook).

As a business owner, learning how to work with reports is valuable and helps you efficiently manage reporting in your QuickBooks file. Next, in Chapter 15, "Reviewing Your Data," p. 576, you learn about specific data reviews in your file that can help with management decisions for your company.

REVIEWING YOUR DATA

This book would not be complete without a few pages of instructions about what reports you should review for your business. These reports are not the only reports you will find useful in QuickBooks, but they are important for you to periodically review in your file.

These reports are only a subset of the many reports in QuickBooks, but accounting professionals typically use them to verify the accuracy of your data. This chapter is devoted to the business owner, helping you properly review your data for accuracy. Each section tells what the review accomplishes and what reports in QuickBooks help with these reviews.

Reviewing the Balance Sheet

The report a business owner is least likely to look at is also one of the most important. To the business owner, the Balance Sheet report shows the balance of assets (what the business owns), liabilities (what the business owes others), and equity (what was put into the business or taken out of the business). Because these numbers are important, a business owner should first review this report.

This section details specific reports to use when reviewing your data. Each report is prepared on accrual basis unless otherwise mentioned. Begin by creating a Balance Sheet report of your data; this is the primary report we use for review.

From the menu bar, select **Reports**, **Company & Financial**, **Balance Sheet Standard**.

Leave the report with today's date on it. You first review your data with today's date before using any other date. In the following instructions, if a different date is needed, the step-by-step details state that. Verify that the top left of the report shows Accrual Basis. If not, click the Customize Report button on the report and select **Accrual Basis** from the Report Basis options.

Figure 15.1 shows a sample data Balance Sheet Standard report.

Figure 15.1

Review your Balance Sheet first, as in this example.

Account Types

Reviewing the account types assigned requires some basic knowledge of accounting. If you're unsure of what to look for, ask your accountant to take a quick look at how your accounts are set up.

Review the names given to accounts. Do you see account names in the wrong place on the Balance Sheet? For example, does an Auto Loan account show up in the current asset section of the Balance Sheet?

To correct the category (account type) assigned, follow these steps:

1. From the menu bar, select **Lists**, **Chart of Accounts**.

2. Select the account in question with one click. From the Account drop-down menu, select **Edit**. On the Edit Account dialog box (see Figure 15.2), you can select the drop-down menu for **Account Type** to change the currently assigned account type.

Figure 15.2
In the Edit or New Account dialog box, you assign the account type for proper placement of financial reports.

Prior Year Balances

You should give your accountant a copy of your Balance Sheet dated as of the last day of your *prior* tax year (or fiscal year) and request that he or she verify that the balances agree with the accounting records used to prepare your tax return. This is one of the most important steps to take in your review because Balance Sheet numbers are cumulative over the years you are in business.

➡ *For more information, see "Accrual Versus Cash Basis Reporting," p. 89.*

You can also create a two-year balance sheet to give to your accounting professional:

From the menu bar, select **Reports**, **Company & Financial**, **Balance Sheet Prev Year Comparison** (see the report in Figure 15.3). If necessary, click the Customize Report button to change the Report Basis.

> **tip**
>
> You might want to give the Balance Sheet Prev Year Comparison report to your accountant using both accrual and cash basis reporting. To change the basis of the report, click the Customize Report button and select the desired report basis on the Display tab.

Figure 15.3
The Balance
Sheet
Prev Year
Comparison
report is a
useful report
to give your
accounting
professional at
tax time.

Bank Account Balance(s)

Compare your reconciled bank account balances on the Balance Sheet report to the statement your bank sends you. Modify the date of the Balance Sheet to be the same as the ending statement date on your bank statement. Your QuickBooks Balance Sheet balance for your bank account should be equal to the bank's ending statement balance plus or minus any uncleared deposits or checks/withdrawals dated on or before the statement ending date.

At tax time, give your last month's bank statement and QuickBooks bank reconciliation report to your accounting professional.

Accounts Receivable

The Accounts Receivable balance on your Balance Sheet report should agree with the A/R Aging Summary Report total (see Figure 15.4).

To create the A/R Aging Summary report, from the menu bar, select **Reports**, **Customers & Receivables**, **A/R Aging Summary or A/R Aging Detail**. On the top of the report, click Collapse to minimize (remove from view) the line detail, making the report easier to view at a glance. The total should match the Accounts Receivable balance on the Balance Sheet report (see Figure 15.1).

Figure 15.4
Use Expand or Collapse at the top of the report to change the level of detail displayed.

Undeposited Funds

The Undeposited Funds amount should agree with funds not yet deposited into your bank account, as shown in the custom report in Figure 15.5 (use today's date on your Balance Sheet report).

Figure 15.5
The amount of funds this report shows should agree with the amount of funds you have not yet taken to the bank.

Create the following custom report to review the Undeposited Funds detail sorted by payment method:

1. From the menu bar, select **Reports**, **Custom Reports**, **Transaction Detail**. The Modify Report dialog box opens.

2. In the Report Date Range box, select **All** (type an **a** to change the date range to All).

3. In the Columns box, select the data fields you want to view on the report; in the Total By drop-down menu, select **Payment Method**.

4. Click the Filters tab; Account is already highlighted in the Choose Filter box. In the Account drop-down menu to the right, choose Undeposited Funds.

5. Also in the Choose Filter box, scroll down to select **Cleared**; on the right, select **Cleared No**.

6. (Optional) Click the Header/Footer tab and change the report title to Undeposited Funds. Click OK to view the report.

Inventory

The Inventory balance on the Balance Sheet report (refer to Figure 15.1) should agree with the Inventory Valuation Summary Asset Value report total (see Figure 15.6). The ending dates of both reports need to be the same.

To create the Inventory Valuation Summary report, from the menu bar, select **Reports**, **Inventory**, **Inventory Valuation Summary**. Chapter 6, "Managing Inventory," has more details on working with inventory reporting.

Figure 15.6
The total of the Asset Value column should agree with the Inventory balance on the Balance Sheet report.

	On Hand	U/M	Avg Cost	Asset Value	% of Tot Asset	Sales
Door Frame (standard interior door frame)	21		12.00	252.00	0.8%	
Hardware						
Brass hinges (standard interior brass hinge)	246	ea	3.00	738.00	2.4%	
Doorknobs Std (Doorknobs Part # DK 3704)	124		26.91	3,337.16	10.9%	
Lk Doorknobs (Locking interior doorknobs Part # DK415)	122		35.27	4,302.35	14.0%	
Hardware - Other	0		0.00	0.00	0.0%	
Total Hardware	492	ea		8,377.51	27.3%	
Wood Door						
Exterior (Exterior door - #P-10981)	16		308.51	4,936.10	16.1%	1
Interior (Interior door - P-187055T)	47		69.90	3,285.17	10.7%	
Wood Door - Other	1		1,750.00	1,750.00	5.7%	
Total Wood Door	64			9,971.27	32.5%	
Total Inventory	1,006	ea		28,683.38	93.5%	
Assembly						
Interior Door kit (complete Interior door)	20		100.00	2,000.00	6.5%	
Total Assembly	20			2,000.00	6.5%	
TOTAL	1,026	ea		30,683.38	100.0%	

Rock Castle Construction
Inventory Valuation Summary
As of December 31, 2017
5:59 PM
12/15/17

Other Current Assets

The Other Current Asset accounts can differ widely by company. If you have employee advances, make sure your employees concur with your records. For any other accounts in the Other Current Asset category, look to documentation within QuickBooks to verify the reported balances.

Do you need an easy report to sort the detail in these Other Current Asset accounts by a list name? In this example, I created a detail report of the Employee Advances account, sorted and sub-totaled by payee (see Figure 15.7). You can create this same report for any of your accounts, sorting in a way that improves the detail for your review.

To create a detail report of your Other Current Asset accounts (in addition to other types of accounts), follow these steps:

1. From the menu bar, select **Reports**, **Custom Reports**, **Transaction Detail**. The Modify Report dialog box displays.

2. On the Date Range drop-down menu, select **All**.

3. In the Columns box, select the specific data you want to see in the report.

4. Also in the Columns box, in the Total By drop-down menu, select **Payee**.

 tip

Reconciling accounts like these can be useful. An example is when an employee pays back the loan in full. Complete the reconciliation for this account when the total of the loans matches the total of the payments, marking each transaction for this employee as Cleared. You can then filter the report for Uncleared only, limiting the amount of information that displays. This results in a beginning and ending balance of net $0.00.

Figure 15.7
Create a custom report to review balances in an Employee Advances account or any other asset account.

5. Click the Filters tab.

6. The Choose Filter box already has selected the Account filter. At the right, in the Account drop-down menu, select the **Employee Advances** account (or select the specific account for which you want to see detail).

7. (Optional) Click the Header/Footer tab and provide a unique report title. Click OK to create the modified report.

Verify the balances reported here with either the employees or outside source documents. If you do reconcile the account, you can filter for those transactions with a cleared status of No. This streamlines the amount of information the report displays.

Fixed Assets

Fixed assets are purchases that have a long-term life and, for tax purposes, cannot be expensed all at once. Instead, they must be depreciated over the expected life of the asset.

Accountants can advise business owners on how to classify assets. If the account balances have changed from year to year, you might want to review what transactions were posted, to make sure they are fixed-asset purchases and not expenses that should be reported on the Profit & Loss report.

If you have properly recorded a fixed-asset purchase to this account category, give your accountant the purchase receipt and any supporting purchase documents for their depreciation schedule records.

If you see a change in the totals from one year to the next, you can review the individual transactions in the account register by clicking Banking, Use Register, and selecting the account you want to review. Figure 15.8 shows the register for Fixed Assets—Furniture and Equipment. If a transaction was incorrectly posted here, you can edit the transaction by double-clicking the line detail and correcting the assigned account category.

Figure 15.8
Use registers for certain accounts to see the transactions that affect the balances.

Accounts Payable

The Accounts Payable balance on the Balance Sheet report should agree with the A/P Aging Summary report total (see Figure 15.9).

To create the A/P Aging Summary or Detail report, from the menu bar, select **Reports**, **Vendors & Payables**, **A/P Aging Summary** or **Detail**. For more information, see Chapter 8, "Managing Vendors."

Figure 15.9
The A/P Aging Summary report total should agree with your Balance Sheet, Accounts Payable balance.

Credit Cards

Your credit card account balances should reconcile with the balances from your credit card statement(s). You might have to adjust your Balance Sheet report date to match your credit card vendor's statement date, or you can request that your credit card company provide you with a statement cut-off at the end of a month.

You should give your accountant a copy of the most recent credit card statement so that he or she can verify the accuracy of your credit card balance.

For more information on working with reconciliation tasks, see Chapter 13, "Working with Bank and Credit Card Accounts."

Payroll Liabilities

The Payroll Liabilities balance on the Balance Sheet report should agree with your Payroll Liability Balances report total. Be careful with the dates here. If you have unpaid back payroll taxes, select a date range of All for the Payroll Liability Balances report. See Figure 15.10.

To create the Payroll Liability Balances report, from the menu bar, select **Reports**, **Employees & Payroll**, **Payroll Liability Balances**. Totals on this report should match your Balance Sheet report for the Payroll Liabilities account.

Figure 15.10
The Payroll Liability Balances report total should agree with the same total on the Balance Sheet report.

Sales Tax Payable

The Sales Tax Payable balance on the Balance Sheet report should agree with the Sales Tax Liability report balance. You might need to change the Sales Tax Payable report date and basis to match that of your Balance Sheet.

To create the Sales Tax Liability report, from the menu bar, select **Reports, Vendors & Payables, Sales Tax Liability**.

Make sure the To date matches that of the Balance Sheet report date. The total should match the Sales Tax Payable total on your Balance Sheet report (see Figure 15.11).

> 🔔 **caution**
>
> If you have set up your Sales Tax Preference as Cash Basis, you cannot compare this balance to an Accrual Basis Balance Sheet report.

Figure 15.11 The Sales Tax Liability report total should match the Sales Tax Payable balance on your Balance Sheet report.

	Total Sales	Non-Taxable Sales	Taxable Sales	Tax Rate	Tax Collected	Sales Tax Payable As of Dec 31, 17
City of East Bayshore	95.00	0.00	95.00		0.29	0.29
State Board of Equalization	53,026.16	40,624.25	12,401.91		957.34	957.34
Multiple taxes from different vendors	-95.00	0.00	-95.00		0.00	0.00
TOTAL	53,026.16	40,624.25	12,401.91		957.63	957.63

Other Current Liabilities and Long-Term Liabilities

Compare any other accounts you have in the Other Current Liabilities and Long-Term Liabilities account types with outside documents from your lending institutions.

Reconcile these accounts the same as you reconcile your bank account, to verify that your balances agree with the lending institution's records.

Equity

Equity accounts differ for each company. Your accountant should review these account balances and make any necessary tax adjustments at year-end or tax time.

> 🔍 **note**
>
> If you have an account named Opening Balance Equity that has a balance, this account should have a zero balance after data file setup is completed. For more information, see "Closing Opening Balance Equity into Retained Earnings," p. 593.

The reports this chapter discusses do not make up an exhaustive, end-all list for reviewing your Balance Sheet, but they are a great start when reviewing your own data or your client's data.

Reviewing the Profit & Loss Report

My experience over the years has been that business owners do not look at the Balance Sheet report often, if at all. However, nearly every business owner I have worked with has reviewed the Profit & Loss Standard report for the business. The reason might be that the Profit & Loss report is easier to interpret than the Balance Sheet report.

Even with simple organization (money in, money out), a careful review of the Profit & Loss report is prudent for the business owner who wants to track how well the business is doing financially. To create a Profit & Loss Standard report, from the menu bar, select **Reports**, **Company & Financial**, **Profit & Loss Standard** (or **Profit & Loss Detail**).

You can review your Profit & Loss report using two methods:

- **Cash Basis**—Income is recognized when received. Expenses are recognized when paid.

- **Accrual Basis**—Income is recognized as of the date of the customer's invoice. Expenses are recognized as of the date of the vendor's bill.

Cash basis reporting offers an incomplete snapshot in time because it shows what cash has changed hands but doesn't show unpaid bills from vendors or uncollected invoices from customers. Additionally, many companies file their annual tax returns using cash basis reports. Nothing is wrong with looking at reports prepared with cash basis accounting. However, I encourage all my clients to consider reviewing the Profit & Loss Standard report in accrual basis.

Accrual basis, although more complex, provides so much more information about the business:

- **Matching Principle**—Revenue (customer invoice) is recorded in the same accounting period as the expenses (vendor bills, paychecks, and the like) associated with services or products sold on the customer's invoice.

- **Seasonal Variations**—Track how your business performs financially—for example, by comparing the same month across multiple years.

- **Tracking Receivables and Payables**—This information helps with both short-term and long-term forecast planning.

With QuickBooks, you can easily change the report from cash to accrual basis by clicking the Customize Report button and manually selecting Cash or Accrual Basis on the Display tab of the Modify Report dialog box.

When reviewing the details of your Profit & Loss Detail report, you might want to look for these types of transactions:

- Monthly charges, such as rent, utility, equipment lease expenses, or other recurring expenses. Verify that the correct number of these charges is recorded, such as 12 monthly payments for rent.

- Credit card expenses reported to the proper expense accounts.

 tip

To review recurring monthly charges, preparing your Profit & Loss by the month is useful. In the Profit & Loss report, from the Columns drop-down menu at the top of the report, select **Month**.

- Nonpayroll payments to owners, which normally are recorded to draw or equity type accounts.

- Purchase of equipment with a significant cost, which should have been recorded to an asset account.

- The principal portion of loan payments for vehicles or equipment; these should have been recorded to liability accounts.

A business owner who takes the time to review the Profit & Loss Detail report can feel more confident that business decisions founded on financials are as accurate as possible.

Other Reviews

You have completed the basic Balance Sheet and Profit & Loss Report reviews. These are important, and you are well on your way to being more confident about the information. This section details other equally important reviews.

Tracking Changes to Closed Accounting Periods

You can "lock" your QuickBooks data and prevent users from making changes to prior accounting periods. (Accountants call this process a soft close.) If you then need to add or modify a transaction in a prior period, the Admin user (or someone with security rights) can return and "unlock" the accounting period.

To have QuickBooks track information for the Closing Date Exception report, you have to set a closing date and, optionally, set specific users' access to adding or modifying transactions on or before this date.

If you have compared your own or your clients' data to prior-year financials or tax returns and the ending balances prior to the closing date have changed, you should view the Closing Date Exception report (available with QuickBooks Premier or Enterprise) to see exactly who made the change and what specific transactions were affected. For more information on working with clients' files, see Chapter 16, "Sharing QuickBooks Data with Your Accountant."

To create the Closing Date Exception report (see Figure 15.12), from the menu bar, select **Reports**, **Accountant & Taxes**, **Closing Date Exception**. If you have not set a closing date, a warning prompt displays.

> **⚟ caution**
> Exceptions, additions, and changes are not tracked unless a closing date has been set for a QuickBooks file.

This report enables you to identify changes that were made to transactions dated on or before the closing date. For modified transactions, the report details both the latest version of a transaction and the earlier version (as of the closing date). If your QuickBooks access rights allow you to change closed period transactions, you can then re-create the original transaction or change the date of added transactions so that you again agree with the ending balance from the previously closed period.

Accounting professionals can consult Appendix A, "Client Data Review," for details on using the Troubleshoot Beginning Balances feature in QuickBooks Accountant.

Figure 15.12
Review the Closing Date Exception report for changes made to transactions dated on or before a closing date.

Using the Audit Trail Report

The Audit Trail report provides details of additions and changes made to transactions, grouping the changes by username. The detail on this report shows the earlier and latest version of the transaction, if it was edited. You can filter the report to show a specific date range to narrow the amount of detail.

The Audit Trail report is available in all desktop versions of QuickBooks. To create the Audit Trail report in Figure 15.13, from the menu bar, select **Reports**, **Accountant & Taxes**, **Audit Trail**.

Figure 15.13
The QuickBooks Audit Trail report helps identify what changes were made to transactions and by which user.

If you find undesired transaction changes, consider setting a closing date password and limiting user security privileges.

➡ *For more information, see "Set a Closing Date," p. 613.*

Using the Credit Card Audit Trail Report

QuickBooks users can stay in compliance with credit card industry security requirements by enabling security around who can view, add, or edit customers' credit card numbers.

You can include or exclude individual users' access to customers' sensitive credit card information. The company accountant also can take advantage of a user type called External Accountant. When this type is assigned to your accountant, he or she cannot view these sensitive customer credit card numbers.

Additionally, when the Credit Card Audit Trail report is enabled, you can track which user viewed, edited, added, or removed a customer's credit card number.

These three steps provide an overview of how to use this feature correctly:

1. Enable the customer credit card protection feature.

2. Select which users are given security rights to view the credit card numbers and which users are not given this privilege.

3. View the new Credit Card Audit Trail report to track viewing, editing, adding, and deleting activity with your customers' credit cards.

The first step to viewing details on the Credit Card Audit Trail report is to enable Customer Credit Card Protection in QuickBooks. To do so, follow these steps:

1. Log in to the data file as the Admin user. From the menu bar, select **Company**, **Customer Credit Card Protection**.

2. Click the Enable button to open the Customer Credit Card Protection Setup dialog box. Type a complex password that is at least seven characters, including one number and one uppercase character. For example, coMp1ex is a complex password. This complex password now replaces the previous Admin password.

3. You also must choose a Challenge Question from the drop-down menu and provide an answer to a question. This question helps you reset your password if you forget it. Click OK.

4. A message box opens, letting you know the next steps and telling you that you will be reminded in 90 days to change the password. Click OK.

5. QuickBooks notifies you that you have enabled Customer Credit Card Protection and details how to allow access by user to the credit card numbers (see step 6). Click OK. You then return to QuickBooks logged in as the Admin user.

6. To select which employees have access to view the full credit card numbers, or to add or change customer credit card numbers, from the menu bar, select **Company**, **Set Up Users and Passwords**, and select the **Set Up Users** option.

7. The QuickBooks login dialog box displays, requiring you to enter the Admin password to gain access to user security settings. Click OK to open the User List dialog box.

8. Select a username and click the Edit button. (Optional) Edit the username or password, or click Next to accept these fields as they are.

9. The Access window for the specific user opens. Choose the Selected Areas of QuickBooks option. Click Next.

10. The Sales and Accounts Receivable access options display. Choose either Full Access or Selective Access; either of these choices combined with a checkmark in the View Complete Credit Card Numbers box (see Figure 15.14) enables the user to view and add, delete, or modify the credit card number. If no checkmark is placed, the user sees only the last four digits of the customer's credit card when recording transactions that use this sensitive information.

> **tip**
>
> When creating a login user for your accountant, select the user type External Accountant. By default, this user type cannot view your customers' stored sensitive credit card numbers.

11. Click Finish if this is the only setting you want to modify, or click Next to advance through additional security settings.

You have now properly enabled the customer credit card protection and granted or removed user access to these confidential credit card numbers.

With this feature enabled, your data file is now tracking critical user activity about your customers' credit card numbers. QuickBooks records when the credit card security was enabled and maintains records of when a user enters a credit card number, modifies a credit card, or even views the Customer Credit Card Audit Trail report (see Figure 15.15).

This Customer Credit Card Audit Trail report is always tracking customer credit card activity, as long as the feature remains enabled. This report can be viewed only by logging into the file as the Admin user. However, you can use your mouse to select the entire report or part of it and then press Ctrl+C to copy the report to the Windows Clipboard. You can then paste the report into Excel or another program if you want to search or filter the report.

Figure 15.14
Option to limit user-specific access to viewing complete customer credit card numbers.

Figure 15.15
The Customer Credit Card Audit Trail report cannot be modified, filtered, or purged.

While not recommended, if you want to disable this setting, you must first log in to the data file as the Admin user and enter the complex password that you created when you enabled the protection. From the menu bar, select **Company**, **Customer Credit Card Protection**, and click the **Disable Protection button**. Click Yes to accept that customers' credit card number viewing, editing, and deleting activity by QuickBooks users is no longer being tracked for audit purposes.

Reporting on Voided/Deleted Transactions

QuickBooks offers flexibility for handling changes to transactions. If you grant users rights to create transactions, they also have rights to void and delete transactions. Don't worry—you can view these voided transaction changes in the Voided/Deleted Transactions Summary (see Figure 15.16) or Voided/Deleted Transactions Detail reports. You can use these reports to view transactions before and after the change, as well as to identify which user made the change.

To create the Voided/Deleted Transactions Summary report, from the menu bar, select **Reports**, **Accountant & Taxes**, **Voided/Deleted Transactions Summary** (or **Voided/Deleted Transactions Detail**).

Figure 15.16
The QuickBooks Voided/Deleted Transactions Summary report quickly identifies which transactions were either voided or deleted, making troubleshooting easy.

Viewing the Transactions List by Date Report

Although the title of Transaction List by Date report doesn't imply as much "power" as the other reports discussed in this chapter, I use this report most often when reviewing a data file.

If you are new to QuickBooks, you will soon learn that the date you enter for each transaction is important. The year you assign to the transaction is the year QuickBooks reports the transaction in your financials. For example, if you record a transaction with the year 2071 instead of 2017, this date can cause your financials not to show the effect until the year 2071.

To create the Transaction List by Date report, shown in Figure 15.17, from the menu bar, select **Reports, Accountant & Taxes, Transaction List by Date**. In the Dates drop-down menu, select **All**.

You can use this report to see both the oldest dated transaction (when the file was started) and the furthest-dated transaction (to identify whether date errors have been made). As with all other QuickBooks reports, you can double-click a specific transaction to change the date, if needed.

Figure 15.17 The QuickBooks Transaction List by Date report can help identify any incorrectly dated transactions.

Fortunately, QuickBooks preferences help avoid transaction dating errors by enabling you to set a warning for date ranges. To open the date warning preference, follow these steps:

1. Log in to the QuickBooks data file as the Admin or External Accountant user.

2. From the menu bar, select **Edit, Preferences**. In the Preferences dialog box, select the **Company Preferences** tab and choose the Accounting preference on the left.

3. Type in the user-defined date warning range you want to work with for past-dated transactions and future-dated transactions. QuickBooks sets the default warnings at 90 days in the past and 30 days in the future. An attempt to enter transactions dated before or after this date range prompts QuickBooks to give the user a warning message (see Figure 15.18).

> ⚡ **caution**
> Be cautious when making changes to the dates, especially if the year in question has already had a tax return prepared on the existing information.

Figure 15.18
Set the Date Warning preference so users are warned when dating a transaction outside an acceptable date range.

> Future Transactions
>
> ⚠ This transaction is more than **30 days** in the future. Are you sure you want to make this change?
>
> Turn off this warning, or change the number of days, in Edit > Preferences > Accounting.
>
> [Yes]   [No]

Troubleshooting Opening Balance Equity Account

QuickBooks automatically records the following transactions to the Opening Balance Equity account:

- Your opening balance transaction when you created a new bank account in the Express Start setup

- Opening balances for other Balance Sheet report accounts created in the Add New Account dialog box

- Inventory total value balances entered in the New Item dialog box

- Bank reconciliation adjustments for older versions of QuickBooks

> 📡 **caution**
>
> Although Intuit offers certain ready-made tools to convert other software to QuickBooks, some might not convert the data as expected. Be sure to verify that the information is correct after the conversion.

Other common transactions that a user might assign to this account include the following:

- Accrual basis opening accounts payable transactions as of the start date

- Accrual basis opening accounts receivable transactions as of the start date

- Uncleared bank checks or deposits (accrual or cash basis) as of the start date

Closing Opening Balance Equity into Retained Earnings

The Opening Balance Equity account should have a zero balance when a file setup is complete and done correctly. When I refer to a completely and correctly set-up QuickBooks file, I assume the following:

- You *are not* converting your data from Quicken, Sage 50 (formerly Peachtree), Small Business Accounting, or Office Accounting. Each of these products has an automated conversion tool available free from Intuit, which eliminates the need to do startup transactions if you convert the data and not just lists.

- Your company *did not* have any transactions prior to the first use of QuickBooks. In this case, you simply enter typical QuickBooks transactions after your QuickBooks start date, with no need for unusual startup type entries.

- Your company *did have* transactions prior to the first use of QuickBooks. You have chosen to enter these transactions one by one as regular transactions. You do not need to record any transactions to the Opening Balance Equity account.

- Your company *did have* transactions prior to the first use of QuickBooks, but there are so many that it is not feasible to re-create them in QuickBooks. Instead, follow the directions in Chapter 3, "Setting Up a QuickBooks Data File for Accrual or Cash Basis Reporting," p. 94.

- You have entered each of your unpaid customer invoices, unpaid vendor bills, and uncleared bank transactions and dated them prior to your QuickBooks start date.

- You have entered and dated your trial balance one day before your QuickBooks start date. (You might need to request the trial balance numbers from your accountant if you are not converting from some other financial software that provides you with a trial balance.)

- When you create a Trial Balance report in QuickBooks dated one day before your QuickBooks start date, it agrees with your accountant's trial balance or with the trial balance from your prior financial software, with the exception that you have a balance in the Opening Balance Equity account.

If you answered yes to each of these assumptions, I expect that your Opening Balance Equity account is equal to the Retained Earnings balance from your accountant's financials or from your prior software, or I assume that the amount matches the Equity section balance if your entity is an LLC or partnership with no Retained Earnings. If it doesn't agree, you need to continue to review the data to identify the errors. If it does agree, you are prepared to make the final entry in your startup process.

To create this closing entry using a General Journal Entries transaction, follow these steps:

1. From the menu bar, select **Company, Make General Journal Entries**.

2. Enter a Date (it should be one day before your QuickBooks start date).

3. Type an **Entry No**.

4. Leaving line 1 of the transaction blank, on line 2 of the Make General Journal Entries transaction (using the example shown in Figure 15.19), decrease (debit) Opening Balance Equity by $38,773.75 and increase (credit) Retained Earnings by the same amount. This action "closes" Opening Balance Equity to Retained Earnings. Click Save & Close.

ACCOUNT	DEBIT	CREDIT	MEMO	NAME	BILLA...	CLASS
30000 · Opening Bal Equity	38,773.75		Reclass to Retained Earnings			
32000 · Retained Earnings		38,773.75	Reclass to Retained Earnings			
Totals	38,773.75	38,773.75				

DATE 12/31/2017   ENTRY NO. 1005   ADJUSTING ENTRY

Figure 15.19
Use a Make General Journal Entries transaction to close Opening Balance Equity to Retained Earnings.

> ## 🔊 caution
>
> Leave the first line of any Make General Journal Entries transaction blank because QuickBooks uses this line as the source line. Any list item in the name column on the first line (source line) of a General Journal Entries transaction also is associated in reports with the other lines of the same General Journal Entries transaction. For more information about working with multiple-line journal entries, see the caution on p. 406 of Chapter 10, "Managing Customers."

5. Click OK to the QuickBooks warning that displays; QuickBooks saves the transaction. The warning advises you that you are posting to a Retained Earnings account and states that QuickBooks has a special purpose for this account. It is appropriate to post this entry to Retained Earnings. This warning is a result of a preference setting you can access from the menu bar by selecting **Edit**, **Preferences**, **Accounting**. Select the **Company Preferences** tab and choose the option to enable Warn when posting a transaction to Retained Earnings prompt. (You must be logged in as Admin or External Accountant user, and you must be in single-user mode to modify this preference.)

When the transaction is saved, create the Balance Sheet Standard report as explained earlier in this chapter and verify that your ending numbers are accurate—that is, they should match your accountant's or your prior software trial balance for the same period. Figure 15.20 now shows the proper Retained Earnings balance, and you no longer have a balance in Opening Balance Equity.

Figure 15.20
The Balance Sheet viewed after "closing" Opening Balance Equity to Retained Earnings.

Reviewing your data file can help improve the accuracy of your tax filings and provide more reliable information for management decisions.

16

SHARING QUICKBOOKS DATA WITH YOUR ACCOUNTANT

One feature that truly sets QuickBooks apart from other business account-ing software is the ease and flexibility of sharing a copy of the data between the business owner and the accounting professional. This chap-ter shares useful details for both the business owner and the accountant.

Overview

Accounting professionals can work more profitably with their clients' files by partnering the Accountant's Copy functionality with the robust Client Data Review feature. The Client Data Review feature is available in QuickBooks Accountant 2014 and QuickBooks Enterprise Solutions Accountant 14.0.

➡ *For more information, refer to Appendix A, "Client Data Review."*

Benefits for the Business Owner

As a business owner, you want to have your accounting professional review your data. After all, you are using this data to make important management decisions. Additionally, you need to provide your data to your accountant for the preparation of your federal and state tax returns.

So what might be some of the benefits of sharing your QuickBooks business data with your accountant? Benefits include the following:

- You can share an Accountant's Copy of your data, which allows your accountant to review and provide timely feedback without interrupting your daily workflow.

- You have less stress because you do not need to prepare multiple reports for your accountant to review.

- You can delegate critical tasks to your accountant, such as reconciling a bank account. (Use the Accountant's Copy file sharing method.)

- Your accountant can use your data to compile the information needed for your tax returns.

- You can choose from multiple sharing methods and select one that is right for your business.

- Periodically having your accountant review your data can save precious time at year's end and provide more accurate financials during the year.

Benefits for the Accountant

Periodically reviewing your clients' data has become more important in recent years, as strict accounting guidelines tighten further. Often your clients are even unaware of these changes.

As an accountant, you can benefit from access to your clients' data by doing the following:

- Review your clients' data at your office at a time convenient for you or your staff.

- Complete key reviewing tasks while enabling your clients to continue their day-to-day transactions. (Use the Accountant's Copy file sharing method.)

- Use the many accountant-specific tools to facilitate this review offered in the QuickBooks Accountant or QuickBooks Enterprise Solutions Accountant, including the Client Data Review feature.

- Complete critical tasks for your client, such as reconciling a bank account, making your services more valued by the client. (Use the Accountant's Copy file sharing method.)

- Provide your clients with more frequent and timely analysis of their data.

This chapter is a guide for how both the business owner and the accountant can share QuickBooks data.

QuickBooks File Types

QuickBooks offers much flexibility in how a business owner or accountant can share a common QuickBooks data file. This chapter discusses details of all the choices offered in facilitating this sharing.

Table 16.1 lists the common QuickBooks file types used for sharing data. Knowing these file types is important as you make decisions about the best method for your business or your clients' data sharing needs.

Table 16.1 QuickBooks File Types

Extension	File Type	Description	QuickBooks Editions*
.QBW	QuickBooks for Windows regular working file	This is the working data file type created when a user creates a new QuickBooks file.	Pro, Premier, Accountant, Enterprise
.QBB	QuickBooks for Windows backup file	The most secure and complete method for protecting your data with a backup.	Pro, Premier, Accountant, Enterprise
.QBM	QuickBooks for Windows portable company file	This is a compressed version of your QuickBooks .QBW data file. Used primarily to email or move the file to another location.	Pro, Premier, Accountant, Enterprise
.QBX	Accountant's Copy (export file)	The business owner creates this to save or send data to the accountant.	Pro, Premier, Accountant, Enterprise
.QBA	Accountant's Copy (converted .QBX file)	QuickBooks creates this file when opening or converting a .QBX file (usually by the accountant).	Premier Accountant, Enterprise Accountant
.QBY	Accountant's Copy (import file)	This is the file the accountant sends to the business owner after making changes.	Premier Accountant, Enterprise Accountant

*Not shown in Table 16.1 are QuickBooks Online and QuickBooks for Mac. Both versions have a different file structure, and neither of them supports the Accountant's Copy feature discussed at length in this chapter.

Choosing a Method to Share Data

QuickBooks offers flexibility in how data is shared between a business owner and the accountant. Different methods can be used at different times during the year, depending on the nature of the changes to be made.

Options available might also be determined by the edition of QuickBooks you use and whether your data is in an older version of QuickBooks. The enhancements made in recent years for sharing your data with your accountant make it a perfect time to upgrade to the newest release.

To compare different QuickBooks products, go to http://quickbooks.intuit.com/product/accounting-software/quickbooks-comparison-chart.jsp and click Desktop Products.

You might even choose to use multiple data-sharing methods during the course of a year, after you know the advantages and limitations associated with each type.

Before choosing an option, review the details of each file type (shown earlier in Table 16.1 and in the sections that follow).

How the QuickBooks Year and Version Affect Your Data Sharing Choices

The choices of how you can share your data with your accountant depend on the version and release year of QuickBooks you and your accountant use.

The QuickBooks product line includes Pro, Premier (general and industry-specific versions), Premier Accountant, Enterprise (general and industry-specific versions), QuickBooks for Mac, and QuickBooks Online.

Additionally, Intuit releases a new QuickBooks version each year, often represented by the year included in the name. For example, QuickBooks Premier 2014 is the Premier version usually released the fall before the stated year. This version is separate from the maintenance release updates QuickBooks provides throughout a year to add functionality and fix issues discovered with a version.

To determine your current version and release, with QuickBooks open, press F2 or Ctrl+1. At the top of the Product Information dialog box is the product name (and industry edition if Premier or Enterprise), year, and release number.

So you can see how the version year can affect your choices for sharing data, in this chapter, I discuss the Accountant's Copy features, which are not available for QuickBooks Online, the QuickBooks for Mac edition, or any QuickBooks desktop product earlier than the 2007 version.

.QBW: Regular Working Copy of the Data

Each client file is originally created in the .QBW file type. Here is a list of some of the advantages and limitations of sharing this type of data file:

- The accountant *cannot* take the file to his office, work in the file, and later merge changes into the business owner's file unless the client agrees not to work in the file while the accountant has possession of it.

- The accountant can use the Send General Journal Entries features if both the client and the accountant are using QuickBooks 2014. The journal transactions are attached to an email and imported by the client by clicking on the attachment. Additionally, such journal transactions are not subject to the Dividing Date restrictions found in the Accountant's Copy file sharing method.

- The accountant has access to all transaction activities.

- The accountant can access this file at the business owner's office or with a remote Internet-assisted program. QuickBooks partners with Remote Access by WebEx, but several others are available in the market, including LogMeIn or GoToMeeting.

- The file can often be too large to send as an attachment in an email.

To open a working copy of the data from the menu bar, select **File**, **Open or Restore Company** and select the **Open a Company File** option.

.QBB: QuickBooks Backup File

This file type remains as it has for years—it's the best choice for securing a data backup of your work. If needed, you can restore this file to a .QBW file. Sharing this type of data file has some advantages and limitations:

- The file cannot be opened first without being restored.

- When restored, the file extension becomes .QBW (see the pros and cons listed earlier).

- Changes made to a restored version of this file type cannot be merged later into the original data file.

To restore a backup file from the menu bar, select **File**, **Open or Restore Company** and select the **Restore a Backup Copy** option.

.QBM: QuickBooks Portable Company File

The .QBM file type has been offered for the past few years; however, it does not replace the usefulness of the QuickBooks .QBB file type. Consider some of the advantages and limitations of sharing this type of data file:

- The compressed file size makes a .QBM a perfect choice for attaching to an email or moving from one computer location to another.

- The file type does not replace a .QBB backup because it lacks some of the needed transaction logs.

- The file cannot be opened until it is restored.

- When restored, the file extension becomes a .QBW (see the pros and cons listed earlier).

- Changes made to a restored version of this file type cannot be merged later into the original data file.

To restore a portable company file from the menu bar, select **File**, **Open or Restore Company** and select the **Restore a Portable File** option.

.QBX: Accountant's Copy (Export File)

As a business owner, if you choose to share your data with your accountant using the Accountant's Copy functionality, you will send the .QBX file type to your accounting professional. Consider some of the advantages and limitations of sharing this type of data file:

- The business owner creates this file type, which enables your accountant to review and make needed changes to your data while you continue recording your day-to-day transactions in the file at your office.

- Any changes or additions your accountant makes can be imported (merged) into your company's data file.

- The accountant's work is protected by a required Dividing Date, preventing the business owner from making changes to transactions dated on or before the Dividing Date.

- The compressed file size makes it a perfect choice for attaching to an email or moving from one computer location to another.

- The file type does not replace a .QBB backup because it lacks some of the needed transaction logs.

- The file cannot be opened; it must be converted to a .QBA file type.

Using QuickBooks Accountant software, from the menu bar, select **File**, **Accountant's Copy** and select the **Open & Convert Transfer File** option.

.QBA: Accountant's Copy (Working File)

Only the accountant works with the .QBA file. Listed here are some of the advantages and limitations of sharing this type of data file:

- This file type is a converted .QBX file. The accountant creates it from within the QuickBooks Accountant or QuickBooks Enterprise Solutions Accountant.

- The .QBA file type is the file the accountant makes changes to. It is converted to a .QBY file for the client to import.

- The accountant can save it to his or her computer and then open and close it as needed while reviewing the file.

.QBY: Accountant's Copy (Import File)

The business owner receives the .QBY file from the accountant, and it includes any accounting changes made to the original .QBX file. Consider some of the advantages and limitations of sharing this type of data file:

- The accountant creates this file type using QuickBooks Accountant or QuickBooks Enterprise Solutions Accountant software.

- The file includes the changes the accountant made to the original .QBX file the business owner provided the accountant.

- The file cannot be opened; it must be imported into the data file that *originally created* the Accountant's Copy data file.

QuickBooks offers your business many options in how you want to share your data with your accountant. Select a solution that works for you and your accountant.

Send General Journal Entries

With QuickBooks Accountant 2014, you have flexibility in choosing what method of file sharing works best for you and your client. When considering a method, your client needs to continue the daily accounting tasks while allowing you to review the data and create journal entries.

With the Send Journal Entry feature, your clients send you either a copy of their working file (.QBW), a backup (.QBB), or a portable company file (.QBM). Your clients can continue to work in their files while you review their copy at your office. This avoids the restrictions imposed when sharing an Accountant's Copy file.

See the section titled "Send General Journal Entries," later in this chapter, for more details.

Data Sharing for the Business Owner

Few business owners with whom I have worked over the years have a college degree in accounting. That situation is exactly what makes QuickBooks so appealing to a growing business—you don't need to be an accountant to use it. However, you need an accountant to review your financials, perhaps at tax time or when you need a statement of your business's financial condition to give to a bank when requesting a business loan.

QuickBooks provides several methods of sharing data with your accountant. Refer to Table 16.1 for details on the QuickBooks file types the business owner can choose.

When Your Accountant Is Using QuickBooks Accountant 2014

If you are using a version of QuickBooks 2013 or 2014 or Enterprise Solutions version 13.0 or 14.0, and you choose to share your data using the Accountant's Copy feature, your accountant can use the QuickBooks 2014 Accountant or Enterprise Solutions Accountant 14.0 versions to open your 2013 or 2014 company file and make changes. Enterprise Solutions Accountant 14.0 can open a Pro or Premier Accountant's Copy (2013 or 2014) and can return the file to clients to open in their Pro or Premier software.

When the file is returned with the accountant's changes, you can import the changes back into your QuickBooks file, even though the accountant used a newer version of QuickBooks. QuickBooks Accountant 2014 and Enterprise Solutions Accountant 14.0 offer a degree of backward compatibility.

If you are sharing any other file type (other than the Accountant's Copy) with your accountant, there is no backward compatibility. When your accountant restores a .QBB (backup) or .QBM (portable) company file in a 2014 version, the file will be updated to 2014; if the file is returned to you, you need to update your QuickBooks version to the same release year as your accountant.

For example, suppose you are currently using a QuickBooks 2013 version. Your accountant is using QuickBooks 2014 Accountant. When your accountant restores a QuickBooks file backup, he or she must update the file to the QuickBooks 2014 release. If your accountant returns the data to you, you will not be able to open it with your QuickBooks 2013 software.

So as you decide which method to use, consider discussing with your accountant the QuickBooks version and release year you are using. QuickBooks accountants who have serviced companies for many years often have several versions of QuickBooks installed.

Keep in mind that QuickBooks Enterprise Solutions presents its own set of special requirements. If you open a backup or portable company file from a Pro or Premier data file with the Enterprise Solutions software, you will no longer be able to open the same data file in its original QuickBooks Pro or Premier edition.

For the most flexibility in sharing data with your accountant, consider using the Accountant's Copy file type, discussed at length in this chapter.

Reviewing Your QuickBooks Data

No matter what method you choose to share your data file with your accountant, one of the most important things you can do is review your data for accuracy, especially in the areas of accounts payable and accounts receivable—areas that you will know better than your accountant.

To begin, pick a chapter of this book that covers the area of QuickBooks you need to review. You might want to start with Chapter 15, "Reviewing Your Data." This chapter shows you quick and easy data checks you can do before your accountant formally reviews your data. Performing this quick review can also help you identify any potential errors for which you will need your accountant's guidance when correcting.

Creating an Accountant's Copy of Your Data

The Accountant's Copy method of sharing your data is the most efficient because it enables your accountant to work in the data file from her office without interrupting your day-to-day work pattern.

You must consider the following before making the choice to use the Accountant's Copy file sharing type:

- If you choose to create an Accountant's Copy, you need to determine how to get the Accountant's Copy data file to your accountant. QuickBooks offers these options:

    - Send an encrypted copy of your data to your accountant via Intuit's secure Accountant's Copy File Transfer Service

    - Attach the saved file to an email

    - Copy it to a storage device such as a USB drive or CD

    - Use an online file sharing service such as YouSendIt or Dropbox

> **⚠ caution**
>
> Only the Admin or new External Accountant user can create an Accountant's Copy or import the .QBY Accountant's Copy import file that contains the changes the accountant made to your data.

- You also are required to set a Dividing Date, as shown in Figure 16.1. The Dividing Date is a specific date in the past that determines the restrictions you and your accountant have when adding or editing transactions.

Figure 16.1
Setting a Dividing Date is required when creating an Accountant's Copy.

The following list briefly identifies the date restrictions with a Dividing Date in place when you share an Accountant's Copy of your data with your accountant. For example, if you choose a sample Dividing Date of 12/31/16, the following restrictions exist:

- **On or Before the Dividing Date**—You (the business owner) cannot add, delete, or modify transactions. The accountant can add, delete, or modify transactions.

- **After the Dividing Date**—You (the business owner) can add, delete, or modify transactions. The accountant can add transactions but cannot delete or modify them.

For more information, see "What the Business Owner Can and Cannot Do," later in this chapter, for any restrictions that affect you, the business owner.

The business owner has the following options for delivering the QuickBooks data file to the accountant:

- **Send to Accountant**—Send an encrypted copy of your data to your accountant via Intuit's Accountant's Copy File Transfer Service (free for the business owner). This is included for the accountant who subscribes to the QuickBooks ProAdvisor program.

- **Save File**—Attach the file to an email or copy it to USB or other portable medium.

Method 1: Using the Send to Accountant

Offered with QuickBooks Pro, Premier, and Enterprise is the option to use a secure, Intuit-hosted site to encrypt and transfer data to your accountant without needing to create a file and attach it to an email.

To send data to your accountant with the secure encrypted file service, follow these steps:

1. From the menu bar, select **File**, **Accountant's Copy**, **Client Activities**, **Send to Accountant**. The Confirm Sending an Accountant's Copy dialog box displays, as in Figure 16.2. This message details the service and what types of shared work are and are not recommended with this type of file.

2. Click Next. The Set the Dividing Date dialog box displays.

3. From the Dividing Date drop-down list, choose one of the date options in Figure 16.1, or choose Custom to select your own Dividing Date.

4. Click Next. The Information for Sending the File (1 of 2) dialog box displays, as in Figure 16.3. Type the email address to notify your accountant, and include your name and return email. Your accountant receives an email notification that your data file is ready to download. The download is available only for 14 days.

5. Click Next. The Information for Sending the File (2 of 2) dialog box displays, as in Figure 16.4.

6. Enter a strong password that is at least seven characters and contains at least one capital letter and one digit. (Optional) Type a note to your accountant, but do not include the password in the communication.

7. Click Send.

note

Before you send the Accountant's Copy to your accountant using the Accountant's Copy File Transfer service, be aware of these limitations.

- Your company file must be less than 200MB.

- A dial-up connection might be too slow to send your file over the Internet.

Send Accountant's Copy   ✕

Confirm sending an Accountant's Copy

This sends an Accountant's Copy to your accountant using Intuit's Accountant's Copy File Transfer service. Your accountant will receive a notification and download your file.   File size and Internet bandwidth limitations

An Accountant's Copy allows

- your accountant to complete a fiscal period
- you and your accountant to work independently
- you to import your accountant's changes into your file

Note: If your accountant needs to set up your books, do daily bookkeeping, or work on payroll, you should create a portable or backup file that you can send instead. To do that, click **Cancel** now, and go to the **File** menu and click **Save Copy or Backup**.

Help me choose

| Back | Next | | Help | Cancel |

Figure 16.2
Confirm that the Accountant's Copy is the appropriate choice for the shared work you and your accountant will be doing.

Figure 16.3
Identify the email address where your accountant should be notified, as well as your own name and email address.

Send Accountant's Copy

Information for sending the file (1 of 2)

Your accountant will be sent a notification e-mail with a link to download the file.

Accountant's e-mail address:

mycpa@cpaurl.com

Reenter the accountant's e-mail address:

mycpa@cpaurl.com

Your name:

Laura Madeira

Your e-mail address:

rockcastle@samplename.com

Figure 16.4
Set a strong password and add an optional note for your accountant.

Send Accountant's Copy

Information for sending the file (2 of 2)

Create file transfer password to encrypt file for security (OK to use your Admin password if it's strong):

••••••••• (At least 7 characters, including at least 1 digit and 1 capital letter)

Reenter password:

•••••••••

Note: Be sure to let your accountant know this password.

Note to your accountant (but do not include file transfer password here):

Please complete the bank reconciliation for December 2016 as part of your review. Thank you!

8. Click OK to the message that QuickBooks has to close all windows to create the Accountant's Copy. Note that QuickBooks also provides an information message only (no action to be taken) that the transfer might take a few minutes, so don't worry if QuickBooks seems unresponsive.

9. Click OK on the QuickBooks Information dialog box that displays, to indicate that the file was successfully uploaded to the Intuit Accountant's Copy File Transfer server.

The QuickBooks title bar identifies your file as having Accountant's Changes Pending, as in Figure 16.5. This title bar change indicates that you have successfully created a file for your accountant to review, edit, modify, and later return the changes to you without interrupting your work.

Rock Castle Construction (Accountant's Changes Pending) - QuickBooks Accountant 2014

Accountant Company Customers Vendors Employees Banking Reports Window Help

Calendar Snapshots Customers Vendors Employees Docs Reports App Center Invoice User License

Figure 16.5
Your QuickBooks title bar indicates whether you have Accountant's Changes pending.

Method 2: Using the Save File Method

Another method is to create the file, save it to your computer, and then email it or provide the file to your accountant on a USB device. To create an Accountant's Copy file of your data that your accountant can review and modify while you continue to do your daily transactions, follow these steps:

1. Close all your active QuickBooks windows. From the menu bar, select **File**, **Accountant's Copy**, **Client Activities**, **Save File**.

2. Choose the Accountant's Copy option, as in Figure 16.6. (The other option includes the Portable or Backup File. These methods do not allow the accountant to export any changes made or allow you to import the changes.)

3. Click Next. The Set the Dividing Date dialog box opens.

4. From the Dividing Date drop-down list, select one of the date options previously shown in Figure 16.1, or choose Custom to select your own specific Dividing Date. For more information on the importance of this date, see "What the Business Owner Can and Cannot Do," p. 609.

Save Accountant's Copy

Confirm Accountant's Copy

Verify that the Accountant's Copy is appropriate for your situation.

◉ Accountant's Copy
  • Use if your accountant is completing a fiscal period.
  • You and your accountant can work independently.
  • Then you import the accountant's changes into your file.

○ Portable or Backup File
  • Use if your accountant needs to set up your books, do daily bookkeeping, or work on payroll.
  • You must either stop working in your company file or manually enter your accountant's changes later.

Figure 16.6
Saving a file as an Accountant's Copy creates a file that your accountant can work in and later merge the changes with your file.

5. Click Next. QuickBooks opens the Save Accountant's Copy dialog box, where you can browse your computer for the location where you want to save the Accountant's Copy export file (.QBX file).

6. Click the Save button. QuickBooks provides the message shown in Figure 16.7, indicating that you successfully created an Accountant's Copy and telling you where the file was saved, as well as other useful information.

Figure 16.7
QuickBooks provides information about where the file was saved.

(Accountant's Copy Created dialog)

> ℹ **You have successfully created an Accountant's Copy file.**
>
> File: C:\Users\Owner\Documents\My Data\Rock Castle 12-31-16.QBX
>
> Dividing Date: 12/31/2016
>
> Next step: Deliver this file to your accountant using e-mail, CD, or some other method.
>
> Click Help for more information about sending the Accountant's Copy to your accountant.
>
> OK   Help

7. Click OK. As Figure 16.5 showed earlier, the QuickBooks title bar now identifies your file as having Accountant's Changes Pending.

8. Send this .QBX file to your accountant as an email attachment, or copy it to a removable data storage device.

What the Business Owner Can and Cannot Do

With the useful features of Accountant's Copy, your accountant can be assured that the information in the file he or she is working in will not change for dates before the Dividing Date.

The following list details what you can and cannot do with your data file while an Accountant's Changes are pending:

- **Transactions**—You can add, edit, and modify transactions with a date after the Dividing Date.

- **Accounts**—You can add a new chart of accounts list item.

- **Subaccounts**—You cannot add a subaccount to an existing account.

- **Editing, merging, or inactivating accounts**—You cannot edit, merge, or inactivate a chart of accounts item (but your accountant can).

- **Editing lists (other than the chart of accounts)**—You can add, edit, and inactivate your list items. If you and your accountant make changes to the same item, the accountant's changes will override your changes.

- **Deleting lists**—You cannot delete or merge list items (your accountant can).

- **Reconciling the bank account**—In the .QBW file with pending Accountant's Copy, if the statement date and all transactions involved in the reconciliation are after the Dividing Date and the accountant didn't reconcile this account in the Accountant's Copy, reconciliation work remains in the .QBW file after the import. Bank reconciliations for dates on or before the Dividing Date are removed when you incorporate your accountant's changes file.

Reconciling While an Accountant's Copy Is Pending

When choosing to use the Accountant's Copy to share your data, you can complete the bank reconciliation only for reconciliations where the bank statement date and all transactions to be cleared are dated after the selected Dividing Date.

From the menu bar, select **Banking, Reconcile,** and select your bank account. The bank reconciliation dialog box opens. In this dialog box, dates entered must follow these guidelines:

- **Statement Date**—Must be a date after the specified Dividing Date
- **Service Charge Date**—Must be a date after the specified Dividing Date
- **Interest Earned Date**—Must be a date after the specified Dividing Date

Your bank reconciliation work will remain after the import of your accountant's changes in these cases:

- None of the transactions you mark as cleared are dated on or before the Accountant's Copy Dividing Date.
- Your accountant did not also complete the bank reconciliation for the same bank account.
- Your accountant doesn't undo any bank reconciliations for this account in the Accountant's Copy.

You might find value in reconciling, even if the Accountant's Copy import will undo it, simply to verify that your bank balances are correct.

Importing Your Accountant's Changes

When you make an Accountant's Copy from your data file, QuickBooks creates a file for you to give to your accountant. Your accountant then works in this file, adding and editing transactions, and even reconciling your bank account. When the accountant finishes with the review, he or she exports the changes for you, which generates a .QBY file, also referred to as an Accountant's Copy Import File.

Your accountant has two options for sending you the file with changes:

- **Send Changes to Client**—This method allows the business owner to incorporate the changes from a menu in QuickBooks. The business owner is not charged for this service, and the accounting professional faces only a nominal fee (included free for the accountant with a subscription to the QuickBooks ProAdvisor program).

- **Create Change File**—The file can be attached to an email or stored on a removable device. No fee is charged to the business owner or the accountant when using this method.

Encourage your accountant to use the Send Changes to Client method—of the two methods, it is the easiest for the business owner.

Method 1: Importing Accountant's Changes from Web

You can tell your accountant used this method if you receive an email from Intuit, providing instructions for incorporating the changes your accountant made to your file. This method does not require attachments to emails or files on flash drives, making it the simplest method to use.

To import changes from the Web, follow these steps:

1. With your QuickBooks data file open, verify that the title bar indicates that the accountant's changes are pending (refer to Figure 16.5). You might also see the message shown in Figure 16.8 when you open your data file.

Figure 16.8
Message when you open the data file indicating that your accountant's changes are pending.

2. From menu bar, select **File**, **Accountant's Copy**, **Client Activities**, **Import Accountant's Changes from Web**. The Incorporate Accountant's Changes dialog box opens, enabling you to view the details of the changes to be imported (see Figure 16.9).

3. Click the plus sign (+) in front of a transaction to see more details about that specific transaction, or click Expand All to see the details of all the transactions.

4. Click Save as PDF or Print to save the details for your future reference.

5. Click the Incorporate Accountant's Changes button when you have finished reviewing the changes.

6. The Accountant Import dialog box opens, instructing you to close any open QuickBooks windows. Click OK.

7. The Save Backup Copy dialog box opens, indicating that you must make a backup of your data before the import. In the Save In drop-down menu, select a location to save the backup file; in the File Name field, type a name if you don't want to accept the default name provided.

8. If a message displays about backing up your data to the same location as your data, read the message and select **Change Location** or **Use This Location**.

9. Click OK to close the message that informs you where the backup was stored. QuickBooks displays a progress indicator while it is incorporating the changes. When QuickBooks finishes, the Accountant's Changes Incorporated dialog box displays.

Figure 16.9
View the accountant's changes and notes before they are incorporated into your data.

Click to expand or collapse the details

10. Click OK in the QuickBooks Information dialog box, which informs you about the PDF file of the changes that QuickBooks created and stored in the same location as your company file.

11. Click OK to close the message that your accountant has been notified that you have imported the changes.

12. Click Print or Save As PDF to store a copy of the changes in addition to the PDF automatically created in step 10.

13. Click Close to close the Incorporate Accountant's Changes dialog box.

The changes your accountant made are now incorporated into your file.

Method 2: Importing Accountant's Changes from File

Use this method if the accountant provided you with a file with an extension of .QBY. Your accountant might have provided it via an email attachment or brought it to your office on a flash drive or other removable device.

To import changes from the transfer file, follow these steps:

1. With your QuickBooks data file open, verify that the title bar indicates that the accountant's changes are pending (refer to Figure 16.5). If the Accountant's Copy message displays, click OK to close.

2. Select **File, Accountant's Copy, Client Activities, Import Accountant's Changes from File.**

3. Browse to the location where you stored the .QBY Accountant's Copy (import file) your accountant sent you.

4. Select the file and click Open. The Incorporate Accountant's Changes dialog box opens, enabling you to view the details of the changes to be imported (refer to Figure 16.9).

5. Click the plus sign (+) in front of a transaction to see more details about that specific transaction, or click Expand All to see the details of all the transactions.

6. Click Print or Save As PDF to save the details for your future reference.

7. Click the Incorporate Accountant's Changes button when you have finished reviewing the changes.

8. The Accountant Import dialog box opens, instructing you to close any open QuickBooks windows. Click OK.

9. The Save Backup Copy dialog box opens, indicating that you must first make a backup of your data before the import. In the Save In drop-down menu, select a location to save the backup file in the File Name field, type a name if you don't want to accept the default name provided. Click Save.

10. Click OK to close the message that informs you where the backup was stored. QuickBooks displays a progressive message that it is incorporating the changes. When QuickBooks finishes, the Accountant's Changes Incorporated dialog box displays.

11. Click OK to the QuickBooks Information dialog box about the PDF file of the changes that was created and stored in the same location as your company file.

12. Click Close after viewing the Accountant's Changes—Incorporated dialog box. (Optional) Click Print or Save As PDF to store a copy of the changes in addition to the PDF automatically created in step 11.

13. Click Close to close the Incorporate Accountant's Changes dialog box.

Set a Closing Date

When the accountant's changes are imported, the Dividing Date and all the restrictions associated with it are removed. The accountant can include with his or her changes a closing date that transfers to your file so you do not inadvertently add, delete, or modify transactions before the closing date. If a closing date was set, you will see the details in the Incorporate Accountant's Changes report you view before importing the changes.

If your accountant did not send back a closing date and password, I recommend that you set a closing date that is the same as the Dividing Date, to protect the accountant's work.

To set a closing date for your file, follow these steps:

1. Log in as the Admin user and, from the menu bar, select **Company**, **Set Closing Date**.

2. The Preferences dialog box displays. Click the Set Date/Password button. The Set Closing Date and Password dialog box displays.

3. Select a closing date, typically the same date used for the Dividing Date.

4. (Optional) Select the **Exclude Estimates, Sales Orders, and Purchase Orders from Closing Data Restrictions** checkbox (see Figure 16.10).

Figure 16.10
Setting a closing date helps protect the accountant's work.

5. Enter an optional password (recommended).

6. Click OK to accept the closing date and optional closing date password.

Setting Employee Security

To be certain the Closing Date control is managed properly, review all users for their specific rights for changing transactions before a closing date.

1. From the menu bar, select **Company, Set Up Users and Passwords, Set Up Users**. This is the menu path for QuickBooks Pro, Premier, or Accountant; QuickBooks Enterprise Solutions has more robust security setting options—for more detail, see Chapter 1, "User Security in QuickBooks Enterprise," p. 59.

2. To view existing security by user, from the User List dialog box you opened in the previous step, select the user with your cursor and click the View User button.

3. The View User Access dialog box opens, as in Figure 16.11. Any user who should not have rights to change closed period transactions should have an *N* appearing in the last menu option in the Create column.

4. After reviewing the access for each employee, if you need to edit this setting for an employee, click Leave to close the View User Access dialog box.

Figure 16.11
You can easily view the user's access rights from one summary window.

Should be "N" to prevent changes to closed period transactions

5. You return to the User List dialog box. With your cursor, select the employee and click Edit User.

6. The Access for User dialog box opens. Choose the Selected Areas option and click Continue through the screens until you reach page 9 of 10 (see Figure 16.12). Click Next (page 10 of 10) to see a summary of the employee's security settings, or click Finish to return to the User List dialog box.

7. Click Close.

Figure 16.12
On the second option, click No to prevent the user from changing transactions in closed periods.

Canceling an Accountant's Copy

It is possible for you to cancel an Accountant's Copy of your data, if necessary. Be sure to discuss this action with your accountant before you make this change. The following are some reasons you might need to cancel the accountant's changes:

- Your accountant has delayed the review of your file.

- You have found corrections you would like to make before the Dividing Date.

- You cannot modify nonposting documents (purchase orders, sales orders, and estimates) dated before the Dividing Date.

- Your accountant needs to work in your file without any transaction restrictions and makes an appointment to come to your office to work or perform the work remotely via the Internet.

Before canceling or removing restrictions on your data file, discuss this option with your accountant. After the Accountant's Copy is canceled, your accountant's changes file cannot be imported into your data file.

To remove the restrictions placed on your file by an Accountant's Copy, select **File**, **Accountant's Copy**, **Client Activities**, **Remove Restrictions** from the menu bar. The Remove Restrictions dialog box displays, warning you that your accountant will no longer be able to import changes back into your file (see Figure 16.13).

After you remove the restrictions from the file, no more data restrictions are imposed by the Dividing Date, and the top bar of your data file no longer displays the Accountant's Changes Pending message.

Figure 16.13
The Remove Restrictions warning displays when canceling an Accountant's Copy file.

Data Sharing for the Accountant

Earlier, Table 16.1 listed the types of QuickBooks files that business owners and accountants have the options of working with. This section discusses the options from the perspective of the accountant.

As the accountant, you want to review the variety of file types and the pros and cons of using each file type for sharing data with your client.

➡️ *For more information, see "QuickBooks File Types," p. 599.*

File Manager 2014

QuickBooks File Manager 2014 (see Figure 16.14) is automatically installed with your QuickBooks Accountant 2014 and Enterprise Accountant 14.0 software. With File Manager, accounting professionals can do the following:

Figure 16.14
File Manager, included with QuickBooks Accountant, manages multiple client files, stores clients' passwords, and can upgrade client files in batch.

- Build a client list that creates a virtual view of your hard drive where your client files are stored. You can store files on a server, on a local hard drive, or both.

- Create user-definable client groups, such as Annual Review Clients, Monthly Review Clients, or Payroll Clients, to name just a few suggestions.

- Save your client file passwords in one place. QuickBooks File Manager will open the clients' files without requiring the password.

- View important information about your clients' files without opening them. You have the following capabilities:

  - Upgrade client files in batch to the newest release—a real time saver.

  - Open your client files from within File Manager, and the correct year's version of QuickBooks opens automatically (you must have that version installed).

  - Back up and restore your File Manager settings, which is useful when you buy a new computer or want to share one employee File Manager settings with another.

You can launch QuickBooks File Manager in multiple ways:

- Click the QuickBooks File Manager desktop icon.

- Launch it from the Accountant Center in your Accountant version of QuickBooks.

- From the menu bar, select **Accountant**, **QuickBooks File Manager**.

- Click the Start button in Windows, and then select Programs, QuickBooks, File Manager.

Using File Manager takes the guesswork out of working with your client's file. It is easy to use and is included with your Accountant version software.

Creating an External Accountant User Type

When you work in a client's file, request that the client create a username specific for you and assign that username the External Accountant type, as in Figure 16.15. Benefits and controls available when working in a client's file as the External Accountant user type include the following:

- The capability to separate the changes you make in the data file from the changes your client makes.

- The option to use the Client Data Review feature efficiently. For more information, see "Client Data Review," p. 695.

- Access to all areas of QuickBooks, except when creating new users, changing a user's access privileges, or viewing sensitive customer credit card numbers.

Figure 16.15
Ask your client to create an External Accountant user type for you as the company accountant.

To create this unique type of user, you must be logged in to the data file as the Admin user, and you or the client must create the new user *before* the client creates the Accountant's Copy file for your use.

You will then use this new login when you begin working with the client's data file.

Preparing Your Client for Data Exchange

As an accounting professional, you probably will be able to choose the method you and your client use to share the data. However, you might not be able to control the condition in which you receive the file. I am speaking specifically of accounting accuracy. Some accounting professionals don't worry much about this until they receive the data file; others might want their client to take certain steps to ensure the accuracy of the data before beginning the review. Encourage your clients to review specific chapters in this book to help better prepare their file for your review, making your review time more profitable.

Ask your clients to review the following in their files before sharing the data with you:

- Accuracy of bank balances

- The open customer invoices in Accounts Receivable

- The unpaid vendor bills in Accounts Payable

Other critical numbers to review are usually easier to reconcile by asking for documents from banks, such as a bank loan payoff statement or comparing the business financials with filed payroll returns.

After your client has reviewed the information and provided the documents you requested, you are ready to choose a method for sharing the data with your client.

Receiving an Accountant's Copy File

After reviewing the advantages or limitations of each file type in the section titled "QuickBooks File Types," you can see that the most effective method is the QuickBooks Accountant's Copy file feature. Using this file type, your clients can continue their day-to-day accounting tasks, and from the convenience of your office, you can review and make needed changes to their data, later importing these changes into the files they have been using.

Discuss the following with your clients before they prepare an Accountant's Copy of their QuickBooks data:

- The Dividing Date selected. As the accounting professional, communicate what date this should be.

- How current are the bank reconciliations in the data file? In the Accountant's Copy, your bank reconciliation work is returned to the client only for statement dates on or before the Dividing Date. Additionally, the client can mark as cleared only items dated after the Dividing Date.

- Verify that the user settings in the data file include restrictions for editing or modifying transactions earlier than the closing date. This step is optional, but when you are working in the Accountant's Copy file, you can send back the closing date with your changes.

- Instruct clients not to cancel or remove restrictions on the Accountant's Changes Pending file without first consulting you.

- Discuss the options for sending this file to you. Owners have these options:

  - Send you an encrypted copy of their data via Intuit's secure Accountant's Copy File Transfer Service, a free service to your client. Accounting professionals pay a nominal fee annually for an unlimited number of uses of the service (free if you are a QuickBooks ProAdvisor). Be sure your client knows the email address where you would like to be notified.

  - Attach the saved file to an email.

  - Copy it to a storage device, such as a USB drive or CD.

🌐 **tip**

If you are using QuickBooks Accountant 2014 or QuickBooks Enterprise Solutions Accountant 14.0, you can convert your clients' QuickBooks 2013 or 2014 Accountant's Copy files (.QBX file extension), work with them in your QuickBooks Accountant 2014 or Enterprise Solutions Accountant 14.0, and return them to your clients to import back into their QuickBooks 2013 or 2014 versions. This feature is available only with the Accountant's Copy file sharing feature and does not apply to other file types.

QuickBooks Accountant can open a Pro or Premier industry-specific edition, and when the files are returned to the clients, they will be able to work again with the files in their product edition.

QuickBooks Enterprise Solutions can open an Accountant's Copy file from a Pro, Premier, or Enterprise file and return the file to the client for use in a Pro, Premier, or Enterprise product.

Method 1: Receiving Accountant's Copy from Client via Web

If your client chooses the Intuit's Accountant's Copy File Transfer secure server to get the data to you, you are notified at the email address the client provides in the transfer process, and you are directed to a secure site to download your client's file. This service offers your client simplicity in getting the data to you while aiding in the encrypted security of the transfer of sensitive data over the Internet.

📶 **caution**

You can download the client's file for only 14 days, so don't delay.

After downloading the file, follow the instructions in the next section for opening and converting the Transfer File (.QBX file extension) to an Accountant's Copy file (.QBA file extension).

Method 2: Receiving Accountant's Copy from Client via File

Have your client follow the steps to create and send you the Accountant's Copy file of the data, as you learned in the section "Create an Accountant's Copy of Your Data."

To work with the Accountant's Copy (.QBX) file type your client sent you or that you downloaded, follow these steps:

1. From the menu bar, select **File**, **Accountant's Copy**, **Open & Convert Transfer File**. The Open and Convert Accountant's Copy Transfer File dialog box displays, as in Figure 16.16. This summary provides you with an overview of the workflow when using an Accountant's Copy of your client's data.

Figure 16.16
Overview of the Accountant's Copy workflow when working with your client's data.

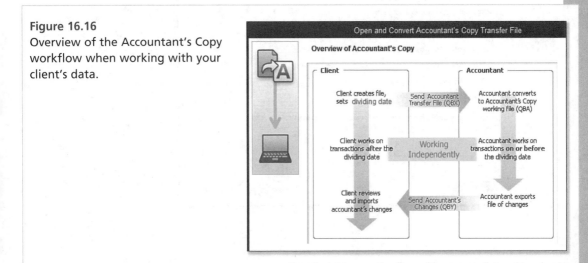

2. Click Next. The Open and Convert Accountant's Copy Transfer File dialog box displays. This provides details on what tasks you can and cannot do when working with an Accountant's Copy. See Figure 16.17. Click Next.

3. Browse to the location where you stored your client's QuickBooks transfer file. Select the file and click Open. If displayed, click OK to the message that you have chosen an Accountant's Copy transfer file.

4. In the Save Accountant's Copy dialog box, select a location and name for the new file. I usually put the accounting period being reviewed in the name, such as <Company Name_YE_12_31_XX.QBA>. Click Save. QuickBooks shows a message that the conversion is taking place.

5. If you have not previously disabled this warning, you will see a message indicating that you are opening an Accountant's Copy; it shows you the Dividing Date that your client chose (see Figure 16.18). Click OK to close.

6. Your QuickBooks Accountant title bar shows that you are working with an Accountant's Copy and shows the Dividing Date for that file (see Figure 16.19).

As the company's accounting professional, you can now review, add, and edit the data file without your clients being able to modify the balances before the Dividing Date—all while the clients continue their day-to-day accounting tasks.

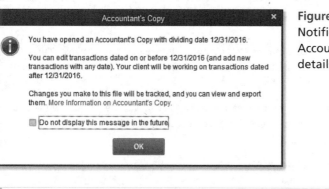

Figure 16.17
Review a summary of the tasks you can and cannot do when working with an Accountant's Copy file.

Open and Convert Accountant's Copy Transfer File

What the Accountant's Copy Can and Can't Do

In an Accountant's Copy, you CAN

- Edit and delete most types of transactions dated on or before the dividing date.
- Add new transactions with **any date** and add most types of list elements.
- Edit existing accounts, vendors and items.
- Merge, delete and reconcile accounts.

In an Accountant's Copy you CANNOT

- Edit or delete existing transactions dated after the dividing date.
- Edit or delete existing list elements, except those listed above.

More details on what you can and can't do

What your client can and can't do

If the Accountant's Copy does not meet your needs, you can convert it to a regular company file. How do I convert an Accountant's Copy to a regular company file?

☐ Do not display this page or the previous one in the future

| Back | Next | | Help | Cancel |

Figure 16.18
Notification that you are opening an Accountant's Copy file, and providing details of the selected Dividing Date.

Accountant's Copy

You have opened an Accountant's Copy with dividing date 12/31/2016.

You can edit transactions dated on or before 12/31/2016 (and add new transactions with any date). Your client will be working on transactions dated after 12/31/2016.

Changes you make to this file will be tracked, and you can view and export them. More Information on Accountant's Copy.

☐ Do not display this message in the future

OK

Figure 16.19
You can be certain you are working in the correct file by looking at the title bar of your Accountant's Copy .QBA file.

Rock Castle Construction (Acct Copy, Div Date 12/31/2016) - QuickBooks Accountant 2014

Accountant Company Customers Vendors Employees Banking Reports Window Help

| Calendar | Snapshots | Customers | Vendors | Employees | Docs | Reports | App Center | Invoice | User License |

Reinstate Warning Dialog Boxes

If you do not see some of the dialog boxes mentioned in this chapter, a user might have selected Do Not Display This Message (or Page, and so on, depending on which dialog box is open), causing future users not to see these messages.

To turn these one-time messages back on, log in to the file as the user for whom you want to reinstate the warnings and follow these steps:

1. From the menu bar, select **Edit**, **Preferences**. In the dialog box that displays, select **General** on the left side.

2. Click the My Preferences tab.

3. Place a checkmark in the Bring Back All One-Time Messages box and click OK.

I often do this task in my client's file (before making an Accountant's Copy), especially if I have found errors that might have been prevented if the user had heeded the warning of a previously dismissed message.

What the Accountant Can Do

Recent releases of the QuickBooks software have greatly improved the capabilities you have with an Accountant's Copy of your client's data.

The restrictions invoked by the Dividing Date your client sets affect your ability to add or edit transactions. If these restrictions prevent you from completing your tasks, you can convert the Accountant's Copy to a working QuickBooks data file (.QBW file extension). However, your changes cannot be imported into your client's file.

> ➥ *For more information, see "Converting the Accountant's Copy to a Regular Company File," p. 629.*

The Accountant's Copy provides a unique feature that helps you determine whether your changes will be sent back to the client's file. Any field that is colored beige will transfer back to your client. If the field is white, you might be able to modify it for your own purposes, but the change will not be sent back to your client.

For example, if part of your correction to your client's file was to modify an existing list item, only the fields in Figure 16.20 would be sent back to your client's data file. All other fields can be modified for your purposes, but they will not transfer back to your client's file. If you and your client make changes to details on the same item, your changes will override the client's when the changes are imported.

The following sections describe more specifically what you, the accountant, can do (with noted limitations) while working in the Accountant's Copy of your client's file.

Changes to these shaded fields will transfer to a client's file

Figure 16.20
When adding or modifying details in the Accountant's Copy, any fields shaded beige (non-white) will be sent back to your client's file.

Accounting Activities

Recent versions of QuickBooks enhance the accounting activities you can do with the client's data when sharing an Accountant's Copy file type:

- **Reconcile the bank statements for dates earlier than the Dividing Date**—You can create and edit transactions necessary to perform the bank reconciliation. Additionally, your changes to a reconciled item will be sent back to the client.

  Your client can reconcile the bank account when the statement date and all cleared transactions are dated after the selected Dividing Date. However, if you also reconcile this account, the client's bank reconciliation work will be rolled back to the transactions cleared status as of the time the Accountant's Copy was created.

- **Set 1099 account mappings**—You can assign the proper chart of account to the Federal Form 1099-MISC Income box.

- **Reconcile the bank statements for dates after the Dividing Date**—You can do this if it helps your review. However, these reconciliations will not be sent back to the client's data. Any transactions added will be sent back to the client.

- **Set tax-line mappings**—This assigns the tax form line to a chart of accounts. Use this feature if you are integrating the QuickBooks data with Intuit's tax-preparation software ProSeries or Lacerte.

QuickBooks Lists

Also enhanced with recent QuickBooks releases is your ability to manage your client's list items when performing data corrections:

- **Chart of Accounts**—No restrictions, including the capability to merge charts of account list items. For more information, see "Merging Duplicated Accounts," p. 134.

- **List Items**—In general, you can add, edit, delete, and inactivate list items you create in the Accountant's Copy.

- **Items List**—For lists with items dated before the Dividing Date, you can edit the Item Name/Number, Subitem, Expense Account, Tax Code, and Income Account, and also make the item inactive. Note that if you and your client both make changes to the same item, the accountant's changes will override that of the client when the changes are imported.

- **Customer, Other Names List**—Add a new Name, edit the Name field, or make the Name inactive.

- **Vendor**—Add a new vendor, edit the Vendor Name and Tax ID fields, and identify a vendor as eligible to receive a 1099-MISC Income form at year end. Additionally, you can assign up to three general ledger accounts on the Account Prefill tab. Your changes will override the same information in the client's file when imported.

- **Employee List**—Add a new employee or edit the Name and Social Security fields only.

- **Class List, Fixed Asset Item**—Merge class list items. Additionally, you can add a new list item or edit the Name, assign a Subclass Of field, or make the class inactive.

- **Sales Tax Code**—Add a new sales tax code, edit the Name and Tax Agency, and make the item inactive. You can create new sales tax items, but the tax rate assigned will not transfer to the client's file.

Transactions

Generally, you can add any transaction type before or after the Dividing Date, with the following limitations on editing, voiding, or deleting:

- **Bills and checks**—Add these types of transactions with dates before or after the Dividing Date. Capabilities to edit, void, or delete are limited to transactions dated before the Dividing Date.

- **Vendor credits**—Add these types of transactions with dates before or after the Dividing Date. Edit, void, and delete capabilities are limited to transactions dated before the Dividing Date.

- **Item receipts**—You can add or delete, but you cannot edit or void transactions before and after the Dividing Date.

- **Bill payments by credit card**—You can add or delete, but you cannot edit or void transactions before and after the Dividing Date.

- **Inventory quantity/value adjustments**—You can add or delete, but you cannot edit or void transactions before and after the Dividing Date.

- **Customer payments**—You can add or delete, but you cannot edit or void transactions before and after the Dividing Date.

What the Accountant Cannot Do

You, the accountant, *cannot do* the following while working in the Accountant's Copy of your client's file:

- Add or modify payroll transactions.

- Add or modify nonposting transactions, such as estimates, sales orders, or purchase orders.

- Add or modify transfers of funds between accounts. Although you cannot use the transfer transaction, you can create the same effect on the accounts with a journal entry or deposit transaction.

- Add or modify the build assembly transaction.

- Add or modify the sales tax payment transaction.

> **note**
>
> If you are working with a client's Accountant's Copy file created from a QuickBooks 2013 version, you can open the file with your QuickBooks Accountant 2014 and return the data to the client in the original QuickBooks 2013 version.

Although you cannot make changes to these types of transactions in your client's file with an Accountant's Copy file type, you can conveniently make these changes in the client's file using remote access via tools such as Webex, LogMeIn, and GoToMyPC.

Returning the Accountant's Copy Change File to the Client

One of the most important features of using the Accountant's Copy to share your clients' data is that when your changes are complete, you can send back updated files for your clients to import into their files.

Set a Closing Date

When your clients import the changes you have made to the Accountant's Copy of their files, the Dividing Date restrictions are removed. If you do not want a client to add or edit transactions before the Dividing Date, make sure you also set a closing date before you export the data for the client.

To set a closing date while working in the Accountant's Copy of your client's data, follow these steps:

1. Log in to the client's Accountant's Copy file. From the menu bar, select **Company**, **Set Closing Date**.

2. The Company Preference dialog box displays. Click the Set Date/Password button. The Set Closing Date and Password dialog box displays.

3. Enter an optional password and a closing date—typically the same date that was used for the Dividing Date.

4. Click OK to accept the closing date and optional closing date password.

The closing date transfers back to the client's file, and the client is not asked to set the closing date. The fact that a closing date was set is included in the information the client previews before incorporating the accountant's changes.

> **note**
>
> If you do not set a closing date as part of your changes, when the client incorporates the changes file, a message displays asking whether the client wants to set a closing date.

If you want your client to have the ability to modify your changes, you might not need to set a closing date for the file.

Review the details of setting a closing date and reviewing each employee's access rights to changing transactions before the closing date.

 For more information, see "Setting Employee Security," p. 614.

Method 1: Send Changes to Client via Web

The Send Changes method is the simplest for your client to use to import. This service is included with a QuickBooks ProAdvisor membership or is available for a nominal annual fee. No fee is charged to the client to accept this file from you.

To return the corrected file to your client after you make all your changes, follow these steps:

1. From the menu bar, select **File**, **Accountant's Copy**, **View/ Export Changes for Client**. The View/Export Changes for Client dialog box displays, as in Figure 16.21.

2. Review your changes and add an optional note for your client.

> **note**

If you have already exported these changes for the client, a message displays informing you that if your client has already imported the previously exported changes file, the client will not be able to import these changes. Click OK if you still want to export the changes.

Figure 16.21
In the View/Export Changes for Client dialog box, you can review your changes and include a note for your client.

Click to collapse the detail

3. If you need to make additional changes or edit the changes you have made to the file, click the X in the top-right corner.

4. If your changes are complete, click Send Changes to Client.

5. Enter your client's email address, your name, and your email address.

6. Click Send.

Intuit sends you an email notifying you that the file was uploaded to the Intuit Accountant's Copy File Transfer secure server. Your client also receives an email notification that the file is available for downloading for 30 days. Encourage your client to follow the instructions in the email to easily incorporate your changes into the data file.

Method 2: Send Changes to Client via File

You might also choose to send the Changes File to the client via a file you can attach to an email or store on a flash drive or other storage device. This method requires more effort from your customers. They must access the file, save it to their computer, and then import the changes into QuickBooks. Consider using the first method of sending the file via the Web, which does not require as many steps.

To create the Changes File (.QBY extension) to give to your client, follow these steps:

1. From the menu bar, select **File**, **Accountant's Copy**, **View/Export Changes for Client**. The View/Export Changes for Client dialog box displays (refer to Figure 16.21).

2. Review your changes and, optionally, add a note for your client.

3. If you need to make additional changes or edit the changes you have made to the file, click the X in the top-right corner.

4. If your changes are complete, click Create Change File. The Save Accountant Changes File to dialog box displays.

5. Browse to the location where you want to save the file, and optionally edit the filename to be saved. QuickBooks creates a file with a .QBY extension.

6. If you have already exported these changes for the client, you will see the message informing you that if your client has already imported the previously exported changes file, the client will not be able to import these changes. Click OK if you still want to export the changes.

7. Click Save. A message displays, letting you know the file was successfully created.

8. Click OK to close the message. QuickBooks returns you to the .QBA file.

To complete the process, simply give this newly created .QBY (Accountant's Copy import file) back to the client. You can copy it to a removable storage device or attach it to an email.

Instruct your client to follow the steps listed in the section "Method 2: Importing Accountant's Changes from File," p. 612. Your client will be able to review your changes in detail before accepting or incorporating the changes into her file.

QuickBooks Remote Access for Accountants

As the accountant, if you want to take more control over the import of your changes into your client's file, as well as for setting the closing date, you might want to consider using a remote access program to log into your client's file through the Internet.

QuickBooks partners with WebEx to bring you a solution that makes it easy to work remotely in your file or your clients' files. You can use this option if you need to make data changes that are not allowed in an Accountant's Copy—for example, making changes to payroll transactions. You can also use this tool to import your changes into your client's data file.

I find working in the remote environment perfect for simplifying the entire process for clients. For more information, select **Accountant**, **Remote Access** from the menu bar in QuickBooks Accountant or QuickBooks Enterprise Accountant.

What to Request from the Client When the Import Is Complete

Clients can import your changes with simple, easy-to-follow instructions if you used the Send Changes to Client method. However, you might want to request a few items from the client after the import to be sure the process completed successfully:

- **Trial Balance**—Review the Trial Balance report as of the Dividing Date to compare it with the same information from your copy of the client's file. From the menu bar, select **Reports**, **Accountant**, **Trial Balance**. Request that clients prepare the report in accrual or cash basis; they might have one as the default setup in their file.

- **Closing Date**—If you want to verify that the closing date was incorporated with your changes, instruct your client to select **Company**, **Set Closing Date** from the menu bar. Doing so opens the Company Preference tab for Accounting Preferences. Have your client verify the closing date (or any date at all). Refer to Figure 16.10.

- **User Security Rights**—Verify with your client the access rights each employee has for changing transactions dated before the closing date. Instruct your client to select **Company**, **Set Up Users and Passwords**, **Set Up Users** from the menu bar. In the User List dialog box that opens, select the employee and the View User tab on the right. A *Y* in the Changing Closed Transactions permission allows that user to add or edit transactions dated before the closing date. If a closing date password was set, the user must type that password first. A creative password that I have used is *call laura*, prompting the client to call me first before making the change.

Converting the Accountant's Copy to a Regular Company File

What can you do if, after beginning to work in the Accountant's Copy, you determine that this file type does not accommodate some of the changes that need to be made? You can convert the client's Accountant's Copy (.QBX) file type to a regular QuickBooks (.QBW) file type by following these steps.

From the menu bar, select **File**, **Accountant's Copy**, **Convert Accountant's Copy to Company File/ QBW**. A message displays, recommending that you contact your client to discuss this change.

You have to make the following decisions:

- Have the client manually repeat your changes in the client's file.

- If the client is going to use your file, the client must stop working in the file she has.

QuickBooks 2014 offers accountants more flexibility than previous versions in how you choose to share and work in your client's data. These improvements help make the workflow for you and your client more efficient, making your accounting business more profitable.

Other Methods of Sharing Data

With QuickBooks Accountant 2014, you have flexibility in choosing what method of file sharing works best for you and your client. When considering a method, your client needs to continue daily accounting tasks while allowing you to review the data and create journal entries.

Send General Journal Entries

Send General Journal Entries is available in QuickBooks 2014. It allows your accountant to share changes to your data easily with an email attachment.

The best practice when using this new feature is to have the business owner send the accountant either a copy of the working file (.QBW), a backup (.QBB), or a portable company file (.QBM). Business owners can continue to work in their files while that accountant reviews the copy at his or her office. This avoids the restrictions imposed when sharing an Accountant's Copy file.

The accountant's journal entries are emailed directly from QuickBooks, with no messy file transfers to worry about. Clients simply click the attachment to import the entries automatically into their file.

The best part about this new feature is that there are no new "tools" to learn for the accountant or your client. For the accountant, just follow these simple steps:

1. For the accounting professional, open or restore the file you have received from the client.

2. From the menu bar, select **Company**, **Make General Journal Entries**. Create the Journal Entry as you normally would. Click Save on the Main tab of the ribbon toolbar.

3. From the displayed Make General Journal Entries transaction, on the Main tab of the ribbon toolbar, click the Send GJEs icon. See Figure 16.22.

4. The Send General Journal Entries dialog box displays. Select a single journal entry or multiple journal entries. If needed, use the Dates or From and To fields to filter the displayed journal entries. See Figure 16.23.

> **note**
>
> To use the Send General Journal Entries method, the business owner must be using a Windows version of QuickBooks 2014 or newer, and the accountant must be using QuickBooks Accountant 2014 or QuickBooks Enterprise Accountant 14.0 or newer.

Figure 16.22
Click the Send GJEs icon to send to your client.

Figure 16.23
Select a single journal entry or multiple entries.

5. Place a check in the box in front of each journal entry you want to send to the client. (Optional) Click Select All or Deselect All.

6. Click the Email as Attachment button. QuickBooks utilizes the email program specified within your QuickBooks preferences. In the example in Figure 16.24, an Outlook email is created with instructions for your client. The journal entries are attached automatically.

QuickBooks creates a ready-made email communication, complete with instructions, and attaches the journal entry or entries. You do not need to browse to find and attach the entries.

The business owner receives the email and clicks the attachment to add to the business owner's file.

Recommend this method to your accountant, if the accountant has been sending a list of journal entries for you to enter manually.

Figure 16.24
Click the attachment to add to the currently open QuickBooks file.

---

caution

Take care not to click more than once on the attachment. QuickBooks allows the import of the attachment more than once, misstating the financials from what the accountant provided. If this happens to you, prepare a report that shows the duplication and click one of the duplicated entries. From the Edit menu, select **Void**.

If the journal entry includes a new general ledger account (chart of account), vendor, customer, or other list item, this new list item will be created in the business owner's file automatically.

If you have more than one QuickBooks company file, it works best to have that company file open before clicking the attachment. If you have the wrong file open, QuickBooks provides a warning message but will not prevent you from incorporating the changes into the wrong file.

Batch Enter Transactions

The improved batch transaction entry feature offers accounting professionals a way to streamline data entry tasks. This feature is also useful for business owners who do batch entry of transactions when using QuickBooks Enterprise. This feature is included only with QuickBooks Accountant 2014 and all versions of QuickBooks Enterprise 14.0.

Use Batch Enter Transactions to add the following to a QuickBooks data file:

- Checks
- Deposits
- Credit card charges or credits
- Vendor bills and bill credits
- Customer invoices and credit memos

Typically, accounting professionals offer services that help clients enter data into QuickBooks. With the Batch Enter Transactions feature, you can do the following:

- Enter transactions in batches on a screen designed for power data entry.

- Paste 1,000+ transactions from Excel and save all at once.

- Enter after-the-fact transactions easily into a customizable data entry grid.

- Configure the batch entry screen, including specifying data fields and column order.

Accounting professionals, follow these steps to use this helpful feature:

1. From the menu bar, select **Accountant**, **Batch Enter Transactions**. A dialog box of the same name displays. For all other Enterprise users, you can access the same feature from the menu bar by selecting **Company**, **Batch Enter Transactions**.

2. From the Transaction Type drop-down menu, select **Checks**, **Deposits**, **Credit Card Charges & Credits**, **Bills & Bill Credits or Invoices & Credit Memos**. I demonstrate entering checks, but the procedure is similar for other permitted transaction types.

3. Select the appropriate Bank Account or Credit Card account.

4. Click the Customize Columns button (see Figure 16.25). You can add or remove data fields and rearrange the order of the fields. This is particularly useful if you are using Excel's copy and paste functionality.

5. Add transactions to the Batch Enter Transactions dialog box by manually entering them or from an Excel worksheet (see Figure 16.26) using the Windows copy and paste functionality.

> **tip**
>
> If your transactions are in Excel, customize the columns of the Batch Enter Transactions dialog box to match those of your Excel spreadsheet. You can then copy the transaction data from Excel and paste it into the Batch Entry screen in QuickBooks.

> **note**
>
> If you are copying data from Excel and the list item does not exist in the QuickBooks file, the item text appears red. See Figure 16.27. Simply click through the field, and you are given the opportunity to add the list item to QuickBooks.

Figure 16.25
Customize the columns to aid in data entry or to match the Excel worksheet you are copying from.

Figure 16.26
Copy and paste transactions from Excel to add to the Batch Enter Transactions dialog box.

Figure 16.27
When adding data from an Excel spreadsheet, fields with values not recognized in QuickBooks appear in red type.

This feature supports transaction entry using the Expenses tab details (shown in these figures) and also supports the Items tab details. However, you can use only one or the other in the same Batch Enter Transactions session.

In effect, this feature allows accounting professionals to automate the process of entering large amounts of data into a client's QuickBooks data file. Access to this in QuickBooks Enterprise gives companies the option of entering data in batch from an Excel spreadsheet.

Client and Accountant Collaboration

As a business owner, how often do you contact your accountant by email or phone to ask a question about specific transactions? Or as an accounting professional, how often do you review your client's data and find yourself making a list of questions about transactions?

New for QuickBooks 2014 is the QuickBooks Client Collaborator. This new feature helps the business owner and the accounting professional efficiently ask transaction-specific questions and track each other's replies.

The accountant initiates collaboration using QuickBooks Accountant 2014 PLUS or QuickBooks Enterprise Accountant 14.0 software. Business owners wanting to collaborate with their accountant using this feature must be using any Windows desktop version of QuickBooks 2014, including Pro, Premier, or Enterprise.

The QuickBooks Client Collaborator includes the following features:

- Capability to create a list of questions associated with specific transactions

- Automated notification to the business owner of the transaction question(s)

- Business owner replies or additional questions added directly inside the QuickBooks file

- Automated notification to the accountant of the business owner replies

- Capability for the accountant to review the business owner's transaction conversation replies and mark them as closed

Specifically, Client Collaborator is a timesaving solution that helps the accountant and business owner converse about specific transactions without leaving the QuickBooks file. Accounting professionals can begin using the feature from any file type from the client, including backup, portable company, accountant's copy, or working copy.

Client Collaborator is a connected service, and the Transaction Conversation List is stored in the "cloud." Access to the Transaction Conversation List is launched from within QuickBooks. The accountant and business owner can both collaborate while working in two different copies of the same file. The transaction conversation is not stored with the actual data file, but it continues as a conversation list for reviews from future copies of the client's file.

Access to Client Collaborator

For the accounting professional, Client Collaborator is included with a subscription to QuickBooks Accountant 2014 PLUS software or QuickBooks Enterprise Accountant 14.0 software. Business owners using QuickBooks Pro or Premier 2014 and QuickBooks Enterprise 14.0 can collaborate with their accountant for no additional fee.

Accounting professionals have two methods for subscribing to the QuickBooks Accountant 2014 PLUS software:

- QuickBooks ProAdvisors with a current, paid membership receive the QuickBooks Accountant 2014 PLUS subscription automatically.

- Accountants can purchase the QuickBooks Accountant 2014 PLUS software, paying in monthly installments or as a yearly fee.

Accountants using QuickBooks Enterprise Accountant 14.0 as part of their ProAdvisor membership automatically have access to the Client Collaborator.

How the Accountant Gets Started

The collaboration experience is initiated by the accountant and accepted by the business owner in just a few easy, automated steps.

1. To begin collaborating, open a transaction as in Figure 16.28 in the business owner's file. From the menu bar, select **Accountant**, **Ask Client About Transaction**.

Figure 16.28
The accountant begins the conversation with a transaction displayed in a copy of the file at the accountant's office.

2. The Sign in to Your Intuit Account window displays. Enter your email or user ID and password.

3. Click Sign In. If you have used this email with other Intuit-connected services, you might be prompted to select your company file (not your client's file).

4. Client Collaborator prompts you to enter your client's email address. This email address will receive automated notifications generated by the Client Collaborator.

5. Click Send, and an automated email notification is sent to the email address specified here. Click Close to the "Your invitation" message.

6. After the client has accepted the accountant's invitation, Client Collaborator generates an email notification (see Figure 16.29) to the accountant using the accountant's email address, as specified by the client. The accountant clicks the link Sign in to <company name> provided in the email.

7. A web browser opens to Client Collaborator. The accountant signs into the Intuit account (not shown). After a successful sign-in, the accountant receives a "You Are Now Connected with Your Client" message.

Collaboration can begin in both the copy of the business owner's file at the accountant's office and the file the business owner is using at the place of business.

These one-time collaboration steps are now complete. This section discusses both the accountant and client actions, but in real life, you have to complete only one; all notifications are automated.

Figure 16.29
QuickBooks Client Collaborator automates notices to both the accountant and the business owner.

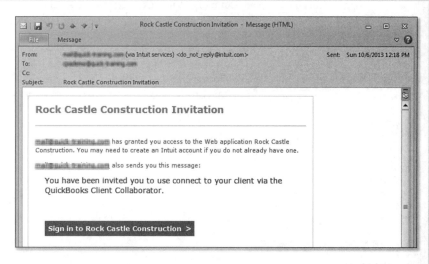

How the Business Owner Gets Started

After the accountant has initiated a request for collaboration, the business owner follows these few steps, all completed conveniently in his or her own copy of the file.

1. The business owner receives an automated email from the accountant with instructions (see Figure 16.30), inviting him or her to join the Transaction Conversation.

Figure 16.30
All communications are automated, saving time for both the accountant and the business owner.

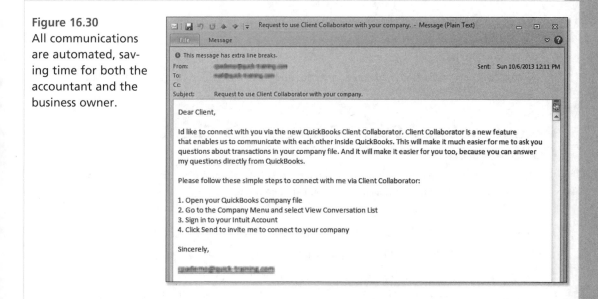

2. From the menu bar, select **Company**, **View Conversation List**, shown in Figure 16.31, and as detailed in the email received. You are then prompted for your Intuit account email or user ID and password.

Company	Customers	Vendors	Employees	Ban
Home Page				
Company Snapshot				
Calendar				
Documents			▸	
Lead Center				
My Company				
Advanced Service Administration...				
Set Up Users and Passwords			▸	
Customer Credit Card Protection...				
Set Closing Date...				
Ask Accountant about Transaction...				
View Conversation List...				
Planning & Budgeting			▸	

Figure 16.31
All communications are accessed by the client directly in the QuickBooks file at their office.

3. The Client Collaborator window displays. Enter the accountant's email address for future communications using Client Collaborator.

4. Click Send. Client Collaborator automatically sends a notification to the accountant, allowing him or her to collaborate with you.

So simple! Business owners get started quickly and from the convenience of their own file. For the accounting professional, there's no need to ask for a new copy of the client's file—the collaboration is all stored in the "cloud."

With all the communication between accountant and client automated, working with Client Collaborator is just smart.

Accountant and Client Converse via Client Collaborator

The accounting professional initiates the request for collaboration. When the business owner accepts the initial invitation, full collaboration can take place.

Accountant Asks Questions

The accounting professional follows these steps to begin collaborating:

1. The accountant opens a copy of the business owner's file for review at the accountant's office. The file copy can be a backup copy (.QBB), portable company file (.QBM), the accountant's copy (.QBA) or even a working copy of the file (.QBW).

2. With a transaction displayed, from the menu bar, select **Accountant, Ask Client About Transaction**. Beginning with maintenance release R3, you can also access this option from the icon drop-down menu on the far right of the menu bar.

> *For more information, refer to "Installing a QuickBooks Maintenance Release," p. 652.*

3. You are prompted to sign in to your Intuit account.

4. The Transaction Conversation window in Figure 16.32 shows the details of the displayed transaction added to the collaborator. Type a comment or question in the space provided. Click Add to Conversation List & Close, or click Add & Open Conversation List.

5. To view the Conversation List as in Figure 16.33, from the menu bar, select **Accountant, View Conversation List**.

note

Client Collaborator stays signed in as long as users are actively adding questions or making comments to the list. After 30 minutes of inactivity, the accountant must sign in again.

Figure 16.32
Accountants ask questions about specific transactions.

Client Collaborator

Transaction Conversation

Privacy Policy

DATE	TYPE	REF#	NAME	AMOUNT
03/01/2012	Bill		Kershaw Computer Services	2,714.00

ENTER COMMENT/QUESTION

Is this the purchase of the new office server?

[Add to Conversation List & Close]   [Add & Open Conversation List]   [Cancel]

6. Click Notify Client, and a single email advises the client that there is a Conversation List to review. The automated email does not include details of the questions and transactions.

7. Optionally, click Close next to a Transaction Conversation to remove it from the list that the client will see. Only the accountant can mark a Transaction Conversation as closed.

The accountant now waits for an automated notification that the client has provided replies to the accountant's comments or questions. No phone calls, no emails to keep track of!

Figure 16.33
The list of questions can be reviewed.

Business Owner Responds to Accountant's Questions

Not only does the accountant work more efficiently, but so does the business owner. No interrupting emails or phone calls addressing questions about transactions—let QuickBooks Client Collaborator do the work!

1. The business owner receives an automated email notification that the accountant has questions.

2. The business owner launches the Client Collaborator from the file by selecting from the menu bar, **Company**, **View Conversation List**.

3. The business owner is prompted to sign into his or her Intuit account with the correct user ID and password.

4. The most recent updated Transaction Conversation List (see Figure 16.34) displays because it is stored in the "cloud," not with the file. The business owner adds comments or additional questions and clicks Add This Message to the Conversation List.

Figure 16.34
The business owner replies to the transaction questions directly in the QuickBooks file.

5. When the business owner has completed his or her replies or comments, he or she clicks Notify Accountant. The accountant receives one email instructing him or her to access the Conversation List from the copy of the client's file the accountant has at the office. The email notification does not include any specifics about the Transaction Conversation.

6. The collaboration comes full circle now, when the accountant receives an automated email notice that there are replies and/or comments from the business owner.

The accountant then uses whatever method he or she has in place to make these changes to the business owner's file. Client Collaborator simply solves the need for discussion about specific transactions.

MANAGING YOUR QUICKBOOKS DATABASE

This reference guide would be incomplete without a detailed discussion of the QuickBooks database and how to manage it. This chapter provides guidelines for both the business owner and the computer professional for managing the QuickBooks database and handling any issues that can arise.

The QuickBooks Database

If you are the typical QuickBooks user, you purchased the software to track the income and expenses of your business. By selecting software for this task, you have advanced from a manual recordkeeping system into the world of database technology.

A database is an automated version of a big file room, with information of different types stored in different cabinets, drawers, and files. Years ago, companies employed file clerks to keep track of paperwork. QuickBooks uses a Database Server to perform similar tasks to a file clerk: organizing and storing the data you create.

Depending on the number of licenses you purchased, you can choose to install the software as a single-user application or install it in a network environment for use by multiple users (see Figure 17.1).

Based on your installation selection, QuickBooks installs either the personal Database Server or the network Database Server to control the flow of data from the QuickBooks application to your QuickBooks Company file. During installation, the computer operating system creates a Windows user account for this server so that it can assign administrative-level access rights to the computer's resources and the QuickBooks files. When you view your list of users for your computer, included is the QBDataServiceUser*xx* (where *xx* defaults to 24 for all QuickBooks 2014 versions). During installation, the QuickBooks Database Server Manager is also installed. This utility is discussed in this chapter on page 648.

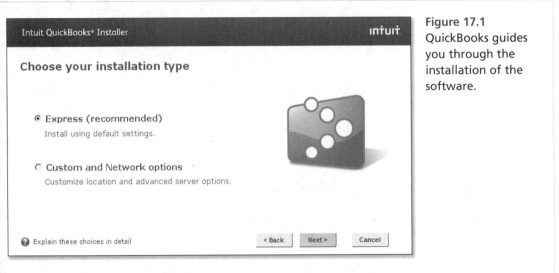

Figure 17.1
QuickBooks guides you through the installation of the software.

System Requirements

Verify that your computer and network hardware meet the minimum requirements for QuickBooks. This list is applicable to QuickBooks 2014 versions, but you might want to check the requirements for your specific version.

Following are supported operating systems for QuickBooks for Windows products:

- Windows 8, either 32-bit or 64-bit versions (must be on R4 or newer maintenance patch), natively installed.

- Windows 7, either 32-bit or 64-bit versions, natively installed.

- Windows Vista, Service Pack 1, including either 32-bit or 64-bit versions, natively installed.

- Windows XP, Service Pack 3 and later, natively installed.

Computer processor, memory, and disk space requirements are as follows:

- Minimum of 2.0GHz processor; 2.4GHz is recommended.

- Minimum of 1GB of RAM for single-user configurations; 2GB of RAM recommended for multiple users. 2GB RAM required for Windows 8 64-bit version.

- Minimum of 2GB of RAM for multiuser configurations; 4GB (or more) is recommended.

- Minimum of 2.5GB of disk space for the application.

- 250MB for Microsoft .NET 4.0 Runtime. Additional space is required for your QuickBooks data files.

 caution

Do not delete QBDataServiceUser24 (or whatever version you are running) from the User's applet within the Control Panel.

note

QuickBooks system requirements, browsers supported, and integrated software capabilities are always changing. For the most current requirements; visit www.quickbooks.com/support and in the search field type "system requirements."

Additional hardware, software, and Internet connectivity requirements include the following:

- Hardware

  - 4x CD-ROM drive required for CD installations

  - 1024×768 or higher screen resolution, 16-bit or higher color

- **Multiuser**—Microsoft Windows XP (SP3), Vista (SP1 with UAC on), Windows 8 (with UAC on), Windows 7 (with UAC on), Windows Server 2003 (SP2), Windows Server 2008, Small Business Server 2008, Windows Small Business Server 2011, Windows Server 2012 (Windows Home Server *not* supported)

- Internet connectivity

  - Internet access with at least 56Kbps connection speed

  - Cable or DSL modem highly recommended over dial-up service

  - Internet Explorer 7, 8, or 9

- Minimum browser requirement—Internet Explorer 7, 8, 9, and 10 with maintenance release 3 or newer, as discussed in this chapter (Firefox and Chrome are not currently supported)

- Software for integration capabilities

  - Word 2003, 2007, 2010, or 2013/365, and Excel 2003, 2007, or 2010 (including 64-bit) for Microsoft Word and Excel integration

  - QuickBooks Contact Sync for Outlook 2003, 2007, and 2010 (including 64-bit) for synchronization with Outlook (downloadable for free at www.quickbooks.com/contact_sync)

    ➡ *To learn more about synchronization with Outlook, see "Using Other Planning and Management Tools," p. 675.*

  - Email Estimates, Invoices, and other forms with Windows Outlook, Outlook Express, and Mozilla Thunderbird, as well as web mail services such as Gmail, Yahoo! Mail, and Hotmail

  - Compatibility with QuickBooks Point of Sale version 10.0

- Capability to import data from Excel and other programs

  - Capability to transfer data from Peachtree 2001–2011, Microsoft SBA 2006, and Microsoft Office Accounting 2007–2009 using the free tool available at http://quickbooks.intuit.com. If converting from Peachtree 2012 or later, only lists and balances are imported, no historical transactions are imported.

  - Capability to transfer data directly from Quicken 2012 through the current version, QuickBooks 4.0 through current version, and Microsoft Excel 2000–2010. Currently, Microsoft Excel 2013 is not supported.

> **🔍 note**
>
> As of the writing of this book, Microsoft Office 2013 is not supported. However, integrated software capabilities are always changing. To see if your version of Office is supported, visit www. quickbooks.com/support and type **"system requirements."**

Antivirus and firewall compatibility considerations include the following:

- Antivirus products (with/without firewalls) software compatibility
  - Symantec/Norton Antivirus, Internet Security, Norton 360
  - McAfee Internet Security, Total Protection, VirusScan Plus
  - Trend Micro PC—cillin
  - ZoneAlarm

- Windows firewall compatibility
  - Windows 7 firewall (all versions)
  - Windows Vista firewall (all versions)
  - Windows XP firewall (all versions)

Express Installation of QuickBooks

Select the **Express** option (see Figure 17.1) when you need to use QuickBooks from a single computer and you want to replace your original version of the software with the new software. QuickBooks Pro and Premier defaults the install of the application and database manager in the `C:\Program Files\Intuit\QuickBooks 2014` folder. QuickBooks Enterprise Solutions defaults to the `C:\Program Files\Intuit\QuickBooks Enterprise Solutions 14.0` folder. You can browse to a location of your choosing for the installation files.

By default, QuickBooks uses the following locations for storing your data file. If you have previously created a file, the default is the last known directory a file was created in, although you can select a different directory:

- **Windows**—`C:\Users\Public\Documents\Intuit\QuickBooks\Company Files`

- **Windows 7**—`C:\Users\Public\Public Documents\Intuit\QuickBooks\Company Files`

- **Windows XP**—`C:\Documents and Settings\All Users\Documents\Intuit\QuickBooks\Company Files`

- **Windows Vista**—`C:\Users\Public\Public Documents\Intuit\QuickBooks\Company Files`

QuickBooks prompts you to enter the license and product numbers; you can find these numbers on a bright yellow sticker on the QuickBooks CD sleeve, or if you have downloaded the software, you will receive an email with the license details. Follow the remaining instructions for installing the QuickBooks software.

Installing QuickBooks for Multiuser Mode

QuickBooks 2014 streamlines the process of installing QuickBooks for multiuser simultaneous access to your company data. As discussed in the introduction, when QuickBooks is going to be used in a multiuser configuration, one computer on your network must act as the QuickBooks Server to host your data files and the QuickBooks Database Server.

Using an actual computer to run Windows Server software as your QuickBooks host is not necessary because QuickBooks runs equally well on peer-to-peer and client/server domain networks. When you install QuickBooks on a network, you should always perform the installation on the computer that functions as the server before installing QuickBooks on any workstations.

During installation, QuickBooks prompts you to select the installation type (see Figure 17.1). Select **Custom and Network Option** for all network installations, including server (host) and workstations (clients). Follow the remaining prompts to select the installation options that best fit your network requirements for the specific computer you are installing. Choices include the following:

- **I'll Be Using QuickBooks on This Computer**—Choose this if you are installing QuickBooks on a computer that will access only the Company files across the network.

- **I'll Be Using QuickBooks on This Computer, AND I'll Be Storing Our Company File Here So It Can Be Shared Over Our Network**—You will possibly run QuickBooks from this machine and have it act as your QuickBooks Server, which hosts your Company files.

- **I Will NOT be Using QuickBooks on This Computer**—You can elect to install only the QuickBooks Database Server and the QuickBooks Database Server Manager Utility on the hosting computer. This install does not require a license.

During the installation, you might be prompted with Validate Your Intuit User ID or with the option to create one. This step is optional. If you choose to enter or create a new account, Intuit populates your registration for you. If you choose to skip entering your User ID, you are prompted to enter your license and product numbers. Follow all additional prompts to complete the installation process.

When all your settings are correct for your network, click Install from the Ready to Install dialog box. As with the Express install, QuickBooks displays a progress bar indicating the status of the install process. The Congratulations dialog box displays when the installation is finalized. You can either launch QuickBooks to begin creating a new file or open an existing file or a practice file.

> **tip**
> Choosing the option I'll Be Using QuickBooks on This Computer, AND I'll Be Storing Our Company File Here So It Can Be Shared Over Our Network is the preferred server option, even if QuickBooks is not routinely used on this machine. Selecting this option allows the QuickBooks application to be opened on the server to perform certain file-related functions, including backup activities.

> **caution**
> If you selected the I Will NOT be Using QuickBooks on This Computer option, you should also review the upcoming section "The QuickBooks Database Server Manager."

➡️ *For more information, see "Getting Started with QuickBooks," p. 35.*

The QuickBooks Database Server Manager

The QuickBooks Database Server Manager Utility is automatically installed if you selected the option I Will NOT Be Using QuickBooks on This Computer. I Will Be Storing Our Company File Here So It Can Be Shared Over Our Network (A License Is Not Required For This Option). This utility launches automatically after the installation completes.

> **note**
>
> The QuickBooks Database Server Manager is needed only if you are using QuickBooks in multiuser mode.

Changing to Multiuser Access

If you initially installed QuickBooks for single-user access and want to change it to multiuser access, follow these steps to enable the Database Server Manager utility:

1. From the menu bar, select **File**, **Utilities**, **Host Multiuser Access**.

2. Click Yes to the Start Hosting Multiuser Access message that displays.

3. Click Yes to the Company File Must Be Closed message. If prompted, click Continue to allow Windows administrator permissions, and click Yes to allow the changes to be made to your computer.

4. Read the information on the Multiuser Setup Information message that displays. Click OK to close.

QuickBooks installs the network database server as a Windows service/process, and it is configured to run under the QBDataServiceUser24 Windows user account. (This is the user account assigned to QuickBooks 2014.)

The QuickBooks Database Server Manager utility gives users access to configure the database server. It is critical that this utility run and be properly configured to permit multiuser simultaneous access to your QuickBooks Company data files.

Opening the QuickBooks Data Server Manager

Your computer might display the utility in your system tray in the lower right of your computer taskbar. If not, you can open the QuickBooks Data Server Manager by following these steps:

1. From the Windows Orb or Windows Start button (lower-left corner of Windows taskbar), click All Programs.

2. Scroll to find and select the QuickBooks folder.

3. Click the QuickBooks Database Server Manager. If prompted, click Yes to the User Account Control Message. The Database Server Manager is launched (see Figure 17.2). The data path this figure displays might differ from your own data path.

The Scan Folders tab consists of two main panels, each performing critical functions. The first is to identify the various Windows folders on the QuickBooks server computer that contain QuickBooks data files. To add folders, click the Add Folder button and use the Windows directory service display to locate all folders appropriate for your network configuration.

Figure 17.2
The Database Server Manager helps configure proper multiuser hosting.

When all folders containing QuickBooks data files display in the top panel, perform a scan of those folders to locate your QuickBooks files; these files then appear in the lower panel. As a result of this scanning process, the Database Server creates a *.QBW.ND file for every QuickBooks Company file. This Network Description file contains critical information about the Database Server's location on your network, including the server name and IP address. When a QuickBooks workstation accesses the Company file, the companion *QBW.ND file advises QuickBooks on where and how to find the Database Server.

The QuickBooks Administrator should also configure the Monitored Drives tab, selecting the computer disk drive(s) containing the folders where QuickBooks Company files are located. The utility then monitors these drives to identify new *.QBW or *.QBA files that might be added to those drives and directories.

➡ *For more information about these named QuickBooks file types, see "Choosing a Method to Share Data," p. 599.*

🌐 tip

If your QuickBooks network suddenly starts suffering from an incapability to connect one or more workstations in multiuser mode to your Company file, you should promptly check to ensure that the QuickBooks Database Server Manager is running and still configured on the hosting computer.

Some Windows updates require a reboot of the computer. The QuickBooks Database Server Manager Service might have been stopped in the process. Contact your IT professional to restart the process. You might also need to perform the Scan function again to locate the data files on your computer.

The Database Server tab displays information about the Database Server, the current QuickBooks Company file(s) in use, and the name of the user logged in. The Updates tab provides information about the current version of the QuickBooks Database Server; it is essential that the Database Server version always match the QuickBooks version in use.

For QuickBooks to operate properly, never close the QuickBooks Database Server Manager unless you must also shut down the server for other reasons. A best practice is to minimize the utility instead.

Windows Permissions Required for QuickBooks

Simply installing QuickBooks for single-user or multiuser configuration does not guarantee that it will work properly. Certain Windows user permissions must be established to ensure proper access. All QuickBooks users must have full control, including read/write privileges for any directory from which Company data files will be accessed.

Setting Permissions in Windows 7 or Windows Vista

To properly configure Windows 7 or Windows Vista user permissions, follow these steps:

1. Using Windows Explorer, locate the folder that contains your QuickBooks Company files.

2. Right-click the folder and select **Properties**.

3. Click the Sharing tab, and then click the Share button.

4. In the File Sharing window, use the drop-down list to select each user that needs access to QuickBooks, and then click Add.

5. In the Permission Level column, click the Read drop-down list and select **Read/Write**.

6. Click the Share button to close the File Sharing window; then in the Properties window, click the Security tab.

7. Click the Edit button for the Group or usernames section.

8. Select the **QBDataServiceUser24 User**.

9. In Permissions for QBDataServiceUser24, select the **Full Control** checkbox in the Allow column and click OK.

10. Click Close.

Setting Permissions in Windows XP Professional

To properly configure Windows XP Professional user permissions, follow these steps:

1. Using Windows Explorer, locate the folder that contains your QuickBooks Company files.

2. Right-click the folder and select **Properties**.

3. Click Sharing, Share This Folder.

4. Click the Permissions button.

5. In the Group or usernames section, select **Everyone**.

6. In the Permissions for Everyone section, select the Full Control checkbox in the Allow column.

Setting Permissions in Windows 8

Before you begin sharing files and folders, make sure you're logged in to Windows as Administrator. Follow these steps to properly set permissions for sharing a folder that resides in local drives or User Profile folders.

1. From the right-click context menu, open Properties.

2. Click the Sharing tab.

3. From the Network File and Folder Sharing tab, click Share to open File Sharing.

4. Select **Everyone** from the drop-down menu and click Add. This adds the Everyone group in the File Sharing list and enables you to change folder access permissions.

5. From the Read drop-down menu, select **Read and Write Permissions** to users.

6. (Optional) Remove the Everyone group from the File Sharing list.

7. Be certain that QBDataServiceUser24User has been included in the permission settings.

8. Click Share to share the folder on the network.

Keeping Your Software Current

Intuit has a service discontinuation policy on its software. Live technical support and add-on business services such as payroll, credit card processing, QuickBooks Email, and online banking will be discontinued for versions three years or older.

Typically, you need to upgrade your software by May 31 each year for versions of QuickBooks three years or older to retain these active services.

Upgrading Your QuickBooks Version

To keep your QuickBooks software supported, you need to upgrade at least every three years—or, if you are like me, you might want to upgrade each year to take advantage of the newest features.

If you are using QuickBooks Enterprise and you subscribe to the annual Full Service Plan, you receive the newest software version each year, in addition to having access to elite technical support.

tip

I recommend selecting **Change the Install Location** during the installation. This retains the previous version of QuickBooks, in case you run into any issues with the new installation.

After you have successfully upgraded your data to the newest version, you can then uninstall the earlier version of the software using Windows Uninstall.

If you have used QuickBooks and you purchase the newest-year edition, you upgrade your QuickBooks file. QuickBooks Pro and Premier both can be upgraded to a QuickBooks Enterprise Solutions file. QuickBooks Enterprise Solutions cannot be downgraded to a QuickBooks Pro or Premier file.

The upgrade process is quite simple. If an earlier installation of QuickBooks is detected, you have the options to upgrade or change the installation location. If you want to upgrade the earlier version, select **Replace the Version Selected Below with the Version I'm Installing Now**. From the drop-down list, select the version you want to upgrade. The Windows path for your current version of QuickBooks displays.

However, if you want to install QuickBooks 2014 without upgrading any existing version, select the **Change the Install Location** option. Select a different location by clicking the Browse button and locating a new installation folder. If the folder you want to use does not exist, click the Create New Folder icon for your installation. Follow the instructions for completing the installation process.

note

Are you worried about changes made to the software when upgrading? No worries—for QuickBooks 2014, you can easily review improvements with the What's New tips.

At any time, from the menu bar, select **Help, What's New** to see the overlay of tips for working with the newest version of QuickBooks.

Installing a QuickBooks Maintenance Release

After a version is released, changes, improvements, and fixes are provided in the form of a maintenance release. Often Intuit offers the release as a manual download only. This is usually during the testing phase, and you might not want to install the update in this phase.

To choose how QuickBooks detects whether a maintenance release exists, follow these steps:

1. From the menu bar, select **Help, Update QuickBooks**.

2. The Overview tab displays on the Update QuickBooks dialog box. Read the provided information. (Optional) Click Update Now if you want to complete the task.

3. Click the Options tab and select from the following:

   ■ **Automatic Update**—If you select Yes, QuickBooks automatically downloads the update and provides a dialog box for you to install the update the next time you launch QuickBooks.

note

An Internet connection is required to download and install the release patches.

- **Shared Download**—If you work with multiusers accessing QuickBooks, select Yes to share the download with the others. This saves time and ensures that other users can access the newly updated file.

- **Download Location**—QuickBooks displays the location and name of the downloaded file.

4. You can then choose which updates to install:

- Payroll, Federal and State Forms Engine

- Employee Organizer

- Maintenance Releases

- Help and Other Updates

5. Click Save if you have made your changes, Revert to return to the original settings, or Close if you have not made any changes. (Optional) Click Help for more guidance.

6. Click the Update Now tab. From this tab, you can choose which updates to install, learn when they were last checked, and view the status.

7. (Optional) Select **Reset Update** to reinstall the entire update, or select **Get Updates**.

8. A progress message displays. Click Close when finished.

To install the newest maintenance release, you might need to close QuickBooks and reopen the software. You can also check the product information window from an open QuickBooks file by pressing F2 or Ctrl+1 on your keyboard; then you can read the Product line at the top (see Figure 17.6).

Protecting Your QuickBooks Database

It is a good practice to protect your QuickBooks data and safeguard it against some unforeseen catastrophic event. In addition to making a backup of your data regularly, you might consider including power protection, virus protection, and computer disk defragmentation.

> **🔍 note**
>
> You can perform a backup with multiple users logged in to the file. However, the backup process will not perform the recommended verification of the data as part of the backup.

Creating a QuickBooks Backup

Even with the best planning and safeguards, unforeseen catastrophic events can happen. Safeguard your company data by creating a regular backup.

Ideally, you should back up your Company files at the end of each session. However, if you are working in a multiuser environment, you should routinely wait until the end of each workday to back up. If your computer has more than one drive, you can back up onto a different disk drive from the one where your QuickBooks data is normally stored. If you have only one hard drive, you should back up onto some type of removable media, such as a USB flash memory drive.

To make a backup of your QuickBooks data, follow these steps:

1. From the menu bar, select **File**, **Back Up Company**, **Create Local Backup**. The Create Backup dialog displays with Local Backup selected.

2. (Optional) Click the Options button. The Backup Options dialog box displays (see Figure 17.3). Setting these options enables preferences for this and future backups.

Figure 17.3
Create a backup of your QuickBooks file for safekeeping.

3. Click the Browse button and browse to select a location to save your backup. It is recommended that you save your backup file to a location other than the location where the data is stored.

4. (Optional) Choose to Add the Date and Time, and to Limit the Number of Backup Copies in the selected folder.

5. Select the **Complete Verification** (recommended) option. For more information, see the section titled "Using the Verify Data Utility" in this chapter.

6. Click OK. If you have selected a location for the backup that is on the same drive where the data is stored, a warning message might display, recommending that you change the location for the backup copy. Click Change Location (recommended) or Use This Location.

7. From the Create Backup dialog box, click Next.

8. Select **Save It Now** and click Next.

> **⚠ caution**
> Complete Verification is available only when the file is in single-user mode when performing the backup.

9. Type a filename for your backup, or accept the default filename.

10. Click Save.

Automating Your QuickBooks Backup

To create a schedule for automatically backing up your QuickBooks data file, follow these steps:

1. Follow steps 1–7 listed in the previous section titled "Creating a QuickBooks Backup."

2. Select one of the following options: **Save It Now and Schedule Future Backups** or **Only Schedule Future Backups**. The Where Do You Want to Backup Your Company File? message displays if you have not previously set your file to back up automatically.

3. If you want QuickBooks to back up automatically when you close the file, you can define how many times you can close the Company file before the automatic backup is done. To do so, select **Save Backup Copy Automatically**....

4. To set a backup on a schedule, click the New button to display the schedule details (see Figure 17.4). Type a description for the backup, browse to the desired location, and define the number of Backup Copies to Keep.

Figure 17.4
Schedule an automatic backup of the QuickBooks file.

5. Specify the Start Time, how often the task is run, and on what specific days.

6. (Optional) Click Store Password if your computer is password protected. Click OK to return to the Schedule Backup dialog box.

7. Click OK to close the Schedule Backup dialog box.

8. Click Finish to save the schedule.

9. Click OK to close the confirmation message that a backup has been scheduled.

Restoring a Backup

If you find you need to restore your data from a backup, follow these steps:

1. From the menu bar, select **File**, **Open or Restore Company**.

2. Select **Restore a Backup Copy**. Click Next.

3. Select **Local Backup**. Click Next.

4. Locate the backup file and click Open.

5. Click Next after reading the message Where Do You Want to Restore the File.

6. Browse to select the location and type a name for the restored file. Click Save.

7. QuickBooks provides a progress bar as the file is being restored. Click OK to the information window that the file was restored successfully.

Protecting the QuickBooks Operating Environment

To prevent an unexpected or unattended shutdown, install an uninterruptable power supply (UPS) on each of your computers running QuickBooks, as well as all network components that connect those computers. An adequately sized UPS can prevent power blackouts, brownouts, and surges. When QuickBooks must be left running unattended, use a Smart-UPS that automatically begins closing open programs and powering down the computer before the UPS battery is depleted.

 tip

Do not plug printers or other appliances into any UPS that is protecting your computers and network components. Often when a printer or other appliance launches, it pulls a significant load of power that can produce a brownout condition within your UPS itself and compromise power protection.

Power Protection

Even if a UPS protects your server and workstation, if the connecting network hardware (switches, hubs, or routers) is not protected, a sudden power event will produce a loss of connection between the QuickBooks client and QuickBooks server; this can result in data corruption. It is recommended that all network hardware also be UPS protected.

Keep your computer safe by preventing power-related corruptions to your QuickBooks and not overloading your UPS with any nonessential computing components.

Virus Protection

The Internet has changed our lives, but one unfortunate side effect has been computer viruses sent via email (or other data transfers). Because of the Internet, computers and networks are not immune from attack. Malware programmers look for weaknesses in the computers of not only big corporations, but also small businesses and individuals, to hopefully steal financial information or wreak havoc and destroy computer applications. Because QuickBooks is the leading financial software on the market, it is a favorite target of many who seek to invade Company files for personal gain.

Good behavior on the part of computer users is not enough to protect your QuickBooks data from attacks. Although surfing certain kinds of websites puts users at higher risks of infection, even legitimate websites can be compromised. Seemingly innocent results in a search engine can open hostile sites that immediately download a computer virus. Some of these viruses collect information from your computer (spyware), and some install malicious (malware) software, but almost all disguise themselves just long enough to take down your data or your network. Even if you never surf the Web, you are still vulnerable as long as you have an open Internet connection or ever access a flash drive or CD.

A high-quality antivirus program is essential if you are running QuickBooks on your computer or over a network. Certain effective programs can run with a minimum of computer resources and block the overwhelming majority of threats. Set your antivirus program to run in an always-on mode and to perform a regular (preferably daily) scan of your computer. Ensure that these programs are up-to-date; you should update your antivirus software to the most current virus definitions before each complete scan. Do not turn off your antivirus software unless you unplug your computer from the Internet and your network.

Many antivirus programs are sold in combination with a variety of Internet and network security features. Be advised that some of these features create additional layers of security that can restrict the capability to connect QuickBooks in a multiuser environment. For a list of compatible antivirus and firewall programs, see the "System Requirements" section of this chapter.

Windows Disk Defragmentation Utility

Fragmentation refers to any condition in which data is not recorded in a logical contiguous order. QuickBooks is subject to two different kinds of fragmentation: disk fragmentation and database fragmentation.

➡ *For more information on database fragmentation, see "Reducing Database File Fragments," p. 669.*

An example of disk fragmentation is when a QuickBooks invoice is recorded on your hard drive adjacent to a picture of your pets. Although it seems ridiculous to anyone who ever worked as a file clerk, this is the normal function of the Windows operating system.

Your QuickBooks Company file can be fragmented on your computer's disk drive just like any of your other files. This occurs when the operating system cannot create or insert new information into the file in one logically contiguous space. Because the Windows operating system does not restrict the writing of data to only contiguous areas of your disk drive, as the total amount of data on your disk drive increases, fragmentation also increases.

Because of fragmentation, the hard drive's disk head must repeatedly move back and forth over the disk when reading and writing various parts of the file. The more the disk head must move from one area to another, the less efficient the disk drive is. This situation lengthens the response time of QuickBooks when trying to find your data.

To correct this type of fragmentation, we must force our Windows computer to rewrite all the parts of files to contiguous space on the hard drive. This is called *defragmentation*. QuickBooks users should routinely run the Disk Defragmentation tool included with Windows software. After running this tool, QuickBooks users should see an increase in the speed of file access and data retrieval.

If your disk drive is less than 10 percent full, run defragmentation three or four times per year. If your disk drive is running at 25 to 30 percent of capacity, perform a monthly defragmentation. If your disk drive is at 50 percent or more of capacity, or if you have a QuickBooks Company file in excess of 50MB, you might need to run defragmentation once a week.

Defragmenting Your Windows 7 Computer Choosing to defragment your computer can lead to a more responsive data file, providing quicker retrieval of data for reporting.

1. In the lower-left corner of your screen, click the Windows Orb or the Start button.

2. Click All Programs.

3. Open the Accessories folder.

4. Open the Systems Tools folder.

5. Click Disk Defragmenter to open the utility in Figure 17.5.

Figure 17.5
Run the defragmenter tool on your computer often.

6. Select the drive you want to defragment.

7. Click Analyze. A dialog box displays after the disk is analyzed, detailing whether you need to perform the defragmentation.

8. To defragment the selected drive(s), click the Defragment Disk button. You can monitor the process in the Current status area (under the Progress column). When the process is complete, the results display.

9. To display more detailed information, click View Report.

10. To close the Disk Defragmenter, click Close.

Optimizing Your Hard Drive in Windows 8   Windows 8 has an entirely different process that includes defragmentation, called Optimize (of hard drives). This tool includes three types of optimization, including Defragmentation, Trim optimization, and Slab consolidation. The type of optimization the tool performs depends on the type of drive being optimized. Windows automatically chooses the optimization processes that are right for your drive(s).

Defragmenting rearranges fragmented data so that a drive can work more efficiently. Trim optimization informs the backing storage which blocks of data are no longer in use; this allows the storage to optimize space and performance for future use. Slab consolidation, used primarily in thinly provisioned drives, rearranges data from sparsely populated slabs to densely populated slabs.

To optimize your hard drive, follow these steps:

1. Open the Search charm, type **defragment**, and then tap or click Defragment and Optimize Your Drive(s).

2. Under Media Type in the Optimize Drives dialog box, pick the type of drive you want to optimize. Then tap or click Optimize and follow the on-screen prompts.

This process can take several minutes to several hours, depending on the size of the drive and degree of optimization needed.

Using Intuit Data Protect Online Backup Service

Intuit Data Protect is a subscription service that automatically backs up your Company file(s) and, optionally, other important files from your computer. When you use Intuit Data Protect as your backup method, all your data needed to restore your Company file is saved to Intuit's secure server. The backup files Intuit Data Protect creates are stored for 45 days, enabling you to restore not only the most recent backup, but also any prior backup during the past 45 days.

After you have set up your Intuit Data Protect subscription, you do not need to establish a backup schedule or perform manual backups. Intuit Data Protect performs a once-a-day backup of every QuickBooks file you have configured for back up. This is unlike the manual backups, which you should do when no one is working in the file. The Intuit Data Protect backups run in the background, enabling you to continue working normally in QuickBooks. If a scheduled backup is missed because your computer is off or can't access the Internet, Intuit Data Protect starts a backup as soon as your computer is turned back on or Internet service becomes available.

To restore a backup made using the Intuit Data Protect Backup service, follow these steps:

1. From the menu bar, select **File**, **Back Up Company**, **Open Online Backup**: **Intuit Data Protect**.

2. From the Backup Status dialog box, click Restore from Backup.

3. Select the file you want to restore, and select the version (date and time) of the backup. Click Continue.

4. Browse to the location where you want your file restored (original or new location). Click Select.

   Intuit Data Protect begins the process of restoring your file(s) to the designated location. This process can take a substantial period of time, depending on the size and number of files you are restoring. Do not attempt to close either Intuit Data Protect or QuickBooks during the restore process.

5. Upon completion, Intuit Data Protect displays a message that the restore completed. Click OK to close the dialog box.

Monitoring Your QuickBooks Database

Because QuickBooks consists of a series of tables that store your accounting records, monitoring your data file from time to time is important, to ensure that your data has integrity and is the proper size and configuration. QuickBooks offers a couple methods to monitor the database, including the Product Information dialog box and the Verify Data utility.

The Product Information Dialog Box

The Product Information dialog box provides valuable information about the health of your QuickBooks file. From an open QuickBooks file, press Ctrl+1 or F2 on your keyboard. The Product Information dialog box provides a wealth of information, including version, product license number, versions used, and much more. See Figure 17.6.

File Size

In Figure 17.6, about halfway down the left side is a section that provides data about the File Size, Total Transactions, Total Targets, Total Links, and DB File Fragments. This information can help you judge whether your data file is becoming too large for efficient processing of transactions and reports.

Many experts debate over the maximum file size of QuickBooks data, and Intuit has not published any formal guidelines regarding file size limits.

To calculate the anticipated growth of a data file, follow these steps:

1. Multiply the number of transactions each month by 2KB to get the monthly growth rate.

2. Multiply that amount by 12 for the annual kilobytes growth per year.

3. Divide that amount by 1024 for the number of megabytes growth per year.

Typically, the file should grow by 30MB per year or less for Pro or Premier, and 50MB per year or less for Enterprise to maintain reasonable performance. Specialized condense features are available in the QuickBooks Accountant editions that can help in removing data from prior years; contact your accounting professional for this service. The age and processing speed of the computer, along with other factors, can also affect the software's performance.

Figure 17.6
With QuickBooks open, press Ctrl+1 on your keyboard to view useful information about the file. Here you can see the number of Data File Fragments shown.

Factors such as the number of lines of detail for each transaction significantly increase the number of links per transaction—this factor alone can greatly impact the size of the database. Based on personal experience, QuickBooks Pro or Premier data files larger than 200MB or QuickBooks Enterprise files larger than 450MB might experience sluggish performance. So many variables impact QuickBooks file performance; naming specifics is not possible.

🔍 note

If you would like more information about QuickBooks file size restrictions, from the QuickBooks support site, visit http://support.quickbooks.intuit.com and search for Knowledge Base article INF12412.

If you find your data file is becoming sluggish, consider starting a new data file or finding companies listed on www.marketplace.intuit.com that will "shrink" your current file. You can contact me at info@quick-training.com for more information on this type of service.

Database File Fragments

As mentioned earlier, file fragmentation can negatively affect the performance of QuickBooks. Because file fragmentation is a normal part of using Windows, we must assume that some fragmentation is also normal. The question becomes, how many file fragments is too many? Some experts say more than 10 fragments is too many; others say 20, and still others say 50.

As a general rule, if the file is performing without issue and file fragments are fewer than 50, you don't need to be alarmed; however, anytime your file exceeds 50 fragments, it is time to reduce fragmentation.

➡ *For more information, see "Reducing Database File Fragments," p. 669.*

QuickBooks List Limitations

As you saw previously in Figure 17.6, the Product Information dialog box includes the List Information section. This section includes the size of the various QuickBooks lists (both active and inactive entries) and is another important database statistic to monitor. QuickBooks lists have been preconfigured to limit the number of entries the database can support.

One of the most significant limitations deals with the number of names you can have in QuickBooks Pro or Premier—the combined limit of customers, employees, vendors, and other names is 14,500. QuickBooks does not permit you to delete any names that have been used in a transaction, and the list limits include both active and inactive entries. This list size restriction can be a serious limitation to a growing business. According to Intuit, QuickBooks Enterprise can support up to 1 million combined names; some performance degradation is likely as you approach this upper limit.

Similar list limits exist for the Items List—14,500 in Pro or Premier, and 100,000 from a functional standpoint for Enterprise. Most other lists in QuickBooks Pro, Premier, or Enterprise are limited to 10,000 entries. One notable exception is the Price Levels list, which is limited to 100 entries in Pro and Premier, and 750 entries in Enterprise.

For QuickBooks Enterprise Solutions 14.0, review Table 17.1 for these specific lists limits.

Table 17.1   QuickBooks Enterprise 14.0 Larger List Limits

List	Pro or Premier	Enterprise 14.0
Items, including inventory items	14,500	>100,000
Chart of Accounts	10,000	100,000
Classes	10,000	100,000
Customer Types	10,000	100,000
Vendor Types	10,000	100,000
Memorized Transactions	14,500	50,000
To Do's	10,000	100,000
Customer Messages	10,000	100,000
Items in a Group or Sales Tax Item (also for Pro, and Premier)	50	50

You can find more details on the list limits for the various versions of QuickBooks by searching for "List Limits" on the Intuit support website, at http://quickbooks.com/support.

📡 **caution**

When running the Verify Data utility, if the Not Responding message displays, do not attempt to close QuickBooks. Let the utility finish before you close it. The following section has more information on the Not Responding message.

Using the Verify Data Utility

The Verify Data utility can detect many forms of data corruption and test the integrity of the database. It also can monitor the health of your Company file. Select this option when creating a backup of your QuickBooks Company file.

Additionally, if you use an external backup or Intuit Data Protect, run the Verify Data utility periodically to check the integrity of your Company file.

To Run the Verify Data Utility

To check the health of your QuickBooks data file, follow these steps for using the Verify Data utility:

1. Close all open windows in QuickBooks.
2. From the menu bar, select **File, Switch to Single-User Mode**. If this option does not appear, you are currently using the file in Single-User Mode.
3. From the menu bar, select **File, Utilities, Verify Data**.

QuickBooks begins to verify your data. The QBWin.log file reports the technical results. For more information, see "The QBWin.log File," p. 665. If data integrity issues are not detected, QuickBooks displays the prompt in Figure 17.7.

Figure 17.7
You see this message when the Verify Data utility detects no problems with the file.

The length of time the process takes depends on the size of your Company file.

Monitoring QuickBooks Performance Using Windows Task Manager

Have you ever encountered the Windows alert that QuickBooks is not responding? This can occur during any prolonged operation, such as when compiling a lengthy or complex report, running one of the internal utilities, or even adding entries to large lists. This usually is a problem with the way Windows reports activity, not with QuickBooks itself. Give the process time—do not get in a hurry, even if you think the process has stopped working.

Follow these steps to see if QuickBooks is still properly working by viewing the process in Windows Task Manager:

1. Place your cursor on an empty section of the Windows taskbar (typically at the bottom) of your computer. Right-click, and then select **Start Task Manager**.

2. From the Windows Task Manager, select the **Processes** tab.

3. Place a checkmark in the box Show Processes from All Users, located near the bottom of the list of processes.

4. Click the header of the Image Name column to sort the list of processes in alphabetical order.

5. Scroll down the list to the process QBW32.EXE. Observe the numbers listed in both the CPU and Memory columns. Watch this process for a minute or more; if either or both of these columns are changing even slightly, QuickBooks is still active and working.

6. To close the Windows Task Manager, click the X in the top-right corner.

After verifying that the process is running and the information referred to in step 5 is valid for your file, you can feel confident that when the task you started is finished, QuickBooks will return to full operation and no longer display the (Not Responding) Windows message.

QuickBooks Database Corruption

Occasionally, your QuickBooks Company file can become corrupted. Database corruption is any damage to a database that impacts its integrity or functionality.

Common Causes of Corruption

Database corruption can result from improper shutdown of QuickBooks, as well as power issues (surges, spikes, and outages). It can also occur as a result of a fatal application (program) error. System hardware, such as bad disk drives or RAID controllers, can corrupt data. Your operating system can produce QuickBooks data fragmentation.

In a multiuser environment, networking components (such as wireless routers) might produce corruption because their failure can break the connection between the application and Database Server.

> **note**
>
> New for QuickBooks 2014, software and hardware performance alerts display prominently on the top-right side of the menu bar. Click the Alerts icon to view the details.

A large QuickBooks file size does not necessarily cause data corruption, although it involves more data in which corruption can occur. Larger files also have more fragmentation and performance issues if your hardware is not meeting the reported minimum requirements. Consider adding computer resources to support your large QuickBooks file and reducing potential data size associated corruptions. For more information, see the section titled "System Requirements" in this chapter.

Signs of Data Corruption

QuickBooks might report data corruption by displaying specific problem messages or error codes. Often the first sign of data corruption does not appear until a QuickBooks user sees an accounting transaction irregularity—for example, when an out-of-balance balance sheet or accounts receivables or payables subledger reports don't reconcile to the general ledger.

If you run the Verify Data utility and your Company file has lost integrity, QuickBooks displays a warning such as the one in Figure 17.8, indicating that you should run the Rebuild Data utility. In addition to the displayed message, the QBWin.log file provides more information.

Figure 17.8
Some database corruption errors require using the Rebuild Data utility.

> **Problem**
> A data problem prevents QuickBooks from continuing.
>
> **Solution**
> Rebuild your data now. Close all windows and choose Utilities and then Rebuild Data from the File menu.
>
> If you see this message again, call Intuit Technical Support.
>
> [Close]

The QBWin.log File

If the Verify Data utility detects an error in your data, you might want to get more information about the specific problem(s) within your data. QuickBooks records operational data, including information related to the Verify Data and Rebuild Data utilities, within a log file called the QBWin.log.

To view the QBWin.log file, follow these steps:

1. With your QuickBooks Company file open, press the F2 key (or Ctrl+1) to display the Product Information dialog box.

2. Now press the F3 key (or Ctrl+2) to display the Tech Help dialog box.

3. Click the Open File tab.

4. Scroll down the list and click the QBWin.log file; then click Open File. The file opens in Windows Notepad (see Figure 17.9).

5. The Verify Data section should be near the bottom of the log, so scroll to the bottom and then scroll back up until you find the Verify portion of the log file, which begins with the following:

= = = = = = = = = = = * BEGIN VERIFY LOG * = = = = =

The QBWin.log file ends with this:

= = = = = = = = = == = = * END VERIFY LOG * = = = = = =

Figure 17.9
Review the QBWin.log file to identify errors that might be causing the error messages.

You can scroll through the log file to view errors detected with the file. I recommend that you contact Intuit technical support or a local QuickBooks professional to read and correct any errors listed.

The QBWin.log file is a snapshot of technical details during the current session of QuickBooks. It contains information about how the program performed when it was started, whether it successfully connected with your Company file, and whether any errors occurred during operations or while performing the verify/rebuild utilities. Your QBWin.log file can contain many different messages; some might represent minor errors, and others might represent more severe forms of database corruption. The QuickBooks Support website contains many Knowledge Base articles that correspond to the various errors. This section covers a few common error messages and possible solutions.

You might want to rebuild the Company file after performing the suggested repairs.

➡ *For more information, see "Rebuilding Your Company File," p. 670.*

Error: Verify Memorized Report List

A corrupted Memorized Report is usually associated with this error. QuickBooks normally repairs this problem if you re-sort the Memorized Report List and then run the Rebuild Data utility. To do so, follow these steps:

1. From the menu bar, select **Reports**, **Memorized Reports**, **Memorized Report List**.

2. In the Memorized Report drop-down list, select **Re-Sort List**.

3. To continue, click OK to the Re-sort prompt.

In some cases, these steps do not correct the corruption; then you must "delete" the affected Memorized Report, re-sort the list, and rebuild the data file.

Error: Verify Names List (Such As Customers)

This form of corruption occurs when one of the Names lists has a database index error. Try re-sorting the Names List and then running the Rebuild Data utility to resolve this type of error.

To access the Names List, follow these steps while logged in to the file in single-user mode:

1. From the menu bar, select **Banking**, **Write Checks**.

2. Place your cursor in the Pay to the Order Of field.

3. On your keyboard, press Ctrl+L.

4. The Names List displays. In the Name drop-down list, select **Re-sort List**.

5. In response to the Re-sort List? message, click OK.

Error: Verify Name (Specific List): Duplicate Name Encountered

QuickBooks might encounter a duplicate name. This can occur if you import data using the IIF (Intuit Interchange Format) import file type or you use a third-party application. Frequently, one name is marked as inactive, or QuickBooks might have inserted an asterisk (*) in front of the duplicate name.

To locate and merge the duplicate names, follow these steps:

1. Find the names that are duplicated.

2. Edit one of the names to make it unique; if QuickBooks has inserted an asterisk (*), remove that character from the name as part of this change. Save the new name.

3. Return to the name you just changed, and edit it again so it is identical to its duplicate; then click Save.

4. QuickBooks displays the Merge dialog box (see Figure 17.10). Confirm the merge of both names by clicking Yes.

5. Run the Rebuild Data utility.

Figure 17.10
Certain lists in QuickBooks let you merge duplicate names.

Error: Verify Target: Transaction Out of Balance

This error usually results when the target record (such as the check detail lines) does not equal the amount of the source record (such as the check total).

To correct this type of error, follow these steps:

1. Open the transaction identified in the `QBWin.log` report.

2. Verify whether the amount in the header (such as check amount) is identical to the total of the amounts in the detail lines. If these amounts are different, you need to correct the erroneous amount(s).

3. Save the corrected transaction.

4. Run the Rebuild Data utility.

Error: Verify Target: Invalid Open Quantity

This error can result when the link between an estimate and sales order and its associated invoice (for partial quantities) is broken.

To relink the transactions, follow these steps:

1. Open the transaction, reported in the `QBWin.log` report.

2. Add a period (.) to an empty detail line of the transaction; this will not change any values for the transaction. However, doing so can help relink the source and target transactions.

3. Save the transaction.

4. Run the Rebuild Data utility.

For more information, see "Rebuilding Your Company File," p. 670.

Repairing List Corruptions

Several of the symptoms associated with data corruption, and `QBWin.log` messages detailed previously, involve problems with the various QuickBooks lists. For many lists, you can re-sort the list simply by opening the list and clicking the list's menu button located at the bottom of the list (such as Items). Before actually re-sorting the list, check the box labeled Include Inactive (if available) and then select the option to change the list view from Hierarchical to Flat (not all lists offer a hierarchical view).

One of the major lists in QuickBooks is a hidden list called the Name List, which is a combined list of all the names (customers, employees, vendors, and other names).

To sort all the name lists at once, follow these steps:

1. From the menu bar, select **Banking**, **Write Checks**.

2. Place your cursor in the Pay to the Order Of field.

3. On your keyboard, press Ctrl+L.

4. The Name List displays. From the Name drop-down list, select **Re-sort List**.

5. In response to the Re-sort List? message, click OK.

Reducing Database File Fragments

The highly compressed QuickBooks Portable Company File can be useful in dealing with some forms of index corruption, as well as fragmentation. When a Portable Company (*.QBM) File is restored, QuickBooks re-creates all indexes associated with the database. In addition, the extreme level of compression applied when the file is produced eliminates file fragments. Therefore, creation and restoration of a Portable File can resolve many file-related issues.

Follow these steps to create and restore a Portable Company File:

1. From the menu bar, select **File**, **Create Copy**. The Save Copy or Backup dialog box displays (see Figure 17.11).

2. Choose **Portable Company File** and click Next.

3. Accept the default location and filename, or select a location to save the file and type a desired name for the file.

4. A few individual progress messages display; click OK for each of them.

5. Upon completion, QuickBooks displays an Information message indicating that the file has been saved and details the designated location. Click OK.

Figure 17.11
Create and restore a Portable Company File to help reduce database file fragments.

6. To restore the Portable Company File, select **File**, **Open or Restore Company** from the menu bar.

7. Select **Restore a Portable File** and click Next.

8. Select the Portable Company File (ending in .QBM) you saved to the desktop (or your alternative location), and click Open.

> 🔒 **caution**
> Always create a backup of your file before attempting this type of file restore.

9. In the Open or Restore Company dialog box, the Where Do You Want to Restore the File dialog displays. Review the message details regarding overwriting your current file, and click Next, as in Figure 17.12.

Figure 17.12
Review this information before restoring your Portable Company File.

10. Click Save and select a save location. Because you are intending to replace your current file, select your current file location and current filename.

11. Click Save. QuickBooks replaces your current file with the data restored from the QuickBooks Portable Company File.

Rebuilding Your Company File

The Rebuild Data utility can repair many QuickBooks Company file issues. The utility attempts to repair or update data found to be corrupted, which can include permanently deleting transactions or list entries that are damaged beyond repair or that compromise the overall integrity of the file.

Before running the rebuild utility, you should gather information for comparison when the rebuild is complete. This should include all summary reports, including the Balance Sheet Standard and Profit & Loss Standard reports. You might also want to process additional reports, such as those for payroll details or checkbook registers.

To use the QuickBooks Rebuild Data utility, follow these steps:

> **⚡ caution**
>
> Never rebuild a Company file on a remote drive or across a network. Always copy the file to a local computer before running the Rebuild Data utility.
>
> Close all unnecessary programs, and turn off your Windows screen saver and any power-saver functions before you start a rebuild.

1. If you use your file in a multiuser install, you need to log in to the file in single-user mode. From the menu bar, select **File**, **Switch to Single User**.

2. From the menu bar, select **File**, **Utilities**, **Rebuild Data**.

3. QuickBooks displays a warning message requiring a backup of the Company file before actually starting the rebuild process. Follow the prompts to save a backup copy of your data.

4. When the backup is completed, the Rebuild Data utility starts. The time required to rebuild the database can vary, depending on the size of your Company file. It is extremely important to permit the utility to finish completely.

5. QuickBooks displays a Rebuild Has Completed message. Click OK.

After the Rebuild Data utility finishes, the data file might still have corrupted transactions that the first pass of the rebuild did not correct. You might need to rebuild your data more than once. As a general rule, if the utility does not resolve an issue within three passes, the database error cannot be fixed using the Rebuild Data utility.

Although severely damaged transactions are usually removed during the rebuild process, you might need to manually correct or delete other transactions that Rebuild Data could not correct and then reenter them. Transactional data removed or corrected is listed in the QBWin.log file, along with corrupted transactions that the Rebuild Data utility cannot correct.

For severe cases of database integrity issues, contact Intuit's Technical Support.

Using the QuickBooks File Doctor

The QuickBooks File Doctor tool helps diagnose and repair several forms of damage that prevent Company files from opening. The tool must be run locally on a corrupted QuickBooks file; you cannot run this tool across a network or a mapped drive.

The QuickBooks File Doctor tool replaces and provides improved problem-solving features over the formerly available QuickBooks Company File Diagnostic tool.

The Company File Doctor tool requires the following:

- You must have an Internet connection.

- The Company file must be smaller than 2GB.

- You must be logged in as the Administrator to run the network diagnostic functions.

- QuickBooks must be in hosting mode. To start hosting from the menu bar, select **File**, **Utilities**, **Host Multiuser Access**.

- If Windows User Account Control is turned on, the File Doctor tool is relaunched with elevated administrator privileges.

- Network diagnostic and repair functionality might not work properly if multiple QuickBooks versions are installed on your computer.

Download the tool from the QuickBooks technical support site: http://support.quickbooks.intuit.com/support and type HOW12723 in the search box. The referenced Knowledge Base article includes general instructions for downloading and using the tool.

1. Install the downloaded QuickBooks Company File Diagnostic Tool, following the instructions provided by Intuit within the Knowledge Base article.

2. Click the installed icon to launch the tool. If you receive a message that the tool will be relaunched with elevated permissions, click OK. Click Yes in response to the User Account Control message. Figure 17.13 shows the dialog box that displays.

Figure 17.13
Use this tool to diagnose and repair a QuickBooks Company file.

3. Click the Browse button to select the QuickBooks Company (*.QBW) file or QuickBooks Accountant's Copy File (*.QBA) that needs to be diagnosed and/or repaired.

4. Click Diagnose File. If required, enter the Admin password. Click OK. QuickBooks displays a Diagnosing Company File progress bar.

5. Select **Yes** if you access your company file from other computers on the network, or else answer **No** to the same message. When the tool has finished the process, three outcomes are possible:

- The problem was found and fixed.

- The problem was found but not fixed. Instructions are provided for different methods of handling this.

- No problem was found. Instructions are provided for additional tools to try, including detailed instructions for network connectivity issues.

> **note**
>
> If the File Doctor finds and fixes a problem, a new copy of your file is created automatically for you to open and use.

The File Doctor also offers advanced settings that can help with the following errors, although it is recommend that you use these advanced settings only with the assistance of Intuit's Technical Support.

- **-6130 Errors**—These errors often occur when you are opening a Company file and the database server terminates.

- **Data Sync Errors**—These errors are related to the QuickBooks Sync Manager that manages the data housed in your desktop software and the data maintained in the Intuit Cloud for applications to which you have granted this access.

Resolving QuickBooks Program File Corruption Issues

Some corruption can be the result of problems with the QuickBooks program files. This can occur during installation when a conflict occurs with some required component, such as Microsoft.NET or even the Windows Registry. Generally, QuickBooks runs normally, but at some point, the program experiences fault errors or might not install an update properly. Usually, you can resolve these problems by repairing the QuickBooks installation.

To repair your QuickBooks program files, follow these steps:

1. From your Windows taskbar, click the Windows Orb or the Start button and select **Control Panel**.

2. In the Control Panel, double-click Programs.

3. In Programs, select **QuickBooks** and choose **Uninstall/Change**.

4. Select **Repair** and click Next. QuickBooks begins the repair, displaying a progress bar during the process.

5. When the repair is complete, click Finish.

This procedure usually (not always) resolves file issues. If it does not work, uninstall QuickBooks and then reinstall it. Use the preceding steps to remove QuickBooks by selecting the Uninstall option instead of Repair.

18

USING OTHER PLANNING AND MANAGEMENT TOOLS

Much can be said about properly setting up your QuickBooks file and recording transactions correctly. However, for this chapter, I want to share with you some lesser-known features that can truly help you manage your business and work more efficiently with QuickBooks.

Planning and Budgeting

Like most business owners I have met, you probably know where your money will be spent each month, yet you might not see the value in writing it down. An old saying is very appropriate here: "When you fail to plan, you plan to fail." This saying couldn't be truer than when it comes to watching your business financials.

QuickBooks makes the task of creating and tracking a financial budget for your business easy. Just follow a few steps, and in no time, you can print useful reports that track actual financial performance and compare it to your original budget.

Create a Budget

The first step is to set up a budget. Follow these steps to begin using this feature in QuickBooks:

1. From the menu bar, select **Company**, **Planning & Budgeting**, **Set Up Budgets**. The Create New Budget dialog box in Figure 18.1 displays.

Create New Budget   ✕

Create a New Budget

Begin by specifying the year and type for the new budget.

[2017] ⬆⬇

Choose the budget type

◉ Profit and Loss (reflects all activity for the year)

◯ Balance Sheet (reflects ending balance)

[Back] [**Next**] [Finish]   [Cancel]

Figure 18.1
Create a Profit and Loss or Balance Sheet budget easily with QuickBooks.

2. Select the year you want to create the budget for.

3. Choose the budget type:

   ■ Profit and Loss

   ■ Balance Sheet

4. Click Next. Select from the following choices (see Figure 18.2):

   ■ **No Additional Criteria**—If you want a simple budget, use this format. I recommend you start with this choice.

   ■ **Customer:Job**—You can create a budget for your customers or jobs here, but a better method might be to use a QuickBooks estimate. For more information, see "Using QuickBooks Estimates," p. 348.

   ■ **Class**—If you are using classes (department tracking), you might want to select the Class budget report. For more information on classes, see "Class," p. 117.

5. Click Next.

> 🔍 **note**
>
> If you have previously created a budget, click the Create New Budget button in the Set Up Budgets dialog box (see Figure 18.4).

Figure 18.2
Choose the type of budget to create.

> Create New Budget
>
> **Additional Profit and Loss Budget Criteria**
>
> ◉ No additional criteria
> ○ Customer:Job
> ○ Class

6. Choose how you want to create a budget from the choices in Figure 18.3.

   ■ **Create Budget from Scratch**—You manually enter the budget amounts. This method requires the most effort on your part.

   ■ **Create a Budget from Previous Year's Actual Data**—The budget is created using the previous year's data, allowing you to modify the budgeted amounts as needed. I recommend starting with this option.

7. Click Finish. QuickBooks creates the new budget. In Figure 18.4, a new budget has been created using actual revenue and expenses from the previous year.

8. Click Save. To close the newly created budget, click OK.

Figure 18.3
Choose from two methods for creating the new budget.

> Create New Budget ✕
>
> **Choose how you want to create a budget**
>
> ○ Create budget from scratch.
> This option lets you manually enter amounts for each account that you want to track.
>
> ◉ Create budget from previous year's actual data.
> This option automatically enters the monthly totals from last year for each account in this budget.
>
> Back | Next | **Finish** | Cancel

Figure 18.4
QuickBooks can create the budget quickly using actual information from the previous year.

Edit a Budget

You can edit budgets at any time to accommodate changes in your business. Additionally, if you created the budget using last year's actual numbers, you can follow these steps to revise the budget information:

1. From the menu bar, select **Company**, **Planning & Budgeting**, **Set Up Budgets** to display your previously saved budget.

2. To view a different budget, click the drop-down list to select the desired budget.

3. To create a new budget, click Create New Budget and follow the steps in the previous section.

4. With your cursor, click in any cell to change the amount budgeted for that category and month.

5. (Optional) With your cursor in a specific cell, click Copy Across. QuickBooks copies that amount to all the columns to the right of your current cursor position.

6. (Optional) With your cursor in a specific cell, click Adjust Row Amounts. You can choose to increase or decrease by a specific percentage or dollar amount. (See Figure 18.5.) You can choose to update the following:

   - **1st Month**—Update budget amounts beginning with the first month in the year.

   - **Currently Selected Month**—Update budget amounts beginning with the currently selected month.

7. Click OK to close the Adjust Row Amounts dialog box. QuickBooks calculates new budget amounts depending on your selections in step 6.

Figure 18.5
Use the Adjust Row Amounts dialog box to quickly change your budget amounts.

8. (Optional) Click Clear and answer Yes or No to the warning message about clearing this page of the budget.

9. Click Save to save your changes as you work.

10. To close the budget, click the X in the top-right corner. You might be asked if you want to record your budget changes. Choose from Yes, No, or Cancel.

> **⚠ caution**
> If you select Clear and then choose Yes, QuickBooks removes all the budgeted amounts for the currently displayed budget.

Print Budget Reports

You now have a budget prepared. Let's see how your current year is progressing by viewing the budget reports included with QuickBooks. From the menu bar, select **Reports**, **Budgets & Forecasts**. You find these reports:

- Budget Overview

- Budget vs. Actual

- Profit & Loss Budget Performance

- Budget vs. Actual Graph

- Forecast Overview (available only in Premier or Enterprise)

- Forecast vs. Actual (available only in Premier or Enterprise)

Figure 18.6 shows a Profit & Loss Budget vs. Actual report.

To display a budget report, follow these steps:

1. From the menu bar, select **Reports**, **Budgets & Forecasts** and choose a report.

2. In the drop-down list, select the year's budget you want to review.

	Jan 1 - Dec 15, 17	Budget	$ Over Budget	% of Budget
Ordinary Income/Expense				
Income				
40100 · Construction Income	447,537.34	397,500.00	50,037.34	112.6%
40500 · Reimbursement Income	2,119.80	0.00	2,119.80	100.0%
Total Income	449,657.14	397,500.00	52,157.14	113.1%
Cost of Goods Sold				
50100 · Cost of Goods Sold	14,766.19	33,000.00	-18,233.81	44.7%
54000 · Job Expenses	165,299.14	228,850.00	-63,550.86	72.2%
Total COGS	180,065.33	261,850.00	-81,784.67	68.8%
Gross Profit	269,591.81	135,650.00	133,941.81	198.7%
Expense				
60100 · Automobile	6,844.94	1,850.00	4,994.94	370%
60300 · Bad debt	0.00	0.00	0.00	0.0%
60600 · Bank Service Charges	125.00	165.00	-40.00	75.8%
60900 · Depreciation Expense	0.00	0.00	0.00	0.0%
61200 · Dues and Subscriptions	0.00	0.00	0.00	0.0%
61500 · Union Dues	0.00	0.00	0.00	0.0%
62100 · Insurance	20,125.09	7,700.00	12,425.09	261.4%
62400 · Interest Expense	1,995.65	550.00	1,445.65	362.8%

Figure 18.6
You can display this report for many time periods, including day, month, and year.

3. Click Next.

4. If the report offers multiple layout options, select the layout of your choice and click Next.

5. Click Finish to prepare the report.

You can also modify the information displayed on this report. Click Customize Report to modify these settings:

- **Report Date Range**—Settings that determine the dates included in the budget details

- **Report Basis**—Accrual or cash basis

- **Columns and Rows**—Settings that determine what data is included in the budget

(Optional) Click the Advanced button and choose Display Only Non-zero Rows or Columns. You might also want to click the Show Only Rows and Columns with Budgets checkbox. See Figure 18.7.

Figure 18.7
Modify the information displayed in the Budget vs. Actual report.

Delete a Budget

If you find it necessary to delete a budget and start over, follow these steps:

1. From the menu bar, select **Company**, **Planning & Budgeting**, **Set Up Budgets**. Your previously saved budget displays in the Set Up Budgets dialog box.

2. From the menu bar, select **Edit**, **Delete Budget**.

QuickBooks Loan Manager

Use the Loan Manager in QuickBooks to track loans you have created in QuickBooks. The Loan Manager helps you track all your loans in one convenient location.

With the Loan Manager, you can do the following:

- View payment schedules
- Set up loan payments
- Analyze different loan payoff scenarios

18

Information to Collect

Before adding a loan to the Loan Manager, you should have the following information about your loans available. This information is usually included on your original finance documents:

- Origination date
- Payment amount
- Payment term
- Escrow amount (if any)
- Interest rate

Getting QuickBooks Ready

Before setting up a loan in the Loan Manager in QuickBooks, you need to set up the following:

- **Create a Loan Payable Account**—Usually, this is a long-term liability account. It displays the balance owed on the loan.
- **Create an Expense Account**—This records the interest paid on the loan.
- **(Optional) Create an Escrow Account**—You can create an escrow account if it is required for your specific loan reporting needs.
- **Create a Vendor Record**—This is the person or institution to which you'll make payments.

If you have previously been using these QuickBooks accounts, make sure the balances in these accounts are up-to-date and agree with your lending institution's balances for the loan. Most businesses use a single interest expense account for all loans.

Setting Up a New Loan

To use QuickBooks to track your loan payment, follow these steps:

1. From the menu bar, select **Banking**, **Loan Manager**.
2. Click Add a Loan and complete the information in Figure 18.8.
3. In the Account Name drop-down list, select the long-term liability account for the loan.
4. In the Lender drop-down list, select the payee.
5. Enter the loan Origination Date.
6. In the Terms drop-down list, select **Weeks**, **Months**, or **Years**. Click Next.
7. Enter the Due Date of Next Payment, Payment Amount, and (optionally) Next Payment.
8. Select the **Payment Period**.
9. (Optional) Choose Yes or No for making an escrow payment, and complete the fields for Escrow Payment Amount and Escrow Payment Account.

Figure 18.8
Complete the account information for the loan.

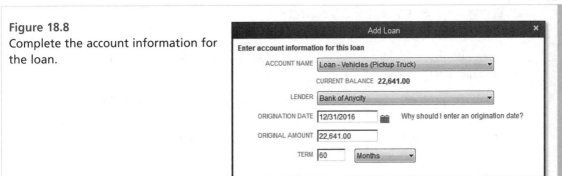

10. (Optional) Select the box to be alerted 10 days before the payment is due. Click Next.

11. Enter the Interest Rate and select a **Compounding Period**.

12. Choose a bank account from the Payment Account drop-down list.

13. Choose the Interest Expense Account and the account for Fees and Charges.

14. Click Finish. QuickBooks displays information in the Loan Manager about the newly created loan. See Figure 18.9.

Figure 18.9
Use the Loan Manager to track long-term loan details.

Setting Up a Loan Payment

To set up a payment for the loan, follow these steps:

1. Select the loan from the list, and click the Set Up Payment button. The Set Up Payment dialog box displays (see Figure 18.10).

2. In the This Payment Is drop-down list, select one of the following options: **A Regular Payment** or **An Extra Payment**.

3. View the Account Information and Payment Information. Modify the Payment Information if necessary.

Figure 18.10
The Loan Manager can create the payment for the loan.

4. Select a **Payment Method,** choosing either Write a Check or Enter a Bill.

5. Click OK. QuickBooks prepares a check or bill with the correct payment information.

Additionally from the Loan Manager, you can do the following:

- Edit the loan details or remove the loan

- View summary information about the loan

- View the payment schedule by payment number

- Access contact information for the vendor, as set up with the original vendor record

- Print the details of the loan

- View multiple "what-if" scenarios, as in Figure 18.11

Figure 18.11
Use the QuickBooks Loan
Manager to analyze different
loan-payoff scenarios.

What If Scenarios	
Choose a scenario	What if I change my payment amount?
	What if I change my payment amount?
Choose a loan	What if I change my interest rate?
	How much will I pay with a new loan?
	What if I refinance my loan?
LOAN - VEHICLES (	Evaluate two new loans

CURRENT BALANCE	22,366.50		
AMOUNT BORROWED	22,641.00		
ORIGINATION DATE	12/31/2016		
MATURITY DATE	12/15/2021		
PAYMENT AMOUNT	359.40	PAYMENT AMOUNT	359.40
PAYMENT PERIOD	Monthly		
INTEREST RATE	4.500 %		
NEXT PAYMENT DATE	02/15/2017		
			Calculate
TOTAL PAYMENTS	$25,414.38	TOTAL PAYMENTS	$0.00
TOTAL INTEREST	$3,047.88	TOTAL INTEREST	$0.00
BALLOON PAYMENT	$4,569.18	BALLOON PAYMENT	N/A

Using the Year-End Guide

QuickBooks offers a ready-made Year-End Guide and checklist to help with your year-end tasks, as Figure 18.12 shows. Keep track of your progress as you get your file ready for your accountant or for tax time.

From the menu bar, select **Help**, **Year-End Guide**. Each task offers a link to more detailed help information. (Optional) Click the Save Checkmarks button so you can keep track of completed tasks.

Figure 18.12
Use the Year-End Guide to help prepare your file for tax time.

Synchronizing QuickBooks Lists with Microsoft Outlook

If you use Microsoft Outlook to manage contact information, you can synchronize your contact data with QuickBooks. You can synchronize the following information:

- Customer and Job contact information

- Vendor contact information

- Other Names list contact information

To begin synchronizing your QuickBooks lists with Microsoft Outlook, follow these steps:

1. Before proceeding with this task, make sure you have a backup of your QuickBooks data and your Outlook contacts.

2. If you have previously installed the Contact Sync tool, you will be prompted to synchronize your contacts.

note
If you delete a contact in Outlook, QuickBooks does not delete that name.

note
If you need help backing up your Outlook contacts, from the QuickBooks Help search box on the icon bar, type **backup Outlook data** and select to search Help. Follow the appropriate links for more detailed information.

3. If you have not previously installed the free Contact Sync tool, from the menu bar, select **File, Utilities, Synchronize Contacts**. The Synchronize Contacts message displays. Click OK to be directed to the website (Internet connection required) to download the tool.

4. Before proceeding with the install, close Outlook. Click the file that was downloaded, and follow the instructions to install.

5. After installing, open Outlook. The Contact Sync Setup Assistant displays. See Figure 18.13.

> **tip**
>
> If you want to have your QuickBooks contacts in a unique folder separate from your other contacts, create the new contact folder in Outlook and select the folder in step 7.

Figure 18.13
Setting up QuickBooks Contact Sync is easy with step-by-step instructions.

6. Click Get Started and review the Begin Setup information. Click Setup.

7. QuickBooks Contact Sync displays the available Outlook folders. If more than one is detected, select the appropriate folder. Click Next.

8. Select from Customer, Jobs, and Vendors to Synchronize. Click Next.

9. (Optional) Select to exclude from synchronization Outlook contacts marked as Personal or Private in Outlook. Click Next.

10. Review the defaults in the Mapping Fields window, as in Figure 18.14. Modify as needed or select **Restore Defaults**. Click Next.

11. If you selected to import Jobs or Vendors, complete the same information detailed in step 10. Click Next.

Figure 18.14
Modify the default mapping of fields from Outlook to QuickBooks.

12. Set an option for resolving any conflicts. Choices include the following:

- Let Me Decide Each Case

- Outlook Data Wins

- QuickBooks Data Wins

13. Click Save. Click Sync Now.

14. QuickBooks displays a Contact Overview Complete. If you selected Let Me Decide Each Case in step 12, click Next to review the list of contacts to be imported.

15. Click to accept the changes (not shown in Figure 18.15) and import the contacts. QuickBooks displays a progress bar.

16. Click Accept. QuickBooks displays a Synchronization Complete Message; click OK to close.

17. You can now view your contacts in Outlook or view your Outlook contacts in QuickBooks. See Figure 18.16.

The tool automatically installs in Outlook a QuickBooks Add-Ins tab (Outlook 2010) or a QuickBooks Toolbar (Outlook 2007 and earlier). From the Add-Ins tab, you can change your Synchronizing Settings or select to Synchronize Contacts.

Figure 18.15
Review the contacts to be imported, if you selected the option in step 12 of Let Me Decide Each Case.

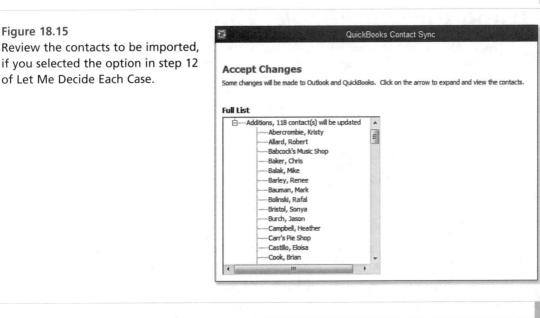

Figure 18.16
QuickBooks and Outlook update with changes to contact details.

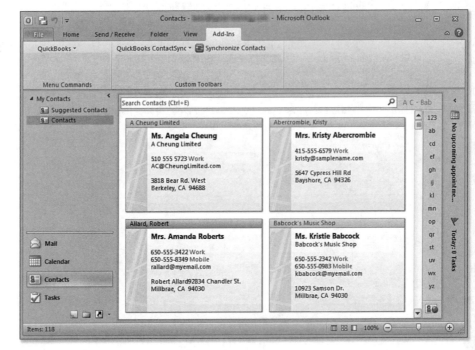

Using the QuickBooks Timer

The QuickBooks Timer is a separate program that can run on its own without QuickBooks. Time recorded with the QuickBooks Timer can be added to customer invoices when you do Time and Expense invoicing.

➡ *For more information, see "Time and Expense Invoicing," p. 363.*

Features of the QuickBooks Timer include the following:

- Track time spent on a task using a clock timer, or enter the time after you have done the work.

- Track time without having access to the QuickBooks data.

- Give a copy of the QuickBooks Timer program to people you want to track time, such as employees or subcontractors.

The basic workflow for using the QuickBooks Timer requires some manual processes, so be sure this is the right solution for you. The process includes the following four steps:

1. After the QuickBooks Timer is installed, the administrator of the QuickBooks file exports the current list of Service Items, Customers and Jobs, Vendors, and Employees.

2. The timekeepers receive this file via email or on a removable storage device such as a USB flash drive. The lists are imported into each individual QuickBooks Timer file.

3. The timekeepers track their time on their own computer and, when completed, export the time to a file attached to an email or USB storage device.

4. The QuickBooks file administrator receives the file(s) and imports the time.

Each time the customers, jobs, vendor, employees, or service list items change, a new export file must be sent and imported by each timekeeper.

Installing the QuickBooks Timer

The QuickBooks Timer install file is located on the program CD-ROM if you ordered a CD or is a free download online. To install it from a CD, follow these steps:

1. Insert the QuickBooks CD-ROM into the computer.

2. Exit the QuickBooks startup if it displays.

3. Click the Microsoft Windows Start button and select **Run**.

4. Enter **D:\QBTimer** (where D:\ is your CD-ROM drive). Click OK.

5. Double-click the Setup file.

6. Follow the Timer installation instructions.

> ⦿ **tip**
>
> Time format can be in decimal (10.20) or minutes (10:12) form. Log in to the QuickBooks data as the Admin user and then, from the menu bar, select **Edit, Preferences, General, Company Preferences tab.**

You can create a CD-ROM with the same install file and provide this CD to other timekeepers who might or might not have access to QuickBooks.

> 🔍 **note**
>
> If you downloaded your QuickBooks program, you will not have a CD to install the Timer from. Follow these directions to download and install the free QuickBooks Timer:
>
> Visit the www.quickbooks.com/support website and, in the search field, type **HOW13261**. You are directed to the appropriate Knowledge Base article, with links and instructions for downloading the free QuickBooks Pro Timer that works with all Windows versions of QuickBooks.

Tracking Time with the Timer

Timekeepers can track time using the QuickBooks Timer even if they do not have access to the QuickBooks data file. However, to be current with the list of customers, jobs, or service items, the QuickBooks Administrator should frequently export the lists as detailed in the previous section.

To begin tracking time using the QuickBooks Timer, follow these steps:

1. Launch the QuickBooks Timer. If you recently installed the Timer, you can launch it by clicking the Start button in Windows and then clicking All Programs, QuickBooks Timer, QuickBooks Pro Timer.

2. In the QuickBooks Pro Timer window, click New Activity.

3. Select the Date, Your Name (timekeeper), Customer:Job, Service Item, and (optional) Class; then enter an optional note, as in Figure 18.17.

4. (Optional) Select **Billable** if this item will be included on a customer's invoice.

5. Click OK. The Timer shows the current activity. Click Start.

Figure 18.17
Enter your time after the service is performed, or click OK to start a stopwatch type of timer for the activity.

6. The QuickBooks Timer now begins a stopwatch type of timer. If instead you are entering your time after the service is performed, enter the time in the Duration field.

7. Click Edit any time you need to change the time recorded.

8. Click Stop to stop the timer, and click Resume to begin timing again. See Figure 18.18.

9. Click Stop when you are done with the selected task.

Figure 18.18
You can choose to use a stopwatch timer to track activities.

Exporting Timer Activities

If you are not entering your time directly into the QuickBooks file, the file administrator needs you to export your Timer activities so that they can be imported into the QuickBooks file. When you are instructed by the QuickBooks administrator to export the Timer activities, follow these steps:

1. From the QuickBooks Timer file menu, select **Export Time Activities**. Click Continue.

2. Select the date you will be exporting activities through. Click OK.

3. Provide a filename and accept the default location for storing the exported lists, or browse to select a location of your choice. The file will have the extension of .IIF (Intuit Interchange Format). Remember this location because you will need to attach this file to an email or copy it to a removable storage device such as a USB flash drive. Click Save.

4. Click OK to close the Data Exported Successfully message.

> **note**
>
> The next time you import Timer activities, QuickBooks remembers where the lists were stored.

Each timekeeper needs to provide this saved file to the QuickBooks administrator for importing into the QuickBooks file.

> **tip**
>
> You can set a preference to have all time activities marked as billable. From the menu bar, select **Edit, Preferences, Time and Expenses** on the Company Preferences tab.
>
> You mark a time activity as billable only if your company wants to include line detail on a customer's invoice for the employee's or vendor's time activities. This is referred to as Time & Expense or Cost Plus billing.

Importing Timer Activities into QuickBooks

One feature of using this free Timer program is that the user does not need to have QuickBooks installed.

When you want the Timer activities included in your QuickBooks data file, you need to import the Exported Timer Activities. Ask each of your timekeepers to follow the instructions listed previously for exporting their Timer activities.

To import the Timer activities received from your timekeepers, follow these steps:

1. Receive your timekeepers' individual QuickBooks Timer Exported Lists files. The files have an extension of .IIF (Intuit Interchange Format).

2. Launch QuickBooks. From the menu bar, select **File, Utilities, Import, Timer Activities**.

3. Click OK to the Import Activities from Timer message.

4. Browse to the location where you stored the Exported Timer Activities from your timekeepers.

5. Select the file. Click Open. QuickBooks displays the QB Pro Timer Import Summary. Click View Report (see Figure 18.19) to see a listing of the Timer activities imported. See Figure 18.20.

You can now include these imported Timer activities on customer invoices, or issue vendor checks or employee checks using the Timer activity totals.

Figure 18.19
View a summary of the imported Timer activities.

Figure 18.20
Details of the imported Timer activities.

A

CLIENT DATA REVIEW

This appendix is provided for accounting professionals using QuickBooks Accountant 2014 or QuickBooks Enterprise Solutions Accountant 14.0. Client Data Review is a tool available with these editions of the QuickBooks software.

Reviewing clients' files can be a time-consuming process. Accounting professionals can save time working with their clients' files using these capabilities of Client Data Review:

- Reclassify hundreds of transactions at once

- Write off multiple open customer invoice balances at once

- Fix incorrectly recorded sales tax payments

- Quickly troubleshoot inventory issues

- Identify changes clients made to the lists in QuickBooks

- Troubleshoot beginning balance changes from year to year

- Apply open vendor and customer credits in batch to charges/invoices

- Clear up balances left in the Undeposited Funds account

After working with the Client Data Review tools you may never want to review a client's file the "old-fashioned way" again!

Introduction: Features and Benefits

Available with QuickBooks Accountant 2014 is the Client Data Review (CDR) feature, in Figure A.1. Accessing CDR tools and features is easier than ever with the customizable Accountant's Center. CDR is a collection of tools and reports that accounting professionals primarily use to streamline the many tasks involved in reviewing, troubleshooting, and correcting a client's QuickBooks data.

Figure A.1 Client Data Review (CDR) is helpful for finding and fixing your client's QuickBooks data entry errors.

The CDR feature is not available for use with QuickBooks Online, or QuickBooks for Mac. However, QuickBooks Online Accountant has its own set of accounting tools similar to the ones in this appendix.

With QuickBooks Accountant software, all the features of CDR work with a QuickBooks Accountant's Copy of your client's file; see Chapter 16, "Sharing QuickBooks Data with Your Accountant."

You can use CDR when working with a client's Accountant's Copy file type (.QBX file extension), but some feature limitations apply. Refer to Chapter 16 for more details on the benefits of working with this file type.

Typically, a best practice workflow using CDR tools is as follows:

1. Review with the client open Accounts Receivable, Accounts Payable, and other balances for which the client has current information.

2. Review your client's data file using the CDR-specific tasks and reports.

3. Make data corrections using CDR tools, and set a QuickBooks closing date.

4. If completing a formal review, select **Mark Review Complete**, letting CDR "store" your period reviewed balances. (The client cannot change these reviewed balances.)

5. Save the details of the review as a PDF.

6. Print the details from the Client Data Review dialog box. Save the details as a PDF. You can also print an Audit Trail of Review, listing the transactions that were added or modified.

7. Begin your next review, and let QuickBooks detail for you any and all changes to balances, transactions, and lists since your last completed review.

> **tip**
>
> You can use CDR features when QuickBooks is in multiuser mode. This means other users in the QuickBooks file can continue with their daily tasks while the accounting professional uses the CDR tools or features to review or make changes to the client's file.
>
> However, only one user can access Client Data Review at a time.

> ➡ *For more information on working with the Accountant's Copy, see Chapter 16 "Sharing QuickBooks Data With Your Accountant" p. 597.*

There are specific tasks and reports that are available only with CDR. The tasks are indicated with the CDR icon. For example, see the icon next to the Troubleshoot Prior Account Balances task, in Figure A.1. Other tasks listed without the icon indicate a feature or report that is available within and outside the CDR functionality.

CDR offers robust tracking of the changes your client makes to the data between your reviews. CDR also offers the following:

- Powerful time-saving tools for finding and fixing client entry errors: Reclassify Transactions, Write Off Invoices, Fix Incorrectly Recorded Sales Tax, Inventory Troubleshooting, Identify Changes to Lists, Troubleshoot Beginning Balance Differences, Match Unapplied Vendor and Customer Credits, and Clear Up Undeposited Funds.

- Troubleshooting beginning balances "saves" the previously reviewed debit and credit balances; the tool then compares this stored balance to the same prior-dated balances in QuickBooks as of today. Your client cannot modify your previously reviewed and stored QuickBooks balances.

- QuickBooks suggests an adjusting journal entry to make your prior-period reviewed balances agree with the current QuickBooks data for that period. You remain in control and can decide whether you want to modify the detail in the journal entry.

- Identify what chart of accounts balances differ, and determine the amount of the difference when compared to your prior period of reviewed financials.

- Track changes to the Items Lists, such as additions, name changes, and even tracking accounts or list items that were merged.

- Track changes made to list items, accounts assigned, or payroll items when a change to a payroll tax rate is made.

- While working with CDR activities, if you have the Open Windows dialog box displayed, you can move efficiently between activities in QuickBooks and the CDR activities. For more information about navigating QuickBooks, see Chapter 2, "Getting Around QuickBooks."

- Conveniently work on CDR in QuickBooks, and modify or add transactions as normal with an immediate refresh of the data in your review.

- You can use the CDR tool while working in a client's Accountant's Copy file-sharing format. All CDR tools and features work with an Accountant's Copy. Other restrictions apply when working with an Accountant's Copy; Chapter 16 details these.

If you are an accounting professional and want to work most efficiently with your client's file, use QuickBooks Accountant 2014 or QuickBooks Enterprise Solutions Accountant 14.0.

Accessing Client Data Review Tools and Features

With QuickBooks Accountant 2014, accounting professionals can access common CDR tools and features in the software multiple ways, including the following:

- **Accountant Center**—Customize this to include the tools you use most with your clients' files.

- **Accountant Menu**—Use individual CDR tools and features without starting a review, or launch a formal dated review.

Before you use CDR, determine whether you need to do a formal review or just efficiently work on troubleshooting and fixing client data entry errors.

If your client has engaged you simply to clean up data entry errors, you might not need to open a review to complete these CDR-specific tasks:

- Reclassify Transactions

- Fix Unapplied Customer and Vendor Credits

- Clear Up Undeposited Funds Account

- Write Off Invoices

- Fix Incorrectly Recorded Sales Tax

tip

As an accounting professional, if you would like to try CDR even if you don't have the Accountant's edition of QuickBooks, you have a way to do so. Have your client create a user login for you in the client's file and assign the External Accountant user type. For more information, see "Creating an External Accountant User Type," p. 618.

When you log in to the client's Pro or Premier 2014 or Enterprise 14.0 data file as an External Accountant user, you then have access to the Accountant Center (which opens automatically, or you can access it from the Company menu). Although this Accountant Center is not customizable, you do have *limited* access to some of the features found only in QuickBooks Accountant software and selected CDR tools, including the following:

- Create a Working Trial Balance

- Reclassify Transactions

- Fix Unapplied Payments and Credits

- Write Off Invoices

In addition, your Accountant Center provides easy access to other common QuickBooks tasks, memorized reports, reconciliation details, and updates especially for the accounting professional.

- Compare Balance Sheet and Inventory Valuation

- Troubleshoot Inventory

- Find Incorrectly Paid Payroll Liabilities

However, if part of your engagement with the client includes using the following CDR tools (detailed later in this chapter), you need to Start Review formally using CDR:

- Troubleshoot Prior Account Balances

- Review List Changes

If your client sends you an Accountant's Copy file with data, you can access the features available with CDR. The benefit of using the Accountant's Copy file is that your client can continue day-to-day operations while you make changes to the data. The file is then sent back to the client to import your changes.

 For more information on working with the Accountant's Copy, see Chapter 16 "Sharing QuickBooks Data With Your Accountant" p. 597.

If your client sends you a QuickBooks 2014 backup file (.QBB extension) or portable company file (.QBM file extension), both of these files, when restored, enable you to use the CDR tool. However, your changes cannot be merged into the data file at the client's office.

> **tip**
>
> You can use many of the CDR tools without opening a dated review. The date range that defaults when using CDR tools is your last fiscal year. However, with most of the tools, you can change the date range manually, if needed.

> **note**
>
> New for QuickBooks 2014, if you are using the QuickBooks Accountant software and your client is using a version of QuickBooks 2014 for Windows, you can send your adjusting journal entries by email for your client to import. For more information, see "Other Methods of Sharing Data," p. 630.

Customizing the Accountant Center

For the accounting professional, a great benefit of using the Accountant version of QuickBooks 2014 or Enterprise 14.0 is the Accountant Center, in Figure A.2. The Accountant Center offers easy access to Client Data Review tools and other accountant features.

You also can access the Accountant Center from a client's 2014 Pro or Premier (nonaccountant) and Enterprise 14.0 file when you, the accounting professional, log into the file as an External Accountant user.

By default, a preference is set to have the Accountant Center open automatically, but you also can access the Accountant Center from the Accountant menu. In a nonaccountant edition of QuickBooks, you can log in as the External Accountant user type and access the Accountant Center from the Company menu. When you log in to the file this way, some of the Accountant Center features are available, but not all.

> **tip**
>
> You need to customize the Accountant Center only once, and your customized view displays with each unique client file opened with your Premier Accountant 2014 software. However, a shortcut won't appear on the Accountant Center if the feature it points to is not enabled in a particular client's file.

Figure A.2
Customize the Accountant Center to include the tools and features you use most when working with your client's data.

The Accountant Center also provides easy access to Memorized Report Groups. You can learn about working with reporting in QuickBooks in Chapter 14, "Reporting in QuickBooks," p. 553.

For accounting professionals, create your own memorized report group and access it from the Accountant Center when working with each client's file.

The Reconciliation panel includes timely information about your client's last reconciliation date—reconciled balance and current balance for all bank and credit card type accounts. Click Refresh to reflect recent changes to the client's data. More information about working with banking activities is in Chapter 13, "Working with Bank and Credit Card Accounts," p. 520.

The Accountant's Update section helps accounting professionals stay informed with important alerts, practice development tips, and links to training opportunities.

If you are using QuickBooks Accountant 2014 or Enterprise Accountant 14.0, practice customizing the Accountant Center with these instructions.

Customize the Accountant Center

Open the Accountant Center from the Accountant menu to customize the Tools section:

1. From the menu bar, select **Accountant, Accountant Center**.
2. Click the Customize link in the Tools panel of the Accountant Center. The Customize Your List of Tools dialog box displays. See Figure A.3.

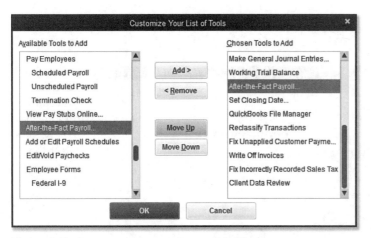

Figure A.3
Customize the Accountant Center to include the tools you use most often.

3. From the Available Tools to Add list, select an action you want to add to the Chosen Tools to Add section and click the Add button.

4. Rearrange the order of the selected tools by selecting one in the Chosen Tools to Add list and then clicking the Move Up or Move Down buttons.

5. (Optional) To remove a tool, click the tool in Chosen Tools to Add, and then click the <Remove button.

6. Click OK to close the Customize Your List of Tools dialog box. Your changes display in your very own Accountant Center.

Customizing the Client Data Review Center

You can customize the list of displayed clean-up tasks in CDR. However, the changes you make affect only the QuickBooks file currently opened. Additionally, some CDR tasks display only if the related feature in QuickBooks is enabled (Sales Tax, for example).

To gain access to the customizing feature, launch the CDR feature. To do so, follow these steps:

1. From the menu bar, select **Accountant**, **Client Data Review**, **Client Data Review**. You can also launch CDR from the QuickBooks icon bar if you are using QuickBooks Accountant 2014 or Enterprise Solutions Accountant 14.0.

2. If this is your first review for this client, the Client Data Review—Start Review dialog box displays, as in Figure A.4. From this dialog box, either accept the default Review Date Range shown or select a date range from the following options in the drop-down list:

   ▪ Last Fiscal Year (your default fiscal year is defined in the QuickBooks Company, Company Information menu)

   ▪ Last Fiscal Quarter

■ Last Month

■ Custom (you choose the From and To dates)

Client Data Review - Start Review

Client Data
Review

QuickBooks
Accountant
Edition

Client
Data
Review

The Client Data Review tool streamlines your client file cleanup tasks. To begin, specify the date range and basis for the review.

REVIEW DATE RANGE

Dates Last Fiscal Year   From the first day through the last day of last fiscal year.

From 01/01/2016 To 12/31/2016

REVIEW BASIS

○ Accrual   ● Cash

Modify Review   Cancel   Help

Figure A.4
When you choose to do a formal review, you select the date range and basis.

3. Select the appropriate **Review Basis**—**Accrual** or **Cash**. This basis defaults from the Reports & Graphs preference setting in the QuickBooks file.

4. (Optional) Click to select to have Task Notes from previous reviews repeat in the new review.

5. Click Start Review. The Client Data Review tasks display as previously shown in Figure A.1.

---

tip

If you find you need to change your default reporting basis, you can do so on the Reports and Graphs tab of the Preferences dialog box (select **Edit, Preferences** from the menu bar). You need to be logged in as the Admin or External Accountant user in single-user mode to change the global preference for reporting basis.

Modifying the Review Date and Basis

The basis shown in the CDR defaulted from the QuickBooks data file preferences when the CDR was first launched, or you might have manually selected the basis on the Client Data Review—Start Review or Modify Review dialog box.

After beginning a review, if you need to change either the review period or the basis, click the Modify Review link in the CDR (top center) to return to the dialog box (refer to Figure A.1).

Customize Cleanup Tasks

You might have some clients who do not need a review of some of the task groups in their QuickBooks data. For example, say you are working in a client's file that does not have to track or pay sales tax.

With CDR, you can remove the tasks you do not need for the specifically open client file. The changes made in one client's file do not affect another client's file CDR tasks.

With Client Data Review open, follow these steps to remove the sales tax task group (or any of the other tasks) from the CDR:

1. Click the Customize Cleanup Tasks link in the center of the CDR dialog box (refer to Figure A.1).

2. The Client Data Review—Customize dialog box displays (see Figure A.5).

Figure A.5
Remove CDR tasks from being displayed in this currently selected client file.

Client Data Review - Customize

Check all Categories or Tasks you wish to see in the Client Data Review

CATEGORIES/TASK
✓ Account Balances
✓   Troubleshoot Prior Account Balances
✓   Reclassify Transactions
✓   Open Working Trial Balance
✓ Review List Changes
✓   Chart of Accounts
✓   Items
✓   Fixed Asset Items
✓   Payroll Items
✓   Review Item Setup
✓   Customers
✓   Vendors
✓   Change Other Name Types
✓ Accounts Receivable
✓   Fix Unapplied Customer Payments and Credits
✓   Clear Up Undeposited Funds Account
✓   Review AR Aging Summary Report
✓   Write Off Invoices

3. Place your mouse pointer on any list item, and click once to deselect that specific task or group of tasks. Clicking again reselects the list item.

4. Click the Restore Defaults button to return to the original settings.

5. Click Help to open the help topic specific for CDR.

6. Click Save Changes or Cancel if you do not want to make the changes.

You have successfully changed the lists of tasks that display for this client's data file only.

> **tip**
>
> If the desired Categories/Task does not display in the Client Data Review—Customize dialog box, it is because for the currently opened QuickBooks file that feature is not currently enabled.

Minimize or Expand Task Groups

You might not want to remove a task completely, but you instead want to minimize it. Figure A.6 shows the task group before being minimized. Figure A.7 shows the same group after being minimized. The Hide and Show Task state for each task group on the CDR is company file dependent. The changes you make in one company file are not made in other QuickBooks client files.

Figure A.6
View before minimizing the Review List Changes task.

Figure A.7
View after minimizing the Review List Changes task.

- **Balances in Client's File**—Debit and credit columns, these amounts are the currently calculated balances in the client's file for an earlier review period.

- **Difference**—Debit and credit columns, the amounts displayed in these columns represent differences between the Balances in Accountant's Records and the Balances in Client's File.

The primary purpose of this task is to provide a window where QuickBooks can compare the prior-year's ending balances (which you used to prepare financials, tax returns, or monthly and quarterly reviews) with what QuickBooks currently shows for that same date range.

Your work is completed in this window when no amounts remain in the difference columns—this indicates that the Balances in Accountant's Records agree with the Balances in Client's File for that same date.

Entering Balances in Accountant's Records

If this is your first time using CDR with your client's data, you first need to enter the Balances in Accountant's Records columns in debit and credit spreadsheet format. You have two options for completing this task:

- Select **Yes** to the message that displays when you begin your first CDR of this file. CDR copies the columns of data from the Balances in Client's File to the Balances in Accountant's Records columns. Simply change any of the values copied to agree with your prior financials. If you select **No** to this message, a Copy Balances button is available at the top left for you to click to complete the task automatically.

- Alternatively, you can manually enter the amounts in the Balances in Accountant's Records columns to agree with your last reported financials or filed tax return.

This is the only time you are required to enter the balances. For future reviews, QuickBooks populates the Balances in Accountant's Records columns with the reviewed balances as recorded when you selected Mark Review as Complete at the bottom right of the CDR center.

The Troubleshoot Prior Account Balances task compares these prior balances to the current balances QuickBooks has for each account for the same earlier date range. QuickBooks is determining for you which accounts have a discrepancy from the last review. You'll spend less time on clean-up tasks with CDR.

Any reported balance differences might have been less likely to occur if you had entered a closing date and password in your client's data file.

Figure A.9 shows a difference for the account Checking (as well as a difference for the account Rent, not shown). The next section details how these CDR-dependent tasks help you locate these differences.

> 💠 **tip**
>
> When working with the Troubleshoot Prior Account Balances task, if a chart of account was marked as inactive in QuickBooks but has a balance in the account as of the date range in the review, the CDR includes that account listing.

View Changed Transactions

If this is your first time using the CDR for a client's data file, QuickBooks will not be able to detail the specific changed transactions in the Differences columns. However, after you choose Mark Review as Complete for the first CDR, QuickBooks begins tracking specific changed transactions from that time forward.

To determine what transactions dated on or before your last completed review date have been modified, double-click any amount displayed in the Differences column. A transaction listing report displays (see Figure A.10). The report identifies for you the specific transactions dated on or before the end of the last review period that have been added, modified, or deleted.

8:10 AM	Rock Castle Construction - Account: 10100 · Checking							
12/15/17	Transactions on/before 12/31/2015 - Changed on/after 01/01/2016							
	No list changes affect this account.							
Last modified by	◇ State ◇	Date ◇	Name ◇	Account ◇	Split ◇	Debit ◇	Credit ◇
Laura (External Accountant)	*Deleted*					0.00	
Admin	Prior	12/01/2015	Reyes Properties	10100 · Checking	63900 · Rent		1,200.00
			Reyes Properties	63900 · Rent	10100 · Checking	1,200.00	

Figure A.10
Using CDR can help you easily identify changes to transactions that affect the beginning balances.

If you double-clicked a difference amount on a specific line, the resulting report is filtered for transactions modified after your last review. You can limit what you see on the report by clicking the Customize Report button on the displayed report. You can filter for Entered/Last Modified dates to see only transactions that changed after you finished your review.

This one feature alone is why accountants should use QuickBooks Accountant 2014. Think of all the time you can save on future reviews of your client's data!

> ## tip
>
> Select the **Only Show Accounts with Different Balances** checkbox if you want to view fewer rows of detail in the Troubleshoot Prior Account Balances task in CDR.

View Suggested Adjustments

When QuickBooks detects any difference between the Balances in Accountant's Records and the Balances in Client's File, CDR suggests an adjusting journal entry for you to review.

To have QuickBooks assist in the preparation of this adjusting journal entry, follow these steps:

1. If QuickBooks detects differences, click the View Suggested Adjustments button. QuickBooks opens the Make General Journal Entries dialog box, marked as an adjusting entry and dated as of the last date of the period under review (see Figure A.11). If your debits and credits are equal in the Review Last Balances columns, this journal entry should also have debits equal to credits for any detected differences.

Figure A.11
QuickBooks prepares an adjusting journal entry to agree with your reviewed balances for the earlier period.

2. If you are working in an Accountant's Copy file, you might also get a notice that any changes made to shaded fields in the journal entry transfer back to the client. Click OK to close this message.

3. Click OK to close the message about automatically numbering your journal entries.

4. Click Save & Close to close the Make General Journal Entries dialog box.

5. Click View Suggested Reversing Entries if, after you make these adjustments, you need to reverse them. This is useful if the client corrected the error in a future accounting period. Or click the Don't Reverse button to close the Reversing Entries dialog box.

6. Click the X in the top-right corner to close the Troubleshoot Prior Account Balances dialog box.

The Troubleshoot Prior Account Balances task is complete when no amounts appear in the Differences column. Optionally, you can enter a task note for the Troubleshooting Prior Account Balances task to document your work or note other necessary actions.

When you click the Mark Review Complete button on the CDR dialog box, CDR transfers the Balances in Client's File columns to the Balances in Accountant's Records columns in the Troubleshoot Prior Account Balances dialog box. The Balances in Accountant's Records amounts *do not* change when clients add, modify, or delete transactions dated in your completed review period.

> **note**
> You cannot save a journal entry transaction unless the totals of the debits and credits are equal.

> **caution**
> If you selected View Suggested Adjustments and you had adjustments to an Accounts Receivable and Accounts Payable account, a warning message displays that you cannot adjust accounts receivable and accounts payable in the same journal entry. Instructions are given to remove one of the lines and the corresponding balancing line, and enter it in a separate journal entry.

Reclassify Transactions

How often have you reviewed your client's QuickBooks data to see multiple transactions posted to the incorrect general ledger account? As an accountant, you probably do not want to spend the time needed to correct each individual transaction. A preferred method might be to create a journal entry transaction, which essentially "reclassifies" the amount out of the incorrect account and into the correct account.

With CDR in QuickBooks Accountant 2014 or Enterprise Solutions Accountant 14.0, you can use the Reclassify Transactions feature. You access this tool from the Accountant Center, from the Accountant menu, or from an opened review using CDR.

From the Accounts panel on the left side of the Reclassify Transactions dialog box, you can do the following:

- Accept or change the defaulted date range. These dates control the transactions that display for reclassifying.

- Accept or change the defaulted basis. This reporting basis defaults from the setting found in Preferences. If you want to change the default preference used, from the menu bar, select **Edit**, **Preferences**. On the left, choose Reports & Graphs and click the Company Preferences tab.

- From the View drop-down list, choose to view Expense, Profit & Loss, or Balance Sheet accounts.

- New for QuickBooks 2014, reclassify the "source" account to another account of the same type. For example, checks were assigned to the incorrect bank account. With Reclassify Transactions, in a single window, you can correctly assign them to the proper bank account.

After selecting a chart of account listing on the left in the Accounts panel, you can filter the transactions displayed on the right in the Transactions panel with these options:

- From the Name drop-down list, leave the default of All, for all active list items. Or select a specific list item from Customers, Employees, Vendor, or Other Names list.

- From the Show Transactions drop-down list, the default of Non-Item-Based (can be reclassified) is selected. Other options include Item-Based (can change only the class) or All to show all transactions.

After reviewing the detailed transactions, you might find that a certain vendor had all transactions assigned to the wrong expense account. For example, in Figure A.12, vendor Cal Gas & Electric had the transactions assigned to the Utilities:Water expense account. This was a mistake made on each check all year. The proper account should have been the Utilities:Gas and Electric expense account.

Before using CDR, accounting professionals would have created a journal entry reducing expenses recorded to the Utilities:Water account and increasing expenses for Utilities:Gas and Electric account. With this CDR feature, reclassifying the transactions is easy by following these steps:

tip

When you select **Include Inactive Names** from the Name drop-down list in the Reclassify Transactions task, you do not affect the transactions displayed. Instead, the list now includes any inactive list items for you to select from.

If you select an inactive name from the list, a message displays from QuickBooks asking if you want to use it once, make it active, or cancel.

For more information on working with lists, see Chapter 4, "Understanding QuickBooks Lists."

Figure A.12
Use the
Reclassify
Transactions
dialog box
to correct
the account
assigned to
multiple
transactions.

Currently viewing

1. With the Reclassify Transactions dialog box displayed (see Figure A.12), select a date range for which you want to review and possibly reclassify transactions.

2. Accept the default Basis, or change it if needed.

3. From the View drop-down list, select the account types you want to review for reclassification.

4. Select a specific chart of account list item. In the Accounts panel on the left, displayed to the right are transactions assigned to that account for the selected date range and basis.

5. (Optional) From the Name drop-down list, select a specific vendor, customer, employee, or other name for which you want to filter the displayed transactions.

6. The Show Transactions drop-down list defaults to display only transactions you can reclassify with this feature. Optionally, you can choose to show item-based transactions. For item-based transactions, you can reclassify only the Class assigned. Or select **All** to see both item-based and non-item-based transactions.

> 🔊 **caution**
> You can reclassify only non-item-based transactions with the CDR tool. If you want to edit the account assigned on item-based transactions, you need to edit the individual item in the original transaction. For more information about working with QuickBooks items, refer to Chapter 4.

7. (Optional) Select the Include Journal Entries checkbox.

8. In step 5, if you selected a specific name from the drop-down list, you might want to select Accounts: **Show All**. CDR displays all transactions for the Name selected for all accounts (not just the account selected on the left).

9. As you make changes to the filters in Reclassify Transactions, the displayed transactions refresh automatically.

10. (Optional) Choose Select All or Deselect All when choosing which transactions to reclassify.

11. For all selected transactions, select the proper general ledger account from the Account To drop-down list. Optionally, you can assign a new Class, if desired.

12. Review your selections and click the Reclassify button. The window data refreshes, displaying the changes made to the transactions.

13. Continue reviewing all the accounts until your review is complete.

14. Press the Esc key on your keyboard or click the X at the top right of the Reclassify Transactions dialog box when you are ready to close.

Open Working Trial Balance

The Working Trial Balance tool has been available for years. It is included with the Premier Accountant and Enterprise Solutions Accountant versions of QuickBooks.

The Working Trial Balance displays the following details (see Figure A.13):

- Account

- Beginning Balance

- Transactions (for the selected date range)

- Adjustments (total of adjusting journal entries)

- Ending Balance

- Workpaper Reference (where you can record specific notes)

The Working Trial Balance provides a window to manage changes to a client's ending balances. You normally use this tool after you have matched the prior-year balances in the Troubleshoot Prior Account Balances task with your records and you need to review and correct the next accounting period.

Click the Make Adjustments button to create an adjusting journal entry and watch the net impact to your client's Net Income change with each saved journal entry change. When you are finished, click the Print button to prepare a report of your work.

Figure A.13
Use the
Working Trial
Balance to
make and
review adjust-
ments to the
client's file in
preparation
for tax filings.

ACCOUNT	BEGINNING BALANCE	TRANSACTIONS	ADJUSTMENTS	ENDING BALANCE	WORKPAPER REFERENCE
10100 · Checking	24,342.03	12,686.07		37,028.10	Need to reconcile, print, file
10300 · Savings	15,600.00	281.03		15,881.03	Reconciled & filed
10400 · Petty Cash	500.00			500.00	
Money Market					
11000 · Accounts Receiva...	2,891.35	-950.97		1,940.38	
12000 · Undeposited Funds		18,470.02		18,470.02	
12100 · Inventory Asset	17,903.00	-7,235.96	-1,035.00	9,632.04	
12800 · Employee Advanc...	770.00			770.00	
13100 · Pre-paid Insurance	4,050.00	893.02		4,943.02	
13400 · Retainage Receiv...	1,796.72			1,796.72	
15000 · Furniture and Equ...	22,826.00			22,826.00	QuickBooks Fixed Asset Manager
15100 · Vehicles	78,936.91			78,936.91	QuickBooks Fixed Asset Manager
15200 · Buildings and Imp...	325,000.00			325,000.00	QuickBooks Fixed Asset Manager
15300 · Construction Equi...	15,300.00			15,300.00	
16900 · Land	90,000.00			90,000.00	QuickBooks Fixed Asset Manager
17000 · Accumulated Depr...	-65,908.69		-44,435.91	-110,344.60	QuickBooks Fixed Asset Manager
Totals	0.00	0.00	0.00	0.00	

Working Trial Balance

Selected Period [Last Fiscal Year ▼] From [01/01/2016] To [12/31/2016] Basis [Cash ▼]

Net Income   47,170.44

☐ Only show accounts with transaction activity   [Make Adjustments...]   [Print...]

Review List Changes

The Review List Changes feature is available only with your QuickBooks Premier Accountant software and is available only when you launch a review using the Client Data Review feature. The
type of changes tracked is specific to each task, as the next several sections detail. Remember, if a
task has the CDR icon in front of it, the task can be accessed only using CDR. If any other tasks are
listed, they link to the respective menu in QuickBooks for that activity.

◎ Chart of Accounts

Chapter 4 covered reviewing the chart of accounts, correcting setup errors, making an account
inactive, and merging like accounts. When a CDR is marked as Completed, these list changes are
also marked with an R for "reviewed" so that, in future reviews, you can conveniently hide those
changes.

Click the Chart of Accounts task in the Review List Changes task group. QuickBooks displays the
Review List Changes dialog box in Figure A.14.

Figure A.14
Easily track your client's changes to the chart of accounts.

The Chart of Accounts tab on the Review List Changes dialog box tracks the following types of changes:

- **Added**—Account Name and Account Type

- **Changed**—Marked Inactive, Name or Account Number changed, Account Type changed, Parent:Subaccount relationship changed, or Tax-Line Mapping changed

- **Deleted**—Account Name and Account Type

- **Merged**—Original Account Name, Destination Account Name, and Account Type

For changes your client has made, which you want to indicate as Reviewed, click the Mark All as Reviewed button. Changes you make to the lists while logged in as the new External Accountant user are automatically marked as Reviewed.

The tabs at the top enable easy access to the remaining tracked list changes. Press the Esc key on your keyboard or click the X on the top right of the Review List Changes dialog box when you have completed this task.

Items

Chapter 4 details methods for finding and troubleshooting item setup errors. This feature tracks changes made to items. When the review is completed, an R is placed next to each line item change to indicate that it has been reviewed. In future Client Data Reviews, you can conveniently hide these previously reviewed changes.

Click the Items task in the Review List Changes task group. QuickBooks displays the Review List Changes dialog box, in Figure A.15.

Figure A.15
Items affect-
ing account-
ing and
reviewing
changes to
these help in
a client's file
review.

> **Review List Changes**
>
> | Chart of Accounts | **Items** | Fixed Asset Items | Payroll Items |
>
> After reviewing, click Mark All as Reviewed to hide reviewed items. To redisplay them, check Include Reviewed items.   How this works
> (View Item List) (Review Item Setup)
>
> **Added**
>
> | REVIEWED | ITEM NAME | ITEM TYPE |
> |---|---|---|
> | | Wood Door With Glass | Inventory Part |
>
> **Changed →**   **→Details of**   Bad debt
>
> | REVIEWED | ITEM NAME | ITEM TYPE | | DATA THAT CHANGED | ORIGINAL VALUE | NEW VALUE |
> |---|---|---|---|---|---|---|
> | | Bad debt | Other Charge | | Item Name | Bad debt | Bad Debt w Sales Tax |
>
> **Deleted**
>
> | REVIEWED | ITEM NAME | ITEM TYPE |
> |---|---|---|
> | | BOM | Group |
>
> **Merged**
>
> | REVIEWED | ORIGINAL ITEM NAME | DESTINATION ITEM NAME | ITEM TYPE |
> |---|---|---|---|
> | | Retainage 2 | Retainage 1 | Other Charge |
>
> ☐ Include Reviewed Items   Mark All as Reviewed

The Items tab on the Review List Changes dialog box tracks the following:

- **Added**—Item Name and Item Type

- **Changed**—The data that changed, with Original Value and New Value

- **Deleted**—Item Name and Item Type

- **Merged**—Original Item Name, Destination Item Name, and Item Type

When you click the Mark All as Reviewed button, the CDR feature places an R in the Reviewed column for each item list change your client made. Changes you make to the list while logged in as the
External Accountant user are automatically marked as reviewed.

Tabs at the top enable easy access to the remaining tracked list changes. Press the Esc key on your
keyboard or click the X on the top right of the Review List Changes dialog box when you have completed this task.

Fixed Asset Items

A business owner using QuickBooks can create a Fixed Asset item type from the Fixed Asset Item
List (select **Lists**, **Fixed Asset Item List** from the menu bar). Then when a purchase is made for the
asset, the respective Fixed Asset item can be recorded on a purchase order, or on the Items tab of
the Enter Bills dialog box or the Write Checks dialog box. This tab tracks changes made to the list of
fixed assets.

Click the Fixed Asset Items task in the Review List Changes task group. QuickBooks displays the
Review List Changes dialog box (see Figure A.16).

Figure A.16
Easily track additions, deletions, and changes to the client's fixed assets.

The Fixed Asset Items tab on the Review List Changes dialog box tracks the following fixed assets:

- **Added**—Displays the Fixed Asset Item Name and Fixed Asset Item Type
- **Changed**—The data that changed, with Original Value and New Value
- **Deleted**—Fixed Asset Item Name and Fixed Asset Item Type

When the Mark All as Reviewed button is selected, the Client Data Review places an "R" in the Reviewed column for each fixed asset item list change your client made. If you are logged in to the file as an External Accountant user type, as you make list changes, they are automatically marked as Reviewed.

Tabs along the top of the Review List Changes dialog box enable easy access to the remaining tracked list changes. Press the Esc key on your keyboard or click the X on the top right of the Review List Changes dialog box when you have completed this task.

Payroll Items

Chapter 11, "Setting Up Payroll," reviewed the purpose of payroll items. Chapter 12, "Managing Payroll," also provided details on correcting payroll setup errors. This feature tracks changes made to payroll items. When the review is completed, an R is placed next to each payroll item change to indicate that it has been reviewed. In future client data reviews, you can conveniently hide these.

This task displays only in a file that has the payroll preference enabled.

Click the Payroll Items task in the Review List Changes task group. QuickBooks displays the Review List Changes dialog box (see Figure A.17).

Figure A.17
See the changes the client made to payroll items throughout the year.

The Payroll Items tab on the Review List Changes dialog box tracks the following payroll items:

- **Added**—Payroll Item Name and Payroll Item Type

- **Changed**—The data that changed, with Original Value and New Value

- **Deleted**—Payroll Item Name and Payroll Item Type

- **Merged**—Original Payroll Item Name, Destination Payroll Item Name, and Payroll Item Type

When you click the Mark All as Reviewed button, CDR places an R in the Reviewed column for each item list change your client made. If you are logged in to the file as an External Accountant user type, as you make list changes, they are automatically marked as Reviewed.

Tabs at the top enable easy access to the remaining tracked list changes. Press the Esc key on your keyboard or click the X on the top right to close the Review List Changes dialog box when you have completed this task.

Review Item Setup

Click the Review Item Setup in the Review List Changes task group. The Add/Edit Multiple List Entries dialog box displays.

From this dialog box, you can make changes to selected item types. Chapter 4, "Understanding QuickBooks Lists," and Chapter 5, "Setting Up Inventory," have more detail about working with the Add/Edit Multiple List Entries.

Customers

In Figure A.18, note that the Customers task in the Review List Changes pane does not have a Client Data Review icon in front of the name. This indicates that CDR is linking you back to the original Customer Center.

Tasks with an icon are only available with CDR

Figure A.18
Tasks without the CDR icon provide quick access to the same menu in QuickBooks.

Refer to Chapter 9, "Setting Up Customers," for more details on how to use the Customer Center to gather information and easily find specific transactions.

Vendors

The Vendors task in the Review List Changes task group also does not have a CDR icon in front of the name. This indicates that CDR is linking you back to the original Vendor Center.

Refer to Chapter 7, "Setting Up Vendors," for more details on how to use the Vendor Center to gather information and easily find specific transactions.

Change Other Name Types

QuickBooks includes another names list that is useful when you are paying a supplier or service provider one time and you are not required to provide a 1099-MISC Income document at the end of the year.

This list is titled Other Names List. If you previously added a name to this list and you later need to change the list name to a vendor or even a customer record, click this task link and make the change as desired. The change is not reversible, so take care with this task.

Accounts Receivable

Reviewing open accounts receivable with your client is an important part of a successful review of a client's file. When errors exist in accounts receivable, the Balance Sheet and Profit & Loss accounts could be misstated.

For a complete review of Accounts Receivable, including the proper process to use in QuickBooks for potentially avoiding the corrections detailed in this section, see Chapter 9, "Setting Up Customers," and Chapter 10, "Managing Customers."

The tasks listed in the Accounts Receivable task group of the CDR help you easily correct client mistakes made when the client recorded a customer payment or completed a deposit but *did not* properly complete the transaction.

Recent versions of QuickBooks discourage this error with messaging that warns the user not to use a Make Deposits transaction to record a customer payment. When recording a customer payment without assigning the payment to an open invoice, QuickBooks provides a message that a credit will be left in the customer's account.

You might want to review the AR Aging Summary report first and then begin the process of using the CDR tools. Properly reviewing your client's data helps you make the most informed decisions about the corrections that might be needed.

Fix Unapplied Customer Payments and Credits

If your client entered a customer payment but did not apply the payment to an invoice, this tool helps simplify the task of assigning the unapplied payment to the proper invoice.

Review the Open Invoices report (select **Reports**, **Customers & Receivables**, **Open Invoices** from the menu bar) before you begin to make corrections. This is especially important if you have more than one Accounts Receivable account in your chart of accounts.

To fix unapplied payments and credits, follow these steps:

1. If you are completing these changes as part of a dated review, from the menu bar, select **Accountant**, **Client Data Review** and launch **Client Data Review**. Then launch the Fix Unapplied Customer Payments and Credits task in the Accounts Receivable group.

2. If you are not completing these changes as part of a dated review, from the menu bar, select **Accountant**, **Client Data Review** and launch the Fix Unapplied Customer Payments and Credits task.

3. If you have more than one Accounts Receivable account, review the details for each by selecting the appropriate Accounts.

4. Select any of the customers on the list (see Figure A.19). With a customer selected on the left, the Invoices and Charges tab displays any unapplied payments and credits (left side) and any open invoices (right side) for that specific customer.

5. On the Invoices and Charges tab, place a checkmark next to the payment or credit in the left pane, and place a checkmark next to the associated open invoice in the right pane to which you want to apply the payment.

Figure A.19
Assign unapplied customer payments or credits to an open customer invoice.

caution

Taxpayers who use cash basis reporting should proceed with caution when using this tool. In cash basis reporting, the date of the Receive Payments transaction is the date revenue is recorded. If a customer payment was dated in the previous filed tax year and was *not* applied to the customer's open invoice, the income from the invoice was not included in cash basis reporting.

When you use CDR to assign the payment to the open invoice, QuickBooks reports the revenue associated with that invoice as of the *date* of the customer payment.

This correction changes prior-period financials. The CDR *does not* recognize the controls associated with setting a closing date. Additionally, QuickBooks *does not* provide any warnings that you are modifying a transaction dated on or before the closing date.

6. If you want to apply only part of the credit or payment, enter the partial amount in the Amt to Apply column.

7. Click the Apply button to assign the payments or credits selected on the left to the selected open invoices on the right. The items are then grayed out to indicate that you have already assigned them.

8. (Optional) Click the Auto Apply All button to apply all the unapplied payments and credits to the invoices on the right.

9. Click Save to begin working on another customer record, or click Save & Close to complete the task.

Recent editions of QuickBooks make recording unapplied credits and payments less likely to occur because of the many warnings provided when the transactions are entered.

Clear Up Undeposited Funds Account

Have you ever worked with a client's data file that had an incorrect undeposited funds balance? Did your client create a separate deposit transaction without assigning the receive payment to the deposit?

The undeposited funds account is a current asset type on the Balance Sheet. It's like using a safe to store checks before you take them to the bank. Customer payments are recorded in QuickBooks, increasing the amount in Undeposited Funds on the Balance Sheet. Later the checks are gathered and added to a single deposit ticket taken to the bank account (more details are provided in Chapter 9, p. 370).

The Clear Up Undeposited Funds Account task can help you assign those undeposited funds to the deposit transaction that was created incorrectly.

Recent releases of QuickBooks make this error less likely to occur with the many warnings provided when the transactions are entered.

It is important to know that this feature works when any of the following conditions apply:

- The Receive Payments transaction was recorded and assigned to the Undeposited Funds account without including the payment in a Make Deposits transaction.

- The Make Deposits transaction was recorded, the Received From column included the Customer or Customer:Job name, and the Account From column has an account assigned, which is typically an income account. See Figure A.20.

Figure A.20
This customer payment was recorded improperly on the Make Deposits dialog box.

- If the Make Deposits transaction did not include a name in the Received From column, CDR reports that deposit transaction in the Clear Up Undeposited Funds Account CDR task assigned to a customer named No Name in Deposit.

To clear up the Undeposited Funds account, follow these steps:

1. If you are completing these changes as part of a dated review, from the menu bar, select **Accountant**, **Client Data Review** and launch Client Data Review. Then select the **Clear Up Undeposited Funds** task in the Accounts Receivable group.

2. If you are not completing these changes as part of a dated review, from the menu bar, select **Accountant**, **Client Data Review**, **Clear Up Undeposited Funds** task.

3. The Show Deposits From field defaults to the review period selected when you started a client data review; if you did not start a formal review, the dates default to your last fiscal year. If needed, change the selected dates and click Refresh to display the changes.

4. The Payers pane on the left displays any customers with transactions that meet the criteria listed previously. With a customer selected, review the payment transaction types on the right.

5. With a customer selected, place a checkmark next to the DEP transaction and also next to the PMT transaction on the right with which you want to associate the payment (see Figure A.21).

Figure A.21
Associate the customer payment in Clear Up Undeposited Funds Account to the incorrectly recorded Make Deposits transaction.

6. Click the Apply button to assign. The list items are grayed out, indicating they have been applied to each other.

7. Click Save to begin correcting records for the next customer, or click Save & Close to complete the task.

You are now ready to move on with your review or continue with additional clean-up tasks. I recommend reviewing the AR Summary report first to get a general idea of the types of corrections you might need to make with the remaining accounts receivable CDR tasks.

> **tip**
> Do you need to return to the original transaction in QuickBooks during your review? Simply double-click the selected transaction.

Reviewing the AR Aging Summary Report

Check the AR Aging Summary report before fixing transactions. An individual transaction can be deceiving if you don't see its relationship with other related transactions.

When you select the Review AR Aging Summary report link, QuickBooks opens the report of the same title.

What exactly are you looking for on the aging report? You might be looking for customer credits that are aged and have not been applied to current open customer invoices. Or perhaps, as in Chapter 10, p. 403, you might want to remove an open balance from a customer's invoice.

I recommend that you use the Open Invoices report instead of the Aging reports. The Open Invoices report shows the transactions listed separately instead of in summary form. The Open Invoices report is not part of the CDR tool set. It is, however, a regularly used QuickBooks report. Because the Open Invoices report shows the current A/R status, if you are reviewing it for a previous date, you need to modify the report to show the open balances as of that earlier date. To do this, follow these steps:

1. From menu bar, select **Reports**, **Customers & Receivables**, **Open Invoices**. This report includes all open invoices, credits, and payments for your customers as of today's computer system date.

2. Review the report with today's date first. This helps you identify what corrections you might want to make using the tasks defined in this section. Reviewing it with today's date also shows whether the correction you might have needed on a previous date has already been entered.

3. If you are reviewing for some date in the past, you can adjust the report to that date by clicking Customize Report in the top-left corner of the report window.

4. From the Display tab, click the Advanced button. In the Open Balance/Aging pane of the Advanced Options dialog box, change the selection to the Report Date option (see Figure A.22). This modification to the report enables you to see each customer's balance detail (see Figure A.23) as of a date in the past.

Figure A.22
You can compare the modified Open Invoices report to the totals on your Balance Sheet report for some time in the past.

Figure A.23
The Open Invoices report easily shows unpaid balances and any unapplied customer credits or payments.

9:46 AM								
12/15/17			**Rock Castle Construction**					
			Open Invoices					
			As of December 15, 2017					
◆ Type ◆	Date ◆	Num ◆	P. O. #	◆ Terms ◆	Due Date ◆	Class ◆	Aging ◆	Open Balance ◆
Remodel								
Payment	12/15/2017	1234						-14,510.00
Invoice	09/12/2017	1058		Net 15	09/27/2017	Remodel	79	14,510.00
Total Remodel								0.00
Total Allard, Robert								0.00
Burch, Jason								
Room Addition								
Invoice	11/25/2017	1083		Net 30	12/25/2017	New Co...		1,005.00
Total Room Addition								1,005.00

Write Off Invoices

Accounting professionals often need to adjust client's Accounts Receivable balances. Perhaps there were several small unpaid finance charge invoices, or over the year the client's customers did not pay the full amount of their invoices.

Creating a customer credit memo and assigning the credit memo to the original open invoice used to be time-consuming for the accounting professional. Often a journal entry was created, correcting the Accounts Receivable balance on the Balance Sheet but leaving the QuickBooks user with extra line details in the A/R Aging Summary or Detail reports.

> **tip**
>
> If the customer's invoice that is being written off included sales tax, make sure the item selected for the write off is a taxable item. This ensures that the Sales Tax Payable account is also reduced, which is important when sales tax is paid on an accrual basis.

The Write Off Invoices feature in Figure A.24 is one convenient window where you can write off balances, review the suggested transaction, and print the details for your customer.

To write off invoices, follow these steps:

1. If Client Data Review isn't already open, from the menu bar, select **Accountant**, **Accountant Center**.

2. Select the **Write Off Invoices** task in the Accounts Receivable task group.

> **tip**
>
> Earlier in this chapter, I recommended that you review the AR Aging Summary report before using the Accounts Receivable CDR tools. However, even if you do not review the report, the Write Off Invoices dialog box shows CREDITS in the Avail Credit/Pmt column if the customer with the open invoice balance also has unapplied credits.
>
> Click the CREDITS link to open the Fix Unapplied Customer Payments and Credits dialog box. Here you can apply the payment to the open invoice as instructed previously.
>
> It might be more appropriate to assign the available credit than to write off the open balance.

Figure A.24
Using CDR's
Write Off
Invoices task
makes remov-
ing open A/R
uncollected
balances easy.

3. If you see the warning that one or more customers in the list have available credits, click OK to close the message. Be sure to do a thorough review of your client's Open Invoices reports, as previously recommended.

4. From the Age drop-down list, choose to show receivables aged over 120 days, receivables aged over 180 days, a Review Period, or a custom date.

5. (Optional) Enter an amount in the Balances Due Less Than box to limit the transactions that display. This is particularly useful when writing off small balances.

6. Select a **To Date**.

7. From the Transaction Type drop-down list, select **All Charges**, **Invoices**, **Finance Charges**, or **Statement Charges**.

8. Click Refresh if you are changing the filters.

9. Place a checkmark next to each transaction for which you want to write off the open balance. (Optional) Click the Select All button or the Deselect All button at the bottom of the screen to simplify the process.

10. From the drop-down lists, select **Write Off Item** and **Write Off Date**. (Optional) Select a **Class**.

11. Click the Preview & Write Off button. CDR displays the Confirm Write Off dialog box (see Figure A.25).

12. Click Write Off when you are done reviewing the invoices, or click Cancel.

13. CDR returns you to the Write Off Invoices dialog box. Press the Esc key on your keyboard to view the Write Off Completed details.

14. Click Save as PDF to print for your records.

QuickBooks creates a Credit Memo transaction using the item and date you selected at the time you created the write off and applies this credit to the original invoice.

You are now finished with the Accounts Receivable tasks. Many QuickBooks preferences guide your clients as they manage undeposited funds and Accounts Receivable transactions. Review Chapters 9 and 10 for more details and other Accounts Receivable troubleshooting suggestions.

Figure A.25
You stay in control of the write off, confirming the balances to be removed.

Accounts Payable

Chapter 7, "Setting Up Vendors," and Chapter 8, "Managing Vendors," offer a complete review of Accounts Payable, including the proper process to use in QuickBooks. Following that procedure potentially avoids the corrections detailed in this section.

The tasks listed in the Accounts Payable section of the CDR feature can help you easily correct client mistakes made when the client has created a vendor credit or bill payment and did not assign it to the open vendor bill.

> **caution**
>
> Item receipts do not display in the CDR tools, but these transaction types are included in your client's open Accounts Payable balances. Review the Unpaid Vendor Bills report (select **Reports, Vendors & Payables** from the menu bar) for any aged item receipts.
>
> Chapter 6 offers more specific details for correcting aged item receipts.

The Review Unpaid Bills report is listed last in the Accounts Payable task group. I recommend reviewing this report and other reports before making corrections with the CDR. Properly reviewing your data helps you make the most informed decision on the corrections that might be needed.

⊚ Fix Unapplied Vendor Payments and Credits

Chapter 7 detailed the proper accounts payable process, which is to use the Pay Bills dialog box to pay vendor bills. Some QuickBooks users might have used the Enter Bills transaction type and later paid that vendor bill using the Write Checks transaction instead of properly using the Pay Bills dialog box.

To fix unapplied vendor payments and credits, follow these steps:

1. If you are completing these changes as part of a dated review, from the menu bar, select **Accountant**, **Client Data Review** and launch Client Data Review. Then select the **Fix Unapplied Vendor Payments and Credits** task the Accounts Payable group.

2. If you are not completing these changes as part of a dated review, from the menu bar, select **Accountant**, **Client Data Review** and launch the Fix Unapplied Vendor Payments and Credits task.

> **⚠ caution**
>
> If any of the checks listed in the left side of the Bills detail have an asterisk(*) in front of the word CHK, this indicates that the expense is marked as billable to the customer. CDR warns you that when you assign the check to an open vendor bill, the expense will no longer be marked as billable.
>
> Chapter 9 has more details about working with billable expenses in the section titled "Time and Expense Invoicing."

3. The Vendors tab at the top left and the Bills tab at the right are selected by default. Select any of the vendors on the list to the left. The Bills pane displays all unapplied vendor credits for the vendor selected on the left. On the right of the Bills pane, any open vendor bills for that specifically selected vendor display.

4. Place a checkmark next to the credit on the left and the open vendor bill on the right to which you want to apply the payment (see Figure A.26).

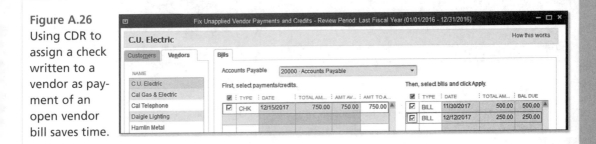

Figure A.26
Using CDR to assign a check written to a vendor as payment of an open vendor bill saves time.

5. Click the Apply button to assign that specific vendor credit transaction to that specific vendor bill. The items selected appear grayed out, indicating that you have assigned them properly.

6. Click Save to begin correcting transactions for another vendor, or click Save and Close to complete the task.

Evaluate and Correct 1099 Account Mapping

Setting up your vendors for proper 1099 status is important. However, be assured that, after reviewing this information, if you determine that the original setup was incorrect, any changes made here correct prior- and future-dated reports and forms.

When you select the link in the Accounts Payable task group for Evaluate and Correct 1099 Mapping, the Preferences dialog box for 1099s displays.

In the preference setting for Tax:1099, you can click the Yes button to select the Do You File option to let QuickBooks know you will be providing 1099 forms to your vendors at the end of the year. A new QuickBooks file defaults with the preference set to Yes for filing 1099-MISC forms.

If this is your first time setting up 1099s in your file, click the link next to If You're Ready to Prepare. The QuickBooks 1099 Wizard displays, as in Figure A.27.

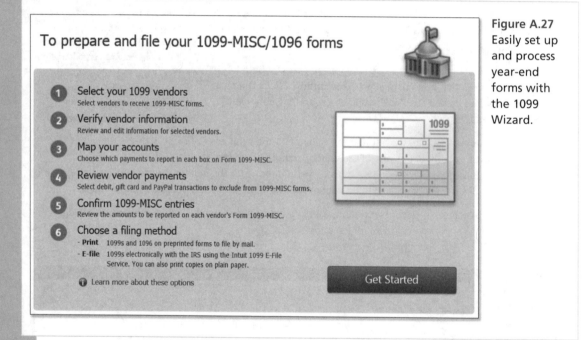

Figure A.27
Easily set up and process year-end forms with the 1099 Wizard.

For more detailed information on setting up your 1099s in QuickBooks, see Chapter 7.

Reviewing the Unpaid Bills Report

One of the first tasks to do with your client is review the Unpaid Bills report, primarily because the client knows best whether the bills that are open are still due and payable to the vendor.

What exactly are you looking for on the aging report? You might be looking for vendor credits that are aged and have not been applied to current open vendor bills. Or, as Chapters 7 and 8 documented, you might see several aged item receipts for vendors that you know your client has paid.

Use the information collected from this report to help determine the corrections that should be made with the tasks listed in the Accounts Payable task group of the CDR.

Sales Tax

This CDR feature not only identifies errors with using the incorrect payment transaction, but also automatically fixes the transaction.

For more information on properly setting up and using sales tax, see Chapter 9.

Before beginning the tasks listed in this section, review the client's settings (preferences) for sales tax (see Figure A.28). Additionally, the Sales Tax task group does not display in the CDR if the Sales Tax feature has not been enabled.

Figure A.28
Review Sales Tax preferences before making any corrections.

After reviewing and correcting your client's sales tax preference settings, you are prepared to begin the following CDR tasks.

Fix Incorrectly Recorded Sales Tax

QuickBooks uses a special Pay Sales Tax dialog box (see Figure A.29) to properly record the sales tax liability payments. When payments are made using other transaction types, such as Write Checks, Pay Bills, or Make General Journal Entries, the Pay Sales Tax dialog box might not reflect the payments accurately.

The Fix Incorrectly Recorded Sales Tax task helps you identify and correct the transaction when a client paid the sales tax liability outside the Pay Sales Tax dialog box. Figure A.30 shows the negative line entry that is included in the Pay Sales Tax dialog box when a Write Checks transaction was created, assigned to the Sales Tax Payable Liability account, and payable to the sales tax vendor. Properly recorded sales tax payments have a transaction type of TAXPMT in the checkbook register.

Figure A.29
Create properly paid sales tax using the Pay Sales Tax dialog box.

When sales tax is paid using a non-sales tax payment transaction type

Figure A.30
The Pay Sales Tax dialog box looks like this when an improperly recorded sales tax payment was made.

What exactly is this tool fixing? The tool identifies and fixes non-sales-tax-payable type transactions used to pay sales tax liability using Void and Replace functionality.

The tool identifies any Write Checks transactions in which the payee is the same as an assigned payee for any sales tax item.

This tool *does not* identify any vendor bills, vendor bill payment checks, or journal entries recording payment for the Sales Tax Liability.

📡 **caution**

This might be a good time to review with your client the vendor names associated with different types of tax payments. Some states might have the same vendor name for multiple agency tax payments.

Suggest that your client use a unique vendor name for each different type of tax being paid. This keeps CDR from possibly correcting a non-sales-tax type of payment made to a vendor.

If this is your first incorrectly recorded sales tax transaction fix, you might want to change the "to" date to include today's date. This ensures that you are seeing all sales tax payable transactions that were improperly recorded using the wrong transaction in QuickBooks.

To fix incorrectly recorded sales tax, follow these steps:

1. If you are completing these changes as part of a dated review, from the menu bar, select **Accountant, Client Data Review** and launch Client Data Review. Then select the **Fix Incorrectly Recorded Sales Tax** task in the Sales Tax group.

2. If you are not completing these changes as part of a dated review, from the menu bar, select **Accountant, Client Data Review** and launch the Fix Incorrectly Recorded Sales Tax task as in Figure A.31.

Figure A.31 Automatically find and fix incorrectly recorded sales tax payment transactions.

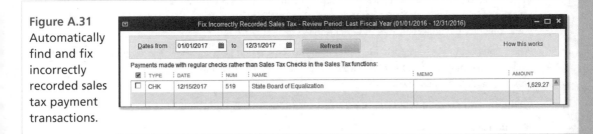

3. Double-click any transaction to see the originally created non-sales-tax payment transaction to make sure it should be changed to a Sales Tax Payment. Make note of the check number or check date.

4. Place a checkmark by each transaction to be fixed. (Optional) Use the Select All button or the Deselect All button to streamline the process.

5. Click Void & Replace (not shown in Figure A.31). CDR then creates a new Sales Tax Payment transaction and voids the original Write Checks transaction or Make General Journal Entries transaction.

6. Click Proceed to the Fix Sales Tax message that displays to continue with the change, or click Cancel to return to the CDR tool.

> **⚠ caution**
>
> If your client has multiple lines recorded on sales tax payable checks, such as including an additional fee for a late payment penalty or other adjustment lines, you might want to use the link for making a manual Sales Tax Adjustment.
>
> The Fix Incorrectly Recorded Sales Tax tool assumes that all lines of the incorrect transaction belong in the Sales Tax Payable account.

> **📶 tip**
>
> With the Void and Replace functionality included in the Fix Incorrectly Recorded Sales Tax tool, you are assured that if your original transaction was marked as cleared in a bank reconciliation, the newly created Sales Tax Payment transaction will be marked as cleared.

7. Click OK to close the message indicating that the transaction(s) have been fixed.

8. Click the X in the top-right corner to return to the CDR Center.

9. Return to your checkbook register (icon on the Home page) and look for the check number or date (or both) to view the original transaction voided and the new transaction created as a Sales Tax Payment type.

Adjust Sales Tax Payable

If you did not use the Fix Incorrectly Recorded Sales Tax tool to correct the client's sales tax records, you might instead want to use this manual Adjust Sales Tax Payable link.

In addition to reviewing fixing transactions, I recommend that you review the Sales Tax Liability reports and your Balance Sheet balance for Sales Tax Payable before and after making corrections to your sales tax payable balances in QuickBooks.

When comparing these reports and the Pay Sales Tax dialog box, make sure each report is using the same accrual or cash basis and is prepared with the same reporting date. For more information on working with the sales tax payable reports in QuickBooks, see Chapter 10.

Compare the following reports to each other for sales tax payable balances:

- **Balance Sheet**—Sales Tax Payable balance. From the menu bar, select **Reports**, **Company & Financial**, **Balance Sheet Standard**. (Optional) Click the Modify button to change the report basis and date.

- **Sales Tax Liability Report**—Sales Tax Payable as of <date> column total. From the menu bar, select **Vendors**, **Sales Tax**, **Sales Tax Liability**.

- **Pay Sales Tax**—Amt. Due column total. From the menu bar, select **Vendors**, **Sales Tax**, **Pay Sales Tax**.

The end result of a properly made sales tax correcting entry or adjustment is that the totals listed in the previously mentioned reports agree.

To adjust sales tax payable, follow these steps:

1. If you are completing these changes as part of a dated review, from the menu bar, select **Accountant**, **Client Data Review** and launch Client Data Review. Then select the **Adjust Sales Tax Payable** task in the Sales Tax group.

2. If you are not completing these changes as part of a dated review, from the menu bar, select **Vendors**, **Sales Tax**, **Adjust Sales Tax Due**.

3. The Sales Tax Adjustment dialog displays (see Figure A.32).

4. Select the Adjustment Date.

5. Type in an Entry No., if desired.

6. Select your Sales Tax Vendor from the drop-down list.

Figure A.32
Use the Sales Tax Adjustment dialog box to adjust QuickBooks Sales Tax Payable properly.

7. Select the Adjustment Account from the drop-down list. As an accounting professional, you should recommend the proper account type to your customer to use for these adjustments.

8. In the Adjustment pane, select the **Increase Sales Tax By** or **Decrease the Sales Tax By** option buttons. Enter an amount for the adjustment.

9. Enter a Memo or select the default memo.

10. Click OK to save the transaction.

QuickBooks creates a Make General Journal Entries transaction with a decrease (debit) or increase (credit) to Sales Tax Payable account, with the resulting debit or credit in the account that was selected in step 7.

The adjustments created remain unapplied in the Pay Sales Tax dialog box until you assign them to your next Sales Tax Payment.

Manage Sales Tax

Click the Manage Sales Tax task to properly set up and work with sales tax in your QuickBooks data file. Manage Sales Tax is also available from a shortcut on the Home page. For more information, see Chapters 9 and 10.

Pay Sales Tax

Click the Pay Sales Tax task to properly pay your sales tax in QuickBooks. For more information, see Chapter 9.

Sales Tax Preferences

Click the Sales Tax Preferences task to define sales-tax-specific preferences that affect your QuickBooks data file. For more information, see Chapter 9.

Inventory

For the accounting professional, this is commonly one area of QuickBooks that is the least understood. Often when working with a client's file with inventory tracking, I see journal entries used to adjust inventory. Although this makes the adjustment to the inventory account balance on the Balance Sheet report, it does not reflect the adjustment in the Inventory Valuation Summary or Detail report.

Why shouldn't you use a journal entry to adjust inventory? Consider that the inventory value on a Balance Sheet is the quantity of an item multiplied by a cost. When you create a journal entry, you can enter an amount for the adjustment, but you cannot associate it with an actual inventory item.

The following sections detail several inventory troubleshooting tools.

Review Inventory Setup

Chapter 6, "Managing Inventory," discusses several topics about the proper processes needed when your clients track inventory in their business.

When you click the Review Inventory Setup link in the CDR Inventory pane, the Add/Edit Multiple List Entries dialog box opens. From here, you can easily add or edit individual or multiple inventory or non-inventory items on the inventory list, as well as other lists.

The Review Inventory Setup is not a CDR-dependent task, but the link in the CDR center makes it easy to correct your client's inventory items.

Compare Balance Sheet and Inventory Valuation

The Compare Balance Sheet and Inventory Valuation CDR task is an inventory troubleshooting tool that helps you "diagnose" transaction errors involving the Inventory Asset account. Chapter 6 introduced you to the importance of comparing your client's Inventory Asset on the Balance Sheet report to the asset total on the Inventory Valuation Summary report.

When transactions are recorded to the Inventory Asset account without assigning an inventory item (such as a Make General Journal Entries transaction, or on the Expenses tab of a Write Checks transaction or an Enter Bills transaction by assigning the Inventory Asset account), the Inventory Valuation Summary report no longer matches the value of the Inventory Asset on the Balance Sheet report.

Another result of improperly recording inventory transactions is the potential for misstating the value of the Cost of Goods Sold, or the cost of the inventory sold to a customer, which affects job costing reports.

To compare the balance sheet and inventory valuation, follow these steps:

1. From the menu bar, select **Accountant**, **Client Data Review** and launch Client Data Review.

2. In the Inventory group, select the **Compare Balance Sheet and Inventory Valuation** task.

3. The CDR tool displays the Inventory Asset account balance from the Balance Sheet for the selected As Of date. (Optional) Click the Balance Sheet link to review the report.

4. The CDR tool displays the total asset value from the Inventory Valuation Summary report for the selected As Of date. (Optional) Click the Inventory Valuation Summary link to review the report.

5. A warning message displays (see Figure A.33) if the asset values reported on the two reports differ.

6. (Optional) Click the Transactions Using Inventory Asset Account but Not Inventory Items link, and the report in Figure A.34 displays. The report displays transactions that affect the Inventory Asset balance on the Balance Sheet but are not properly affecting an inventory item.

7. (Optional) Click Review Inventory Setup to open Add/Edit Multiple List Entries.

8. (Optional) Click New Item to create a new inventory item.

9. (Optional) Click Adjust Inventory Quantity/Value on Hand to properly adjust inventory.

There should be no difference listed if the proper type of transaction was used to adjust inventory.

Figure A.33
The Compare Balance Sheet and Inventory Valuation task is useful when troubleshooting Inventory Asset account discrepancies.

General Journals should not be used to adjust inventory balances

Figure A.34
CDR makes it easy to locate transactions that are affecting the Inventory Asset but not using the proper transaction type.

10. (Optional) Click Item List to modify an item.

11. To close, press the Esc key on your keyboard or click the X in the top-right corner.

If you find these types of errors in your accounting for inventory, you instead should create an inventory adjustment to replace them with. QuickBooks continues to report a difference between the reports if journal entries are recorded to the Inventory Asset account.

Troubleshoot Inventory

Chapter 6 provides useful information on troubleshooting issues surrounding inventory. One of the issues that chapter discussed is the effect on the company's financials when inventory goes negative.

Negative inventory results when QuickBooks has recorded a higher quantity of inventory sold than is available to sell. This process might seem acceptable for some clients if they are waiting for back-ordered product but want to collect the payment from the customer in advance. Chapter 5 details better methods for handling back orders and other issues, which can result in negative inventory values and misstated financials.

Chapter 6 also explained that if an inventory item is marked as inactive, the resulting inventory value does not display on the Inventory Valuation Summary report. If a client truly has inventory in stock but is not selling it, the Inventory Valuation Summary report would be misstated.

With the Troubleshoot Inventory feature (see Figure A.35) in QuickBooks Accountant, the new Troubleshoot Inventory CDR task replaces many of the reports and processes that previously had to be reviewed in diagnosing inventory valuation errors. In fact, this tool is so valuable in detecting errors such as negative inventory and finding inactive items with a quantity on hand (to name just a couple) that, as accounting professionals, we should encourage our clients to upgrade to QuickBooks 2014.

Figure A.35
Easily identify inventory with a negative quantity, and help your clients better manage their inventory processes.

All users in QuickBooks Premier 2014 and QuickBooks Enterprise Solutions 14.0 have access to the Inventory Center, which offers the ability to list any items that have negative inventory.

To review your client's inventory using the Troubleshoot Inventory CDR task, follow these steps:

1. If you are completing these changes as part of a dated review, from the menu bar, select **Accountant**, **Client Data Review** and launch Client Data Review. Then, in the Inventory group, select the **Troubleshoot Inventory** task.

2. If you are not completing these changes as part of a dated review, from the menu bar, select **Accountant**, **Client Data Review** and launch the Troubleshoot Inventory task.

3. From the Show Items drop-down list, select **Filtered By**, **All**, or **All Active**. This helps display specific data for your review of your client's inventory.

4. Place a checkmark in any combination or all of the following:

   ■ Qty Bought/Built = 0

   ■ Qty Sold/Used = 0

   ■ Negative Quantity

   ■ Inactive Items with Qty on Hand

   ■ % Markup less than <enter the %>

5. The default date range is the same as the selected Review Period. (Optional) You can change the dates.

6. Click Refresh if you are changing the filters or dates to show current data.

7. (Optional) Click Columns to Display to modify the content that is displayed.

8. Inventory items that match your selected filter criteria display. The column End Qty displays the number of units in stock as of the To date selected. Next to the End Qty column, a green circle symbol displays if there is no negative inventory. A yellow caution symbol displays if inventory items have a negative inventory quantity.

9. Select the option for **Alert If There's Negative Inventory As Of the "To" Date** or **Any Time in Date Range**.

10. (Optional) Place a checkmark in the box in front of any inventory item, and then click the Make Selected Items Inactive button to mark the inventory item as inactive.

11. (Optional) Click Adjust Inventory Quantity/Value on Hand to adjust the ending inventory balances to the client's physical inventory counted totals. The next section has more information.

If your review using the CDR tools and features has identified inventory errors, be sure to read Chapter 6, which has sections on troubleshooting inventory in QuickBooks.

Adjust Inventory Quantity/Value on Hand

Before you perform this task, you need to know the actual ending quantity and value for each inventory item. You determine this by completing a physical inventory count. Without this important step, you might make an adjustment that the actual count does not support. To create a list for the warehouse personnel to count inventory, select **Vendors**, **Inventory Activities**, **Physical Inventory Worksheet** from the menu bar.

Quantity Inventory Adjustment

The most common type of inventory adjustment is the Quantity Inventory Adjustment. Adjust Quantity/Value on Hand is not a CDR tool, but is accessible from the Vendors, Inventory Activities menu or from an opened Client Data Review. If you use this feature often, you can also add this to your Accountant Center.

For more details on properly using the Quantity Inventory Adjustment transaction, see Chapter 6. The next section discusses a different type of inventory adjustment, called a Value Adjustment.

Value Inventory Adjustment

When deciding whether to use a Quantity on Hand or Value Adjustment transaction, be sure of the net result you want to obtain. A value adjustment does not change the quantity on hand, but it assigns a new average cost by dividing the units in inventory by the new value.

Timing is important when doing a valuation adjustment. Value adjustments, if appropriate, should be carefully considered for their impact on the company's resulting financials.

Value Inventory Adjustment transaction is a less common type of inventory adjustment. Adjust Quantity/Value on Hand transaction is not a CDR tool, but is accessible from the Vendors, Inventory Activities menu or from an opened CDR. If you use this feature often, you can add this to your Accountant Center.

Payroll

To have QuickBooks automatically calculate payroll, you or your client need to purchase a payroll subscription from Intuit. When payroll is not prepared properly, many of the QuickBooks payroll transactions and calculations will not work correctly or at all.

➡ *For more detailed information on the payroll subscriptions offered, as well as details on the proper payroll process, see Chapter 11.*

The CDR tasks for payroll help you find payroll errors and set defaults in your client's file, to help avoid future mistakes.

---

tip

As the accountant, your ability to make changes in a client's payroll setup, as well as adjust payroll transactions, is possible only in these circumstances:

- You are working in a client's working data file (.QBW file extension). You cannot make changes to payroll transactions when working in an Accountant's Copy file copy.

- You are working onsite or while remotely logged in to the client's file (via the Internet), and your client has a current paid payroll subscription. The payroll features available are limited by the payroll subscription the client owns.

- You are working with the client's file at your place of business, and you have a paid payroll subscription from Intuit. Accounting professionals providing payroll services for their clients can benefit from using the QuickBooks Enhanced Payroll for Accountants subscription. See Chapter 11 for more details.

Find Incorrectly Paid Payroll Liabilities

Chapter 11 offered details on the proper methods for preparing payroll and paying the accrued liabilities. Some QuickBooks users might choose to use the Write Checks transaction when preparing their payroll liability payments. Incorrectly prepared payments adjust the balance sheet balances but are not reflected accurately in the Payroll Center. However, over the past several years, payroll liability payment errors are less likely to occur because of improved error messaging that encourages QuickBooks users to prepare these liability payments properly.

This CDR task delivers another timesaving tool: It helps the accounting professional easily and quickly find payroll liability payments that were recorded incorrectly.

When you select the menu or link in CDR to Find Incorrectly Paid Payroll Liabilities (Payroll Group), QuickBooks prepares a report titled Payroll Liabilities Paid by Regular Check. Figure A.36 displays the results in true debit and credit format for each item found. This report finds a Write Checks transaction that was payable to a payroll item vendor.

Use the details from this report to determine the account to which your client has recorded these payroll liability payments. Did the client record them to the payroll liabilities account or select an expense account by mistake? For more details on troubleshooting payroll, see Chapter 12.

Figure A.36
This CDR
report finds
incorrectly
paid Payroll
Liability
Payment
transaction
types.

After you determine the account where the original entries were posted, you can complete a Payroll Liability Adjustment by following these steps:

1. From the menu bar, select **Employees**, **Payroll Taxes and Liabilities**, **Adjust Payroll Liabilities** to open the Liability Adjustment dialog box in Figure A.37.

2. Enter the Date and the Effective Date. Both should be dated in the quarter you want to make the change.

3. Select **Company** for the adjustment. Do not select Employee here because the amounts calculated and paid are correct—just the type of transaction used to make the payment is incorrect.

4. Assign a Class if your business tracks different profit centers.

Figure A.37
Correct payroll
liabilities paid
incorrectly with a
Liability Adjustment.

5. Click the Accounts Affected button. When determining which option button to select in the Affect Accounts? dialog box, take these suggestions into consideration:

- **Do Not Affect Accounts**—Select this option if the payroll liabilities and expenses are correct on the financial statements and you want to affect only totals in the Payroll Center and totals used in QuickBooks-prepared state and federal payroll forms.

  - **Affect Liability and Expense Accounts**—Select this option if the payroll liabilities and expenses are incorrect on the financial statements and you want to affect the financials as well as the Payroll Center totals and the amounts used in QuickBooks-prepared state and federal payroll forms.

6. Click OK.

7. QuickBooks might open another dialog box with the default account that will be affected. You can specify the account used on the original tax payment transaction being corrected.

8. Click OK to save the transaction.

9. Review the balances in the affected accounts to make sure the adjusting transactions have been entered correctly.

You can check this and other details of your client's payroll setup by completing Run Payroll Checkup, which Chapter 11 covers.

Review Payroll Liabilities

Conveniently, from within CDR, you have access to the Employee Center: Payroll Center. From the displayed dialog box, you can view multiple month calendars, your upcoming scheduled payroll processing dates, due dates and amounts for paying your payroll liabilities in a timely fashion, and even links to processing the quarterly and annual forms for federal filings and most state filings.

▶ *To learn more about using the Payroll Center, read Chapter 11.*

Review Employee Default Settings

QuickBooks CDR provides easy access to another feature that has been well hidden. Reviewing employee defaults helps your client process payroll with fewer mistakes, making future payroll reviews less time-consuming.

▶ *You can learn more about setting these employee defaults in Chapter 11.*

Enter After-the-Fact Payroll

No longer is entering after-the-fact payroll time-consuming. From within CDR, the accounting professional has access to this important feature. You or your client must have an active payroll subscription. If you or your client does not have an active payroll subscription, the After-the-Fact Payroll task will not display in the Payroll task group. Keep this in mind if you are working at the client's site or are remotely logged in to the client's data file.

Payroll transactions entered through the After-the-Fact Payroll processing are included in all the federal and state forms totals that the QuickBooks payroll subscriptions prepare.

Bank Reconciliation

You can troubleshoot bank reconciliation issues with your client's data in many ways. With QuickBooks Accountant 2014, you have access to the Accountant Center (see Figure A.2), which displays timely information about your client's bank and credit card reconciliations.

 Learn more about completing and troubleshooting your client's bank reconciliations in Chapter 13, p. 541.

Reconcile Accounts

You can use the Reconcile Accounts link in the Bank Reconciliation task group of the CDR feature to troubleshoot or complete your client's monthly bank reconciliation. If you are working with a client's Accountant's Copy file, you can reconcile the bank account and have these reconciliations incorporated into your client's data.

➡ *For more details on this topic, see Chapter 16.*

In my years of working with clients' QuickBooks files, the bank reconciliation is the task I most frequently see not completed at all or not done correctly, yet it is one of the most important tasks when you want to look at trusted financials. The CDR feature helps you, the accountant, work with your client's data file when reviewing or completing the bank reconciliation.

Locate Discrepancies in Bank Reconciliation

After reviewing the client's previous bank reconciliations, you might determine that the beginning balance, which was once correct, is no longer correct. Perhaps your client modified, voided, or deleted a previously cleared transaction.

The Locate Discrepancies in Bank Reconciliation report helps you easily find these. The report is added to the CDR, Bank Reconciliation group:

1. From the menu bar, select **Accountant**, **Client Data Review** and launch the Client Data Review feature.

2. In the Bank Reconciliation group, select the **Locate Discrepancies in Bank Reconciliation** task.

3. The Previous Reconciliation Discrepancy report displays. For each transaction on this report, you see the modified date, reconciled amount, type of change (amount added or deleted), and financial effect of the change (see Figure A.38), grouped by bank statement date.

🔔 caution

Troubleshoot your beginning balance differences with the Previous Reconciliation Discrepancy report before you complete the next month's reconciliation. Doing so is important because QuickBooks removes all details from the discrepancy report when you complete a new reconciliation. This is because QuickBooks determines that you have solved the issue, or you would not have completed the next month's bank reconciliation.

Figure A.38
View details of previously cleared transactions that have been modified or deleted.

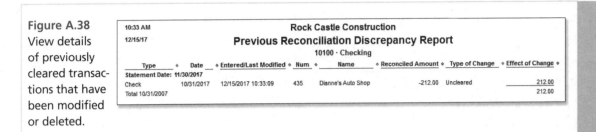

You can add the username to the report details to help identify who made the change to the transaction:

1. From the displayed Previous Reconciliation Discrepancy report, click Customize Report.

2. On the Display tab, place a checkmark on Last Modified By in the Columns box.

3. Click OK.

After reviewing the Previous Reconciliation Discrepancy report, you can prepare the Voided/Deleted report to help determine how to correct the transaction(s). To prepare this report, from the menu bar, select **Reports**, **Accountant & Taxes**, **Voided/Deleted Transactions Summary** (or Detail).

The Voided/Deleted report does not track discrepancies caused by changing the bank account associated with a transaction or changing a transaction amount. However, now the Client Data Review, Review List Changes task tracks changes made from adding, deleting, or even merging charts of accounts and other list items in QuickBooks.

Reviewing Missing Checks

The Missing Checks report is useful when reviewing the accuracy of your client's bank account data. This report can help you determine whether any check transactions are missing or duplicated.

The Review Missing Checks link is conveniently included in the Bank Reconciliation cleanup tasks. In the Specify Account dialog box, select the appropriate bank account from the drop-down list.

The resulting Missing Checks report shows all transactions that are withdrawals from (that is, credits to) the bank account and that have a reference number. Transaction types include check, bill payment, sales tax payment, liability payment, paycheck, and general journal entry type transactions, presented in order by their reference number (see Figure A.39).

Look for any breaks in the detail with a "***Missing or ***Duplicate" warning.

Figure A.39
The Missing Checks report can help you determine whether you need to enter any missing transactions before you reconcile.

Miscellaneous

This section of the CDR can be one of the most useful to you because it shows you how to set preferences to make your client's work more accurate and how to set a closing date, to prevent or discourage a user from making changes to your reviewed data. If you are working with a client's Accountant's Copy, you can set the Closing Date and optional Closing Date Password, which are then incorporated back into the client's file.

Setting Closing Date and Password

QuickBooks offers flexibility for accounting professionals who want to protect prior-period data and those who need or want to make changes to prior-period accounting records.

What exactly is a "closed" accounting period? Well, a business can decide to close a month when a task such as bank reconciliation is done or a sales tax return is filed, or a business can close once a year when the data is finalized for tax preparation. Because QuickBooks does not require you to close the books, it is a decision of the accounting professional and business owner (see Chapter 16).

The option of setting a closing date and password makes it easy to protect prior-period transactions from unwanted modifications. With additional user-specific security settings, the business owner and accountant can also manage who has the privilege to make changes to transactions dated on or before a specific closing date.

Step 1: Setting the Date and Assigning the Password

The first step in controlling changes to closed accounting periods is to set a closing date and, optionally (although recommended), a closing date password the user must provide when adding, deleting, or modifying a transaction dated on or before the closing date.

Another important reason for setting a closing date is to track additions, modifications, or deletions to transactions dated on or before a closing date. The Closing Date Exceptions report does not track these changes when a closing date is not set.

To set the closing date and, optionally, a password (different from the Admin or External Accountant password) from an open Client Data Review, follow these steps:

1. Click the Set Closing Date and Password link in the Miscellaneous group of the CDR center. The Accounting—Company Preferences tab of the Preferences dialog box opens.

2. Click the Set Date/Password button. The Set Closing Date and Password dialog box displays.

3. (Optional) Select the checkbox titled **Exclude Estimates, Sales Orders, and Purchase Orders from Closing Date Restrictions**. These transactions are nonposting, and changes made do not affect your financials.

4. Enter a closing date and optional password. Consider using your phone number as the password or using **Call Accountant**, to encourage your client to call you before making changes to closed period transactions.

5. Click OK to close the Set Closing Date and Password dialog box.

6. If the No Password Entered warning displays, select **Yes** to add or edit users, or **No** to close the warning.

7. Click OK to close the Preferences dialog box.

Setting a closing date is only the first step. Next, you must set user-specific privileges for users to whom you want to allow access for adding, deleting, or modifying a transaction dated on or before the closing date.

Step 2: Setting User-Specific Security

To be certain the closing date control is managed properly, review all users for their specific rights to change transactions, up to and including a closing date. To view the following menu, you need to be logged in to the file as the Admin user (the External Accountant user type does not have the capability to create new users or change permissions for existing users):

1. From the menu bar, select **Company, Set Up Users and Passwords, Set Up Users**. The User List dialog box opens.

2. To view a user's existing security privileges (other than the Admin or External Accountant user) from the User List dialog box, select the user and click the View User button. You can view in summary form the security settings for that user (see Figure A.40).

3. Any user who should not have rights to changing closed-period transactions should have an N in the last setting of Changing Closed Transactions.

4. After reviewing a user's existing security privileges, if you need to edit the setting referenced earlier, click Leave to close the View User Access dialog box.

5. QuickBooks returns you to the User List dialog box. Select the username and click the Edit User button.

6. On the Change User Password and Access dialog box, optionally modify the username or password. Click Next to continue.

7. The User Access dialog box for the specific user displays. Choose **Selected Areas** and click Next to continue through each of the security selections until you reach the selections on Page 9 of the dialog box (see Figure A.41).

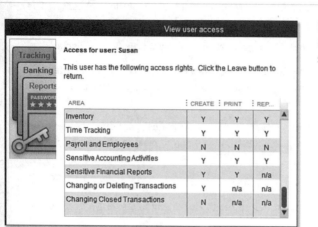

Figure A.40
Review in summary form the user's security privileges.

Figure A.41
With QuickBooks, you set controls to keep users from changing transactions on or before a set closing date.

With the ease of doing client reviews, and now the security of knowing your hard work is documented and protected with a closing date, your future reviews should take even less time to complete. This gives you more time to help your client with important management decisions.

Review QuickBooks Preferences

Don't forget during your review to manage properly the many useful preferences that help you and your client work more efficiently and accurately in the QuickBooks data file.

QuickBooks offers two types of preferences:

- **My Preferences**—Choices selected on this tab are being defined only for the currently logged-in user. If you are setting preferences for your client, you should log in with the client's username and then set the desired My Preferences. These settings can be changed while in a multiuser environment (when others are in the data file).

- **Company Preferences**—Preferences set on these tabs are global for all users in the QuickBooks data file. Often these preferences can be set only when you are in single-user mode, meaning that other users cannot be working in the file when you set the Company Preferences. Both the Admin and the new External Accountant type user can modify Company Preferences.

You should review certain preferences specific to accounting. As the trusted accounting professional for your client, you benefit by reviewing each of the available preferences, including the following:

- Accounting
- Bills
- Calendar
- Checking
- Desktop View
- Finance Charge
- General
- Integrated Applications

- Items & Inventory
- Jobs & Estimates
- Multiple Currencies
- Payments
- Payroll & Employees
- Reminders
- Reports & Graphs
- Sales & Customers

- Sales Tax
- Search
- Send Forms
- Service Connection
- Spelling
- Tax: 1099
- Time and Expenses

Of the preferences, those that can enhance the accounting accuracy of a QuickBooks file are discussed in more depth in the related chapter. For example, Chapter 9 details the Sales & Customer preferences that improve the client's accuracy in QuickBooks.

Condense Data from Previous Periods

If you find that the client's data has become "sluggish" or has grown too large to manage efficiently, you might want to consider using the Condense Data feature. The Condense Data feature is greatly enhanced for the QuickBooks Accountant and QuickBooks Enterprise Solutions Accountant editions. Specifically, these software versions can do the following:

- Remove transactions before a specific date and, optionally, create a report showing which transactions were removed

- Remove all transactions, but keep lists and preferences

- Remove transactions outside a date range (to prepare a period copy of the company file)

After choosing from one of these data removal options, the accounting professional can then choose from these options:

- Create One Summary Journal Entry for All Transactions Prior to the Specified Cut-Off Date.

- Create a Summary Journal Entry for Each Month.

- Don't Create a Summary. This option removes all transactions before the stated date, regardless of status. Removed transactions are not replaced with a journal entry.

When condensing involves inventory, the accounting professional has these choices:

- Summarize Inventory Transactions (recommended if the goal is to reduce file size)

- Keep Inventory Transaction Details

As with any process of removing data, you should create a backup first, in case the process does not provide the expected results. Some limitations arise when using this tool—namely, current year payroll transactions are not removed.

 For more information, see Chapter 17, "Managing Your QuickBooks Database," for details on file size management.

With a password set and preferences reviewed, your next review of your client's data should take even less time using the CDR.

Finishing a Client Data Review

You can leave the CDR open for as long as it takes you to finish. When you close out of a task, your work is saved. Additionally, as you are working, you can conveniently select a QuickBooks menu outside the Client Data Review, and CDR refreshes automatically, including transactions created and modified.

(Optional) As you work through the many tasks, you can record an overall note for the review or individual notes assigned to specific tasks.

Saving the Review as a PDF

You can print the details of your CDR to paper or save as a PDF file. Figure A.42 shows the information included with this document:

- Company Name

- Review Period (Last Fiscal Year, Quarter, Month, or Custom)

- Date Printed

- Dates Included in This Review

- Basis: Accrual or Cash

- Client Data Review Notes

- Cleanup Tasks and Subtasks

- Status

- Task Notes

- Filename and Path (where the PDF format of the report is stored)

Figure A.42
Print the details of the review or save them to PDF for your paper files.

Rock Castle Construction

Review Period: **Last Fiscal Year**   Date Printed: **12/15/2017**

Dates: **01/01/2016 - 12/31/2016**   Basis: **Cash**

Review Notes:

```
Provide copy of review notes when completed to:

Bob Smith
CFO
Rock Castle Construction
bob@rockcastleconstruction.com
```

Cleanup Tasks	Status	Task Notes
Account Balances		
Troubleshoot Prior Account Balances	Completed	
Reclassify Transactions	Completed	
Open Working Trial Balance	In Progress	
Review List Changes		
Chart of Accounts	Completed	
Items	Completed	
Fixed Asset Items	Completed	11/15/16 Client purchased a new Dell Server, request purchase documents.
Payroll Items	Completed	
Review Item Setup	Not Started	
Customers	Not Started	
Vendors	Not Started	
Change Other Name Types	Not Started	
Accounts Receivable		
Fix Unapplied Customer Payments and Credits	Completed	
Clear Up Undeposited Funds Account	Completed	
Review AR Aging Summary Report	In Progress	
Write Off Invoices	Completed	Provide list of invoices to client
Accounts Payable		
Fix Unapplied Vendor Payments and Credits	Completed	
Evaluate and Correct 1099 Account Mapping	Completed	
Review Unpaid Bills Report	Completed	
Sales Tax		
Fix Incorrectly Recorded Sales Tax	Completed	
Adjust Sales Tax Payable	Completed	
Manage Sales Tax	Completed	
Pay Sales Tax	Completed	
Sales Tax Preferences	In Progress	
Inventory		
Review Inventory Setup	Not Started	
Compare Balance Sheet and Inventory Valuation	Completed	
Troubleshoot Inventory	Completed	
Adjust Inventory Quantity/Value On Hand	In Progress	
Payroll		
Find Incorrectly Paid Payroll Liabilities	Completed	
Review Payroll Liabilities	Completed	
Review Employee Default Settings	Completed	
Enter After-The-Fact Payroll	Completed	
Bank Reconciliation		
Reconcile Accounts	Completed	
Locate Discrepancies in Bank Reconciliation	Completed	
Review Missing Checks	Completed	
Miscellaneous		
Set Closing Date and Password	Completed	
Review QuickBooks Preferences	Completed	
Condense Data from Previous Periods	Completed	

Mark Review Complete

When you have completed all tasks in the CDR and you click the Mark Review Complete button, QuickBooks does the following:

- Provides the option to set a closing date and password.

- Changes the Prior Review Period dates in the Troubleshoot Account Balances task.

- In the Troubleshoot Account Balances task, QuickBooks transfers your final reviewed balances to the Last Review Balances column. (These amounts will not change even if a customer makes a change to a transaction dated in that review period.)

- Provide the option to carry over task notes to the next review.

Specific to the Troubleshoot Account Balances task, you do not have to Mark Review as Complete for each review. However, your ending balances are recorded only in the Last Review Balances column when you mark the review as completed. Marking a review as completed still gives you the option to reopen a previously closed review.

Reopen Completed Review

After marking a review as complete, and before you start the next review, you have the option to reopen the previously marked completed review, as in Figure A.43. After you start a new review, you no longer have the option to reopen the previously completed review.

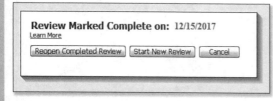

Figure A.43
Before starting a new review, you have the option to open a previously closed review.

Reporting on Review Activity

Also available on the CDR center is a link to the Audit Trail of Review report (see Figure A.44). You can use this report to detail the transactions you have added, modified, or deleted during your review. The Audit Trail report does not report on changes made to list items.

Additionally, if you used the new External Accountant type of login access, you have all the rights of the Admin user (except adding or modifying users and viewing sensitive customer credit card information), and you can see your changes separate from the Admin or other users on this report.

The Audit Trail report provides details of additions and changes made to transactions, grouped by username. The detail on this report shows the previous versions of the transaction and the latest version of the transaction, if it was edited. The Audit Trail report defaults to changes made as of today's date. You can modify this filter date for your needs.

Figure A.44
The QuickBooks
Audit Trail
report helps
identify what
changes were
made to trans-
actions and by
which user.

The Audit Trail report can be lengthy to review. However, if as an accountant you try to track down specific user activity with transactions, it can be a useful report because it groups the changes by username.

If you find undesired transaction changes, consider setting a closing date password and setting specific user security privileges, as detailed earlier in this chapter.

Creating an External Accountant User

Setting up a QuickBooks user for each person who enters data provides a level of control over the sensitive data to be viewed by this user and gives access to specific areas in QuickBooks. For additional control, you can assign a user-specific password.

When you create a new user (or edit an existing user) in QuickBooks, you can assign that user as an External Accountant.

As an accounting professional using the CDR, you might want to request that your client create a username for you and assign the new External Accountant type. If you then log in to the client file with this new user type, you benefit from the following:

- You have complete Admin access (but you cannot create or edit users or view sensitive customer credit card numbers).

- You can filter reports such as the Audit Trail in Excel for a specific username, enabling you to see your transactions separate from the client's transactions.

- Client Data Review distinguishes in the dialog box whether your login is the new External Accountant type (see Figure A.1).

- You have access to Accountant Center, plus limited accountant and CDR tools when logging in to a client's QuickBooks Pro, Premier, or Enterprise 2014 nonaccountant edition file.

If you are reviewing your client's data using the Accountant's Copy file type, or if you are not given the Admin login, this new External Accountant has to be created before your client creates the Accountant's Copy or has you review data files.

To create an External Accountant, follow these steps:

1. Open the QuickBooks data file using the Admin user (the default user QuickBooks creates with a new QuickBooks file), and enter the appropriate password, if one was created.

2. From the menu bar, select **Company, Set Up Users and Passwords, Set Up Users**.

3. Enter the Admin user password if one was originally assigned. Click OK.

4. The User List dialog box opens; it lists the current users set up for this file.

5. Click the Add User button to create a new user, or select an existing username and click the Edit User button.

6. The Set Up (or Change) User Password and Access dialog box opens.

7. In the User Name field, type the name you want the user to be identified by in the file.

8. In the Password field, enter an optional password. In the Confirm Password field, retype the password for accuracy.

9. (Optional) Click the box Add This User to My QuickBooks License. (See the Explain link for more details.)

10. Click Next. You might receive a No Password Entered message, click Yes or No to creating a password. If you selected Yes, you are returned to step 8.

    (Optional) Select **Do Not Display This Message in the Future**. The Access for User:<username> dialog box opens.

11. Select the option for **External Accountant** (see Figure A.45).

Figure A.45
Ask your client to create an External Accountant type user for your login.

12. Click Next.

13. QuickBooks provides a warning message, confirming that you want to give this new user access to all areas of QuickBooks except customer credit card numbers. Select **Yes** to assign the new External Accountant type privileges to this new or existing user.

14. The Access for User:<username> dialog box opens. The message restates that the new External Accountant user will have access to all areas of QuickBooks except sensitive customer credit card data. Click Finish to complete the process.

B

QUICKBOOKS STATEMENT WRITER

Overview

QuickBooks Statement Writer, formerly known as Intuit Statement Writer, is an extremely powerful and flexible reporting tool available for no additional fee with QuickBooks Accountant 2014 and all QuickBooks Enterprise Solutions 14.0 versions. Accounting professionals can use QuickBooks Statement Writer to prepare professional Generally Accepted Accounting Principles (GAAP)–compliant financials from QuickBooks data.

QuickBooks Statement Writer uses Microsoft Excel as the platform for creating customized financial reports from QuickBooks data. Additionally, QuickBooks Statement Writer keeps the statements synchronized with changes in the QuickBooks data. You can also add supporting documents created in Word and include them in your customized financials.

QuickBooks Statement Writer works with Excel 2003 or newer. (*Note:* It does *not* work with Microsoft Office 2003 Standard, 2003 Student Edition, or 2003 Small Business Edition.) Improved for QuickBooks 2014, QSW works with both the 32-bit and 64-bit installs of Excel 2010.

Terms

The following terms help you when working with the QuickBooks Statement Writer:

- **QSW**—QuickBooks Statement Writer.

- **Statement**—Specific financial statement, such as a Balance Sheet or Income Statement.

- **Documents**—Addition to Statement created with Word, such as a cover sheet or letter.

- **Statement Writer Report**—Collection of statements and documents.

> 🔍 **note**
>
> The QuickBooks Statement Writer feature replaces the Intuit Statement Writer (ISW) and Financial Statement Designer (FSD) reporting tools used in earlier versions of QuickBooks.
>
> As of the writing of this edition, Microsoft Office Suite 2013 is not yet supported.

Workflow

Working with the QSW tool involves three main steps:

1. Open the QuickBooks file that contains the data, using your QuickBooks Accountant 2014 or QuickBooks Enterprise Solutions 14.0 software (all editions).

2. Use the Report Designer for a step-by-step approach to creating a Statement Writer Report.

3. Output the customized financials to Microsoft Excel, and use common Excel features or functions to add customization.

Benefits

Benefits of using QSW include the capability to do the following:

- Create customized, professional financial statements from your client's QuickBooks data without manually typing data into Excel.

- Include multiple financial statements and supporting documents in a single QSW Report.

- Use one of the many templates provided to create your own statements. Templates come in a variety of formats for the Balance Sheet, Income Statement, Cash Flow Statement, Retained Earnings Statement, and Budget to Actual Statements.

- Use Microsoft Excel (2003, 2007, or 2010) as the platform for customizing and utilizing all the additional features and reporting flexibility available in Excel.

- Refresh customized financials with current QuickBooks data without leaving the Excel QSW Report.

- Combine multiple QuickBooks account lines into one line on financial statements without changing your client's QuickBooks data.

- Add your own rows or columns of detail.

- Drill down to QuickBooks data and make changes to transactions within the QSW tool.

- Easily view and add any missing accounts not included in the current statement.

- Create charts and graphs using Excel functionality.

- Add supporting documents, such as a cover sheet or compilation letter created in Microsoft Word, and you have a complete set of financials ready to print.

- Share your customized reports with clients as an Excel spreadsheet or PDF-formatted document.

Getting Started

To launch QSW from your QuickBooks Accountant 2014 or QuickBooks Enterprise Solutions 14.0 software, follow these steps:

1. From the menu bar, select **Reports**, **QuickBooks Statement Writer**. If you are using QuickBooks Accountant or QuickBooks Enterprise Accountant software, you can also launch QSW from the Accountant Menu or the Accountant Center.

> **note**
> If you are prompted to install an update, you might need to restart your computer to finish the update process.

➤ *For more information, see "Customizing the Accountant Center," p. 699.*

2. If prompted, select **Download Update** and then select **Install Update**. If you are not prompted, skip to step 5. Some computer systems require additional setup. If prompted with the User Account Control or other messages, follow the prompts to run QSW. You have to do these additional setup steps only once.

3. Select **Yes** to the Install Shield Wizard, and follow all prompts to install the update. Click Close to the QSW Update Manager message that you have the most current version.

4. The main QSW screen displays (see Figure B.1).

Figure B.1
The QuickBooks Statement Writer main screen offers easy access to all the features.

The following sections detail the different global preferences that you can set in QSW.

Preferences & Formats

From the Preferences & Formats menu, you set global preferences and settings for customized reports prepared from all your client's files.

General Preferences

The General Preferences settings dialog box opens when you launch Preferences & Formats from the main QSW screen. These settings permit you to take these actions:

 note

Selecting OK on the General Preferences dialog box closes Preferences and returns you to the main QSW screen.

- Accept the default location for your stored reports or browse to a location of your choice

- Accept the default location for storing QSW templates or browse to a location of your choice

- Choose to manually configure network permissions (advanced setting)

- Run Diagnostics Now, which checks to see if your system, QuickBooks, and QSW are configured correctly

- Reset all warnings

- Reset defaults

Optionally, select **Apply** as you make changes. Next, select the **Your Details** menu tab to the left.

Your Details

Complete Firm Name, Address, and other fields on the Your Details tab. The information you enter here appears for all client files you open with this registered copy of QuickBooks. See Figure B.2.

Click the blue text to access help content about the currently displayed window.

General Preferences

Your Details

Your Details

Formatting

Styles

Resources

Your Details

Watc

Enter your information to appear in documents ───────────

Click on blue text for quick help content

Firm Name: John C. Smith, CPA

Name: John C. Smith

Address: 100 Emerald Creek Center

Suite 200

City: Anytown

Phone: 555-111-2222

Email: jsmith@johncsmithcpa.com

Website: www.johncsmithcpa.com

Federal EIN: 11-1111111

Document Templates

«Accountant_Firm_Name»
«Accountant_Address1»

555-222-3333

Create your own custom reports using Word Templates. Insert QSW fields, and we will automatically populate them with your firm and client information.

Figure B.2
Enter your firm information once to have it included with each client's customized financial reports.

Formatting

On the Formatting tab, you can define the following global settings (see Figure B.3) for formatting all QSW statements. You can override these settings on individual statements when needed.

- **Automatic Underlines**—When total or subtotal rows are added to a statement, underlines are added upon refresh.

- **Show**—You can set defaults for displaying or not displaying decimals, column headers, inactive accounts, and zero-balance accounts.

- **Show Zero Balances As**—Set the default format for displaying any cell with a zero balance.

- **Show Negative Numbers As**—Choose from several options for displaying negative numbers on reports.

- **Divide All Data By**—You choose here whether to round up or down the displayed amount.

Click the Reset Defaults button to return to the original formatting settings. Click Apply to save your changes. Click OK to close and save changes.

> 🔊 **caution**
>
> Data formatting preferences display in Excel, but not while working in the QSW Report Designer.

Figure B.3
Set default format settings for all QSW statements.

Styles

You use styles to format the font, font size, bold, italic, and justification of the text, as in Figure B.4. On the Styles tab, select any style(s) and change the format as desired.

Figure B.4
Styles set default font type and size. You can save style settings for reuse with other statements.

After customizing your style, from the More drop-down list, select **Save as New Style Set**. Enter a Style Set Name; this customized Style will be available the next time you create a new QSW statement.

Resources

Select the Resources tab for a listing of QSW resources and contact information. Additionally, use this menu to download Intuit-provided statement and document templates.

Using the Report Designer

With the global preferences set, you are now prepared to create customized financials for your clients using QSW.

To begin using QSW, open your client's file in your QuickBooks Accountant 2014 or QuickBooks Enterprise 14.0 software (all versions), and launch QSW (as previously instructed).

You can use the ease of the QSW Report Designer to customize the financial report before creating it in Excel. You can further customize the report after you've exported it to Excel from the QSW.

Report Content

The Report Content tab displays when you launch QSW and select **Design New**. From this dialog box, you select your Report Date from predefined periods or choose a Custom Date range. You can change this date range later without returning to this dialog box.

Select from Accrual or Cash Basis. From the Statement and Document Templates panel, select the desired template. With the template selected, click the arrows in the center to add or remove statements and documents, as well as arrange their order in the Financial Report Contents pane. See Figure B.5.

Finally, you are required to provide a name for the report. These reports are stored in the default location defined in preferences.

➡️ *For more information, see "General Preferences,"*
p. 756.

Click Next to advance to the next task of customizing the columns of data to include in the report.

tip

While in the QSW Report Designer, on the Headers & Formatting tab, hold down the Ctrl key on your keyboard when selecting multiple headers, labels, or cells. Then at the top right, select the More drop-down list and choose to Switch Style Set. After making these changes, from the More drop-down, you can choose Save as New Style Set or Set as Default.

note

Each template in the Financial Report Contents column becomes a worksheet within a single Excel workbook.

You do not need to worry about the order the statements or documents are added to the Financial Report Contents. When you are ready to print the financials, you specify the print order within Excel.

Figure B.5
You can later modify the Report Date and Basis you define here using the Statement Writer Report.

Columns

Figure B.6 shows the Columns tab. A separate tab is created for each included statement or document. Click a specific statement to display data from the currently opened QuickBooks file (if a document is selected, instructions for modifying documents are provided).

Figure B.6
Use the QSW Report Designer to customize the column properties in the selected statement.

Features of customizing columns include the capability to do the following:

- Drag to insert columns. You can choose from several types of columns, including Blank, QuickBooks Data, Variance, and Total columns, to mention just a few.

- Refresh the data displayed in the QSW Report Designer, change the position of columns, remove columns, and modify the column header or dates from the toolbar.

 tip

Right-click a column within a report for a shortcut menu containing many of the Columns functions.

Click the Undo icon on the toolbar (see Figure B.6) to undo the last action. Click Next to advance to the Rows/Accounts tab. Alternatively, click the Rows/Accounts tab at the top the QSW Report Designer dialog box to access this tab directly.

Rows/Accounts

Figure B.7 shows the Rows/Accounts tab. A separate tab (worksheet) is created in Excel for each included statement or document. Click a specific statement to display data from the currently opened QuickBooks file (if a document is selected, instructions for modifying documents are provided).

Figure B.7
Right-click to modify the currently selected row(s).

Features of this tab include the capability to do the following:

- Drag to insert rows. You can choose from several types of rows, including Blank/Custom, Account, and a variety of Total row options.

- Use the following toolbar buttons to modify rows and accounts: Refresh, Move Up, Move Down, Insert Row, Delete Row, Combine Accounts, and Separate Accounts.

- Easily identify missing or new rows by selecting the Show: Missing/New option button in the lower-left corner.

On the left side of the toolbar, click the Undo icon to undo the last action. Refer to Figure B.6. Click Next to advance to the Headers & Formatting tab. Alternatively, click the Headers & Formatting tab at the top of the QSW Report Designer dialog box to access this tab directly.

tip

Combine rows by selecting multiple rows with the Ctrl key on your keyboard. From the Rows/Accounts toolbar, select **Combine Accounts**.

Headers & Formatting

Figure B.8 shows the Headers/Footers Formatting tab. A separate tab is created for each included statement (tab) or document.

Click a specific statement to display data from the currently opened QuickBooks file (if a document tab is selected, instructions for modifying documents are provided).

Features of this tab include the capability to do the following:

- Drag to insert header and footer fields. You can choose from several types of fields, including Statement Ending Date, Date Prepared, Basis, and Page #, to name just a few.

- Use the Header & Formatting toolbar buttons to cut, copy, and paste fields and change the font, size, and properties of a field.

- Use QSW Smart Underlines. Statement Writer will automatically adjust total and sub-total underlines upon refresh. If you prefer to maintain all underlines yourself, uncheck this box. For more information, click the blue text to display help content. See Figure B.8.

Figure B.8
Hover your cursor over blue text to view help content for that feature.

Click the Undo icon on the toolbar to undo the last action, as in Figure B.8. Click Next to advance to the Review & Finish tab. Alternatively, click the Review & Finish tab at the top of the QSW Report Designer to access this tab directly.

Review & Finish

If this is your first time creating the report using Report Designer, on the Review & Finish tab, a separate tab is created for each included statement or document for review. Click a specific statement to display the customized formatting (if a document is selected, instructions for modifying documents are provided).

Select a specific statement and, from the toolbar, choose the Memorize Current Statement. You can then reuse this customized statement with new financial reports.

Choose, Memorize Report Group from the toolbar to save the group of selected statements for use with a newly created financial report from another client's data.

Click Create Report to send your customization into Excel.

QuickBooks launches Excel and adds the customized formatting you created in the Designer. Each statement is an individual worksheet tab in a single Excel workbook. See Figure B.9.

> ### note
>
> If you are returning to the Report Designer from a previously prepared QSW Report, you will not see the individual statement tabs at the top. Instead, you have to select the desired statement in the Excel QSW and then select the Report Designer icon from the QSW Document Actions pane toolbar to modify.

Figure B.9
QSW uses Excel 2003, 2007, or 2010 for the completed report.

Opening a Previously Created Report

When a user clicks Open Report from the main QSW dialog box, the five most recently accessed reports for the currently opened company file display. Optionally, a user can select Browse to Open, which, by default, looks to the same folder where the current reports are stored.

After selecting a report from the list or browsing to a report, QSW launches the report in Excel. If your system prompts you, select Yes to any prompts to trust the source of the file. (Your version of Excel might have security settings that will not recognize the .QSM extension of the QSW stored report without your granting permission to trust the file type.)

Creating a New Report from a Memorized Report

You can create a new report from an existing report, by first making a copy of the original report as detailed in these steps:

1. Click the Copy From button on the main QSW dialog box to reuse a previously memorized statement or report group.

2. Click Browse. QSW defaults to the location where the most recent QSW Report was stored. If necessary, browse to another location to find the report with the .QSM extension.

3. With the Source Report selected, click Open. The Copy From dialog box displays the Source Report location and the Destination Folder. Provide a New Report Name, and click Copy.

4. Select or deselect the option to Open New Report.

Modifying a Statement Writer Report in Excel

Now that you have created a Statement Writer Report, you might find that you need to customize the content for future reports or for use with other clients' data files.

You can use several methods to edit an existing Statement Writer Report:

- Return to the Report Designer.

- Use the Document Actions pane.

- Use the QSW icons on the Excel Add-Ins ribbon (or Excel 2003 toolbar).

- Right-click a report column, row, or cell in Excel.

You might use one or all of these methods. The next sections provide additional details on working with each of these methods.

> **note**
>
> If you have multiple statements in your report, you need to select the desired statement in Excel that you want to modify in Report Designer. Only the first time you created your QSW Report does each statement display as an individual tab on the Report Designer, Review & Finish tab.

Method 1: Using the Report Designer

When you created the original Statement Writer Report, you most likely used the Report Designer. You can return to this familiar tool to make edits to your existing Statement Writer Report.

From a displayed Statement Writer Report in Excel, click the Design icon on the Document Actions pane toolbar (see Figure B.10).

Figure B.10
Access the Report Designer from the toolbar in the Document Actions pane.

Click to return to the Report Designer

If you have made formatting edits while in Excel, answer Yes or No to the warning message that displays. If you select Yes, the Report Designer for the current Statement Writer Report opens.

➡ *For more information, see "Using the Report Designer," p. 759.*

Method 2: Using the Document Actions Pane

You can edit an existing Statement Writer Report in several ways. One method involves accessing the many editing tools from the Document Actions pane.

The Document Actions pane, in Figure B.11, displays only when you launch QuickBooks and then open a Statement Writer Report from within the QSW. QSW assigns the file extension of .QSM to these reports, and you cannot open them directly with Excel.

You can find most, if not all, of the functionality detailed to this point in the chapter by selecting one of the drop-down menus from the menu bar in the Document Actions pane.

The Documents Action toolbar includes frequently used actions (see Figure B.11).

You can make more detailed edits by selecting one of the expandable panes for Report, Statement, Row, Column, and Cell Properties, depending on the change you need to make.

Figure B.11
Use the Document Actions pane to add to or edit the Statement Writer Report.

🔍 note

Are you having trouble viewing the Statement Writer pane in Microsoft Excel as it's shown in Figure B.11? First, be sure you have opened the QSW Report from within the QuickBooks file. If you still do not see the Statement Writer pane, you might have inadvertently closed it.

Depending on which version of Excel you have (supported versions include 2003, 2007, and 2010), reopening the Statement Writer pane requires different steps. In Excel 2010, select the **Statement Writer** ribbon in the Tools section and click the Show QSW Pane. In Excel 2007 and 2003, select the **Add-Ins** tab; select **View, Toolbars**; and place a checkmark next to QuickBooks Statement Writer. With Excel 2003, you might have to make the toolbar visible. Hover your mouse over the icons to find the icon that will reinstate your Statement Writer pane (see Figure B.19).

Find Missing Accounts

Identifying new accounts your client created since the last time you prepared a Statement Writer Report used to be a daunting task. Now it is easier than ever.

From the toolbar in the Document Actions pane, select **Edit**, **Show All Accounts**. The All Accounts dialog box displays, as in Figure B.12. Any missing accounts from the customized financials display in red. Optionally select to show only the Missing accounts.

Figure B.12
Has your client added new accounts since you prepared your last report? Locate them efficiently with the All Accounts dialog box.

To review or add the missing account(s), follow these steps:

1. After reviewing the missing accounts, click Close on the All Accounts dialog box.
2. From the Row Properties, choose to add a new account row, or highlight with your cursor an existing row you want to add the missing account(s) to.
3. With your cursor on the row you want to add the account(s) to, from the toolbar in the Document Actions pane, select **Edit**, **Show All Accounts**.
4. Select the missing account(s).
5. Click the Add to Current Row button. As you complete this for each missing account(s), you will no longer see any accounts in red.
6. Click Close to return to the modified Statement Writer Report.

Report Properties

The term QSW uses for a collection of statements is a Statement Writer Report. When you need to make global changes to all statements within a report, use the Report Properties. With Report Properties (previously shown in Figure B.10), you can manage the following:

- **Documents**—Add or modify supporting documents.

- To learn more, see "Working with Supporting Documents," p. 774.

- **Report Date**—Select from predetermined dates or choose a custom date.

- **Basis**—Specify whether you want to use accrual basis or cash basis reporting.

- **Header/Footer Content**—Designate whether you want your changes in Excel to supersede changes you made in Report Designer.

- **Refresh from QuickBooks**—Restate the entire QSW Report (multiple statements) with updated QuickBooks data.

Statement Properties

When you need to modify properties that affect a single statement, not just a specific row or cell, use the Statement Properties task from the QSW Document Actions pane. The Statement Properties task (see Figure B.13) controls changes made to the currently selected financial statement.

Figure B.13
Modify a selected statement from the Statement Properties panel.

- **Class Filter**—Filter for all classes, a specific class, or multiple classes.

- **Jobs Filter**—Filter for all jobs, specific jobs, or multiple jobs.

- **Zero-Balance Accounts**—When selected, show accounts with a zero balance; when not selected, hide accounts with a zero balance.

- **Balance Sheet Round-Off**—Assign the account to use for any rounding differences.

- **Refresh from QuickBooks**—Restate the currently selected statement with updated QuickBooks data.

- **Edit Header/Footer**—Change to the Header/Footer.

- **Delete Statement**—Remove a statement from a QSW Report.

Row Properties

To make a change to a specific row without affecting other rows, review the features of the Row Properties task of the QSW Document Actions. The Row Properties, in Figure B.14, affect formatting for the selected row and offer the following functionality when selecting a blank row:

- **Type**—Change the type of data represented in the cell, including Blank, Captions, Headings, Account (QuickBooks data), and Total types. For more information, see Table B.1.

- **Name**—Change the label of the cell (with the cell selected). The default is the account name.

Figure B.14
Use the Row Properties options to control the data you view in a particular row.

- **Manage Accounts**—Select from the following:

  - Combine accounts from selected rows.

  - Add accounts by number, type, or name.

  - Separate accounts that were previously combined.

  - Remove accounts.

  - Override zero-balance settings (from Statement Properties).

  - Reverse all the positive and negative numbers in the row.

- **Insert Rows**—Insert new rows. Choose from Blank, Captions, Headings, Account (QuickBooks data), and Total types.

- **Delete**—Delete the currently selected row. You have to use the QSW Delete Column function because the Excel worksheet is protected from using the Excel Delete command.

> **tip**
>
> To change the text in a row label, you can either make the change directly in the Row Properties pane with the row selected or simply type the new text directly into the appropriate cell of the spreadsheet. Entering new text using either of these options updates the Row Properties pane and the row label viewed for the statement.

Combine Account Rows

QuickBooks offers users a lot of flexibility when working with a chart of accounts. Often several chart of account list items might have been created since your last review of the data. The QSW tool enables you to create customized financials grouping accounts together, without affecting the client's original chart of accounts.

To combine account rows, follow these steps:

1. With the QSW statement open and your Ctrl key pressed, click to highlight any two or more cells you want to combine into a single row. In the example in Figure B.15, the cells for Checking, Savings, and Petty Cash are selected.

Use the control key on your keyboard to select multiple rows

Figure B.15
Combine multiple QuickBooks account rows into one row in the customized financials. No change is made to the QuickBooks file.

2. With multiple cells selected that you want to "roll up," select **Combine Accounts from Selected Rows** from the Manage Accounts drop-down list. (Optional) Click the Combine Accounts icon from the Excel Add-Ins ribbon.

3. Rename the label either in the Row Properties task or directly in the Excel cell. Figure B.16 shows that the row was renamed to Cash and Cash Equivalents.

Figure B.16

Multiple cash rows are now included in a single row. Mouse over the row to see the accounts included.

4. Hover your mouse over the row to see a note of the accounts that the new cell total includes.

To separate the accounts, in step 2, choose the Separate Accounts menu choice.

One of the most efficient uses in customizing your client's financials is the capability to combine like rows of data into a single row. This makes your financials more professional in appearance, without affecting the client's chart of accounts.

Table B.1 provides some technical information on the characteristics of the different row Total types:

Table Appendix B.1   Row Total Specifications

Total Row Type	Behavior
Total 4	Inserts a Total 4 row.
	The row is inserted, and the total is the sum of all accounts above this line and after the previous total.
	An underscore appears below the last value in the Total 4 group of accounts.
	The row takes on the Total 4 Style.
Total 3	Inserts a Total 3 row.
	All accounts and Total 4s above the current row and below the previous secondary caption or Total 3 row are included.
	An underscore appears below the last value in the Total 3 group of accounts.
	A blank row is inserted above the Total 3 row.
	The row takes on the Total 3 Style.

Total Row Type	Behavior
Total 2	Inserts a Total 2 row.
	All Total 3s above the current row and below the previous secondary caption are included.
	An underscore appears below the last account and Total 3 value in the secondary group.
	A blank row is inserted above the Total 3 row.
	The row takes on the Total 2 Style.
Total 1	Inserts a Total 1 row.
	All accounts and Total 2s, 3s, and 4s within the group above the new row and below the previous Total 1 or primary caption are included.
	A double underscore appears below the last value in the Total 1 row.
	A blank row is inserted above the Total 1 row.
	The row takes on the Total 1 Style.

Column Properties

Use the Column Properties pane (see Figure B.17) to change the properties of the selected column in the QSW statement. The options available in the Column Properties pane change depending on the type of column that is current when the pane is selected.

- **Type**—Choose the type of data in the column: Blank, Accounts (the column or statement header), Variance, % of the Whole, Summary Total, and Grand Total. Each type has its own unique column property options.

- **Heading**—Control the heading title of the currently selected column.

Depending on what type of column you have selected, the following menu options change:

- **Period**—Change the accounting period for the currently selected column.

- **Show Data**—Select to display past years for the same accounting period. Use this for side-by-side analysis.

- **Filter for Class**—If you are using class tracking, select all classes, a combination of classes, or a single class.

- **Filter for Job**—Filter for all jobs, a combination of jobs, or a single job.

- **Insert Column(s)**—Add columns from the specified allowed types. Types include Blank, Account Numbers, QuickBooks Data, Variance, % of the Whole, Summary Total, and Grand Total.

- **Delete**—Click to select the column you want to delete, and then click the Delete Column button on the Column Properties pane. You have to use the QSW Delete Column function because the Excel worksheet is protected from using the Excel Delete command.

Figure B.17
Place your cursor in a column and then, from the Column
Properties panel, control the contents of that column.

Cell Properties

The Cell QSW actions vary by the type of cell selected. In Figure B.18 an account balance cell is selected. Cell Properties include these:

- **Current Cell**—Indicates the cell reference for the currently selected cell

- **Cell Type**—Determined and set by either row or column properties

- **Temporary Balance Override**—Defines a manual amount for an account cell

- **Override Date**—Overrides the selected date for a specific cell so that the date range differs from the rest of the statement data

- **Reset Date**—Returns the cell date to match the date assigned to the entire statement

- **Insert Field(s)**—Adds any of the following information to a selected blank cell:

  - Accountant Information
  - Client Information
  - Basis

  - Statement "From" Date
  - Statement "To" Date
  - Formatted Statement Date

Figure B.18
Use Cell Properties to manage the information displayed in a specific data cell.

Method 3: Using the Excel Add-Ins Ribbon Icons

You can also access selected editing functions from the Excel Add-Ins ribbon icon, in Figure B.19.

Figure B.19
Reinstate the QSW Document Actions pane and other activities from the QSW toolbar in Excel.

Working with Supporting Documents

Another feature of the QuickBooks Statement Writer 2014 tool is the capability to create supporting documents to the customized statements.

You can add two types of supporting documents to your QSW statement:

- **Documents From Templates**—Created from templates that merge accountant and client information from the company file with present text. These documents are created with Word and have the file extension .dot.

- **Documents From My Computer**—Word documents you have already created that do not contain merged information. There are no limitations to the content of these documents.

You can add documents from templates or documents stored on your computer. Templates are both those that are shipped with the QSW product and those you can download directly from Intuit. For access to ready-made reports for download, click the Help menu in QuickBooks Statement Writer. Scroll down the Get Started with QSW section that displays and look for a section titled "Helpful Resources."

The following sections detail how to create or modify existing document templates and then attach them to your Statement Writer Report. When you complete your client's customized financials, you can specify the order in which the documents should print.

Overview

You can add or modify the provided supporting document templates, or you can create them on your own using Microsoft Word. Supporting documents can be a combination of text (your own manually typed content) or dynamic data fields from the QuickBooks file, which are selected from a predefined list. For example:

> We have audited the accompanying statement of assets, liabilities, and equity—(cash, income tax basis) of «Client Company Name».

In the previous text, the first part of the sentence is manually typed text. The field name is **Client Company Name**. The chevrons («») are required and are added automatically by Microsoft Word. When the final report is printed, the data from QuickBooks (in this example, the Client Company Name) is replaced where the field name is listed in the template.

When you are creating a template with merged fields, you use a Microsoft Word .dot file. The only time you open the .dot file is when you need to modify the template details. When the final report is prepared, the field names refresh with current data from the QuickBooks file you are using with QSW.

Adding or Modifying a Supporting Document

You might have added a supporting document when you created the Statement Report using the Report Designer. In Figure B.5, a Cover Letter document was added to the Financial Report Contents in Report Designer. If you did not add documents during the Report Designer setup, you can add them from the Document button in the Report Properties panel (see Figure B.20).

To add or modify a supporting document, follow these steps:

1. Open a Statement Writer Report. From the Document Actions pane, expand the Report Properties panel.

2. Click the Documents button. The Add or Modify Supporting Documents dialog box displays any documents currently included in the Statement Report.

3. Click Add, to choose to add From Templates or From My Computer.

4. If you select From Templates, the Insert Documents dialog box displays (see Figure B.21).

5. Select the desired document template on the left, and click the arrow pointing to the right to include the document in the Financial Report Contents.

Figure B.20
View, add, open, rename, and delete supporting documents.

Figure B.21
Insert ready-made supporting documents or ones you created.

6. Click OK. The new document displays in the Add or Modify Supporting Documents dialog box.

7. (Optional) With a document selected, click Rename or Delete.

8. To modify a selected document, click the Open button. QSW automatically launches Word.

Using templates saves you time by creating customized financial templates you can use with multiple clients' Statement Writer Reports.

Using the QSW Toolbar in Word

QSW adds a toolbar to Word to help you properly create supporting documents.

To access the toolbars in Word 2003, select **View**, **Toolbars**, and place a checkmark next to QuickBooks Statement Writer. In Word 2007, select the Add-Ins ribbon; the QSW toolbar displays (see Figure B.22). As of this writing, QSW is not compatible with Word 2013.

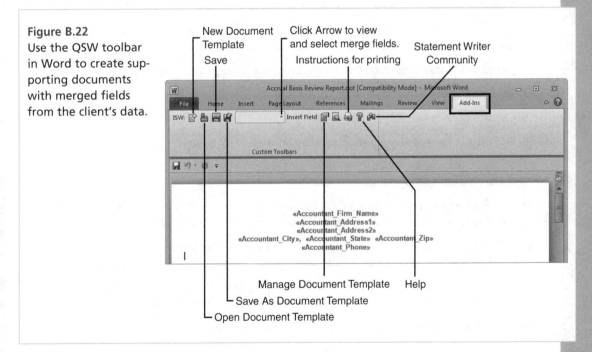

Figure B.22
Use the QSW toolbar in Word to create supporting documents with merged fields from the client's data.

Editing an Existing QSW Supporting Document

You might find it necessary to edit the text or fields in an existing QSW supporting document. You can access the Microsoft Word .dot templates directly from a QSW Report, or you can browse to the stored templates directly from within Word.

To edit an existing QSW supporting document, following these steps:

1. Launch the QSW tool from within QuickBooks.

2. From the Document Actions pane, Report Properties, click the Documents button.

3. A list displays any supporting documents currently assigned to this QSW Report (see Figure B.20). Select a supporting document, and then click the Open button and skip to step 9. If no supporting documents are listed, go to step 4.

4. Click the Add button and select **From Templates**.

5. The Insert Documents dialog box displays (see Figure B.21). Select a specific document and, in the center of the window, click the arrow pointing to the right to add the selected document to the Financial Report Contents pane.

6. (Optional) Select **Show**, **All Documents**, **Intuit Documents**, **Custom Documents**, or **Custom Template Groups** to filter for specific documents to choose from.

7. Repeat step 5 until you have added the necessary documents to your QSW Report. Click OK to close the Insert Documents dialog box.

   The Add or Modify Supporting Documents dialog box displays, with a list of added documents.

8. Click the Rename button if you want to give the document a new name for this QSW Report.

9. Click the Open button. QSW opens the .dot template in Microsoft Word.

10. Edit the text as needed using Word's editing functions.

11. To add or edit merged data fields in Word 2003, click the QSW toolbar. For Word 2007 and 2010 users, click the Add-Ins ribbon.

12. With your mouse in the location on the document where you want to add the merged field, select the desired field from the Insert Field drop-down menu (see Figure B.23).

13. When you are finished with your edits on the QSW toolbar, click the Save button to save over the original document. Click the Save As button to save the document with a different name.

14. When you click Save As, the Save As—Document Template dialog box displays. Provide a Name for the template and choose a Type from the drop-down list (see Figure B.24).

15. Click OK to close the Save As—Document Template dialog box.

Figure B.23
Add QuickBooks data fields to customized document templates.

Figure B.24
Save your new supporting document as a template to be used with other client files.

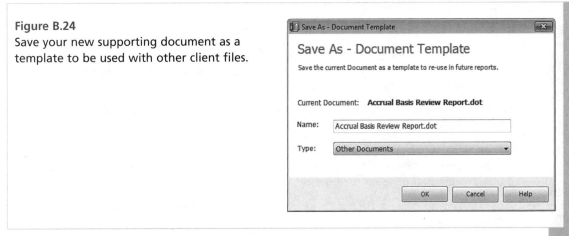

Creating a New QSW Supporting Document

You can optionally create your own supporting document templates and store them on your computer.

To create a new QSW supporting document, follow these steps:

1. Open Microsoft Word 2003, 2007, or 2010.

2. Add the text or images as needed using Word editing functions.

3. To add or edit merged data fields in Word 2003, click the QSW toolbar. For Word 2007 or 2010 users, click the Add-Ins ribbon.

4. With your mouse in the location in the document where you want to add the merged field, select the desired field from the drop-down list items.

5. Click the Insert Field link (see Figure B.23) on the QSW toolbar.

6. When you are finished with your edits on the QSW toolbar, click the Save button to save over the original document. Click the Save As button to save the document with a different name.

7. When you click Save As, the Save As—Document Template dialog box displays (refer to Figure B.24). Provide a Name for the template and choose a Type from the drop-down list.

Now that you have created a new supporting document, you can attach the document to your QSW Report so you can print a complete set of customized financials for your clients. Read the next section to learn more about attaching supporting documents.

Printing or Exporting a Statement Writer Report

In the previous section, you learned how to add or modify supporting documents to your QSW Report, making it a complete set of custom financials ready to print. QSW creates a PDF of the complete report set so you can print, send via email, and store for future reference.

To print or export a Statement Writer Report, follow these steps:

1. Launch the QSW tool from within QuickBooks.

2. If you have just opened your QSW Report, the QuickBooks data has automatically refreshed. If you have been modifying the QSW Report or QuickBooks data, refresh the data by clicking the Refresh button on the Document Actions pane.

3. From the Document Actions pane, select **Save As**, **QSW Report**, **Excel Workbook**, **Template Group**, or **PDF**.

4. If you selected Save As PDF, the Create PDF dialog box displays (see Figure B.25). The Available Report Contents show each of the statements and supporting documents you have included in this QSW Report. On the left pane, select a statement or document to include in your PDF.

5. Use the arrow pointing to the right to include the selected statement or document in the PDF Contents pane.

6. Select an item in the PDF Contents pane, and use the up or down arrows to organize the print order for your financials.

Figure B.25
You define the print order of the documents when creating a PDF.

7. (Optional) Select Set As Default Order so you do not have to make these choices again.

8. (Optional) Select Open PDF upon Save.

9. Click Create.

10. Select **Save As Excel Workbook**. QSW opens a Windows Explorer window.

11. Browse to the computer folder where your Excel workbook should be saved, and give the workbook a filename. Click Save.

Accounting professionals can use QSW to create financial reports that include statements and supporting documents. These reports can be saved as templates for use with other client files and for updating with future dated information.

> **⚠ caution**
>
> When you export your QSW Report to Excel, it is no longer linked to QuickBooks, so you cannot update or refresh it.

C

QUICKBOOKS ENTERPRISE SOLUTIONS FEATURES

QuickBooks Enterprise Solutions offers robust features for growing businesses with complex needs. This appendix provides details on using these unique features found only in the QuickBooks Enterprise Solutions software.

For the inventory-specific features, if you are new to inventory management in QuickBooks, you might want to first review Chapter 5, "Setting Up Inventory," and Chapter 6, "Managing Inventory." These two chapters provide the basics for managing inventory in QuickBooks.

If your business currently uses QuickBooks Pro or Premier, you can review this appendix to see what additional features would be available to you if you upgraded to QuickBooks Enterprise Solutions software.

 For more information, see "Upgrading Your QuickBooks Version," p. 651.

QuickBooks Enterprise Customization

New for QuickBooks Enterprise Solutions 14.0 is the capability to customize the fields of data displayed on expense transactions. Expense transaction types that you can customize include Write Check, Enter Bill, Bill Credit, Credit Card Charge, and Credit Card Credit.

The need for customizing an expense transaction varies for each company using QuickBooks; perhaps the ultimate purpose is to report on expense activity using some variable that was previously not found in QuickBooks.

For example, this might come in handy for a restaurant required to report on the ounces of liquor purchased or a manufacturer that wants to track the weight of items purchased. These purposes and many others can be easily accomplished when adding custom-defined fields to the expense transactions.

Custom Fields

Custom fields are offered in QuickBooks Pro, Premier, and Enterprise. However, in Enterprise, users have more options when creating custom fields; including the following (see Figure C.1):

- **Choose Field Attributes**—Text, numbers with or without decimals, date, phone, and user-defined multichoice list.

- **Required Field**—Field required on a transaction, list, or both.

Custom fields provide the flexibility to add specialized information to data that QuickBooks already tracks about your customers, your vendors, your employees, and items that you purchase and sell. An advantage is the capability to create a user-defined drop-down list of values.

When using QuickBooks Enterprise software, you can create the following custom-defined fields:

- **Items List**—Up to 15 custom-definable fields.

- **Customer/Vendor/Employee Lists**—Up to 12 custom-definable fields, limited to a total of 30 for these three lists combined.

You might consider using custom fields to track weight, color, or size for products you buy and sell. Some uses for custom fields within the customer list might include recording a route number or preferred shipping method. The uses are really endless.

The following instructions detail how to add a custom field to an item. Follow these basic instructions if you are adding a custom-defined field to a vendor, customer, or employee list name.

1. From the menu bar, select **Lists**, **Item List**.

2. With your cursor, select the item you want to define custom fields for; on your keyboard, press Ctrl+E to edit the item.

3. Click the Custom Fields button to the right. Custom Fields For (name of item) displays.

> **note**
>
> You can use custom fields to hold special values that you enter in a customer's invoice. Some QuickBooks-compatible programs use custom fields to hold calculated values. For example, CCRQInvoice (by CCRSoftware) can calculate the total quantity of items ordered in an invoice or calculate the total weight of items in an invoice, using custom fields to hold the item weight and to store the calculated totals: See www.ccrsoftware.com/ CCRQInvoice/InvoiceQ.htm.

Figure C.1
QuickBooks Enterprise permits you to define custom fields with specific attributes.

4. Click the Define Fields button to the right. Set Up Custom Fields for Items displays.

5. In the Label field, type a name to identify the field on transactions.

6. Place a checkmark in the Use column for Fields You Want to Use box.

7. From the What Kind of Data drop-down list, choose the attribute for the Defined Field.

8. Place a checkmark in the Trans field to require use on sales transactions. The Select Required Item Types dialog box displays.

9. Place a checkmark next to the item types you want this newly custom-defined field to be used with. Click OK to close.

10. Place a checkmark in the List field to require data when creating new items. Click OK to close the Set Up Custom Fields for Items dialog box.

11. Complete any required fields.

12. Click OK to close the Custom Fields for the selected item.

🔊 **caution**
You cannot remove a checkmark in the Use column of the Custom Fields dialog box if the same field is included in a sales transaction template. First remove the field from the template, then remove the checkmark from the Use column.

Information you enter into the fields can be for your use only, or you can prefill fields within certain transactions when you enter a name or item on the form, as in Figure C.2. You can also include data from customized fields in your reports.

➡ *For more information, see "Customizing QuickBooks Forms," p. 339.*

QuickBooks treats the information you enter into a custom field the same way it treats information you enter into any other field. If you memorize a transaction that has a custom field, QuickBooks memorizes what you entered in the field along with the other details of the transaction. If you export a list that contains data in custom fields, QuickBooks exports that data along with the other data from the list.

Now that you have learned how to add custom-defined fields to your Enterprise data, you can add these fields to expense transactions, a new feature for QuickBooks Enterprise 14.0.

> ### 📡 caution
>
> Including custom fields in reports can be tricky. Two types of reports exist—summary and detail. A summary report shows only the value of a custom field associated with the list record. A detail report shows the custom field associated with a transaction. Because the custom fields can be changed on the transaction, you might find the value in a custom field assigned to the list to be different than what was used on a transaction.

Customize Expense Transactions

New for QuickBooks Enterprise 14.0 is the capability to add custom-defined fields in addition to the Sales Rep field to expense transactions. This customization feature is new for expense transactions. We have had the ability to add these fields to sales transactions for many years.

You can customize the following expense transactions exclusively in QuickBooks Enterprise 14.0:

- Write Check
- Enter Bill
- Bill Credit
- Credit Card Charge
- Credit Card Credit

Follow these steps to customize any of these transaction types. The instructions given here and the images provided are of a vendor bill; however, the steps are the same for any of the mentioned transaction types.

1. From a displayed Enter Bill (or any of the mentioned expense transaction types), right-click with your mouse on the grid detail as in Figure C.2.

2. Select **Customize Columns** from the list that displays.

3. Customize Columns—Enter Bills displays, as in Figure C.3.

4. From the left side, select from Available Columns and click the Add> button. The field selected is added to Chosen Columns on the right.

> ### 🔍 note
>
> You can customize the fields of data displayed on either the Expenses tab or the Items tab of the referenced expense transactions types in this section.

Figure C.2
Right-click on the expense transaction grid to customize the columns.

Figure C.3
Add custom-defined and Sales Rep fields to expense transactions.

5. (Optional) From Chosen Columns on the right, select a field and choose <Remove to remove that field from being visible on the transaction. Fields that are grayed out are required, and you cannot remove them.

6. (Optional) From Chosen Columns on the right, select a field and choose Move Up or Move Down to determine the order the fields display from left to right.

7. (Optional) Click Default to reset the values.

8. When completed, click OK to save your changes. The field selected now displays on the expense transaction, as Figure C.3 shows.

After adding data to these fields, you can include them in reports, making QuickBooks Enterprise software the right choice for companies with complex reporting needs.

QuickBooks Enterprise Inventory

In addition to the unique features this appendix discusses in detail, other features exclusive to QuickBooks Enterprise include the following:

- Customizable reports using QuickBooks Statement Writer, to harness the power of Microsoft Excel.

  ➡ *To learn more, see "QuickBooks Statement Writer," p. 753.*

- ODBC connectivity for applications such as Microsoft Access, Microsoft Excel, and other ODBC-aware programs. To get started, in QuickBooks Enterprise, select **File**, **Utilities**, **Set up ODBC**, and follow the onscreen documentation. Existing ODBC users report that the functionality works well with Microsoft Excel.

- Support for more users, locations, and company files. QuickBooks Enterprise scales up to 30 simultaneous users and tracks thousands of customers, vendors, and inventory items.

  ➡ *For more information, see Table 17.1, p. 662.*

- Safeguarded sensitive business data. This gives you more granular control over QuickBooks security settings for employees, which allows you to finely tailor access to just the information employees need to do their jobs.

  ➡ *To learn about user security, see "User Security in QuickBooks Enterprise," p. 59.*

Accessing Inventory Features and Reports

QuickBooks Enterprise makes it easy to access the many tasks and reports needed to manage the inventory needs of your business. Flexibility in accessing these tasks permits you to pick a method that works best for you (see Figure C.4).

Figure C.4
You can add custom fields to sales forms and expense transactions, and include them in reports.

Custom field added to sales form

Inventory Center

The Inventory Center is available in QuickBooks Premier, Accountant, and QuickBooks Enterprise Solutions. In QuickBooks Enterprise, the Inventory Center includes the capability to edit the cost, sales price, markup, and margin without opening the individual item record. Additionally, in Enterprise only, you have the option to store an image of the item, as Figure C.5 shows. However, currently you cannot use this image on transactions or include it in reports.

➡ *To learn more, see "Inventory Center," p. 212.*

Figure C.5
Use the Inventory Center for all your inventory needs.

Inventory Access from the Menu Bar

QuickBooks Enterprise users can access features and reports from an Inventory-specific menu on the menu bar (see Figure C.6).

Figure C.6
QuickBooks Enterprise includes an Inventory-specific menu on the menu bar.

Auto Create Purchase Orders

The Auto Create Purchase Orders feature available exclusively in QuickBooks Enterprise helps you restock your items in record time. In earlier versions of QuickBooks, you reviewed your inventory reorder reports and then created a single purchase order at a time.

New for QuickBooks Enterprise 14.0, the Auto Create Purchase Orders capability now suggests a quantity to purchase. The suggested Quantity factors in the Quantity Available and Quantity on Purchase Orders and then compares this to the Reorder Point, Max value for the item.

Follow these instructions for creating multiple purchase orders from the inventory stock reports:

1. From the menu bar, select **Reports**, **Inventory**, **Stock Status By Vendor** or any of the other stock status reports. You can also access this feature from the Inventory Reorder reports found in the Manufacturing and Wholesale edition of Enterprise. See Figure C.7.

Figure C.7
Access the
Auto Create
Purchase
Orders capa-
bility from
the inventory
stock status
or reorder
reports.

2. (Optional) Select the **Use Avail Qty to Reorder** checkbox. Selecting this checkbox might include additional items you need to reorder.

3. Click the Create Auto PO's button at the top of the displayed report. A dialog box of the same name displays (see Figure C.8).

4. Select a date to assign to the multiple purchase orders.

5. If you are tracking multiple inventory locations, optionally select a **Ship To Site**. If you do not select a Ship To Site at this time, you will be required to select the Ship To Site when receiving the items into inventory.

6. Place a checkmark next to the item(s) you will be creating purchase orders for.

7. Select a **Class** if you are tracking departmental profit centers.

> **note**
>
> When multiple items are selected with the same vendor assigned, QuickBooks creates a single purchase order for that vendor that includes each of the selected items.

Figure C.8
Select the
items you
will be creat-
ing purchase
orders for.

8. Accept the default vendor selected (this default is the vendor assigned to the item record), or optionally select a different vendor from the drop-down menu in the Vendor column.

9. In the Qty to Order column, accept the suggested quantity or change this as needed for the number of items you want to order.

10. In the lower right, add a checkmark if you choose to Show Purchase Orders After Saving.

11. Click Create PO's. The Create Auto PO's dialog box closes automatically.

If you selected Show Purchase Orders After Saving, QuickBooks displays the Open Purchase Orders report filtered for today's date. QuickBooks adds the memo "Auto created" to each purchase order. See Figure C.9. This helps users identify which purchase orders were created using the Auto Create PO's feature.

Figure C.9
When view-
ing the Open
Purchase
Orders report,
the memo
line indicates
whether they
were auto
created.

Working with Assemblies

Assemblies are useful when you want to select individual component items used in the manufacture of a finished good. Using assemblies depletes the inventory for the components and tracks the on-hand quantity for the finished good. Inventory Assemblies are available only with QuickBooks Premier (all editions), Accountant, and Enterprise (all editions).

➡ *To learn more, see "Working with Assemblies," p. 195.*

Automatically Build Subassemblies

For some industries, inventory assemblies can have subassemblies as components. To complete the final assembly, QuickBooks must have on hand the required quantity of the subassemblies. QuickBooks Enterprise improves the process of working with assemblies by allowing users to first have QuickBooks build the subassemblies. In QuickBooks Premier, the other edition of QuickBooks that offers assemblies, users must know to build the subassemblies first.

To use this exclusive feature of automatically building subassemblies, follow these instructions:

1. From the menu bar, select **Inventory**, **Build Assemblies**.

2. From the Assembly Item drop-down, select the assembly you want to build.

3. For assemblies that have other assemblies listed in the Components Needed to Build detail, place a checkmark next to Automatically Build Required Subassemblies. See Figure C.10.

4. QuickBooks builds the needed subassemblies before attempting to build the selected build assembly.

5. If there are not enough components to build the subassembly, QuickBooks offers the choice of either Mark the Build as Pending or Cancel the Build Assembly.

6. Click either Build & Close or Build & New.

For companies that manage inventory and use assemblies with subassemblies, this feature can save time and improve accuracy when working with inventory.

Figure C.10
Automatically building subassemblies first saves time.

Replace or Remove Components in Assemblies

QuickBooks Enterprise improves the process of adding or removing components in an assembly. Only in QuickBooks Enterprise can users choose to automatically remove or replace components in multiple assemblies easily. In QuickBooks Premier, if a component is used in multiple assemblies and needs to be removed or replaced, users have to manually edit each assembly that includes that component.

Follow these steps to automatically replace or remove a component in all the assemblies it is associated with.

1. From the menu bar, select **Lists**, **Item List**.

2. With your cursor, select the item (component) that needs to be removed or replaced in assemblies.

3. Right-click with your cursor and select **Assemblies Where Used**. See Figure C.11.

4. The Assemblies Where Used dialog box displays with the same item already selected in the Where Used Item drop-down field. At the bottom of the dialog box are any assemblies listed where the component is used. See Figure C.12.

5. If you are replacing the item, in the Replacement Item drop-down field, browse to select the new item, or click Add New at the top of the list and follow the prompts.

Figure C.11
New for Enterprise 14.0, you can view all assemblies a component is included in.

Figure C.12
You can easily manage the replacement or removal of components in an assembly.

6. (Optional) If you are simply removing the component from the assemblies and will not be replacing it, leave the Replacement Item field blank.

7. The grid detail at the bottom of the dialog box lists any assemblies for which the selected part is a component. Click to select which assembly to edit, or click Select All in the lower left.

8. Click the Replace button in the lower right to replace the item (or remove the item without a replacement item).

9. QuickBooks displays a successful QuickBooks Information window. Click OK to close the window and return to Assemblies Where Used for the selected part. Click Close to close the window and return to the Item List.

Managing assemblies and being able to easily substitute or remove components are compelling reasons to use QuickBooks Enterprise if your company manages inventory assemblies.

Options for Autocalculating the Assembly Cost Field

Another related assembly improvement included exclusively with QuickBooks Enterprise is the capability to set a default for handling the Cost field on an Item record (see Figure C.13).

Figure C.13
Enterprise offers options for what is recorded in the Cost field of an assembly.

QuickBooks uses the Cost amount in the Cost field on an inventory assembly item record in the following ways:

- To prefill the cost field on all purchase transaction forms, such as purchase orders, bills, and checks.

- To set the sales price of this inventory assembly item if you're using a default markup percentage.

- To adjust this inventory assembly item's price by a percentage of the unit cost.

- To adjust this inventory assembly item's price by a fixed amount above the unit cost.

■ To display a cost on the Item Listing and Price List reports. If you build the item yourself, the Avg. Cost is the total of the costs of all the items in the Bill of Materials. However, you're still responsible for filling in the Cost amount yourself.

■ When you create a new inventory assembly and enter an existing On Hand quantity, QuickBooks calculates the Total Value for the Asset Account by multiplying the Cost you enter by the On Hand quantity.

■ To calculate the initial Avg. Cost of the inventory assembly when you first create the item. The initial Avg. Cost is the initial Total Value divided by the initial On Hand quantity.

caution

This cost is *not* used to calculate the actual cost on reports such as Profit & Loss. For reports, QuickBooks uses the calculated average cost based on your purchases of the components (or the assembly itself, if you purchase it directly from a vendor). To learn more about average cost, refer to "Reviewing the Recorded Average Cost Valuation," in Chapter 6, p. 217.

Follow these steps to set a global default for the Cost field on an assembly or to manually assign a cost:

1. Log in to the file as the Admin user and, from the menu bar, select **Edit**, **Preferences**, **Items and Inventory**.

2. Select the **Company Preferences** tab.

3. Click the Automatic Cost & Price Updates button, as in Figure C.14.

Figure C.14
Set global preferences for how the cost field in an assembly is calculated.

4. In the For Assembly Items box, choose between these two options:

■ **Use Auto-updated BOM Cost as Assembly Cost**—This choice takes the total of the costs for each component and adds the total in the Cost field on the assembly record (refer to Figure C.13).

■ (Optional) **When BOM Cost Changes, Update Sales Price**—if you selected Auto-update BOM Cost as Assembly Cost, you can also choose here to have the sales price update when component costs change. This can be valuable in ensuring that your price is adequately covering your costs.

However, even if you select a global preference, you can override that preference on specific assemblies. Your choices include these:

- **Use Total BOM Cost**—This is the sum total of what all the components (items) cost, as recorded on each individual item record.

- **Use Global Preference**—This will default the selection to the preference set. To select or edit this global preference from the menu bar, select **Edit**, **Preferences**, **Items and Inventory**. On the Company Preferences tab click the Automatic Cost & Price Updates button.

- **User Defined Cost**—With this choice you manually enter a cost amount. However, this is not the cost used in preparation of your Profit & Loss report—it only helps calculate automatic price updates.

Sales Order Fulfillment Worksheet

If you track inventory items in QuickBooks and use sales orders, the Sales Order Fulfillment Worksheet (see Figure C.15) can help you decide which sales orders to fulfill when you don't have enough quantity on hand to fulfill them all. It does this by letting you create different what-if scenarios to see how fulfilling one set of sales orders affects your ability to fulfill others.

The Sales Order Fulfillment Worksheet is available with the following editions of QuickBooks:

- QuickBooks Enterprise (all editions)

- QuickBooks Accountant

- QuickBooks Premier Manufacturing and Wholesale

- QuickBooks Premier Retail

Figure C.15
The Sales Order Fulfillment Worksheet can help you choose which orders to fulfill first.

Enable Inventory and Sales Orders

To use this feature, you need to first enable Inventory and Sales Orders. From the menu bar, select **Edit**, **Preferences**, **Items & Inventory**. On the Company Preferences tab, select **Inventory and Purchase Orders Are Active**. You must be logged in to the file as the Admin or External Accountant user.

Using the Sales Order Fulfillment Worksheet

You can use the Sales Order Fulfillment Worksheet to see at a glance which sales orders you can fulfill. To access the Sales Order Fulfillment Worksheet, from the menu bar, select **Customers**, **Sales Order Fulfillment Worksheet**. The worksheet includes the following tables of data:

- **Sales Orders**—Provides a single-row listing of all sales orders not yet fulfilled. You can sort this table of data by any of the following means:
  - Sales Orders Chosen for Fulfillment First
  - Sales Orders That Can Be Completely Fulfilled First
  - By the Date the Sales Order Was Entered
  - By Ship Date
  - By Order Number
  - By Customer:Job
  - By Open Amount
  - By Amount That Can Be Fulfilled
  - Partially Invoiced Sales Orders First
- **Details of Sales Order**—QuickBooks displays the line-item detail for the currently selected sales order.

Status icons in the Fulfillable column in both tables in the worksheet indicate whether the sales order, specific items, or specific assemblies can be completely or partially fulfilled:

- **Solid green circle**—In the sales orders table, this indicates that you have enough inventory to fulfill the entire order. In the details table, it indicates that you have all of an individual item needed to fulfill the order.
- **Half-full orange circle**—In the sales orders table, this indicates that you can fulfill only part of the order. In the details table, this indicates that you have enough of an individual item to only partially fulfill the order.
- **Red X**—This indicates that you are out of stock for that order in the sales orders table or for an individual item in the details table.

Follow these steps to complete the process:

1. Place a checkmark next to the sale order(s) you want to fulfill.

2. In the Print Your Work section, select print **Pick Lists**, **Packing Slips** and/or **Sales Orders**. These printouts are used to fulfill inventory and create invoices.

3. Select **Print**. QuickBooks opens the Print dialog box for you to select your printer. Click Print.

4. QuickBooks displays a message confirming that the documents printed successfully. Place a checkmark in the Reprint column next to any document you need to reprint. Click OK.

5. QuickBooks displays a warning message about invoicing your sales order to decrease your inventory levels. Click OK after reading the message.

6. Gather the printed documents and locate the individual sales orders in QuickBooks.

7. Click Create Invoice from the Main tab of the ribbon toolbar for each individual sales order.

Enhanced Inventory Receiving

Enhanced Inventory Receiving (EIR) is a preference that enables an optional workflow for improving how you receive and pay for inventory. With Enhanced Inventory Receiving, item receipts increase inventory and the inventory offset (current liability) account until the vendor bill is received and entered.

When you turn on EIR, you receive and pay for items in QuickBooks in a completely different way:

- Item receipts don't increase accounts payable.

- Vendor bills don't affect inventory.

- Vendor bills associated with item receipts no longer replace item receipts.

To set up your file to track purchasing this way, QuickBooks changes the effect on accounting for past transactions during the EIR setup. It is recommended that you first evaluate whether EIR is right for you. To help you decide, ask yourself the following questions:

- Do you receive one bill that covers multiple item receipts?

- Do you receive multiple bills for one item receipt?

- Are your inventory quantities skewed when you enter a bill and QuickBooks automatically changes the date of the item receipt?

> **⚠ caution**
>
> If you turn on EIR, you can't turn it off. You should read and understand these important considerations before you turn it on.

> **🔍 note**
>
> When EIR is not enabled QuickBooks does the following:
>
> - The inventory asset account is increased when a vendor bill including inventory items is recorded.
>
> - When a vendor bill is associated with an item receipt, the item receipt no longer is a separate document. Instead, it is converted to a vendor bill.

- Do you pay for items before you receive them but don't want your inventory quantities to increase? If you don't use EIR, QuickBooks increases inventory quantities when you enter a bill for inventory items.

- Do you want to separate the receiving department (item receipts) from the accounts payable department (enter and pay bills)? If you don't use EIR, QuickBooks converts item receipts to a bill when you receive the bill.

> **⚡ caution**
> Third-party applications that affect inventory might not work as expected with EIR. Check with the vendor before you enable this feature.

If you answered "yes" to any of these questions, consider using EIR. However, it's important that you read the following cautionary points before you begin because you can't turn off EIR:

- When you turn on EIR, QuickBooks changes past transactions. Converting to EIR can take up to a few hours, depending on the size of your company file. If you have a large company file, you might consider condensing your company data before turning on EIR.

   ➡️ *For more information on the size of a company data file, see Chapter 17, "Managing Your QuickBooks Database."*

- EIR separates item receipts from bills. This creates a new process for receiving and paying for items. This new process also comes with some restrictions.

- You can't turn off EIR (see Figure C.16). After it's on, you must use the new EIR process for receiving and paying for items. A safe practice is to create a backup of your file before you begin. If after trying EIR you find that it doesn't work for you, restore your backup.

- When using EIR, if you receive a bill with different item costs compared to the related item receipt, QuickBooks automatically changes the item cost on that item receipt. QuickBooks makes this change even if the item receipt is in a closed period.

Figure C.16
You cannot reverse the Enhanced Inventory Receiving setting, so be sure to back up your data before the conversion.

Changes Made When You Enable EIR

Take care when deciding whether to use Enhance Inventory Receiving. Considerations include the following:

- **Past transactions**—With EIR turned on, bills do not increase inventory quantities. This means that QuickBooks has to create an item receipt for every bill that included items. This increases the number of transactions in your company file.

- **Accounts Payable balance**—If you haven't received a bill for an open item receipt, the amount no longer shows up in Accounts Payable. This is correct because you haven't received the bill yet. QuickBooks shows only the amount in Accounts Payable when you receive the bill. To understand what QuickBooks does with the value of open item receipts, review "The Accounting Behind EIR" section in this appendix.

- **Small rounding error to average cost**—When QuickBooks creates the new item receipts, it recalculates inventory average cost. These item receipts change the order of inventory transactions within each day. This change in transaction order can sometimes result in minor changes to the average cost of an item.

Workflow When Using EIR

Enabling Enhanced Inventory Receiving requires a slightly different workflow, as detailed next:

- **Without EIR**—You can receive and pay for inventory in two ways:

  - **A single transaction**—Enter a bill for inventory items that increases your inventory on hand and increases Accounts Payable.

> **note**
>
> This new process applies only to vendor bills. You can still increase inventory quantities and pay for items with checks and credit card charges.

  - **Two transactions**—Enter an item receipt to receive the inventory. Inventory is increased along with Accounts Payable; however, the item receipts do not display in the Pay Bills dialog box. When the vendor bill is recorded, the same item receipt is converted to a vendor bill.

- With EIR, you must enter two separate transactions, and they can be entered in any order:

  - An item receipt to receive items

  - A bill to pay for the items

Restrictions When Using EIR

Enhanced Inventory Receiving imposes the following restrictions:

- You can't enter negative items on item receipts or bills.

- The Item Receipt transaction no longer includes an Expenses tab, as Figure C.17 shows.

- If you create a purchase order for non-inventory items, you must receive them with an item receipt to close the PO.

- You can no longer mark items as billable on item receipts.

Figure C.17 Item receipts created using EIR enabled do not include the Expenses tab.

The Accounting Behind EIR

QuickBooks automatically creates a new account (Other Current Liability) called the Inventory Offset account. QuickBooks completes the following accounting with an item receipt and vendor bill, detailed in Tables C.1 and C.2:

Table C.1   Item Receipt Accounting

Debit	Credit
Inventory Asset account	Inventory Offset account

Table C.2   Vendor Bill Accounting

Debit	Credit
Inventory Offset account	Accounts Payable

After enabling EIR, QuickBooks provides a summary of the transactions and their value affected by the change, as Figure C.18 shows.

Figure C.18
QuickBooks provides a summary of the changes made to the file after enabling Enhanced Inventory Receiving.

If you enter items directly on a check or credit card charge, QuickBooks does the same accounting as before: debiting Inventory Asset and crediting the bank or credit card account.

Automatic Cost & Price Updates

As Figure C.19 shows, you can use the Automatic Cost & Price Updates Preference to determine how you handle item cost changes.

To set preferences for handling cost and price updates, follow these steps:

1. Log in to the file as the Admin user or External Accountant user in single-user mode.

2. From the menu bar, select **Edit**, **Preferences**, **Items & Inventory**, and then select the **Company Preferences** tab.

3. Click the Automatic Cost & Price Updates button. The Automatic Cost & Price Updates dialog box displays.

4. You can set the following global preferences (see Figure C.19):

   ▪ **If Item Cost Changes on a Purchase**—Always Update the Item Cost, Never Update Item Cost, or Ask About Updating the Item Cost.

   ▪ **When Item Cost Changes**—For the sales price: Always Update Sales Price, Never Update Sales Price, or Ask About Updating Sales Price.

   ▪ **Markup**—Choose Percent Over Cost or Amount Over Cost. You can override this preference individually within individual inventory item records.

Figure C.19
Set global preferences for automatically handling cost and sales price changes. You can override these settings on the individual item record.

Automatic Cost & Price Updates

FOR ALL ITEMS

Markup | Percent over Cost

FOR NON-ASSEMBLY ITEMS

If item cost changes on a purchase | Ask about updating item cost

When item cost changes | Ask about updating sales price

FOR ASSEMBLY ITEMS

☐ Use auto-updated BOM cost as assembly cost.

☐ When BOM cost changes, update sales price.

OK   Cancel

Assigning Markup Defaults per Item

The previous section detailed the options for setting a global preference for handling markups when a cost of item changes. This helps your business make sure you are earning the expected markup on your products and services.

Follow these steps to manage the markup individually for each item on your item list, as in Figure C.20:

1. From the menu bar, select **Lists, Item List**.

2. Double-click an item to display the Edit Item dialog box. You can also define these settings when creating a new item.

3. Click the Edit Markup button to the right. The Edit Markup dialog box displays.

4. From the Type of Markup drop-down list, choose from the following:

   - Percent Over Cost

   - Amount Over Cost

   - Use Default (Percent Over Cost), or whatever your preference setting was

5. Edit the Cost, Sales Price, and Markup Percent fields as desired.

6. From If Item Cost Changes on a Purchase, choose from Always Update Item Cost, Never Update Item Cost, Always Ask About Updating the Item Cost, or Use Default.

7. When Item Cost Changes, for the sales price, choose from Always Update Sales Price, Never Update Sales Price, Always Ask About Updating Sales Price, or Use Default.

8. Click OK twice to save your changes.

Figure C.20
Enterprise includes the capability to manage markup defaults individually for each item.

QuickBooks Enterprise with Advanced Inventory

Advanced Inventory is a collection of advanced inventory management features, all detailed in this section of the appendix. Advanced Inventory is an annual subscription and requires the user to also have an active Full Service Plan for QuickBooks Enterprise. For more details on current pricing for Advanced Inventory and the Full Service Plan, visit Intuit's website, http://enterprisesuite.intuit.com/.

Your Advanced Inventory subscription enables additional features within QuickBooks Enterprise. You don't have to install or learn additional software, and you can manage a number of sophisticated inventory scenarios.

Multiple Inventory Locations

In addition to tracking inventory in multiple warehouses, you can track inventory in different staging areas within a single warehouse, on service trucks, and on consignment, for example.

Before using Enterprise or before Multiple Inventory Locations tracking was available, you might have used one of these alternative methods of tracking multiple inventory locations:

- Using multiple items (or subitems) for the same part

- Using a custom-defined field

- Using class tracking

- Using Microsoft Excel

Although this list is not exhaustive, note that you should take care when you begin to use the Multiple Inventory Locations feature when you have been tracking it in some other way.

To find more details about making the switch to using Multiple Inventory Locations, from the menu bar, select **Help**, **QuickBooks Help** and, in the search field, type **Multiple Inventory Locations**. Click the How to Switch from Another Method of Tracking Multiple Inventory Sites link, and click the Show More Results link.

Assign a Starting Inventory Site

When you first set up Multiple Inventory Locations in QuickBooks Enterprise, you must create a temporary site (for example, you might name it **Starting Inventory**). QuickBooks assigns all past inventory transactions to this site when you first enable Multiple Inventory Locations. You can later transfer items to their actual sites and bin locations. You can also rename this temporary site later.

To enable Multiple Inventory Locations, follow these steps:

1. Log in to the file as the Admin or External Accountant user in single-user mode.

2. From the menu bar, select **Edit**, **Preferences**, **Items & Inventory** and click the Company Preferences tab.

3. Click the Advanced Inventory Settings button to display a dialog box of the same name.

4. Click the Multiple Inventory Locations tab if it is not already selected.

5. Place a checkmark in the Multiple Inventory Sites Is Enabled checkbox.

6. QuickBooks displays the Enable Multiple Inventory Sites dialog box (see Figure C.21). Read the information and then assign your Beginning Inventory Site.

7. From the Inventory Site drop-down menu, select **Add New**. QuickBooks displays the New Inventory Site dialog box.

8. Type a name for the site; as mentioned previously, you might want to name this site **Starting Inventory**. Complete any of the remaining fields as desired. Click OK to close.

9. You return to Enable Multiple Inventory Sites. Click the Continue button. You return to the Advanced Inventory Settings preferences.

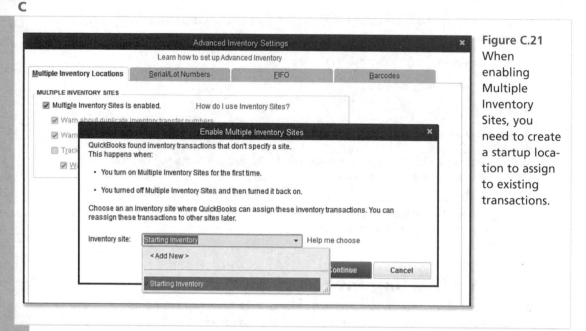

Figure C.21
When enabling Multiple Inventory Sites, you need to create a startup location to assign to existing transactions.

10. (Optional) Select any or each of the following:

- Warn About Duplicate Inventory Transfer Numbers

- Warn per Site If Not Enough Inventory to Sell

- Track Bin Locations Within Inventory Sites (row, shelf, or bin) and the additional Warn Per Location If Not Enough Inventory to Sell. If selected, a message displays that, to get started, QuickBooks assigns all the items to a bin named Unassigned. Later you can transfer your items to their correct bins. See Figure C.22.

> **note**
> You can add more sites or rename existing sites later from the menu bar by selecting **Lists, Inventory Site List**.

Figure C.22
Define warning preferences and the capability to track subsite locations for row, shelf, or bin tracking.

note

You might encounter a message that items were automatically placed in a row, shelf, or bin titled Unassigned. QuickBooks found inventory transactions that don't specify a site (or bin location, if you track bin locations). Reasons you might see this message include the following:

- You imported your accountant's changes. When you created the Accountant's Copy of your file, QuickBooks required you to turn off Multiple Inventory Locations. However, your accountant modified or added inventory transactions in the Accountant's Copy. Now QuickBooks must assign these transactions to a site (and bin location, if you track bin locations).

- You turned Multiple Inventory Locations back on. Multiple Inventory Locations was turned off in this file. Since then, QuickBooks hasn't assigned a site (or bin location, if applicable) to any inventory transactions.

Add an Inventory Site and Bin Locations

After creating your initial starting inventory site, you can add sites and bin locations, if you track bin locations.

1. From the menu bar, select **Lists**, **Inventory Site List**.

2. From the Inventory Site drop-down, select **New**.

3. In the Name field, type the name of the location.

4. If this is a bin location (row, shelf, or bin), select the **This Is a Location Within Site** checkbox. Then click the drop-down arrow and select a site (warehouse). See Figures C.23 and C.24.

5. Enter the appropriate information.

6. Click Next to add another location, or click OK if you're finished.

tip

For added efficiency, you can add multiple Inventory Sites using Add/Edit Multiple List Entries. From the menu bar, select **Lists**, **Add/Edit Multiple List Entries** and select **Inventory Sites** from the List drop-down.

Figure C.23
Add inventory sites.

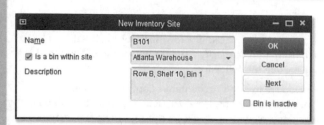

Figure C.24
Row, shelf, or bin tracking using sublocations of inventory sites.

Edit an Inventory Site and Bin Locations

You might find it necessary to edit an existing inventory site. You can even rename an existing site, if needed. Follow these steps:

1. From the menu bar, select **Lists**, **Inventory Site List**.

2. Double-click an inventory site or bin location from the list.

3. Change the information as needed.

4. Click OK.

 tip

You can also choose to use the Lists, Add/Edit Multiple List Entries feature from the menu bar to efficiently add or edit the Inventory Site list.

Transferring Between Locations

Use the Transfer Inventory dialog box to transfer inventory between locations, as in Figure C.25.

You can do this between sites (warehouses) to accomplish these goals:

- Replenish items at a location

- Transfer items from your home warehouse to your satellite locations

- Transfer items to a loading dock or ship

You can also do this between bin locations (row, shelf, or bin) to replenish items in a row, shelf, or bin.

Follow these instructions to transfer inventory from one location, row, shelf, or bin to another:

1. From the menu bar, select **Inventory**, **Transfer Inventory**.

2. In the Date field, enter the date of the transfer.

3. In the Reference No. field, enter the appropriate transfer number. If you have a physical form for the transfer, use the number in this field.

4. (Optional) Click the Class drop-down arrow and select a class.

5. Click the Transfer From drop-down arrow and select an inventory site (warehouse).

6. Click the drop-down arrow to select the other inventory site (warehouse).

Figure C.25
Use the Transfer Inventory dialog box for moving inventory from one location, row, shelf, or bin to another.

7. Select the inventory items to transfer to the site:

   ■ To select individual items:

      ■ Click in the Item column.

      ■ Click the drop-down arrow and select an inventory item.

   ■ To search for or select multiple items:

      ■ Click Find & Select Items.

      ■ (Optional) Enter a search term in the Find field and click Search.

      ■ Click the left column to select or clear inventory items.

      ■ Click Add Selected Items.

8. If you track bin locations, in the first Location column, click the drop-down arrow, and then select the bin you're transferring from.

9. In the Qty to Transfer column, enter the number to transfer for each item.

10. If you track bin locations, in the second Location column, click the drop-down arrow, and then select the bin you're transferring to.

11. (Optional) In the Memo field, enter the reason for this transfer, such as **Transfer opening quantity to site**.

12. (Optional) Click the Prefill Qty to Transfer with Quantity on Hand checkbox.

13. (Optional) Click the Print button to print a copy of the transfer for your records.

14. Click the Save & Close button.

> **note**
>
> If you're transferring between bin locations, you still need to enter a site in the Transfer From and To fields (in most cases, this will be the same site). You specify the bin locations in the fields below.

Duplicating Inventory Transfer Transactions

You cannot transfer inventory from one site to multiple sites in the same transfer transaction. If you need to enter multiple inventory transfers, QuickBooks lets you duplicate previously recorded inventory transfers.

To duplicate a previously recorded inventory transfer, follow these steps:

1. Open an existing transfer.

2. With the transfer displayed, from the menu bar, select **Edit**, **Duplicate Inventory Transfer**.

3. Change the details of the transfer as necessary.

4. Click the Save & Close button.

Reporting Inventory by Site

QuickBooks Enterprise makes it easy to report on inventory by site, shelf, bin, or row.

1. From the menu bar, select **Reports**, **Inventory**.

2. Choose from the following reports:

   - Serial Numbers in Stock by Site

   - Items by Bin Location (see Figure C.26)

   - Quantity on Hand by Site

   - Inventory Valuation Summary by Site

   - Inventory Stock Status by Site

   - Pending Builds by Site

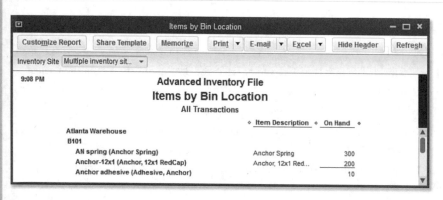

Figure C.26
Report on inventory by warehouse, row, shelf, and bin.

Serial/Lot Numbers

With a subscription to QuickBooks Enterprise with Advanced Inventory, you can track serial numbers or lot numbers. You can't track both, so decide which you want before you begin.

Select serial numbers if the following applies to your business:

- You buy and sell inventory items that have unique serial numbers.
- You keep track of which customers bought specific serial numbers.
- You want to know which serial numbers are in stock.
- You need a report that shows the invoices related to a specific serial number (this helps you track down a serial number's history for a warranty).

Select lot numbers if the following applies to your business:

- You buy items in lots.
- You keep track of which customers bought items from a specific lot.
- You need a recall report in case you have to track all the items from a specific lot (such as which items are in inventory and which customers purchased them).

Turn On Serial or Lot Number Tracking

Follow these instructions to begin using this feature:

1. Log in to the file as the Admin or External Accountant user in single-user mode.
2. From the menu bar, select **Edit**, **Preferences**, **Items and Inventory**, and then select the **Company Preferences** tab. See Figure C.27. Make sure Inventory and Purchase Orders Are Active is selected.
3. Click the Advanced Inventory Settings button. A dialog box with the same name displays, as in Figure C.27.
4. Click the Serial/Lot Numbers tab.
5. Click Enable Lot or Serial Numbers.
6. Select **Serial Numbers** or **Lot Numbers**.
7. (Optional) Select which transactions should display serial or lot numbers.
8. (Optional) Under Default settings for inventory and assembly items, click the drop-down arrows to set your preferences for warnings for all inventory and assembly items.
9. Click OK.
10. In the Preferences dialog box, click OK to save your changes and close.

> **note**
> You can override global warnings set in preferences for each inventory and assembly item in the New or Edit Item dialog box.

Figure C.27
Use these preferences when enabling serial or lot number tracking.

After you turn on serial or lot number tracking, QuickBooks adds a serial or lot number field to most transaction types (see Figure C.28), including the following:

- Purchase Transactions

    - Item Receipts

    - Bills

    - Credit Card Transactions

- Write Checks

- Sales Transactions

    - Invoices

    - Credit Memos

    - Sales Receipts

    - Sales Orders and Pending Invoices. However, QuickBooks doesn't remove these numbers from what's available to sell. The serial/lot number moves to the invoice or sales receipt when the sale becomes final.

You can also assign serial/lot numbers when you build assemblies and adjust inventory.

🔍 note

You can edit templates to add or remove serial/lot numbers on printed forms. Serial/lot numbers always appear on the screen.

On printed forms, multiple serial numbers appear in the description, separated by commas. The lot number appears in its own column.

〰️ tip

If you buy or sell multiple items with serial numbers, enter all the serial numbers on the same line. Separate serial numbers with a space or comma.

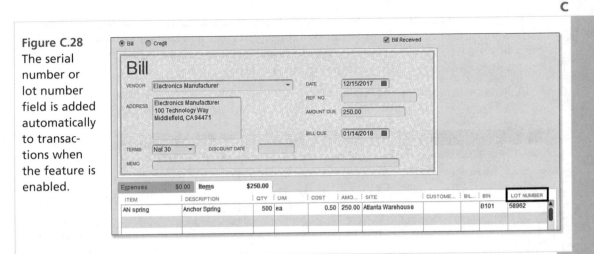

Figure C.28
The serial number or lot number field is added automatically to transactions when the feature is enabled.

Beginning to Track Serial or Lot Numbers

You don't have to assign serial or lot numbers to existing inventory to start tracking serial or lot numbers. If you have many different items with serial numbers in stock, you might choose not to enter all your serial numbers in QuickBooks right away. It's okay to continue your current method of tracking while slowly moving to QuickBooks by entering all newly purchased or assembled items with serial numbers as you acquire them. Eventually, your QuickBooks data will include all your serial numbers.

The following steps detail multiple methods for assigning serial numbers to existing inventory. First, gather information about the serial/lot numbers associated with your current inventory on hand. Use the Adjust Quantity/Value on Hand window to assign serial (or lot) numbers to existing inventory:

1. Select **Inventory, Adjust Quantity/Value on Hand**.

2. From the Adjustment Type drop-down menu, select **Serial Number**.

3. Select an **Adjustment Date** and **Inventory Site**.

4. (Optional) Assign a Reference No., Customer:Job, and Class.

5. (Optional) Select **Find & Select Items**, a useful feature for selecting multiple items at one time.

> ![tip icon] **tip**
>
> For another method useful for adding your initial serial numbers, from the menu bar, select **Lists, Add/Edit Multiple List Entries**.

6. From the Item field, begin typing the item name, or click the drop-down arrow and select it from the list.

7. In the Add Serial Numbers column, type the serial number; if you are adding multiple serial numbers, separate them with a comma. See Figure C.29.

8. (Optional) One method for adding serial numbers to existing inventory is to use the drop-down menu in the Add Serial Numbers column and select **Quick View for Serial Numbers**. In this dialog box, you can efficiently copy and paste serial numbers from Excel or manually type them. See Figure C.30.

9. (Optional) Another method for adding serial numbers to existing inventory is to open the drop-down menu in the Remove Serial Numbers column and select **Add Multiple Serial Numbers**. In this dialog box, you can enter multiple serial numbers with ease. See Figure C.31. Click Add Selected Numbers to add them to the Transfer Inventory dialog box.

10. Repeat steps 6 and 7 for each item as needed. When finished, click Save & Close.

Figure C.29
Are you using serial number tracking for the first time? Simply type the serial numbers and separate them with a comma.

Figure C.30
Use Quick View to efficiently add multiple serial numbers (or lots) for a single inventory item.

Figure C.31
To select multiple serial numbers for transfer, use Add Multiple Serial Numbers from the Serial Number drop-down menu.

Paste Serial or Lot Numbers from Excel

You can paste serial numbers from Excel or a comma-delimited file into a QuickBooks transaction. In Excel, copy the serial numbers. In QuickBooks, click the Add Serial Numbers column.

If your serial numbers are separated by commas or spaces, paste them directly into the field. If your serial numbers are a column in Excel, click the drop-down arrow and select **Quick View for Serial Numbers**. In the Serial Numbers column, right-click and select **Paste** to add the new numbers.

If your serial numbers are in a row in Excel, you can easily transpose them into a transaction column in Excel. To copy and paste serial numbers from Excel, follow these steps:

1. In Excel, copy the serial numbers.
2. Click the Excel column where you want to put the serial numbers.
3. Right-click and select **Paste Special**.
4. Select **Transpose**. Use the Transpose function outside the block of cells from which you are copying data.
5. Click OK to accept.

To manually update lot numbers in QuickBooks, follow these steps:

1. Select **Inventory, Adjust Quantity/Value on Hand**.
2. Click the Adjustment Type drop-down arrow and select **Lot Number**.

3. Click the Item field. Enter the item name, or click the drop-down arrow and select it from the list.

4. Enter the lot number.

5. In the New Count column, enter the number of items in that lot.

6. To assign a different lot number to more of the same item, or to assign a different lot number to a different item, repeat steps 3 to 5.

7. When finished, click Save & Close.

8. To verify your setup, run the Serial/Lot Numbers in Stock report.

Reporting on Lot Numbers

If you track lots and need to know where items from a specific lot are, follow this two-step process:

1. Find out how many items from a particular lot are still in inventory.

   ■ From the menu bar, select **Inventory, Inventory Center** to open the Inventory Center.

   ■ From the list on the left, select the item.

   ■ On the right side of the window below Recall Information, click Quantity on Hand by Lot Number. The Quick View window appears and shows the quantity on hand for each lot number associated with the item. See Figure C.32.

   ■ When finished, click Close.

 note

If you are tracking serial numbers (not lot numbers), you can use these same steps for reporting on serial numbers.

Figure C.32
Use the Inventory Center to gather information about where lots are currently stored.

2. Research which customers purchased items from the lot:

- Under Recall Information, click Transaction List by Lot Number.

- Click the Item drop-down arrow and select the item from the list.

- Click the Lot drop-down arrow and select a lot number.

- Click OK. QuickBooks lists all transactions that include the lot, including assemblies and sub-assemblies.

You can also report on lots (or serial numbers). From the menu bar, select **Reports**, **Inventory**, **Lot Numbers in Stock by Site**, as in Figure C.33. Another report is the Transaction List by Lot Number report.

Figure C.33
Report on Lot Numbers in Stock by Site

First-In, First-Out (FIFO) Inventory Costing

FIFO (First-In, First-Out) is a method of calculating the value of inventory sold and on hand. When you turn on FIFO, QuickBooks calculates inventory values based on the assumption that the first inventory items received are the first sold.

Without turning on FIFO, QuickBooks uses average costing as the means for determining the cost of inventory sold.

➡ *For more information, see "Reviewing the Recorded Average Cost Valuation," p. 217.*

> **note**
> You can start tracking FIFO on any date. If you later decide to turn off FIFO, click to clear the Use FIFO Starting On checkbox. QuickBooks again calculates inventory value using the average cost method.

Enabling First-In, First-Out Inventory Costing

1. From the menu bar, select the **Edit**, **Preferences**, **Company Preferences** tab.

2. On the left side of the Preferences window, select **Items & Inventory**.

3. Click the Advanced Inventory Settings button.

4. In the Advanced Inventory Settings dialog box, select the **FIFO** tab. Place a checkmark in the Use FIFO Starting On box and choose a date. QuickBooks recalculates all inventory-related transactions, starting with the date you enter.

5. Click OK.

6. In the Preferences window, click OK.

Reports Affected by FIFO Inventory Costing

When you enable FIFO inventory costing, the following report values are adjusted:

- Inventory valuation reports

- Balance sheet reports

- Profit & Loss reports (cost of goods sold)

- FIFO Cost Lot History Report

> **🔍 note**
>
> The FIFO Cost Lot History by Item report is included in your inventory reports only if you have enabled FIFO costing.

➡️ *To learn more, see "Inventory Reporting," p. 211.*

When FIFO costing is enabled in QuickBooks Enterprise, the FIFO Cost Lot History by Item report efficiently tracks the inventory acquisition (purchase, customer return, inventory adjustment, and so on) along with its cost. This provides users with information so they can see that the oldest (first in) cost lot is being disbursed first.

To prepare this report after enabling FIFO costing, follow these instructions:

1. From the menu bar, select **Reports**, **Inventory**, **FIFO Cost Lot History by Item**. See Figure C.34.

Figure C.34
Prepare the FIFO Cost Lot History for details about the calculations done behind the scenes.

2. To filter for specific item(s), click the Customize Report button at the top left of the displayed report. The Modify Report dialog box displays.

3. Click the Filters tab. In the Filter pane, select **Item**.

4. From the Item drop-down, scroll to find the specific item or items.

5. Click OK on the Modify Report dialog box to prepare the report filtered for the select Item or Items.

Barcodes

Increase efficiency and reliability for all inventory data entry by scanning items and serial numbers without touching a keyboard. QuickBooks automatically puts the information into the right field. If you don't have barcodes, QuickBooks creates them for you.

Overview—Working with Barcodes

Using barcodes in QuickBooks makes data entry faster and easier. You assign barcodes to items. Then you can scan barcodes when you buy or sell items. You can also scan barcodes to adjust the quantity of items on hand.

What barcode scanners does QuickBooks support? QuickBooks supports most USB and Bluetooth scanners. When you purchase or evaluate a scanner, look for the following specifications:

- Support for EAN-13 and Code-128 barcodes

- Capability to produce a single carriage return at the end of the barcode

To test your scanner using Windows Notepad, follow these steps:

1. On the Windows desktop, select **Start**, **Accessories**, **Notepad**.

2. Scan an item with your barcode scanner. You should see the barcode number, one per line in Notepad, as in Figure C.35.

Figure C.35
Test the barcode scanner first in Notepad, making sure it scans with a hard return after each item.

QuickBooks accepts UPC/EAN-13 barcodes. Specifically, a valid barcode can be between 5 and 30 characters in length and contains the following character types:

- Numbers (0–9)

- Letters (a–z and A–Z)

- Space

- Minus sign (–)

- Plus sign (+)

- Period (.)

- Full stop (.)

- Colon (:)

- Forward slash (/)

> 🔍 **note**
>
> Barcodes are case sensitive. For example, 123456A is different from 123456a.
>
> Barcodes QuickBooks generates begin with QB:. You can't create your own barcodes that begin with QB:.

Important: If the barcode is to be used as a serial or lot number, it must adhere to these rules:

- It can't contain spaces.

- It can't consist entirely of numbers. That is, it must contain other character types (for serial or lot numbers only).

- It must be between 6 and 13 characters in length.

Set Up Barcode Scanning

Before you can begin scanning items into QuickBooks, you need to enable the Barcode Scanning feature. Follow these instructions:

1. From the menu bar, select the **Edit**, **Preferences**, **Company Preferences** tab.

2. On the left side, select **Items & Inventory**.

3. Select **Advanced Inventory Settings** and click the Barcodes tab.

4. Select the **Enable Barcode Scanning** checkbox.

5. Click Open Barcode Wizard. If you already track barcodes in QuickBooks, QuickBooks moves the barcode you currently track into a custom-defined field for you. Just click the drop-down arrow and select the field you currently use for barcodes.

6. If you don't currently track barcodes in QuickBooks, leave the selection as I Don't Currently Track Barcodes in QuickBooks.

> 〰️ **tip**
>
> Barcodes that QuickBooks generates begin with QB:. Edit the barcode name to remove the QB:, and also change or remove barcodes that QuickBooks automatically generated for parent (top-level) items.

Importing Barcodes

If you track barcodes outside QuickBooks (in Excel, for example), you can import them using Add/Edit Multiple List Entries. From the menu bar, select **Lists**, **Add/Edit Multiple List Entries**, as in Figure C.36.

➡️ *For more information, see "Using Add/Edit Multiple List Entries," p. 166.*

Figure C.36
Use the Add/Edit Multiple List Entries feature to quickly scan in new barcodes or manually enter them.

Use your scanner to add the barcode to new items

Using Barcodes to Complete Transactions

You can scan barcodes while filling out sales or purchasing forms, to speed data entry. While working in a sales or purchasing form, simply scan a barcode; QuickBooks automatically places the barcode in the correct field on the form.

If QuickBooks doesn't automatically place the barcode in the correct field, QuickBooks might not support your scanner. However, you can still use your scanner for data entry by following these steps to first disable barcode scanning and then set a preference for how data advances between fields:

1. Turn off barcode scanning.

2. From the menu bar, select the **Edit**, **Preferences**, **Company Preferences** tab.

3. Click Advanced Inventory Settings.

4. Click the Barcodes tab.

5. Click to remove the checkmark from the Enable Barcode Scanning checkbox.

6. In the Advanced Inventory Settings window, click OK.

7. In the Preferences window, click OK.

8. From the menu bar, select the **Edit**, **Preferences**, **Company Preferences** tab.

9. At the left of the Edit Preferences window, click General.

10. On the My Preferences tab, select the **Pressing Enter Moves Between Fields** checkbox.

11. In the Preferences window, click OK.

To use your barcode scanner, click the field you want to enter information into, and then scan the barcode.

Print Barcodes to a Report

Follow these steps to print a report that lists the barcodes in your company file, for ease in scanning:

1. From the menu bar, select **Reports**, **Inventory**, **Item Barcodes**.

2. At the top of the report window, click Print. See Figure C.37.

3. In the Print Reports window, change your printer settings as needed.

4. When you're ready to print the report, click Print.

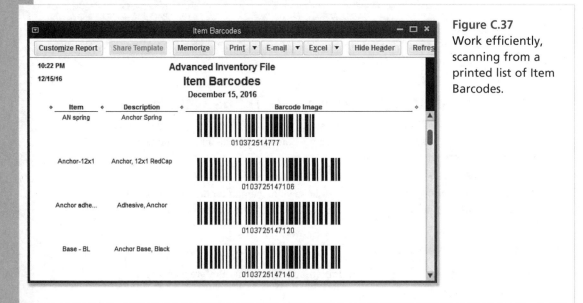

Figure C.37
Work efficiently, scanning from a printed list of Item Barcodes.

Print Barcode Labels

Follow these steps to print barcodes to affix to your products:

1. From the menu bar, select **File**, **Print Forms**, **Labels**. The Select Labels to Print dialog box displays as in Figure C.38.

2. Select the **Item Barcodes** option. From the drop-down list, select the item you want to print barcodes to labels for. Your choices are as follows:

- All Items

- Multiple Items

- All Items by type, including All Services, All Inventory Items, and so forth

3. Click OK to open the Print Labels dialog box.

Figure C.38
Print a barcode to
label stock.

Select Labels to Print	

Print labels for Names from

- Name — All names
- Customer Type — All Customer Types
- Vendor Type — All Vendor Types
- Item Barcodes — All inventory items
- with Zip Codes th...

OK
Cancel
Help

All parts
All other charges
All discounts
All sales items
All sales tax
All payments
All inventory items
All assembly items
All inventory and assembly items
All fixed asset items
All except fixed asset items

Sort labels by   Name
☐ Print labels for inactiv...
☐ Print Ship To address
☐ Print labels for jobs
☑ Include item descript...

Installation Labor	Service	Installation, Initial Labor
Installation Repair	Service	Installation, Repair Labor
Labor	Service	Direct Labor per build
Upfront Deposit	Service	Customer up front deposit
AN spring	Inventory Part	Anchor Spring
Anchor-12x1	Inventory Part	Anchor, 12x1 RedCap

4. From the Label Format drop-down list, select the type of label being printed. See Figure C.39.

5. Click Print.

 note

This barcode printing capability includes only basic barcode printing functionality. For example, users cannot specify the size of the barcode, add a box around the barcode, or assign characteristics such as spacing and density to the barcode. Additionally, you cannot add other fields, such as the manufacturer's part number or other information.

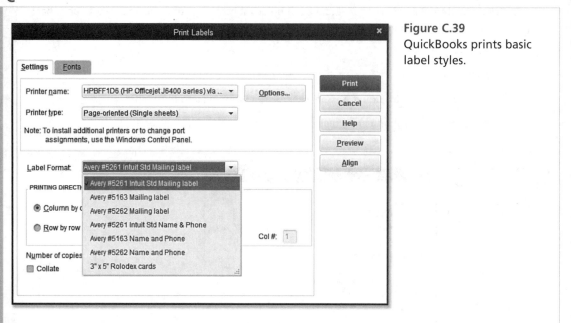

Figure C.39
QuickBooks prints basic label styles.

QuickBooks Enterprise with Advanced Pricing

Exclusively for QuickBooks Enterprise 14.0 is Advanced Pricing. Advanced Pricing is a subscription-based feature charged annually, and it also requires a current Full Service Plan. The feature replaces the free Price Levels, discussed in the previous section, with much more sophisticated automated price settings.

For more information see, "Price Rules," p. 335.

Advanced Pricing provides the capability to have QuickBooks automatically apply the following:

- Manufacturer discounts

- Scheduled promotions with future start dates

- Thousands of price rules or combinations of rules

With Advanced Pricing, QuickBooks automatically changes the prices of items on sales forms according to the rules you create. Each price rule can contain multiple conditions that must be met before QuickBooks changes the sales price.

Price Rules

After purchasing Advanced Pricing, follow these steps to set up a Price Rule:

1. To enable Advanced Pricing, from the menu bar, select **Edit**, **Preferences**, **Sales & Customers**. From the Company Preferences tab, select **Enable Advanced Pricing** and choose your option for handling price rounding. See Figure C.40.

Figure C.40
Advanced Pricing is a new subscription feature that is enabled in Preferences.

2. If your file previously had Price Levels, a message displays about QuickBooks converting these to Price Rules. Click to dismiss the message. It would be prudent at this time to review the details of the former Price Levels that are now Price Rules.

3. To create a new Price Rule, from the menu bar, select **Lists, Price Rules**. The New Price Rule window displays (see Figure C.41).

4. From the Price Rule drop-down list at the bottom of the Price Rule List, select **New**.

5. Type a Price Rule name and description.

6. Provide conditions for the newly created Price Rule. These conditions can be any combination of the following:

   ■ Customer Name, Type, Job Type, or Custom Fields

   ■ Item Name, Item Type, or Preferred Vendor

   ■ Class

   ■ Sales Rep

Figure C.41
Price Rules offer sophisticated autopricing for customer purchases.

7. Select a Date Range if this promotion is for a specific period of time.

8. Specify the price to be a percentage or amount decrease or increase over the item's current base price. The base price is determined by the item's Sales Price or Rate, depending on which item type you are assigning. Or you can choose to calculate the decrease or increase from the cost recorded on the item's record.

9. In the Options section, you can select any Price Overrides. When selected, you can specify a specific price for selected items that will be used instead of the Price Rule decrease or increase.

10. Select Exclusive Rule when you want this rule to not be combined with any other rules used in calculating the price for items on sales forms.

11. Click OK when finished.

You can view and edit your Price Rule List from the menu bar by selecting **Lists**, **Price Rule List** (see Figure C.42).

> **🔍 note**
> Subscribers must also have a current paid Full Service Plan (FSP) with their Enterprise software. Enterprise Certified ProAdvisors can access the feature for free; otherwise, the cost is $399 annually as of this writing. This fee includes both Price Rules and the Quantity Discount feature. New Enterprise Certified ProAdvisors must call ProAdvisor Support to activate the features.

Figure C.42
Price Rules replace the formerly titled Price Levels feature.

NAME	DESCRIPTION	PRICE ADJUSTM...	START DATE	END DATE
Commercial	Pricing for Commercial Customers	-10.0%	09/12/2013	12/31/2013
Door Replacement Special			09/12/2013	
Industrial		-15.0%	09/12/2013	
Kitchen Upgrade Package			09/12/2013	
Pretell Real Estate Rates			09/12/2013	
Residential		-5.0%	09/12/2013	
Sept New Cust Discount	September New Customer Discount	-10.0%	09/01/2013	09/30/2013

Price Rule ▾   Reports ▾   ☐ Include inactive

Quantity Discount

Also included with the Advanced Pricing subscription is Quantity Discounts. With Quantity Discounts, you can reward your customers for making bulk purchases. For example, QuickBooks can charge different prices when a customer buys 10 to 19 items, or 20 to 29 items, or 30 or more items.

After purchasing Advanced Pricing, follow these steps to set up a Quantity Discount and assign it to a specific item (product or service):

1. Enable Advanced Pricing. From the menu bar, select **Edit**, **Preferences**, **Sales & Customers**. From the Company Preferences tab, select **Enable Advanced Pricing** and choose your option for handling price rounding.

2. If your file previously had Price Levels, a message displays about QuickBooks converting these to Price Rules. Click to dismiss the message.

3. To assign Quantity Pricing to an item from the menu bar, select **Lists**, **Item List**. From the list that displays, with your cursor double-click an item to open the Edit Item dialog box.

4. With the item record displayed, click the Qty Discount button on the right to open the Quantity Discount window for the selected item (see Figure C.43).

5. Type an amount in the Qty From column.

6. Enter a Discount %, and the New Rate column calculates automatically.

7. (Optional) Enter the New Rate amount; the Discount % calculates automatically.

8. Select a Discounts Effective date.

9. Click OK when completed.

> **⚑ caution**
> For the Quantity Discount feature to work properly, your item must have an amount recorded in the Rate (or Cost) field of an Item record.

Advanced Pricing can help companies that want QuickBooks to automatically calculate pricing specials or discounts.

Figure C.43
Quantity Discounts reward customers for making larger purchases.

QuickBooks Enterprise Reporting

QuickBooks Premier (industry editions) and QuickBooks Enterprise (industry editions) share many of the same unique reports. However, some distinct differences in reporting arise when using QuickBooks Enterprise 14.0. This section details these unique reports.

Job Work in Process (WIP) Summary Report

This new report provides much-needed details for any industry that needs to report revenue based on a percentage of completion computation for their jobs.

One industry in particular, the construction industry, uses this type of calculation to determine the amount of revenue to record in its year-end financials.

This report is also valuable for reviewing over- or underbillings on jobs.

> **note**
> This report provides only accrual-based figures. Also, if Act. Cost exceeds Est. Cost, reported (%) Complete column is reported at 100%.

To prepare this report, follow these steps:

1. From the menu bar, select **Reports, Jobs, Time & Mileage, Job WIP Summary** (see Figure C.44).

2. (Optional) To filter for specific jobs, from the displayed report, click the Customize Report button.

3. (Optional) Select the **Filters** tab and choose **Name** from the list of fields to filter on.

4. (Optional) To the right, from the Name drop-down, select the specific Customer:Job, or choose **Multiple Names**.

5. (Optional) If you selected Multiple Names, place a checkmark next to each Customer:Job you want included in the report.

6. Alternatively, if you have been using the Job Status field on the Customer or Job record, you can now filter for Job Status, selecting it from the Choose Filter list of fields.

Figure C.44
New report in Enterprise used to calculate over- and underbillings.

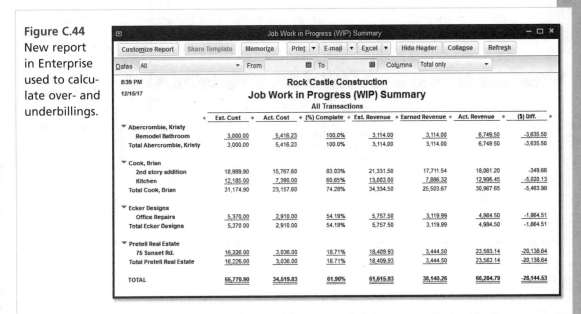

TOTAL | 55,770.90 | 34,519.83 | 61.90% | 61,615.93 | 38,140.26 | 66,284.79 | -28,144.53

	Est. Cost	Act. Cost	(%) Complete	Est. Revenue	Earned Revenue	Act. Revenue	($) Diff.
Abercrombie, Kristy							
Remodel Bathroom	3,000.00	5,416.23	100.0%	3,114.00	3,114.00	6,749.50	-3,635.50
Total Abercrombie, Kristy	3,000.00	5,416.23	100.0%	3,114.00	3,114.00	6,749.50	-3,635.50
Cook, Brian							
2nd story addition	18,989.90	15,767.60	83.03%	21,331.50	17,711.54	18,061.20	-349.66
Kitchen	12,185.00	7,390.00	60.65%	13,003.00	7,886.32	12,906.45	-5,020.13
Total Cook, Brian	31,174.90	23,157.60	74.28%	34,334.50	25,503.67	30,967.65	-5,463.98
Ecker Designs							
Office Repairs	5,370.00	2,910.00	54.19%	5,757.50	3,119.99	4,984.50	-1,864.51
Total Ecker Designs	5,370.00	2,910.00	54.19%	5,757.50	3,119.99	4,984.50	-1,864.51
Pretell Real Estate							
75 Sunset Rd.	16,226.00	3,036.00	18.71%	18,409.93	3,444.50	23,583.14	-20,138.64
Total Pretell Real Estate	16,226.00	3,036.00	18.71%	18,409.93	3,444.50	23,583.14	-20,138.64

Committed Costs by Job Report

This report provides a more comprehensive view of a Customer or Job potential profit or loss. The report includes Estimated Costs minus Actual Costs minus Committed Costs (open monetary value on purchase orders) minus Unpaid Wages to arrive at Remaining Cost.

Using this report requires that you are setting up estimates for your jobs.

➡ *For more information, see "Using QuickBooks Estimates," p. 348.*

To prepare this report, follow these steps:

1. From the menu bar, select **Reports, Jobs, Time & Mileage, Committed Costs by Job** (see Figure C.45).

> 🔍 **note**
>
> The Committed Costs column is the dollar value of any open purchase order amounts for that job.
>
> The Unpaid Wages amount is equal to the hours on a timesheet multiplied by the employee's hourly rate (not including any burdened costs). After the payroll check is prepared, the Unpaid Wages amount is removed from this report and reported in the Act. Cost column.

2. (Optional) To filter for specific jobs, from the displayed report click the Customize Report button.

3. (Optional) Select the **Filters** tab and choose **Name** from the list of fields to filter on.

4. (Optional) To the right, from the Name drop-down, select the specific Customer:Job, or choose Multiple Names.

5. (Optional) If you selected Multiple Names, place a checkmark next to each Customer:Job you want included in the report.

6. Alternatively, if you have been using the Job Status field on the Customer or Job record, you can now filter for Job Status, selecting it from the Choose Filter list of fields.

Figure C.45
The report includes open balances on purchase orders and a timesheet payroll estimate.

Combine Reports from Multiple Companies

Another report feature that is exclusive to QuickBooks Enterprise is the capability to prepare combined financial reports for multiple QuickBooks Enterprise files. This feature is not new; it has been available for many years.

This feature works best if the companies share a similar chart of accounts. QuickBooks Enterprise uses Microsoft Excel to join the reports into one Excel workbook.

A column is prepared for each company file, and each unique chart of account is on a row. For example, if multiple companies all use account number 1000 for a bank account, combining reports creates one row for account 1000 and includes a unique column for each company file's data that is combined.

To combine reports, follow these steps:

1. Open your first QuickBooks Enterprise company file for which you want to report combined financials.

2. From the menu bar, select **Reports**, **Combine Reports from Multiple Companies**.

3. The Combine Reports From Multiple Companies dialog box displays (see Figure C.46).

Figure C.46

With Enterprise, you can combine financial reporting of multiple files.

4. At the right, click the Add Files button and browse to find the file(s); click the Open button. QuickBooks adds the path of the newly added file to the dialog box. Continue until you have selected all the desired files.

5. Next, in the Select Reports for Combining box, choose from these options:

   ▪ Balance Sheet Standard

   ▪ Balance Sheet Summary

   ▪ Profit & Loss Standard

   ▪ Statement of Cash Flows

   ▪ Trial Balance

   ▪ Profit & Loss by Class

   ▪ Sales by Customer Summary

6. Set a report date range.

7. Select a report basis of either Accrual or Cash.

8. Type a Company Name that is included on the prepared reports.

9. (Optional) Click the Excel Options button to define the formatting of the Excel workbook.

10. When ready, click the Combine Reports in Excel.

11. QuickBooks opens each selected QuickBooks file, one after another. If you have login credentials, enter them when prompted.

12. QuickBooks launches Excel and prepares the consolidated report for you. See Figure C.47.

Figure C.47
Financial reports are consolidated into an Excel worksheet.

note

This method of consolidating reports in Excel does not allow you to make changes in the Excel worksheet and have those changes be sent to the file. After the report is created, there is no longer any connection to the selected QuickBooks files.

D

QUICKBOOKS SHORTCUTS

These Windows and QuickBooks keyboard shortcuts help you work more efficiently in QuickBooks. With these shortcuts, you can keep your hands on the keyboard and minimize the time you might otherwise waste when using a computer mouse to activate a command or move to a field on a transaction.

Editing QuickBooks Transactions and Lists

Use these shortcuts to save time editing a transaction or list in QuickBooks.

Key	Action
Ctrl+Del	Deletes the selected line in a transaction
Ctrl+Insert	Inserts a blank detail line in a transaction above the selected line
Ctrl+N	Creates a new transaction or list item when you have a list or transaction window open
Ctrl+D	Deletes the current transaction or list item
Ctrl+E	Edits the selected list item or transaction within an item list or register
Alt+S	Saves the selected transaction and opens a new transaction of the same type
Alt+N	Saves the selected transaction and advances to the next same-type transaction
Alt+P	Saves the selected transaction and advances to the previous same-type transaction
Alt+A	Saves the selected transaction and closes that transaction type
+	Within date fields, increments the date one day at a time; within other fields, such as check or invoice number, increments the transaction number by one
−	Within date fields, decreases the date one day at a time; within other fields, such as check or invoice number, decreases the transaction number by one
Ctrl+right arrow	Advances to next word in a field
Ctrl+left arrow	Advances to previous word in a field

Opening QuickBooks Dialog Boxes and Lists

With an open QuickBooks file, use these shortcuts to open a variety of dialog boxes and lists.

Key	Action
F1	Opens QuickBooks Help
F2	Displays QuickBooks diagnostic information
F3	Opens Search dialog box for company file information and transactions (different from the Ctrl+F search)
F4	Opens the QuickBooks Technical Support Helper, where you can provide technical information to an Intuit QuickBooks support agent when troubleshooting a database issue
Ctrl+W	Opens the Write Checks dialog box
Ctrl+Q	Opens a QuickReport for the selected saved transaction or list item

Key	Action
Ctrl+Y	Opens a Transaction Journal report for the selected transaction
Ctrl+L	From a displayed transaction, with a data field selected, opens the drop-down fields belonging to that list
Ctrl+J	Opens the Customer Center
Ctrl+A	Opens the Chart of Accounts list
Ctrl+I	Opens the Create Invoices dialog box
Ctrl+R	Opens the Use Register dialog box
Ctrl+P	Displays print options on an open transaction, report, or list
Ctrl+D	Deletes the selected transaction or list item
Ctrl+F	Launches the Find dialog box, or with an open transaction, displays Find filtered for that specific transaction type
Ctrl+H	Opens the Transaction History dialog box on a displayed transaction

Memorized Transactions

Use these keyboard shortcuts to save repeating transactions or to open the Memorized Transaction list.

Key	Action
Ctrl+M	Opens the Memorize Transaction dialog box from a displayed transaction
Ctrl+T	Opens the Memorized Transaction list

Standard Text Editing

These shortcuts make adding or modifying text more efficient.

Key	Action
Ctrl+Z	Undoes typing or changes made in a field
Ctrl+X	Cuts (deletes) selected text
Ctrl+C	Copies selected text
Ctrl+V	Pastes selected text
Del	Deletes a character to the right
Backspace	Deletes a character to the left

Opening QuickBooks Data Files

These shortcuts change how QuickBooks starts.

Key	Action
Ctrl	Before launching QuickBooks, press and hold the Ctrl key on your keyboard when clicking on the QuickBooks icon on your desktop. The No Company Open dialog box displays, where you can select from other listed data files. This shortcut is useful if you have trouble opening the last company file you accessed.
Alt	Before launching QuickBooks, press and hold the Alt key on your keyboard when clicking on the QuickBooks icon on your desktop. QuickBooks launches without opening the dialog boxes that were open when you exited QuickBooks. This can be useful if your file takes a long time to open.

QuickBooks Date Shortcuts

Use these shortcuts to efficiently change dates on transactions or reports.

Key	Action
+	Plus key, next day
–	Minus key, previous day
T	Today
W	First day of the week
K	Last day of the week
M	First day of the month
H	Last day of the month
Y	First day of the year
R	Last day of the year
Alt+down arrow	In a date field, opens the calendar; in a list field, displays the drop-down list
[	For same date in previous week
]	For same date in next week
;	For same date last month
'	For same date next month
Date Fields	Dates can be entered into date fields without manually typing the date format

Miscellaneous Shortcuts

Be sure to try these—they will save you time as you work with QuickBooks transactions.

Key	Action
Shift+Tab	Returns to previous field
Esc	Closes most open windows
Alt+Tab	Toggles between open dialogs in windows
Ctrl+Enter	Saves the currently displayed transaction
Alt+F4	Closes QuickBooks
Ctrl+F4	Closes a QuickBooks dialog box when Esc will not close it
Ctrl+Tab	Advances through your open QuickBooks dialogs
Home	Returns to first character in a field
End	Advances to the last character in a field
Tab	Advances to the next field
Ctrl+Tab	Advances to the next open dialog box
Ctrl+Page Up	Returns to the top of a long dialog box
Ctrl+Page Down	Advances to the bottom of a long dialog box
Ctrl+F6	Toggles between open dialog boxes (moves between items on the Open Windows list)
Shift+Ctrl+F6	Advances to the previous open dialog box

INDEX

Numbers

1099-MISC payments

entering midyear balances, 298

tracking and reporting, 275-285

A

access rights, users, 59

Account Balances setting (Company Snapshot), 555

Account Balances task group (CDR), 705-713

Balances in Accountant's Records columns, 707

fixing unapplied customer payments and credits, 719-720

Reclassify Transactions feature, 710-712

Troubleshoot Prior Account Balances tool, 706-709

Working Trial Balance tool, 712-713

account types, Balance Sheet reports, 576-577

Accountant Center, customizing to include CDR (Client Data Review) tools, 698-701

Accountant menu, CDR (Client Data Review), accessing, 698

accountants

data sharing, 616-630

Client Collaborator, 634-641

creating External Accountant user types, 618

File Manager 2014, 617-618

permissions, 623-626

external, creating login for, 56

Accountant's Copy, 597-598, 603-604

canceling, 616

converting to company file, 629-630

creating, 604-609

reconciling while pending, 610

returning change file to client, 626-629

accounting, 87

accrual basis, 89-90

setting up data file for, 94-106

cash basis, 89-90

setting up data file for, 94-106

checklist, 92-93

Company Preferences, 79-80

Enhanced Inventory Receiving (EIR), 803-804

financial reports, 91

accounting checklist, 92-93

balance sheets, 91

income statements, 91-92

statements of cash flows, 92

matching principle, 87-89

periods

condensing data from previous, 747-748

setting closing date and password, 744-746

Accounting preferences, 232-233

accounts, 88

bank

reconciling, CDR (Client Data Review), 742

Write Check transactions, 520-528

charts of accounts, 108

adding new, 110-112

assets, 108

assigning subaccount relationships, 136-137

cost of goods sold, 109

equity, 109

expense, 110

income, 109

liabilities, 109

making inactive, 133-134

merging duplicated, 134

modifying, 135-136

removing subaccount relationships, 138

required, 133

credit card
  entering charges, *529-531*
  liabilities account, *109*
  reconciling, *538-552*
  reconciliation reports, reviewing previous, *548*
  transactions, *542-548*

accounts payable, 247
accrual and cash basis accounting, *100-103*
aged open item receipts, removing, *289-290*
applying vendor credits, *259-262*
bartering services with vendors, *293-294*
correcting errors, *285-293*
credit card bills, paying and recording, *301-302*
data file information, *94*
entering purchase orders, *251*
Form 1099-MISC payments, entering midyear balances, *298*
liabilities account, *109*
making general journal adjustments, *290-293*
paying vendor bills, *256-259*
preferences, *232-240*
prepayments, recording, *295-298*
recording vendor bills, *251-254*
recording vendor credits, *254-256*
reporting, *265*
  1099-MISC payments, *275-285*
  cash basis balance sheet, *272-274*
  reconciling Balance Sheet Accounts Payable balance, *265-267*
  reviewing aged open item receipts, *268-270*
  reviewing item setup, *270-272*
  Unpaid Bills Details report, *267-268*
reporting aged, *223*
reviewing, *223*
taking discounts on bills, *262-264*
transactions, *247-248*
  memorizing recurring, *299-300*
workflow, *249-251*

Accounts Payable balance (Balance Sheet report), 583

Accounts Payable task group (CDR), 726-729

Accounts preference (Accounting), 232-233

accounts receivable
accrual and cash basis accounting, *95-97*
assets account, *108*
correcting errors, *402-418*
Customer Center, *318*
  adding customers, *319-323*
  finding customer transactions, *323-324*
  modifying customers, *319-323*
data file information, *94*
estimates, *348-349*
preferences, *304-305*
  Checking, *308*
  Finance Charge, *309-310*
  Jobs & Estimates, *310-311*
  Payments, *306-307*
  Reminders, *311*
  Reports & Graphs, *312-313*
  Sales & Customers, *307-308*
  Sales Tax, *314-315*
  Send Forms, *315-316*
  Spelling, *316*
  Time & Expenses, *316-317*
processes, *346-347*
reporting, *381-382*
  A/R Aging Summary, *382-383*
  Collections Center, *391-393*
  Income Tracker, *388-391*
  Missing Invoices report, *393-394*
  Open Invoices report, *383-384*
  reconciling totals, *385-386*
  viewing balance on cash basis balance sheets, *386-388*
sales orders, *349*
year-end adjusting journal entries, recording, *432*

Accounts Receivable task group (CDR), 719-726
AR Aging Summary report, *722-724*
Clear Up Undeposited Funds Account task, *720-722*
Write Off Invoices dialog box, *724-726*

accrual basis accounting
versus cash basis accounting, *89-90*
setting up data file for, *94-106*
startup transactions
  accounts payable, *100-103*
  accounts receivable, *95-97*
  bank account statement balance, *103-105*
  uncleared bank checks, *105-106*

activities

Timer

exporting, 692-693

importing, 693

tracking time spent, 691-692

users, reporting, 65

Add Available Time/Costs to Invoice for the Selected Job preference (Sales & Customers), 308

Add Icon Bar Item dialog box, 71-73

Add New Account dialog box, 110-112, 135

Add the People You Do Business With dialog box, 43

Add/Edit Multiple List Entries dialog box, 734

adding

multiple list entries, 122-124

payroll items, 475-477

adjusting inventory, 205-211

quality adjustments, 207-209

value adjustments, 209-211

adjustments, reconciling, 551-552

Admin user, 75

Advanced Import, Excel worksheets, 126-129

Advanced Inventory subscription (QuickBooks Enterprise Solutions), 155, 806-826

barcodes, 821-826

completing transactions, 823-824

importing, 823

printing labels, 824-826

printing to reports, 824

scanning, 821-822

FIFO (First In, First Out) costing, 819-821

multiple inventory locations, 806-812

adding sites and bin locations, 809

assigning starting sites, 807-809

duplicating inventory transfer transactions, 812

editing site and bin locations, 810

reporting by inventory by site, 812

transferring between locations, 810-811

serial/lot numbers, tracking, 813-819

Advanced Pricing subscription (QuickBooks Enterprise Solutions), 156, 334, 826-829

price rules, 335-336, 827-829

quantity discounts, 336-338, 829

Advanced Setup or Detailed Start option, creating files, 45-49

aged accounts payable, reviewing, 223

aged item receipts, reviewing, 219-223

aged open item receipts

removing, 289-290

reviewing, 268-270

Aging Reports preference (Reports & Graphs), 237, 312, 560

Annual Interest Rate preference (Finance Charge), 309

antivirus software, 657

A/P Aging Summary, reconciling Balance Sheet Accounts Payable balance, 265-267

A/R Aging Summary, reviewing, 382-383, 722-724

assemblies, inventory, 160-161, 793-798

autocalculating Cost field, 796-798

automatically build subassemblies, 793

list items, 4.102

replacing or removing components, 794-796

Assess Finance Charges on Overdue Finance Charges preference (Finance Charge), 309

assets, balance sheets, 91

assets account, charts of accounts, 108

Assign Check Numbers dialog box, 434

Assign Sales Tax Codes preference (Sales Tax), 314

Audit Trail of Review report, 697, 750-751

Audit Trail option (Reports, Accountant & Taxes), 65

Audit Trail report, reviewing, 588

Auto Create Purchase Order feature (Enterprise), 791-792

Auto-Check the "Email Later" preference (Send Forms), 315

Autofill Payee Account Number in Check Memo preference (Checking), 235

Automatic Cost & Price Updates dialog box, 804-805

Automatically Assign General Journal Entry Number preference (Accounting), 233

Automatically Open Drop-Down Lists When Typing preference (General), 236

Automatically Recall Information preference (General), 236

automating, backups, 655-656

average cost, inventory, 189
    calculating, 217
    prior purchase transactions, 224-226

B

backorders, handling, 196-200

Backup Options dialog box, 654-656

backups
    automating, 655-656
    creating, 653-656
    Intuit Data Protect online backup service, 659-660
    restoring, 656

Balance Sheet Accounts Payable balance, reconciling A/P Aging Summary report total, 265-267

Balance Sheet reports
    account types, 576-577
    Accounts Payable balance, 583
    Accounts Receivable balance, 578-579
    bank account balances, 578
    credit card account balances, 584

Equity accounts, 585
fixed assets, 582-583
Inventory balance, 580
Other Current Assets accounts, 581-582
Other Current Liabilities and Long-Term Liabilities account types, 585
Payroll Liabilities balance, 584
prior year balances, 577
reviewing, 575-585
Undeposited Funds, 579-580

balance sheets, 91
    comparing, 734-736

bank accounts
    assets account, 108
    debit charges, entering, 529
    deposits, recording, 373-376
    entering bank debit charges, 529
    reconciliation reports, reviewing previous, 548
    reconciliations, 742
        CDR (Client Data Review), 742
        completing multi-month/ year, 545
        locating discrepancies, 548-549
        restarting previously completed, 550
        undoing, 550-551
    reconciling, 538-540
        adjustments, 551-552
        determining if reconciled, 541-542
        troubleshooting, 541-552
    statement balance, 103
    transactions
        identifying uncleared, 544-545
        verifying that all have been entered, 542-544

transferring funds between, 532
uncleared transactions, reviewing, 546-548
Voided/Deleted Transactions Summary reports, reviewing, 549-550
Write Check transactions, 520-528

Bank Acct No. field (Add New Account), 112

bank ending balance, data file information, 94

Bank Feeds, 235, 532-537
    configuring, 533-534
    managing, 534-537
    renaming rules, 537

barcodes
    completing transactions, 823-824
    importing, 823
    printing labels, 824-826
    printing to reports, 824
    scanning, 821-822

basic invoices, creating, 352-355

Batch Enter Transactions, 632-634

batch invoices, 355

Batch Summary dialog box, 357

Begin Reconciliation dialog box, 538-540, 545

Best Selling Items setting (Company Snapshot), 556

bills, 181
    accounts payable, removing, 289-290
    credit card
        paying, 531
        paying and recording, 301-302

paying vendor, 256-259

payment without proper process, 285-287

vendor, 182-190

  creating purchase orders, 182-186

  entering, 189-190

Bills preferences, 233-234

bonuses, taxable, paying, 507-508

bounced checks, recording, 434-437

budgets

creating, 676-677

deleting, 681

editing, 678-679

printing reports, 679-681

business identification numbers, federal and state required, 451

C

Calculate Charges From preference (Finance Charge), 309

Calendar view, 234

canceling Accountant's Copy, 616

cash basis accounting

setting up data file for, 94-106

startup transactions

  accounts payable, 100-103

  accounts receivable, 95-97

  bank account statement balance, 103-105

  uncleared bank checks, 105-106

versus accrual basis accounting, 89-90

cash basis balance sheets, reconciling Balance Sheet Accounts Receivable balance, 386-388

CDR (Client Data Review), 695, 739

Account Balances task group, 705-713

  Balances in Accountant's Records columns, 707

  minimizing/expanding, 704

  Reclassify Transactions feature, 710-712

  Troubleshoot Prior Account Balances tool, 706-709

  Working Trial Balance tool, 712-713

Accountant Center, customizing to include tools, 699-701

accounting periods

  condensing data from previous, 747-748

  setting closing date and password, 744-746

Accounts Payable task group, 726-729

  minimizing/expanding, 704

Accounts Receivable task group, 719-726

  AR Aging Summary report, 722-724

  Clear Up Undeposited Funds Account task, 720-722

  fixing unapplied customer payments and credits, 719-720

  minimizing/expanding, 704

  Write Off Invoices dialog box, 724-726

Audit Trail of Review report, 750-751

Bank Reconciliation task group, 742

  minimizing/expanding, 704

cleanup tasks, customizing, 702-703

Compare Balance Sheet and Inventory Valuation task, 734-736

customizing, 701-705

Employee Center: Payroll Center, 741

External Accountants, creating, 751-752

features, 696-698

  accessing, 698-699

Find Incorrectly Paid Payroll Liabilities, 739-741

finishing reviews, 748-750

Mark Review Complete button, 750

QuickBooks preferences, reviewing, 746-747

reopening reviews, 750

review date and basis, modifying, 702

Review Inventory Setup, 734

Review List Changes feature, 713-718

  Chart of Accounts tab, 713-718

  Customers task, 718

  Fixed Asset Items tab, 715-716

  Items tab, 714-715

  Other Names List, 718

  Payroll Items tab, 716-717

  Review Item Setup tab, 717

  Vendors task, 718

review tasks, assigning status and notes to, 705

Sales Tax task group, 729-733

Troubleshoot Inventory feature, 736-738

Vendors, Inventory Activities, Physical Inventory Worksheet, 738

Change Check Date When a Noncleared Check Is Printed preference (Checking), 235

charges, entering, 529

charts of accounts, 107-108

accounts, 108

    adding, 110-112

    assets, 108

    assigning subaccount relationships, 136-137

    cost of goods sold, 109

    creating payroll, 452-453

    equity, 109

    expense, 110

    income, 109

    liabilities, 109

    making inactive, 133-134

    merging duplicated, 134

    modifying, 135-136

    removing subaccount relationships, 138

    required, 133

    errors, finding and fixing, 132-138

preferences, 121-122

Chart of Accounts dialog box, 134-135

Chart of Accounts tab (Review List Changes), 713-714

Checking preferences, 234-235, 308

checks, 181

    bounced, recording, 434-437

    Missing Checks report, 742

printing, 526-528

writing, 523-526

Choose Billable Time and Costs dialog box, 363, 366

classes, lists, 107, 117-119

Classify Cash preference (Reports & Graphs), 312

cleanup tasks, CDR (Client Data Review), customizing, 702-703

Clear Up Undeposited Funds Account task (Accounts Receivable), 720-722

Client Collaborator, 634-641

    accessing, 635

Client Data Review (CDR). *See* **CDR (Client Data Review)**

Closing Date Exception report, 65, 744

    tracking changes to, 587

Closing Date preference (Accounting), 233

closing dates, accounting periods, setting, 744-746

codes, sales tax

    assigning to customers, 332-333

    assigning to products or services, 330-332

    creating, 329-330

Collapse option (Report window), 563

Collections Center, 307

    enabling, 391-393

columns, Troubleshoot Prior Account Balances tool, 706-707

Columns option (Report window), 563

Columns tab (Report Designer), 760-761

Committed Costs by Job report, 831-832

company files

    creating new files from, 49-50

    opening, 83-85

    Portable Company File, creating and restoring, 669-670

    rebuilding, 670-671

Company Preferences, 79, 458

    accounting, 79-80, 232-233

    Bills, 234

    Checking, 235

    Finance Charge, 309

    General, 236

    Graphs, 237

    Jobs & Estimates, 310

    Payments, 306-307

    Reminders, 236-237, 311

    Reports, 237

    Reports & Graphs, 312-313, 560-562

    Sales & Customers, 307-308

    Sales Tax, 314-315

    Send Forms, 315

    Tax:1099, 238

    Time & Expenses, 239, 316-317

Company Snapshot, 553-556

    customizing, 554-556

    defaulting as Home page, 556

Compare Balance Sheet and Inventory Valuation task (CDR), 734-736

condensing data from previous accounting periods, 747-748

Contact Info dialog box, 41

Contact Sync tool, 686-689

Contributed tab (Report Center), 492

corruption, database, 664
common causes, 664
File Doctor, 671-672
QBWin.log file, 665-668
rebuilding company file, 670-671
reducing file fragments, 669-670
repairing list, 668
resolving program file issues, 673
signs, 665

Cost field, inventory assemblies, autocalculating, 796-798

cost of goods sold account, charts of accounts, 109

Create Credit Memos/ Refunds dialog box, 380

Create Invoices dialog box, 350-352, 363, 377

Create New Budget dialog box, 676-677

Create Progress Invoice Based on Estimate dialog box, 363

credit card accounts
entering charges, 529-531
liabilities account, 109
reconciliation reports, reviewing previous, 548
reconciling, 538-540
completing multi-month/ year, 545
determining if reconciled, 541-542
troubleshooting, 541-552

transactions, 181
identifying uncleared, 544-545
uncleared, 546-548
verifying that all have been entered, 542-544

Credit Card Audit Trail report, reviewing, 589-591

credit card bills
paying, 531
paying and recording, 301-302

credit card deposits, recording less a discount fee, 375-376

credit memos
correcting errors, 411-412
recording, 405
recording and applying, 376-378
sales tax, issuing, 442-443

credits
applying vendor, 259-262
unapplied, fixing, 727
unapplied customer, fixing, 719-720
vendor, recording, 254-256
vendors, misapplied, 288

.CSV files, exporting reports to, 571-573

Custom Pricing preference (Sales & Customers), 308

Customer Center, 318
customers
adding, 319-323
finding transactions, 323-324
modifying, 319-323
jobs, adding, 319-323

Customer Credit Card Audit Trail option (Reports, Accountant & Taxes), 65

customer inventory returns, handling, 200-201

Customer Return Materials Authorization forms (QuickBooks Premier 2014), 153

customer types, lists, 107, 120

customers, 381
accounts receivable
correcting errors, 402-418
estimates, 348-349
preferences, 304-317
processes, 346-380
reporting, 381-394
sales orders, 349
bounced checks, recording, 434-437
correcting payments, 407-410
creating payment terms, 338
credit memos, recording and applying, 376-378
Customer Center, 318
adding, 319-323
finding transactions, 323-324
modifying, 319-323
customizing Home page for, 304
invoices
creating, 350-363
progress invoicing, 360-363
removing open balances, 403-407
time and expense invoicing, 363-366
Lead Center, 325-327

payments, recording, 370-372

price level lists, creating, 333-334

refunding overpayment, 379-380

sales receipts, recording, 367

sales tax, 327

   assigning to, 332-333

   assigning to products or services, 330-332

   assigning to codes, 332-333

   creating codes, 329-330

   creating group items, 328-329

   creating items, 327-328

   paying, 398-402

sales tax payable reports, 394-398

statement charges, recording, 369

tracking deposits, 438

undeposited funds account errors, correcting, 426-431

as vendors, 432-434

Customers task (Review List Changes), 718

Customers Who Owe Money setting (Company Snapshot), 556

Customize Columns dialog box, 139

Customize Data Layout tool, customizing forms, 343-346

Customize My Forms Wizard, 340-342

Customize Report button, modifying reports, 564-565

customizing

   Company Snapshot, 554-556

   data displayed on Home page, 76-77

icons, 75-76

Left Icon Bar, 72-73

Top Icon Bar, 71-72

D

Damaged Goods logs (QuickBooks Enterprise Solutions), 155

Damaged Goods logs (QuickBooks Premier 2014), 153

data, display, customizing, 76-77

data files

   cash basis and accrual accounting, setting up for, 94-106

   information collection, 94

   opening, 83-85

   keyboard shortcuts, 838

Data Server Manager, opening, 648-650

data sharing, 597-598, 630

   accountants, 616-630

   Client Collaborator, 634-641

   converting Accountant's Copy to company file, 629-630

   creating External Accountant user types, 618

   File Manager 2014, 617-618

   permissions, 623-626

   preparing client for data exchange, 619

   receiving Accountant's Copy files, 619-623

   requests upon import completion, 629

   returning Accountant's Copy change file to client, 626-629

   Accountant's Copy

   canceling, 616

   reconciling while pending, 610

   Batch Enter Transactions, 632-634

   business owner, 603-616

   Client Collaborator, 634-641

   creating Accountant's Copy of data, 604-609

   importing accountant's changes, 610-615

   permissions, 609-610

   reviewing data, 604

   choosing method, 599-603

   file types, 599-603

   Send General Journal Entries, 630-632

database, 643-644

   corruption, 664

   common causes, 664

   File Doctor, 671-672

   QBWin.log file, 665-668

   rebuilding company file, 670-671

   reducing file fragments, 669-670

   repairing list, 668

   resolving program file issues, 673

   signs, 665

   monitoring, 660-664, 660

   Product Information dialog box, 660-663

   Verify Data utility, 663

   Windows Task Manager, 663-664

protecting, 653-660

   creating backup, 653-656

   Intuit Data Protect,
   659-660

   operating environment,
   656-659

Database File Fragments section (Product Information dialog box), 662

Database Server, 643-644

Database Server Manager, 648-650

   multiuser access, changing to, 648

Date Warnings preference (Accounting), 233

dated payments, undeposited funds accounts, removing, 429-431

dates, keyboard shortcuts, 838

debit charges, entering, 529

Default Date to Use for New Transactions preference (General), 236

defragmentation, 657-659

depositing

   refunds of payroll liabilities, 514-515

   vendor refunds, 300-301

deposits

   correcting errors, 412-418

   tracking customer, 438

desktop view, My Preferences, 80-81

dialog boxes

   Accountant's Copy feature, 606-607

   Add Icon Bar Item, 71-73

   Add New Account, 110-112, 135

Add the People You Do Business With, 43

Add/Edit Multiple List Entries, 734

Assign Check Numbers, 434

Automatic Cost & Price Updates, 804-805

Backup Options, 654-656

Batch Enter Transactions, 632-634

Batch Summary, 357

Begin Reconciliation, 538-540, 545

Chart of Accounts, 134, 135

Choose Billable Time and Costs, 363, 366

Client Data Review—Customize, 703

Client Data Review—Start Review, 701

Client Data Review—Start Review or Modify Review, 702

Contact Info, 41

Create Credit Memos/Refunds, 380

Create Invoice, 363

Create Invoices, 350-352, 377

Create New Budget, 676-677

Create Progress Invoice Based on Estimate, 363

Customize Columns, 139

Edit Customer, 395

Edit Markup, 805

Edit Role, 60-61

Enter Bills, 255, 257

Enter Payroll Information, 483

General Preferences, 756

Make General Journal Entries, 708

My Company, 40, 54-55

No Company Open, 38

Open and Convert

Accountant's Copy Transfer File dialog box, 621-622

Open or Restore Company, 83

opening, keyboard shortcuts, 836

Pay Bills, 260

Pay Bills or Write Checks, 108

Pay Sales Tax, 419, 729-730

Payment Summary, 258-260

Payments to Deposit, 373

Payroll Item List, 478-479

Preferences, 79, 360, 455-458

Print Checks, 259

Print Labels, 825

Product Information, 660-663

Receive Payments, 371, 379, 404

Reconcile—Account, 545

Reconcile—Account Name, 539

reinstating warning, 623

Review and Create Paychecks, 483

Review List Changes, 713-718

Save Backup Copy, 611

Select Previous Reconciliation Report, 548

Send General Journal Entries, 630-632

Set the Dividing Date, 606

Specify Invoice Amounts for Items on Estimate, 361

Time/Enter Single Activity, 481

Transfer Inventory, 810-811

Troubleshoot Prior Account Balances, 709

Undo Previous Reconciliation, 550-551

Unit of Measure, 178

User List, 56

Using Group, 359

View User Access, 614-615

How can we make this index more useful? Email us at indexes@quepublishing.com

ViewMyPaycheck, 485-487

Write Check, 520-528

Write Off Invoices, 724-726

direct connect method, downloading transactions, 533-534

discount items, lists, 114

discounts, taking on bills, 262-264

disk defragmentation, 657-659

Display preference (Calendar), 234

Display tab (Customize Report), 564-565

Do You Create Estimates? preference (Jobs & Estimates), 310

Do You Do Progress Invoicing? preference (Jobs & Estimates), 310

Document Actions pane (QSW), modifying reports in Excel, 765-774

documents, 754

Don't Print Items that Have Zero Amount preference (Jobs & Estimates), 310

downloading transactions, 533-534

E

EasyStep Interview. *See* **Advanced Setup or Detailed Start option**

Edit Customer dialog box, 395

Edit Markup dialog box, 805

Edit Role dialog box, 60-61

editing

budgets, 678-679

inventory items, 161

  changing prices, 170-172

  individual, 162-166

  multiple list entries, 166-168

multiple list entries, 122-124

payroll items, 475-477

QSW supporting documents, 777-779

e-filing, tax payments and forms, 497

EIR (Enhanced Inventory Receiving), 800-804

accounting, 803-804

considerations, 802

restrictions, 802-803

workflow, 802

emailing, reports, 573-574

Employee Center, employees, setting up, 469-474

employees

classifying workers as, 450

paychecks, adjusting, 508-509

paying, 479-487

  liability payments, 487-489

  preparing paychecks, 482-483

  printing paychecks, 484

  ViewMyPaycheck, 485-487

reviewing default settings, CDR (Client Data Review), 741

setting up, 469-474

time, entering, 480-482

employer identification numbers, 451

Enhanced Inventory Receiving (EIR), 800-804

accounting, 803-804

considerations, 802

restrictions, 802-803

workflow, 802

Enter Bills dialog box, 255, 257

Enter Bills transaction, 520

Enter Opening Balance field (Add New Account), 112

Enter Payroll Information dialog box, 483

Entering Bills, Bills Are Due preference (Bills), 234

Enterprise Solutions, 783

Advanced Pricing subscription, 826-829

customization, 784-788

  expense transactions, 786-788

  fields, 784-786

inventory, 788-805

  accessing features and reports, 788-790

  Advanced Inventory subscription, 806-826

  assemblies, 793-798

  assigning markup defaults per item, 805

  Auto Create Purchase Order feature, 791-792

  Automatic Cost & Price Updates preference, 804-805

  Enhanced Inventory Receiving (EIR), 800-804

  Sales Order Fulfillment worksheet, 798-800

reporting, 830-834

    combining reports from multiple companies, 832-834

    Committed Costs by Job report, 831-832

    WIP (Work in Process) summary reports, 830-831

entries, lists, adding/editing multiple, 122-124

equity, balance sheets, 91

equity account, charts of accounts, 109

errors

    accounts receivable, correcting, 402-418

    charts of accounts, finding and fixing, 132-138

    sales tax, correcting, 419-424

estimates, 181, 304

Evaluate and Correct 1099 Mapping (Accounts Payable task group), 728

Excel

    exporting reports to, 571-573

    pasting serial/lot numbers from, 817-818

    payroll reports, 492-493

    QSW reports, modifying, 764-774

Excel Add-Ins ribbon icon (QSW), modifying reports in Excel, 774

Excel data, adding to QuickBooks utility, 124-129

existing files, creating new files from, 49-50

expense accounts, charts of accounts, 110

Expense Breakdown setting (Company Snapshot), 555

expense transactions, customizing, QuickBooks Enterprise Solutions, 786-788

Expenses tab (Write Check), 521-523

exporting

    QSW reports, 779-781

    report templates, 570-571

    reports

        to .CSV file, 571-573

        to Excel, 571-573

    Timer activities, 692-693

Express Start, creating files, 39-44

External Accountant user types, creating, 618

external accountants

    creating, CDR (Client Data Review), 751-752

    creating login for, 56

F

Favorites tab (Report Center), 492

features, CDR (Client Data Review), accessing, 698-699

federal identification numbers, 451

fields, customizing, QuickBooks Enterprise Solutions, 784-786

FIFO (First In, First Out) inventory costing, 151

    Advanced Inventory subscription, 819-821

File Doctor, 671-672

File Manager 2014, 617-618

File Size section (Product Information dialog box), 660-661

file types, QuickBooks, 599-603

filed payroll returns, payroll summary reports, comparing, 500

files

    company

        opening, 83-85

        rebuilding, 670-671

    creating, 38-50

        Advanced Setup or Detailed Start option, 45-49

        from existing files, 49-50

        Express Start, 39-44

    fragments, reducing, 669-670

    Intuit Interchange Format (IIF), importing, 169-170

    opening, keyboard shortcuts, 838

    program, resolving corruptions, 673

    QBWin.log, 665-668

filing tax payments and forms, 497

Filters tab (Customize Report), 565

Finance Charge Account preference (Finance Charge), 309

Finance Charge preferences, 309-310

financial reports, 91

    accounting checklist, 92-93

    balance sheets, 91

    income statements, 91-92

    statements of cash flows, 92

Financial Statement Designer (FSD). *See* **Statement Writer (QSW)**

Find Incorrectly Paid Payroll Liabilities (CDR), 739-741

First In, First Out (FIFO) inventory costing, 151
> Advanced Inventory subscription, 819-821

Fix Incorrectly Recorded Sales Tax tool (Sales Tax task group), 732-733

Fixed Asset Items tab (Review List Changes), 715-716

fixed assets
> assets account, 108
> Balance Sheet reports, 582-583

Fonts & Numbers (Customize Report), 565

Form 1099-MISC payments
> entering midyear balances, 298
> tracking and reporting, 275-285

Format preference (Reports & Graphs), 312, 562

Formatting tab (General Preferences), 757-758

Formatting tab (ribbon toolbar), 351

forms
> customizing, 339-346
>> *Customize Data Layout tool, 343-346*
>> *Customize My Forms Wizard, 340-342*
> tax, filing, 448

forms (tax), 494-497
> filing, 497
> preparing and printing, 494-496

fragments, files, reducing, 669-670

FSD (Financial Statement Designer). *See* **Statement Writer (QSW)**

G

GAAP (Generally Accepted Accounting Principles), 753

general personal preferences, 81-82

General preferences, 235-236

General Preferences settings dialog box, 756

Generally Accepted Accounting Principles (GAAP), 753

Grace Period preference (Finance Charge), 309

Graphs Only preference (Reports and Graphs), 237, 313, 559

Graphs preferences, 237

group items, 194
> creating, 175
> lists, 114

groups (report), 565-569
> creating, 565-566
> managing memorized, 568-569

groups items (inventory), 160-161

H

Header/Footer tab (Customize Report), 565

Headers & Formatting tab (Report Designer), 762

Help, Learning Center Tutorials, 79

Hide Header option (Report window), 563

Home page, 74-77
> customer activities, customizing for, 304
> customizing
>> *data display, 76-77*
>> *icons, 75-76*
> Left Icon Bar, 72-74
> menu bar, 68-69
> Open Windows list, 77-78
> payroll workflow, 480
> title bar, 67-68
> Top Icon Bar, 69-72
>> *customizing, 71-72*
> vendor activities, customizing for, 231-232

I

icons, customizing, 75-76

identification numbers, federal and state required, 451

IIF (Intuit Interchange Format) files, importing, 129-131, 169-170

importing
> Advanced Import, Excel worksheets, 126-129
> barcodes, 823
> Intuit Interchange Format (IIF) files, 129-131, 169-170
> report templates, 570-571
> Timer activities, 693

income, 88

income account, charts of accounts, 109

Income and Expense Trend Graph setting (Company Snapshot), 555

Income Breakdown setting (Company Snapshot), 555

Income Payments preference (Payments), 307

income statements, 91-92

Income Tracker, 388-391

incorrectly recorded sales tax, fixing, 729-732

independent contractors, classifying workers as, 450

indirect costs, allocating to jobs through payroll, 509-514

installing

    maintenance release, 652-653

    QuickBooks

        Express option, 646

        for multiuser mode, 647

    Timer, 691

    uninterruptable power supply (UPS), 656

Intuit Data Protect online backup service, 659-660

Intuit Interchange Format (IIF) files, importing, 129-131, 169-170

Intuit Payroll Experts option, 448

Intuit Statement Writer (ISW). *See* Statement Writer (QSW)

inventory, 88, 151-152, 205

    accessing features and reports, QuickBooks Enterprise Solutions, 788-790

adjusting, 205-211

    quality adjustments, 207-209

    value adjustments, 209-211

adjusting quantity and value, CDR (Client Data Review), 738

Advanced Inventory subscription, 155, 806-826

    barcodes, 821-826

    FIFO (First In, First Out) costing, 819-821

    multiple locations, 806-812

    serial/lot numbers, 813-819

Advanced Pricing subscription, 156

assemblies, 160-161, 793-798

    autocalculating Cost field, 796-798

    automatically build subassemblies, 793

    list items, 133

    replacing or removing components, 794-796

Average Cost method, 151

backorders, handling, 196-200

comparing balance sheets and valuation, CDR (Client Data Review), 734-736

cost and price updates, handling, 804-805

customer returns, handling, 200-201

enabling preferences, 156-159

Enhanced Inventory Receiving (EIR), 800-804

Intuit Interchange Format (IIF) files, importing, 169-170

items, 152, 159

    adding, 161-180

    changing prices, 170-172

    creating inventory assemblies, 173-175

    editing, 161-180

    group, 160-161, 175, 194

    inventory assemblies, 160-161, 195-196

    non-inventory parts, 160

    parts, 160

    receiving into, 187-189

lack of prior average cost, 227-230

management, 88

markup defaults, assigning per item, 805

Multiple Unit of Measurement preference, 177-180

negative, handling, 224-230

paying for, 190-192

physical inventory count, performing, 206-207

prior average cost, 224-226

processes, 180-181

purchase orders, 152

    Auto Create Purchase Order feature, 791-792

QuickBooks Enterprise Solutions features, 153-156

QuickBooks Premier 2014 features, 153

QuickBooks Pro 2014 features, 152-153

reporting, 211

    Inventory Center, 212-213

    Inventory Valuation Summary report, 214-216

    Report Center, 213-214

    reviewing aged accounts payable, 223

    reviewing aged item receipts, 219-223

    reviewing recorded average cost valuation, 217-219

reviewing setup, 734

Sales Order Fulfillment worksheet (QuickBooks Enterprise Solutions), 798-800

selling, 193-194

transactions, 181

vendor bills, 182-190

troubleshooting, CDR (Client Data Review), 736-738

vendor returns, handling, 203

Inventory Center, 153, 789-790

reporting inventory, 212-213

inventory part items, lists, 114

Inventory Reorder reports (QuickBooks Enterprise Solutions), 155

Inventory Valuation Summary or Detail report, 734

Inventory Valuation Summary report, 214-216

Invoice Options preference (Time & Expenses), 239

invoices, 181

creating, 350-363

basic, 352-355

batch, 355

memorized transaction groups, 358-360

multiple sales tax rates on one, 441-442

progress invoicing, 360-363

removing open balances, 403-407

time and expense invoicing, 363-366

Invoicing Options preference (Time & Expenses), 317

ISW (Intuit Statement Writer). *See* **Statement Writer (QSW)**

item lists, 107

customizing view, 139-140

errors, finding and fixing, 139-150

Item Listing report, 140-141

Profit & Loss report, 142-144

reviewing, 139-140

item receipts, reviewing aged, 219-223

item receipts with bill, 181

item receipts without bill, 147

items, 112-113, 152, 159

adding, 115-117, 161

individual, 162-166

multiple list entries, 166-168

non-inventory parts, 164-166

parts, 162-164

changing prices, 170-172

correcting one-sided, 144-147

creating as subitems, 149-150

discount, 114

editing, 161

individual, 162-166

multiple list entries, 166-168

group, 114, 160-161, 194

creating, 175

Intuit Interchange Format (IIF) files, importing, 169-170

inventory assemblies, 114, 160-161, 195-196

creating, 173-175

inventory part, 114

making inactive, 147-148

merging, 148-149

Multiple Unit of Measurement preference, 177-180

non-inventory parts, 114, 160

other charge, 114

parts, 160

payment, 114

payroll

adding and editing, 475-477

reporting about, 478-479

setting up, 475-479

receiving, 187-189

reviewing setup, 270-272

sales tax, 114, 327-328

sales tax group, 114

service, 113

subtotal, 114

Items tab (Review List Changes), 714-715

Items tab (Write Check), 521-523

J

Job Status Descriptions preference (Jobs & Estimates), 310

job WIP (Work in Process) summary reports, 830-831

jobs, Customer Center, adding, 319-323

Jobs & Estimates preferences, 310-311

K

keyboard shortcuts, 835

data files, opening, 838

dates, 838

dialog boxes, opening, 836

lists

editing, 836

opening, 836

memorized transactions, 837

text editing, 837

transactions, 839

editing, 836

L

labels, barcodes, printing, 824-826

Lead Center, 325-327

Learning Center Tutorials, 79

Left Icon Bar, 72-74

Open Windows list, 77-78

liabilities

balance sheets, 91

comparing balances to balance sheet, 497-499

finding incorrectly paid, CDR (Client Data Review), 739-741

payroll, depositing of liabilities, 514-515

reviewing, 741

liabilities account, charts of accounts, 109

liability payments, preparing, 487-489

LIFO (Last In, First Out), inventory, 151

List Limitations section (Product Information dialog box), 662-663

lists, 107-108

charts of accounts, 107, 108

adding accounts, 110-112

assets account, 108

assigning subaccount relationships, 136-137

cost of goods sold account, 109

equity account, 109

expense accounts, 110

finding and fixing errors, 132-138

income account, 109

liabilities account, 109

making accounts inactive, 133-134

merging duplicated accounts, 134

modifying accounts, 135-136

preferences, 121-122

removing subaccount relationships, 138

required accounts, 133

classes, 107, 117-119

corruptions, repairing, 668

customer types, 107, 120

editing, keyboard shortcuts, 836

entries, adding/editing multiple, 122-124

Excel data, adding to QuickBooks utility, 124-129

Intuit Interchange Format (IIF), importing, 129-131

items, 107, 112-113

adding, 115-117, 161-168

changing prices, 170-172

correcting one-sided, 144-147

creating as subitems, 149-150

customizing view, 139-140

discount, 114

editing, 312

finding and fixing errors, 139-150

group, 114, 160, 175, 194

Intuit Interchange Format (IIF) files, importing, 169-170

inventory assembly, 114

inventory part, 114

Item Listing report, 140-141

making inactive, 147-148

merging, 148-149

Multiple Unit of Measurement preference, 177-180

non-inventory part, 114, 160

other charge, 114

parts, 160

payment, 114

payroll, 475-479

Profit & Loss report, 142-144

receiving, 187-189

reviewing, 139-140

reviewing setup, 270-272

sales tax, 114, 327-328

sales tax group, 114

service, 113

subtotal, 114

limitations, 662-663

managing, 120-131

opening, keyboard shortcuts, 836

price level, creating, 333-334

reporting on, 132

synchronizing with Outlook, 686-689

Loan Manager, 681-685

collecting information, 682

configuring, 682

setting up payments, 684-685

tracking payments, 682-683

loan payments

setting up, 684-685

tracking, 682-683

Locate Discrepancies in Bank Reconciliation report, 742

long-term liability, liabilities account, 109

lost paychecks, reprinting, 506-507

lot numbers

pasting from Excel, 817-818

reporting on, 818-819

tracking, Advanced Inventory subscription, 813-819

M

Main tab (ribbon toolbar), 350-351

maintenance release, installing, 652-653

Make General Journal Entries dialog box, 708

Manage Sales Tax task (Sales Tax task group), 733

Mark Finance Charge Invoices "To Be Printed" preference (Finance Charge), 309

Mark Review Complete button (CDR), 750

markup defaults, inventory, assigning per item, 805

matching principle of accounting, 87-89

maximum sales tax, 439-440

Memorized Report List, verifying, 666

memorized report lists/groups, managing, 568-569

memorized reports, 569-570

creating reports from, QSW (QuickBooks Statement Writer), 764

Memorized tab (Report Center), 492

memorized transactions

groups, 358-360

keyboard shortcuts, 837

menu bar, 68-69

merging list items, 148-149

Minimum Finance Charge preference (Finance Charge), 309

misapplied credits, vendors, 288

Miscellaneous preference (Sales & Customers), 307

Missing Checks report, 742

Missing Customer Invoices report, generating, 393-394

multi-month/year reconciliations, completing, 545

multiple list entries, adding/editing, 166-168

Multiple Unit of Measurement preference, 177-180

multiuser access, Database Server Manager, 648

multiuser mode, QuickBooks, 647

My Company dialog box, 40, 54-55

My Preferences, 79

Accounting, 233

Calendar, 234

Checking, 235, 308

desktop view, 80-81

General, 81-82, 235-236

Graphs, 237

Reminders, 236-237, 311

Reports, 237

Reports & Graphs, 559

Sales & Customers, 308

Send Forms, 315

Spelling, 82, 316

Time & Expenses, 239-240

N

Names List, 666

negative inventory, handling, 224-230

network Database Server, 643-644

Never Update Name Information When Saving Transactions preference (General), 236

No Company Open dialog box, 38

Nonconfoming Material reports

QuickBooks Enterprise Solutions, 155

QuickBooks Premier 2014, 153

non-inventory parts, 160

adding, 164-166

notes, CDR review tasks, assigning to, 705

O

Office Accounting, converting from, 52-54

one-sided items (lists), correcting, 144-147

Online Payroll subscription, 449

Open and Convert Accountant's Copy Transfer File dialog box, 621-622

open balances, invoices, removing, 403-407

Open Invoices report, 383-384

open item receipts

removing aged, 289-290

reviewing aged, 268-270

Open or Restore Company dialog box, 83

Open the Make Deposits preference (Checking), 308

Open Windows list, 77-78

opening
company files, 83-85
Data Server Manager, 648-650

Opening Balance Equity accounts
closing into retained earnings, 593-595
troubleshooting, 593

opening balances, data file information, 95

operating environment, protecting, 656-659

operating income, 88

optimization hard drives in Windows 8, 659

other charge items, lists, 114

Other Current Assets accounts (Balance Sheet report), 581-582

Other Names List (Review List Changes), 718

Outlook, synchronizing lists with, 686-689

overpayment, refunding, 379-380

P

parts, inventory, 160
adding, 162-164

passwords, accounting periods, setting, 744-746

Pay Bills dialog box, 260

Pay Bills or Write Checks dialog box, 108

Pay Sales Tax dialog box, 419-420, 729-730

Pay Sales Tax task (Sales Tax task group), 733

payable sales tax, adjusting, 732-733

paychecks, 447-448
adjusting employee paychecks, 508-509
preparing, 447-448, 482-483
printing, 447-448, 484

paying
credit card bills, 529-531
employees, 479-487
taxable bonuses, 507-508
for inventory, 190-192
sales tax, 398-402

Paying Bills, Automatically Use Credits and Discounts preference (Bills), 234

payment items, lists, 114

Payment Summary dialog box, 258-260

payment terms, creating, 338

payments
dated, removing from undeposited funds accounts, 429-431
loan
setting up, 684-685
tracking, 682-683
recording, 370-372
unapplied, fixing, 727
unapplied customer, fixing, 719-720

Payments preferences, 306-307

Payments to Deposit dialog box, 373

payroll, 445, 491
accounts, creating in the chart of accounts, 452-453
allocating indirect costs to jobs through, 509-514
allowing Intuit Payroll expert preparation, 448
comparing liability balances to balance sheet, 497-499
comparing summary report to filed payroll returns, 500
data file information, 94
depositing refunds of payroll liabilities, 514-515
employees
adjusting paychecks, 508-509
classifying workers as, 450
entering time, 480-482
paying, 479-487
setting up, 469-474
entering after-the-fact, CDR (Client Data Review), 741
finding incorrectly paid liabilities, CDR (Client Data Review), 739-741
Home page, workflow, 480
items
adding and editing, 475-477
reporting about, 478-479
setting up, 475-479
liability payments, preparing, 487-489
limiting access to, 63
lost paychecks, reprinting, 506-507
Online Payroll subscription, 449
paychecks, preparing and printing, 447-448

paying taxable bonuses, 507-508

Payroll Setup Interview, 458-466

preferences, 455-458

 Company Preferences tab, 458

 Payroll & Employees— Company Preferences tab, 455-457

 Time & Expenses— Company Preferences tab, 458

process, 446-447

recording

 employee loan payment and repayment, 501-505

 outside service, 515-517

reports

 Excel, 492-493

 reconciling to business financials, 500-501

 Report Center, 491-492

reviewing liabilities, CDR (Client Data Review), 741

Run Payroll Checkup diagnostic tool, 466-469

state filing requirements, 451-452

subscription services, selecting and activating, 447-449

summary reports, comparing to filed returns, 500

tax forms, 494-497

tax tables, updating, 449-450

troubleshooting, 497-501

vendors, setting up payroll tax, 454-455

ViewMyPaycheck, 485-487

Payroll & Employees— Company Preferences tab (Preferences dialog box), 455-457

Payroll Item List dialog box, 478-479

Payroll Items tab (Review List Changes), 716-717

Payroll Liabilities balance (Balance Sheet report), 584

payroll services, recording payroll, 515-517

PDF files, saving CDRs (Client Data Reviews), 748-749

Peachtree, converting from, 52-54

performance, monitoring, Windows Task Manager, 663-664

permissions

data sharing

 accountants, 623-626

 business owner, 609-610

setting up, 55-59

Windows, 650-651

personal Database Server, 643-644

Personal Preferences, My Preferences,79

Accounting, 233

Calendar, 234

Checking, 235, 308

desktop view, 80-81

General, 81-82, 235-236

Graphs, 237

Reminders, 236-237, 311

Reports, 237

Reports & Graphs, 559

Sales & Customers, 308

Send Forms, 315

Spelling, 82, 316

Time & Expenses, 239-240

physical inventory counts, performing, 206-207

Portable Company File, creating and restoring, 669-670

preferences, 79

accounts payable, 232-240

 Bills, 233-234

 Checking, 234-235

accounts receivable, 304-305

 Checking, 308

 Finance Charge, 309-310

 Jobs & Estimates, 310-311

 Payments, 306-307

 Reminders, 311

 Reports & Graphs, 312-313

 Sales & Customers, 307-308

 Sales Tax, 314-315

 Send Forms, 315-316

 Spelling, 316

 Time & Expenses, 316-317

banking, 520

credit card management, 520

inventory, enabling, 156-159

Multiple Unit of Measurement, 177-180

My Preferences, 79

 Accounting, 232-233

 Calendar, 234

 Checking, 235, 308

 desktop view, 80-81

 General, 81-82, 235-236

 Graphs, 237

 Reminders, 236-237, 311

 Reports, 237

 Reports & Graphs, 559

 Sales & Customers, 308

 Send Forms, 315

 Spelling, 82, 316

 Time & Expenses, 239-240

payroll, 455-458

   Company Preferences tab, 458

   Payroll & Employees— Company Preferences tab, 455-457

   Time & Expenses— Company Preferences tab, 458

   Tax:1099, 237-238

Preferences & Formats menu (QSW), 756-759

Preferences dialog box, 76, 79, 360

preformatted Excel spreadsheets, entering data into, 124-126

prepayments, recording, 295-298

Pressing Enter Moves Between Fields preference (General), 236

Previous Year Income Comparison setting (Company Snapshot), 555

price level lists, creating, 333-334

Price Rules (Advanced Pricing), 335-336

pricing

   Advanced Pricing subscription, 826-829

     price rules, 827-829

     quantity discounts, 829

   inventory items, changing, 170-172

Print Account Names on Voucher preference (Checking), 235

Print Checks dialog box, 259

Print Labels dialog box, 825

print queues, customer invoices marked to print, eliminating, 418

printing

   barcode labels, 824-826

   barcodes to reports, 824

   budget reports, 679-681

   checks, 526-528

   lost paychecks, 506-507

   paychecks, 447-448, 484

   QSW reports, 779-781

   tax forms, 494-496

processes, payroll, 446-447

Product Information dialog box, 660-663

products, sales tax codes, assigning, 330-332

products and services, 88

Profit & Loss report

   item lists, 142-144

   reviewing, 586-587

program files, resolving corruptions, 673

progress invoicing, 360-363

Prompt Me to Modify Report Options Before Opening a Report preference (Reports and Graphs), 237, 559

Prompt Me to Modify Report preference (Reports & Graphs), 313

purchase orders, 152, 181

   Auto Create Purchase Order feature (Enterprise), 791-792

   creating, 182-186

   entering, 251

Q

.QBA files, 599, 602

.QBB files, 599-601

.QBM files, 599-601

.QBW files, 599-601

QBWin.log file, 665-668

.QBX files, 599-602

.QBY files, 599, 602

QSW (QuickBooks Statement Writer), 753

   benefits, 754-755

   Document Actions pane, modifying reports in Excel, 765-774

   Excel Add-Ins ribbon icon, modifying reports in Excel, 774

   launching, 755-756

   Preferences & Formats menu, 756-759

   Report Designer, 759-763

     Columns tab, 760-761

     Headers & Formatting tab, 762

     modifying reports in Excel, 765

     Report Content tab, 759

     Review & Finish tab, 763

     Rows/Accounts tab, 761-762

   reports, 754

     creating from memorized, 764

     exporting, 779-781

     modifying in Excel, 764-774

     opening, 764

     printing, 779-781

supporting documents, 774-775

   adding or modifying, 775-777

   creating, 779

   creating with Word toolbar, 777

   editing, 777-779

workflow, 754

quality adjustments, inventory, 207-209

Quality Discounts (Advanced Pricing), 829

QuickBooks, 35, 67

file types, 599-603

installing

   Express option, 646

   for multiuser mode, 647

maintenance release, installing, 652-653

preferences, reviewing, 746-747

sample data, 37-38

system requirements, 644-646

versions, 35-36

   upgrading, 651-652

Windows user permissions, 650-651

QuickBooks Enterprise Solutions, 783

Advanced Pricing subscription, 826-829

customization, 784-788

   expense transactions, 786-788

   fields, 784-786

inventory, 788-805

   accessing features and reports, 788-790

   Advanced Inventory subscription, 806-826

   assemblies, 793-798

   assigning markup defaults per item, 805

   Auto Create Purchase Order feature, 791-792

   Automatic Cost & Price Updates preference, 804-805

   Enhanced Inventory Receiving (EIR), 800-804

   Sales Order Fulfillment worksheet, 798-800

reporting, 830-834

   combining reports from multiple companies, 832-834

   Committed Costs by Job report, 831-832

   WIP (Work in Process) summary reports, 830-831

user security, 59-64

Quicken, converting from, 50-52

R

Rebuild Data utility, 665-666

rebuilding company file, 670-671

receipts, sales, recording, 367

Receive Payments dialog box, 371, 379, 404

Receive Payments preference (Payments), 306-307

receiving items into inventory, 187-189

Recent tab (Report Center), 492

Reclassify Transactions feature (Account Balances task group), 710-712

Reconcile Accounts link (Bank Reconciliation task group), 742

reconciliation reports, reviewing previous, 548

reconciliations

adjustments, 551-552

bank or credit card accounts, 538-540

determining, 541-542

locating discrepancies, 548-549

multi-month/year, completing, 545

restarting previously completed, 550

troubleshooting, 541-552

undoing, 550-551

recorded average cost valuation, reviewing, 217-219

recording

employee loan payment and repayment, 501-505

vendor bills, 251-254

vendor credits, 254-256

refunding overpayment, 379-380

refunds of payroll liabilities, depositing, 514-515

refunds, vendors, depositing, 300-301

reinstating warning dialog boxes, 623

Reminders preferences, 236-237, 311

Reminders setting (Company Snapshot), 556

renaming rules, Bank Feeds, 537

Report Center, 557-559

    payroll reports, 491-492

    reporting inventory, 213-214

Report Content tab (Report Designer), 759

Report Designer (QSW), 759-763

    Columns tab, 760-761

    Headers & Formatting tab, 762

    modifying reports in Excel, 765

    Report Content tab, 759

    Review & Finish tab, 763

    Rows/Accounts tab, 761-762

Report window, modification options, 563

reporting. *See also* **reports**

    accounts receivable, 381-382

        Collections Center, 391-393

        Income Tracker, 388-391

        Missing Invoices report, 393-394

        Open Invoices report, 383-384

        A/R Aging Summary, 382-383

        reconciling totals, 385-386

        viewing balance on cash basis balance sheets, 386-388

    inventory, 211

        Inventory Center, 212-213

        Inventory Valuation Summary report, 214-216

        Report Center, 213-214

        reviewing aged accounts payable, 223

        reviewing aged item receipts, 219-223

        reviewing recorded average cost valuation, 217-219

on lists, 132

QuickBooks Enterprise Solutions, 830-834

reports

    AR Aging Summary, reviewing, 722-724

    Audit Trail, reviewing, 588

    Audit Trail of Review, 697, 750-751

    Balance Sheet

        account types, 576-577

        Accounts Payable balance, 583

        Accounts Receivable balance, 578-579

        bank account balances, 578

        credit card account balances, 584

        Equity accounts, 585

        fixed assets, 582-583

        Inventory balance, 580

        Other Current Assets accounts, 581-582

        Other Current Liabilities and Long-Term Liabilities account types, 585

        Payroll Liabilities balance, 584

        prior year balances, 577

        reviewing, 575-585

        Undeposited Funds, 579-580

    budget, printing, 679-681

    Closing Date Exception, tracking changes to, 587

    Closing Date Exceptions, 744

    combining from multiple companies, 832-834

    Committed Costs by Job, 831-832

    Company Snapshot, 553-556

    Credit Card Audit Trail, reviewing, 589-591

    dates, keyboard shortcuts, 838

    emailing, 573-574

    exporting to .CSV file, 571-573

    exporting to Excel, 571-573

    groups, 565-569

        creating, 565-566

        managing memorized, 568-569

        templates, exporting/ importing, 570-571

    Inventory Valuation Summary or Detail, 734

    Locate Discrepancies in Bank Reconciliation, 742

    lot numbers, 818-819

    memorized, 569-570

    Missing Checks report, 742

    modifying, 563

        Customize Report button, 564-565

        Report window, 563

    payroll

        Excel, 492-493

        items, 478-479

        reconciling to business financials, 500-501

        Report Center, 491-492

    printing barcodes to, 824

    Profit & Loss, reviewing, 586-587

    QSW (QuickBooks Statement Writer)

        creating from memorized, 764

        exporting, 779-781

        modifying in Excel, 764-774

        opening, 764

        printing, 779-781

    Report Center, 557-559

report groups, 565-569

  creating, 565-566

  managing memorized, 568-569

Reporting Preferences, 559-562

templates, exporting/ importing, 570-571

Transaction List by Date, viewing, 592

Undeposited Funds Detail, 426-431

Unpaid Bills Details, reviewing, 728-729

user activity, 65

Voided/Deleted Transactions Summary, 591

  reviewing, 549-550

WIP (Work in Process) summary, WIP (Work in Process) summary reports, 830-831

Reports & Graphs preferences, 312-313, 559-562

Reports preferences, 237

Reports Show Items By preference (Reports and Graphs), 237

Reports tab (ribbon toolbar), 351-352

Reports-Show Accounts By preference (Reports & Graphs), 312, 560-561

Reports-Show Items By preference (Reports & Graphs), 312, 560

reprinting lost paychecks, 506-507

researching vendor transactions, 246-247

Resources tab (General Preferences), 757-758

restoring backups, 656

restrictions, Enhanced Inventory Receiving (EIR), 802-803

returns, customer inventory types, handling, 200-201

revenue, 88

Review & Finish tab (Report Designer), 763

Review and Create Paychecks dialog box, 483

Review Inventory Setup (CDR), 734

Review Item Setup tab (Review List Changes), 717

Review List Changes feature (CDR)

  Chart of Accounts tab, 713-718

  Customers task, 718

  Fixed Asset Items tab, 715-716

  Items tab, 714-715

  Other Names List, 718

  Payroll Items tab, 716-717

  Review Item Setup tab, 717

  Vendors task, 718

review tasks, CDR (Client Data Review), assigning status and notes to, 705

reviews (CDR)

  finishing, 748-750

  reopening, 750

ribbon toolbar, creating invoices, 350-352

roles, users, setting up and modifying, 60-63

Routing Number field (Add New Account), 112

Rows/Accounts tab (Report Designer), 761-762

Run Payroll Checkup diagnostic tool, 466-469

S

Sales & Customers preferences, 307-308

Sales Forms preference (Sales & Customers), 307

Sales Order Fulfillment worksheet (QuickBooks Enterprise Solutions), 153, 155, 798-800

sales orders, 181, 304, 349

Sales Orders preference (Sales & Customers), 308

sales receipts, 181

  recording, 367

sales tax, 327

  adjusting payable, 732-733

  codes

    assigning to customers, 332-333

    assigning to products or services, 330-332

  correcting errors, 419-424

  incorrectly recorded, fixing, 729-732

  issuing credit memos, 442-443

  items

    creating, 327-330

    group, 114, 328-329

    lists, 114

  managing, 733

  maximum, 439-440

  multiple rates on one invoice, 441-442

payable reports, 394-398

paying, 398-402, 733

Sales Tax Liability report, 420-424

tracking, 304

Sales Tax Liability report, 420-424

Sales Tax preferences, 314-315

Sales Tax Preferences task (Sales Tax task group), 733

Sales Tax task group (CDR), 729-733

sample data, 37-38

Save Backup Copy dialog box, 611

Save File method, creating Accountant's Copy, 608-609

Save Transactions Before Printing preference (General), 236

scanning barcodes, 821-822

security

antivirus software, 657

users

access rights, 59

QuickBooks Enterprise, 59-64

setting up, 60-64

modifying roles, 60-63

Select Default Accounts to Use preference (Checking), 235

Select Previous Reconciliation Report dialog box, 548

selling inventory, 193-194

Send Email Using preference (Send Forms), 316

Send Forms preferences, 315-316

Send General Journal Entries, 630-632

Send to Accountant method, creating Accountant's Copy, 605-608

Send/Ship tab (ribbon toolbar), 351-352

serial numbers

pasting from Excel, 817-818

tracking, Advanced Inventory subscription, 813-819

service items, lists, 113

services, sales tax codes, assigning, 330-332

Set the Dividing Date dialog box, 606

Set Up Sales Tax Item preference (Sales Tax), 314

sharing data, 597-598, 630

accountants, 616-630

Client Collaborator, 634-641

converting Accountant's Copy to company file, 629-630

creating External Accountant user types, 618

File Manager 2014, 617-618

permissions, 623-626

preparing client for data exchange, 619

receiving Accountant's Copy files, 619-623

requests upon import completion, 629

returning Accountant's Copy change file to client, 626-629

Accountant's Copy

canceling, 616

reconciling while pending, 610

Batch Enter Transactions, 632-634

business owner, 603-616

Client Collaborator, 634-641

creating Accountant's Copy of data, 604-609

importing accountant's changes, 610-615

permissions, 609-610

reviewing data, 604

choosing method, 599-603

file types, 599-603

Send General Journal Entries, 630-632

shortcuts (keyboard), 835

data files, opening, 838

dates, 838

dialog boxes, opening, 836

lists

editing, 836

opening, 836

memorized transactions, 837

text editing, 837

transactions, 839

editing, 836

Small Business Accounting, converting from, 52-54

Sort By option (Report window), 563

sorting transactions, 547-548

Specify Invoice Amounts for Items on Estimate dialog box, 361

Spelling preferences, 82, 316

spreadsheets (Excel), entering data into preformatted, 124-126

Start with Payee Field on Check preference (Checking), 235

starting inventory sites, assigning, Advanced Inventory subscription, 807-809

startup transactions

  accounts payable, 100-103

  accounts receivable, 95-97

  bank account statement balance, 103-105

  uncleared bank checks, 105-106

state identification numbers, 451

statement charges, recording, 369

Statement of Cash Flows preference (Reports & Graphs), 561-562

Statement Writer (QSW), 753, 754

  benefits, 754-755

  Document Actions pane, modifying reports in Excel, 765-774

  Excel Add-Ins ribbon icon, modifying reports in Excel, 774

  launching, 755-756

  Preferences & Formats menu, 756-759

  Report Designer, 759-763

    Columns tab, 760-761

    Headers & Formatting tab, 762

    modifying reports in Excel, 765

    Report Content tab, 759

    Review & Finish tab, 763

    Rows/Accounts tab, 761-762

  reports, 754

    creating from memorized, 764

    exporting, 779-781

    modifying in Excel, 764-774

    opening, 764

    printing, 779-781

  supporting documents, 774-775

    adding or modifying, 775-777

    creating, 779

    creating with Word toolbar, 777

    editing, 777-779

  workflow, 754

statements (QSW), 754

  supporting documents, 774-775

    adding or modifying, 775-777

    creating, 779

    creating with Word toolbar, 777

    editing, 777-779

statements of cash flows, 92

status, CDR review tasks, assigning to, 705

Styles tab (General Preferences), 757-758

subaccount relationships, charts of accounts

  assigning, 136-137

  removing, 138

subassemblies, automatically building, 793

subitems, creating list items as, 149-150

subscription services, payroll, selecting and activating, 447-449

subtotal items, lists, 114

Summary Report Basis preference (Reports & Graphs), 312, 560

summary reports, payroll, comparing to filed returns, 500

Summary Reports Basis preference (Reports and Graphs), 237

supporting documents (QSW), 774-775

  adding or modifying, 775-777

  creating, 779

    with Word toolbar, 777

  editing, 777-779

system requirements, 644-646

T

task groups, CDR (Client Data Review), minimizing/expanding, 704

Task Manager (Windows), monitoring performance, 663-664

tasks, tracking time spent, Timer, 691-692

tax forms, 494-497

  filing, 448, 497

  preparing and printing, 494-496

tax tables, updating, 449-450

Tax:1099 preferences, 237-238

taxable bonuses, paying, 507-508

taxes. *See also* **sales tax**
year-end checklist, Year-End Guide, 685-686

templates, reports, exporting/importing, 570-571

text editing keyboard shortcuts, 837

Time & Expenses preferences, 239-240, 316-317

Time & Expenses—Company Preferences tab (Preferences dialog box), 458

time and expense invoicing, 363-366

Time Format preference (General), 236

Time Tracking preference (Time & Expenses), 239, 316

Time/Enter Single Activity dialog box, 481

Timer, 690-693
activities
exporting, 692-693
importing, 693
tracking time spent, 691-692
installing, 691

title bar, 67-68

tools
CDR (Client Data Review), 695
Account Balances task group, 705-713
customizing, 701-705
features, 696-698
Review List Changes feature, 713-718
Contact Sync, 686-689
File Doctor, 671-672
Run Payroll Checkup, 466-469

Timer, 690-693
Verify Data, 663

Top Customers by Sales setting (Company Snapshot), 555

Top Icon Bar, 69-72
customizing, 71-72
Open Windows list, 77-78

Top Vendors by Expense setting (Company Snapshot), 556

tracking serial/lot numbers, Advanced Inventory subscription, 813-819

Transaction List by Date report, viewing, 592

transactions. *See also* **specific transactions**
accounts payable, 247-248
Batch Enter Transactions, 632-634
completing, barcodes, 823-824
dates, keyboard shortcuts, 838
downloading, 533-534
editing, keyboard shortcuts, 836
Enter Bills, 520
expense, customizing, 786-788
finding customer, Customer Center, 323-324
keyboard shortcuts, 839
memorized, keyboard shortcuts, 837
memorizing recurring, 299-300
sorting, 547-548
startup
accounts payable, 100-103
accounts receivable, 100-103

bank account statement balance, 103-105
uncleared bank checks, 105-106
types, 181
uncleared
identifying, 544-545
reviewing, 546-548
vendor bills, 182-190
creating purchase orders, 182-186
entering, 189-190
vendors
finding, 245-247
researching, 246-247
verifying that all have been entered, 542-544
Write Check, 520-528

Transfer Inventory dialog box, 810-811

transferring funds between bank accounts, 532

Troubleshoot Inventory feature (CDR), 736-738

Troubleshoot Prior Account Balances tool (Account Balances task group), 706-709

troubleshooting
inventory, CDR (Client Data Review), 736-738
Opening Balance Equity accounts, 593
payroll, 497-501
prior account balances, 709, 706-709
reconciliations, 541-552

Turn Off Online Payments preference (Payments), 307

tutorials, 79

U

unapplied customer payments and credits, fixing, Account Balances task group (CDR), 719-720

unapplied vendor payments and credits, fixing, 727

uncleared bank checks, recording, 105-106

uncleared checks and deposits, data file information, 94

uncleared transactions
identifying, 544-545
reviewing, 546-548

undeposited funds account errors, correcting, 426-431, 720-722

unemployment identification numbers, state, 451

uninterruptable power supply (UPS), installing, 656

Unit of Measure dialog box, 178

Unpaid Bills Details report, 267-268
reviewing, 728-729

Upcoming Events & Past Due Settings preference (Calendar), 234

updating tax tables, 449-450

upgrading QuickBooks, 651-652

UPS (uninterruptable power supply), installing, 656

Use Class Tracking for Transactions preference (Accounting), 233

User List dialog box, 56

users
Admin, 75
external accountants, creating login for, 56
reporting activity, 65
security
access rights, 59
QuickBooks Enterprise, 59-64
setting up, 63-64
setting up and modifying roles, 60-63
setting up, 55-59

Using Group dialog box, 359

V

valuation, comparing, 734-736

value adjustments, inventory, 209-211

vendor bills, 182-190
creating purchase orders, 182-186
entering, 189-190

Vendor Center, 240-242
adding and modifying vendors, 242-245
finding transactions, 245-247

vendor inventory returns, handling, 203

vendors, 231, 265
accounts payable, 247
applying vendor credits, 259-262
correcting errors, 285-293
entering purchase orders, 251
paying bills, 256-259
preferences, 232-240
recording bills, 251-254
recording credits, 254-256
taking discounts on bills, 262-264
transactions, 247-248
workflow, 249-251
accounts payable
reporting, 265
cash basis balance sheet, 272-274
reconciling Balance Sheet Accounts Payable balance, 265-267
reviewing aged open item receipts, 268-270
reviewing item setup, 270-272
tracking and reporting 10990MISC payments, 275-285
Unpaid Bills Details report, 267-268
aged open item receipts, removing, 289-290
bartering services, recording, 293-294
bills
payment without proper process, 285-287
removing, 289-290
as customers, 432-434
customizing Home page for, 231-232
misapplied credits, 288
prepayments, recording, 295-298
refunds, depositing, 300-301
setting up payroll tax, 454-455
transactions, researching, 246-247
Vendor Center, 240-242
adding and modifying vendors, 242-245
finding transactions, 245-247

Vendors, Inventory Activities, Physical Inventory Worksheet, 738

Vendors task (Review List Changes), 718

Vendors to Pay setting (Company Snapshot), 556

Verify Data utility, 663-665

Versions, QuickBooks, 35-36
    upgrading, 651-652

View Suggested Adjustments button (Balances in Accountant's Records), 708-709

View User Access dialog box, 614-615

ViewMyPaycheck, 485-487

views
    Calendar, 234
    item lists, customizing, 139-140

virus protection software, 657

Voided/Deleted Transactions Detail option (Reports, Accountant & Taxes), 65

Voided/Deleted Transactions Summary report, 65, 591
    reviewing, 549-550

W-Z

Warn About Duplicate Bill Numbers from Same Vendor preference (Bills), 234

Warn About Duplicate Check Numbers preference (Checking), 235

Warn About Duplicate Estimate Numbers preference (Jobs & Estimates), 310

Warn When Deleting a Transaction or Unused List Item preference (General), 236

Warn When Editing a Transaction preference (General), 236

Warn When Posting a Transaction to Retained Earnings preference (Accounting), 233

warning dialog boxes, reinstating, 623

web connect method, downloading transactions, 533

When Do You Owe Sales Tax? preference (Sales Tax), 314

When Do You Pay Sales Tax? preference (Sales Tax), 314

Windows disk defragmentation utility, 657-658

Windows Task Manager, monitoring performance, 663-664

WIP (Work in Process) summary reports, 830-831

withholding tax identification numbers, 451

Word QSW toolbar, creating supporting documents, 777

Work in Process (WIP) summary reports, 830-831

workers, classifying as employees, 450

workflow
    accounts payable, 249-251
    Enhanced Inventory Receiving (EIR), 802
    payroll, Home page, 480

Working Trial Balance tool (Account Balances task group), 712-713

worksheets (Excel), Advanced Import from, 126-129

Write Check transactions, 520-528
    Expenses tab, 521-523
    Items tab, 521-523
    printing checks, 526-528
    writing checks, 523-526

Write Off Invoices dialog box, 724-726

writing checks, 523-526

year-end adjusting journal entries, recording, 432

Year-End Guide, 685-686

Your Details tab (General Preferences), 756-757

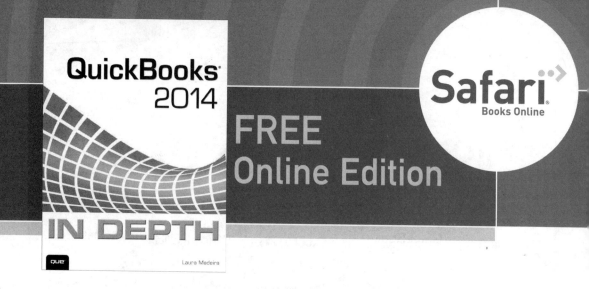

Your purchase of *QuickBooks 2014 In Depth* includes access to a free online edition for 45 days through the **Safari Books Online** subscription service. Nearly every Que book is available online through **Safari Books Online**, along with thousands of books and videos from publishers such as Addison-Wesley Professional, Cisco Press, Exam Cram, IBM Press, O'Reilly Media, Prentice Hall, Sams, and VMware Press.

Safari Books Online is a digital library providing searchable, on-demand access to thousands of technology, digital media, and professional development books and videos from leading publishers. With one monthly or yearly subscription price, you get unlimited access to learning tools and information on topics including mobile app and software development, tips and tricks on using your favorite gadgets, networking, project management, graphic design, and much more.

Activate your FREE Online Edition at
informit.com/safarifree

STEP 1: Enter the coupon code: WVGKYFA.

STEP 2: New Safari users, complete the brief registration form.
Safari subscribers, just log in.

If you have difficulty registering on Safari or accessing the online edition,
please e-mail customer-service@safaribooksonline.com